The
Pursuit of
Oblivion

The
Pursuit of
Oblivion

*A Global History
of Narcotics*

Richard
Davenport-Hines

W. W. NORTON & COMPANY

New York · London

YUMA COUNTY
LIBRARY DISTRICT

(928) 782-1871
www.yumalibrary.org

Copyright © 2002, 2001 by Richard Davenport-Hines

First published as a Norton paperback 2004
Originally published in Great Britian in 2001 by Weidenfeld & Nicolson,
The Orion Publishing Group Ltd, under the title *The
Pursuit of Oblivion: A Global History of Narcotics, 1500–2000*

For information about permission to reproduce selections from this
book, write to Permissions, W. W. Norton & Company, Inc.,
500 Fifth Avenue, New York, NY 10110

Manufacturing by Courier Westford
Book design by Molly Heron
Production manager: Anna Oler

Library of Congress Cataloging-in-Publication Data

Davenport-Hines, R. P. T. (Richard Peter Treadwell), 1953–
The pursuit of oblivion : a global history of narcotics / Richard
Davenport-Hines.
p. cm.
Includes bibliographical references and index.
ISBN 0-393-05189-7
1. Drug abuse—History. 2. Narcotics—History. 3. Drugs of abuse—History.
4. Drug traffic—History. 5. Narcotics, Control of—History. I. Title.

HV5801 .D25 2002
363.45'09—dc21   2002071908
ISBN 0-393-32545-8 pbk.

W. W. Norton & Company, Inc.
500 Fifth Avenue, New York, N.Y. 10110
www.wwnorton.com

W. W. Norton & Company Ltd.
Castle House, 75/76 Wells Street, London W1T 3QT

1 2 3 4 5 6 7 8 9 0

For

AJH

Contents

✌⟊❧

History is the most dangerous concoction the chemistry of the mind has produced. Its properties are well known. It sets people dreaming, intoxicates them, engenders false memories, exaggerates their reflexes, keeps old wounds open, torments their leisure, inspires them with megalomania or persecution complex, and makes nations bitter, proud, insufferable and vain.

History can justify anything you like. It teaches strictly nothing, for it contains and gives examples of everything.

—Paul Valéry, *Regards sur le Monde Actuel*

Hidden worlds haunt our imagination. The underworld of criminals; the Underground; the *demi-monde* (occupied in part by the inhabitants of polite society, wearing as it were, their Hyde aspects.)

The world of the gods; Shangri La; Middle Earth; the world through the Looking-Glass.

The Mafia; the Establishment; the System; the great conspiracy of the left; the great conspiracy of the right.

Of these five apparently normal, respectable citizens, one is a ruthless murderer who disembowelled Sir Toby with the ornamental Javanese paper-knife!—At once they all five become deep, interesting in their very uninterestingness.

—Michael Frayn, *Constructions*

The need to go astray, to be destroyed is an extremely private, distant, passionate turbulent truth, and has nothing to do with what we call substance.

—Georges Bataille, *Le Coupable*

Prologue

*The desire to take medicine is perhaps the greatest feature
which distinguishes man from animals.*
—SIR WILLIAM OSLER

*Every kind of addiction is bad, no matter whether
the drug be alcohol, morphine or idealism.*
—CARL JUNG

ITSUBISHIS, 007S, DOVES, New Yorkers, California Sunrises, M&Ms, Dennis the Menaces, Rhubarb and Custards, Snowballs, Blue Butterflies, McDonalds, Flatliners, Shamrocks, Swans, Swallows, Turbos, Phase Fours, Refreshers, Love Hearts, Riddlers, Pink Elephants—these are some of the alluring brand names of Ecstasy available on the illegal British drug market at the start of the twenty-first century. The ingredients of each type of tiny pill vary according to their colour, size and the pictograms stamped on them. The diversity of the branding demonstrates the vigour of the business and the dynamism of the market.

The international illicit drug business generates $400 billion in trade annually, according to recent United Nations estimates. That represents 8 per cent of all international trade. It is about the same percentage as tourism and the oil industry. Yet many of the chief substances of this illicit business have been used for thousands of years to treat physical pain or mental distress as well as for pleasure. This book explores how licit medicines became the commodity of the world's greatest illicit business.

11

Intoxication is not unnatural or deviant. Absolute sobriety is not a natural or primary human state. Drugs are variously swallowed, smoked, injected and inhaled. Though, at times, politicians speak or journalists write of drugs as if their characteristics collectively cohere, they fall into very different categories, with discrete powers and effects.

NARCOTICS relieve pain, induce euphoria and create physical dependency. The most prominent are opium, morphine, heroin and codeine.

HYPNOTICS cause sleep and stupor; examples include chloral, sulphonal, barbiturates and benzodiazepines. They are habit-forming and can have adverse effects. These side effects are shared with tranquillisers, which are intended to reduce anxiety without causing sleep.

STIMULANTS cause excitement, and increase mental and physical energy, but create dependency and may cause psychotic disturbance. Cocaine and amphetamines are the pre-eminent stimulants, but others include caffeine, tobacco, betel, tea, coffee, cocoa, qat and pituri.

INEBRIANTS are produced by chemical synthesis: alcohol, chloroform, ether, benzine, solvents and other volatile chemicals.

HALLUCINOGENS cause complex changes in visual, auditory and other perceptions and possibly acute psychotic disturbance. The most commonly used hallucinogenic is cannabis (marijuana). Others include LSD, mescaline, certain mushrooms, henbane and belladonna.

The working of these substances only began to be understood correctly by researchers in the last three decades. The human brain transmits pulses of electrical activity along nerve fibres connecting one nerve cell, or neuron, to another. These nerve cells are the source of neural activity in the brain. The transmission of the signal from cell to cell involves neurotransmitters—that is, pulses of chemical signal molecules. Neurotransmitters excite or inhibit nerve cell firing, and are recognised by specific receptors, which are specialised proteins located in the cell membranes of target cells. Minute quantities of neurotransmitter chemicals are released: serotonin, which makes people feel satisfied, dopamine which arouses pleasurable feelings, and noradrenaline are crucial neurotransmitters so far as many controversial drugs are concerned. Cocaine and amphetamines, for example, can be enjoyable because their use causes neurotransmitters to release noradrenaline and dopamine. Morphine acts on three distinct receptors—called collectively the opiate receptors—which have been known only since the

1970s. In the same decade a group of neurotransmitters collectively called the endorphins were found to act as opiate receptors and block both sensory and emotional pain.

It is easy to summarise these facts, but more challenging to encapsulate the passions that drugs arouse. Feelings range from giggly enthusiasm or nonchalance at one extreme to the deepest dread of corruption, violence, pollution and death. Drugs are often the recourse of people who are bored or sad or angry—that is, they are part of the repertoire of human moods and needs. People use them to retreat from a brutal environment, or as a salve to assuage guilt and anxiety, or as a trick to vex their elders. Opiates can provide a way of re-inventing oneself as a remote, pitiless and superior being. They provide the semblance of control with the reality of degradation. They are for people for whom existence seems to be an implacable enemy. Taken together, stimulants, hallucinogens, tranquillisers and painkillers provide every extreme of love rush and death wish, of opening and closure, of rebuilding and demolition, of exterior energy and interior implosion, the pursuit of destiny against an attempted suspension of the future. Drugs are full of dizzying incongruities and contradictions. They illustrate the maxim of the Danish physicist Niels Bohr (1885–1962) that profound truths can be recognised by the fact that the opposite is also a profound truth, in contrast to trivialities, where opposites are absurd. Any substance that has the power to do good also has the power to do harm.

Being 'on drugs' can be represented as a depraved appetite, a wretched obsession, escapism for fugitives; or as a search for transcendental visions and mystical excitement. Drug-users encrypt meaning and invent their own fabulous mythologies. Drug-taking can be claimed as a search for utopian protocols, or as the sure route to an ethical wasteland. Toxic side effects become a game for some drug-users. Many of them are put under surveillance, and ostracised as members of a threatening underclass; but a few users (rock stars, fashionable models or poets) are allowed an aristocratic status.

This book is a history of drug-taking and therefore a history of emotional extremes. It tells the story across five centuries of addicts and users: monarchs, prime ministers, great writers and composers, wounded soldiers, overworked physicians, oppressed housewives, exhausted labourers, high-powered businessmen, playboys, sex workers, pop stars, seedy losers, stressed adolescents, defiant schoolchildren, the victims of the ghetto, and happy young people on a spree. Its later chapters are set in the cities and suburbs of the United States, in London and Paris, and in the countryside of almost every part of the world, especially South America, Eastern Europe, North-West Africa and South-East Asia. Although it is primarily a history of people and of places, it is also the history of one bad idea: prohibition.

It describes how prohibition policies have turned licit, if dangerous, medicines into the world's most lucrative and tightly organised black market. Essentially prohibition has been a technique of informal American cultural colonisation. Back in 1875 San Francisco responded to the growing phenomenon of middle-class youngsters smoking opium in the opium shops frequented by Chinese labourers and a few underworld types by passing a prohibitive city ordinance. Other cities and states in the western USA passed similar legislation during 1876–90. These laws were the first that criminalised drug-users—the people operating or using the opium shops—rather than regulating the supply of substances. The smoking of opium by social delinquents or adolescent rebels in the USA was followed in the 1890s by similar illicit recreational use of cocaine in American cities. The social use of cocaine by underworld characters and delinquent young men going through the stresses of adolescence began the transformation of our view of drug-users from eccentrics with a specialised vice into evil criminals and menacing enemies of society. The US Opium Exclusion Act of 1909 began diverting drug-users from the more innocuous opium-smoking to the more destructive intravenous use of heroin. The US Harrison Narcotic Act of 1914 provided the model for drug prohibition legislation throughout the Western World. By the early 1920s, the conception of the addict was changing from that of a middle-class victim accidentally addicted through medicinal use, to that of a criminal deviant using narcotics (or stimulants) for pleasure. The policies of the Federal Bureau of Narcotics promoted the growth of criminal underworlds and subcultures. Criminals were provided with a new commodity in which to deal after the raising of alcohol prohibition. The official American orthodoxy constituted a highly generalised half-truth, which suppressed the reality of some drug-users controlling their habit, holding down good jobs, and leading prosperous lives, while enforcing on other addicts the part of the degraded, dying creature that society required them to play. The American attitudes and policies generated by the Harrison Act were crude and counterproductive.

The United States has claimed the leadership of the global anti-drugs wars since 1909, and its prohibitionist legislation has provided the model for international drug-control agreements. The prohibition policies of the USA have escalated into the global Wars on Drugs associated since 1969 with the Nixon, Reagan and Bush administrations. The American approach can be summarised as requiring unconditional surrender from traffickers, dealers, addicts and occasional recreational users. That surrender has not occurred. American prohibition policies have failed and failed again and still continue to fail. Despite this lack of success, the US Drug Enforcement Administration has convinced governments around the world that it has unrivalled expertise. Successive Washington administrations have cajoled European states into adopting these failed tactics, and imposed them in the Third World.

In Britain, before 1914, the supply of drugs was regulated under the Pharmacy Acts, but not severely repressed. When the slaughter began in Flanders, society women included half-grains of morphine with the handkerchiefs and books they parcelled up for soldiers at the Front. Department store catalogues still listed morphine and heroin pastilles. Emergency wartime legislation apart, Britain's criminal laws against illicit drug possession date from 1920, and its problems with recreational drug fashions began only around 1950. The most critical moments in the development of British drug scenes occurred when the British authorities inappropriately adopted American punitive strategies in the mid-1960s and in the early 1980s. Badly behaved or rebellious British youngsters aping the antics of American brats were of secondary importance in these phases.

Here are some facts to show what eighty years of prohibition have achieved:

- The United Nations Drug Control Program reported in 1997 that 141 million people had used cannabis in the previous year (about 3 per cent of the world's population). There were 30 million amphetamine-users, 13 million cocaine-users and 8 million heroin-users.
- World production of opium *trebled* and of coca *doubled* between 1985 and 1996.
- 10–15 per cent of illicit heroin and 30 per cent of illicit cocaine is

intercepted. Drug-traffickers have gross profit margins of up to 300 per cent. At least 75 per cent of illicit drug shipments would have to be intercepted before the traffickers' profits were hurt.

- A kilogram of heroin in Pakistan cost an average of $2720 in 2000. The same kilogram can be sold for an average of $129,380 in the United States.

- A kilogram of coca base in Colombia costs an average of $950. Its US price in 1997 was nearly $25,000, with a street price of $20 to $90 a gram.

- The United Nations reported in 1999 that over the previous decade inflation-adjusted prices in Western Europe for cocaine and heroin fell by 45 per cent and 60 per cent respectively. Comparable US figures were 50 per cent for cocaine and 70 per cent for heroin.

- At the end of the twentieth century it cost the US $8.6 billion a year to imprison drug law violators.

- Despite the rise in US federal spending on the drug war from $1.65 billion in 1982 to $17.7 billion in 1999, over half of US adolescents had tried an illegal drug before they graduated from high school.

- An estimated 14.8 million Americans were current users of illicit drugs in 1999. The highest number of current illicit drug-users was in 1979, when the estimate was 25.4 million.

- 10.9 per cent of US youths aged twelve to seventeen had used illicit drugs within the past thirty days in 1999. Again the rate was highest in 1979 with 16.3 per cent.

- In 1999 an estimated 208,000 Americans were current users of heroin: a tripling of the figure since 1993. The average age of heroin-users at first use of the drug was twenty-one.

- There were an estimated 991,000 new inhalant users in the US in 1998. This figure had risen by 154 per cent from 1990. Sixty-two per cent of first-time inhalant-users in 1998 were aged between twelve and seventeen.

- At least 45 million Europeans (18 per cent of those aged fifteen to sixty-four) have tried cannabis at least once; 15 million have used cannabis in the past twelve months.

- In the European Union up to 5 per cent of people aged sixteen to thirty-four have used amphetamines and/or ecstasy, and up to 6 per cent have tried cocaine at least once; but heroin experience is under 2 per cent in young European adults.

- Most acute drug-related deaths in Europe involve opiates, often combined with alcohol or tranquillisers. Some European governments report significant numbers of adolescent deaths from inhaling volatile substances, but death from cocaine, amphetamines and ecstasy are uncommon throughout Europe.
- Variations in drug-use statistics of the member states of the European Union suggest little direct association between prevalence of illicit drug use and national policy: countries seem to have similar, often moderate levels of use regardless of whether the laws are restrictive or not.
- Britain has a far severer regime over possession of illicit drugs than most other European countries, but also has among the highest consumption rates. Forty per cent of its young adults have used cannabis (together with Denmark the highest percentage in Europe); 16 per cent of its young adults have tried amphetamines; and 8 per cent ecstasy.
- About 25 per cent of the British population aged between sixteen and sixty-nine have tried an illegal substance at some time: this amounts to about 10 million people.
- Drug use among young British people increased until the early 1990s, but has now levelled off.

This book is a history, not a contemporary polemic; but it marshals evidence that conflicts with many assumptions of the prohibitionists. It indicates that it is not a drug itself that drives an addict to crime but the need for the drug. It is not the supply of a drug that turns a user into a criminal but the illicitness of that supply. Enforced abstinence and punitive treatment of users are generally ineffective. Drug-suppliers are not averse to the risks posed by law enforcement, and never have been, because higher risks always raise the potential profits. Criminal sanctions against drug-trafficking may be well intentioned, and may enjoy temporary or localised success; but overall the primary role of these laws is as business incentives. Prohibition creates an irresistibly lucrative opportunity for entrepreneurs willing to operate in illicit business. It is the policy of idealists who cannot appreciate that the use of drugs often reflects other sets of human ideals: human perfectibility, the yearning for a perfect moment, the peace that comes from oblivion.

The
Pursuit of
Oblivion

ONE

Early History

IN THE 1670s an English merchant seaman called Thomas Bowrey (1649?–1713) was plying his trade along the coast of Bengal together with other English sailors. They saw the local people amusing themselves with a drink called *bhang*—dried and crushed cannabis seeds and leaves mixed in fresh water—and determined to try the concoction. Eight or ten of them each bought a pint of *bhang* in the bazaar for the equivalent of sixpence. Bowrey's record of what happened is apparently the earliest first-hand account of recreational cannabis written by an Englishman. Although sailors are not usually decorous in their pleasures, Bowrey's compatriots worried about seeming foolish in public and were conspiratorial in arranging their party. Perhaps, in a puritan age, they did not like to be seen as too happy in taking their pleasures. They recruited a local fakir to protect and monitor their experiment. After each sailor had drunk his *bhang*, the fakir went outside, fastening all the doors and windows, so 'that none of us might run into the Street, or any person come in to behold any of our humors thereby to laugh at us'. Most of the English drug-takers enjoyed their escapade, as Bowrey recounted, although their dignity was forfeited:

> It Soon tooke its Operation Upon most of us, but merrily, Save upon two of our Number, who I Suppose feared it might doe them harme not beinge accustomed thereto. One of them Sat himselfe downe Upon the floore, and wept bitterly all the Afternoone, the Other terrified with feare did runne his head into a great Mortavan Jarre, and continued in that Posture 4 hours or more; 4 or 5 of the number lay upon the Carpets (that were Spread in the roome) highly Complimentinge each Other in high termes, each man fancyinge himself noe lesse than an Emperour. One was quarralsome and fought with one of the wooden Pillars of the Porch, until he had left himselfe little Skin upon the knuckles of his fingers. My Selfe and one more Sat sweatinge for the Space of 3 hours in Exceedinge Measure.

Meanwhile, their protector became absurdly intoxicated in the street, 'callinge us all Kings and brave fellows, fancyinge himselfe to be at the Gates of the Pallace at Agra, Singinge to that purpose in the Hindostan Languadge'.[1] Bowrey knew that the drug could be smoked in tobacco—'a very Speedy way to be besotted'—or chewed, but the pleasantest way was drinking. 'It Operates according to the thoughts or fancy of the Partie that drinketh thereof, in Such manner that if he be merry at that instant, he Shall Continue Soe with Exceedinge great laughter . . . at Every thinge.' However, if 'taken in a fearefull or Melancholy posture, he Shall keep great lamentation and Seem to be in great anguish of Spirit'.[2]

Bowrey's *bhang* trials were more significant than he could imagine. The English customers in the Indian bazaar presaged drugs as internationally traded commodities with fluctuating levels of supply, demand and consumption. Their party was a pioneering episode in Western use of medicinal substances to satisfy curiosity and the desire for oblivious joy; increasingly, and markedly from the nineteenth century, people have explored the possibilities of prescribed medicines providing heightened pleasure or reduced sensibility. Already, in the 1670s, puritan self-consciousness had turned such experimental pleasures into an illicit pursuit. Both the excitement of clandestine drug use and the hostility to drug-related hedonism were to increase exponentially from the mid-nineteenth century under the influence of American puritanism and European industrialisation. Bowrey's companions at his *bhang* party were also exemplary. Their behaviour was variously joyful, mindless, psychotic and violent. The sailor who fancied himself an emperor, and his distracted colleague who hid his head inside the jar, provided prototypes of Western behaviour that have endured over three centuries.

Opium is the foremost psychoactive substance known to humanity; but cannabis, also known as marijuana or hemp, is also of great antiquity and has been the most prevalent hallucinogenic. This plant, which is a member of the mulberry family, has two significant species catalogued by Linnaeus in 1753. The most common is *Cannabis sativa*, which is gangly, loose-branched, can reach a height of twenty feet and is productive of fibre and inferior seed oil. *Cannabis indica* grows to three or four feet in height, is densely branched, shaped like a pyramid and yields higher quantities of intoxicating resin. The plant perhaps originated north of Afghanistan, but it was long ago dispersed across the world. It flourishes both as a weed and under cultivation in a variety of soils and climates in both hemispheres. Hemp seeds have been found in Neolithic sites in Germany, Switzerland, Austria and Romania. Hemp was known as *haenep* in Old English, and by other names across the world: *hashisch* (or *hashish*) in Arabia, France and parts of Asia and Africa; *bhang, ganja* or *charas* in India; *grifa* in Spain and Mexico; *anascha* in Russia; *kendir* in Tartar; *konop* in Bulgaria and *konope* in Poland; *momea* in Tibet; *kanbun* in Chaldea; *kif* in North Africa; *dawamesk* in Algeria; *liamba* or *maconha* in Brazil; *bust* or *sheera* in Egypt, and *dagga, matakwane* and *nsangu* in South Africa.

The plant's geographic diversity arose because the stems of the male plant were used to make rope and textiles before the development of synthetic fibres. In China hemp is called *ta-ma*, meaning 'great fibre', although early Chinese pharmacopoeias recognised its hallucinogenic possibilities by the first century BC. Hieron, ruler of Syracuse, the Greek city on Sicily, imported hemp from the river valley of the Rhône for use in shipbuilding around 470 BC; a thousand years later François Rabelais's father cultivated hemp for rope-making near Chinon. The plant was known in India for its sedative and hallucinogenic effects by the first century BC. Three varieties of cannabis preparations developed in India: the cheapest and least potent was *bhang*, the drink tested by Bowrey's merchant seamen, prepared from ground leaves, seeds and stems; *ganja*, prepared from the flowers of cultivated female plants, was two or three times as potent; *charas* was pure resin (the equivalent of hashish in the Middle East). Indians used cannabis to cure dysentery, headaches and venereal diseases; but it collected a strong recreational following. Garcia d'Orta (1501–68), who was a Portuguese physician at Goa, published a treatise there in 1563 containing the earliest clinical description of cholera together with an analysis of the effects of hashish, datura and opium.[3] However, hemp in the seventeenth century remained associated by Europeans with the punishment of villainy. 'I have a most unconquerable antipathy to Hemp,' declares a miscreant in Shadwell's play *The Libertine* (1675). 'Hanging is a kind of death I cannot abide.'[4]

A sticky gold resin exuded from the flowers of the female plant contains the chemical compound responsible for cannabis's hallucinogenic and medicinal properties. Botanists believe that this resin serves to protect the plant from heat and drying out during reproduction (resin is not secreted after the fruits have ripened), and the plants with the highest resin content grow in regions such as the Middle East, India and Mexico. Overall the plant contains over 460 known compounds, but only tetrahydrocannabinol (THC) is actively hallucinogenic. In a complex and dose-dependent manner, THC affects the central nervous system, and produces alterations in mood and cognition. THC's effects include dizziness, diminished physical co-ordination, sensations of bodily heaviness, food cravings (particularly for sweets or junk food), accelerated heartbeat, disorientated thought patterns, disturbed memory, distorted temporal and spatial perception, and increased sociability, relaxation or euphoria. In 1990 researchers at the National Institute of Mental Health at Bethesda, Maryland published their discovery of receptors located in the human brain and neural cell lines that are stimulated by THC. These receptors are chiefly located in the cerebral cortex and in the hippocampus, the loci of higher thinking and memory. This discovery raised the suggestion that human bodies produce a version of the compound.

Centuries earlier, in 1678, two Englishwomen in northern Bengal saw a beggar 'pounding some of those intoxicating Leaves, which they had a Fancy to taste, enticed, either by the Colour of the Leaf, which was of a charming Green, or by one of those fantastical Whims, which possess Women some times'. Their servant brought each woman a small glass of *bhang* diluted with sugar and cinnamon. 'They begun to be affected with that mad and comical Drunkenness, which is the infallible Effect of that Potion, then they were taken with a Laughing Fit, and with a Humour of Dancing, and telling Stories, without either Head or Tail, till the Potion had perform'd its Operations.'[5] The French traveller Jean Chardin (1643–1713) thought that cannabis smoked with tobacco was less harmful than *bhang*. The latter was so 'pernicious' to the brain that in India 'none but the Scum of the People drink of it'. Itinerant beggars used it three or four times a day as 'by Virtue of that Drink, they walk more Briskly and Nimbly'. Chardin, whose account of his travels was reprinted in translation in London in 1705 and at Amsterdam in 1711, lived for several years in Persia under the Shah's patronage. He explained that *bhang* was drunk in coffee houses:

> between three and four a-Clock in the Afternoon, you see them full of Men, who seek in that infatuating Liquor some Relief to their Troubles, and some abatement of their Misery; the Use of it becomes Mortal in Time, like that of Opium, especially in the cold Countries, where its mischievous Property sinks the Spirits so much the more; the constant use of it alters their Complexions, and weakeneth wonderfully both the Body and the Head . . . The Habitual Use of the Stuff is also as dangerous as that of Opium; those who have once contracted an Habit of that Drink, being no longer able to live without it, and being so knit to it, that they would die for Want of it.[6]

The discrepancies between Bowrey's and Chardin's accounts of *bhang*—the contrast between the playful tone of the English sailor and the admonitory disapproval of the French jeweller—have persisted ever since.

In the century after Bowrey and Chardin visited Bengal, cannabis became better known among Europeans as a drug consumed by Arabs and Indians either because they were feckless or because they needed some intoxicant to make them oblivious of their privations. According to the Hanoverian surveyor Carsten Niebuhr (1733–1815), who was the sole survivor of the first scientific expedition to Arabia funded by King Frederick V of Denmark in the 1760s,

> the lower people are fond of raising their spirits to a state of intoxication. As they have no strong drink, they, for this purpose, smoke

Haschisch, which is the dried leaves of a sort of hemp. This smoke exalts their courage, and throws them into a state in which delightful visions dance before their imagination. One of our Arabian servants, after smoking Haschisch, met with four soldiers in the street, and attacked the whole party. One of the soldiers gave him a sound beating, and brought him home to us. Notwithstanding this mishap, he would not make himself easy, but still imagined, such was the effect of this intoxicant, that he was a match for any four men.[7]

This cultural perception of cannabis was, however, tentative until the early nineteenth century, when the French occupation successively of Egypt and Algeria increased European knowledge of the drug.

Other widely dispersed plants were known to provide hallucinogenic experiences, including the fly agaric mushroom (*Amanita muscaria*) and datura, and there were popular stimulants such as qat. Such substances had localised importance in cultures across the world, but after opium poppies and hemp plants, coca leaves were historically by far the most important psychoactive substance. The coca plant (*Erythroxylum coca*) is a hardy bush or shrub with golden-green leaves containing a small amount of nicotine and larger amounts of cocaine among its fourteen alkaloids (alkaloids are compounds producing physiological effects in their consumers). It grows to a maximum height of two metres and can be harvested three times a year. Although coca plants thrive in hot, damp sites, such as forest clearings, the most desirable leaves are obtained from drier, hillside localities. The leaves are ready for plucking when they break on being bent, and are then dried in the sun. Coca has grown wild in the Andes Mountains, especially near what are now the states of Colombia and Bolivia, for thousands of years. Archaeological evidence from Ecuador and Chile suggests that chewing coca leaves is a habit of over 2000 years' duration. The local indigenous inhabitants would moisten the leaves in their mouths, and wedge them between their cheek and gums. The alkaloids in the leaves act directly on the central nervous system to alleviate hunger, thirst and weariness. The amount of cocaine alkaloid absorbed in this way is much lower than in pure extracts of the plant. In the thirteenth century AD the Peruvian Incas extolled coca as a sacred plant, handed down by the gods, and burnt it to honour their idols. In 1505 the Italian Amerigo Vespucci (1454–1512), who was a navigator on Spanish voyages to the Caribbean and South America in 1497–8, described encounters with a coca-chewing race:

> They were very brutish in appearance and gesture, and they had their mouths full of the leaves of a green herb, which they continually chewed like beasts, so that they could hardly speak; and each had round his neck two dry gourds, one full of that herb which they had in their mouths, and the other of white flour that appeared to be powdered lime. From time to time they put in the powder with a spindle which they kept wet in the mouth. Then they put stuff from their mouths from both, powdering the herb already in use. They did this with much elaboration; and the thing seemed wonderful, for we could not understand the secret, or with what object they did it.[8]

Vespucci concluded that these people used the herb to avert thirst.

The commodification of coca began with the arrival of the Spanish *conquistadors* in Peru. They used coca to increase the productivity of the workers whom they enslaved to mine silver under punitive conditions at Potosí, at an altitude of nearly 14,000 feet. Spanish imperial silver requirements were crucial to the integration of coca-growing into the local economy. Coca plantations were transferred from Inca ownership to Spaniards, and landowners were permitted to pay their taxes with coca leaves. In 1539 the Bishop of Cuzco imposed a tithe of one tenth of the value of the coca crop in his diocese, which was the centre of coca production and the source of most supplies to Potosí. Spanish missionaries believed that the solace provided by chewing coca leaves was a hindrance to the conversion of natives to Christianity, and in the 1550s the Spanish viceroy tried to limit the acreage under coca cultivation, encouraging the substitution of food crops. The Seville physician Nicolás Monardes (*c*.1510–88) described the coca plant in his *Historia Medicinal de las Cosas*, which was translated from Spanish to Latin in 1574. An 'Englished' version of Monardes's book, entitled *Joyfull Newes out of the Newe Founde Worlde*, was published in London in 1577. By chewing the leaves of coca and tobacco together, they 'make them selves dronke', in the translator's words. 'Surely it is a thyng of great consideration, to see how the Indians are so desirous to bee deprived of their wittes.'[9] Another Spaniard, Father José de Acosta (1540–1600), who was sent as a Jesuit missionary to Peru in 1571, estimated that the annual Peruvian coca traffic was then worth half a million dollars. Indeed the plant was exchanged as currency. The human cost of harvesting coca leaves had already prompted suggestions that the crop should be eliminated, as Acosta described in his *Historia Natural y Moral de las Indas* (1590), which was translated into Italian (1596), French (1597), Dutch (1598), German (1601) and English (1604). Acosta reported that coca imbued the Indians with 'force and courage'. A handful of leaves enabled them to survive for days without meat. Great care was needed in coca cultivation. The harvested crop was lain in long, narrow baskets transported by troops of sheep from the valleys of the Andes. The severity of the climate, and the hardships of the work, killed many coca labourers. There was therefore discussion among the Spaniards 'whether it were more expedient to pull up these trees, or to let them growe, but in the end they remained'.[10]

Coca could not be grown in Europe until the first heated greenhouses were installed in the University of Leiden's botanical gardens in 1709. The gardens' superintendent Herman Boerhaave (1668–1738) had some knowledge of coca, but this was probably derived from published texts, for the first known samples were shipped to Europe by the French botanist Joseph de Jussieu (1704–79) as late as 1750. Coca's properties became better known when the Bolivian city of La Paz was besieged during an Indian uprising in 1781. The garrison subsisted upon coca after other provisions were exhausted and thus demonstrated the plant's nutritive and supportive powers. In 1787 the Jesuit Antonio Julián (b. 1722) suggested that coca be used to protect Europe's poor against hunger and thirst, and to support 'working people . . . in their long-continued labours'.[11] In a treatise of 1793 Pedro Nolasco similarly urged the supply of coca leaves to European seamen both to strengthen their labours and as a substitute for alcohol. Cocaine, the psychoactive alkaloid in coca leaves, was not identified until the 1860s.

Despite the global prevalence of cannabis and the ultimately dispersed use of coca, the pre-eminent place in any history of drugs must be assigned to opium. The use of this drug in early modern Europe provides the beginning of a historical continuum from which most of the world's drug attitudes and experiences derive. Opium was probably the first drug discovered by early man. Certainly its use must antedate alcoholic spirits, which require knowledge of distillation in production: by contrast opium is obtainable from poppies by a simpler process of harvesting and preparation. The drug deserves specially detailed consideration.

Although there are twenty-eight genera of the poppy, and many more individual species, opium is associated with *Papaver somniferum*. This Latin name, meaning sleep-inducing poppy, is its botanical classification, which was coined as recently as 1753 by the Swedish botanist Carl von Linné (1707–78), better known as Linnaeus. Although most poppies produce milky juice, and contain compounds called alkaloids, which may produce pronounced physiological effects when consumed by humans or animals, only this species (with one other close relation in the poppy family) contains the alkaloid morphine. It is morphine that gives *Papaver somniferum* its special powers, which were recognised thousands of years before the alkaloid itself was isolated from raw opium in 1804. Jean Chardin described the harvesting of opium poppies in seventeenth-century Persia:

> tho' there are Plenty of *Poppies* in other Countries, yet they have in no other Place so much Juice, and so strong, as they have here. This Plant is four Foot high, its Leaves very white, it is ripe in the Month of *June*, and they then extract the Juice from it; they slice it in the Head, and the *Persians* by way of Superstition, always make twelve Slices of it, in Memory of the twelve *Imams*, three Incissions one just by another, all at one time, with a little Bill, that has three Edges, like the Teeth of a Comb. There comes out of it a kind of viscuous or thick Juice, which they gather together at the dawn of Day, before the Sun appears; and this is so strong, that the People who gather it together seem like dead People, taken up out of their Graves, being livid, meagre and trembling as if they had the Palsie.[12]

Although opium poppies are usually white, they may be crimson, pink, pale purple or variegated. The exuded juice that is obtained by incising the poppies' pods resembles milky-white drops, but coagulates and turns brown on exposure to the air. Raw opium is sun-dried for several days, and when the water content has evaporated, the residual sticky, malleable, dark-brown solid is moulded into lumps, cakes or bricks. In this form it can be stored for several months. Raw opium must undergo further processing before it can be consumed. It is cooked in boiling water, sieved to remove impurities, boiled again, and reduced until it is a clean brown fluid. This liquid opium (as it is called) is then slowly simmered until it becomes a thick brown paste called 'cooked', 'prepared' or 'smoking' opium. Cooked opium is dried in the sun until it acquires the consistency of dense modelling clay: it is much purer than raw opium.

One can only guess at the early history of *Papaver somniferum*. Knowledge of its properties may have originated in Egypt, the Balkans or the Black Sea. It was apparently first domesticated about 8000 years ago in the western Mediterranean, but it is impossible to identify all the areas of the world in which it was systematically cultivated. The oldest written language in existence, Sumerian, which was first attested in southern Mesopotamia around 3100 BC, contained an ideogram denoting the opium poppy as 'the plant of joy'.[13] The ethnologist Richard Rudgley (b. 1961) has suggested that at about the same time opium infusions were introduced to Egypt from Bronze Age Cyprus for medical use and for obtaining mind-altering effects in ceremonies (possibly also as an aphrodisiac). In a papyrus of 1552 BC Theban physicians were advised on the use of opium in about 700 different concoctions, including one for sedating troublesome children. Arab traders introduced opium to Persia, India, China, North Africa and Spain. Homer recounted in the *Odyssey* how when Telemachus was entertained by Menelaus, king of Sparta, in the thirteenth or twelfth century BC, and memories of the dead warriors of the Trojan war made the company weep, Menelaus's wife Helen intervened. 'Into the bowl in which their wine was mixed, she slipped a drug that had the power of robbing grief and anger of their sting and banishing all painful memories. No one who had swallowed this dissolved in wine could shed a single tear that day, even for the death of his mother and father, or if they put his brother or his own son to the sword and he was there to see it done.'[14] Helen's nepenthe, which obliterated grief and anxiety, was probably a solution of opium in alcohol.

Arab, Greek and Roman physicians were familiar with the dangers of opium poisoning. Nicander of Colophon in the second century BC described the unconsciousness of someone who had drunk too deeply of opiate concoctions: 'Their eyes do not open but are bound quite motionless by their eyelids. With the exhaustion an odorous sweat bathes all the body, turns cheeks pale, and causes the lips to swell; the bonds of the jaw are relaxed, and through the throat the laboured breath passes faint and chill. And often either the livid nail or wrinkled nostril is a harbinger of death.' Nicander recommended speedy treatment for someone in such a coma: 'Forthwith rouse him with slaps on either cheek, or else by shouting, or again by shaking him as he sleeps, in order that the swooning man may dispel the fatal drowsiness.'[15] The fatal possibilities of opiates dissolved in drink were well known to malefactors too. The Roman emperor Nero used opiates to kill Britannicus, whose throne he usurped in AD 55.

Early Egyptian texts recorded the use of opium to alleviate the pain of wounds and abscesses, and Pliny the Elder (AD 23?–79) stated that the Romans used opium to treat elephantiasis, carbuncles, liver complaints, epilepsy and scorpion bites. The writings of Galen (AD 130–c.200), the Greek who was the most distinguished physician of antiquity after Hippocrates, describe the opium use of the Roman emperor Marcus Aurelius (AD 121–80). Marcus Aurelius, whose reign Gibbon extolled as 'the period in the history of the world during which the condition of the human race was most happy', was a practising Stoic philosopher but no mere quietist.[16] His *Meditations*, which resonate with the chord of an inexhaustible private serenity, recommended moderation in thought and action: his drug habits reflected this precept. The dosage of the opium-based electuary compounded with dollops of honey was adjusted daily by the imperial physician to satisfy Marcus Aurelius's desire for sleep without compromising his capacity to fulfil his duties as emperor. He was a ruler of strenuous energy whose worst characteristic as a leader—excessive tolerance of other men's vices—was perhaps attributable to the anaesthetised indifference of opiates. Galen reported that the emperor could distinguish the quality of the ingredients in his opiate concoctions, and reduce his consumption when necessary for the execution of his imperial duties. This is not the uncontrolled conduct of someone whose drug use has escalated into addiction requiring increasing dosages.[17]

Opium long served as an ingredient of the four standard general palliatives: mithridatium, theriaca, philonium and diascordium. In the sixteenth century, however, the number of medical recipes using opium began to increase. Physicians and pharmacists devised a host of new opium tinctures that were listed in pharmacopoeias. Philippus Aureolus Theophrastus Bombast von Hohenheim (1490–1540), the German physician who worked under the name of Paracelsus, reputedly coined the word 'laudanum' for his secret remedy, which was one-quarter opium compounded with henbane, crushed pearls and coral, amber, musk and more exotic substances, including (he claimed) derivatives from stag's heart, from a unicorn and from a cow's intestine (called bezoar stone). Given his exaggerated claims for his curative powers, it is apt that one of his names was Bombast. 'Many an old wife or country woman doth often more good with a few known and common garden herbs, than our bombast physicians, with all their prodigious, sumptuous, far-fetched, rare conjectural medicines,' Robert Burton (1577–1640) noted in *The Anatomy of Melancholy* (1621). 'We are careless of that which is near us, and follow that which is afar off, to which we will travel and sail beyond the seas'.[18] By 1660 in England, so the distinguished physician Thomas Willis (1621–75) complained, 'there was a Swarm of Pretenders to Physick; whereof each brags of his own peculiar Laudanum, which they give in every Distemper.' The promiscuity of the quacks' prescriptions was 'pernicious'.[19]

The word 'laudanum' came to be fixed as meaning a solution of opium in alcohol, like Helen of Troy's nepenthe so familiar to all classically educated men. During the sixteenth century, however, classical history's influence on Western people's attitudes to drugs was augmented by a new literary genre. The publication of travellers' tales began raising curiosity among educated people about opium's non-medicinal uses by Islamic peoples. In 1546 a French naturalist, Pierre Belon (1517–64), who had travelled in Asia Minor and Egypt, reported, 'There is no Turk who would not buy opium with his last penny; he carries it on him in war and peace. They eat opium because they think that they thus become more daring and have less fear of the dangers of war. In war-time such quantities are purchased that it is difficult to find any left.'[20] From Belon's time opium was associated with Ottoman warriors, although fatuity and indolence were as often associated with the drug in early English anecdotes.

Cristóbal Acosta (c.1515–c.92), a Spanish physician and surgeon, in 1582 published a treatise on the drugs and medicines of the East Indies, which was translated into Latin and French. Acosta reported that opium was used throughout the East Indies both as medicine and food consumed 'in the way that a worker looks upon his bread'. In Malabar he had known an official, who was scribe to the local king: 'a very wise and lively man, very capable and shrewd, and he consumed five drams daily, which he would do in front of me'. Acosta nevertheless recognised the dangers of opium: it 'has the effect of stupefying the user, or if he uses it carelessly, killing him'. He reported an example of its powers which he had witnessed when returning to Portugal, 'sailing across the sea from the Cape of Good Hope', in a ship with Turkish, Parsee and Arab captives. These prisoners had a hidden stash of opium. 'When they had consumed it all, one of them, a good and wise man, a Turk by appearance, from Aden, told me, since I had charge of the sick and the wretched, that if he did not give them opium, they would not survive two days, and were in danger of dying, through the constant habit they had formed when young of consuming it.' Acosta had no opium, and settled with the Turk that instead the captives would be given draughts of wine that would be increased daily. As a result, all the prisoners survived, 'and in under a month, they did not want the wine, and neither needed nor desired opium'. Acosta had the prurience often characteristic of writers on opium: 'It is also used for sexual purposes,' he explained. 'Although this is repellent, they make so much use of it that it is the most common and familiar remedy for the vile sons of Venus.' He cautioned, however, that 'the stupefying effect of opium renders men impotent if they use it too much': this was 'notorious not only among our medical students but also amongst the Arab, Parsee, Turkish, Corazon, Sundasi, Malayan, Chinese and Malabar doctors'. Acosta observed that imaginative men who took opium to enhance their sexual performance often instead suffered premature ejaculation, because the combination of imagination and opium overheated them. For unimaginative men, though, opium was helpful.

> They are able to complete the act slowly. Since women for the most part do not expel semen like men, so the slower he is, so she is better able to control her own nature, and for this reason, it often happens that they climax together, so for this reason opium-eating is a bonus. And it must be said that although opium with its great coldness slows down and almost closes up the channels along which the genital seed comes from the brain, it is this effect that brings delight to the lovers.[21]

It was not only Spanish and Portuguese traders who brought new perspectives to opium in Europe. Official relations between England and the Ottoman Empire began in the 1580s with the establishment of an English trading organisation known from 1592 as the Levant Company. By 1600 there were English mercantile communities in the cities of Constantinople, Izmir and Aleppo. The Islamic Ottoman Empire was thus one of the earliest non-Christian cultures in which the English established outposts. These pioneers seldom assumed racial or economic superiority: indeed in some cases they praised the population in country districts as more couth than their counterparts among English yokels. They were seldom as hostile to Muslim culture as to Roman Catholicism. English travellers to these outposts began remitting reports of opium during the first decade of the seventeenth century. William Biddulph, preacher to the English merchants at Aleppo after 1600, reported that Turkish men congregated in coffee houses, 'more common than Ale-houses in England', to take 'Opium, which maketh them forget themselves, and talke idle of castles in the air, as though they saw visions, and heard revelations'.[22] The poet George Sandys (1578–1644), recalling his journey from Venice to Constantinople in 1610, found the coffee houses more exotic than an English ale-house: many kept catamites to entrap their customers. 'The Turkes are also incredible takers of Opium . . . carrying it about them both in peace and in warre; which they say expelleth all feare, and maketh them couragious: but I rather thinke giddy headed.'[23] Such tales were popularised by Samuel Purchas (1577?–1626), the vicar of a Thames-side parish who met many seafarers coming to the port of London, and published their stories in two successful books of 1613 and 1619.

Other nationalities produced comparable voyagers' tales. The Italian Pietro Della Valle (1586–1652), who married a Syrian Christian and became a pioneering European explorer of Persia, described opium in 1622. Most Persians ate opium daily 'in such quantity that it is surprising it should not kill them, some eating as much opium as would equal a walnut in size'. They supposed 'it is good for their health, and relieves the spirits, making them forget all care; this it actually does, seeing it possesses a great stupefying quality'.[24] Chardin, the French jeweller who became a favourite of the Shah, gave a similarly authoritative account: 'That drug is pretty well known in our Country to be a Narcotick in the highest Degree, and a true Poison. These *Persians* find it entertains their Fancies with pleasant visions, and a kind of Rapture; those who take it, begin to feel the Effects of it an Hour after; they grow Merry, then swoon away with Laughing, and say, and do afterwards a thousand Extravagant Things, like buffoons and jesters.' Chardin appreciated the need of opium-eaters to repeat and increase their dosage, and their anguish if they tried to renounce their reliance on the drug: 'As little so ever as one Accustoms himself to those Poppy Pills, one must constantly use them, and if one misses taking them but one Day, it is discern'd in one's Face and Body, which is cast into such a languishing State, as would move any one to Pity. It fares a great deal worse with those, in whom is rooted the Habit of taking that Poison, for if they forbear it, they endanger their Lives by it'. Prompted by these fatalities, the Persian government had unsuccessfully tried to discourage the use of opium. 'It is so general a Disease', Chardin concluded, 'that out of ten Persons, you shall not find one clear from that ill Habit.'[25]

The seventeenth century was not only an era of expanding international travel but of important medical discovery. The English physician Thomas Sydenham (1624–89), once called 'the Shakespeare of medicine', made major contributions to the history of narcotics. In the 1650s he had studied at the medical faculty at Montpellier, the capital of Languedoc. Montpellier's physicians specialised in cordials, and reproached their Parisian counterparts for excessive bloodletting and purging; the southern school preferred tonics to heroic measures. Sydenham's reputation rested partly upon his expertise in cordials. His moderate cordials were made of borage, lemon, strawberry, treacle, and syrups of cloves, lemon juice or other substances. Stronger cordials comprised Gascoigne's powder, bezoar, hyacinth, Venice treacle and the like.[26] But crucially, in the 1660s, Sydenham prepared an alcoholic opium tincture that he popularised under the name of laudanum. It is not to be confused with the solid opiate compound upon which Paracelsus had bestowed the same name a century earlier. His formula was two ounces of opium and one ounce of saffron dissolved in a pint of Canary or sherry wine, and mixed with a drachm of cinnamon powder and of cloves powder, before being left in a vapour-bath for two or three days.[27] This medicine had a particular attraction for physicians. As his contemporary Thomas Willis explained, 'whereas an Opiate Pill (which was no less famous for doing hurt than good) was a terrour to some People, a Dose of Liquid Laudanum may be better concealed (if it be necessary, and the Patient averse to it) and when it is poured into other liquor, may go for a Cordial rather than a sleeping Medicin'.[28]

Sydenham was eloquent in extolling laudanum. In his *Medical Observations Concerning the History and the Cure of Acute Diseases* (published in Latin by London printers in 1676, and rapidly reprinted in Amsterdam) he inserted a heartfelt digression during a discussion of dysentery. 'Here I cannot but break out in praise of the great God, the giver of all good things, who hath granted to the human race, as a comfort in their afflictions, no medicine of the value of opium, either in regard to the number of diseases it can control, or its efficiency in extirpating them,' he apostrophised.

> So necessary an instrument is opium in the hand of a skilful man, that medicine would be a cripple without it; and whosoever understands it well, will do more with it alone than he could well hope to do with any single medicine. To know it only as a means of procuring sleep, or of allaying pain, or of checking diarrhoea, is to know it only by halves. Like a Delphic sword, it can be used for many purposes besides. Of cordials, it is the best that has hitherto been discovered in Nature. I had nearly said it was the only one.[29]

With opiates, as with newly discovered drugs of later centuries, fool-hardy prescriptions by physicians aroused patients' physiological dependence. This was partly what Sydenham meant by the 'anomalous accidents' that arose from rash doctoring. He warned of the treacherous nature of opiates and the dangerous contingencies of their use. Excessive drugging was as stupid and futile as surrounding 'a monarch with a body-guard of foreigners'.[30] For this reason, despite his zeal, Sydenham tried to limit his use of laudanum. 'If, after the fever, the strength of the patient was broken, and worn out (and this was commonly the case with hysterical women), I tried to call back the spirits by a small dose of laudanum. This remedy, however, I seldom repeated'.[31]

Meanwhile Thomas Willis, the physician who discovered saccharine diabetes, devised his own alcoholic opium tincture to treat delirium, convulsions, gout, kidney-stones, irregular bowels, vomiting, colic, pleurisy and respiratory disorders. It worked, he thought, by 'defeating some of the animal spirits' in the brain and inducing healthy sleep, 'the most cordial Remedy'.[32] Opium disciplined fevers and disease—'so many are there, and such different cases, wherein, whilst the animal spirits, like wild Horses, run up and down, or leap over their bounds, they ought to be restrained or reduced by Opiates, as with a bridle'— but was inadvisable for use on patients with tuberculosis, ulcered lungs, palsy and apoplexy.[33] Although Sydenham had warned against contingent dangers in the medical use of opium, it was Willis who first articulated—explicitly, repeatedly and emphatically—the perils of indiscriminate use. 'The Angelical face of Opium' was dazzlingly seductive, 'but if you look upon the other side of it . . . it will appear altogether a Devil', he warned. 'There is so much poison in this All-healing Medicin, that we ought not to be by any means secure or confident in the frequent and familiar use of it.' People who had taken 'an excessive or unseasonable Dose of it, have either shortened their lives, or made them ever after troublesom and unhappy by the hurt it hath doth to their principal faculties'. Opium's perils made it all the more deplorable to Willis that in Restoration England there was 'no Empirick, no dull Piss-Doctor, nor any pitiful Barber, but professeth himself a Laudanist'.[34] In mild illnesses 'that Physician is a sneaking Fool that draweth them [opiates] into practice' for it was likely to result in 'destructive Tragedies'.[35] Like Chardin, he warned of users' tendency to rely on increasing doses. 'There was a woman who was persuaded by her doctor to take one or two grains of London laudanum every other night,' he told Oxford medical students. 'Finding relief from it she continued to employ this remedy and gradually increased the dose, a grain at a time, till she reached twelve grains. For nature, accustomed to the remedy, refuses to yield to a smaller amount; and the patient could not bring on sleep or feel any relief if a smaller dose was substituted.'[36]

Other researchers investigated opium in the seventeenth century. Sir Christopher Wren (1632–1723) and Robert Boyle (1627–91) in 1656 experimentally injected opium into dogs using a hollow quill attached to a bulb. In 1664 Samuel Pepys (1633–1703) attended 'an experiment of killing a dogg by letting opium into his hind leg'.[37] German researchers, Johann Daniel Major (1634–93) and Johann Sigismund Elsholtz (1623–88), also experimented with canine opium injections, but like their English counterparts they were more interested in techniques of application than in the pharmacology of opium. Despite these seventeenth-century trials, the administration to humans of opiates by injections under the skin was not mastered until the 1840s. Daniel Ludwig (1625–80), who as court physician to the Duke of Saxe-Gotha made a special study of the volatility of salts, obtained a medicinal substance by dissolving opium in an acid and then saturating the solution with an alkali. It has been suggested that the resulting 'Magisterium Opii', as Ludwig named it, was identical to the substance rediscovered in 1804–6, and known thereafter as morphine.[38] Further experimental work on opium was undertaken by William Courten (1642–1702) at Montpellier, Johann Gottfried Berger (1659–1736) at Wittenberg, Abraham Kaau Boerhaave (1715–98) at The Hague, and at Göttingen by Albrecht von Haller (1708–77) and Johann Adrian Theodor Sproegel (1728–1807). Among Sydenham's French contemporaries the royal physician-pharmacist Moses Charas (1619–98) compiled his *Pharmacopée Royale* containing several opium recipes. Nicholas Lémery (1645–1715), author of the *Dictionaire ou traité universel des drogues simples*, also published a recipe for opium in his textbook, which was published in English as *A Course of Chymistry* in 1677.[39] Pierre Pomet (1658–99), Louis XIV's chief druggist, described opium in his textbook of 1695, which was translated into English as *A Compleat History of Drugs* (1712). 'It composes the Hurry of the Spirits, causes Rest and Insensibility, is comforting and refreshing in Great Watchings and strong Pains; provokes Sweat powerfully; helps most Diseases of the Breast and Lungs; as Coughs, Colds, Catarrhs, and Hoarseness; prevents or allays spitting of Blood, vomiting, and all Lasks of the Bowels; is specifical in Colick, Pleurisies and hysterick Cases.'[40] To judge from the warnings of Lémery, more widespread and ambitious use of narcotics in France as in England meant that physiological dependence was raised in an increasing number of patients.[41]

Opiates aside, there was continuous business in drugs and potions purporting to alleviate or cure the experience of being human. 'Every city, town, almost every private man hath his own mixtures, compositions, receipts [recipes],' Robert Burton wrote in 1621 of the pharmaceutical cures of melancholy.[42] The English playwright Aphra Behn (1640–89) satirised the naïvety of people who hoped to find a drug that was a panacea for human existence.

Behold this little Viol, which contains in its narrow Bounds what the whole Universe cannot purchase, if sold to its true Value; this admirable, this miraculous Elixir, drawn from the Hearts of Mandrakes, Phenix Livers, and Tongues of Maremaids, and distill'd by contracted Sunbeams, has besides the unknown Virtue of curing all Distempers both of Mind and Body, that divine one of animating the Heart of Man to that Degree, that, however remiss, cold, and cowardly by Nature, He shall become Vigorous and Brave.[43]

Behn knew men's supreme wishes: immorality, and (like Christóbal Acosta's East Indian opium-eaters) a pounding sexual drive (which is what 'vigorous and brave' meant).

This desire for pharmaceutical improvement of the human experience occurred at a time of great changes in the mentalities of educated western Europeans. These changes were crucial in the making of what later came to be described as addiction. A few members of the prosperous European classes were becoming more susceptible to the attractions of mind-altering substances. Human character did not suddenly become depraved; but among some of Sydenham's seventeenth-century contemporaries there arose a new mentality that was to have increasing influence over human attitudes to hallicinatory, stimulating, narcotic and inebriating substances. 'The unexamined life is not worth living,' Socrates had declared at the dawn of the Western tradition; but educated Europeans in the seventeenth century began advancing this self-awareness as an accompaniment to their developing sense of personal identity. In 1599, the lawyer Sir John Davies (1569–1626) wrote a long poem on the subject of self-knowledge and the soul. His 'Nosce teipsum', which means 'Know thyself', marks the beginning of a process that became central to the increasing use of psychoactive drugs. Early in the poem Davies asked,

For how may we to others' things attaine,
When none of us his owne soule understands?
For which the Divill mockes our curious braine,
When, 'Know thy selfe' his oracle commands.

Davies's view of selfhood suited an age of exploration. It seemed intolerable to learn about the material world while remaining ignorant about the inner:

> *All things without, which round about we see,*
> *We seeke to knowe, and how therewith to doe:*
> *But that whereby we reason, live and be,*
> *Within our selves, we strangers are thereto.*

One couplet resembles a declaration of resolve for modern humankind:

> *My selfe am center of my circling thought*
> *Onely my selfe I studie, learne and know.*[44]

There is no self-pity in Davies, but plenty in his ideas that would draw the self-pitying of future generations into destructive courses with drugs.

A line of poetry written in 1684 by Thomas Traherne (1637–74)—'A secret self I had enclos'd within'—is recorded by the *Oxford English Dictionary* as the first occasion in which the word 'self' took its modern meaning of 'a permanent subject of successive and varying states of consciousness'. The more complex introspective temper gathering force in the seventeenth century—foreshadowed in the poetic ideas of Sir John Davies—can be traced in the advancing vocabulary of the age. The *OED*'s earliest dates of usage for new English words are highly suggestive: self-knowledge (1613), self-denial (1640), self-fearing (1646), self-examination (1647), self-destructive (1654), self-contradiction (1658) and self-conscious (1687). Many of these words bore negative connotations: they indicated a failure to control selfhood or selfishness. Awareness of personal singularity (often accompanied by emotional caprices) spread among Europe's leisured classes. 'Learn, Madam, that the greatest cruelty is to torment ones self,' the French essayist Seigneur de Saint-Evremond (1613–1703) advised a self-indulgently unhappy duchess in 1683.[45] This high valuation of personal consciousness—self-absorption is perhaps a truer description—reached its apogee in the twentieth century. It is exemplified by the protagonist of M. Ageyev's *Novel with Cocaine*—an ambitious, self-destructive student living in Moscow *circa* 1917. 'During the long nights and long days I spent under the influence of cocaine ... I came to see that what counts in life is not the events that surround one, but the reflections of those events in one's consciousness.' Ageyev's cocainist is the solipsistic culmination of the injunction to know your Self. 'All of a man's life—his work, his deeds, his will, his physical and mental prowess—is completely and utterly devoted to, fixed on bringing about one or another event in the external world, though not so much to experience the event in itself as to experience the reflection of the event on his consciousness.'[46]

This late seventeenth-century preoccupation with altered human consciousness was exemplified by John Locke (1632–1704) in his influential *Essay Concerning Human Understanding* (1690). Locke argued that the human mind had no innate principles, but rather was as blank as paper or as malleable as wax, to be inscribed or moulded by experience. 'If a Child were kept in a place, where he never saw any other but Black and White, till he were a Man, he would have no more *Ideas* of Scarlet or Green, than he that from his Childhood never tasted an Oyster, or a Pine-Apple, has of those particular Relishes.'[47] The use of experience by intelligent people comprised their true education, and could enable them to settle the rules by which they lived. Individuals could improve or re-invent themselves by cultivating their awareness rather than pursuing self-knowledge or exploring their inner being. 'If we were to take wholly away all Consciousness of our Actions and Sensations, especially of Pleasure and Pain,' Locke declared, 'it will be hard to know wherein to place personal Identity.'[48] As he declared, '*Self* is not determined by Identity ... which it cannot be sure of, but only by identity of consciousness.'[49] Not until the nineteenth century did speculative curiosity about human consciousness tempt Europeans to experiment with mind-altering substances; but Locke's ideas provide one starting point for the historical continuum that led Balzac to test the possibilities of cannabis, Freud those of cocaine, Auden of amphetamines and Huxley of mescaline. Similarly the introspection of Davies's 'Nosce teipsum', which had been so swiftly vulgarised into the moody self-absorption of Saint-Evremond's duchess, had huge implications for the imaginative life, personal affections and inward hopes of Europeans and Americans. It was in the nineteenth century that these began to have extensive consequences for the history of drug use.

Narcotics, though, in the Age of Reason retained their privileged position in European culture. Opiates continued both to diminish human ills and to augment them: laudanum alleviated sickness, and caused it. Medicines, in short, corrupted as they cured.

TWO

Opium during
the Enlightenment

Cur'd yesterday of my Disease
I died last night of my Physician.
—MATTHEW PRIOR

It banishes melancholy, begets confidence, converts fear into boldness,
makes the silent eloquent, and dastards brave. Nobody, in desperate
circumstances, and sinking under a disrelish for life, ever laid violent hands
on himself after taking a dose of opium, or ever will.
—JOHN BROWN

A NEW PHASE IN the history of opiates was opened in 1700 by the publication by the Welsh physician John Jones (1645–1709) of his medical treatise entitled *Mysteries of Opium Reveal'd*. Sydenham and Willis had written in Latin as a way of reserving their expertise for their professional colleagues, but Jones wrote in vivid English prose, at a time when medical guides were being issued with commercial appeal to the reading public. *Mysteries of Opium Reveal'd* was intended to promote the use of the drug, and to share Jones's zealously collected expertise. His summary of attitudes at the beginning of the eighteenth century in many ways held good throughout that century. This was a period when the rejection of classical Graeco-Roman medicine was leading to more experimentation, and less caution by some experimenters.

The galenes prescribed by such ancient physicians as Andromachus or Galen had been thought to work by raising the patients' spirits. This principle of galenes resembled the theory of opiate remedies propounded by Jones: 'Pain is often taken away by Opium by the Diversion and Relaxation caused by Pleasure, and its Inconsistencies with Pain.'[1] His enthusiasm for opium was that of a user with a stable or controlled intake: 'It Prevents and takes away Grief, Fear, Anxieties, Peevishness, Fretfulness,' he averred. The drug made 'millions' of its consumers 'at the same time more serene, and apt for the Management of Business, and near Dispatch of Affairs'.[2] Like drug promoters in other ages Jones attributed aphrodisiac powers to his preferred substance. He assured his readers that opium 'causes a great Promptitude to Venery, Erections &c', which was why 'the Infidels of Turky, and the Eastern Nations (especially where Polygamy is allow'd) use Opium so much'. This was 'notorious in all (or most) Countries from Greece to Japan inclusively'. Jones confided that 'several Merchants, Factors and Travellers, now living in London, can attest . . . the same, upon Experience in their own Bodies . . . whose Words I do not repeat, partly for Modesty's, partly for Brevity's sake'.[3] More prosaically, Jones recommended opium for gout, dropsy, catarrh, asthma, dysentery, cholera, measles, smallpox, colic and other ailments. He reported that it reduced or stopped vomiting, hiccoughs, convulsions and contractions (including in childbirth), moderated hunger, alleviated menstruation pains, prevented some haemorrhages, and induced 'Growth of the Breast, Penis, and increase of Milk', 'Venereal Dreams' and 'Nocturnal Pollutions'.[4] He was puzzled by the contradictions inherent in his wonder-drug: 'It stupifies the Sense of Feeling, yet irritates that Sense to Venery'; 'It causes Stupidity, and Promptitude in Business; Cloudiness, and Serenity of Mind'; 'It causes a furious Madness, yet composes the Spirits above all things'. Although it 'raises very weak People (when nothing besides will do it) yet it kills other weak People'.[5]

Jones did not shirk the destructive possibilities of opium. He described, too, 'the Effects of a long, and lavish Use of Crude Opium' as 'a dull, moapish, and heavy Disposition (as in old Drunkards) except it be during the Operation of Opium'.[6] He believed—or desired to believe—in the possibility of using the drug (as Marcus Aurelius had done) to arouse sensations of well-being without increasing dosages. Human vice he blamed for the misfortunes associated with opium: 'There is nothing so good, whereof an intemperate Use is not mischievous, God having so ordered it to deter from, and punish Intemperance . . . Therefore ill Effects are not always to be imputed to the viciousness of the Things used, but frequently of the Person that imprudently uses them.'[7] His account of withdrawal symptoms was realistically unattractive: 'Great, and even intolerable Distresses, Anxieties and Depressions of Spirits, which in few days commonly end in a most miserable Death, attended with strange Agonies, unless Men return to the use of Opium; which soon raises them again.' His advice for those trying to withdraw from dependency recalled Cristóbal Acosta's account of weaning Turkish and Arabian captives from opium by making them drink wine for a month: 'If they have not Opium, or will not take it, they must use Wine very plentifully, and often, as a substitute to the Opium, tho' it does not perform half as well.'[8]

The opium used by Jones and his medical colleagues was not cultivated in Europe. As the Irish physician Samuel Crumpe (1766–96) explained, it was 'generally imported from Persia, Egypt, Smyrna and other parts of the Levant, in cakes of from four ounces to a pound weight; which are sometimes covered with the dried leaves of the poppy'. The opium 'when cut, appears of a dark brown colour; when reduced to powder, of a yellowish brown'. Crumpe found 'its smell is peculiar, faint and disagreeable; and its taste bitter, pungent and acrimonious'.[9] Turkish opium was prepared with 'rich syrups and juices, to render it palatable and less intoxicating', according to James Dallaway (1763–1834), the English physician at Constantinople in the 1790s. 'It is either taken with a spoon, or hardened into small lozenges, stamped with the words, "Mash allàh", literally, "the work of God".'[10] Little if any Indian opium reached the British Isles, although some opium may have been remitted to other European powers, such as Portugal and the Netherlands, from their Asiatic possessions. The export of Indian opium to China by European merchants was, however, already lucrative in the eighteenth century.

Earlier, in 1557, the Chinese had permitted Portuguese traders to establish an outpost at Macao, on the western side of the estuary of the Canton river, some thirty-five miles from Hong Kong. From Macao in the early seventeenth century the Portuguese began selling the Chinese small quantities of opium cultivated in their settlement at Goa, on the western coast of India. This was the first non-Arabic opium imported by the Chinese, who knew the drug as a medicine. Gradually, during the seventeenth century, opium became a significant trading commodity in the Far East. Around 1610, the Dutch established trading settlements on Java from which recreational opium-smoking seems to have spread. A visitor to the island in 1689 saw primitive smoking dens where the drug was being smoked with tobacco. The opium habit also became established on the Chinese island of Formosa (now Taiwan), where the Dutch established a brief suzerainty in the mid-seventeenth century. Some of the Chinese colonists who supplanted the Dutch became recreational opium-smokers, and spread the habit in the coastal Chinese province of Fukien.

Portuguese ships began regularly carrying chests of Indian opium through Macao into China around 1700. Subsequently the English used Penang in the Malacca Straits as an outlet for Indian opium. Although consumption of the drug remained localised in the southern Chinese coastal provinces, its association with foreign traders (more than its destructive properties) provoked the Peking government to issue the first edict against opium in 1729. Under this edict, dealers and keepers of opium shops were to be strangled. Intermediaries were liable to a hundred blows with a bamboo cane, and were then confined for days or weeks either with a heavy wooden yoke encircling their necks, or in a sort of caged pillory in which they often died; survivors were then banished a thousand miles from home. All those implicated in opium-trafficking—from boatmen, bailiffs and soldiers to corrupt customs officers and complacent magistrates—were subject to punishment. The Peking authorities did not scruple to exploit the opium trade despite their prohibitions and penalties: they imposed an import duty in 1753. In the eighteenth century the habit was not an obtrusive international issue. It certainly did not seem important to Sir George Staunton (1781–1859), the child prodigy who was the only Chinese-speaking member of the British diplomatic mission to Peking in 1792. Staunton barely mentions opium in his memoirs and essays on China, although he opposed the traffic in later life.

Queen Elizabeth I had in 1600 granted a monopoly to the East India Company of trade with lands beyond the Cape of Good Hope and Magellan Straits which was controlled by a Court of Directors in London. These directors, several of whom enjoyed intimate relations with British political leaders, permitted the supply of opium from territories under their control. However, in 1733 they prohibited their ships from carrying the commodity, which they judged was contraband in China as a result of the edict of 1729. Despite this prohibition, the total annual opium trade between India and China was by 1760 reckoned at about 1000 chests. This trade was chiefly derived from the ancient city of Patna, the rich commercial centre of Bihar. Opium made from the poppies cultivated in the surrounding area was highly esteemed for smoking. In 1756 a dispute arose between the English factory near Calcutta and the Nawab of Bengal. Robert Clive (1725–74), commanding a small military force, waged a brilliant campaign in Bengal that proved the foundation of British power in India. In 1763 Clive's forces took Patna, which was held for the East India Company. The company swiftly asserted its monopoly of the opium trade, excluding native, Dutch and French merchants who had previously been able to buy from poppy-cultivators in competition with the British. After 1763, the company's servants at Patna recognised China's 300 million inhabitants as a huge potential market and developed their own remunerative opium businesses. However, to comply with the London directors' interdiction against contraband, they sold the drug to private exporters, and had no direct part in smuggling it into China.

As Bengal became entrenched as the first British territorial possession in India, the privileges of the Patna officials were increasingly resented. In 1772 Warren Hastings (1732–1818) was installed as Governor of Bengal with instructions from the East India Company to reform its administration. The following year he transferred the opium trade to a new monopoly. Henceforth, the Bengal government paid advances to peasant cultivators who undertook to sell their products exclusively to the official agency at a fixed price. The raw opium was refined to a standard quality, and each brick was stamped with the company's mark. It was then sold at auction in Calcutta. Hastings never countenanced a free trade in opium: the commodity was subject to sharp price fluctuations and therefore highly speculative; unregulated trade would have disturbed the precarious social balance of Bengal and thus jeopardised the stability that his policies were enforcing. Moreover, Hastings needed to raise revenues for his administration, and no possibility seemed as lucrative as the opium trade. He stated his view clearly: 'Opium is not a necessity of life but a pernicious article of luxury, which ought not to be permitted except for purposes of foreign commerce only, and which the wisdom of the Government should carefully restrain from internal consumption'.[11] In other words, Hastings did not want his Indian subjects poisoned by a drug that, nevertheless, it was expedient to export for revenues. The ban by the London Court of Directors on their vessels smuggling opium did not prevent other ships from carrying Indian opium to China under the British flag. There were incentives for this trade beyond the East India Company's revenue needs. Although Western consumers were eager buyers of Chinese teas and silks, few Chinese had a taste for European products. Silver specie was the main item exchanged by Europeans for teas and silks; but Indian opium provided an additional means of adjusting the trading discrepancy. The opium traffic with China continued despite the London directors reiterating in 1782 that it was 'beneath the company to engage in . . . a clandestine Trade', and prohibiting the export of opium to China on the company's account.[12] The directors considered that their hands were clean; but by the time Hastings left the subcontinent in 1785 opium was yielding half a million pounds annually to their company.

In the previous year responsibility for India had been divided between the Court of Directors and a new ministerial department for East Indian affairs, called the Board of Control, which was charged with superintending and controlling the resolutions of the Court of Directors. Both the directors and government ministers had a pressing need of revenues: the opium monopoly became indispensable to the maintenance of the Indian fiscal system. Hastings' successor as Governor General, the Marquess Cornwallis (1738–1805), found that the poppy-cultivators in Bengal were so exploited that they would only continue production under compulsion. He proposed ending the state monopoly so as to protect these peasants from oppression, but was overruled by William Pitt (1759–1806), the Prime Minister, who argued that the East India Company's prosperity depended on the China trade.[13] Pitt's concern at the amount of silver bullion being used to pay the Chinese for tea ensured that the status quo was preserved. This anxiety about the depletion of British bullion reserves became keener after the outbreak of war with France in 1793.

Chinese consumption of opium gradually shifted in the eighteenth century from *madak* to the more potent *chandu*, which had a higher morphine content. By the 1790s the opium habit had spread northwards and westwards from the southern coastal provinces. It became fashionable among rich youths and then among young clerks and government officials. In response to these trends, an imperial proclamation of 1799 prohibited throughout China the importation or use of opium together with the cultivation of poppies. 'The Celestial Empire', declared an edict directed at foreigners, 'does not forbid you people to make and eat opium, and diffuse the custom in your native place. But that opium should flow into the interior of this country, where vagabonds clandestinely purchase and eat it, and continually become sunk into the most stupid and besotted state . . . is an injury to the manners and minds of men.'[14] The import of opium nevertheless continued to rise, and became an increasing international issue during the nineteenth century.

Back in Britain, pharmacological research had been stimulated by the publication in 1742 of 'A Dissertation on Opium' by Charles Alston (1683–1760), Professor of Botany and Materia Medica at the University of Edinburgh. His work adumbrated three lines of research which were pursued during the next half-century: attempts to establish opium's mode of action; investigation of opium's effects on heart activity and blood circulation; and the identification of effective opium therapies. Alston undermined the existing orthodoxy that opium rarefied the blood by arguing that it acted not on the brain, or the blood, but on the nerves.[15] His theories seemed to be supported by contemporary experimental evidence; but in the nineteenth century it was established that opium was absorbed and conveyed in blood circulation.[16] The Scottish physician John Brown (1735–88) was more influential even than Alston. The purity of his Latin style in his *Elementa Medicinae* (1780) ensured for him an attentive reading abroad, especially in Italy and Germany. His book was translated into English, and published at Philadelphia; there were editions issued at Copenhagen, Milan and elsewhere; the French translation converted Napoleon Bonaparte to the so-called Brunonian system of medicine. His master-stroke was to associate most diseases with debility, and correctly to denounce many of the prevalent lowering techniques of medicine as mistaken. In *Elementa Medicinae* Brown extolled opium as the strongest and most superior stimulant. He taught his medical students in Edinburgh, and argued in print, that laudanum raised patients to the degree of excitability upon which he believed the vital processes depended. (He himself suffered from gout, which he attributed to asthenia—meaning the diminution of vital power—and treated with opium.) His followers administered opium preparations in an attempt to raise the vitality of patients exhibiting debility. Rash prescriptions of opium by Brown and his followers caused a host of those 'anomalous accidents' against which Sydenham had warned: many patients became addicted, and some Brunonians ruined themselves with self-ministrations.

Contrary to Alston and Brown, the physician George Young (1691–1757) argued in his *Treatise on Opium* (1753) that opium's good effects 'depend on its soporific qualities'.[17] Young was a valetudinarian who lavished opium on his own ailments, and habitually used twenty drops of laudanum, taken at bedtime, as a cough suppressant. He attributed his improvement to a restful night's sleep, but one may suspect that his body became wracked with coughs as a pretext justifying his self-dosing with opium. 'I have often had my cough seemingly cured in the morning, by the laudanum which I took the preceding night; but it returned in the afternoon, when the effect of the opium was over: yet opium was still the cure.'[18] Young regretted that 'opium has already got into the hands of every pretender to practice, and is prescribed every day, not only by charitable and well meaning ladies, but even by officious and too ignorant nurses'. This was dangerous because, as he warned, 'opium is a poison by which great numbers are daily destroyed; not, indeed, by such doses as kill suddenly, for that happens very seldom, but by its being given unseasonably'.[19]

Young's treatise was intended as a home manual, which makes his attitude to women all the more pointed. In his representation they were silly and unreliable. As mothers they failed.

> Some children are crammed every day by their fond mothers with varieties of jellies, sweetmeats and preserves. To those, when their digestion is quite spoiled, we often add many stomach boluses and draughts; and all this betwixt their meals, at which they are never stinted. A constant looseness is the usual effect: in which case, if the mother conceals the confects and restoratives from the knowledge of the doctor, he will be too apt to prescribe . . . *laudanum*, when chalk and water, with a spare diet, would be much more proper. Thus the child grows gradually more pale, thin, and lax . . . till some new disease is brought on, or the physician discovers the mismanagement of the mother, and corrects it.[20]

Two centuries later a leading physician, Sir Almroth Wright (1861–1947), declared in 1912:

For man the physiology and psychology of women is full of difficulties. He is not a little mystified when he encounters in her periodically recurring phases of hypersensitiveness, unreasonableness, and loss of the sense of proportion. He is frankly perplexed when confronted with a complete alteration of character in a woman who is child-bearing. When he is a witness of the tendency of woman to morally warp when nervously ill, and of the terrible physical havoc which the pangs of a disappointed love may work, he is appalled. And it leaves on his mind an eerie feeling when he sees serious and long-continued mental disorders developing in connexion with the approaching extinction of a woman's reproductive faculties. No man can close his eyes to these things; but he does not feel at liberty to speak of them.[21]

This medical view of womankind was already clear in Young's representation in the eighteenth century. It is crucial to the history of narcotics. Opium was deployed to regulate women's feelings and to contain their behaviour in patterns that male physicians would understand. Young regarded his women patients, in another phrase of Wright's, as 'always threatened with danger from the reverberation of her physiological emergencies'. A typical case study catches his attitude:

> One Mrs.——, that was weakly, with a very delicate habit, a low, sunk pulse, cold extremities, and a desponding mind, received more benefit from opium alone than I could well believe: it not only suspended her menstrual flooding, but all her fears and gloomy ideas. All her friends advised her to lay aside the use of opium, lest it should by habit become necessary, but she whispered privately, that she would rather lay aside her friends.

She continued to take opium until some months into her pregnancy. 'Now she keeps it by her for a day of distress, i.e. desponding fits'.[22] For menstruation Young recommended laudanum drops: nothing could rival opium when 'the nerves [were] unstrung, the heart beating for fear of they know not what, the mind presaging and apprehending everything that is bad'.[23] Young treated the nausea of pregnant women as 'a nervous disease', for which he prescribed 'five drops of liquid laudanum frequently in mint or cinnamon-water, or in claret boiled with spices . . . yet in a more advanced state of pregnancy I think opium is improper'.[24] As to hysteria, Young administered 'four grams of opium to a gentlewoman who lost the use of her reason on a sudden, by the barbarous treatment of her husband, and she was cured by that single dose'.[25]

'Vapours'—described by the fashionable Bath physician George Cheyne (1671–1743) as 'Hysterical and Hypochondriacal Disorders'—were mostly associated with women. According to Cheyne in his classic study *The English Malady* (1733), the most troublesome symptoms of this illness were restlessness, moodiness and insomnia. Some patients with vapours could take opiates with little harm. 'There are others, to whom they give a little dozing or dead Sleep, yet when their Force is worn off, they leave a Lowness, Disspiritedness, and Anxiety, that even over-balances the Relief of Quiet they bring.' Recourse to laudanum or opiates, therefore, should be limited to 'extreme Cases' and never be continued 'longer than absolute Necessity requires'. Opiates ought always to be blended with aromatic medicines which 'possibly may hinder their destructive Effects'.[26] However, patients who used opiates to treat physical illness discovered that they abated emotional pain. In 1787 the Duchess of Devonshire (1757–1806) had an attack of stomach cramp after eating oysters, 'but proper care & two slight doses of laudanum removed it'.[27] This was harmless, but she resorted to opiates as sedatives, too. 'For God's sake try to compose yourself,' implored her mother at a time when the duchess was 'distress'd and agitated' by her amours. 'I am terrified lest the perpetual hurry of your spirits, and the medicines you take, to obtain a false tranquillity, should injure you.'[28]

Opium was an acknowledged means of alleviating the suffering of dying patients. 'I am sometimes gloomy,' Samuel Johnson (1709–84) confided shortly before his death, but small doses of opium were 'useful' in improving his mood.[29] 'A dying man can do nothing easy,' said Benjamin Franklin (1706–90), whose excruciating pains from gout, stone and respiratory failure were eased by opium in his final years.[30] The role of opium among the terminally ill interested Young. He suspected that opium made his cancer patients 'die sooner than they would have done without it'. This may have been a relief; but he was unimpressed by the effects of opium on patients with advanced tuberculosis.

The people of rank, who must have something prescribed for every ailment, and believe that we have a cure for every symptom, grow impatient if the physician does not abate their cough, and give them some rest for the night. Opium, and nothing but opium, will do this: they take it in many different shapes, and find it of service in making them cough less and sleep more; therefore they continue it, become slaves to it, and must have the dose gradually increased. They moan and struggle under its influence all night, and in the day-time have their heads confused. In their last ... days, they are struggling for breath, their memory fails, and they are half delirious, and attended with a constant diarrhoea ... The poor man, without opium, sinks into the grave with ease both of mind and body, if compared with those splendid persons, who commonly die delirious.[31]

Young's patients were typical in requesting specific drugs from their physician, and in trying to settle with him the doses they desired. Not only was self-medication common; but gullible or overwrought individuals continued to seek human perfectibility from pharmaceutical technology. Paracelsus, among others, had boasted of a universal panacea that would indefinitely prolong life. Francis Bacon (1561–1626) claimed that by mixing myrrh with human blood he discovered the secret of immortality. As an accompaniment to their newly refined sense of Self, Europeans from the late seventeenth century began trying to tune their characters, or to extend their longevity, as if they were machines that might be improved by adjustments and oils. This was part of the recurrent tendency to pathologise the human condition: 'Life is an incurable disease,' as Abraham Cowley (1618–67) had declared in 1656.[32] In the eighteenth century there were innumerable quacks peddling nostrums which purported to transform human nature; they were the Age of Reason's equivalent of New Age gurus and herbalists of the late twentieth century, although they sometimes displayed the marketing ruthlessness of latter-day drug barons. The soi-disant Chevalier d'Ailhoud, for example, made a fortune peddling what he claimed guaranteed immortality. It contained several drugs that poisoned the health of his dupes. The soi-disant Count Cagliostro claimed to be 200 years old as the result of drinking his cordial, 'The Balm of Life'.[33] Such despicable impostures encouraged physicians' preference for relying on their own experience rather than adopting new pharmacological ideas. The investigations of alchemists also stimulated quackery. Urine, for example, had long fascinated alchemists because of its golden colour and its formation of symmetrical crystals of micro-cosmic salt. In 1669 a Hamburg alchemist, by heating fermented urine for several months, first isolated phosphorus. Half a century later, in 1719, the discovery of phosphorus in brain tissue provided a new opportunity for European quacks. The element's association with both the genitals and the brain resulted in its promotion as an aphrodisiac and tonic by pharmacists and mountebanks—sometimes in poisonous quantities.[34]

As few medicines at this time could do more than alleviate symptoms or reduce pain, there was an understandable hankering that dosages might be increased with impunity. Alston expected that by 'customary use' Europeans would acquire a higher tolerance of opium.[35] Young was similarly optimistic that 'if a long and confirmed habit of taking opium can divest it of its narcotic quality, it will probably be found a valuable drug'.[36] Yet at the end of the eighteenth century there was no system for assessing any drug's effects on human temperament. There was indeed no agreement whether opium was a stimulant, a depressant or a hallucinogenic: as late as 1843 a prominent English toxicologist advised that 'a judicious and well-directed narcotic', which restores the body by giving healthy sleep, 'may be correctly considered as a stimulant'.[37] However, expert controversies in the eighteenth century mattered less to the reputation of opium than practical experience among the laity. Opiates were becoming more widely used and more widely mistrusted by educated people. In the 1780s, when the fashionable poet Anna Seward (1742–1809) wrote her 'Sonnet To The Poppy', opiates were seen as snares for the vulnerable:

> So stands in the long grass a love-crazed maid,
> Smiling aghast; while stream to every wind
> Her garish ribbons, smeared with dust and rain;
> But brain-sick visions cheat her tortured mind,
> And bring false peace. Thus, lulling grief and pain,
> Kind dreams oblivious from thy juice proceed,
> Thou flimsy, showy, melancholy weed.[38]

Despite the enthusiasm of Jones and the Brunonians, opium-users were not reputed for their universal brilliance. When Sir Robert God-schall (1692–1742), the Lord Mayor of London, presented a petition to the House of Commons, Horace Walpole (1717–97) commented that his speech was 'so dull, one would think he chewed opium'.[39] Other orators, however, resorted to opium more successfully. The great criminal defence lawyer Thomas Erskine (1750–1823) habitually prepared for special efforts in court by taking an 'opium-pellet'.[40] Opium tranquillised his nerves, enabling him to reach his highest powers as an advocate without stumbling through nervousness. He may have regarded the pellets as stimulants, but their use ruined him neither professionally nor personally, for in 1806 he was appointed to the highest legal office, that of Lord Chancellor, with a peerage. The pellets may, however, have contributed to Erskine's notorious self-absorption. Byron's verdict on him still stands: 'the most brilliant person imaginable;—quick, vivacious, and sparkling, he spoke so well that I never felt tired of listening to him, even when he abandoned himself to the subject of which all his dear friends expressed themselves so much fatigued—*self*'.[41]

The lives and deaths of opium-users told varied stories. Its use could destroy the promise and allure of the young. 'I am very sorry for the state of poor Lady Beauchamp,' Horace Walpole wrote of a gloriously rich heiress (recently married to the son of a powerful marquis) a few months before her death in 1772 aged twenty-two. 'Opium is a very false friend.'[42] Samuel Johnson similarly regarded the drug as a useful servant but a dangerous master: he once appeased 'a very troublesome cough' with opium 'in larger quantities than I like to take'.[43] Opium concoctions were used to ease travel-sickness. Jane Austen's mother, a clergyman's wife suffering 'from the exercise and fatigue of traveling', was comforted by a pharmacist who recommended twelve drops of laudanum at bedtime.[44] Restless little children were dosed with it during wearisome journeys in confined coaches. The Earl of Bessborough (1758–1844), preparing in 1793 for a journey to Naples, packed a medicine chest including laudanum to pacify his six-year-old son who accompanied him.[45] Little harm from opium befell the boy, who after a long parliamentary career was created Baron de Mauley.

William Wilberforce (1759–1833), the philanthropic politician who campaigned against slave-trading, in 1788 suffered such agonising intestinal pains and digestive breakdown that his friends despaired of his survival. After a physician, with the utmost difficulty, convinced him to take small doses of opium, he recovered, but for the remaining forty-

five years of his life the drug remained indispensable to him. He feared
that if he abandoned opium, he would relapse into intestinal troubles;
but stomach pains perhaps provided him with an excuse for his habit.
Once, when asked why his fingers were so black, Wilberforce explained
that it was from taking opium before making a long speech: 'To that',
he said, 'I owe all my success as a public speaker.'[46] He was too sane and
fulfilled in his work to submit to the urge for increased dosages, but
though he was never broken by his habit, he was untruthful about it.
'If I take but a single glass of wine', he claimed, 'I can feel its effects,
but I never know when I have taken my dose of opium by my feelings.'[47] This is hard to believe.

Though Wilberforce's opium habit was never used to besmirch him,
that of Robert Clive, afterwards Lord Clive of Plassey, whose military
prowess and political ruthlessness entrenched the East India Company's
power, has been used to denigrate him by those who have deplored the
consequences of his work. In 1752 Clive fell ill with severe spasms of
abdominal pain, accompanied by acute biliousness; he suffered from
gallstones exacerbated by chronic malaria. These abdominal attacks,
which continued through his life, often had bouts of nervous prostration as their sequel. He was given opium to kill the pain of the gallstones, and resorted to the drug when depressed, but does not seem to
have taken it constantly, in escalating doses, like an outright addict. He
died during a terrible recurrence of illness in 1774. Having taken a
purge for constipation, his pain returned with such violence that in a
paroxysm of agony he thrust his penknife into his throat.[48] Rumours
immediately began circulating that his death was an opium fatality; as
recently as 1968 a distinguished historian wrongly described him as
having died of an overdose, taken deliberately or in error, as the result
of the depression that both caused and resulted from his 'addiction'.[49]
The thought of opium was secretly cherished by another great mili-
tarist. In 1758, after the defeat in battle of his army by the Austrians,
King Frederick II of Prussia ('Frederick the Great') (1712–86) confided in an adviser: 'How I detest this trade to which the blind chance
of my birth has condemned me; but I have upon me the means of ending the play, when it becomes unbearable,' he said, opening his tunic to
display a little oval golden box hanging by a ribbon on his chest. It contained eighteen opium pills—'quite sufficient', he said, 'to take me to
that dark bourn whence we do not return'.[50]

These cameos of eighteenth-century drug use all involve the prosperous classes. Perhaps the most significant aspect of opium and the poor is that the drug still had no role in defining European criminality or misconduct. The Amsterdam-born physician and political philosopher Bernard Mandeville (1670–1732), who settled in London and wrote *The Fable of the Bees* (1714), provides evidence on this point. He recognised that the maintenance of civil order depended upon enforcing social definitions. It was not religious leaders who controlled the 'appetites' and subdued the 'dearest inclinations' of mankind, 'but the skilful management of wary politicians'.[51] The politicians' skill lay in docketing people, and then flattering or subjugating them according to their labels. 'Industrious good people, who maintain their families and bring up their children handsomely, pay taxes and are several ways useful members of society' were among 'the political offspring which flattery begot upon pride'.[52] To maintain the social hierarchy, it was necessary to devise a subspecies, or what in the late twentieth century was called an underclass. Politicians, wrote Mandeville, needed to stigmatise some social groups as 'abject, low-minded people that, always hunting after immediate enjoyment, were wholly incapable of self-denial, and without regard to the good of others had no higher aim than their private advantage; such as being enslaved by voluptuousness'. Yet drug-users were not in Mandeville's century incorporated within the politicians' category of human 'dross'.[53] Laudanum was not socially vicious, like gin, in Mandeville's opinion, although he regarded the drug with ambivalence. In his *Treatise of the Hypochondriack and Hysterick Passions* (1711), he depicted its workings as incompletely understood; the reaction of patients to its administration was variable; and it was so seductive that many physicians preferred to discount its attendant perils.

If opium subcultures were invisible or even non-existent in Europe, they were routinely reported in eighteenth-century travellers' tales from the Middle East. These tales continued to be a cultural influence on Western perceptions of opium. Assumptions of cultural superiority were not brutally assertive. The French philosopher Charles-Louis, Baron de Montesquieu (1689–1755), whose fictional correspondence attributed to two well-born Persians visiting Paris and Venice was first published in the Netherlands in 1721, made no facile show of European primacy. In these *Persian Letters*, one of Montesquieu's travellers from the Middle East compared wine with opium. Wine was 'Nature's most fearsome gift to men', the Persian decided. 'If there is anything has discredited the lives and reputations of our monarchs, it is their intemperance, which is the deadliest source of their injustice and cruelty'. Opium seemed preferable. Montesquieu commended 'Orientals' for seeking 'as diligently for remedies against unhappiness as for those against the most dangerous diseases'. The absolute prohibition of alcohol was presented as counterproductive: 'The human mind is contradiction itself: dissolute and licentious, we furiously rebel against the rules; and the Law, designed to make us juster, often does nothing but make us guiltier.'[54]

The decade after the foundation of the Levant Company had seen a proliferation of travellers' tales familiarising readers with the phenomenon of recreational opium use. But eighteenth-century English accounts of the Ottoman Empire were significantly less tolerant of self-destructive opium use than the voyagers of the early seventeenth century. Sir James Porter (d. 1786), for fifteen years British Ambassador at Constantinople, thought the Turks had an inherent depravity that in late twentieth-century jargon would have been termed addictive personality. Despite prohibition, 'the vice of drinking gains ground with the Turks, and imperceptibly creeps from the lower to the higher stations: perhaps in this instance, as in many others, restraint may quicken appetite and enflame desire'. Porter observed that, from religious scruples or fear of discovery, miscreants 'frequently change their wine to opium, which is equally intoxicating, and perhaps attended with worse consequences, both to the corporeal and mental faculties'. His distaste was, he felt, widespread in Constantinople where opium use was held 'a despicable practice'.[55]

Porter's contemporary Alexander Russel (d. 1768) was physician to the British Factory at Aleppo. In his experience European interest in the recreational Islamic use of drugs exaggerated the extent of the phenomenon. 'I could never find the custom of taking Opium was so general in Turkey, as commonly believed in Europe,' he reported. 'It prevails indeed more at Constantinople than at Aleppo, where happily it is held almost as equally scandalous as drinking wine, and practised by few openly, except by persons regardless of their reputation.'[56] James Dallaway, who served as both chaplain and physician to the British Embassy in Constantinople, agreed in 1798 that 'intoxication with this noxious drug is certainly less prevalent than we have been informed.'[57]

Recreational opium-users at Aleppo were pictured by Russel as fools whose misconduct presaged the breakdown of social barriers and class hierarchies, which were considered essential to peace and prosperity. 'The Grandees sometimes divert themselves with persons of inferior rank, who happen to be immoderately addicted to opium,' he explained. On one occasion he saw an intoxicated servant become deluded into believing that he was a man of privilege and wealth.

> He placed himself in a corner of the Divan, talked familiarly with the master of the house, entered into a detail of ideal business, ordered persons brought before him to be drubbed, or imprisoned, disgraced some of the officers in waiting, and appointed others. In the midst of all these extravagancies, a page, who had been instructed beforehand, getting unperceived behind him, made a loud and sudden clatter with the window shutter. In a moment the enchantment was dissolved. The unfortunate [servant] was seized with universal tremulation, his pipe fell from his hand, and, awaking at once to the horror of his condition, he fell to his [opium] as his only resource under such a reverse of fortune.[58]

The drug's physical ill effects were clear to Russel as a physician: 'Persons immoderately addicted to this pernicious practice', he wrote, 'seldom arrive at old age . . . but losing their memory, and by degrees their other faculties, they . . . sink miserably into an untimely grave'. Few were able to withstand the 'thousand hypochondriac evils' of withdrawal.[59]

Similarly the Frenchman François, Baron de Tott (1733–93) in 1784 described a square in Constantinople called Teriaky Tcharchissy, or the Market for Opium Takers, where every day, towards evening, 'the lovers of this Drug' converged from surrounding streets. Along one side of the square was a long row of little shops shaded by an arbour protecting small sofas laid out by the shopkeepers to accommodate their guests. Opium pills were distributed to the customers, who swallowed them with water.

> An agreeable Reverie, at the end of three quarters of an hour, or an hour at most, never fails to animate these Automatons; causing them to throw themselves into a thousand different Postures, but always extravagant, and always merry. This is the moment when the Scene becomes most

interesting; all the Actors are happy, and each returns home in a state of total Irrationality, but likewise in the entire and full enjoyment of Happiness not to be procured by Reason. Disregarding the Ridicule of those they meet, who divert themselves by making them talk absurdly, each imagines and looks and feels himself possessed of whatever he wishes.[60]

It is significant that in the accounts of both Russel and de Tott the opium-eaters imagine themselves to be more prosperous than in reality: as with heroin or crack cocaine in the late twentieth century, drug use had some association with social deprivation or economic disadvantage. Europeans regarded the Middle Eastern misuse of opium as equivalent to the labouring poor destroying themselves with gin. 'It is as disgraceful in Turkey to take too much opium, as it is with us to get drunk,' Samuel Johnson thought.[61] Dallaway confirmed that any Turk 'who is entirely addicted to it, is considered with as much pity or disgust as an inveterate sot is with us'.[62] Yet by the end of the eighteenth century, throughout Western Europe, the policing powers of neighbourhood shaming were receding in congested manufacturing districts. 'It is almost impossible', warned a Parisian secret agent in 1798, 'to maintain good behaviour in a thickly populated area where an individual is, so to speak, unknown to all others and thus does not have to blush in front of anyone.'[63] This development would raise huge anxieties in the next century.

By 1800 the dangers of prolonged medicinal use of opiates were as notorious as their sedative powers. There was no consensus about how narcotics worked, but a powerful international supply network was well established. Drug subcultures were not seen as part of European civilisation, but were reported, projected and re-imagined in Islamic societies. The denizens of these underworlds pursued their destructive courses: unmanly foreigners congregated to play out their unchristian and estranging charades. And meanwhile, in Europe, the wretched urban poor, it seemed, were forgetting how to blush with shame.

THREE

The Patent Age
of New Inventions

This is the patent age of new inventions,
For killing bodies and for saving souls.
—LORD BYRON

The more civilised men become, the more they become actors.
They want to put on a show, and fabricate an illusion of their own identities.
—IMMANUEL KANT

WESTERN ATTITUDES TO drugs were transformed from the 1820s. In that decade De Quincey's *Confessions of an English Opium Eater* became a cult book; the recently discovered alkaloid morphine became popular with physicians and their patients; and the controversy surrounding the opium trade with China intensified. Later, in the 1840s, hashish became a regular diversion for a flamboyant minority of Frenchmen, who thought of themselves as an exclusive but subversive elect and savoured the drug as a means of self-expression. Although the reputations of a few drug-users changed attitudes, European scientific advances, industrialisation and colonialism also affected consumption. Specifically, an interest in cannabis developed among British physicians in India, and as a result of the French occupation of Algeria.

The possession of drugs for non-medicinal use was not subject to criminal prosecutions until the twentieth century (except in a few US cities from the 1870s). Nevertheless at a time when neighbourly opinion remained a reasonably effective regulator of private behaviour

(except in congested urban slums), drug usage began to be stigmatised
as socially offensive. As early as 1814 opium was indicted as 'the pernicious drug' by a member of the English intelligentsia who had seen it
ruin a friend: 'the wild eye! the sallow countenance! the tottering step!
the trembling hand! The disordered frame!'[1] By the 1840s addicts were
depicted in medical case studies as culprits 'incapable of self-control',
whose 'self-inflicted, self-purchased curse' could have no happy earthly
end.[2] Speaking of opium in 1843, the Sinologist Sir George Staunton
condemned 'the perversion for the purposes of vicious luxury, of a poison, the legitimate use of which is exclusively medicinal'.[3]

The possibility of regulating domestic supplies of opium was aided
by the foundation of the Pharmaceutical Society of Great Britain in
1841, but only accomplished with the passage of the Pharmacy and
Poisons Act of 1868. The cost in 1815 of East Indian opium, in its dry
state, was about three guineas per pound, and of Turkish opium, eight
guineas. One grain of opium was the equivalent of 25 drops of laudanum. A medical analgesic dose was one or two grains—25 or 50
drops—every six hours. As in the eighteenth century, most opium sold
and used in England during the nineteenth century came from Turkey.
Of 50,000 kilograms of opium imported in 1827, 97.2 per cent came
from Turkey; 23,000 kilograms were imported in 1840, of which 65.2
per cent came from Turkey, 24.6 per cent from India, with Egypt and
France supplying the small residue. East Indian opium was reputedly
weaker, and more often adulterated.

Early nineteenth-century changes in the use of narcotics, and the
intensification of disapproval of their conspicuous use, occurred in a
newly mechanised environment. Industrialised economies provided a
distinct and unprecedented context for drugs. 'The society of modern
England', reported a London periodical in 1839, 'seems to be governed
by two leading feelings, the desire for wealth as the instrument of this
world's pleasures, and a fretful, gloomy and desponding uneasiness
about the path to happiness in the next'. The causes of these bad feelings were clear:

> The difficulties which beset the struggle for existence, the aggregation
> of the population into large towns, the universal pre-occupation of
> mind on the routine habits of a sordid industry, the disciplining of man
> to the minute restraints of complicated laws, are among the principal

facts which contribute to this result . . . the daily and constant thoughts of the people turn on questions of money and of money's worth . . . the prevalence of uneasy sensations, the constant anxieties, the absence of all pleasures, and more especially of domestic pleasures, arising out of difficulties and uncertainties respecting the means of existence, sour the temper, and deprave the heart; throwing men either upon a course of vicious and brutal indulgences, or the excitements of fanaticism.[4]

As a reaction to the secularising tendencies of this newly mechanised age, addiction in the early nineteenth century became more closely identified with sin and the self-creation of private hells. Addicts were represented as self-tormenting devils lost in eternal damnation. Coleridge saw addiction as the infernal self-torture of sinners: 'chained by a darling passion and *tyrannic* Vice in Hell, yet with the Telescope of an unperverted Understanding descrying and describing Heaven and the road thereto to my companions, the Damn'd'. He thought that 'Hell mean[t] . . . the state & natural consequences of a diseased Soul, abandoned to itself or additionally tortured by the very organic case which had before sheltered it.'[5]

These changes—with their long-term implications for human behaviour and policing—evolved in a European culture where privileged people were usually trusted in their use of opium while the poor were mistrusted. When Lord Melville (1742–1811) was impeached in 1805 on charges of corruption, his wife retreated to bed 'only supported by laudanum'.[6] In Paris, too, noblewomen were not necessarily covert when seeking solace with opiates. The Duchesse d'Abrantés (1785–1838) smoked opium cigarettes in her disappointed widowhood. She was the relict of Napoleon's Maréchal Junot, who had been exiled to the Illyrian provinces, where he once sent two battalions of Croatian troops to rid Dubrovnik of a nightingale; later he defenestrated himself. Her salon was favoured by the Parisian *beaux ésprits*. 'The visitor was sure to meet there with all the living remains of Bonapartism, and a sprinkling of those authors and artists whose genius, like their toilettes, was of a more ultra-republican bias and mode.'[7] Her cigarettes were an assuaging caress to her feelings rather than delinquency. The behaviour of Lady Melville and the Duchesse d'Abrantés was not considered shameful; but there was heavy disapproval about similar habits filtering down to the poor. 'The practice of taking Opium is dreadfully spread,' the poet Samuel Taylor Coleridge (1772–1834) lamented in 1808. 'Throughout Lancashire & Yorkshire it is the common Dram of the lower orders of People—in the small Town of Thorpe the Druggist informed me, that he commonly sold on market days two or three Pound of Opium, & a Gallon of Laudanum—all among the labouring Classes. Surely, this demands legislative Interference.'[8] For the prosperous classes, though, he thought publicity was preferable to legislation. In 1816 he railed against the protective discretion afforded addicts in high places. 'Who has dared blacken Mr. Wilberforce's good name on this account? Yet he has been for a long series of years under the same necessity. Talk with any eminent druggist or medical practitioner, especially at the West End of the town, concerning the frequency of this calamity among men and women of eminence.'[9]

This calamity indeed afflicted one individual of supereminence: the monarch himself depended on laudanum. George IV (1762–1830) had been an intelligent, spirited boy who matured into a robust and beautiful youth. He deserves credit as the only successful architectural and artistic patron from an otherwise direly philistine family; but he needed profusion in everything, and became a corpulent voluptuary before he was thirty. His use of laudanum became obtrusive in 1811 when he was still Prince of Wales. During the autumn of that year, while he was acting as Regent during his father's incapacitating illness, his efforts to recruit more congenial ministers were foiled. His extravagances had by this time inextricably ensnared him in debt. Then, in November, he wrenched his ankle while dancing the highland fling. This accident provoked a general collapse. Lying constantly on his stomach in bed, he took 100 drops of laudanum every three hours. As the courtier Sir William Fremantle (1766–1850) reported, 'He will sign nothing, and converse with no one on business.' Although the Prince's brother, the Duke of Cumberland (1771–1851), protested it was 'all sham', Fremantle felt 'He is so worried and perplexed by all the prospect before him, and by the necessity which now arises of taking a definitive step, that it has harassed his mind, and rendered him totally incapable, for want of nerves, of doing anything.'[10] There is no doubting the reality of the Prince's breakdown, or of his dependence on opium as a salve. He suffered, so his physician Sir Walter Farquhar (1738–1819) said, 'such agony of pain all over him it produces a degree of irritation on his nerves nearly approaching to delirium'.[11] The Prince recovered from this crisis of 1812, but his voracity, and the reluctance of his physicians to frustrate his wishes, meant that his laudanum consumption spasmodically but steadily rose.

After his succession to the throne in 1820, his habits became ungovernable. His binges of cherry brandy and laudanum divided his medical advisers: Sir William Knighton (1766–1836) thought laudanum 'will drive him Mad'; Sir Henry Halford (1766–1844) 'says spirits will drive him mad, if Laudanum is not given; and that he will take it in larger doses if it is not administered in smaller'.[12] These debaucheries did not improve his manners. Charles Greville (1794–1865), clerk to the Privy Council, found him 'a spoiled, selfish, odious beast, [who] has no idea of doing anything but what is agreeable to himself'.[13] By 1827 the king was nearly blind, with cataracts in both eyes; gout made it difficult for him to hold a pen. The prospect of ministerial conferences agitated him. He needed, for example, 100 drops of laudanum before he could face the Foreign Secretary, Lord Aberdeen (1784–1860).[14] Politicians and courtiers chronicled his ruinous greed with contemptuous wonder. 'What do you think of His breakfast yesterday for an Invalid?' Wellington asked in April 1830. 'A Pidgeon and Beef Steak Pye of which he ate two Pigeons and three Beef-Steaks, Three parts of a bottle of Mozelle, a Glass of Dry Champagne, two Glasses of Port [&] a Glass of Brandy! He had taken Laudanum the night before, again before this breakfast, again last night and again this Morning!'[15] Two months later the king died.

His chief physician, Sir Henry Halford, later endorsed a memorandum prepared by the surgeon Sir Benjamin Brodie (1783–1862) as part of the campaign against the Chinese opium trade. This declaration constitutes an authoritative medical commentary on the destruction of George IV's powers by opium. 'However valuable opium may be when employed as an article of medicine', its habitual use had 'most pernicious consequences—destroying the healthy action of the digestive organs, weakening the powers of the mind, as well as those of the body, and rendering the individual who indulges himself in it a worse than useless member of society'.[16] George IV was admired by few of his subjects. His obituary in *The Times* conveyed the indignant disapproval of a nineteenth-century manufacturing nation. He 'could never be made to comprehend the value of money'; he never saved; it was grievous that the head of state, who should be an example to his people, lived with such 'woeful spirit of waste and prodigality'. His profligacy besmirched the new capitalism; as an improvident consumer he personified 'all the vices by which an advanced, and affluent, and corrupt society is infested'. *The Times* provided no obsequies for him. 'There was never an individual less regretted by his fellow creatures than this deceased king,' it thundered. 'What eye has wept for him? What heart has heaved one sob of unmercenary sorrow?'[17] George's habits—including his opium habit—scarcely accorded with the properties of middle-class Europeans in an epoch of accelerated industrialisation (notoriously the effects of opium were not conducive to saving or productivity). He seemed—to borrow Brodie and Halford's damning phrase that was so eloquent of early nineteenth-century attitudes—'worse than useless'. Historians have underrated the part in raising British disapproval of drug-users played by George IV, with his ostentatious opium habit and sumptuous pavilion at Brighton displaying its pagodas resembling an oriental potentate's harem.[18]

It is agreed, though, that the financial complications surrounding the death of a Scottish nobleman—an aristocrat of uncommonly ancient lineage, living in unusually poor circumstances—altered attitudes to opium in Britain. Traditionally, insurance offices have used their financial power to discriminate between their customers, and to enforce conduct that supports or promotes capitalist productivity. Traditionally, too, they have used their privileged position to try to evade payments on policies. 'The offices all looked with horror upon opium-eaters,' a lifelong *habitué* (who lived to the age of seventy-four) reported of this period. 'Fourteen offices in succession, within a few months, repulsed me as a candidate for [life] insurance on that solitary ground of having owned myself to be an opium-eater.' He thought their attitude was as unreasonable as any other prejudice. 'Habitual brandy-drinkers met with no repulse . . . yet alcohol leads into daily dangers.'[19] During George IV's reign, an insurance company decisively signalled its objections to opium, and began a far-reaching medical debate.

In 1826 John, thirty-first Earl of Mar (1772–1828) insured his life for £3,000 as security for money lent to him by a Scottish bank. Mar had recently succeeded his father in the earldom, but his ancestral estates had been dismantled. His discovery in 1827 that he was penniless turned him into a bedridden recluse. Mar, who had been taking opium for thirty years, was by this stage buying two or even three ounces of laudanum daily. After his death of jaundice and dropsy in 1828, the Edinburgh Life Assurance Company refused to pay on its policy, having received information 'that the Earl was addicted to the vice of opium-eating in a degree calculated to shorten life'. The company claimed that Mar should have mentioned his habit when the policy was effected; they would either have declined to insure him, or have raised the premiums, accordingly they repudiated the policy. Mar's creditors, who sued to recover their £3,000, argued in court 'that his health was broken up, not before the insurances were effected and from opium-eating, but at a later period, and simply by the gloomy state of his affairs; and they denied that he was addicted to the use of opium, or if it was so, that his health suffered in consequence'.[20] Edinburgh Life Assurance lost the case because it had been careless in establishing the earl's habits when granting the policy; but a slow-smouldering controversy had been sparked.

The expert witnesses who testified at the trial included the Scottish physician and toxicologist Sir Robert Christison (1797–1882), who doubted that habitual opium use was consistent with health or long life. Nevertheless ten case histories of confirmed opium-users that he collected indicated (as he recognised) that opium-eaters could live to old age. The pharmacologist Jonathan Pereira (1804–53) supported Christison's position by opposing the assumption that 'because opium in large doses, when taken by the mouth, is a powerful poison, and when smoked to excess is injurious to health', its moderate use was necessarily detrimental.[21] A London surgeon countered with six cases of his own indicating that 'this detestable habit' shortened life.[22] Other commentators recognised that the health and longevity of opium-users varied according to such factors as their prosperity, temperament and physique. William Marsden (1754–1836) reported that soldiers in Sumatra, and others in the bazaars, who used opium to excess, 'commonly appear emaciated; but they are in other respects abandoned and debauched. The *Limun* and *Batang Assei* gold-traders, on the contrary, who are an active, laborious class of men, but yet indulge as freely in opium as any others whatever, are, notwithstanding, the most healthy and vigorous people to be met with on the island.'[23] An Englishman living at Penang in the Malacca Straits in the 1840s doubted that prosperous Chinese, 'who have the comforts of life about them', had their lives foreshortened by 'private addiction to this vice, so destructive to those who live in poverty'.[24] The idiosyncratic reactions of different individuals to opium were well known to physicians.[25] Thus the novelist Sir Walter Scott (1771–1832), who took laudanum for crippling stomach cramps, found that 60 or 80 drops disagreed 'excessively' with him, and produced a heavy hangover.[26] By contrast 80 drops had 'no effect, except a slight giddiness in the head' on John Harriott (1745–1817), the Thames Police magistrate who experimented with laudanum. 'I have seen extraordinary effects from opium abroad, and heard much of its potency as a drug, at home; I was consequently surprised at its inefficacy with myself.'[27]

A greater cultural impact in the 1820s even than the Mar case was the publication of *The Confessions of an English Opium Eater* (serialised in a magazine in 1821, and issued as a book during the following year). Its author, Thomas De Quincey (1785–1859), had been reared by his widowed mother, a chilly, scornful and vigilant moralist, whose outlook might be symbolised by an admonitory wagging finger. He had a fatalistic expectation of retribution, fitted easily into the contempt of stronger individuals and felt uncomfortable in accepting personal responsibility. There was a streak of spiritual masochism in his fantasies, which led him into acts of self-mortification; but the worst that can be said against him is that in adulthood he retained an almost puerile helplessness. He did not make himself his own man, but for too long ordered his life as a reprisal against his mother. De Quincey first used opium in 1804 while suffering from facial neuralgia. The physical relief was immediate, and he continued using laudanum first for physical pains and then to mitigate material hardships and emotional distress. Next he incorporated it into his recreations: he regularly set aside one evening a week to attend concerts and operas under the influence of laudanum, which he found stimulated the 'sensual pleasure' of music.[28] These musical opium evenings established De Quincey as among the first Europeans consciously to take a drug to enhance aesthetic pleasure rather than to desensitise pain.

Narcotics users sometimes adopt extreme emotional attitudes, or claim intense emotional experiences, to mask their deficiencies in conventional feelings. They relish secret rites as a substitute for human commitment. Some enjoy a self-image as isolated individuals haunting dark places. The anonymity of great cities succours their egotism, as the opium-smoker Sir Edward Bulwer-Lytton (1803–73) recognised in 1827: 'He who lives surrounded by the million never thinks of any but the one individual—himself.'[29] It was with similar feelings that De Quincey, after drinking laudanum, explored London slums. On these wanderings he was gratified to be an observer who had preserved his incognito; he relished the feeling of solitude in the midst of a crowd. He went to live among literary intellectuals in Edinburgh, where he was acclaimed as a prodigious conversationalist; but the expectations of his admirers drained his physical and nervous strength: he tried to recover his depleted powers by drugs. Depressed by poverty, and oppressed by a sense of personal doom, he could not be long separated from his decanter of laudanum. By 1815 De Quincey's daily dosage was 320 grains (8000 drops of laudanum), though it was reduced subsequently. His opium dreams aroused 'shadowy terrors that settled and brooded over my whole waking life'. An extract from his account of one of these nightmares—dating from 1818—evokes his guilty horrors:

> I was stared at, hooted at, grinned at, chattered at, by monkeys, by paroquets, by cockatoos. I ran into pagodas, and was fixed for centuries at the summit, or in secret rooms; I was the idol; I was the priest; I was worshipped; I was sacrificed. I fled from the wrath of Brama through all the forests of Asia; Vishnu hated me; Seeva lay in wait for me. I came suddenly upon Isis and Osiris; I had done a deed, they said, which the ibis and the crocodile trembled at. Thousands of years I lived and was buried in stone coffins, with mummies and sphinxes, in narrow chambers at the heart of eternal pyramids. I was kissed, with cancerous kisses, by crocodiles, and was laid, confounded with all unutterable abortions, amongst reeds and Nilotic mud.[30]

De Quincey returned to London in 1821, where he strove to escape penury by a determined revival of his journalism. The first product of this resolve was the serial publication of *The Confessions of an English Opium Eater*. Supremely these *Confessions* were written to meet his imperative need of money. De Quincey consequently needed to accommodate, if not bolster, the sentiments of his middle-class readers. His *Confessions* won popularity precisely because they were steeped in the spirit of the 1820s. He made the waste of money, by himself and others, into a recurrent lament of his memoirs. His technique set the pattern for later individuals who wanted to transgress, shock or rebel without abandoning utterly the moral rules of their time. Notably he repudiated the traditional model of oriental drug-users stupefying themselves for pleasure: 'Turkish opium-eaters, it seems, are absurd enough to sit, like so many equestrian statues, on logs of wood as stupid as themselves.'[31] Instead he advocated productivity as earnestly as any life-insurance office. Conspicuously, amidst all the self-abasement of his *Confessions*, De Quincey took pride in one fact: 'We, in England, more absolutely than can be asserted of any other nation, are not *fainéans*: rich and poor, all of us have something to do.' He set in contrast indolent Spanish dukes, exhibiting 'undisguised evidences of effeminate habits operating through many generations', or Italian peasantry, 'idle through two-thirds of their time'.[32] Bulwer-Lytton echoed him in 1846: 'Labour is the very essence of spirit . . . the most useless creature that ever yawned at a club, or counted the vermin on his rags under the suns of Calabria, has no excuse for want of . . . purpose.'[33] Similarly their fellow opium-eater Coleridge acclaimed the happiness 'produced by effective Industry, by monuments of well spent Time', and inveighed against 'the indolence' associated with 'the dire self-punishing Vice of Opium'.[34] Yet despite the rueful self-mortification of the *Confessions* De Quincey could not appease mid-Victorian moralists. His 'habit of diseased introspection'—this 'hurtful practice of unceasingly speculating on his own emotions'—made him 'the most unhealthy and abnormal mind to be found among modern writers', according to the *Athenaeum* in 1859.[35] The trouble was that De Quincey, like many other drug-users, had a sense of identity that was often unstable, improvised, disintegrating and discontinuous. Habitual users of narcotics seldom fit into the bourgeois sense of human identity as a serious business, stable, abiding and continuous, requiring the assertion of one true cohesive inner self as proof of health and good citizenry.

By mid-century 'the ordinary British prejudice against opium', according to Sir William Des Vœux (1834–1909), 'was strengthened by the perusal of De Quincey's *Confessions*'.[36] Whereas Des Vœux found the book estranging, others were attracted by its morbid tone. In people who have 'a morbid craving for *something*, exactly what is not known', claimed an American physician who specialised in treating addiction, 'reading such a book as that of De Quincey's would create a longing . . . that has a certain ending in a life's bondage'.[37] The French author Alfred de Musset (1810–57) published an inaccurate translation of *Confessions* that influenced his compatriot Hector Berlioz (1803–69) when composing his *Symphonie Fantastique* (1830), with its powerful opium dream section. In a later generation the poet Francis Thompson (1859–1907) resolved to experiment with opiates after studying the *Confessions*; the book graduated into a (misleading) primary source on the opium habit by the late nineteenth century.

De Quincey's experiences can be compared with those of his French novelist contemporary, Charles Nodier (1780–1844). Nodier was scarred by his adolescence during the Terror. As a youth he narrowly survived huge doses of opium taken to stimulate his literary inspiration. His first novel, *Le Peintre de Salzbourg, journal des émotions d'un coeur souffrant (The painter of Salzburg, journal of the emotions of a suffering heart)* (1803), recalls the tortured evolution of the protagonist's feelings in Goethe's *Wilhelm Meister* (1796). Nodier believed that individual development was sacred, and was one of the earliest Romantics to seek enhanced states of mind and transcendent feelings through drugs. Narcotics were enlisted not in pursuit of oblivion, but in an odyssey of self-discovery. On one occasion his reputation as an opium-eater saved him from grave difficulties. When, in 1804, he was arrested for publishing an anti-Napoleonic squib, family friends (including the *préfet* of Doubs and the mayor of Besançon) extricated him from prison by excusing his indiscretions as symptoms of the 'near-insanity' of an irresponsible addict. In his maturity Nodier was tormented by his accurate presentiments of a great new literature that he recognised he was not gifted enough to lead. Nevertheless, by the 1820s, he had abandoned opium as an aesthetic crutch and found new creative springs by fictionalising the past events of his life. The only remnant of his old habit was his love of pharmacological diversity. To the end he continued tinkering with his body and testing untold quantities of outlandish nostrums.[38] His character remained as segmented as De Quincey's: he was, during different phases of his life, a botanist, an entomologist, a philologist, a learned bibliophile, a civil servant in Illyria, a scholar of folklore, a dabbler in the supernatural, a gambler and a literary hoaxer.

Another literary opium addict of this period was Samuel Taylor Coleridge. He claimed that his drug dependency arose from prolonged therapeutic treatment for swollen knees and indigestion. 'By a most unhappy Quackery . . . & thro' that most pernicious form of Ignorance, medical half-knowledge, I was *seduced* into the use of narcotics, not secretly but (such was my ignorance) openly & exultingly as one had discovered & was never weary of recommending a grand Panacea—& saw not the truth, till my *Body* had contracted a habit.'[39] Such protests were disbelieved by the poet laureate Robert Southey (1774–1843), who was brother-in-law of Coleridge's wife: 'Every person who had witnessed his habits, knows that for . . . infinitely the greater part, inclination and indulgence are its motives.'[40] Coleridge never alluded to the pleasures of opium, but only to the painful effects on mind and body of abandoning or reducing his dependency on the drug. He made repeated efforts, under medical supervision, to renounce opium, but always failed. There was a spiritual masochism in his character (as there was in De Quincey's) that needed a detested yet despotic master. 'Often have I wished to be thus trodden and spit upon, if by any means it might be an atonement for the direful guilt, that (like all others) first *smiled* on me, like Innocence! Then crept closer, and yet closer, till it had thrown its serpents folds round and round me, and I was no longer in my own power!'[41] He constantly harked on his subjugation. His habit was 'the worst and most degrading of Slaveries', he declared in 1816, 'a specific madness which leaving the intellect uninjured and exciting the moral feelings to a cruel sensibility, entirely suspended the moral Will'.[42] Yet he knew himself that these histrionics were addictive too. As he declared in 1811, 'Never let it be forgotten either by the framers or dispensers of criminal law, that the stimulus of shame, like other powerful medicines, if administered in too large a dose, becomes a deadly narcotic poison to the moral patient!'[43]

At times he yearned for a new drug to revive his spirits: he imagined 'a Gymnastic Medicine' (like amphetamines in the twentieth century) that would set his mind racing.[44] Having nearly died in 1813 of an overdose, he was removed to a medical household at Bristol, where his laudanum consumption was lowered in minute reductions. A burly manservant was installed in his room to restrain him from secret opium-dosing or violent acts. Soon afterwards, in the spring of 1814, Coleridge sent several long letters to friends confessing his addiction. Making a semi-public rigmarole of his predicament seems to have given him some ease and strength. 'I had been crucified, dead, and buried, descended into *Hell*, and am now, I humbly trust, Rising again, tho' slowly and gradually,' he wrote in May 1814. 'I have in this one dirty business of Laudanum a hundred times deceived, tricked, nay, actually & consciously LIED.'[45] For a man who idealised the Truth he had one heartbreaking trait: deceit. 'The slave of stimulants', Dorothy Wordsworth (1771–1855) called him in 1810; 'his whole time and thoughts, (except when he is reading, and he reads a great deal), are employed in deceiving himself, and seeking to deceive others.'[46] He himself recognised this when he wrote in 1804: 'Let me live in *Truth*— manifesting that alone which *is* . . . but o! I am very, very weak—from my infancy have been so—& I exist for the moment!'[47]

In 1816 Coleridge installed himself in the Highgate household of a physician, James Gillman (1782–1839), who regulated his opium consumption. He was known to the local youths as 'Gillman's Softie', and was thought 'half-baked' by their elders. For many years he deceived Gillman, and procured clandestine supplies of the drug from a local druggist named Dunn, who admired him warmly. 'But mark!' Dunn told his apprentice in 1824. 'You must never tell anybody anything about him, nor even that he takes laudanum. Never speak of him, unless you can help it, except to me; for if you do, I don't know what the consequence may be.' Coleridge charmed both the apprentice and chemist, who refused the Gillmans' request in 1828 that the poet should no longer be supplied: Dunn 'boldly declared his persuasion that without laudanum Coleridge would soon languish, fail & die'.[48] They had succumbed to the addict's manipulative powers. Coleridge was devious in satisfying his desires; at his worst he was slothful, possessive, parasitic, irresolute and self-absorbed. His opium excesses were often accompanied by drunken sprees, hysterical accusations and screaming fits. Sir Walter Scott tried to excuse Coleridge's bad behaviour with the phrase, 'a man of genius struggling with bad habits'.[49] It is nearer the truth that Coleridge was a man of bad habits struggling with genius.

Coleridge was an extremist. Perhaps Prosper Mérimée (1803–70) was a more representative literary drug-user of this period. Always oversusceptible to the opinions and antics of his friends, Mérimée understood the meaning of Stendhal's motto for the post-Napoleonic era: Hide your self. He cloaked his feelings when young under the pose of a cold, smooth, raffish and foul-mouthed cynic. With the studied and dominating diction of an actor, he protected himself with a series of segmented identities for use with his different sets of friends: his segmentations had much more ruthless control than De Quincey's. His drug usage was similarly controlled and demarcated. As a traveller in the Middle East, his experiences were relaxed, pleasurable and humorous. At Tyre in 1841 'we indulged ourselves deliciously for two days doing *kef* ... having the best view in the world from our divan and nourished by first-rate kebabs', he wrote to a Paris friend. There were comedies of drug tourism too:

> The Pasha of Smyrna, my excellent friend Osman, who wears a frock coat just like you or me, but crouches on a cushion of six inches' diameter, tells me what a wonderful invention European newspapers are. They while away the time. I say to him, but you have the pipe which does that better. Yes, the pipe is good [he replies], but sometimes when you smoke it brings you sad thoughts, instead of which, if you read the newspapers, you can think of nothing at all.[50]

In France Mérimée needed sedation to cope with the strain of living; he insulated himself from the discomfort of human feelings with the help of drugs. Nevertheless, even on days when he was attacked by 'a swarm of blue devils', he retained enough sense to fight self-absorption. 'My task is to forget my *Self* as much as possible'.[51]

Narcotics and hallucinogens for him were not a symptom of self-hatred, a way to flirt with self-destruction or a means of enhanced consciousness. They were the devices whereby a clever, self-conscious and disillusioned man deadened his aggressive resentment of the people with whom he was professionally involved. As Inspector of Historic Monuments, Mérimée travelled France saving such masterpieces as the papal palace at Avignon or the Roman amphitheatres at Orange and Arles from vandalism or squatters. His good work days lifted his spirits and improved his self-respect.[52] However, his duties were sometimes mind-numbing in their provincial stupidity: at Apt, for example, the local worthies made him admire a foxhole that they attested was a druidic monument. As he explained to a Spanish noblewoman in 1846,

> I am horribly sad when I set out on my tours, and this time more than ever. The weather is superb, and I have consumed hashish to make myself cheerful, but in vain. I have been told that I would see paradise

and the Old Man of the Mountain's houris; but I saw nothing at all. You know that hashish is an extract from an intoxicating drug with which Orientals make themselves for hours at a time the happiest people on earth. This particular drug is not customary with us.[53]

For many years Mérimée used laudanum to cope with the frustration of his duties as a courtier to Napoleon III. 'We have sweated blood and water to amuse Her Majesty: balls, picnics, charades, etc.,' he wrote during a state visit by Queen Sophia of the Netherlands. He was required to act as a jester—writing witty sycophantic verses to the queen and performing in charades for Empress Eugénie—as well as to overeat at banquets before squeezing into tight breeches. He could only contain his resentment by stupefying himself: 'I'm . . . half-poisoned through having taken too much laudanum,' he confessed to a friend.[54] Mérimée feared that without laudanum he would be sterilised by irritable boredom. In later life, when he was the prey of asthma and emphysema, he shifted his preference to ether.

Not all drug-users were so fortunate. Lord Dufferin and Clandeboye (1794–1841) overdosed on the steam packet *Reindeer* while crossing the Irish Sea from Liverpool to Belfast. Just before embarking, he had bought from a quayside chemist some morphine pills, of which he took a fatal quantity. There were suspicions of suicide; but his family preferred to believe that the chemist was flustered while compounding the prescription by the *Reindeer*'s bell clanging a warning across the wharf, and therefore made the pills incorrectly.[55] Certainly opiates were so notorious as a means of deliberate 'self-destruction' that many chemists would only sell them in small rations so as to impede suicidal customers. A physician at Charing Cross Hospital in 1842 publicised the attempted suicide of a youth who, having been upset by his girlfriend, was found insensible in a Soho doorway after taking opium that he had been forced by suspicious chemists to procure in small quantities at different shops.[56] Opiates were associated with homicide, too. The profligate French physician Edme-Samuel Castaing (1796–1823) poisoned his friend Hippolyte Ballet (1799–1822) with morphine, shared the inheritance with Hippolyte's brother Auguste Ballet (1798–1823), and having persuaded his accomplice to bequeathe him the spoils, murdered him with morphine too.[57] There is a deathbed scene in Harrison Ainsworth's best-selling novel *Rookwood* (1836) where Sir Piers Rookwood is making his dying speech longer and more explicit than suits his wife. An attendant entering the room finds her 'glaring at him like a tigress—so savage—so full of spite and malice'. She instructs the attendant to administer laudanum to the baronet as a settler. ' "Give him laudanum," whispered Lady Rookwood; "here is the phial, it will abridge his sufferings."—"Oh, no—no!" said Sir Piers, with a look of horror, which I shall never forget, and struggling for utterance—"no drugs—no drugs—let me live, if only for a few moments." '[58]

European pharmacology decisively changed in the early nineteenth century. The morphine pills used by Castaing had only recently been marketed as the result of advances in the study of alkaloids made by several eager young Frenchmen and one crankier Austrian. In 1803 Jean-François Derosne, a French manufacturing chemist, began producing a salt marketed as Sel Narcotique de Derosne containing the alkaloids later known as narcotine and (in smaller quantities) morphine. His compatriot Armand Seguin (1767–1835) isolated the active principle of opium during the following year. Then, using Derosne's salt, Friedrich Wilhelm Sertürner (1783–1841) began investigating the composition of raw opium with the intention of isolating its sleep-inducing factor. Sertürner was an apothecary's assistant in Hanover who conducted his investigations on primitive equipment in spare moments snatched from his job. By these means he isolated a white crystalline substance that, as he reported in 1805–6, was more powerful than opium. This substance he named 'morphium', in allusion to the Greek god of dreams and sleep, Morpheus. Sertürner had an ardent passion for firearms, developed extreme hypochondria and latterly was obsessed with a life element he named 'zoon' and by a theory about the coldness of sunlight. Partly in consequence of these unprepossessing eccentricities, it took a decade, and the republication of his findings in 1817, before the significance of his morphium received attention. Thereafter, under the name of morphia, Sertürner's alkaloid was hailed as a drug ten times more potent than opium. Meanwhile the French physician François Magendie (1783–1855) began studying the toxic action of vegetable drugs in 1809. Profiting from improved laboratory techniques and more accurate analysis, 'the illustrious Magendie', as Bulwer-Lytton called him, became one of the most influential nineteenth-century physiologists.[59] He was among the experts testifying at Castaing's trial.[60] His translated *Formulary for the Preparation and Mode of Employing Several New Remedies* (1823) improved English medical awareness of morphine's powers. His colleague Pierre-Joseph Pelletier (1788–1842) isolated a whole range of important active compounds from drugs, including emetine (from the ipecac root, in 1817), strychnine (the alkaloid discovered in St Ignatius' beans in 1818), quinine (the alkaloid identified in cinchona bark in 1820) and caffeine (coffee and coca beans, tea leaves and kola nuts, in 1821).

Pierre-Jean Robiquet (1780–1840), the Parisian pharmacist and chemist who discovered the alkaloids narcotine and codeine, perfected an extraction process for morphine. The new substance was promoted both as an efficient painkiller and as a cure for opium *habitués*. Thomas Morson (1800–1874), a London retail pharmacist who had studied in Paris, where he was impressed by the discoveries of Magendie and Pelletier, began producing commercial morphine in the parlour behind his shop in Farringdon Street in 1821. The Darmstadt pharmacist Heinrich Emanuel Merck (1794–1855) started wholesale morphine production around 1825; Macfarlan & Company of Edinburgh began to manufacture the alkaloid in the early 1830s. Morphine entered the *London Pharmacopoeia* in 1836: by the 1840s the drug was widely accepted. It confirmed the British preference for Turkish opium supplies. 'In repeating Sertürner's and Robiquet's experiments, I obtained from good Turkey opium nearly three times the quantity of morphia yielded by the same weight of East India opium,' the Professor of Materia Medica at London University reported.[61] It was partly for this reason that little Indian opium was imported to Britain, its consumption being confined to China and other Asian countries. Yet, despite the inferiority of Indian opium, it was responsible for a decisive change during the 1820s in British comments on the drug.

Interest in opium-taking—whether prompted by the vices of George IV, De Quincey's *Confessions* or other causes—was sustained by the contention surrounding the export traffic in Indian opium. Public debates about Chinese opium culture supplanted the historic interest in oriental travellers' tales, and became the medium for vehement disapproval of recreational opium use. Despite the imperial edicts that were issued from Peking in 1799–1800 declaring opium contraband throughout China, and forbidding its sale, trade in the drug had steadily swollen. Increasing amounts of Malwa opium, produced in the independent Maratha native states of central and western India, began to reach Macao. The Governor General of Bengal banned the export of Malwa opium from Bombay in 1805; but the traffic soon resumed through Portuguese outlets such as Goa. Despite a further Chinese edict of 1809 forbidding the import of opium, an American brig brought the first cargo of Turkish opium to the Canton river in 1811. An East India Company vessel followed in 1817. Malwa opium was selling in China at this time for about £330 for each chest; this depressed the selling price of Bengal opium from its peak of £888 to less than £440. Henceforth the opium trade was highly competitive. The value of opium imported into Canton and Macao was £737,775 in the season of 1817–18 rising to £2,332,250 in 1822–3. By 1819, when an opium mart was opened at Bombay, opium-smuggling had assumed a magnitude that the most determined camouflage and bribery could not hide. Each season more traders unconnected with the East India Company appeared at Canton and Macao.

In 1819 the Marquess of Hastings (1754–1826), then Governor General and Commander-in-Chief in India, oversaw the most extensive changes in the opium supply system since 1773. The old policy of restricting output and maintaining prices was discarded. In order to support the Bengal opium revenues, it was determined that the East India Company would buy all Malwa opium that came on to the market, and would sell it in China, even if this meant competing against its own Bengal opium. This decision was represented as a patriotic scheme to exclude foreigners from sharing in a lucrative business. Its real effect was to create a potentially illimitable supply. Historians have suggested that the Indian government could in the 1820s have abolished the Bengal monopoly and prohibited poppy cultivation in British India. Although opium would still have been trafficked in China, consumption of the drug might not (so it has been argued) have grown so bloated during the nineteenth century. The suppression of poppy cultivation in every remote field was, however, an impossibility. It is true, though, that some officials wished to reduce British India's reliance on opium revenues. The 'manly and virtuous' Indian administrator Sir Charles Metcalfe (1785–1846) thought 'the good name lost' by Hastings's policy was 'greater than any pecuniary gain can warrant'.[62]

Lord William Cavendish Bentinck (1774–1839), who was appointed Governor General of Bengal in 1827, is reckoned among the great holders of that office. It was during his rule that the British first began to debate whether and how far they should try to change Indian traditions and social organisation. Bentinck found that two-thirds of opium exported was smuggled, and only one-third belonged to the Company. After weighing the alternatives, his administration in 1830 abandoned all restrictions on the growth or transit of Malwa opium, but imposed a transit tax pitched to produce revenue without diverting trade. Then, with the intention of shoring up revenues, he sponsored an expansionist policy whereby fifteen new districts were developed for poppy cultivation between 1831 and 1839.[63] Opium sales were the third highest source of Indian revenues by the financial year 1831–2. Within five years opium production tripled. Prices declined as output rose: during the 1830s prices averaged half as much as for the 1820s, although some of this reduction is attributable to the resistance of the Chinese government rather than to a glutted market.

British expansion of Indian opium cultivation seemed regressive to some administrators responsible for developing Asiatic economies. The accomplished young imperialist Sir Stamford Raffles (1781–1826) lamented in 1817 that opium use in Java, where he had been lieutenant governor, had 'struck deep into the habits and extended its malign influence to the morals of the people, and is likely to perpetuate its power in degrading their character and enervating their energies, as long as the European governments, overlooking every consideration of policy and humanity, should allow a paltry addition to their finances to outweigh all regard to the ultimate happiness and prosperity of the country'. Despite its prevalence, opium use was 'still reckoned disgraceful, and persons addicted to it are looked upon as abandoned characters, and despised accordingly'.[64] In the 1830s, the Swedish soldier-diplomat Count Björnstjerna (1779–1847) publicly denounced the 'immoral' Indian Empire for exporting 15,000 to 20,000 chests of 'noxious' opium (worth two or three million pounds sterling), 'with which the Chinese are yearly poisoned'.[65] Björnstjerna deplored the resultant degradation of India as much as that of China's consumers. Bentinck's opium policy seemed incompatible with the agricultural reforms that he instituted in Assam in north-west India. Assam was bounded on the north by the Himalayas, and on the east by the Burmese frontier. It was plundered by Burmese troops who had been invited there in 1816 by a claimant to the throne. After further disorder, Assam, with its men massacred, women abducted and economy ruined, came under direct British rule in 1826. Twelve years later it was incorporated into Bengal (upon which its western border trenched), and Bentinck's administration decided to revive the local economy and palliate local miseries by establishing tea cultivation. This required the recruitment of labour from other regions. The Scottish superintendent of tea culture at Assam pleaded during the 1830s for the suppression of Assamese poppy cultivation together with the prohibition of opium imports:

> If something of this kind is not done, and done quickly too, the thousands that are about to emigrate from the plains into Assam will soon be infected with the Opium-mania—that dreadful *plague* which has depopulated this beautiful country, turned it into a land of wild beasts, with which it is overrun, and has degenerated the Assamese from a fine race of people to the most abject, servile, crafty, and demoralized race in India. This vile drug has kept, and does now keep down the population: the women have fewer children than those of other countries, and the children . . . in general die at manhood; very few old men being seen in this unfortunate country in comparison with others. Few but those who have resided long in this unhappy land know the dreadful and immoral effects which the use of Opium produces on the native. He will steal, sell his property, his children, the mother of his children, and finally, even commit murder for it. Would it not be the highest of blessings, if our humane and enlightened Government would stop these evils by a single dash of the pen, and save Assam, and all those who are about to emigrate into it as Tea cultivators, from the dreadful results attendant on the habitual use of Opium? We should in the end be richly rewarded by having a fine healthy race of men growing up for our plantations, to fell our forests, to clear the land from jungle and wild beasts, and to plant and cultivate the luxury of the world. This can never be effected by the feeble opium-smokers of Assam, who are more effeminate than women.[66]

His words reflected the new attitudes to opium in an age of acquisition. Meanwhile, in 1833, the British government, at the behest of its merchants, abolished the East India Company's monopoly of trade in China. Chinese ports were opened to new mercantile interests who were eager to exploit the huge, undeveloped market. With the brutal impatience of newcomers, these merchants immediately claimed trading privileges that the Chinese were unwilling to concede. The most powerful of the new merchant houses arose from the partnership of William Jardine (1784–1843) with his fellow Scot, James Matheson (1796–1787). Jardine had studied medicine at Edinburgh before becoming a ship's surgeon with the East India Company. The ships' officers were allotted cargo space for private trade, and when Jardine's trading profits surpassed his earnings as a surgeon, he abandoned medical work. From 1818 he travelled regularly from Bombay to Canton on the supercargo *Sarah*, of which he was co-owner. Acting initially as a commercial agent for Indian opium merchants, Jardine lived at Canton from 1822 until 1839. In his first year as a drug-dealer he sold 649 chests of Malwa opium for $818,000. He joined with Matheson to deal in opium in 1828—'the safest and most gentlemanlike speculation I am aware of', as he declared in 1830—although the famous firm of Jardine, Matheson & Company was not registered until 1832.[67] From 1834 the firm supplied smuggled opium and piece goods along the Chinese coast.

The cultural incomprehension separating the Peking government from the British free traders raised considerable tensions. More than ever, after 1834, the opium trade (although still officially prohibited) became a source of great profit to the private traders. Peking ordered the expulsion of the opium-importers in 1836, but Jardine (by now the most influential Briton at Canton) refused to leave. Instead Matheson circulated his free trade manifesto, *The Present Position and Prospects of British Trade with China* (1836). 'The number of British boats employed in illicit traffic had greatly increased,' Charles Elliot (1801–75), the naval officer who was British plenipotentiary at Canton, recounted in 1838. When opium was delivered, there were 'disgraceful riots . . . in which fire-arms were used'. Dozens of Chinese were strangled 'for their traitorous intercourse with foreigners' while 'the prisons were full of persons charged with similar offences, and that, in short, the illicit trade carried on was daily assuming a very serious aspect'.[68] There was resentment, too, among the natives at the impunity of foreign merchants under regulations whereby Chinese opium-dealers were punished with such cruel severity.

In 1839 the central government at Peking sent a special commis-

sioner to Canton charged with suppressing the opium traffic. He compelled the foreign merchants there to surrender 2000 cases of opium
worth upwards of £4,000,000 ($9,000,000 Chinese). These stocks
were burned. Sixteen foreign merchants (including Matheson) were
detained. Foreign merchants were required to give bonds not to import
the drug in future. All trade was meantime prohibited. Jardine, who had
recently retired from Canton, reached London in time to incite the
Foreign Secretary, Lord Palmerston (1784–1865), to a military
response. The opium issue exacerbated Anglo-Chinese relations, but
neither the war of 1839–42, nor its sequel in 1856–60, was primarily
fought to prevent the Peking government from prohibiting imports of
the drug. Opium, observed former US President John Quincy Adams
(1767–1848) in 1841, 'is a mere incident to the dispute, but no more
the cause of the war than the throwing overboard the tea in Boston
harbor was the cause of the North American revolution'.[69] Palmerston's diplomatic instructions of May 1841 were equally clear that the
British government 'make no demand in this [opium] matter, for they
have no right to do so. The Chinese Government is fully entitled to
prohibit the Importation of Opium, if it pleases; and British Subjects
who engage in a contraband Trade must take the consequences of
doing so.'[70] Nor does opium figure in the Treaty of Nanking, by which
fighting was terminated in 1842.

William Gladstone (1809–98) was one of the politicians whose consciences were affronted by opium-trafficking. He stood 'in dread of the
judgements of God upon England for our national iniquity towards
China', and thought that opium policy had been wrong since the era
of Hastings and Bentinck.[71] In a parliamentary speech of 1840, Gladstone denounced the 'unjust' war that had broken out 'to protect an
infamous contraband traffic'. If the British flag 'were never to be
hoisted except as it is now hoisted on the coast of China, we should
recoil from its sight with horror, and should never again feel our hearts
thrill . . . when it floats proudly and magnificently on the breeze'.[72] Yet
it is likely that Gladstone himself was under the influence of the poppy
when he delivered his superb peroration in 1840; for he often took laudanum in his coffee before addressing the House of Commons. Like
the criminal lawyer Thomas Erskine, described previously, Gladstone
found that opiates appeased his nerves before a great speech, and sustained his self-possession during the period of speechifying. Lord Ran-

dolph Churchill (1849–95) indeed compared Gladstone's oratory to 'the taking of morphia! The sensations . . . are transcendent; but the recovery is bitter'.[73]

The strategic course of the first Anglo-Chinese War counts for little in a history of narcotics. The chief effect of the Treaty of Nanking— triggering the process that destroyed the Manchu dynasty's primacy and led to the partitioning of China into spheres of foreign domination in 1898—is equally peripheral. It is the publicity effect of the campaign that must be reckoned with. Attitudes to the Orient and to opium were permanently changed. Queen Victoria (1819–1901) henceforth regarded 'the East' as 'very barbarous, cruel and dangerous'.[74] Certainly the lurid images of Chinese opium dens that were propagated from the 1840s resulted in less tolerance of British opium-users. As an Englishman reported from Malacca in 1842,

> The smoking shops are the most miserable and wretched places imaginable: they are kept open from six in the morning till ten o'clock at night, each being furnished with from four to eight bedsteads, constructed of bamboo-spars, and covered with dirty mats and rattans. At the head of each is placed a narrow wooden stool, which serves as a pillow or bolster; and in the centre of each shop there is a small lamp, which while serving to light the pipes, diffuses a cheerless light through the gloomy abode of vice and misery. On an old table are placed a few cups and a tea-kettle, together with a jug of water, for the use of smokers.[75]

His memoir contained an ominous detail about opium price movements. 'In Penang excessive duties have increased the thirst for opium; and what is worse they have quadrupled the number of murders and other crimes committed in order to obtain the means of procuring the drug!!' He averred that opium-smoking was encouraged among the Chinese as a deterrent to homosexuality. 'Parents are in the habit of granting this indulgence to their children, apparently to prevent them from running into other vices still more detestable, and to which the Chinese are more prone than, perhaps, any people on earth.'[76]

Such comments had powerful effects in an era during which male productivity had become both an economic compulsion and cultural fetish. The bad reputation of Chinese opium-users was increasingly fastened on to their British counterparts. The identification of opium consumption as an effete and luxurious custom, which was incompatible with the hopes of a progressive, industrialising and aggressive Western power, reflected a prevalent anxiety about habits, conditions and public health in Britain's new industrial towns and cities. The state of an industrialising nation was summarised by Coleridge in 1818. 'Great oppression on the part of the Rich,' he wrote. 'On the part of the Poor, clubbing; debauchery; sedition; loss of all private & all public social duties.'[77] For Carlyle, in 1829, it was an 'Age of Machinery, in every outward and inward sense of that word'.[78] Time became a commodity in the industrialised economies; procrastination was anathematised. The French social thinker Comte Claude-Henri de Saint Simon (1760–1825) urged that industrial leaders should replace archbishops as the spiritual directors of the nation, that productive labour would bring human redemption, and that the chief purpose of society was to organise citizens to produce useful objects. His disciples established a journal, *Le Producteur*, in 1826 and gained considerable influence with a *mentalité* that was profoundly antagonistic to slacking or drug-taking. One French Saint-Simonien claimed in 1844 that

> quiet enjoyment is almost exhausting for a working man. The house in which he lives may be surrounded by greenery under a cloudless sky, it may be fragrant with flowers and enlivened by the chirping of birds; but if a worker is idle, he will remain inaccessible to the charms of solitude. However, if a loud noise or a whistle from a distant factory happens to hit his ear, if he so much as hears the monotonous clattering of the machines in a factory, his face immediately brightens. He no longer feels the choice fragrance of flowers. The smoke from the tall factory chimney, the booming blows on the anvil, make him tremble with joy. He remembers the happy days of his work.[79]

The idea that opium was feminising, or appealed to effete men, became more explicit. The London toxicologist Anthony Todd Thomson (1778–1849) observed in 1831 that the use of opium for 'exhilarating the spirits has long been common in Turkey, Syria, and China; and of late years, it has unfortunately been adopted by many, particularly females, in this country'.[80] John Paris (1785–1856), a physician at Westminster Hospital, similarly remonstrated in 1843 that 'the votaries of fashion in this town have been in the habit of taking opium to sustain their powers under repeated dissipation'.[81] Male effeminacy was not identified with sexual preferences until the late nineteenth century, but instead with dandies like Bulwer-Lytton 'learned in the *savoir vivre*'. An actor described him in 1836:

> Called on Bulwer, whom I found in very handsome chambers in Albany, dressed, or rather *déshabillé*, in the most lamentable style of foppery—a hookah in his mouth, his hair, whiskers, tuft, etc., all grievously cared for. I felt deep regret to see a man of such noble and profound thought yield for a moment to pettiness so unworthy of him. His manner was frank, manly and cordial in the extreme—so contradictory of his appearance.[82]

One of the questions asked of physicians in industrial districts during the 1830s by the officials of the Factories Inquiry Commission was: 'Is the use of opium, as an article of luxury, frequent amongst the factory operatives?' It is significant that the non-medicinal use of opium by the labouring poor was characterised as a 'luxury', as if it was equivalent to the indulgence of George IV or Bulwer-Lytton, rather than a palliative for the misery of their lives. The officials' worries were discounted by expert opinion. A Manchester physician responded that he had 'been at pains to ascertain' that 'opium in any form is rarely (if ever) used by the operatives as an article of luxury'. A surgeon at Derby agreed: 'Not very frequent in this town; most of the opium-eaters I am acquainted with are not factory hands, but indolent persons.'[83]

Nineteenth-century women became laudanum delinquents as a way of coping with their subordination in patriarchal households. Gladstone's family, for example, was rent by an oppressed female addict. His sister Helen (1814–80) had been dismayed when in the 1830s her fiancé announced that his parents would not sanction their marriage. The atmosphere of the Gladstone household was always too strenuous and fatiguing for her nerves, but when her emotional circumstances became unbearable, she sought solace in Roman Catholicism. Her father and brother ardently opposed her conversion. She sought release from her powerlessness in constant travel, accompanied by her personal physician, and by another kind of escape, over which she found it difficult to maintain her control: opiates. It was as if she retaliated on her family controllers by punishing them with an angry, disruptive and embarrassing addiction. In 1845 Gladstone journeyed to Baden-Baden to try to coax his sister into abandoning her habit and returning to her family. 'She was in danger of death!' he reported. 'She is poisoned much in body and, more, in mind, by the use of that horrible drug'. His idea of repairing her 'moral disorganization' was to read a history of Christian martyrs in Japan to her, and an Italian book of devotions. Later she took volumes by Protestant divines from the family library for use as toilet paper. Her brother found the books, as she doubtless wanted, in her water closet: 'some torn up, the borders or outer coverings of some, remaining—under circumstances which admit of no doubt as to the shameful use to which they were put', as he remonstrated. Yet after the family relented, and Helen Gladstone was able to live as a Roman Catholic, she renounced laudanum for long periods.[84]

Opiates were not the only abused substances. 'It is very remarkable how the lower classes love physic,' a titled woman gossiped in 1819. 'Our cook . . . ruins herself in Antimonial Wine and emetics of the strongest nature; no remonstrance can deter her from pouring every species of quackery down her unhappy throat.'[85] Poor and disenfranchised people gobbled down quacks' nostrums that they could ill afford. In 1837 Thomas Holloway (1800–1883), who was working in the City of London as a commercial agent for foreigners, realised the potential profits to be made in patent medicines and started marketing Holloway's Family Ointment. By 1851 he was spending over £20,000 a year on advertising: his self-medicaments were marketed with such care that he became a millionaire. Holloway was among the more scrupulous traders. 'Shame on the age in which we live,' declaimed a surgeon in 1845. In his town, Leeds, the working classes shopped on Saturday night for 'pills and drops as regularly as in meat and vegetables, and in the public market place . . . are to be seen, in creditable juxtaposition, one stall for vegetables, another for meat, and a third for *pills!*'[86]

As poorer people became more extravagant and incautious about drugs, so the rich and educated classes became more wary. The use of opium by pregnant women provides an example. In 1806 an old noblewoman sent a message to Lady Caroline Lamb (1785–1828), wife of the future prime minister, Viscount Melbourne (1779–1848): 'If Lady Car Lamb should be breeding, I hope she will wear the laudanum plaister on her back which has done such wonders'.[87] Laudanum continued to be administered to pregnant prime-ministerial wives. 'They are always so kind as to call Sarah's horrid bad temper—excitement,' a friend wrote in July 1827 of Lady Goderich (1793–1867) whose husband became Prime Minister a few months later. 'She would not hear of the slightest contradiction, and . . . was quieted at last by a quantity of Laudanum, beside her own way to satisfy her.'[88] Goderich's 'whining' about his wife's health exasperated George IV, and shocked Charles Greville: 'She never left him any repose—sent for him twenty times a day, even from the midst of Cabinets, and he was weak and silly enough to give way to her fancies, for she had persuaded him that she should die if she were thwarted, which would be the best thing that could happen to him, for she is ridiculous, capricious and tiresome.'[89] Lady Goderich, whose daughter had recently died, was far advanced in pregnancy, but her son was unharmed by the tranquillising of his mother.

By the 1840s attitudes to opium use in pregnancy had changed. The future poet Elizabeth Barrett (1806–61) had been prescribed low dosages of laudanum at the age of fifteen after complaining of spinal pains. Her drops became her crutch: 'Opium—opium—night after night!—and some nights even opium won't do,' she exclaimed in 1839.[90] In the grief following the drowning of her brother in 1840, 'her ambiguous illness worsened, she declined into downright invalidism, sustained by opium and the care (tender, complacent, sinister) of her family', in the summary of the critic Daniel Karlin (b. 1953).[91] She was treated by a leading London physician, Frederick Chambers (1786–1855), 'a part of whose office it is, Papa says, "to reconcile foolish women to their follies"'.[92] Her justification of her opium habit seems honest.

It might strike you as strange that I who have had no pain . . . should need opium . . . But I have had restlessness until it made me almost mad . . . the continual aching sense of weakness has been intolerable . . . as if one's life, instead of giving movement to the body, were imprisoned undiminished within it, & beating & fluttering impotently to get out, at all the doors and windows. So the medical people gave me opium, a preparation of it, called morphine & ether—& ever since I have been calling it . . . my elixir, because the tranquillising power has been so wonderful.[93]

In 1845 a younger poet, Robert Browning (1812–89), initiated a correspondence with her that blossomed into a love affair. She was candid about her habit ('I think better of sleep than I ever did, now that she will not easily come near me except in a red hood of poppies'), and recognised that it was a measure of Browning's love that he so deprecated it.[94] They married in 1846; when she became pregnant, she was able to reduce but could never completely renounce opium consumption. She therefore felt 'unspeakable rapture' when her baby was pronounced perfect: she had expected 'a puny, sickly infant', because 'one of the great London physicians' had 'predicted evil' attributable to opium use during her pregnancy.[95]

Many poor English parents were unable to be so scrupulous or protective. Instead they administered soothing syrups and patent medicines—Mother Bailey's Quieting Syrup, Mrs Winslow's Soothing Syrup, Street's Infant Quietness, Batley's Sedative Solution, McMunn's Elixir, Godfrey's Cordial, Daffy's Elixir, Atkinson's Infants' Preservative and Dalby's Carminative—to their children. Excessive dosing with these products killed countless infants and older children. The physician at Derby General Infirmary testified to the Factory Commission in 1834 that 'many mothers employed in mills' gave opiates such as Godfrey's Cordial, Daffy's Elixir, or laudanum so that their infants slept during the mother's absence. His counterpart at Salford and Pendleton Royal Dispensary opined 'that opium is unknown as an article of luxury among factory operatives'. However it caused infant fatalities. 'Mothers who work from home are obliged during the day to leave their infants under the care of some neighbour who not uncommonly takes charge of three or four. The infant becomes irritable, laudanum is administered to induce sleep, the child awakes fretful and feverish, more laudanum is administered, the consequences of which manifest themselves in no long period.'[96] Leonard Horner (1785–1864), who was appointed as a factory inspector in 1833, reported, 'In one street in Manchester alone there were three druggists who sold five gallons a week of each of these drugs—one was called Godfrey's Cordial, and the other (significantly enough) Atkinson's Quietus.'[97] The penal reformer the Revd John Clay (1796–1858) testified that in 1843 in the Lancashire manufacturing town of Preston 1600 families bought Godfrey's Cordial or similar injurious compounds. Clay knew of one Preston burial club of which 64 per cent of the members died aged under five years.[98]

English chemists stocked opium pills, opium soap, lead and opium pills, opiate lozenges, opiate plasters, opium enema, opium liniment, and other products such as vinegar of opium. Apart from patent medicines, most opium preparations were sold in jugs or bottles, and could be collected from shops by children sent on an errand by their mothers. A famous bottled medicine of this kind was Dover's Powder, a mixture of ipecacuanha and powdered opium long ago devised by a pupil of Sydenham's called Thomas Dover (1660–1742), and originally prescribed for gout. Yorkshire, Cambridgeshire and Lincolnshire were notorious for opium use by their labouring poor; but cities such as Manchester, and the smaller manufacturing towns of Lancashire, also had an unenviable reputation, which may have been false.[99] One English locality was specially known for its domestic poppy cultivation. The Fen District—covering north Cambridgeshire, east Huntingdonshire, west Norfolk and south Lincolnshire—was low-lying, marshy, damp and unhealthy. The labouring poor of the Fens were liable to rheumatism, neuralgia and the malarial disease called ague; they had a high mortality rate. Opium poppies had been grown locally for centuries to provide herbal cures. The resemblance of this dank, miserable area to another great poppy-growing district was noted by Lord William Bentinck, who had lived in both places. 'Bengal', he said, 'is almost a facsimile upon a gigantic scale of the Great Level of the Fens.'[100] The inhabitants of remote country districts would go into market towns such as Wisbech on Saturdays, and crowd into the shops to buy their opium. More opium was sold in the cathedral city of Ely than any other drug. Country shopkeepers, general dealers, market stalls and hawkers travelling from village to village also provided it to the Fen people. Those who lived in villages or small towns consumed less opium than inhabitants of remote hamlets and isolated farms. The latter often shared the drug with their farm animals.

Wars tend to increase the number of drug-users. It is possible that some combatants who had been wounded in the Napoleonic Wars, and were given opiates to deaden the pain, became habituated. In addition the French military may sometimes have been pepped up with drugs. An English physician certainly claimed in 1843 that French army surgeons had administered opium with cayenne pepper to revive exhausted soldiers.[101] If this practice was widespread, it is bound to have aroused dependency; but the most historically significant increase in drug experimentation among the French did not occur among the common soldiery. Hashish became the affectation of a few authors, and their emulators among the *flâneurs* of Paris.

The 1830s and 1840s were the inaugural epochs of Parisian bohemianism—Murger's *Scènes de la vie de Bohème* were published in 1851—when artists and idlers freed themselves from family restraints and burdensome routines to pursue an improvising, self-centred existence. The Parisians who in the 1840s discovered hashish resembled Californian pot-heads of the 1960s. They wanted unconditional love, and demanded permission to act out childish fantasies. 'Don't force me to do anything, and I'll do everything. Understand me, and don't criticise me.'[102] So Gustave Flaubert (1821–80) wrote aged twenty-five. The French hashish-eaters hoped that drugs would reconcile their conflicting desires. 'When I was a child I wanted to be a military pope, and sometimes to be an actor,' wrote Charles Baudelaire (1821–67). 'Even when quite a child, I felt two conflicting sensations in my heart: the horror of life and the ecstasy of life.'[103] They wanted to assert their individuality—to make themselves heroes—in a mechanistic age. Their aesthetics as much as their personal habits were intended to defy middle-class conventions; they revelled in the public role of culprits; they were thrilled when charged with outraging public morals, for notoriety increased their celebrity. Like mischievous children, they put themselves in anomalous positions, in which they could be decried as criminals by the authorities while their admirers could indignantly proclaim their innocence. Although they violated middle-class customs, they recoiled from the lives of the labouring poor, and indeed their constant tilting against respectability and public order were an affirmation of the importance of ordered society. Their acts of rebellion were seldom more than theatrical gestures of bourgeois disgruntlement. When Charles Nodier entered 'Come to overturn your Republic' under the heading 'Purpose of Visit' in a hotel register at Geneva, it was in exasperation at nothing more oppressive than the proliferation of 'Keep off the grass' signs in the local parks. Charles-Augustin Saint-Beuve (1804–69) turned up for a duel grasping a pistol in one hand and an umbrella in the other. The concession of Victor Hugo (1802–85) to his wife after taking a mistress in 1834 was to buy into a pension scheme.[104]

The French writers made their lives into public spectacles intended to impress their friends and outrage their opponents. Flaubert conceded in 1846 that his 'basic nature' was 'that of a mountebank'.[105] Jules

Vallès (1832–85) called Baudelaire 'a ham actor'.[106] Neither the motives nor the achievements of these creative young Frenchmen were invariably contemptible. They were sincere in desiring to extend their emotional experiences and to enhance their aesthetic awareness: they embraced suffering; they minimised the value of repose. 'There is nothing worse than the life of an oyster,' Mérimée adjured in 1843. 'The repose of which you sometimes speak admiringly, just like that of hashish, which gives the superior satisfaction of this sort, is nothing in comparison with the bliss "which is almost a torment".'[107] Honoré de Balzac (1799–1850) similarly explained in 1846 that he tried hashish because he wanted to make 'a study upon myself of this very extraordinary phenomenon'. He modelled his approach on the pharmacological and psychological self-experimentation of Sir Humphry Davy (1778–1829) and the Brunonian physician Thomas Beddoes (1760–1808).[108]

Supremely these French bohemians were 'the orphans of liberty disinherited by Napoleon', as Nodier said.[109] Almost a million Frenchmen (half of whom were aged less than twenty-eight) had died between the Revolution in 1789 and the Battle of Waterloo in 1815. The younger surviving intellectuals reacted against the crude savagery of soldiers and rampaging revolutionary mobs: they came into their imaginative powers after the great myth-making revolutionary period, and needed to devise their own personalised myths. Yet the Bourbon restoration of the 1820s connoted sobriety, prudence and stultification. Although the Orléanists were swept to power in 1830 on a wave of popular enthusiasm, their reforming impulses were soon dispelled, and by 1840 France was in the grip of a bourgeois reaction. The young intelligentsia replaced the violence of the outer world with turbulent introspection. They rejected leaden, lugubrious facts for unruly, mettlesome fantasy. 'We were not only troubadours, rebels and Orientals', Flaubert wrote of his youth, 'above all else, we were artists.' The troubador-rebels intoxicated themselves as a way of estranging themselves. Like De Quincey and Nodier in the first decade of the nineteenth century, they heightened their aesthetic or emotional responses even as they felt alienated. When Eugène Sue (1804–57) gave a cigarette (purportedly hashish, perhaps opium-tinged) to Balzac before a performance of Rossini's *La Gazza Iadra*, the novelist's observation became detached from his capacity for human recognition. 'The music came to me through shining clouds, stripped of all the imperfections that human works contain.' The orchestra seemed 'a vast . . . incomprehensible, mechanism . . . since all I could make out were the necks of the double basses, the daring of the bows, the golden curves of the trombones, the clarinets, the finger-holes, but no musicians. Just one or two powdered wigs, motionless, and two swollen faces, grimacing.'[110]

The fashionable curiosity about hashish among a few influential Parisians originated in the vainglorious brutality of Napoleon's occupation of Egypt in 1798–1801. Although French officers penalised the sale or use of cannabis, awareness of the drug's existence was suddenly raised by first-hand exposure. Napoleon's Egyptian adventure resulted in many new fashions in France—some ephemeral, such as fire-dogs shaped like sphinxes, and some more enduring, like hashish. News of the drug's properties spread from France across Europe. A later adventitious sequence of events enhanced French knowledge of hashish. Algeria, on the North African coast, had long lain under the suzerainty of Turkish military rule. In 1827, during an audience, the French consul was so rude that the reigning Dey of Algiers flicked him with a fly whisk. After an interval of three years, the regime of Charles X, which was striving to regain its grip of domestic affairs, determined to revive its reputation by a patriotic adventure overseas. An expeditionary force was sent to Algeria to avenge the earlier insult to French honour. Pleasure boats carried fashionable sightseers to observe the naval bombardment of Algiers, from which the Dey was soon expelled, although Charles X was also dethroned in July 1830. The historian and statesman François-Pierre-Guillaume Guizot (1787–1874) later told an Englishman: 'Cupidity created the germ of *your* distant empire, vanity created ours.'[111] Most of Algeria was subsequently subdued and colonised by the French. By 1841 over 37,000 Frenchmen (mostly ex-soldiers) had settled there. In 1848 Algeria, including its vast empty Saharan territories, was integrated into France, and subdivided among three administrative *départements*. This colonial foray, like the earlier occupation of Egypt, familiarised many Frenchmen with hashish. Victor Hugo's collection of exotic poems, *Les Orientales* (1829), had already excited worries about the irrational feelings and unorthodox behaviour associated with both the drug and Islamic society; but hashish's public profile was inexorably raised as the colonisation of Algeria developed. 'Hashish is replacing champagne,' Théophile Gautier

(1811–72) declared in 1845: 'we believe we have conquered Algeria, but Algeria has conquered us.'[112]

For the intelligentsia hashish seemed more alluring because of its association with primitive cultures. They recoiled aghast from the newly mechanised Europe. 'Civilisation, that shrivelled runt of human aspirations', so Flaubert railed in 1837, 'that bitch, inventor of railways, prisons, enema pumps, cream cakes, of royalty and the guillotine.'[113] In 1849 he accompanied Maxime du Camp (1822–94) on a Middle Eastern tour. Travel for both men provided opportunities to experiment with sex, opium and hashish. 'Nowhere has better brothels than Cairo,' Flaubert boasted. He described 'sitting on the divan smoking our pipes' and in a relaxed reverie watching two dancing men, 'a pair of rogues, somewhat ugly, but charming in their corruption, in the calculated depravity of their gaze, and in the effeminacy of their movements'. He visited bath-houses to test the pleasures of sodomy: 'Travelling for our edification . . . we have considered it as our duty to try this mode of ejaculation.'[114] Returning to provincial France, Flaubert lost the boldness of a young man on a foreign spree. 'These drugs always arouse in me a great craving,' he later told Baudelaire. 'I still possess some excellent hashish compounded by the pharmacist Gastinel. But it frightens me, for which I reproach myself.'[115] Nevertheless he redevised his drug experiences in his fiction, with the homosexuality discreetly erased. In *L'éducation sentimentale* Flaubert described a Parisian courtesan of 1848 whose protector had fantasies of the harem: 'Rosanette appeared, dressed in a pink satin jacket, white cashmere trousers, a necklace of Eastern coins, and a red smoking cap, round which was twined a spray of jasmine'. Indicating a platinum-tubed hookah resting on a purple divan, she explains, 'The prince likes me like this, and I have to smoke this contraption.' For Flaubert, as for some other people, drug paraphernalia had an erotic charge. Rosanette displays herself smoking opium before a suggestible young man:

> Shall we try it? Would you care to?
> A light was brought. The zinc furnace was hard to kindle, and she began to stamp with impatience. Then suddenly she grew languid; and she lay motionless on the divan, with a cushion under her armpit. Her body was twisted a little; one knee was bent and the other leg outstretched. The long snake of red morocco lay on the floor in rings and coiled

about her arm. She pressed the amber mouthpiece to her lips and looked at Frederic with half-closed eyes, through the clouds of smoke that surrounded her. Her breathing made the water gurgle, and she murmured from time to time.[116]

The seductiveness of this scene reinforced the association of drugs with sexiness that had been popularised by Alexandre Dumas (1802–70) in *The Count of Monte Cristo* (1844). This great romantic novel, beloved by generations of European schoolboys, included luxuriant descriptions of Aladdin inhaling hashish supplied by Sinbad: 'His body seemed to acquire an airy lightness, his perception brightened in a remarkable manner, his senses seemed to redouble their power, the horizon continued to expand . . . with all the blue of the ocean, all the spangles of the sun, all the perfumes of the breeze.' A vivid dream scene reaches a climax in an underground chamber where statues of beautiful courtesans suddenly come to life.

> He gave way before looks that held him in a torturing grasp and delighted his senses as with a voluptuous kiss . . . Then followed a dream of passion like that promised by the Prophet to the elect. Lips of stone turned to flame, breasts of ice became like heated lava, so that . . . love was a sorrow and voluptuousness a torture, as burning mouths were pressed to his thirsty lips, and he was held in cool, serpent-like embraces. The more he strove against this unhallowed passion the more the senses yielded to its thrall, and at length, weary of a struggle that taxed his very soul, he gave way and sank back breathless and exhausted beneath the kisses of those marble goddesses, and the enchantment of his marvellous dream.[117]

A new drug fantasy had been imagined for mass readers.

Théophile Gautier is more closely identified with the history of hashish than Flaubert or Dumas. He was introduced to the drug at the Hôtel Pimodan on the Quai d'Anjou, Île Saint-Louis, by the dilettante painter Ferdinand Boissard de Boisdenier (1813–66). In a boudoir adjoining Boissard's rooms there a melodramatic secret society called the Club des Haschishins met monthly. The club's pantomimic rites were modelled on an Oriental order, commanded by an autocrat called the Vieux de la Montagne, or Prince of Assassins, but its 'fantasias' were usually completed by eleven, when everyone went quietly to bed. Visitors to the club included the caricaturist Honoré Daumier (1808–79), the painter Paul Chenavard (1808–95), the writer Gérard de Nerval (1808–55) together with the sculptor Jean-Jacques Pradier (1790–1852) and his wife Louise Darcet (who partly inspired Flaubert in devising the character of Emma Bovary). The presence of women added an erotic tinge to the evenings. A note survives from 1848 in which Gautier invited Pradier 'to sample hashish' at a fantasia: 'You could probably have the great satisfaction of observing the effects of this drug on an elegant woman, and compare her intoxication with the ecstasies of Louise.'[118] Boissard, who was a pharmacist's son, was a meticulous host at each 'Oriental feast'. His hashish parties were not the only ones in Paris. Gautier was also invited (in 1847) to a rival 'confianza', organised by the ophthalmologist Édouard Tallien de Cabarrus (1801–70), to which the painters Théodore Chassériau (1819–56) and Eugène Delacroix (1798–1863) were also bidden.[119]

As early as July 1843 Gautier published an article, 'Le Hachich', recounting his first experiment with the drug. (Later he wrote *Le Club de Haschischins* and *La Pipe d'Opium*). The article described his experiences after eating some hashish cooked with 'butter, pistachios, almonds, or honey to make a jam which somewhat resembles apricot paste, and is not of a disagreeable taste'. Drug-users writing about their experiences are invariably self-centred, but Gautier's article—in which he takes the part of an histrionic proselytiser—is a crucial document in the early promotion of cannabis, and deserves to be quoted in all its grandiloquence: 'It seemed to me that my body was dissolving and becoming transparent. I could see very clearly in my chest the hashish which I had eaten in the form of a glittering emerald; my eyelashes were elongating indefinitely'. He felt engulfed in a 'kaleidoscope' of 'precious gems of all colours, of arabesques, of floral patterns [which] renewed themselves unceasingly'. Occasionally he glimpsed the other guests, 'but disfigured, part men, part plants, with the pensive airs of an ibis, standing on one foot, or of an ostrich flapping its wings so funnily that I became hilarious in my corner'. After a half-hour interval, a new 'vision' began. 'A swarm of millions of fluttering butterflies whose wings flapped like fans'; gigantic flowers in crystal chalices, lilies of gold and silver. Gautier's hearing became 'prodigiously enhanced; I could hear the noise of colours. Greens, reds, blues, yellows reached me in perfectly distinct sound-waves. A glass overturning, a creak of the chair, a muttered word, all resonated for me like cracks of thunder.' Then, hearing phrases from Rossini's *Barber of Seville* and Donizetti's *Lucia di Lammermoor*, he 'swam in an ocean of sonority'. Finally, while Gautier was experiencing a vision of 'perfect symmetry', 'the magic paste was suddenly assimilated with great force in my brain, so that I became completely mad for an hour'. In this state he envisioned 'a living loco-motive with the neck of a swan terminating in the mouth of a serpent, spurting fire, with monstrous legs composed of wheels and pulleys; each pair of legs was accompanied by a pair of wings, and on the tail of the animal, one could see an ancient Mercury'.[120]

Gautier's pioneering article perhaps influenced Dumas in writing *Monte Cristo*. Certainly it was used by Dr Joseph Moreau de Tours (1804–84) in his treatise *Du Hachisch et de l'aliénation mentale, études psy-chologiques* (1845). Just as the eighteenth-century opium zealot Dr John Brown had amassed a school of Brunonians, so Moreau in the nine-teenth century collected a cell of hashish assassins. He pursued his researches jointly with the epidemiologist Louis-Rémy d'Aubert-Roche (1810–74). During the 1830s D'Aubert-Roche had toured Egypt, Arabia, the Red Sea, Abyssinia and the Ottoman Empire inves-tigating plague and typhus, and in 1840 published an essay on the use of hashish to treat the plague. Another essay by him on hashish was published in 1843. Doubtless it was D'Aubert-Roche who skulked in anonymity in Gautier's article of 1843: 'Doctor ★★★, who has travelled extensively in the Orient, and is a confirmed hashish eater, went first, and took a stronger dose than the rest of us; he saw the stars in his plate, and the firmament at the bottom of the soup tureen; then he turned his nose to the wall, talked to himself, roared with laughter, his eyes lit up with deep jubilation.'[121] The ideas of Moreau, who later published a treatise on hysteria, attracted Balzac. He read Moreau's *Du Hachisch* in order to improve his description of Lucien de Rubempré's hallucina-tions in *Splendeurs et misères des courtisanes*. 'It's an idea which I've had too', he informed Moreau, 'to research the roots of madness by explor-ing our momentary aberrations or exaltations.' Balzac sampled hashish at a 'fantasia' held at the Hôtel Pimodan. According to his account, 'I withstood the hashish and didn't experience all the phenomena; my brain is so resilient that I needed a stronger dose than the one I took. Nevertheless, I heard some celestial voices and saw some heavenly paintings.'[122] This was written to impress a woman: in truth his performance was more craven. According to Baudelaire and Gautier, Balzac merely scrutinised, sniffed and handed back a sample of hashish. Like many other first-time experimenters with drugs, Balzac thought he wanted to propel himself into a vortex of excitement, and then found that he did not.

Hashish was only a phase in Gautier's life, but it symbolised an experimental broad-mindedness that affronted nineteenth-century respectability. 'His principal foible was a propensity for certain *risqué* subjects, and it would certainly have been better for him and for others if *Mademoiselle de Maupin* had never seen the light,' declared an obituarist in 1872.[123] Hints of drugged reveries in contemporary literature were often deprecated. *Palm-Leaves* (1844), a poetic sequence on the Islamic world written by the politician Richard Monckton Milnes (1809–85), afterwards Lord Houghton, was faulted for its passive, luxurious tone. 'His poems want those flashing, cleaving, bolt-like passages, that earnestness and heart,' complained one English reviewer. 'All here is calm, equable and placid . . . it is all a dreamy vision.'[124] Although Monckton Milnes did not permit himself any explicit references to opium or hashish, the suggestion of psychoactive drugs was evident.

French medical interest in hashish focused on the psychological influence of the drug, although D'Aubert-Roche explored its possibilities as a prophylactic against the plague. But British physicians, working in India, were more concerned with the curative properties of what they significantly preferred to call cannabis. According to one nineteenth-century report, '*Cannabis indica* must be looked upon as one of the most important drugs of Indian Materia Medica.'[125] *Bhang* was prescribed by native practitioners for colds and applied in the form of poultices; *ganja* and *charas* were inhaled to treat brain fever, cramps, convulsions in children, headache, hysteria, neuralgia, sciatica and tetanus. Hemp drugs were recommended for a huge range of ailments: hydrophobia, ague, remittent fever, cholera, dysentery, phthisis, erysipelas, gonorrhoea, flatulence, diarrhoea, dyspepsia, piles, prolapsed anus, hay-fever, asthma, bronchitis, diabetes, rheumatism, gout, scabies, guinea-worm and boils. In some cases hemp drugs must have harmed patients—disastrously for bronchitic patients, the drug was mixed with tobacco—but many European physicians were impressed by hemp's effects on convulsive children, neuralgia, tetanus, hydrophobia (rabies) and dysentery. The crucial figure in the adoption by European practitioners of hemp preparations used by native doctors was the Irish-born, Edinburgh-trained physician Sir William Brooke O'Shaughnessy (1809–89), who changed his name to O'Shaughnessy Brooke on receiving the accolade of knighthood. His pioneering paper 'On the preparations of the Indian hemp, or *gunjah* (*cannabis indica*) in the treatment of tetanus and other convulsive diseases' was first published in a Calcutta medical journal, and more influentially summarised in the *Lancet* in 1840.[126] But the future belonged to the *flâneurs* at the Hôtel Pimodan.

FOUR

Nerves, Needles and
Victorian Doctors

Whipping and abuse are like laudanum:
you have to double the dose as the sensibilities decline.
—HARRIET BEECHER STOWE

I feel myself torn apart by the craze for analysis that the
chemical philosophy of our age induces in us. We no longer say,
'What do I know?', like Montaigne, but 'What for?'
—HECTOR BERLIOZ

ODERN DRUG HISTORY began in the 1820s, but there were continuous developments throughout the nineteenth century. The political context of Indian opium exports to China changed in the 1850s; hypodermic syringes were perfected in the same decade, and were popularised in Europe and the USA by the 1870s; and in consequence the *Morbid Craving for Morphia* (to use a book title of 1878) became a recognised problem. The American Civil War of 1861–65, the Austro-Prussian war of 1866 and the Franco-Prussian war of 1870–71 raised levels of addiction among combatants. Physicians refined their theories of addiction by studying the deaths and blighted lives of drug-consumers. These developments occurred during the Victorian apotheosis. In England, so the French critic Hippolyte Taine (1828–93) reported in the 1860s, 'there is nothing beyond work conscientiously done, useful production, and a secure and convenient comfort in one's own home'.[1] The Berlin physician Eduard Levinstein (1831–82) summarised his national *Zeitgeist* when he wrote admiringly in the 1870s of a type of morphine addict who did not let his habit become the centre of his attention: 'who is, on the contrary, mostly absorbed by his art or profession; who fulfils his duties to his government, to his family, and his fellow citizens in an irreproachable manner'.[2] In the USA the claims of work, good citizenry and spiritual uplift were given a similar priority.

The most important changes resulted from the development of hypodermic syringes, and their use in treating neuralgic and chronically ill patients. The late eighteenth-century European discovery of inoculation had revived interest in intravenous medicine. Techniques of opiate injection were slowly developed. In 1836 Dr G.V. Lafargue of St Emilion reported pushing a vaccination lancet, which had been dipped in morphine, under a patient's skin so as to administer morphine into the bloodstream. Lafargue regarded this inoculation as a means of local medication; he used it to cure his own facial neuralgia. In the same decade the American physician Isaac Taylor used a blunt-nozzled syringe to administer morphine. The Irishman Dr Francis Rynd (died 1861) in 1844 cured a woman of neuralgia by injecting a solution of morphine from a gravity-fed bottle attached to a hollow needle. Both Lafargue and Rynd made their injections into the most painful nerves, and regarded their techniques as a type of local anaesthesia directed at the seat of pain. Helen Gladstone in the 1840s apparently sometimes took opiates with the help of a needle: this is the presumed meaning of her brother recording her self-accusation in 1845 of 'self-murder—treating the arm as a kind of Cain's mark'.[3] Conceivably she procured a little syringe constructed by Mr Ferguson of Giltspur Street, London, whose elegant workmanship was praised by an Edinburgh physician, Dr Alexander Wood (1817–84).[4] Proceeding independently of Rynd, Wood developed a hypodermic procedure, using a syringe constructed on the model of a bee-sting, which he publicised in papers of 1855 and 1858. Wood injected his patients in the arm, as a form of local anaesthesia, and believed that he had solved the problem of morphine addiction. It was his idea that taking opiates through the mouth, and the act of swallowing, created an appetite, like other forms of food or drink. He became convinced that if the drug was injected rather than swallowed, patients would not hunger for it. He was mistaken. Several of Wood's patients became dependent on hypodermic administration of morphine. The story that Wood's wife, Rebecca Massy, was amongst the earliest of these addicts, and soon died of a morphine overdose, has been repeated by those who believe he should have suffered retribution. It is a myth: she outlived him, and survived until 1894.

A London doctor, Charles Hunter (1835–78), further advanced this therapeutic revolution. In 1858 he reported that he had abandoned Wood's method of injecting morphine into the most painful area affected by neuralgia, and was injecting into cellular tissue of the neck, arm and other bodily parts. It was Hunter who coined the word 'hypodermic' to distinguish it from the local injection system that Wood had named 'subcutaneous'. A controversy arose as to whether injections of morphine were more effective when localised near the seat of pain; it took several decades for Hunter's view to prevail. No one seems to have injected morphine intravenously until the twentieth century, when American drug-users were turned by prohibition legislation from opium-smoking to heroin injections in the period after 1910. Hunter recommended hypodermic medication of morphine for general therapies and as a nerve tonic in cases of exhaustion or depression. Morphine injections avoided the gastric irritation that accompanied orally administered opiates. Westminster Hospital's Francis Anstie (1833–74), who was founding editor of the influential periodical *The Practitioner*, endorsed Hunter's procedures. 'Of danger', Anstie wrote in 1868, 'there is absolutely none.'[5]

Morphine was first injected in Germany in 1856 into a neuralgic woman who had previously been treated in Edinburgh by Wood.[6] In the 1860s Felix von Niemeyer (1820–71), professor of Pathology and Therapeutics and Director of the Medical Centre at the University of Tübingen in the kingdom of Württemberg, first observed that this treatment of neuralgia was creating addiction. 'The introduction of hypodermic injections', he explained in a major textbook, 'was a great event, and . . . an immense advance in treatment,' but unfortunately the new procedure was abused. 'I know many physicians who never go out to their practice without a syringe and a solution of morphine in their pocket, and who usually bring the morphine-bottle home empty.' If injections were continued, and doses increased, patients became dependent. 'They feel dull, and complain of an indefinable weakness, discomfort, trembling etc. Some describe their state as resembling a hangover [*Katzenjammer*].'[7] Niemeyer's pioneering remarks were supported in articles of 1874–76 by Alfred Fiedler (1835–1921), who suggested that morphine addiction was attributable to an emotional disturbance to which some individuals were specially predisposed. The Viennese psychiatrist Maximilian Leidesdorf (1815–89) published a comparable article on morphine withdrawal in 1876. Abstinence sickness was more acute with hypodermic users, as the Bavarian toxicologist Hermann von Boeck (b. 1843) warned:

> It is easier to cure a morphine-eater of his passion than a morphine-injector; frequently our only resource is physical violence; for instance, I know a case in which a young doctor could only be cured of giving himself morphine injections by being actually shut up in a room for more than a week. He resisted like a maniac, scratched at the walls with his nails, wept and shrieked from misery, ate nothing, and was unable to sleep, had diarrhoea, etc. At last, after some days of unmerciful treatment, he began to feel better, to sleep, to eat.[8]

Eduard Levinstein, who as superintendent of the asylum at Schöneberg made a speciality of his drug-dependent inmates, published a monograph, *Die Morphiumsucht* (1877), which was translated into English as *Morbid Craving for Morphia* (1878), mentioned earlier. Medical men who had instructed patients with painful, protracted illnesses how to inject morphine themselves were 'the originators and propagators of this disease', he wrote. These professional colleagues 'must not be blamed for acting as they did', as they were intending to relieve their patients' suffering and were unaware 'of the attendant danger'. But he condemned talkative patients for praising morphine as a remedy to one another, and thus spreading 'the evil'.[9] Levinstein was emphatic that people's 'morbid craving for morphia injections . . . results from their natural constitution, and not from a certain predisposition'.[10] It could happen to anyone.

The first English warnings about hypodermic morphine addiction came in 1870 from the Yorkshire physician whom George Eliot (1819–80) took as the model for Dr Lydgate in *Middlemarch* (1871). As recently as the previous year (Sir) Clifford Allbutt (1836–1925) had advocated the hypodermic injection of morphine as a 'marvellous remedy' for dyspepsia and for relieving the distress of cardiac disease. 'Injected morphia seemed so different to swallowed morphia, no one had any experience of ill effects from it, and we all had the daily experience of it as a means of peace and comfort, while pain on the other hand was certainly the forerunner of wretchedness and exhaustion.'[11] He soon repented his early zeal, and by 1870 suspected morphine injections, 'though free from the ordinary evils of opium eating', of arousing cravings attended by restlessness and depression. Allbutt had read Niemeyer's observations, which supported his own clinical experience. He had in Yorkshire nine neuralgic women patients who had been injecting morphine for up to three years. 'They seem as far from cure as they ever were, they all find relief in the incessant use of the syringe, and they all declare that without the syringe life would be insupportable.' Allbutt feared 'that now the hypodermic use of morphia is brought into sensational novels as a melodramatic device, it may indeed be said to have reached the heights of fashion'.[12] Following these negative reports, the chemist C. R. Alder Wright (1844–94) began trying to isolate a powerful but non-addictive alternative to morphine. In 1874 he boiled morphine with acetic anhydride, and obtained a substance that received little further attention. It was only in 1898 that a German commercial laboratory first marketed his discovery: the story of heroin, as the substance was ultimately named, will be reserved for later chapters.

Levinstein's advice that morphine injections should be discontinued as soon as the disease receded did not address the dangers if patients were chronically ill and renewed their injections to relieve recurrent symptoms. Indeed, though this was less well understood, an individual need only consume opiates continuously for ten days to a fortnight to arouse physiological dependence: a patient ill even for a fortnight was at risk. Levinstein was adamant that patients must never be left with hypodermic syringes to use themselves. Painful diseases and insomnia made convalescents nervous, depressed and self-pitying so that they magnified the importance of every trifling bodily change that a healthy person would ignore. If morphine injections had helped during the worst phase of illness, and they had ready access to a syringe, few could resist when they were worried by aches or the recurrence of a restless night.[13] In Prussia decrees dating from 1800–1801 prohibited the sale of opium and its preparations to the general public, and ordered that prescriptions containing opium should not be repeated without the knowledge and renewed order of the physician. A German imperial decree of 1872 sought to restrict the supply of morphine by pharmacists. Despite these regulations, chemists and druggists continued selling morphine to the German public, and renewed prescriptions for morphine injections without physicians' knowledge.[14] Similarly, when the level of fatal opium overdoses in Britain in the 1860s roused the General Medical Council against self-medication with opiates, the Pharmaceutical Society lobbied to protect the profits of druggists. The resultant Pharmacy Act of 1868 was a compromise that scarcely reduced the number of accidental and suicidal opiate deaths, although the number of children dying from opiate overdoses fell (20.5 fatalities per million of the population in the mid-1860s to 12.7 per million in 1871 and 6.5 per million in the mid-1880s). People who could afford to consult physicians had little difficulty in obtaining opiates by medical prescription; opium-based patent medicines were excluded from the 1868 Act, and were still available to the poor over druggists' counters, although no longer from general dealers. The 1868 Act rested on voluntary self-regulation, and was no more strictly enforced than the German imperial decree four years later.[15]

European experience with morphine injections was replicated in the USA. On a visit to Edinburgh in 1856 the American obstetrician Fordyce Barker (1817–91) was given a hypodermic syringe, which he afterwards used in New York. During the late 1850s the surgeon Edward Warren (1828–93) began administering morphine under the skin using a lancet and a syringe, and thus established his claim to be a pioneer of American hypodermic medication. However, hypodermic syringes were not accepted as part of the general equipment of American physicians until the 1870s. The doyen of American addiction history, David Courtwright, argues that American opium addiction was by mid-century becoming a serious medical problem. He suggests that the treatment with opiates of patients during the American cholera epidemics of 1832–33 and 1848–54, and the dysentery epidemic of 1847–51, contributed to this situation. Many American physicians repeated the mistakes noted by Niemeyer and Levinstein in Germany. Even if they failed to make addicts of their patients by repeated administration of morphine in excess of ten days, they trusted the patient or the patient's carers with the drug, its accompanying syringe and instructions on their use. There were no controls on the patient increasing the frequency and amount of doses.[16] As the American medical writer Horace Day asked in 1868, 'where is the patient who has learned the secret of substituting luxurious enjoyment in place of acute pain by day and restless hours by night, that can be trusted to take a correct measure of their own necessities?'[17] The danger of addiction was reduced when patients attributed their suffering at morphine withdrawal to their illness; but increased if patients knew that their distress was caused by the withdrawal of morphine. Similarly the risk of addiction was increased where patients knew the name of the drug that had alleviated their symptoms. 'Those who have once experienced the rapid and unfailing relief of the subcutaneous injection are no longer content to await the action of the more uncertain remedies to which they had formerly been accustomed,' as an English physician noted in 1875.[18]

The prescription of opium or morphine for chronically ill patients, with such diseases as asthma, bronchitis, diarrhoea, dysentery, malaria, arthritis and rheumatism, thus often aroused addiction. 'None who have not known long chronic illness can conceive of the misery enforced idleness inflicts on a man used to active life,' the Philadelphia neurologist Silas Weir Mitchell (1829–1914) explained. 'This death of ennui is the most efficient bribe which opium offers.'[19] It was recognised by non-medical people that opiate-based treatments for chronic illness sometimes proved fatal. The treatment for chronic illness of Comte Louis Mathieu Molé (1781–1855), a former French prime minister, created a drug dependency until finally he died of the 'remedy' that had kept him alive.[20] Some patients who, knowing this danger, refused opiates were nevertheless surreptitiously administered them. 'The ignorant distrust of opium' was widespread, declared an English laudanum-drinker in 1868. 'Every doctor in large practice finds himself, now and then, obliged to deceive his patients.'[21] The correlation of addiction with chronic illness is shown by the low addiction rate among blacks in nineteenth-century USA. Slaves, ex-slaves and descendants of slaves were deterred from consulting physicians by poverty and the lack of black practitioners; few of them anyway lived long enough to contract chronic illness. By contrast white southerners, who could afford physicians and suffered such chronic diseases as malaria and diarrhoea, became dependent on opium or morphine. The correlation of addiction with chronic illness also meant that few young Europeans or Americans became dependent on opium or morphine as the result of reckless prescriptions for chronic illness; such addiction more typically began with middle age.[22] The relief given to the chronically ill by opiates tempted them to use the drug to relieve anxiety. 'They drown their anger, their domestic sorrows, and their business cares', according to Levinstein, until a permanent need of morphine was roused. Thereafter with 'their morally and physically miserable life, they again and again make use of another injection of this poison, in the hope of forgetting the misery brought on by themselves'.[23]

Families developed traditions of taking opium or morphine. Aurore Dupin, Baronesse Dudevante (1804–76), who is best known as the novelist George Sand, described in 1873 how she treated bronchitis in her family with minimal doses of morphine taken every evening for a week or more. 'It's so easy and swift! You feel the improvement after two or three days.'[24] No permanent habits were aroused in her family. Louis-Joseph Berlioz (1776–1848), a distinguished physician of the Dauphiné who introduced acupuncture to Europe, depended on opium (ostensibly taken for gastritis). It did not perceptibly disrupt his life, and probably encouraged his son Hector Berlioz in his use of opiates. The composer used laudanum, ostensibly for abdominal pains, but in reality for surcease. 'I must take my . . . ten drops of laudanum and forget things until tomorrow,' he once wrote. ' "Gods of Oblivion." '[25] His frequent experiences of 'nervous exaltation' he compared to 'the sensations brought on by opium'.[26] Opium's influence on his *Symphonie Fantastique* (Fantastic Symphony) and his opera *Les Troyens* (The Trojans) was enriching, and drugs do not seem to have had a destructive effect on his daily life.

The English novelist Wilkie Collins (1824–89) was less fortunate. He had seen the pain of his father's protracted fatal illness relieved by an opium preparation called Batley's Powder: when he in turn succumbed to rheumatism and gout in 1862, he resorted to laudanum despite knowing its dangers.[27] Laudanum soon had mastery over him, as indicated by a letter of 1869:

My doctor is trying to break me of the habit of drinking laudanum. I am stabbed every night at ten with a sharp-pointed syringe which injects morphia under my skin—and gets me a night's rest without any of the drawbacks of taking opium internally. If I only persevere with this, I am told I shall be able, before long, gradually to diminish the quantity of morphia and the number of nightly stabbings—and so

emancipate myself from opium altogether. I am ashamed to bore you
with these trumpery details.[28]

This treatment failed, and Collins wrote of himself in 1885: 'Laudanum—divine laudanum—was his only friend.'[29] He always carried a
small silver flask of laudanum with him, kept a decanter of laudanum
at home, and drank a wineglass of laudanum before bed. Morphine he
sometimes injected too. Opiates recur in his novels. In *No Name*
(1862), Magdalen Vanstone, a girl usurped of her inheritance, sits up all
night at a window, holding a laudanum bottle, wondering about suicide. In *Armadale* (1866) the 'she-devil' Lydia Gwilt also stays up late
one night. She is so anxious about the outcome of her devious schemes
that she takes laudanum, that 'comforter' of 'all the miserable wretches
in pain of body and mind'. Next morning, with recovered self-possession, she crows in her diary: 'I have had six delicious hours of oblivion;
I have woke up with my mind composed; I have written a perfect little letter to Midwinter; I have drunk my nice cup of tea, with a real
relish of it; I have dawdled over my morning toilet with an exquisite
sense of relief—and all through the modest little bottle of drops, which
I see on my bedroom chimney-piece at this moment. "Drops, you are
a darling! If I love nothing else, I love you!" '[30] The plot of *The Moonstone*, which Collins dictated under the influence of laudanum in 1868,
revolves around the effects of opium administered to an insomniac.
Another character, who has become addicted to opium as a result of
chronic disease, describes nightmares that were surely versions of
Collins's own: 'a dreadful night; the vengeance of yesterday's opium
pursuing me through a series of frightful dreams'.[31] Unlike Berlioz,
Collins's creative powers were ultimately dulled by opiates. They worsened his tendency to fussy self-absorption, especially about his health.

In the eighteenth and early nineteenth centuries the treatment of
stomach pains with opiates was the chief cause of serious drug dependence. However, the treatment of neuralgia probably raised Victorian
levels of morphine addiction more than any other condition. Morphine killed the pain of this nervous affliction, pacified highly strung
people and quelled the physical symptoms. The earliest clinical description of neuralgia is a French account of the *tic douloureux* in 1756. By
the mid-nineteenth century the word was used to cover a range of
complaints whose origins and actions often remained obscure. The

word covered such diverse ailments as shooting pains in the nerves, sciatica (then known as rheumatic neuralgia), herpes, toothache, migraine, nervous angina and symptoms produced by secondary syphilis. Muscular rheumatism was sometimes confused with neuralgia. In many patients wet weather and raw winds were an aggravation. Apart from cases where neuralgia arose from malaria or rheumatism, which were usually curable by quinine and sulphur baths respectively, it was a chronic disease. As late as 1876 the neurologist Wilhelm Erb (1840–1921), a forester's son from the Rhenish Palatinate who became a medical professor at Heidelberg, stressed 'our profound ignorance' of the nature of neuralgia, which he ranked as 'among the most common of neuroses' and attributed to 'hereditary neuropathic predisposition'.[32]

In some cases neuralgia was the body's protest against overexertion. Berlioz succumbed while working on his last great work, the opera *Les Troyens*. As he described in 1858, 'I'm living in hell; my neuralgia doesn't give me a moment's rest. Every day at nine in the morning I have violent colics which endure until two or three in the afternoon; spasms in the chest; in the evening pains in the neck of the bladder with redoubled spasms. And depression to darken the rising sun, disgust with everything!'[33] Electrotherapy brought no cure, and Berlioz's resort to opiates is surely reflected in the climax of *Les Troyens* entitled 'The Gods of Oblivion'. In other cases, neuralgia could carry a stigma with employers. A gentleman's valet in George Eliot's novel *Felix Holt* (1866) was neuralgic. 'Next to the pain itself he disliked that anybody should know of it: defective health diminished a man's market value'. Accordingly he used opium to quell his nervous pains, and 'consoled himself ... by thinking that if the pains ever became intolerably frequent a considerable increase to the dose might put an end to them altogether'.[34]

Despite such cases, Francis Anstie, author of *Neuralgia* (1871), was surely correct to attribute the Victorian neuralgic crisis to the damaging effect on people's nerves of aggressive moral training and policing. 'A positively poisonous influence upon the nervous system, especially in youth, is the direct result of efforts, dictated often by the highest motives, to train the emotions and aspirations to a high ideal, especially to a high religious ideal,' he warned. This idealism was inculcated either by the public-school ethos—'education which deliberately dwarfs the nervous energy, with the hope of preserving the mind from the contamination of unbelief and of sinful passion'—or by the 'Puritan' system which sought to purify people by perpetual introspective self-reproach.

> The lessons which our psychologists are rapidly learning, as to the evil effects on the brain of an education that promotes *self-consciousness*, are sorely needed to be applied to the pathology of nervous diseases generally, and of neuralgia among the rest. Common sense and common humanity, when united with the physician's knowledge, cry out against the system under which religious parents and teachers subject the feeble and highly mobile nervous systems of the young to the tremendous strain of spiritual self-questioning upon the most momentous topics. More especially is such a practice to be condemned in the case of boys and girls who are passing through the terrible ordeal of sexual development; an epoch which . . . is peculiarly favourable to the formation of the neurotic habit; and I must emphatically state my belief that among the seriously minded English middle classes, more especially, whose life is necessarily colourless and monotonous, the mischief thus worked is both grave and widely spread.[35]

Taine endorsed this view of Christianity in Victorian Britain—'it subordinates ritual and dogma to ethics; it practices "self-government", the authority of conscience and the cultivation of the will'—in terms equally applicable to American puritanism.[36]

Morphine addiction was interlaced with Victorian sexual attitudes. Neuroses were recognised by the early 1870s as frequently sexual in origin—attributed to sexual excess as well as to sexual frustration—and opiates were deployed in the medical battle against them. The Victorians furiously loathed masturbation, perhaps because unlike other sexual acts it could never be sentimentalised. Anstie believed that masturbating boys became 'self-centred, and often suffer, not merely from fanciful fears and fanciful pains, but from actual neuralgia'. The migraine torment of boys 'addicted to bad practices' was analogous to 'hysteria in little girls under similar circumstances'.[37] Erb agreed that sexuality induced illness:

> The *sexual periods of life* are of great importance to the development of neuralgia. The profound influences exerted upon the nervous system by the genital organs during and after puberty, the great revolution that is effected in the entire organism, owing to the awakening of sexual activ-

ity, the extreme irritation of the nervous system from overpowering desire, and the exhaustion from over-frequent or unnatural gratification, are only too fruitful causes of those changes in the nutrition of the nervous system which occasion the neuropathic predisposition. Thus we see that the period of puberty and of the grand climacteric, that the occurrence of the menses, that pregnancy and the puerperal period, are particularly fruitful in the production of neuralgic affections, and we see, too, that sexual excesses, and particularly the vice of masturbation so frequently practised by both sexes in the present day, are often punished by the development of neuralgic complaints.[38]

Women accounted for 68 per cent of Anstie's neuralgic patients and about 70 per cent of the cases in a German study of neuralgia, Die Hypodermatische Injection (1867) by Albert Eulenberg (1840–1917). Erb was sure that 'unconscious excitations, even in chaste and pure-minded persons' predisposed patients to neuralgia; 'little experience in the treatment of the somewhat more matured woman of the better educated classes is required to demonstrate the truth of this statement'.[39] The phenomenon of the 'Rampant Spinster', as Collins called it, was a commonplace among the Victorian laity, who connected sexual frustration with nervous disease, and laughed at the double entendres thrown up by unconscious desires. Readers smirked at the unwitting self-revelation of the purity-campaigning spinster who exclaims in The Moonstone (1868): 'How soon may our own evil passions prove to be Oriental noblemen who pounce on us unawares!'[40] The Rampant Spinster was thought by the French to be a peculiarity from across La Manche: 'those bigoted fanatics, those stubborn Puritans, whom England breeds in such numbers, those pious and insufferable old maids, who haunt all the tables d'hôte in Europe, who ruin Italy, poison Switzerland, and render the charming towns of the Riviera uninhabitable, introducing everywhere their weird manias, their petrified manners, their ineffable smell of clothes, and a peculiar smell of rubber, as if they were put in a waterproof case over night'.[41]

Early writers had promoted opiates as aphrodisiacs, but nineteenth-century sexual ethics were sometimes so ardently puritanical that sexual abstinence would sound like a libidinous activity. Opiates' power to subdue erotic urges was stressed. Levinstein's male morphine addicts discarded sexual activity or became impotent, he reported from Berlin in the 1870s. The erotic atmosphere of the period was so strained that some bachelors with the morphine habit welcomed this propensity in the drug: 'In case there should be any desire for sexual intercourse during a free interval, they overcame it by an injection of morphine'.[42] Since Anstie advised 'that the continuance of sexual intercourse after the powers naturally begin to wane, is extremely pernicious in its tendency to revive latent tendencies to neuralgia',[43] it is probable that morphine was administered to some older neuralgic men with the intention of rendering them impotent.

Syphilis was among the chronic diseases for which opium was prescribed. The French poet Baudelaire suffered from this sexually transmitted infection, and from its opiate treatment. 'When I was very young I got poxed,' he told his mother bluntly in 1861. 'Now it's returned in a new form, with skin blotches, and an extraordinary lassitude in all my joints.'[44] The prescribed medical treatment brought 'depravity of the senses', as he wrote, for opium became 'a source of morbid sensuality'.[45] His association of women with his syphilis and its opiate sequel is evident in his prose poem 'La Chambre Double' ('The Double Room'). 'Here in this world, cramped but so disgusting, only one familiar object cheers me: the phial of laudanum; an old and terrifying friend; like all women, alas, prolific in caresses and betrayals,' he wrote. All he had left were 'Memories, Regrets, Spasms, Fears, Anguish, Nightmares, Rages and Nerves'.[46] Baudelaire became obsessed with trying to protect his poetic gifts from contamination, whether by the outer world or by the syphilis that finally destroyed his intelligence and killed him. His perceptions were those of a dissolving personality: imminent chaos panicked him. The numbness of depression he tried to replace with the creative force of spiritual masochism. It was in this mood that he compiled *Les Paradis artificiels (Artificial Paradises)* containing his 'La poème du haschisch' ('The Poem of Hashish') followed by a commentary on translated extracts from de Quincey's *Confessions*. Given his experience of medication and disease, he bitterly repudiated the approach of Moreau and Gautier dating from the 1840s. 'It is time to leave on one side all that juggling . . . born in the smoke of infantile brains.'[47] Baudelaire avowed that 'poisonous stimulants seem to me not only one of the most terrible and sure means of the Prince of Darkness for enlisting and enslaving deplorable humankind, but also one of his most perfect devices'.[48] Consumers of these drugs sacrificed their autonomy and came to resemble automata. Yet the ethics of *Les Paradis artificiels* were not clear to some of its most intelligent admirers. Flaubert found the book 'very noble, very discriminating and very searching', but had a reservation about its 'leaven of Catholicism', as he told Baudelaire. 'I would have preferred that you did not condemn hashish, opium, excess, because you don't know what will be made of that condemnation later.'[49] Flaubert's intellectualisations made him deaf to the grief of a dying man, and blind to the anguish of a chronically ill man enervated by his medicines.

Syphilis was a chronic disease associated with sexuality; womanhood might have been reckoned as a chronic illness, at least as far as nine-teenth-century medical practice was concerned. Women with 'female complaints' were often given opium or morphine. It is significant that Fordyce Barker, who imported the first hypodermic syringe to the USA in 1856, held the chair of clinical midwifery and diseases of women at Bellevue Hospital College in New York, and was founding President of the American Gynaecological Society in 1876. Hypoder-mic medication became instrumental in male regulation of women; hypodermic addiction became notorious as a female characteristic. One example of male medical suspicion of women's bodies may be quoted from a European. Sir Thomas Clouston (1840–1915), the Orca-dian who was appointed Physician Superintendent of Royal Edin-burgh Asylum in 1873, believed that he and his fellow physicians were 'priests of the body and the guardians of the physical and mental qual-ities of the race'. According to the *British Medical Journal*, his asylum management 'came to stand for all that was good scientifically and medically, as well as for all that was humane and efficient'.[50] Yet Clous-ton, who specialised in addiction, was prejudiced about women. 'The risks to the mental functions of the brain from the exhausting calls of menstruation, maternity, and lactation, from the nervous reflex influ-ences of ovulation, conception and paturition, are ruinous if there is the slightest original predisposition to derangement,' he warned. Boarding-school education for girls was 'responsible for much nervous and mental derangement, as well as for difficult maternity'. If 'all the brain energy' was 'used up in cramming knowledge', then 'young ladies' would 'seldom have more than one or two children, and only puny ones at that, whom they can't nurse, and who either die in youth or grow up to be most feeble-minded'. Clouston believed that 'for the continuance of the race there would be needed an incursion into lands where educational theories were unknown, and where another rape of the Sabines was possible'.[51] Male anxieties about women's bodies were crucial in the decision to deploy morphine to subdue and regulate.

The most common female affliction was dysmenorrhoea, which was subdivided between painful menstruation (congestive dysmenorrhoea) and uterine colic (dysmenorrhoea proper). The Bavarian professor Karl Schroeder (1838–87) reported that uterine pains, in particular, 'may be so intense that the women believe they will go mad'. Narcotics were administered in stubborn cases (although Schroeder noted that 'the English attribute special efficacy to Indian hemp in dysmenorrhœa').[52] Dysmenorrhoea, according to Anstie, was an example of 'neuralgia connected with sexual difficulty', which was often cured by marriage.[53] If the woman was unmarriageable, then morphine would serve. Paradoxically, child-bearing was regarded as a disturbance to middle-class women's mental balance.[54] Injections were prescribed for morning sickness, puerperal fever and postnatal depression, and cravings for morphine ensued.[55] Babies must have been born with a morphine dependence, although this was not prominently reported.

Vaginismus, too, was treated with morphine, especially when the patients were newly married women.[56] An American physician, reporting a woman morphine addict in 1871, noted that to mitigate her vaginismus, 'the husband (an apothecary) had supplied her freely with morphine, and so by-the-by the habit became perpetuated'.[57]

Nineteenth-century medical attitudes to women's sexuality reflected the domestic circumstances in which more prosperous women lived. Discussing 'the miserable monotony of the lives led by a large section of the middle classes in England', Wilkie Collins in 1866 recognised that women were yoked under 'the established tyranny of the principle that all human happiness begins and ends at home'. Some women enjoyed their domestic regimes, or adjusted to them. Lady Cowell-Stepney (1847–1921), for example, was sincere in extolling 'the Blessedness of Motherhood, and the supreme duty of women to their husbands and children' to behave 'without disturbing the sacred quietness of Home'.[58] (She, however, obtained a judicial separation from her husband after twenty-eight years of marriage.) Other women, who chafed at the boredom and frustration, used morphine or other opiates to drug themselves into a functional passivity that made life bearable.

Foiled by the moral certainties and financial powers of the men around her, Collins's character Lydia Gwilt reflects that 'a man, in my place, would find refuge in drink'. As a woman, she 'can't drink', and instead controls her frustration with laudanum. She resolves to 'darken my bedroom, and drink the blessing of oblivion from my bottle of Drops' so as to survive 'weary, weary hours'.[59] An alternative to oblivion was hysteria, that expression of anguish at finding one's desires are unobtainable. Morphine injections were not only used by prosperous women to relieve their nerves or subdue incipient hysteria, but were administered to them with similar sedative purposes by their male physicians. Addiction became identified with gender; the hypodermic habit was feminised. The physician in *The Moonstone* of 1868 believed himself temperamentally predisposed to the opium habit: 'Some men are born with female constitutions—and I am one of them.'[60] A survey of fifty druggists in Chicago in 1880 found 235 habitual opium customers, of whom 169 were women (generally using morphine).[61]

Addicts' misbehaviour became more widely censured in the third quarter of the nineteenth century. 'If opium-eating is a vice', one of its physician-consumers had claimed in 1851, 'it never betrays its victims into those gross and sensual excesses which make the drunkard the pest of society.'[62] Such apologetics had little weight by the 1870s. 'She was cunning and artful, and would almost always study out some plan to get the morphia,' the American physician Judson Andrews (d. 1894) wrote of a seamstress (1841–71) who was eventually killed by the accumulated effects of injected morphine: 'she often threatened to take her own and her mother's life, and became very difficult to control'.[63] Another delinquent case was reported from Scotland in 1875. The Lochmaben druggist's assistant was spotted leaving his counter by a local woman, 'a confirmed laudanum drinker', who was 'in the habit of watching when no-one was in the shop, and entering and taking laudanum'. She hurried in, gulped a bottle, and was dead in two hours, having taken cantharides instead.[64] These miscreants had their fictional counterparts. In *The Wyvern Mystery* (1869), the Irish novelist Sheridan Le Fanu (1814–73) devised a Dutch villainess Bertha Velderkaust suffering from neuralgia. Her function in the novel is to personify 'the malice, fury and revenge of outraged egotism'. In addition to a strong appetite for brandy, she uses opiates to relieve her pains, thus presenting a 'maddening picture of degradation and cruelty'. Le Fanu's image of the addict depends sometimes on Christian notions of sin ('it was not only that she was cold and hard, but she was so awfully wicked and violent') and sometimes on medical models of insanity ('she's sly, and she's savage, and . . . a bit mad').[65]

Class distinctions were sustained in other judgements of addicts. One English physician condemned poor addicts, but excused those 'among the middle classes of society, who resort to the use of opium, under the pressure of severe mental distress . . . or heart-rending recollections'.[66] Yet the dishonesty of middle-class addicts was notorious. Wilkie Collins, travelling in the Engadine, found with 'horror' that he had exhausted his laudanum supplies. He and a German-speaking friend 'represented themselves to be doctors and so obtained from chemists at Coire, and afterwards at Basle, the maximum supply the Swiss law allowed, and so reached Paris without the catastrophe Collins described in alarming words'.[67] Mrs von C. (b. 1842), who became addicted after being prescribed morphine for an abscess on her breast after childbirth, was admitted to a German hydropathic establishment for a morphine cure in 1874. There her allowance was reduced to one diluted dose, but as she was permitted to move freely inside and outside the institution, with her servant, 'she injected secretly during the night the same dose as before'.[68] Such incidents made Levinstein insist that his addict patients understand that they must 'forego the exercise of their own free will and submit, without opposition, to the orders of the medical attendant'.[69] His Munich colleague von Boeck similarly cautioned that morphine-users were 'untrustworthy, and are very regardless of truth, especially when questioned about their habit'.[70]

Physicians were notoriously tempted to treat their own headaches, insomnia and anxiety with opium and morphine. Long hours, interrupted nights, anxious cases, demanding patients, professional arrogance, money worries and domestic discord all contributed to the notorious phenomenon of addicted medical men. 'Our profession pays dearly,' as Clouston lamented: 'has not every country doctor had to turn out of bed and drive many weary miles, many a stormy night, [and] not because his patient was worse then than he had been on the previous day?'[71] It was partly as a result of such working conditions that, as von Boeck complained in the 1870s, 'a considerable number of morphine injectors have sprung up—chiefly young doctors—who carry on this pernicious practice'.[72] Levinstein, for example, in 1875 successfully treated a physician who had begun injecting morphine 'in order to overcome the worry and anxiety, which he caused himself through the undeserved self-accusation of having made a mistake in his profession'.[73] The majority of male addicts in the USA were physicians: a conservative estimate suggested that up to 10 per cent of American medical men were 'opium inebriates', while other estimates were double that percentage.[74] As in Britain, country doctors, with their gruelling duties over large areas, were reportedly the most prone to addiction. 'The demoralising effects of the vice were conspicuous and unmistakable,' Alonzo Calkins declared of one such case. 'No sooner did opium enter in than conscientiousness walked out. No longer appreciating the moral value of truth, this man would falsify over and over statements he had deliberately made, exhibiting a perversion of spirit that the most cautious contradiction only aggravated.'[75]

There were many cases of fatal indiscretion in the use of morphine in medical households. A Brighton physician, James Crombie (1844–83), was criticised by the *British Medical Journal* in 1873 for inventing an inhaler for the self-administration of chloroform vapour: 'The practice of inducing sleep by the self-administration of anaesthetics . . . has been found to be pernicious, dangerous and unfortunately attended with fatal consequences.'[76] Crombie, however, proved an intractable and resourceful proselytiser. Lamenting that 'the dearness and delicacy of the syringe' had hindered the hypodermic use of morphine by the poorer classes, he devised a cheap method of subcutaneous treatment. He coated a fine silk thread with morphine, which he deposited beneath the skin by drawing the thread through the opening made by the needle.[77] Crombie, who in 1875 published a monograph, *Pain: its cause and cure*, found morphine fatally attractive. He died of a self-administered overdose supposedly taken to ensure sleep after a surgical operation on his wrist. The *Lancet* commented that his inquest shows 'how important it is, not only to forbid even a professional patient to treat himself with a deadly drug, but to take care that such is not within his reach'.[78] Physicians' wives often succumbed to careless use of morphine. The death at Carlisle of a young doctor's wife Annie Macleod (1848–73) provides a tragic example. For some nights she had sat with their son, who had been ill with typhoid. When finally she had a chance to rest, she was too overwrought for sleep. Her husband therefore repeatedly administered morphine in glasses of port at intervals over three hours. She then fell into a coma 'so alarming that Dr Macleod sought additional medical aid, but all efforts to restore the patient were unsuccessful'.[79]

Some English physicians believed that the teetotallers' crusade against alcoholic spirits had increased opium use in rural districts by driving poor people to a cheap substitute intoxicant.[80] However, there is no evidence that opium addiction or the misuse of ether were higher in 'dry' areas of the USA. Although it was indecorous for American women to drink alcohol, etiquette was openly or secretly breached by women in remote country districts and by seafarers' wives separated for long periods from their men.[81] Despite the emphasis on deportment, some fashionable women found in alcohol or morphine a defence against the febrile rivalry of their milieu. The strains of high society were all too recognisable. 'Individually the people are nice enough, and wonderfully kind and civil, but their jealousy and abuse of each other is stupendous,' the Marquess of Dufferin and Ava (1826–1902) recorded after visiting New York in 1874. 'Every American lady seems ashamed of her best friend. Indeed one is constantly made to feel as though one was living in the Servants Hall.'[82] Drug *habitués* of course were not all nervous women, rich debauchees, slum dwellers or ruined members of medical households. Financial speculators became identified with the habit in this period. Wall Street brokers countered 'one sort of excitement, the gold-fever, with another, a stimulating opiate', it was reported in 1871.[83] Mrs B., a New Yorker aged twenty-five who regularly visited the stock exchange, syringed morphine into her rectum. 'The operation was repeated several times in the day, and abroad as well as at home; any by-place serving as a convenience, a side-room in a broker's office, or a nook in a secluded street'. All her attempts at abstinence failed.[84]

Anstie believed that certain individuals were temperamentally predisposed to addiction. In *Stimulants and Narcotics* (1864) he distinguished two classes of users. There was 'the unwary man' who used opiates to treat pain or illness, and was persuaded that increased doses would increase the relief. Such cases were not characterised by a 'desire to be drunk' or for oblivion. By contrast the 'genuine debauchee' loved to be intoxicated and craved escape 'from all the actual surroundings of life' into 'a fool's Paradise, filled with illusions of sensual delight'. In Europe, until after 1950, Anstie's category of the unwary—people who became addicted to opiates as a result of medical treatment—over-whelmingly outnumbered the debauchees. By the end of the twenti-eth century, this latter category dominated the drug problems of the Western world. Anstie judged that debauchees increased their con-sumption of alcohol, opium or coca because their 'debased moral nature loves the unnatural delights which can only now be obtained by such increase'. He considered this debasement inherent in the individual's own character rather than dependent upon the progressive action of the drug. Debauchees were 'born either with a distinct tendency to sensu-alism, or with a peculiar susceptibility to certain external impressions.'[85]

This theory of the sensuality of the addictive personality disregarded a recognised feature of nineteenth-century narcotic addiction: the sus-ceptibility of some war combatants. Despite the identification by the 1870s of opiate habits with women (over 60 per cent of American opium and morphine addicts were female), the problem was also regarded as 'the army disease'.[86] Sick and wounded soldiers and veter-ans became addicted after being given careless amounts of these drugs, or came to depend upon them as much from the emotional as the physical suffering of combat. Just as some individuals are more suscep-tible than others to submitting the control of their lives to a drug habit, so some people find it harder than others to recover from the emo-tional suffering of wartime. The *behaviour* of addicted individuals (as opposed to the origin of their addiction) is not exclusively governed by physiological need; the propensity to and management of combat stress is equally variable between individuals. In the wake of the Viet-nam War, the term Post-Traumatic Stress Disorder was coined by the American Psychiatric Association in 1980 to describe the behaviour of traumatised people, which psychiatrists would call neurotic, and the laity would consider self-destructive or disorderly. This represented no new insight. The emotional damage caused by battle scenes was clearly recognised in the nineteenth century. During the 1820s the British government responded to the problem of ex-soldiers from the French wars roaming the countryside in an aggressive, offensive or eccentric manner. The ex-combatants' habit of exhibiting their disgusting wounds, or other bodily parts, to women led to provision in the Vagrancy Act of 1824 that 'ever person wilfully, openly, lewdly and obscenely exposing his person with intent to insult any female ... shall be deemed a rogue and a vagabond'.[87]

One episode from the Crimean War, waged against Russia by British, French and Ottoman forces, shows the emotional damage inflicted in battle. In 1854, at the Battle of Inkerman, over a quarter of the British force of 8500 men were killed or wounded while the Russians lost some 11,000 soldiers out of 42,000 on the field of battle. General Sir George Higginson (1826–1927), who fought there in the Grenadier Guards, was asked about Inkerman twenty years later. 'He remembers very little about the battle,' his questioner recorded. 'When they marched back and joined the detached companies, he remembers nothing but the men bursting into tears. They were hysterical all night.'[88] In another account Higginson described the British Commander in Chief, the Duke of Cambridge (1819–1904) 'almost moved to tears' after Inkerman. He recalled, too, the Earl of St Germans (1835–1911) standing by his brother's corpse 'paralysed with grief and indifferent to the danger, exposed as he was to shot and shell'. Afterwards, when 'famished comrades' crowded into Higginson's tent, 'so high had been the nervous tension during the whole of the day that we found ourselves laughing'.[89] Lord Forth (1834–61), who killed himself with laudanum, might be counted among the Crimean War's nervous casualties. He broke down after resigning his commission, aged only twenty, and after the death of his mistress, raved with grief, drank three-quarters of a pint of brandy and fatally swallowed a half-bottle of laudanum.[90]

About four million troops participated in the American Civil War between April 1861 and the Confederate surrender in April 1865. The North probably lost 360,000 soldiers in battle, or from disease and wounds, while the South lost 258,000. An estimated 375,000 were wounded. The involvement of civilians and their resources was as unprecedented as the new technologies enlisted in this first of modern wars: machine guns, mass production ordnance, photography, balloon observations, anaesthesia. Opium poppies were cultivated in both Union and Confederate territories. The drug was used to treat endemic dysentery, and as a preventive against malaria and diarrhoea. Ten million opium pills were issued to Union soldiers alone. Additionally 2,841,000 ounces of opium powders and tinctures were issued to the Union forces. They were often administered promiscuously. Courtwright cites a Confederate physician who asked every patient about his bowels, and handed a plug of opium to each soldier who said his bowels were loose. A surgeon-major of the Union forces habitually undertook diagnosis perched astride his horse, and would pour morphine into the palm of his hand, from which the soldiers on the ground licked it out.[91] 63,000 veterans of the war were left with chronic diarrhoea; it is probable that many of them were treated with opium or morphine, and became dependent on them. Morphine was used more sparingly as an anaesthetic. Nevertheless the narrator of an autobiographical novel by the American physician Weir Mitchell, describing his war service as 'assistant surgeon in the wards of a hospital to which were sent most of the bad cases of wounded nerves', commented that 'sixty thousand hypodermic injections of morphia were given and needed' annually 'in this abode of torment'. After being shot in the neck by a Confederate bullet, Mitchell's physician receives hypodermic shots of morphine, and after recovering from his wounds, finds he cannot abstain from the drug: 'If any man want to learn sympathetic charity, let him keep pain subdued for six months by morphia, and then make the experiment of giving up the drug. By this time he will have become irritable, nervous and cowardly. The nerves, muffled, so to speak, by narcotics, will have grown to be not less sensitive, but acutely, abnormally capable of feeling pain, and of feeling as pain a multitude of things not usually competent to cause it.' Ultimately Mitchell's narrator endures an agonising withdrawal, leaving him 'forever tender to those who are under despotic rule of this and other as hurtful habits'.[92]

The stunned and blank condition of people after an ugly, savage war is familiar. They have confronted in their immediate experience the evil and nihilism of which humankind is capable. Narcotics relieve the pain of this recognition. As Horace Day wrote in 1868, the Civil War aggravated the opium habit. 'Maimed and shattered survivors from a hundred battle-fields, diseased and disabled soldiers released from hostile prisons, anguished and hopeless wives and mothers, made so by the slaughter of those who were nearest to them, have found, many of them, temporary relief from their sufferings in opium.'[93] According to Courtwright, it is impossible to establish the numbers of Civil War survivors who became addicted, especially as veterans concealed their addictions to avoid jeopardising their pensions. He notes, however, that Civil War veterans were dying out by 1900, forty years after the war, in which period US imports of opium and morphine fell per capita.[94]

Prussian militarism also raised the level of addiction. Morphine injections were rare in Germany until the war against Austria of 1866, when the technique's 'marvellous action in relieving pain, and the calming effect it had upon the sick and wounded ... paved the way for its adoption', according to Levinstein. After 1866 public enthusiasm for morphine injections quickly spread until the technique was used 'without the slightest discrimination, and very soon this narcotic remedy was used to remove every abnormal sensation'. Numerous inmates at Levinstein's *Maison de Santé* had come to grief through reckless use of morphine after 1866. Some were soldiers who had become addicted to morphine after being treated for gunshot wounds sustained in action.[95] Non-combatants also became dependent on morphine because of war experiences. A Dresden woman who had been administered morphine in 1865 when she had gallstones, resorted to the injections again during the war of 1870–71, to try to overcome her anxiety about the daily dangers to which her male relations were exposed. Levinstein's attempted cure failed.[96]

Although hypodermic syringes were the most important new feature of narcotic history in this period, traditional means of drug consumption continued to flourish. Laudanum was drunk, and pipes were smoked. European and American attitudes towards opium were more affected by the unpopularity of Chinese immigrants than by any other factor; but India's opium traffic with China remained a source of shame to many Europeans. James Legge (1815–97), who was a Christian missionary in the Orient before becoming the first Professor of Chinese at Oxford University, found in China that 'every man had his own narrative of evils, deaths, suicides, misery, ruin, that [opium] had produced'.[97] Although the drug traffic aggravated Anglo-Chinese tensions, it was less contentious than the desire of the Western powers to force the opening of China to foreigners. The Anglo-Chinese Treaty of Nanking was followed in the 1840s by commercial treaties reluctantly conceded by the Peking government to the USA, France, Belgium and Sweden. These arrangements, however, dissatisfied all the signatories. The Chinese believed that they had been coerced into extreme concessions, and were little disposed to respect the claims and grievances of 'barbarians'. They withheld from the Europeans and Americans rights to travel in the interior of China, or to live outside the five treaty ports, and resisted the accrediting of foreign diplomats to the government in Peking.

In 1856 the Chinese authorities arrested the Chinese crew of a British-registered ship. This incident was taken in London as the reason for escalating diplomatic tension, although the mutiny of the Bengal native army early in 1857 delayed the outbreak of outright war.

The mutiny had lasting repercussions on opium policy. During 1858 the old system of rule for India, with responsibility shared between the East India Company and the Board of Control, was abolished. The territories, revenues and troops of the Company were transferred to the Crown; a Secretary of State, assisted by a council of fifteen experts, assumed control; and the Governor General became the first Viceroy of India. British opponents of the opium traffic found that these administrative reforms undermined their campaigns. The opium trade officially became a matter of Indian imperial government revenues (in 1876 the title of Empress of India was conferred on Queen Victoria). Few members of parliament cared about India, or attended debates on Indian policies, which restricted opportunities for parliamentary indignation. Once the mutiny had abated, an Anglo-French military expedition was sent to China to wage what was misleadingly called the Second Opium War. Western troops seized Canton, and temporarily enforced Chinese submission. Many progressive figures and evangelical moralists, who regarded the opium trade as the greatest evil of recent British imperial history after slave-trading, were horrified. The philanthropist MP Robert Fowler (1828–91) typically prayed in 1857 'that God, in His mercy, would lead my beloved country to cease this nefarious traffic'.[98] In the diplomatic negotiations that culminated in the Treaty of Tientsin, the British demanded the extension of trade facilities for foreigners, but evinced no desire for exclusive trade privileges in China. A favourable modification of the tariff system was secured, including a tariff rate for opium, the imports of which were thus formally recognised. Among other parts of the settlement, the residence in Peking of foreign diplomats was conceded; foreigners were permitted to travel in the interior; Christian missionaries were sanctioned; foreign merchant vessels were allowed on the Yangtze river; trade regulations were developed. 'It seems to me', Mérimée told an English friend, 'that China is going to become like America in the sixteenth and seventeenth centuries, a ground for European exploitation; everybody is going to pillage their part of the cake, and then is going to fight over the cake-plate.'[99]

The focus moved in the 1870s on to the influence of Chinese opium shops, or 'dens', in London, California and elsewhere. Chinese addicts were widely dispersed abroad and highly visible. Already in British Guiana during the 1860s Sir William des Vœux saw skeletal Chinese beggars who represented the miserable results of opium-smoking.[100] During the same decade the number of Chinese settling in London began to increase (an estimated 147 in 1861 had risen to over 600 by 1880). They were concentrated in Poplar and Stepney.[101] Their opium shops were initially fascinating rather than repellent to judge from the visits in 1869 of Charles Dickens (1812–70) and the Prince of Wales (1841–1910). Dickens, who visited Chi Ki's premises in New Court, off Victoria Street, in Bluegate Fields, drew on this experience when months later he wrote the opium den scene in *The Mystery of Edwin Drood*: its images were as enduring as the hashish dreams in Dumas's *The Count of Monte Cristo*. One evening in 1872 a party of Frenchmen—including the artist Gustave Doré (1832–83), a young Bonaparte princeling and the Prince Imperial's tutor—went slumming in Whitechapel under the protection of a Scotland Yard escort. They found an early association of the London drug underworld with unemployment. In Bluegate Fields they visited

> the room in which *Edwin Drood* opens. Upon the wreck of a four-post bedstead (the posts of which almost met overhead, and from which depended bundles of shapeless rags), upon a mattress heaped with indescribable clothes, lay, sprawling, a Lascar, dead-drunk with opium; and at the foot of the bed a woman, with a little brass lamp among the rags covering her, stirring the opium over the tiny flame. She only turned her head dreamily as we entered. She shivered under the gust of night air we had brought in, and went on warming the black mixture. It was difficult to see any humanity in that face, as the enormous grey dry lips lapped round the rough wood pipe and drew in the poison. The man looked dead. She said he had been out since four in the morning trying to get a job in the docks—and had failed.[102]

This scene seemed very estranged from the conventional productivity of Victorian Londoners. 'London wears a dismal exterior to the eye of the foreigner, because all London is hard at work,' noted one of the

Frenchmen, who thought the intense, self-mortifying habits of highly paid barristers epitomised the national peculiarity: 'their luncheon is in a sandwich box; so that Nature's cravings may not rob them of an hour in the best part of the precious working time'.[103] The imaginative influence of Chinese opium-smoking was international. The French novelist Octave Mirbeau (1848–1917) went to Paris in 1869 to try his luck as a drama critic:

> He met somebody just back from Cochin-China who told him that everything that Baudelaire had written about opium-smoking was nonsense, that on the contrary a charming contentment was to be procured that way; and the enticer gave him a pipe and a Cochin-China robe. And there he was for those four months, in his flowered garment, smoking pipe upon pipe, up to 124 daily, and at most eating a soft-boiled egg every 24 hours. Ultimately he attained complete self-annihilation, confessing that opium provided some hilarity after a small number of pipes, but that when that passed, the smoker was left in an indescribably sad void. It was then that his father, to whom he had written that he was in Italy, discovered him, took away his robe and lodgings, and walked him, like a real down-and-out, all over Spain for months.[104]

In the USA the cultural impact of Chinese opium-smoking was even more important. The California gold rush of 1848 created a high demand for Chinese indentured mine-workers. Young male peasants went to America with the intention of working there temporarily, earning money to support their families in China, repaying their creditors and amassing enough to return to their native villages. (The few Chinese women who accompanied them worked as prostitutes.) Some of these Chinese had used opium before embarking for America, but their new circumstances were conducive to addiction. Conditions in the California camps were harsh physically and emotionally. The inmates were often desperate to escape on sprees—whether to a Chinese store or laundry in a little adjacent mining town or to San Francisco's Chinatown—where they lost themselves in gambling, whoring and opium. Some Chinese users in the USA smoked only occasionally, on feast days, or other special occasions; so long as the duration of their

binge was under ten or fourteen days, they did not become physiologically dependent. Indeed, as only a small fraction of the morphine content was inhaled up the pipe, subtle and seductive though the fumes
might be, opium-smoking could not be as destructive as morphine injection. Figures on Chinese opium-smoking in the USA are
impossible to ascertain. The New York physician Harry H. Kane (1854–
1906), who was one of the most reliable American medical authorities
on opium, estimated in 1882 that 20 per cent of Chinese in America
smoked opium occasionally, and 15 per cent daily.[105] Kane's figures are
probably conservative (although higher estimates are evidently sensationalised). Daily smokers found their habit impossible to relinquish,
which was ruinous for them and enriching for the pushers. By about
1880, as Courtwright charts, the maximum daily income of a Chinese
labourer scarcely exceeded a dollar: the daily cost of the drug was about
fifty cents. The opium-smoker could not earn money while he was
smoking, so that it swiftly became impossible for him to remit funds
home, or to have any hope of returning to China himself. As his anxiety and depression worsened, his needs for opium's oblivion intensified. This benefited his creditors, by whom he was indentured as
labour, and under whose control he remained until his debts were
cleared. His cycle of despair also enriched the secret criminal societies,
called tongs, that controlled opium supplies.

Chinese 'dens' became a focus of international contempt. Sir George
Birdwood (1832–1917), an Anglo-Indian physician who believed that
smoking opium was 'absolutely harmless', nevertheless deplored the
sole opium shop that he found in Bombay: 'it was only the lowest of
the people who used it for smoking', he said, 'only riff-raff Chinese'.[106]
Similarly in 1868 a recovering American morphine addict, who
claimed for himself 'high moral sentiment, and a keen sense of intellectual enjoyment', disparaged 'the miserable and grovelling Chinese,
who are fed on [opium] almost from the cradle' and smoke it in their
dens.[107] Yet in the very same year—according to an apocryphal but
plausible story—opium-smoking made its great racial breakthrough in
the USA. 'The first white man who smoked opium in America', Kane
wrote in 1882, 'is said to have been a sporting character, named Clendenyn. This was in California, in 1868. The second—induced to try it
by the first—smoked in 1871. The practice spread rapidly and quietly
among this class of gamblers and prostitutes.'[108] 'Clendenyn' may have

been a misspelling of the (Irish) surname of D. R. Clendening, a retired major of the US army, who lived in San Francisco in the late 1860s. Kane reported that American opium-smokers were far more sociable than solitary morphine-users secreted in their homes; the den was a sanctuary where novices were taught the complicated techniques of preparation and smoking while *habitués* could sleep, eat, chatter and socialise. They were strictly self-policed—stealing from a drowsy smoker was never tolerated—and provided a national underworld network, for shady characters could find an opium 'den' in most western American towns, where they could congregate with *confrères*. Smoking shops frequented by non-Chinese *habitués* were soon flourishing in three Nevada towns: Carson City (which became the capital when Nevada acquired statehood in 1864), Reno (a town that flourished after the Central Pacific railroad was built through it in 1868), and Virginia City (a mining boom-town with a 30,000 population, six churches and a hundred saloons). Similar dens opened (soon after 1876) in Chicago, St Louis, New Orleans and New York City.

All the difficulties met by twentieth-century drug enforcement agencies were represented in the phase immediately after 1876. Opium-smoking attracted people who found pleasure and security in surroundings that the majority found vicious or degrading. 'It's part of the disease to want to get way down in the mud,' mused police officer James Mahoney, who led raids on dens in San Francisco in 1881. 'It may sound strange, but I have had men who could easily buy their own outfit and the purest opium tell me that when the longing comes on them, they cannot satisfy it except in a low Chinese den; that the idea of smoking good opium in a clean pipe and in their own rooms doesn't seem to fit the bill'.[109] Subsequent campaigners against drug use have seldom been able to understand or accommodate the implications of Mahoney's insight. Initial reports of the white American opium-smokers of the early 1870s indicate that they were predominantly young men (occasionally young women) drawn from the social margins: gamblers, whores, pimps, hoodlums, young clerks and errand boys.[110] High anxieties that the rich and effete would succumb to the habit were soon raised; by the mid-1870s the desire to protect the youngsters of middle-class families had become paramount. In consequence San Francisco in 1875 and Virginia City in the following year passed the earliest ordinances against opium shops. As a Virginia City physician explained, the smoking of opium in his locality had been confined to the Chinese until 'a sporting character who had lived in China ... spread the practice among his class, and his mistress, "a woman of the town", introduced it among her *demi-monde* acquaintances, and it was not long before it had widely spread ... among the younger class of boys and girls, many of the latter of the more respected class of families'. It was then that 'the necessity for stringent measures became apparent'.[111] During the next fifteen years, eleven western states introduced legislation against opium-smokers: Nevada (1877), South Dakota and North Dakota (1879), Utah (1880), California and Montana (1881), Wyoming (1882), Arizona (1883), Idaho and New Mexico (1887) and Washington (1890). These laws were significant as the first drugs legislation to criminalise users rather than to regulate substances. Typically the California statute imposed a fine of up to $500 and six months imprisonment on individuals operating or using opium shops. Legislators at this time did not distinguish between supply and consumption. Their legislation was ineffective, and sometimes counterproductive. In California the 'dens' favoured by non-Chinese were targeted. Californian police action in the early 1880s did not eradicate opium-smoking, but instead drove some *habitués* to congregate in small groups in cheap lodging houses while others revelled in confrontation with the authorities. 'The very fact that opium-smoking was a practice forbidden by law seemed to lead many who would not otherwise have indulged to seek out the low dens and patronise them, while the regular smokers found additional pleasure in continuing that about which there was a spice of danger,' Kane commented a year later: 'it seemed to add zest to their enjoyment.'[112]

By 1882 Kane was reporting that American opium-smokers were no longer predominantly drawn from the hoodlum element, but included merchants, actors, leisured gentlemen, sportsmen, telegraph operators, mechanics, ladies of good families, actresses, prostitutes, married women, and single girls. For Kane one trait united them all: American national character; 'essentially a nervous people, prone to go to excess in every thing, gladly welcoming narcotics and stimulants, we go to very decided excess in matters of this kind'.[113] These opium-smokers were not Emerson's optimistic, self-reliant, resolute, controlled and nature-loving American pioneers, but their inverse; they showed irrestraint, indecision, dependence and a taste for urban living. As an

English addict later wrote, 'the effect of opium on a vivacious, nervous, mean, cowardly Frenchman, on an Englishman with his congenital guilty conscience or on an American with his passion for pushing everything to extremes . . . is almost certain to produce disaster'.[114] American moral ruggedness, with its clear-cut certainty about the difference between right and wrong, compounded the difficulties in discouraging drug abuse. It has always been incomprehensible to American puritans that a profound truth is recognisable by the fact that the opposite is also a profound truth; still less that, as George Sand recognised in 1871, 'every abuse secretes its opposite'.[115] One lesson of the late 1870s and early 1880s is that the need for moral hygiene carries an equivalent need for moral dirt. Police officer Mahoney knew this in his way; so did Dr Kane. There were significant divergences in the quarter-century after 1860 between European and American responses to opium-smoking. In both continents it was regarded as an unhealthy habit: whereas European commentators on opium 'dens' tended to convey this undesirability by focusing on aesthetic objections to the habit, Americans often treated it as an issue of moral authority. It was doubtless for this reason that opium-smoking became for the first time an issue of parental authority: the American city ordinances of 1875–6 were partly an attempt to buttress that authority in response to perceived problems in supervising young middle-class people. American morality was not dissevered from the ideas of British and German Protestants, but its vehemence contributed to the most important tendency to emerge from the USA at this time: a new manner of propagandist rhetoric. European commentators had often been complacent about the dangers of opiates, while the expert exceptions (Levinstein, say, or Allbutt) were meticulous in confining themselves to issues of fact and proof. In the USA, by contrast, some anti-drugs campaigners indulged in fatally counterproductive scare tactics.

These scare tactics derived both from the prevailing Christian culture and from the imperatives of business competition. American newspapers had few scruples in their battle for readers. Their journalism was competitive rather than factual: stunts, scares, scandals and shrieking headlines were all weapons in the circulation war. The foremost practitioner of this technique was the mining heir William Randolph Hearst (1863–1951), who took over the San Francisco Examiner in 1887. Hearst had 'a prurient hanker' for 'the lowest common denominator' and typified 'the slummer [who] sees only the streetwalkers, the dopeparlors, the strip acts and goes back uptown saying he knows the working class districts'.[116] Significantly the earliest English exponents of American reporting were the London evening newspapers strenuously competing with one another for the same finite readership. Sensational disclosures, vehement language and unscrupulous stunts characterised the rival editorships in the 1880s of Sir George Armstrong (1836–1907) of the *Globe*, W. T. Stead (1849–1912) of the *Pall Mall Gazette* and Frank Harris (1856–1931) of the *Evening News*. The more sedate and scrupulous tone of the *St. James's Gazette* ensured that this fourth evening newspaper never prospered in London. There was a reliable vein of salaciousness among Americanised journalists: Stead's notorious article 'The Maiden Tribute of Modern Babylon' (1885) was proof of Hearst's maxim 'Girls Make News'. Anecdotes about white women being lured into Chinese dens were part of the same phenomenon. Typically, from San José, the bustling trading centre for the Californian goldmines, a journalist in 1881 denounced 'the poor young fool' who, 'deceiving father, mother and employer', visits 'a joint'. He abhorred the San Franciscan boys and girls who 'sneak out of vile alleys in the Chinese quarter and elsewhere . . . into the beautiful sunshine and refreshing sea-breeze, with such expressions of weariness, duplicity, vice and recklessness combined on every face'. After several paragraphs of scarifying sensationalism, doubtless intended to horrify his older readers and to deter the young from visiting dens, he concluded that in ninety-nine cases out of a hundred, 'opium-smoking . . . means the mad-house or the morgue, and not far off, either'. Similarly, about the time of Hale's report in San José, Raymond Lluellyn (1842–86) reported on cannabis for the commuter readers of the most conservative of London's evening newspapers, the *Globe*. 'Hasheesh-smoking', he claimed in the exaggerated tone of American journalism, 'produces a tendency to most diseases that the flesh is heir to. A long puff at the deadly pipe is followed by a violent fit of coughing, and often by spitting of blood, and it has been found to furnish the mad-doctor with as many cases as opium.'[117] A more realistic report of three students at Trinity College, Cambridge, who in 1886 took hashish in 'Turkish Delight' stated that they 'lost their sense of time to such an extent that three weeks seemed to have passed during the time they were vomiting'.[118]

Kane, who detested drug addiction, pounced on the inaccuracies of newspapers catering to the prototypical Moral Majority. The San José journalist might be well intentioned, 'but he makes a grave mistake, made by so many others who have written in the same tone upon this subject, i.e., that of saying a great deal that is untruthful and exaggerated, knowing it to be so, and hoping thus so to work upon the feelings of the reader as to disgust him with the subject and prevent his being led into temptation'. Kane was convinced that such writing caused 'more harm than good in the majority of cases' and that 'the plain, unvarnished truth . . . based on facts' was far preferable. Many who read such warnings, and nevertheless tried the pipe, 'find its effects unlike those described, gather from the habitués and see with their own eyes that the statement regarding the mad-house and the morgue is absurd.' They conclude that 'everything else written by the same author is untruthful'.[119] The prescience of Kane's criticism of corrupt rhetoric cannot be overstressed. Slippery journalists, and self-promoting public moralists, with their lies and distortions about drug effects, were to inflict immeasurable harm on the Western world in the ensuing 120 years.[120]

FIVE

Chemistry

The only good we discover in life, is something that
produces an oblivion of existence.
—MADAME DE STAËL

The majority of humankind only enjoy life
by forgetting that they are alive.
—MAURICE MAETERLINCK

MORPHINE, HYPODERMIC SYRINGES and Chinese dens
were far from providing all drug experiences of this period.
In the mid-nineteenth century both curiosity about and the
use of other stimulants and sedatives diversified and grew apace. This
variety satisfied the needs of human nerves. The age-old uses of
tobacco, alcohol, Indian hemp and the kava of the South Sea Islanders
convinced the physician Sir Benjamin Brodie that there was a basic
'instinct' requiring stimulants or sedatives for the human nervous system.[1] Opiates retained their pre-eminence; but in the second half of
the nineteenth century, there were other copious and appealing substances to be swallowed or inhaled. Some, like coca, had a long pedigree; others were recent discoveries of German science.

The accounts of coca leaves by the Swiss zoologist Johann Jacob von
Tschudi (1818–89) and the German naturalist Eduard Pöppig
(1798–1868) gained international attention in the mid-nineteenth
century. So did the treatise on coca published in 1859 by an Italian
physician, Paolo Mantegazza (1831–1910); an abstract was translated for

the Pharmaceutical Society of London in 1860. Tschudi described the cultivation and consumption of coca leaves, although his only personal trial with the drug was a failure. He thought coca, if consumed habitually, was a useful aid for workers, but that in excess it ruined productivity: 'An inveterate *coquero*, or coca chewer, is known at the first glance. His unsteady gait, his yellow-coloured skin, his dim and sunken eyes encircled by a purple ring, his quivering lips and his general apathy, all bear evidence of the baneful effects of the coca juice when taken in excess.' Mine and plantation owners allowed labourers to interrupt work three times a day for *chacchar* (chewing). 'He who indulges for a time in the use of coca finds it difficult, indeed almost impossible, to relinquish it.' Some prominent white citizens of Lima chewed coca leaves, but never openly, 'because among the refined class of Peruvians, the *chacchar* is looked upon as a low and vulgar practice, befitting only to the labouring Indians'. European visitors to Peru had also acquired the habit. Tschudi knew an Italian and 'a Biscayan who were confirmed *coqueros*'. In the sordid silver-mining town Cerro de Pasco, with its shifting population of Spanish, German, English, Swedish, American and Italian fortune-hunters, 'there are societies having even Englishmen for their members, which meet on certain evenings for the *chacchar*'. Europeans took sugar with their coca leaves.[2]

In 1857 Tschudi gave some leaves to the Göttingen chemist Friedrich Wöhler (1800–1882) who supervised an unsuccessful attempt to identify the active principle in coca. A new sample was obtained in 1859, which Wöhler passed to his student Albert Niemann (1834–61) for analysis. Niemann isolated cocaine from coca leaves, as he announced in his doctoral thesis of 1860. His discovery was reported in several international journals but (perhaps because of his premature death) little further scientific interest was taken in the subject until the early 1880s. The Darmstadt chemists Merck, pioneers of the commercial production of morphine, adopted Niemann's technique to begin producing cocaine in 1862, but demand was so slight that as late as 1884 their total annual cocaine production was under half a kilogram. Frederick Schroff, who personally tested cocaine, reported in a Viennese journal in 1862 that its use was inadvisable on account of its depressing aftermath. Tomés Moreno y Maiz, a Peruvian physician living in Paris who published a treatise on his cocaine experiments in 1868, was the first to hint that it might be used as an anaesthetic. In 1880 the Russian physician Vassili von Anrep (1852–1925), who was then working in Paris, renewed Moreno's suggestion, and also proposed its use to treat melancholia. However, the chief sequel to Niemann's report was more hucksterish.

The Corsican Angelo Mariani (1838–1914), who had trained as a pharmacist, developed a tonic in which Bordeaux wine was laced with extracts of coca leaves. He began selling his Vin Mariani in 1863. He promoted it as a drink for babies, the elderly and everyone else, sending free samples to French physicians, who began prescribing it as a pick-me-up. As a result Vin Mariani, with its distinctive bottle, enjoyed an increasing vogue until the end of the century. Coca extract was also contained in his Pâté Mariani, Pastilles Mariani and non-alcoholic Thé Mariani. His lavish promotional effort perhaps stimulated curiosity in the 1870s about the effects of coca leaves on sportsmen. In 1876 the American walking champion Edward Weston (1839–1929) covered 109.5 miles in twenty-four hours to win an English contest. He was accused of having chewed coca leaves throughout the race, but denied the charge. During trials he chewed coca leaves under the advice of his American medical adviser, he admitted, but 'they acted as an opiate, and forced me to sleep'. For the contest he had eschewed them.[3] This was the first occasion when the use of drugs to enhance sporting performance became controversial; the practice was not considered ignoble or shameful: despite Weston's avowal that coca made him sleepy, other competitive walkers in Europe and the USA were induced by the publicity to chew coca leaves. The veteran toxicologist Sir Robert Christison experimented with coca on two occasions. In 1875, at the age of seventy-seven, he walked fifteen miles in a day, and prevented hunger, thirst and fatigue by chewing coca leaves. In 1876, aged seventy-nine, he climbed to the summit of a small mountain in the Highlands, which left him exhausted; but having chewed the leaves for half an hour, he descended without weariness.[4] Similarly a Devon physician reported using coca extract when out with his gun. 'Filling my flask with the coca tincture, instead of with brandy', he reported in 1876, 'down went the birds right and left. "Eureka", I said to myself; "the coca has made me a steady shot." '[5] These sporting successes raised the tantalising possibility that coca leaves could enhance productivity. An army surgeon, Theodor Aschenbrandt, in 1883 published a medical paper reporting his successful use of cocaine to revive the physical powers of exhausted Bavarian soldiers.

Whereas coca had a long history, other important substances were discovered by the Hesse-Darmstadt-born chemist Justus von Liebig (1803–73). During the 1830s he investigated the constitution of ether, alcohol and their derivatives. As a result he discovered a new drug chloral (obtained by dry chlorine acting on ethylic alcohol), synthesised chloroform, and advanced understanding of ether's properties. Oscar Liebreich (1839–1908) introduced chloral hydrate as a surgical anaesthetic in a treatise published at Berlin in 1869. The drug began to be prescribed in Germany, Britain and elsewhere for insomniacs instead of opiate draughts. Hughes Bennett (1812–75) undertook a trial of chloral on fifty-two patients at Edinburgh Royal Infirmary around 1869. He reported that by producing a healthier sleep than opiates it was 'highly serviceable to the physician'.[6] George Balfour (1823–1903), an authority on cardiac disease who had trained in Edinburgh and Vienna, reported in 1870 on his successful use of chloral to treat coughs, pains and insomnia.[7] Chloral was recommended as a tonic for melancholia and to treat general paralysis of insanity (tertiary syphilis). Levinstein in Berlin began substituting it for morphine when trying to break addicts of their habit. But an ominous sequel was soon evident. The sanitary reformer Sir Benjamin Ward Richardson (1828–96) warned as early as 1871 of the prevalence of the chloral habit. Drawing on data from four commercial firms, he estimated that the equivalent of 36 million narcotic doses of chloral had been supplied since August 1869. Drunkards were substituting the drug for alcohol. It was used without medical supervision by sufferers from neuralgia, and other chronic diseases, to relieve pain. Worried, grieving or care-worn individuals took chloral for sleep, and continued until occasional use became persistent.[8] Chloralism was not extensive among women, and the poor could not afford it, but by 1879 it was 'widespread', so Richardson again warned, 'among the men of the middle class, among the most active of these in all its divisions—commercial, literary, medical, philosophical, artistic, clerical'. Chloral disturbed the digestion, natural tendency to sleep and nervous system, so that heartbeats became 'irregular and intermittent, and the mind excited, uncertain and unstable'. Richardson insisted that chloral was 'purely and absolutely a medicine', and that if its use was not guided by a physician, 'it ceases to be a boon and becomes a curse'.[9]

There had been accidental overdoses and suicides.[10] A young London physician, Edward Amphlett (1848–80), of Charing Cross Hospital, died of an overdose. 'Like other medical men who accustom themselves to the use of this dangerous drug without due advice, he had grown incautious,' the British Medical Journal warned.[11] In Amphlett's case there were suspicions of suicide. He had recently been jilted by his fiancée: her letters, testified his brother, 'were enough to drive the deceased mad'.[12] Around 1876 Germany's Ministry for Clerical, Educational and Medical Affairs ordered the police to issue public notifications warning of chloral poisoning.[13] Professor Rudolf Boehm (b. 1844), who had worked in a Bavarian psychiatric clinic, thought that considering the short time since chloral was marketed, 'the great number of these unfortunate cases . . . ought to furnish a strong motive for the exercise of caution in prescribing its use'.[14]

Whereas many people who had become therapeutically addicted to opiates did not wreck their capacity to fulfil family duties or to work productively, chloral made its *habitués* dysfunctional at home and in workplaces. It accordingly seemed more deplorable. This attitude is clear from a case history published in 1877. A shopkeeper initialled F.S.P. (b. 1830) had around 1870 been medically prescribed chloral hydrate and potassium bromide to relieve retention of urine. He took these drugs for some six years without his friends observing any hurtful effects, but later admitted that chloral 'had enslaved him to some extent, as he felt a desire for its sedative effect apart from its medicinal action, somewhat akin to the drink-craving of the habitual tippler'. After six years F.S.P. was administered chloral to allay breathlessness and procure sleep during a bout of bronchitis. His recovery from bronchitis was rapid, but business cares, and his brother's death, depressed him, and he sought oblivion in chloral. For many months he continued transacting business, carrying about a chloral bottle from which he took a dose every hour or half-hour. Each dose sedated him within five to ten minutes, and lasted from thirty minutes to an hour. Chloral imbued F.S.P. with

a calmative soothing feeling; and with each dose a dreamy sense of comfort and *bien-être* stole over him . . . He complained of no headache, vertigo, or active sense of depression as a result of the drug, but a feeling of lassitude and nervous debility and exhaustion arose, together with an inaptitude for work, and incapacity for continuous thought. He became irritable and peevish, and when anything occurred to annoy him, chloral was his sole panacea . . . As he abandoned himself to the fascination of chloral eating, and the 'tyrant custom' grew upon him, his friends observed, together with his intellectual enfeeblement, a distinct moral alienation, a perversion of his whole affective life and character. He became untruthful, deceitful, the natural affection for his wife and children became diluted, a diseased dislike taking its place. He grew irritable and passionate, and at times threatened violence to his wife. In spite of her entreaties he would leave the house and wander aimlessly about the streets, not knowing whither he went. He became regardless of duty and self-respect—in short, he had drifted imperceptibly into moral insanity.

When F.S.P. was admitted to the Royal Edinburgh Asylum he was 'almost imbecile in manner', and subject to 'fleeting delusions on various subjects, as that the Queen took a special interest in him'. No chloral, narcotics or soporifics were permitted him; instead he was ordered to take a strychnine tonic and as much open-air exercise as he could bear. This cure, together with 'asylum discipline', enabled his discharge after three months.[15]

A survey by Kane around 1880 of 107 physicians in the USA reported 135 patients with a chloral craving. Seventy-seven cases were known to be men (including clergymen, physicians, editors, clerks and farmers), most of whom had been drunkards; and thirty-six women (mostly married, but some prostitutes and hospital nurses). It can be tentatively extrapolated that for every physician in the USA there was at least one chloral *habitué*. 'Both males and females formed the habit through taking it for insomnia and mental depression, dependent on family troubles, business failures and the like. Some through hearing or reading of its magical effects and trying it to satisfy themselves.'[16] Chloral was popular with insomniacs, although its effects were seldom admired by the insomniacs' acquaintances. The 'bad health' of the diabetic tenth Duke of Bedford (1852–93) was 'aggravated by an indolent habit, and sleeplessness, leading to the habitual use of chloral', according to Lord Derby (1826–93). Nevertheless though the duke was 'sluggish in body . . . he seemed active enough in mind'.[17] The adolescent Parisian André Gide (1869–1951) was prescribed chloral for insomnia in 1882–83. It stupefied him, and in manhood he railed against the physician whom his mother had consulted: 'This for a brain scarcely formed! I hold him responsible for all my weakness of will and memory in later life. If one could sue the dead, I would take him to court. I can hardly contain my anger at the thought that every night, for weeks on end . . . the bottle . . . was put entirely at my disposal and I could take as much of it as I liked.'[18]

The German writer Karl Gutzkow (1811–78) became enslaved and was ultimately destroyed by chloral. This important dramatist, whose nine-volume novel *Die Ritter vom Geiste* (*The Night of the Spirit*) (1850–51) presented a powerful portrait of mid-nineteenth century Prussian society, personified the violent nervousness of his age. Under the cumulative influence of chloral, taken to quell his obstinate insomnia, he became hypersensitive, developed persecution mania and in 1865 attempted suicide. Despite resuming work, he continued to suffer from nervous infirmities, which he tried unavailingly to relieve by moving restlessly from one German town to another. His accidental death occurred one night when, in a chloral stupor, he overturned an oil lamp that he had left too near to a sofa. Although he was woken by the smoke, it overpowered him before he could escape the room, where he was found in the morning suffocated.[19] After the Franco-Prussian war of 1870–71, in which he served as a bearer, the health of the philosopher Friedrich Nietzsche (1844–1900) was similarly debilitated by insomnia. He was prescribed chloral by his physicians, 'took immoderate doses of the drug, and in this way at least accelerated his mental ruin', according to the Prussian physician and pharmacologist Louis Lewin (1850–1929).[20]

Chloral also wrecked the life of the poet and painter Dante Gabriel Rossetti (1828–82), whose wife Lizzie had taken a laudanum overdose in 1862. The grieving, guilt-ridden widower, as his protégé Sir Hall Caine (1853–1931) recalled, had suffered insomnia for years, but was cautious in his use of opiates. 'Then he heard of the then newly-found drug, chloral, which was of course accredited at the beginning with all of the virtues and none of the vices of other known narcotics.' He hoped it would

save him from days of weariness and nights of misery. Eagerly he procured it, and took it nightly in small doses of ten grains each;

it gave him pleasant and refreshing sleep. He made no concealment of the habit; like Coleridge under similar circumstances, he
rather elected to talk of it. Not yet had he learned the sad truth,
too soon to force itself upon him, that this dreadful drug was an
evil power with which he was to fight, almost down to his dying
day, a single-handed and losing battle.[21]

Like Gutzkow seven years earlier, Rossetti in 1872 developed chloral-
induced paranoid delusions; like Gutzkow he attempted suicide (by
laudanum). On one occasion, with the encouragement of his physician
John Marshall (1818–91), Rossetti accompanied Caine and a nurse on
a rural rest cure. They travelled behind the drawn blinds of a special
railway carriage; when the murk and stuffiness of the journey sent his
two minders to sleep, Rossetti sneaked a bottle of chloral from Caine's
bag. As soon as they reached their destination, Rossetti announced he
was going to bed, but shortly afterwards, when Caine 'opened his door
without knocking', he surprised Rossetti in the act of drinking the
chloral removed from the bag. Caine spent the night pacing 'on tiptoes
in the corridor outside his door listening for the sound of his breathing, in terror lest it should stop'. Rossetti reacted with an 'almost cruel'
laugh when caught by Caine, but afterwards displayed disarming
remorse. Although since leaving London he had drunk enough chloral
to destroy all the other members of the household combined, 'Rossetti
awoke fresh and in good spirits towards the middle of the afternoon,
breakfasted heartily and then took a turn about the house.'[22]

Similar deceptions were perpetrated on the French critic Louis
Ganderax (1855–1940) by his chloral-addicted friend, Marc-Adrien
('Albert') Delpit (1849–93), the New Orleans-born novelist. The two
men once visited Nice together, on an attempted cure, sharing a bedroom so that Ganderax could keep Delpit under surveillance. Delpit
insisted on going to a theatrical show one night, and despite his suspicions, Ganderax agreed. At the theatre, while they were having their
tickets checked, Delpit disappeared. Ganderax ran to the hotel, found
him with a flask of chloral which he threw into a chamber pot, at
which in exasperation Delpit knocked him down. On another
attempted cure, Delpit retired to bed early, claiming he was tired. Later
Ganderax discovered him 'in his night-shirt, with the bedside table
overturned, reeling and stuttering, completely drunk on chloral'.[23] The

burden on such companions as Ganderax was onerous. Caine became ill under 'the constant fret and fume of this life of baffled effort, of struggle with a deadly drug that had grown to have a separate existence in my mind as the existence of a fiend'.[24] When Rossetti's health began to fail, he was limited to a single bottle at bedtime, which aggravated the strains on Caine.

> The power of the dose was now decreasing rapidly, and hence it came to pass that towards four o'clock in the leaden light of early dawn Rossetti would come to my room and beg for more. Let those who never knew Rossetti censure me, if they think well, for yielding at last to his pathetic importunities. The low, pleading voice, the note of pain, the awful sense of a body craving rest and a brain praying for unconsciousness, they are with me even yet in my memories of the man sitting on the side of my bed and asking for my pity and my forgiveness.[25]

Another new and less destructive substance was amyl nitrite, a volatile liquid discovered by the French chemist Antoine-Jérôme Balard (1802–76). The inhalation of even a small quantity accelerates the heart's action, pumping blood through the body, giving the sensation of throbbing in the head or of pounding excitement. After 1859 Ward Richardson promoted its use. He believed that amyl nitrite would be useful in tetanus while the physiologist Arthur Gamgee (1841–1909) hoped it would help with cholera. During the late 1860s Sir Lauder Brunton (1844–1916) researched the drug under the Leipzig physiologist Carl Friedrich Wilhelm Ludwig (1816–95). Brunton established that when a healthy person inhaled amyl nitrite (putting the phial to one nostril, closing the other nostril with a finger) the pulse quickened, blood vessels dilated, and the blood pressure fell; in angina the reverse occurred, with the drug opening the vessels delivering blood to the heart.[26] Soon the inhalation of a single drop of amyl was applauded for resuscitating new-born infants.[27] Sir James Crichton-Browne (1840–1938), medical director of an asylum in Yorkshire, published a report on amyl nitrite in 1874.[28] An English country physician reported that the effects of inhaled amyl nitrite in relieving women's pains after childbirth was 'simply magical'. He also found the drug 'invaluable in the sickness of pregnancy and in obstinate cases of dysmenorrhoea'.[29] A physician at Evansville, Indiana, described in 1880 the case of a woman who swallowed a spoonful of the liquid. After an emetic was used, she vomited 'great quantities of fluid from her stomach, which saturated the whole room with an amyl-like odour'. With 'her eyes glassy and rolling vacantly in their sockets', her breathing and her pulse became imperceptible: she was 'the most limpid, limber, relaxed body imaginable', but recovered after flagellation and coffee containing opium.[30]

The drug became associated with neurotic cases. Francis Anstie in 1870 reported a case of angina pectoris relieved by amyl nitrite. His patient was a highly nervous gentleman who suffered from spasmodic asthma, facial neuralgia and dangerous angina attacks. However, during an angina spasm, 'the sufferer took one long and powerful inspiration through one nostril from a half-ounce bottle of the drug. After a pause of a few seconds, the characteristic flushing of the face and sense of fullness in the head were induced, and the patient instantly passed from agony into a state of perfect calm repose'. Anstie suspected the patient's angina was 'purely neurotic': certainly the drug (with its brief but violent head sensations) seems to have served in neurotic cases.[31] Ford Madox Ford (1873–1939) centred his novel *The Good Soldier* (1915) on a highly strung American bride who wants to prevent her husband discovering that she is not a virgin. She feigns a heart attack on her wedding night, announces that she has angina and thereafter goes about with a vial of amyl nitrite so as to emphasise that she is not strong enough to consummate the marriage.

The drug was pleasantly exciting for many patients. In 1875 a physician at the Middlesex Hospital reported on its use to alleviate neuralgia in anaemic young women. 'I wish you would let me take that little bottle out with me; I have tried all sorts of things, and never found anything do me so much good as that,' declared one young woman whom the drug relieved. The eager curiosity surrounding new chemical therapies in Victorian households is indicated by his anecdote concerning another patient. This patient's sister 'one day sniffed at the amyl bottle, probably because I had especially cautioned my patient against allowing any of her sisters to use it; and immediately her face became most painfully flushed, and she felt sufficiently uncomfortable to prevent her repeating the experiment'.[32] It was surely as early as the 1870s— although this has not been documented—that amyl nitrite-users discovered that the rush of blood caused by inhaling increased the sexual excitement of men, and in many cases agreeably postponed but ultimately enhanced their orgasms. Perhaps rather later some men also found that it relaxed their anal sphincters, enabling them more comfortably to be sodomised. In the twentieth century amyl nitrite became established in much of the Western world as one of the most recreational of substances. The heavy masturbation of the neurotic adolescent Marcel Proust (1871–1922) was surely increased by his bedtime custom of inhaling 'two amyl capsules' to prevent night attacks of asthma.[33]

Another popular male aphrodisiac was arsenic. From Styria (covering southern Austria and northern Slovenia) arsenic-eaters were reported in the 1820s. A description of their habits by Tschudi published in a Viennese medical journal in 1851 was summarised in several English magazines. In 1855 a woman called Jane Wooler, living near Darlington, died of arsenic poisoning. After a sensational trial, her husband (a retired merchant) was acquitted of murder. The defence hypothesised that having read of the arsenic-eaters of Styria, 'who are said to use arsenic habitually, after the manner of the opium-eater, for the purpose of clearing the skin, heightening the complexion, and improving the wind, Mrs. Wooler may have secretly resorted to this practice, and died from giving it up'. Sir Robert Christison, a prosecution witness, discounted this theory with contempt, believing that the Styrian reports were 'pure fable'.[34] In 1864 two British physicians, Joseph Rutter (1834–1913) of Brighton and R. Craig Maclagan (1839–1919) of Edinburgh, visited the region to investigate. Outside Styria, elsewhere in the Hapsburg Empire, the existence of arsenic-eaters was unknown or disbelieved. As Maclagan reported, 'The people who eat arsenic have the idea that it is regarded as a bad habit, and therefore one to be concealed as much as possible, just like opium-eating in this country; and they have the additional reason for concealing the practice, that from the strictness of the laws regarding the sale of poisons, they cannot get the arsenic by open purchase, as the opium-eater in this country can get his laudanum, and therefore they are generally obliged to purchase it from illicit dealers'. The two British physicians interviewed several Styrians including Joseph Flecker, a forty-six-year-old tailor in the village of Liegist, 'a muscular, healthy-looking, clear-complexioned man', who had been taking arsenic for fifteen years without (he claimed) vomiting or stomach irritation. Flecker told them that when he had a long distance to walk, he took a larger dose, which put him in good spirits for about eight days. However, if he stopped arsenic for a fortnight, he felt lassitude, stiffness and a craving for the drug.[35] In 1878 Bernhard Naunyn (b. 1839), medical professor at Königsberg in Prussia, confirmed that in Styria numerous 'arsenic-eaters' acquired in youth the habit of eating up to six grains daily, 'and yet arrive at an advanced age and remain in good health'.[36]

Reports of the Styrian habit spread fatally. A physician from Halifax, Nova Scotia, published a detailed account of a patient who had died in 1862. His patient was a strong, muscular photographer aged thirty who about four years before his death had begun taking arsenic after reading a newspaper article about Styria. The physician, who had treated the photographer in 1861 for a chronic syphilitic throat, was summoned eighteen months later when the patient was stricken with intense stomach pains. Early in the consultation the patient asked if his suffering might be attributable to his arsenic habit: 'It has never before injured me; but the idea has just struck me that it may be the cause of all the mischief'. This remark was probably untruthful, for his friends said that he had suffered dyspepsia with a peculiar pinkish complexion for years. Discussing his drug habit the patient stated that his 'genital organs had, he thought, been stimulated by the arsenic', and the physician independently 'learned that for a long time he had been *notorious* for his amorous propensities'. His life could not be saved, and in death his remains became horribly corrupted. A few hours after his death large amounts of blood flowed from his mouth and nose.

> When seen twenty-four hours after his decease, the whole body was enormously swollen and disfigured. The abdomen was distended to the utmost limits. All the voluntary muscles were excessively rigid . . . There was great lividity of countenance, and the skin of the face had a glistening appearance . . . Both emphysema and capillary congestion were general to the surface of the body, and air could be freely detected by touch wherever sought. The penis and scrotum were black and swollen from decomposition and gaseous distention. On puncturing these parts and making pressure, the confined air or gas escaped through the venous oozing, in rapidly succeeding bubbles.[37]

The most prominent nineteenth-century arsenic *habitué* was Charles-Auguste, Duc de Morny (1811–65). An illegitimate son of Queen Hortense of Holland, Morny was the most resplendent capitalist in France. The British Prime Minister Sir Robert Peel (1788–1850) described him as 'a spick and span man of considerable aplomb, and . . . one of the greatest speculators in the world'.[38] It was Morny who engineered the *coup d'état* of 1851 by which his half-brother Napoleon III seized power. A few hours before the arrests of the generals and deputies, which Morny had engineered, he went to the opera where he was asked by a lady what he would do 'in case the Assembly was swept away'. He replied with ruthless honesty, 'I should side with the broom'.[39] He was an audacious politician, a furiously busy capitalist and sexually ambitious. Among his speculations in the 1860s was the development of the Normandy coastal village of Deauville into a luxurious resort. His coadjutors in this project included an Irish physician named Sir Joseph Oliffe (1806–69). Oliffe had begun life in humble circumstances, but having graduated in medicine from the Paris Faculty in 1840, he married into the Cubitt family, which had developed Belgravia for the Marquesses of Westminster. With the Cubitts' backing, he built up a large practice which his appointment as Physician to the British Embassy extended.[40] He accumulated a grateful crowd of rich patients by dispensing arsenic-based pills that revived the failing virility of middle-aged men. Morny's biographer described Oliffe as 'the miracle-worker with the arsenical pearls, the . . . comfort of men who needed a crack of the whip before . . . rendering homage to a wife after they have exhausted themselves with a mistress'.[41]

Alphonse Daudet (1840–97) depicted Oliffe in his novel *Le Nabab (The Nabob)* (1877) as Dr Robert Jenkins, 'the busiest man in Paris', who looks 'square-shouldered, sturdy and sound as oak', and dispenses the famous 'Jenkins pearls, globules with an arsenical basis'.[42] Daudet (who was a member of Morny's household) described 'the patients of this fashionable doctor: the pink of society, many politicians, financiers, bankers, *deputés*, a few artists, all the over-ridden men of Parisian high-life, pale, with shiny eyes, saturated with arsenic like gluttonous mice, but insatiable of poison and life'.[43] It was the task of Jenkins to 'supply the fuel . . . to heat up' jaded or impotent men.[44] The arsenic made them priapic: 'they died standing like men of the world'.[45] Foremost among these patients in *Le Nabab* is the magnificent Duc de Mora, nonchalant and worldly, with 'that reputation as a conquering Don Juan, which he must needs support at any price'.[46] In business and politics Morny was cynical and mistrustful, yet in his desperation to maintain his sexual energies he became Oliffe's dupe. By the mid-1860s he could not abstain from arsenic. 'The illness of M. de Morny is anaemia complicated by the absurd remedies of an English doctor,' Mérimée wrote in 1865. 'M. de Morny is dead exhausted, not of any illness, but . . . to all his moral and physical fatigues, he joined the habit of dosing himself in the English manner, which was probably even more dangerous than the rest.'[47] A few days later Morny died. 'The duke craved his aphrodisiac pearls so as to [have the powers to] deceive his wife,' according to a biographer who branded Oliffe 'a dangerous criminal'.[48] Daudet likened Oliffe/Jenkins to Castaing, the French physician who had been the first to use morphine as a murder weapon.[49]

Despite this tragedy, arsenic was listed, together with cannabis, strychnine and phosphorus, as an aphrodisiac in Sir Richard Quain's *Dictionary of Medicine*, which sold 33,000 copies in its first edition of 1882.[50] Lewin reported 'many' arsenic-eaters in Austria, France, England and Germany: 'sometimes they began taking the drug out of curiosity, sometimes after having read some book on the subject, or more frequently out of pure imitation, the cause of so many absurd actions in the world'. Arsenic was a fashionable cosmetic, and widely used by women and girls in certain European boarding schools where it was added to the food under medical supervision. Lewin also described actresses and 'servants of Venus vulgivaga' as arsenic-eaters. 'A fresh complexion, a round form, smooth skin and shining hair are attractions which lead to the use of arsenic.' In the southern states of the USA male and female arsenic-eaters, known as 'Dippers', put doses in their coffee.[51]

It was perhaps from the example of the dippers that arsenic became the cherished substance of James Maybrick (1839–89). This Lancashire cotton-broker, who had long lived in the USA, was by the 1870s addicted to arsenic, which he procured without medical prescription for self-administration in increasing measures. He used it as an aphrodisiac, as he did strychnine. He had the arsenic added to a small bottle of tonic provided almost daily by a compliant Liverpool chemist. To quote the reported testimony of the chemist, 'when he came into the shop I used to receive the order merely by a motion or sign by him, and I used to make it up. I put in 75 per cent more at the last than the original quantity of arsenic. I began with a trifle over four drops and ended with seven. He used to ask for this from two to five times a day. He got it most frequently towards the end.'[52] Maybrick was morbidly anxious about his health, and yet when he consulted a physician about dyspepsia, he suppressed any mention of his arsenic habit, which (as with the Nova Scotia photographer) it was unbearable to think of relinquishing. Two months before his death, when he 'blurted out' to the Liverpool merchant Sir James Poole (1827–1903) that he relished 'poisonous medicines', Poole replied, 'How horrid; don't you know, my dear friend, that the more you take of these things, the more you will require, and you will go on until they carry you off.'[53] This advice proved unavailing. Maybrick was taken ill after taking a double dose of strychnine as a stimulant before going to Wirral races, and died after a fortnight. It is likely that gastro-enteritis rather than homicide killed him—his physicians treated him in his last weeks with strychnine, arsenic, jaborandi, cascara, henbane, morphine, prussic acid, papaine, iridine and other toxic substances—but a murder trial ensued. He had married an Alabama woman, Florence Chandler (1862–1941), who was convicted of his murder. 'The papers', as the Earl of Derby recorded,

> for the last few days have been full of a poisoning case at Liverpool, which will be one of the 'causes célèbres'. The criminal is a Mrs. Maybrick, American by birth, young, and who had married a man double her age. She had an intrigue with one Brierley, which her husband suspected, and this supplied the motive. She poisoned him with arsenic, choosing ingeniously a drug which he was in the habit of taking medicinally. The trial lasted a week: [Sir James FitzJames] Stephen tried the case. Of her guilt no reasonable doubt can be entertained: but for some reason her cause has been taken up by the Liverpool mob, who insulted and hooted the judge, and would have tried a rescue had not a strong force of police been on the spot.[54]

This represents the authorities' public version of events; in truth Florence Maybrick was convicted and sentenced as a punishment for her adultery. Certainly her husband's arsenic habit was not unusual. His chemist testified to having other customers—businessmen from Liverpool Exchange—who regularly bought 'pick-me-ups' containing arsenic: 'I have had as many as sixteen follow each other . . . several times a day.'[55]

Ether provides the rare case of a drug that was first used as a stimulant and later realised to have medicinal value. As early as the thirteenth century the action of mixing sulphuric acid with alcohol was known to produce an intoxicating substance, which became known as ether after 1730. In the early nineteenth century public speakers used it as an aid to oratory. At a dinner in 1827 the English politician William Huskisson (1770–1830) mentioned that the Earl of Liverpool (1770–1828), the Prime Minister since 1812, and the former Foreign Secretary in his administration, Lord Castlereagh (1769–1822), 'both took ether, as an excitement, before speaking'.[56] Mainly, though, the drug was taken for pleasure. In 1842 Crawford Long (1815–78), a doctor in Jefferson, Georgia, whose house was a social centre for young people of the district, was approached by his friends. They had got into the habit of inhaling nitrous oxide ('laughing gas') from bladders, and found the resultant antics one of the few sources of amusement locally. Laughing gas was difficult to transport, and therefore hard to procure, not only in Jefferson, but generally, which limited its hedonistic use.[57] Long was asked to supply nitrous oxide, but had none. He knew, however, that moderate amounts of ether produced exhilarated spirits and a warm glow throughout the body. Larger amounts produced numbness, pricking sensations, sensual distortions and concluded (if enough was inhaled) in unconsciousness. Accordingly he provided controlled amounts of the drug, and started a fad for 'ether frolics' in Jefferson. 'Youths and maidens inhaled and gyrated and tumbled about in semi-intoxication,' as an English physician later summarised. 'Long noticed the bruises or cuts or damage incurred during ether frolics were unfelt by the youthful bacchanals, and it was borne in upon him that a like immunity to pain might obtain even when the cuts were deeper and inflicted by the surgeon's knife.'[58] To test this idea Long excised a neck tumour from a patient using ether as an anaesthetic in 1842; its success justified him in using ether during further documented surgical operations, although the heavy demands of his country practice prevented him from reporting his success until 1849.

Another American physician meanwhile independently introduced ether into surgery in 1846. Soon after news of this success had crossed the Atlantic, the Scottish surgeon Sir James Simpson (1811–70) tested ether. He thought the smell would be too repugnant for his medical speciality, women in labour, and determined to make a trial of chloroform, which had first been synthesised in 1831. Simpson in 1847 inhaled some in his dining room, 'sank into a narcotic sleep beneath the table, and on awakening knew the world was enriched by the discovery of the greatest and best of anaesthetics'.[59] He forthwith introduced it into surgical practice. 'What a beautiful instance Chloroform is of a discovery made from *purely* scientific researches, afterwards coming almost by chance into practical use,' the naturalist Charles Darwin (1809–82) enthused in 1848. Two years later he used it himself when his wife was giving birth to their seventh child. 'I was so bold during my wife's confinement', he wrote happily, 'as to administer Chloroform, before the Dr. came & I kept her in a state of insensibility of $1^1/2$ hours & she knew nothing from first pain till she heard that the child was born. It is the grandest and most blessed of discoveries.'[60] Chloroform anaesthesia in childbirth was attacked on theological grounds ('In pain you shall bring forth your children': Genesis 3: 16) until in 1853 it was administered by Simpson to Queen Victoria (1819–1901) at the delivery of her youngest son. Thereafter it was vindicated in Britain as an effective analgesic, although its use in childbirth was still associated by some men with bad mothering. To convey his disapproval of a selfish Belgian, Daudet in 1877 described her as 'giving birth to children for whom she never cared, whom she never saw, and for whom she had not even suffered—for she used to be delivered under chloroform'.[61]

The choice in anaesthesia lay between chloroform and ether. Hallucinations often ensued after the first whiffs of chloroform, some patients became excited, and they could asphyxiate or suffer heart failure if chloroforming be pushed too far. As one German expert recalled, almost no other substance 'combines, within so narrow a compass, properties at once so salutary and so deadly'.[62] However, as the Scottish surgeon Arthur Fergusson McGill (1846–90) noted in 1873, ether often aroused 'great struggling', requiring three or four assistants to hold down the patient; when patients revived, they often resembled 'noisy drunkards.'[63] Ether was also used under medical supervision as a marital aid. Schroeder in

1875 reported that in the USA 'ethereal cohabitation' was practised as a cure of vaginismus: 'The wife is anaesthetized, and while she remains in a state of narcosis the husband performs coitus, with a view of inducing conception, in order that recovery may be brought about by parturition.'[64] Some individuals acquired the ether habit as a result of medical treatment, including 'a society lady' who was reduced to sleeping on public benches and street beggary by her uncontrollable craving.[65]

Both new anaesthetics, but especially ether, were used mischievously. During the late nineteenth century 'etheromania' became common. The drug's effects varied according to the consumer's sensibility. 'Illusions of sight and hearing, dreams of paradisal happiness', as Lewin listed, 'the hearing of pleasant music, visions of beautiful women and lascivious situations, and many other illusions may be experienced, enduring for some time and leaving behind them the remembrance of a wonderful dream.' Most consumers drank ether, but a minority inhaled its fumes like chloroform abusers. Although *habitués* could tolerate increasingly high doses, death occurred if inhalation was prolonged. Lewin reported the case of 'an ether-inhaler [who] indulged in the mania when driving in a carriage in order to conceal his addiction to the drug. He slowly inhaled the ether, thus prolonging the state of excitation, during which he quarrelled and fought with the coachman, frequently rendering police intervention necessary.'[66]

Ether was used as an intoxicant in Ireland in the second half of the nineteenth century. The habit began in the 1840s, captured certain northern market towns during the 1850s, reached a climax of popularity around 1869, declined after 1876 and revived in the 1880s. A physician from Ballymoney, County Antrim, suggested in 1890 that in the country people had been driven to ether as the best substitute for poteen after the Inland Revenue suppressed illicit distilleries. The parish priest at Knockloughrin first encountered ether-drinking in 1865: doctors had prescribed it as medicine, some of them sold it to the people as a general stimulant, and then the public houses took it up. Although habitual ether-drinkers became irritable, capricious, negligent and lazy, and often succumbed to gastric disorders or nervous prostration, Irish Roman Catholic priests supposedly encouraged parishioners to abandon alcohol in favour of supposedly more innocuous ether. A strenuous Irish temperance campaign was started by Father Theobald Mathew (1790–1856), who incited tens of thousands to pledge themselves to total abstinence from alcohol. This tradition, which survived until the 1950s, perhaps created more ether *habitués* than excessive prescriptions by Irish physicians. By general consent, 'the centre point and spring of ether drinking', in the phrase of the Revd Edward Gallen, was a few miles to the south of his parish of Maghera in County Londonderry, at Draperstown. It was the work of one disreputable shopkeeper. According to the doctor at nearby Magherafelt, in the late 1840s 'an unqualified medical man named Kelly practised at Draperstown, and kept a drug store. He drank more whisky than was good for him; he was prevailed upon to give up the whisky, and then used the ether, and taught the people to use it also.' Gallen agreed that Kelly, having little other business, 'gave draughts of ether as a stimulant cheaper than whisky to healthy people. The evil soon spread.'

From Draperstown ether reached other southern towns in County Londonderry, especially Cookstown, a market town in County Tyrone, a few miles to the south, as well as poverty-stricken farming districts such as Pomeroy.[67] More ether was consumed in this small area of Ireland than throughout England (dreary Lincolnshire was the only English county with a reputation for ether drinking). Draperstown and Cookstown on market days stank of ether vapour, as did the carriages of the local railway. In 1890 Ernest Hart (1836–98), editor of the *British Medical Journal*, began a campaign against the Irish ether 'evil', fearing the possible 'importation of this vice' into England.[68] The ether craze in Ireland disappeared once the drug was included on the list of poisons (as Hart advocated), and only supplied by pharmacies on prescription.

Ether drinking was not a problem in Mediterranean wine-drinking countries, and had only a temporary fashion in Germany during the worst of the Weimar inflationary period. Holidaying Norwegians, however, habitually drank ether during the early twentieth century. It was drunk profusely, when mixed with alcohol, by the poorer peasants of Galicia (the area of Poland lying on the northern slopes of the Carpathian mountains). 'In these cases a kind of morbid stupidity develops which in serious cases renders thought impossible,' Lewin judged. He also reported that by the 1890s there was 'an epidemic among the Lithuanian inhabitants' of the districts surrounding Memel, the seaport which was the most northern town in Prussia and the centre of the Baltic timber trade:

> On market days the smell of ether exhaled by the drinkers is noticeable at every turn. When, on the road between Heydekrug and the neighbouring villages, a carriage with noisy inmates drawn by a madly galloping horse which the intoxicated driver is unmercifully beating, passes the wayfarer, a strong smell of ether can be ascertained in the rush of air. When the market is closed, many men and women can be seen reeling about. Even children are habituated to ether at a very delicate age. School children have suffered mentally to a large extent in consequence. Whole families have been ruined by habitual consumption of ether.[69]

It is notable that life in Draperstown, Galicia and Memel was so harsh and futile that it was seldom worth remaining fully conscious.

German physicians, pharmacists, hospital attendants and druggists frequently indulged in chloroform oblivion. There were several cases of chloroformism related to morphine addiction. Lewin treated a colonel who had tried to break his morphine habit by constantly sniffing at a handkerchief soaked in chloroform. Withdrawal from chloroform proved as harrowing as from morphine.[70] The German authority Boehm in 1878 similarly described one addict as exhibiting 'extreme moral depravity, a sort of moral insanity'. The patient betook himself to chloroform when morphine stopped helping him to sleep, 'he laid in bed nearly all day, and chloroformed himself whenever he awoke. At last he accidentally fractured both thighs; these had to be amputated, and this was done under chloroform, which acted very nicely for this purpose. He finally sank with symptoms of general marasmus [body wasting away]'.[71] Patients undergoing chloroform withdrawal suffered hallucinations of sight and hearing, broke everything they could seize hold of, hurled themselves about and screamed until their fury had exhausted them; vomiting, diarrhoea and cardiac weakness were accompanying symptoms. Most patients, it should be stressed, did not abuse ether or chloroform. The anaesthetic effects of such substances were unattractive to people with fulfilled lives. Indeed many occasional medicinal consumers found the drugs unpleasant. Caroline Tainter Buel (1830–73) of Detroit was afflicted by painful headaches following an inflammation over her eyes in 1864. Her physician first prescribed 'morphine, which only gave a temporary relief', as she reported. As a final resort she took chloroform, but found the effects 'terrible—I was deathly sick, and lame from constant retching'.[72]

In 1856 a compound of chloroform and morphine was marketed to treat cholera, diarrhoea, coughs, influenza, stomach chills, neuralgia, rheumatism, bronchitis and other ills. Until the 1890s 'Dr. Collis Browne's Chlorodyne', as it was known, enjoyed a vogue which created an unknown number of *habitués*. The working class, with its tradition of self-medication to avoid physicians' fees, bought the concoction largely; its devotees also included Theophilus Marzials (1850–1920). Marzials, who was of Venetian extraction, was appointed to the British Museum Library in 1870, but became better known as the composer-lyricist of the 'Creole Love Song', 'Twickenham Ferry' and 'Ask Nothing More of Me, Sweet'.[73] He enjoyed flitting after youths—'he appears & disappears like a sprite, always eloquent and always bizarre',[74] wrote a friend who glimpsed him in Venice—but became dependent on Collis Browne's Chlorodyne. Perhaps this was because he was not fulfilled as a librarian. His doctor reported in 1882 that librarianship was 'calculated to depress his vital and mental powers, and to deteriorate his health',[75] and after his early retirement he chafed at the memory of the 'irritating surveillance, the pedantry and red-tapeism of those weary alien sodden years at the Museum'.[76] Marzials's drug habit (or the emotional strains of which it was a symptom) disrupted his life: he was often late for work or away ill. He was more fastidious than the market traders of Draperstown or the careering horsemen of Memel; but his reasons for self-stupefaction were not very different.

With such experience of the ready perversion of new medicinal substances and techniques by hundreds of thousands of nineteenth-century addicts, physicians should have become cautious about the destructive powers of medicines. Yet in 1884 an Austrian medical man started promoting a new and marvellous stimulant that would, among other powers, cure morphine addiction. It was a momentous mistake: the marvel was called cocaine.

SIX

Degeneration

Hurrah for the unprecedented work and for the
marvellous substance, for the first time!
—ARTHUR RIMBAUD

When one seeks to pursue virtues to extremes, vices emerge.
—BLAISE PASCAL

HORTLY BEFORE THE end of the American Civil War a Georgia
druggist named John Pemberton (1831–88) was shot, slashed
with a sabre and scarred for life by the Yankees. Later, in 1872, he
went bankrupt. He started suffering from rheumatism and recurrent
stomach pains. Whether as a result of treating his wounds, of his chronic
illness, or to appease his business worries, he became reliant on morphine. His displeasure with his habit made him eager to believe the
claims of American medicine-makers that their coca products could be
used to wean people from morphine addiction. These claims rested on
the belief that narcotics were antagonised by stimulants (including caffeine and cocaine), and that it would therefore be possible to withdraw
addicts from morphine by the use of coca. In 1884 Pemberton began
selling his own concoction of wine, kola nuts and coca leaves. Both
coca leaves and kola nuts contain a higher proportion of caffeine than
coffee or tea, and he hoped that his stimulating Wine Coca would
relieve his morphine dependency. He advertised Pemberton's French
Wine Coca in these terms in 1885:

152

All who are suffering from any nervous complaints we commend to use that wonderful and delightful remedy, French Wine Coca, infallible in curing all who are afflicted with any nerve trouble, dyspepsia, mental and physical exhaustion, all chronic and wasting diseases, gastric irritability, constipation, sick headache, neuralgia ... It has proven the greatest blessing to the human family, Nature's (God's) best gift in medicine. To clergymen, lawyers, literary men, merchants, bankers, ladies, and all whose sedentary employment causes nervous prostration, irregularities of the stomach, bowels and kidneys, who require a nerve tonic and a pure, delightful, diffusable stimulant, will find Wine Coca invaluable, a sure restorer to health and happiness. Coca is a most wonderful invigorator of the sexual organs and will cure seminal weakness, impotency, etc., when all other remedies fail. To the unfortunate who are addicted to the morphine or opium habit, or the excessive use of alcoholic stimulants, the French Wine Coca has proven a great blessing.[1]

Pemberton foresaw that temperance campaigners would impair his profits from a wine-based tonic. In 1886 he concocted a new drink of coca, kola and other ingredients (but without wine) shortly before his home town of Atlanta became the first major US city to impose Prohibition. The name given to this new substance became the most famous brand name of the twentieth century. In reaction to racist panic in the southern United States about black men taking cocaine before raping white women, the Coca-Cola Company during 1901–2 decocainised its drink shortly ahead of its home state of Georgia prohibiting the sale of cocaine in any form. For the next seventy years, as cocaine ruined the reputation of coca leaves, the Coca-Cola Company insisted that the drink's name was a poetic and alliterative fancy rather than descriptive of its original ingredients.

Like Pemberton, the Detroit pharmaceutical company Parke, Davis claimed in the early 1880s that their tincture of coca could be used to cure morphine addiction. Coca preparations were included in the company's range of products together with Bolivian coto bark as a remedy for diarrhoea and kava-kava from the Sandwich Isles as a remedy against gonorrhoea, gout and rheumatism. One of the company's owners controlled a medical journal called the *Therapeutic Gazette* and ensured that its contents served as a sales adjunct to his business. In

1880 this periodical published a report by William H. Bentley (d. 1907), a physician of Valley Oak, Kentucky, describing how he had used the Parke, Davis tincture to cure opium addiction and alcoholism.[2] Dr Edward Huse (d. 1900) of Rockford, Illinois, in the same year and in the same tainted source reported substituting Parke, Davis tincture for laudanum when treating a patient who had become addicted after treatment for rheumatic fever. The *Therapeutic Gazette* also quoted the *Louisville Medical News*: 'One feels like trying coca, with or without the opium habit. A harmless remedy for the blues is imperial.'[3]

These puffs, or paid testimonials, gulled an indomitably ambitious young Viennese, Sigmund Freud (1856–1939), who had been obliged to abandon his research career for unglamorous work in Vienna General Hospital. His failure to fulfil his early promise was irksome; but he was more heavily oppressed by his need to achieve the professional status and financial security that would enable him to marry. He had earlier befriended the pathologist Ernst von Fleischl-Marxow (1847–91), who had acquired a morphine habit following surgery. 'He is a thoroughly excellent person,' Freud wrote of his colleague in 1882. 'Wealthy, skilled in all games and sports, with the stamp of genius in his manly features, good-looking, refined, endowed with many talents and capable of forming an original judgement about most things, he has always been my ideal.'[4] Freud unwittingly destroyed this paragon. Fleischl-Marxow's difficulties interested him, and he began ruminating about morphine addiction. He craved instant medical celebrity, and decided that coca might fulfil his ambitions. 'A German has tested this stuff on soldiers and has reported that it has really rendered them strong and capable of endurance,' he wrote to his fiancée in April 1884. He ordered some Merck cocaine with the intention of testing it on cases of heart disease and nervous exhaustion, particularly as suffered by Fleischl following the withdrawal of morphine. 'We do not need more than one such lucky hit to consider setting up house. But, my little woman, do not be too sure that it will come off.'[5]

Early in May he gave Fleischl-Marxow cocaine as a substitute for morphine. 'I take very small doses of it regularly against depression and indigestion, and with the most brilliant success,' he was soon crowing to his fiancée. 'I expect it will win its place in therapeutics, by the side of morphine but superior to it.'[6] In this elated mood he rushed into publication of his essay 'Uber Coca' ('On Coca'). It discussed using cocaine as a general stimulant, as a remedy for indigestion, for the wasting and malnutrition associated with such diseases as anaemia and tuberculosis, for typhoid and diabetes, as a treatment for psychosis and depression, and as a way of raising tolerance to mercury in syphilitics. 'Uber Coca' is a collection of anecdotes and cursory summaries of recent research in Europe and the USA with little evaluative content. Hitherto Freud had specialised in zoology: his meagre knowledge of his new subject was clear from his blunders. His statement that cocaine has an anaesthetic effect when brought into contact with skin was misleading: the drug has a mild anaesthetic action on the skin itself, but no effect beneath unbroken surfaces, because it cannot penetrate to the nerves and thence to the brain. The authorities cited in 'Uber Coca' understood that cocaine must be injected under the skin to obtain anaesthetic effects; and Freud's mistake surely indicates that he had skimped reading the references he was citing. Indeed it is doubtful that he would have cited seven articles from the quasi-corrupt *Therapeutic Gazette* if he had read them conscientiously; possibly he reproduced citations without consulting the texts. Certainly Freud rushed pell-mell. He finished his draft on 18 June 1884 (having first taken the drug as recently as 30 April) and published his conclusions in July. 'I am as strong as a lion, gay and cheerful,' he reported on 19 June in a mood of cocainised exaltation: 'I am very stubborn and very reckless and need great challenges; I have done a number of things which any sensible person would be bound to consider very rash. For example, to take up science as a poverty-stricken man, then as a poverty-stricken man to capture a poor girl—but this must continue to be my way of life: risking a lot, hoping a lot, working a lot.'[7]

Freud's rashness at this time included the statement in 'Uber Coca' that 'repeated doses of coca produce no compulsive desire to use the stimulant further; on the contrary one feels a certain unmotivated aversion to the substance.'[8] His treatment of Fleischl-Marxow's morphine addiction with cocaine had not exchanged one addiction for another, he claimed; 'it does not turn the morphine addict into a *coquero*; the use of coca is only temporary'.[9] Fleischl-Marxow had only been taking cocaine for about a month when Freud issued his confident assurance; he was soon a confirmed *coquero*, and enthralled to the drug for the few years of life that remained to him. This is perhaps the most shameful aspect of 'Uber Coca'. No physician of the 1880s could intelligently

give such an assurance after only a month of tests. The misfortunes that
had followed the hypodermic use of morphine, and the abuse of anaesthetics such as ether, should have forewarned Freud against such a
resounding endorsement of cocaine. The recent example of chloral
should have been a supreme deterrent of any ready claim that a non-
addictive substitute for morphine had been found. Fifteen years earlier
Levinstein of Berlin had abandoned his trial of substituting chloral for
morphine after finding that he was arousing chloralism in patients who
continued to crave morphine. This was the closest precedent, but the
general experience of chloralism since the 1860s should have inhibited
Freud's claims. 'In the early days of chloral one point claimed in its
favour was a freedom from risk of "habit", a claim long ago exploded,'
as the Brooklyn physician Jansen Mattison (c.1845–1911) observed in
1887.[10] It is chloralism that convicts Freud of selfish stupidity over
cocaine. Other drug-researchers showed more scrupulous care. The
German toxicologist Louis Lewin, who pioneered European experiments with the hallucinogenic peyote cacti (*anhalonium lewinii*) after
1886, praised 'this marvellous plant', but warned that it might be habit-
forming and that 'anhalonism, like morphinism, produces a modification of the personality by a degradation of the cerebral functions'.[11]
The English writer Havelock Ellis (1859–1939) was equally cautious
when promoting peyote in the 1890s. In an essay that was peyote's
English equivalent of 'Uber Coca', Ellis concluded that 'habitual consumption . . . would be gravely injurious'.[12]

In the final and shortest section of 'Uber Coca', Freud alluded to the
possibility of cocaine's use in anaesthesia.[13] He suggested to the ophthalmologist Leopold Königstein (1850–1924) that a cocaine solution
might relieve the pain of patients with trachoma and similar eye diseases; but when they tested this hypothesis, Königstein's pharmacist
neutralised the anaesthetic effects by mixing too much acid with
Merck's cocaine. This accident discouraged Freud from further explor-
ing the drug's anaesthetic properties: he was too eager for celebrity and
its rewards to organise systematic research. As a result it fell to his colleague Carl Koller (1857–1944) to win the glory that Freud desired: in
the autumn of 1884 Koller announced his discovery that the pain of
eye surgery could be prevented by a few drops of cocaine solution. He
first confirmed this discovery by touching his own cocaine-numbed
cornea with a pin. His breakthrough transformed eye, nose and mouth

surgery. Freud did not immediately realise that Koller's discovery was the triumph of cocaine research: he still believed that his startling lust for fame would be satisfied by his successes with the drug. In January 1885 he was trying to cure facial neuralgia with cocaine ('I am so excited about it, for if it works I would be assured for some time to come of attracting the attention so essential for getting on in the world').[14] A few days later, assessing his chances of promotion, he assured his fiancée that his prospects were encouraging: 'coca is associated with my name'.[15]

Fleischl-Marxow rapidly became dependent on cocaine, and then began taking morphine and cocaine simultaneously. This was not acknowledged by Freud when, in March 1885, he read a paper to the Psychiatric Society of Vienna. He described Fleischl-Marxow's 'rapid withdrawal from morphine under cocaine', and averred that 'no cocaine habituation set in; on the contrary, an increasing antipathy to the use of cocaine was unmistakably evident'. He specifically commended injections of cocaine as a cure for morphine addiction 'without any fear of increasing the dose'.[16] Yet by the spring of 1885 Fleischl-Marxow was consuming huge amounts of cocaine: he spent 8000 marks on the drug in three months. Freud knew this well enough, for in June 1885 he wrote to his fiancée stating that Fleischl-Marxow had been damaged by cocaine and warning her against the drug. Despite this knowledge, he published his claim that cocaine could cure morphine addiction in a leading medical periodical on 7 August.

Freud's conduct drew the scorn of the psychiatrist Albrecht Erlenmeyer (1849–1926). Erlenmeyer's earliest report that cocaine was useless in treating morphine withdrawal was published in Germany in July 1885, and summarised in English in October.[17] 'This therapeutic procedure', he wrote in the 1887 edition of his textbook on morphine addiction,

> has lately been publicly trumpeted and praised as a veritable salvation. But the greater the fuss made about this 'absolutely precious' and 'totally indispensable' route to health, the less efficacious it proved to be . . . It was simply a question of propaganda expounded by individuals without any truly scientific experience, as objective analysis of the question easily demonstrated. But they persisted despite the warnings, and ended up with the sorry and frightening result that use turned into abuse.[18]

Freud retaliated against Erlenmeyer in his essay 'Craving for and Fear of Cocaine' (July 1887). Recognising that his reputation was compromised, he adapted his literary technique accordingly: in 1884 he had been bold and direct, but by 1887 he was wily and temporising. He had taken lavish amounts of the drug himself without becoming dependent, and was sincerely convinced that Fleischl-Marxow was exceptional in his craving for cocaine; but his new essay was nevertheless disingenuous. Although he had eagerly sought publicity in 1884 for his cocaine work, in 1887 he blamed pamphlets issued by the Merck Company, and an article in the *Deutsche Medizinalzeitung*, for publicising cocaine among physicians and morphine addicts. (Levinstein had similarly railed against the publicity given after 1866 in Germany to hypodermic injections of morphine.) Freud asserted—falsely—that 'all reports of addiction to cocaine and deterioration resulting from it refer to morphine addicts, persons who, already in the grip of one demon are so weak in will power, so susceptible, that they would misuse, and indeed have misused, any stimulant held out to them'.[19] In 1885 he had stressed that 'subcutaneous injections . . . are quite harmless'.[20] He did not mention this advice when in 1887 he blamed the practice for arousing addiction. Later, more obnoxiously, in *The Interpretation of Dreams* (1899), he blamed Fleischl-Marxow, 'my unfortunate friend who had poisoned himself with cocaine', for his own addiction and death. Freud asserted that Fleischl-Marxow had injected cocaine despite being advised by Freud to take the drug orally only while morphine was being withdrawn. 'I had never contemplated the drug being given by injection,' he dishonestly protested.[21] Altogether, in the cocaine episode, Freud behaved like a charlatan. His self-promotional techniques set the pattern for his later claims about psychoanalysis: doubtful conclusions drawn from second-hand anecdotes; falsified data; lying about the outcome of treatment; disastrous incursions into the lives he treated; resolute management of his own public reputation; degrading other people's criticisms by treating them as resistance to his own; insistent and persuasive blame of others for the results of his shortcomings.

As a result of the interest aroused by Freud and Koller, Merck's cocaine production increased from 0.4 kilogram in 1883 to 1673 kilograms in 1884 and 83,343 kilograms in 1885. Prices rose dramatically. In December 1884 a British pharmaceutical firm sold 0.2 kilogram to

European buyers for £250. Drug manufacturers strove to improve their supplies of coca leaves. The German chemical firm of Boehringer & Soehn of Mannheim sent a chemist to Lima in 1884 to organise a Peruvian laboratory, which began production of crude cocaine in 1885. Parke, Davis sent a botanist to Bolivia in 1885. Cultivation in Peru and later Colombia was expanded. British needs were supplied from Ceylon by the late 1880s, and coca cultivation was systematically organised in the Dutch East Indies around 1900. Cocaine rapidly became one of the most important pharmaceutical products in Europe and the USA.

Initially cocaine's possibilities thrilled many physicians. After Koller's discovery was reported in the *Lancet* on 4 October 1884,[22] British doctors began trying it as a local anaesthetic. 'The effect was marvellous,' Sir Henry Butlin (1845–1912) reported in November after it was used (in a 20 per cent solution) before the cauterisation of his nasal passages.[23] Cocaine, declared a patient after undergoing surgery at the Western Ophthalmic Hospital in the same month, 'was a great deal better than that beastly ether'.[24] A country doctor in Westmoreland found that injecting cocaine into the arm acted like a charm in cases of neuralgia of the head and face where morphine had failed.[25] The London pharmaceutical chemist William Martindale promptly marketed coca lozenges (to be sucked at two or three hourly intervals) to relieve 'hunger, thirst, fatigue, exhaustion, distaste for food, depression and indigestion'.[26] American medical practitioners explored other uses for cocaine. Dr Bickerton Winston (d. 1904) of Hanover, Virginia, tried the drug 'in the case of a virgin eighteen years old, who was suffering from vaginismus, hoping that with the aid of the drug, he would be able forcibly to distend the ostium vagina'. More significantly, in the winter of 1884, within a week of hearing of Koller's discovery, the New York surgeon William Stewart Halsted (1852–1922) together with two associates Richard Hall (d. 1897) and Frank Hartley (d. 1913) began experimenting with cocaine on themselves, their colleagues and medical students. They discovered that injections of cocaine into or near a nerve produced local anaesthesia in the area served by that nerve. Within a year Halsted's group had used nerve-block anaesthesia before performing over one thousand surgical procedures that had hitherto been impossible. Halsted visited Vienna General Hospital in 1885 and instructed European physicians in cocaine anaesthetics. Meanwhile, in

1885, one of his associates, the neurologist Leonard Corning (1855–1923), successfully used cocaine as a spinal anaesthetic. These advances exacted a painful personal tax. Hall became dependent on cocaine, abandoned his New York practice, and withdrew to Santa Barbara; he seems never to have escaped the habit. Halsted and several of his assistants also became *habitués*. Halsted's career was in ruins by 1886 when a medical friend resolved to wean him from cocaine by sailing with him on a schooner to the Windward Islands and back. When they returned to the USA Halsted's vitality and charm were dimmed, but he recovered his working equilibrium to become the first Professor of Surgery at the Johns Hopkins School of Medicine (1892). His senior colleagues there knew that he had abandoned cocaine only by substituting morphine. He relied on this substance until his death.

The New York neurologist William A. Hammond (1828–1900) extolled the hypodermic use of cocaine to treat depression and neuralgia in 1887. He had performed trials on himself and others, and recommended it. Like Freud he thought the drug's reputation had been unfairly spoiled by a minority of 'morphia eaters' who had tried to cure themselves by using cocaine without stopping the morphine, 'an exceedingly bad combination'.[27] Freud and Hammond were correct insofar as cocaine does not arouse physical dependence or abstinence sickness. But as Thomas Clouston noted in 1890, cocaine's effects are so transient that the dose must be increased faster—that is, administered in quicker succession—than other drugs.[28] Whereas the craving for opiates was usually at its most implacable when habitual consumers were suffering abstinence sickness, the craving for cocaine was usually most intense immediately after taking the drug, when the cocainist was feeling euphoric. This appetite for increasingly frequent doses of cocaine engendered emotional dependence in some consumers, as shown by the harrowing account given in 1887 by Dr Hugh M. Taylor of Richmond, Virginia, of a young physician whom he had recently treated. His patient had been prescribed cocaine for a kidney ailment. After some two years of taking it hypodermically, 'gradually the size of the dose and its frequency had to be increased as his system became habituated to its effects, or as his depraved nervous system demanded a larger supply'. Eventually the man broke down, was put under restraint and his supply withdrawn. When Taylor saw him, 'almost his first utterance was an appeal for the return of his syringe and permission to continue the use of cocaine . . . He could not live without cocaine, and . . . did not hesitate to threaten his own and other lives if his request was not granted. His legs and arms were thick with needle punctures, and the blood specks on his underclothes showed the frequency of the dose'. After he escaped from the institution where Taylor had placed him, his brothers shut him up in their country house, under guard, for six weeks until his cravings had gone.[29]

Opium-eaters and even morphine addicts often managed to maintain their habits without jeopardising their employment or domestic stability, but the deteriorating physique and conduct of cocaine-users (like chloral addicts) was considered more obnoxious. After being consulted in the cases of two cocainists whose difficulties were secondary to morphinism, Clifford Allbutt concluded that 'the slavery of coca is worse than that of morphia; it is more destructive of mind and body, and harder to put aside. The morphinist still retains some desire to defeat his enemy, and is filled with gratitude, at any rate for the time, when the cure is complete. The cocainist, on the other hand, is so reduced in intelligence that he neither desires emancipation nor feels any thrill of joy when released; his brain is so bemused that he cares nothing for freedom.' Allbutt deplored the 'ghastly automatism', or abasement of individuality, produced by cocaine: 'Few persons would fall into this pit were it not that the use of coca has been recommended, most unfortunately in my opinion, as a means of escape from morphinism.'[30]

Jansen Mattison, Director of the Brooklyn Home for *Habitués*, was the most prominent anglophone to follow Erlenmeyer's lead in warning against cocaine, and became the most knowledgeable American on the subject. From February 1887 he reported periodically on deaths and adverse complications arising from cocaine toxicity. Only three years after the publication of 'Uber Coca' Mattison was warning that cocainism was developing far more swiftly than chloralism had done in the USA. Mattison issued the following advice:

I think it for many, notably the large and enlarging number of opium and alcohol *habitués*, the most fascinating, seductive, dangerous, and destructive drug extant; and while admitting its great value in various disordered conditions, earnestly warn all against its careless administration in these cases, and especially insist on the great danger of self-injecting,

a course almost certain to entail added ill. To the man who has gone
down under opium, and who thinks of taking to cocaine in the hope of
being lifted out of the mire, I would say, 'Don't', lest he sink the deeper.
I have yet to learn of a single instance in which such an effort reached
success.[31]

American physicians heeded Mattison's warnings. A survey in 1891 of
forty-two Philadelphia physicians found that only two discounted the
possibility of a cocaine habit. Only eleven had treated or personally
knew anyone abusing cocaine. Writing of this period, the historian
Joseph Spillane records the sophisticated response of US doctors to
cocaine. They avoided indiscriminate prescriptions, and were attentive
to the effects of dosage, as well as means and context of administration,
on therapeutic results.[32] Informed French medical opinion supported
Mattison. At the Congress on Forensic Medicine held in Paris in 1889
Dr Auguste-Alexandre Motet (1832–1909) and Dr Paul Brouardel
(1837–1906) concurred that cocaine was 'more dangerous' than morphine because 'three times more rapid in its effect'.[33] However, the prohibition of cocaine was nowhere advocated.

Cocaine and morphine were combined under medical orders—
when the former US President Ulysses Grant (1822–85) was dying of
cancer, his doctors treated him with injections of brandy and morphine, together with applications of cocaine—but also illicitly by
delinquents and rebels.[34] One of the earliest such addicts was Ambroise
Aristides ('Jacques') Damala (1855–89). Damala—the French-educated
son of a rich Greek—was handsome, with dark eyes and ferocious
moustaches. In the early 1880s, when he was settled in Paris, supposedly studying for a diplomatic career, he held parties at which the
guests cavorted naked in baths of champagne; he gained a reputation
for exuberant bisexuality. Soon he was injecting morphine, and then
was introduced by a fellow addict to her sister, the acclaimed actress
Sarah Bernhardt (1845–1923). They married in 1882, but separated in
the following year after Bernhardt had thrown out his morphine and
syringes. She continued, however, to protect him, 'even when the morphine fiend had become his fast friend',[35] and even after he began
injecting cocaine too. Until shortly before his death at the age of
thirty-four he lived in a squalid Parisian *entresol*, where he lay in bed
surrounded by the accoutrements of his addiction.[36] Damala had a

counterpart in the early history of psychoanalysis: Otto Gross (1877–1920). The son of a criminologist and judge whose repressive conduct may have given Kafka the germ of his idea for *The Trial*, Gross was a charismatic Freudian pioneer. Addicted to morphine and cocaine by early manhood, he paraded his addiction as if he was mandated to misbehave. He was as licentious as Damala, but constructed a theoretical justification for his irregularities. Promiscuity, he counselled, would help patients: 'The true healthy state for the neurotic is sexual immorality.'[37] His repudiation of patriarchy led him to anarchist politics, and to the serial seduction of married women, including Frieda von Richthofen (afterwards wife of D. H. Lawrence) and her sister, who bore him a son. When he was committed to a Swiss asylum for a withdrawal cure in 1908, he fled over the wall in search of drugs. This had some metaphoric value, for the lives of addicts like Damala and Gross displayed the repetitive breaking of bounds. 'Too bad he had to go to pot,' Freud said.[38]

There was little stigmatisation of cocainists until the mid-1890s. Of all nationalities the Scottish apparently were quickest at individual blame. 'The newest born of all drug cravings is that for cocaine,' the Edinburgh alienist Thomas Clouston reported in 1890. 'It required two of the latest discoveries of science—the hypodermic needle and the extraction of cocaine from the coca-leaf—combined, to create this new vice-disease.' He described the case of 'N.O., a young professional man of intellectual attainments far above the average, and of very industrious habits' who began using cocaine 'at first sparingly for its stimulant effect to enable him to do his work'. N.O. was soon injecting at least 45 grains daily, and developed paranoid delusions. 'When I saw him first . . . he was utterly dirty and untidy—how all the manias take the outward polish off a gentleman!' Clouston withdrew cocaine supplies, and N.O. appeared to acquiesce in his treatment. 'He was plausible, full of promises, cocksure of not again taking to the drug, and suave towards those who had control of him to a suspicious degree. But the strength of his resolution and the intensity of his craving were soon tested by his taking secretly to his old habit on the first opportunity he had. Every kind of excuse and evasion was practised.'[39] Cocaine, for Clouston, was 'the acutest and most absolute destroyer of inhibition and of the moral sense generally that we yet know'.[40] For him loss of control was synonymous with vice.

The use of cocaine in medicines supplied to physicians had diminished by the early 1890s as a result of adverse reports by authorities such as Mattison and Clouston. Proprietary medicines with cocaine ingredients were consequently more energetically marketed direct to the public. By the mid-1890s the British pharmaceutical firm Burroughs, Wellcome recommended tabloids containing cocaine for singers and public speakers wishing to improve their voices. In the USA sufferers from hay fever and sinus pains were recommended nasal sprays containing cocaine solutions (usually about 5 per cent). Cocaine snuffs, which were cheaper than sprays, were pushed at the public as physicians turned away from the medical use of cocaine. Pharmaceutical businesses at the end of the nineteenth century could manufacture, promote and distribute their products on an unprecedented scale. In the case of cocaine, they tried to increase consumption regardless of medical warnings about its dangers, and encouraged consumption for purposes that ran counter to medical orthodoxy. The most notorious of these products was Ryno's Hay Fever and Catarrh Remedy, which was recommended in the USA during the 1890s for 'whenever the nose is "stuffed-up", red and sore'. Its cocaine content was 99.9 per cent. 'It is ruining our boys,' one father complained to the US Bureau of Chemistry. 'I have a son that has been using it and have tried for the last year to break him from it, but no use as long as he can get it and there are others that use it more and are worse than my son.'[41] By the late 1890s many influential Americans considered that the popular consumption of cocaine menaced public safety and jeopardised public health. Accordingly the control of cocaine was incorporated into efforts to regulate the marketing of pharmaceutical products.

Englishmen of this period used cocaine to improve working productivity rather than for amusement. Only one English cocaine coterie has been chronicled during the late 1890s. Allan Bennett (b. 1871), a highly strung asthmatic who had trained as an analytical chemist and later became a Buddhist monk in Ceylon, was intrigued by consciousness-altering substances: he swallowed opium, injected morphine and inhaled chloroform in monthly cycles. He shared his discovery of cocaine with the young mountaineer Aleister Crowley (1875–1947).[42] Both of Crowley's parents were puritanical Plymouth Brethren against whom he spent his life reacting. Like Bennett, too, he pursued a life-long quest for varieties of religious experience. However, the two young men had few compatriots with similar habits until shortly before the First World War.[43] Allbutt, who in 1897 had 'never seen a case of cocainism in which the drug was sought from the beginning for its own sake', knew that 'the habit is said to prevail, chiefly in the form of hypodermic injection, in Paris and the United States'.[44]

American cocaine use, and attitudes to its users, were distinctive. Initially, after 1886, habitual consumers were regarded not as culpable or depraved but as suffering the consequences of misjudgements by their physicians or pharmacists, or from their own rash self-medication. However, after 1893 both medical and lay comment in the USA became more hostile to both suppliers and users. A craving for the drug was seen as the result of a series of voluntary choices rather than as a blameless misfortune. The cocaine habit was reconceived as a vice. Concern about *habitués* who had been initiated by medical prescriptions became secondary to anxiety about cocaine sniffing and injection in the American underworld. Cocaine joined the other vices—the smoking of opium and tobacco, and the drinking of alcohol— favoured by prostitutes, pimps, gamblers and hoodlums in American towns and cities. The scale of the problem is indicated by a reliable estimate that by 1900 over half of the prostitutes imprisoned at Fort Worth, Texas, were cocaine-users. In such places cocainism may by 1900 have exceeded opiate addiction.[45] In this milieu the use of cocaine (as of heroin after 1910) resembled initiation into Freemasonry. Recruits were introduced to arcane rites and a subculture of clandestine kinship. Like adultery, such drug use moved its practitioners into an outlawed state of altered feelings ('adultery' probably derives from the Latin words '*ad*' and '*alter*' meaning 'to' and 'another'). The nineteenth-century representation of adultery as dragging women down was a precursor to the Mattison and Clouston view of cocaine destroying free will and dragging its users into an irretrievable oblivion of dependence. Certainly a free use of drugs was associated with freer sexuality. George Santayana (1863–1952), in his novel *The Last Puritan*, depicted Peter Alden, a young Boston Brahmin of the 1890s, who degrades his class by consorting with 'muckers'. He admires their fornication: 'When a mucker has a best girl, without even marrying her, it's very likely that he can have her.' After qualifying as a physician, Alden retains some 'mucker' habits by indulging in cocaine and opium: 'a little deliberate weakness in prescribing for himself what was most agreeable at the moment, without caring for the remoter consequences'.[46]

In 1896 a physician described a 'cocaine joint disguised as a drugstore' in St Louis, Missouri. Despite well-stocked shelves, it seldom sold anything other than cocaine at a dime per package.

> A pair of portiers covered a back door of the prescription counter, which was kept locked. The interior of this room was dark and contained chairs and two long benches ...A peep into the room ... disclosed the forms of a dozen or more, mostly of the lower class of prostitutes, black as well as white, upon the benches and floor ...The crowd which fills this man's coffers began coming as early as nine o'clock in the evening and at two or three o'clock in the night his room was full.[47]

By 1900 many druggists voluntarily declined to sell cocaine in large amounts, or to certain types of customer. Their self-restraint accentuated the specialised and geographically specific network between cocaine suppliers and their clients. A New York police investigation of 1909 identified sixty-three such drugstores, mainly in the Tenderloin District (lying between Fifth and Ninth Avenues from Madison Square to 49th Street, and cluttered with theatres, bars, gambling houses and brothels). There was a similar concentration of sales outlets in other cities. Tunnel Street in Pittsburgh was known as 'Cocaine Street', for example. Drugstores in the vice district of Chicago sold appreciably more cocaine than drugstores elsewhere in the city. Except in vice districts, or marginal urban areas, cocaine-retailers were monitored by their neighbours. In consequence, before legislatures began to regulate access to cocaine, its distribution system was closed to those without connections. Retailers developed long-term relationships with customers whom they could trust to behave discreetly, while buyers sought suppliers known to provide unadulterated cocaine without risk of police involvement. The arcane slang associated with cocaine—calling it *coke*, *snow*, or *brighteye*, for example—helped to conceal transactions from social and legal sanctions.[48] The cocaine retail system thus went underground into a *demi-monde* celebrated in the anonymous song about the prostitute 'Cocaine Lil' who sniffed so much at 'a snow party' that 'it knocked her dead'. This is an extract from the lyrics:

She had cocaine hair on her cocaine head.
She wore a snowbird hat and sleigh-riding clothes.
She had a cocaine dress that was poppy red.
On her coat she wore a crimson, cocaine rose.

Big gold chariots on the Milky Way,
Snakes and elephants silver and gray,
O the cocaine blues they make me sad,
O the cocaine blues make me feel bad.[49]

The greater avidity for cocaine in the USA must be attributable to cultural influences. All the most important problems in drug history since the 1860s could be resolved by a clear answer to one question: what is so distinctive about the United States? Why has this great country had such a persistent and pervasive drugs problem, which has come to dominate—sometimes inappropriately—global policies on drugs? One pointer is that in the late 1870s and early 1880s the frequenting of opium shops in California, Nevada and elsewhere was seen as an issue of adolescent rebellion against parental authority, and made the object of local scrutiny accordingly. This development, which seems to have been unprecedented in the Western world, was not constructive in forming calm and mature views about illicit drugs—whether by young people or their elders. Another key to the invidious pre-eminence of the US is the most famous sentence in its history, introducing the Declaration of Independence in 1776. 'We hold these truths to be self-evident, that all men are created equal, that they are endowed by their creator with certain inalienable Rights, that among these are Life, Liberty and the pursuit of Happiness.' Only in the USA was personal happiness, or individual fulfilment, enshrined with such formality as a human entitlement; only there were national beliefs, values and norms centred on this idea of inalienable emotional rights. In Europe the formulations were very different. Few people imagined that there was a human right to happiness, although many recognised a Christian duty to be grateful for life, and public figures insisted that citizenship required an acknowledgement of duties. The European emphasis was not, as in the USA, on personal feelings but on possessions. In the maxim attributed to Constantine Phipps, Marquess of Normanby (1797–1863), 'property has its duties as well as its rights'.[50] The high expectations raised in the USA by a right to happiness were unrealistic, and have inevitably been confounded. Some Americans have numbed their disappointment by taking drugs: when the pursuit of happiness has failed them, they have gone in pursuit of oblivion. Other Americans—like many Europeans—have sought artificial happiness in drugs when they have failed to attain what the Declaration of Independence averred the Creator intended for them. The 'self-evident' truths of 1776 are central to American culture, and can seem an inducement to act on self-indulgent impulse. Moreover, the introspective American puritan tradition, with its emphasis on self-examination of conscience, has aggravated the tendencies to self-absorption.

It was perhaps as a consequence of this self-centredness that Americans considered themselves as a people peculiarly susceptible to nervous exhaustion. The Philadelphia neurologist Weir Mitchell, who published *Wear and Tear; or, Hints for the Overworked* as early as 1871, developed the popular Weir Mitchell Rest Cure whereby nervously exhausted patients (especially women) were prescribed bed rest and a rich but bland diet. 'The savage does not feel pain as we do,' Mitchell later averred. 'In our process of being civilised, we have won, I suspect, intensified capacity to suffer.'[51] His fellow American nerve specialist George Beard (1839–83) had in 1869 coined the term 'neurasthenia', a phenomenon attributed in his *American Nervousness, its cause and cures* (1881) to the competitive stresses of an industrial age. Beard's ideas were soon a commonplace: 'Americans are the most nervous people in the world,' announced John Pemberton, the inventor of Coca-Cola, in an advertisement of 1885.[52] In this period the USA produced its own version of the Comte de Saint-Simon, whose ideas had such impact on the French in the 1820s. Frederick Winslow Taylor (1856–1915), the progenitor of mass production Taylorism, who was known for his catchphrase 'Down with dawdling', eventually had nightmares of being surrounded by machinery, and died, after a nervous breakdown, furiously winding his watch in the dark hours of the morning. Taylorism was part of the boundless publicity surrounding busy-ness. 'I fancy that any given thousand Americans do more work in a year than as many of a like group of English,' Mitchell wrote in 1893. 'The gospel of play needs to be preached in this land of ours.'[53] In every continent through the ages men and women have used drugs as an aid to work, sometimes to stimulate their productivity, and in other cases to desensitise themselves against the physical or mental distress of their workplace. The USA is not an exception: American drug habits were an inseparable part of the American business economy.

As the craze for opium-smoking spread among white Americans in the late 1870s it was suggested that a streak of ruffianism in the national character fostered underworld drug habits. Recalling in 1896 the early opium-smoking scene in New York, Stephen Crane (1871–1900) reported that 'the sporting class adopted the habit quickly. Cheap actors, race-track touts, gamblers and the different kinds of confidence men took to it generally.' The characters in the 'Cocaine Lil' song who were nicknamed Hasheesh Nell, Hophead Mag, Dopey Slim, the Poppy Face Kid and the Sleighriding Sisters were representative of this American urban milieu of the 1890s. Drug habits, though, were not confined to lower-class criminals: some rich men, too, were fond of a spree. Until 1894, there was a palatial 'joint' catering to such delinquents on New York's 42nd Street. It was especially a sanctuary for fugitives from the higher echelons of American business. 'An occasional man from Fifth Avenue or Madison Avenue would there have his private "layout", an elegant equipment of silver, ivory, gold. The bunks which lined all sides of the two rooms were nightly crowded and some of the people owned names which are not altogether unknown to the public.'[54] The eighteen sensational books with such titles as *The Bankers, Their Vaults and the Burglars* published under the name of the Chicago private detective Alan Pinkerton (1819–84) promoted the reputation in Europe of fierce, marauding crooks leaving a trail of misdeeds across the USA. The *Spectator* in 1890 cited 'the "hoodlums" of California [and] the "larrikins" of Australia' as part of 'a new disorderly class'.[55] Europe, however, was considered less corrupt. 'All the vice, meannesses and ignominies of the Old World reproduce themselves in the so-called New World, and become more vulgar, more ignoble, more despicable than in their original hemisphere,' according to a self-righteous Englishwoman in 1895. 'The man who lives in a shanty built of empty meat and biscuit tins on the plains of Nevada or New South Wales is by many degrees a more degraded form of humanity than his brother who has stayed amongst English wheat or Tuscan olives or French vines or German pine-trees: many degrees more degraded, because infinitely coarser and more brutal, and more hopelessly soaked in a sordid and hideous manner of life,'[56] This was provocatively expressed; but it represented a widespread feeling that the USA was foremost in the atrocities of gang violence. Drug habits were a feature of this environment.

The context for drugs was different across the Atlantic. There seemed during the 1880s and 1890s to be a strange and intolerable atmosphere hanging over Europe: the effluvium of nervous degeneration and the diffused, sinister exhalation of decadence. It resembled Matthew Arnold's view of England:

> *The weary Titan, with deaf*
> *Ears, and labour-dimm'd eyes,*
> *Regarding neither to right*
> *Nor left, goes passively by,*
> *Staggering on to her goal.*[57]

Fin de siècle anxieties took their grip. 'A common infirmity is visible throughout modern Europe,' Henry Keene (1825–1915) diagnosed in 1888. 'From their hard-living, easy-going, carnal forefathers, what a change to the nervous, excitable men of this century, with their restless craving for novelty and their ready despondency.'[58] European anxieties about human regression were raised by the Italian criminologist Cesare Lombroso (1836–1909); but Parisian psychiatrists did most to popularise the concept of *dégénérescence* in the late nineteenth century. In 1892 the psychologist Alfred Binet (1857–1911) wrote of the degenerate in terms analogous to the drug addict: 'he is dominated by an idea, or by a group of fixed ideas, which tend to give his whole existence its special orientation'. Despite this emotional isolation, 'he may be seen to go, come, do, act, as if his senses and intelligence are fully operative'.[59] The Hungarian physician Max Nordau (1849–1923), who settled at Paris in 1880, was the most influential of Lombroso's admirers. His *Entartung* (1893), published in an English translation of 1895 as *Degeneration*, raised an aesthetic, moral and racial panic. It was chiefly a diatribe against Egotists, by whom he meant aesthetes or any flamboyant forms of individualist, and people who failed to use their will to control their emotional disposition; but other public enemies were denounced. A nation that regularly resorted to alcoholic drinks, tobacco, opium, hashish or arsenic would, he warned, 'rapidly descend to the lowest degrees of degeneracy, to idiocy, to dwarfishness'.[60] Social progress required 'ever tenser self-restraint'. His prescribed 'treatment' for 'the diseases of the age' was ruthless: 'characterization of the leading degenerates as mentally diseased; unmasking and stigmatizing of their imitators as enemies to society; cautioning the public against the lies of these parasites'.[61] Nordau's model of hygienic policing was like a paradigm for the late-twentieth-century War on Drugs.

In the prevailing atmosphere of cultural panic, the obscure causes and ineffectual treatment of drug-cravings made the phenomenon seem more disturbing than ever. As the dread of decay, dirt, passivity and submission intensified, anxieties about pollution and corruption particularly focused on syphilis. Morphine's use in the treatment of tertiary syphilis accentuated the drug's association with degeneration. Alphonse Daudet (1840–97), the French author who suffered from tertiary syphilis, found the pain in his limbs 'atrocious', he said in 1884, 'as if a railway train was crushing his foot'.[62] By 1891 Daudet was injecting himself with morphine every hour.[63] Another French writer who was destroyed by syphilis in this period, Guy de Maupassant (1850–93), developed delusions about his treatment in the clinic where he was confined in 1892. He imagined 'a conspiracy against him of doctors, who lie in wait for him in the corridor to inject him with morphine, the drops of which will make holes in his brain'.[64] The fear and repulsion with which passivity was regarded in the 1890s connected the hostility both to narcotics and homosexuality. Nordau hated Oscar Wilde (1854–1900), author of that great text of *fin de siècle* decadence, *The Picture of Dorian Gray* (1891), yet both men accepted as a symptom of late-nineteenth-century degeneration that human beings felt impelled to take destructive and addictive drugs. The addict's cycle of craving and relapse seemed essentially degenerative. Wilde's character Dorian Gray epitomised the antibourgeois spirit, and not just because he owned great houses in Nottinghamshire and Grosvenor Square. 'He used to wonder at the shallow psychology of those who conceive the Ego in man as a thing simple, permanent, reliable and of one essence. To him, man was a being with myriad lives and myriad sensations, a complex multiform creature that bore within itself strange legacies of thought and passion.' These sentiments are supremely antibourgeois, and characteristic of a type of addict whose life seems distracted and chaotic to others. Certainly, for Wilde, it exemplified Gray's degenerative course that he visited Chinese opium shops in East London because 'the twisted limbs, the gaping mouths, the staring lustreless eyes, fascinated him. He knew in what strange heavens they were suffering, and what dull hells were teaching them the secret of some new joy.'[65]

Jeremiads about degeneracy did not impress everyone. 'I like the original types, the extravagants, the unpredictables, whom the physiologists call the degenerates,' Octave Mirbeau wrote in Les Vingt et un Jours d'un Neurasthénique. Their non-conformity made them 'an oasis in this dismal and monotonous desert which is bourgeois life'.[66] Sir Clifford Allbutt similarly withstood the degeneracy panic. 'The outcry of the modern neurotic has made itself heard rather unduly of late,' he wrote in 1895. The belief that nervous maladies were proliferating he attributed 'to nervous debility, to hysteria, to neurasthenia, to the fretfulness, the melancholy, the unrest due to living at a high pressure, to the whirl of the railway, the pelting of telegrams, the strife of business, the hunger for riches, the lust of vulgar minds for coarse and instant pleasures, the decay of those controlling ethics handed down from statelier and more steadfast generations'. Yet for Allbutt 'all this talk of decadence is a wild absurdity'. The fault of Europeans in the 1890s was 'not that our superficial nerves are too keen, but that . . . we leave vast inner tracts of the nervous system uncultivated . . . in callousness and stupidity'.[67]

It was to treat the severe affliction of insomnia, which blighted lives in every generation, that a white crystalline substance called Sulphonal (diethyl-sulphone-dimethyl-methane) was developed in Germany around 1886 and marketed as a sleeping draught.[68] It was initially hailed with enthusiasm. 'Sulfonal is a "hypnotic", which is free from the incalculable dangers of the "narcotic" remedies such as the opiates and chloral,' reported the Pall Mall Gazette in 1889.[69] However, by 1890 William Henry Gilbert (1860–1906), an English physician working in the spa town of Baden-Baden, had observed adverse reactions:

> Three cases of sulphonalism came under my observation and treatment during the past season. All three were middle-aged ladies of good social standing, who had been advised by their medical attendant to take about two grammes of sulphonal whenever they could not sleep. This had been going on for three to five months, and the use of the drug had become a perfect mania—so much so that the absence of it caused

symptoms similar to those experienced when overcoming the morphia habit. A feeling of intense dizziness, weakness of thought and memory, tottering gait as under the influence of alcohol, inability of writing straight (unsteady characters and an ascending line), loss of appetite and general weakness caused the patients to seek medical aid. The complexion of these formerly healthy women had become somewhat sallow-looking, and the eyes rather dim and expressionless.[70]

Dr Casarelli of Pisa noted the favourable action of sulphonal in diabetes at about the same time as Dr Breslauer, director of a private lunatic asylum near Vienna, reported the deaths of five women patients (out of seventy-seven) to whom he administered sulphonal.[71] These accidental deaths quickly filtered into popular culture. 'I gave him some sulfonal in a phial,' the murderer confesses to the Home Secretary in *The Big Bow Mystery*, a detective novel published in 1892 by the Anglo-Russian Israel Zangwill (1864–1926). 'It is a new drug, which produces protracted sleep without disturbing digestion, and which I use myself.'[72] The effect of such soporifics, wrote Allbutt in 1897, was 'to weaken the will and the intelligence, and slacken the control of the emotions'. They were a common means of suicide. A 'wholly sane friend' of his, who used sulphonal too lavishly to counteract insomnia, hallucinated that 'there were little red butterflies in the streets, which settled on the pavement or flitted in the air as they were disturbed by the stick or foot-step of the passer-by'.[73] In the mid-1890s the Earl of Rosebery (1847–1929) relied on sulphonal to cope with the strains of being Prime Minister. 'If he takes "Sulfonell", he sleeps fairly well; and he is much less depressed,' a confidante noted in 1895.[74] Later he seems to have used cocaine to enliven his public appearances. 'Rosebery made rather a curious speech the other day in the House of Lords,' Lord George Hamilton (1845–1927) gossiped. 'I am informed, by those who watch him, that the impression is he takes some drug before speaking, which makes him brilliant for the moment, but exceptionally flabby and invertebrate for the remainder of the day. He has got very big, and looks very much like the fat boy in Pickwick.'[75]

The dishonesty of drug *habitués* remained notorious. They pretended to be cured when in truth their cravings were incorrigible. They were devious in obtaining supplies. Early in 1889 stringent police orders were issued in Berlin in response to several recent cases of morphine misuse. New instructions were imposed on chemists governing their sale of morphine, and wholesale druggists were forbidden to sell morphine to anybody excepting doctors and chemists. It was hoped these precautions would stop people going from one chemist to another using the same morphine prescriptions.[76] A few months later Auguste Lutaud, the French gynaecologist who had compiled a manual of medical jurisprudence, reported with his medical colleague Paul Descoust on the abuse of morphine, 'which had become much more general during the last ten years'. After being introduced to the drug under the supervision of physicians, some patients were procuring and injecting morphine without medical authority. Despite severe sentences pronounced against dispensing chemists for illegally selling it in Paris and elsewhere, many 'morphiomaniacs' bought from wholesalers or commission agents so as to escape medical surveillance, obtain unlimited supplies and pay less for their drugs. In both Berlin and Paris there were problems with forged prescriptions.[77] In Britain the Pharmacy Act of 1868 was not strictly enforced. 'Anybody could get opium who likes,' an English chemist confided in 1893. In places 'where the use of opium for non-medicinal purposes is common, the druggists had the opium made up in packets ready for their customers'.[78]

'The strange and at once the dangerous element in the use of morphia', reflected the *Journal of Mental Science* in 1888, 'is that it tempts, not only by causing the *habitué* to forget all troubles, but that it actually renders him or her, for the time being, actually more capable— truly a Satanic guise'. The journal endorsed Erlenmeyer's research conclusions that 'the cultured classes, and doctors in particular, are amongst the chief victims', with next place taken by army officers.[79] One case of a cultured man succumbing to morphine's Satanic guise was given in the 1890s by Sir Lauder Brunton, the early proponent of amyl nitrite. It is a story of surreptitious acts and of clandestine heroism.

> The largest quantity that I have ever met with was in the case of a Member of Parliament, who took 24 to 32 grains of morphine subcutaneously every day; 24 grains was the minimum, 32 grains the maximum. He used to take the syringe with him to the House of Commons, and while sitting with his arms quietly crossed he stuck the needle into his biceps and injected morphine, or he had his hand lying apparently quiet on his thigh and made the injection. He used to carry a syringe ready

charged in his waistcoat pocket. This man was not to blame at all . . . because it was the very fineness of his character which led to his acquiring the habit.

He began taking morphine during a serious illness of his daughter's when his anxiety and insomnia were preventing him from arguing his cases successfully in court. His need for the drug steadily increased.

> He made a very brave attempt to give it up, and the suffering he went through was simply awful. He was told that he would have to go through hell to rid himself of the habit, and the poor man said one day, 'Yes, doctor, but there are grades in hell, and I have got down to a very low one.'[80]

Brunton did not name this barrister MP, who conceivably was the Solicitor General in the Rosebery government, Sir Frank Lockwood (1846–97). 'Lockwood's well-spring was mirth—his mirth gushed out of him and affected everyone—it was a general enjoyment, irresistible, contagious, eminently natural,' according to Rosebery. Yet there were shadows in his life. 'He had of course his ups and downs,' wrote his friend Augustine Birrell (1850–1933). 'He knew enough about human nature to know that it was deeply wounded somewhere, and sorely in need of a healer'. Lockwood was obsessed with death—'Frank had died a hundred deaths before his time came,' said the actress Madge Kendal (1848–1935)—and spent the last months of his life heavily depressed, convinced (despite all his physicians said) 'that it was all over with him'.[81] He succumbed to heart failure when influenza supervened upon kidney disease.[82]

Unlike Brunton's patient, women drug-users continued to be stigmatised as weak and manipulative. 'There are many kinds of fool, from the mindless fool to the fiend-fool, but for the most entire capacity to make a household wretched, there is no more complete recipe than a silly woman who is to a high degree nervous and feeble, and who craves pity and likes power,' wrote Weir Mitchell in 1887.[83] Drug habits were often attributed to female silliness, as shown by a paper on the dangers of morphine read to the British Gynaecological Society in 1895 by Dr Henry Macnaughton Jones (1844–1918). Macnaughton Jones had for many years been a professor of midwifery in Ireland before settling in London in 1883 as an obstetrical and gynaecological specialist. His two-volume *Diseases of Women* reached its ninth edition in 1904. Like Clouston he regarded the craving for narcotics as the result of a defective self-control that could be foretold in early life. He believed that the insubordinate nature of women's bodies aggravated the paralysis of volition manifest in drug-cravings. Neurotics could not control their nerves, especially 'when the unequal struggle occurs between the sovereignty of an enfeebled, indeterminate will, and the rebellious and more masterful emissaries—the woman's "lower passions and lower pains" '. Like most Victorian physicians Jones mistrusted the spinster. 'In the single woman of the neurotic type, we are more likely to meet with those erotic thoughts, desires and practices that still further enervate her nervous system and enfeeble her central control.' He offered a stereotype of married women who were both his professional bane and incipient addicts.

> With her, every twinge is 'agonising' . . . and once let her evolve 'uterus and ovary' on the brain, and whether these organs be diseased or not, they are made responsible for every ill her peccant flesh is heir to . . . She may suffer from congestive dysmenorrhœa and overalgia, her uterus may be as flabby as her brain, and her ovary be as fertile in aches as her imagination is in fanciful illusions. Her voluptuosity is not limited to her appetites of palate, and is not infrequently manifested in various sexual abuses. She fancies she sleeps for many hours less than she actually does, and hence is often seeking for some new, when she has already exhausted every conceivable variety of reputed, hypnotic.

According to Macnaughton Jones, both the frustrated spinster and the self-indulgent wife were 'found constantly as representatives of the habit of morphinism'. Citing Dr L.-R. Régnier, the author of *L'intoxication chronique par la morphine* (1890), he observed that when morphine was readily obtainable, women recommended its use to one another and even subcutaneously injected it into their friends. 'Thus the habit becomes contagious, and there is even a morbid delight felt in the act of puncturing, not alone herself, but others.'[84] Such reports seem to have inspired Robert Hichens (1864–1950) in his morphine novel *Felix* (1902), in which Lady Caroline Hurst takes pleasure in injecting both her best friend and her dog. *Felix* also features a Parisian *morphineuse*, 'an old woman who makes a profession of injecting morphia into the smart women and *demi-mondaines* who frequent her house'. Purportedly the *morphineuse*'s establishment existed, and was described to Hichens by Dr Henri Guimbail of Ivry-sur-Seine; its description in the novel surpasses for horror any fictional descriptions of opium dens.[85]

Young women with wills of their own were encouraged to feel guilty. The identification of drug misuse with rebellious adolescents was becoming marked. The *Journal of Mental Science* in 1889 printed a long, self-critical memoir written by a middle-class woman aged twenty-one recovering from laudanum addiction. The authenticity of the document was vouchsafed. Its author had surely had her feelings worked upon, for it is a paradigm of medical men's attitudes to women. The anonymous author was conditioned with shame. In her remorse she presented herself as the sort of Egotist whom Nordau denounced in *Degeneration*.

> There was no excuse for my taking it, brought up by such a mother, and with such a constant example of unselfishness before me in all the rest of the family. All my tastes and fancies were gratified; as mother says, when I take a whim into my head, the whole house is turned upside down. When I came home from school, I insisted on practising [music] seven hours a day, and the family put up with it, though it was a great infliction to them. It would have been better for me if they had not done so, for I was naturally so tired-out at night that I could not sleep, and knowing that sleep would come easily with a little laudanum, it was difficult to resist taking it.

She accepted that her ruin was attributable to scholastic ambitions that were inappropriate in a young woman: she should have conformed to her mother's model of domesticity: 'I'm quite sure I would never have had neuralgia, if it had not been for stewing up for exams. Mother was always writing to tell me not to do them, but I did not feel it my duty to obey her on that point, as what does one go to school for, if not to learn; and to own oneself beaten by a headache would surely show a very weak mind.'[86] The misery of addiction was the well-deserved penalty for her insubordination. 'No one need think that they will escape without punishment . . . sooner or later retribution is sure to follow.'[87] She submitted to the cure because her parents very firmly told me that this was my last chance, that they would not stand any more of it, and that had it been any of the others they would have been sent away at once, but as they considered themselves to blame for having over-indulged me, they were going to give me another trial, and try what a different system would do. The different system began by being very strict; only two hours a day practising, no French novels, tea only three times a day, and not to be allowed out at night this winter. As to the other arrangements, they soon fell through; after having let a girl have pretty much her own way for nearly twenty-two years, it is rather much to expect her to give up all at once so much that she has been accustomed to.

Although parental discipline was thus triumphantly vindicated for the alienists of the *Journal of Mental Science*, it is refreshing to note that the young opium-eater's spirits were not entirely broken by the cure. Months afterwards she still suffered backache from abstinence pangs, and noted acerbically that 'our medical man, who is a bright specimen of the country doctor . . . when asked to explain what that meant, said, "perhaps her corsets are too tight" '.[88] Drug-users, of course, were treated punitively regardless of age or gender. Allbutt in 1897 protested against the 'violent futilities' visited by his medical colleagues on unconscious patients who had taken accidental or deliberate opiate overdoses:

It is the custom, a custom in which I have loyally taken my part during many a weary hour, to 'arouse' the patient by bullying him. He is cuffed, dragged up and down the room by relays of enthusiasts, pinched, singed (Charcot's brûlures), flipped with wet towels, bawled at, and racked by electric currents strong enough to drive an omnibus. Now, although these measures do, no doubt, animate a medical student with his first real sense of doing some good in the world, yet . . . they are as useless as bar-barous . . . to be dismissed with other medieval instruments of torture as curiosities for the *Illustrated Short History of Medicine* of the twentieth century.[89]

Opium houses in the USA, Europe and Australia were represented as haunts of prostitution where Chinese men seduced middle-class white girls, and where white prostitutes went to turn tricks. This appears improbable. 'It kills all lustful inclination,' said Ellen, a prostitute *habitué* of an Australian opium shop, under questioning by the Royal Commission on Chinese Gambling and Immorality in 1891. 'If you were lying down on a bunk smoking opium alongside a Chinaman who was also smoking opium, the probability is that he would not care to have intercourse with you?' she was asked. 'Not if he had the opium habit he would not,' she replied. 'The man who has the opium habit is not like another man; he does not care for women.'[90] Mei Quong Tart (1850–1903), the leading Chinese merchant and philanthropist at Sydney, toured Chinese camps in New South Wales to study opium habits. In *A Plea for the Abolition of the Importation of Opium* (1887) he insisted that the prohibition of opium in Australia would improve the quality of immigrants and thus reduce racial antagonism. If opium was prohibited, Chinese labourers would no longer emigrate, and immigrants to Australia would be confined to those who would behave as good citizens.[91] Similar thinking led to the Chinese Exclusion Act enforced in the USA from 1896 until 1942. This sought to exclude opium-smokers from the Land of Opportunity by restricting the immigration of Chinese to scholars, highly qualified professional men and the rich.

The unintelligibility of Chinese habits, languages and mannerisms to most Americans, Australians and Europeans could seem menacing. Fanciful literary images of Chinese opium shops steadily accumulated after the publication of Dickens's *Mystery of Edwin Drood*. Accounts from real life were often less lurid. Lady Theodora Guest (1840–1924), a tourist who was guided through San Francisco's Chinatown by a local detective in 1894, found the experience intimidating yet humdrum.

> We were next taken to a terrible place; an opium den; down a long underground dark passage to a place that looked like a wine-cellar, or still more a mushroom-house, all shelves, with a passage between them. They were in three rows, I think, one over the other, and in these shelves lay creatures huddled up, smoking opium. Each had a long pipe, and a little lamp; and, with perfect indifference to us, heated and rolled up his little balls of opium, which were put into the pipe, and, after two or three ecstatic whiffs, had to be renewed . . . It certainly was rather horrible; but in no way as degrading a sight as that of the ordinary European drunkard.[92]

Lady Theodora's reaction was typical of the British governing classes of
the 1890s. In Allbutt's words, 'opium-smoking, whether in Europe or
elsewhere, suffers condemnation not because of the direct mischief of
it, which may or may not be great, but of the degrading circumstances
of its pursuit; in Eastern towns it is the resource of the scum of the
earth.'[93]

An authoritative account of New York City's opium-smoking scene
was provided in 1896. Stephen Crane estimated that there were 25,000
opium-smokers in New York divided between Chinatown and the
Tenderloin district. As a result of campaigns to shut 'dens', opium-
smokers had retreated to private apartments after 1894; attempts to
police 'these little strongholds' of the underworld would always be ineffective because opium-smokers were so discreet.[94] In his Sherlock
Holmes story, 'The Man with the Twisted Lip' (1889), Sir Arthur
Conan Doyle (1859–1930) had pictured the opium-smoker as 'an
object of mingled horror and pity to his friends and relatives . . . with
yellow, pasty face, drooping lids, and pin-point pupils, all huddled in a
chair, the wreck and ruin of a noble man.'[95] Although Crane acknowledged the mendacity and self-delusion of opium-users, he repudiated
such lurid propaganda. 'The "fiends" can easily conceal their vice. They
get up from the "layout", adjust their cravats, straighten their coat-tails
and march off like ordinary people, and the best kind of expert would
not be able to bet that they were or were not addicted to the habit.'[96]
Weir Mitchell had noted the irrepressible human propensity to strike
postures as a form of self-reassurance that one is alive: 'A man . . . must
have an audience, or make believe to have one, even if it is only himself'.[97]
Such behaviour was obtrusive among New York's opium-smokers.
Addicts ('habit-smokers', Crane called them) despised the 'sensation-
smoker' who occasionally liked to go slumming for squalid thrills. 'This
latter is a person who has been won by the false glamour which sur-
rounds the vice and who goes about really pretending that he has a
ravenous hunger for the pipe. There are more "sensation-smokers" than
one would imagine.'[98]

Opium shops in the USA and Europe were less contentious than
opium cultivation and smoking in China. The quality and quantity of
opium produced by Chinese poppy-cultivators rose appreciably after
1870 because native-grown opium could be smoked seven or eight
times compared with at most three times with imported drugs. By the

mid-1880s opium poppies were cultivated in all but two provinces of China: Szechuan was the chief producer, closely followed by Yunnan (where one-third of cultivation was estimated to be poppy). In 1890, as a ploy to reduce Indian imports, the Chinese imperial government revoked all edicts prohibiting the cultivation of opium poppies. Meanwhile, the Society for the Suppression of the Opium Trade—under the chairmanship of the Quaker businessman Sir Joseph Pease (1828–1903)—never relented in its opposition to the traffic. In 1891 Pease's parliamentary motion that the Indian opium revenue was 'morally indefensible', that the Indian government should confine future poppy cultivation to medicinal opium, and the transit of Malwa opium across British territory should be prohibited, was carried by 160 votes to 130. It was not, however, until 1893 that Gladstone's government agreed to appoint a Royal Commission to investigate the subject. The Secretary of State for India, the Earl of Kimberley (1826–1902), deprecated 'the anti-opium fanatics',[99] and believed 'prohibition and suppression of opium is simply impossible in China, and the right course is to levy a heavy duty on it, as we do on alcoholic liquors'. He judged alcohol and opium 'very much on a par.'[100] Kimberley has often been said to have packed the Commission with former officials of the Indian government who were tolerably certain to support the status quo. The historian Martin Booth, for example, declares that 'bar one, the commission members were all pro-opium government supporters'.[101] This is untrue. The chairman of the Commission, Earl Brassey (1836–1918), was 'a man of robust patriotism, who thoroughly understands the management of a yacht in dirty weather, and who would make an excellent First Lord of the Admiralty in any administration for which he was not too honest', according to a colleague.[102] He was an independent-minded man who approached his task without preconceptions. Neutrality can also be attributed to the medical member of the Commission, Sir William Roberts (1830–99), a high-principled Methodist who was president of the pharmacology section of the British Medical Association. 'He always looked back on his experience in India on this Commission as one of the most interesting events of his life,' recalled a colleague. 'He took a broad view of the opium question, largely founded on the result of his keen observation of its supposed ill-effects while in India.'[103]

Other Commissioners admittedly held strong beliefs about opium.

The colliery-owner and former Liberal MP Arthur Pease (1837–98) was a member of the council of the SSOT and brother of its president. A maverick Liberal MP, William Caine (1842–1903), who was Secretary of the Anglo-Indian Temperance Society, was also nominated by Kimberley but was prevented by illness from accompanying Brassey to India.[104] Another Liberal MP and temperance campaigner was Henry Wilson (1833–1914), who was an inveterate opponent of vice and militarism. Conversely, Anglo-Indian officials on the Commission saw their duty, in the words of Sir James Lyall (1838–1916), 'to get an expression of opinion, of native opinion in particular, which will carry sufficient weight to enable the question to be shelved'.[105] Lyall tried (with mixed results) to draw native witnesses into declaring that the suppression of the opium trade would result in another Indian mutiny. The Director General of the Post Office in India, Sir Arthur Fanshawe (1848–1931), was a more subdued supporter of the status quo. The retired Indian administrator Sir Lepel Griffin (1840–1908) accepted Kimberley's nomination despite regarding 'a Royal Commission on Opium as an absurdity'. Griffin would have no truck with changing opium policy. 'The anti-opium agitation of Sir Joseph Pease and his friends is one of the most immoral in modern history.' The SSOT existed to alleviate 'the dullness of middle-class English life . . . by the glory of a holy war against vice in Asia'. He approached his duties as a Commissioner armed with adamant views: 'To satisfy their desire for meddling in other people's business and their . . . religious mania, the anti-opiumists would risk the bankruptcy of the Indian Empire and the grave discontent of its people.'[106]

The Commissioners began hearing evidence in London in September 1893, travelled east in November, and held public sittings across India between December 1893 and February 1894. Over 29,000 questions were asked of 723 witnesses: the verbatim reports of their testimony covered over 2500 closely printed pages. Their report was published in April 1895. 'Condensed into a nutshell, the report may be said to assert that everything is for the best in the best of all possible worlds, and that it is impossible to prohibit the use of opium in India, even if it was desirable, and it is not desirable,' in the summary of the journalist W. T. Stead.[107] The Commissioners reported that it was unnecessary to prohibit poppy cultivation and opium manufacture in British India. Such a prohibition, if extended to the protected Indian states adjacent to British territory, would be an unprecedented act of interference that would surely be resisted. The evidence of the Anglo-Indian witnesses and the Report of the Commissioners have not been treated generously by most historians.[108] There are some sustainable objections to the Royal Commission's proceedings, such as its negligence when investigating the impact of opium-smoking on Malaysian health. Carl Trocki's study of opium's impact on Chinese society in the nineteenth-century Straits Settlements concludes that the British Empire was 'in the pathogenic sense, systematically dependent' on opium. He argues 'that the decline of the empire really began when the British got out of the opium business'.[109]

Perhaps; but it is crude to represent that officials were so resolved to preserve Indian government opium revenues that their conduct was immoral. The loss of opium revenue, derived from exports to China and other sales, was considered undesirable; but it was not an isolated or overriding factor in deliberations. There were powerful cultural assumptions at work, which may not be approved by all commentators a century later, but which were not discreditable. Few nineteenth-century physicians had finer judgement than Sir Clifford Allbutt. In the 1890s he believed that 'all people, civilised or uncivilised' required substances 'to soothe the nervous system, to restore it after fatigue', and that opium was used 'in many Oriental countries not as an idle or vicious indulgence, but as a reasonable aid in the work of life'. His views did not reflect racial contempt towards Oriental people, for he juxtaposed their drug habits with the case of one of his most respected patients:

> A gentleman, who consulted me frequently in later life, took a grain of opium in a pill every morning and every evening for the last fifteen years of a long, laborious and distinguished career. A man of great force of character, concerned in affairs of weight and of national importance, and of stainless character, he persisted in the habit—which, indeed, I never was so presumptuous as to endeavour to suppress—as one which gave him no conscious gratification or diversion, but which toned and strengthened him for his deliberations.[110]

Anglo-Indian experts, who had a similar outlook to Allbutt, should not be scorned. In the words of Sir John Strachey (1823–1907), a member of the Council of India and a former acting Viceroy, 'we who have spent all our lives in India are not all fools and imposters'.[111] Most of the Commissioners and officials regarded chronic and inescapable sobriety as an affliction; they shared a fatalistic view of the life prospects of Asians; they mistrusted the dogmatic confidence of the SSOT and temperance campaigners that the consumption of intoxicating substances could be suppressed by forceful policing of producers and consumers. They were wary of making drug-taking a throttle-valve of crime. They foresaw in the 1890s that one result of opium and Indian hemp being proscribed would be an increase in smuggling and criminal gangs: these activities would be hard to control, and would have a contaminating social and political influence. Corruption would accompany Prohibition, as the administrative class understood. The suppression of non-medicinal opium consumption 'would be a terrible harassment to the people', declared Sir Dennis FitzPatrick (1837–1920), Lieutenant Governor of the Punjab. 'We have in this country to work through ill-paid underlings, and they will always take every opportunity of worrying the people and extorting money from them, and I shall look with very great apprehension upon the creation of an army of hungry understrappers that we should have to call into existence, in order to make even a feeble attempt to prevent the smuggling of a thing which is so small in bulk as opium.'[112] The evidence heard by the Commission about Indian opium-eaters simply did not accord with the views of the SSOT, and Arthur Pease, the Commissioner who sat on that society's council, so changed his views as a result of his visit to India that he was required to resign from the society. The majority report (from which only Wilson dissented) struck a practical, even admirable balance between human nature and governmental powers in the 1890s. It was not a counsel of perfection.

Lord Brassey was impressed by the testimony of Dr Henry Martyn Clark (c.1856–c.1905) who trained in medicine at Edinburgh before taking charge of the largest medical mission in the world at Amritsar in the Punjab in 1882. The mission had undertaken 88,961 visits in 1893, and Clark (who spoke all the vernaculars) was one of the most informed Europeans on Indian health. He was a fair-minded realist whose testimony deserves to be given precedence in this history. Clark had no personal knowledge of China, but accepted the consensus that opium harmed its people. However he emphasised that almost all opium in China (as in the Straits Settlements) was smoked, whereas in the Punjab it was habitually eaten and seldom smoked. There was therefore 'not the slightest parallel between China and India', and it was 'absolutely wrong in point of fact to say that opium is working the ruin, harm and mischief in this country that it is said to work in China'. Clark testified that opium was 'a bad habit' with 'a great tendency to enslave man', but warned that as it was impossible for any government to prevent the growth, manufacture, supply and use of drugs, an attempted suppression would be counterproductive: 'we should have the opium traffic *plus* smuggling'. Prohibition would increase opium consumption because 'it is impossible to force a moral measure against the moral or immoral sense of the people on whom it is to operate'. Clark judged many accounts 'of the evil done to opium-eaters by the habit . . . very greatly exaggerated indeed, and they can in no sense apply to moderate users of this drug'. He estimated from his Indian medical experience that about 14 per cent of hospital patients used opium. 'It is used by all classes of the community, Hindus, Sikhs, Mahomedans, outcasts, low castes, no castes; and it is also used by women,' sometimes in enormous quantities. Some users lose weight, but 'in the great majority of cases—no such results appear. While it does not do any good, it does not appear to do the slightest harm. The people who use it are hale and hearty, fit for work and exposure, and the habit seems to interfere with neither their longevity nor their health'. Clark had seen many patients who had been using opium for thirty, forty or forty-five years. 'I know old men now doing a good day's work who began the habit as lads . . . and I am bound to say they appear to me not a bit the worse'. Indian-based life assurance offices, 'guided by the medical men', did not 'impose a higher rate upon opium eaters'.[113] As opium was freely available for eating, it was not much associated with criminality. 'There is no such thing as a murderous opium maniac, or a man under its influence assaulting people,' he testified. 'The train of moral evils' attributed to opium, 'such as neglect of home, of children, of business, ruin of families', was not evident to him. No peasantry was 'hardier and thriftier and more careful than our Punjab peasants . . . yet amongst this class you will find an immense number of opium-eaters. They are very frequently beggared by their marriage customs and so forth, but never by opium'. According to Clark, 'the fact that a man takes moderate doses of opium does not of necessity imply that he forms the opium habit'.[114]

He was, however, passionately opposed to the dosing of children with opium. It was occasionally used for infanticide, he thought. 'It is supposed to strengthen the child against cold, but the real fact of the matter is it is given to the child to keep quiet'. It was besmeared on the child's tongue, or put upon the nipples or fingernail of the mother, which the child sucked. Child development was hindered by this 'pernicious' practice. 'I know nothing more woeful in life than to see an opium baby, a poor shrivelled little thing, with its face in wrinkles, and a curious old mannish expression about it, horribly quiet, and wasting almost before your eyes.'[115] Instead of Prohibition, Clark advocated government programmes of harm reduction to introduce 'moral training in all our schools and colleges to teach men to be men, and not to be enslaved by any habit.'[116]

The Royal Commission, like the contemporary enquiry into Indian hemp drugs, strove to respect the cultural variations between the social norms of Europeans and Asians. Its consensus was that if in Europe one respected the distinction between different habits of alcoholic consumption—abstinence, moderate and excessive—one should show equivalent respect for the different habits of consumption of opium or hemp drugs in Asia. There was cultural tact in the Anglo-Indian testimony. 'The Indian labourer who takes his opium has no means of solacing himself after the day's work; he has no theatres, no music halls, no clubs, no societies, no gin shops,' testified Sir William Moore (1828–96), the retired Surgeon General.[117] The redoubtable Miss Sturmer, who could read and write in Hindi and managed her own estate in Azimgarh district, reported that 'the opium cultivators are our most industrious and satisfactory tenants'.[118] She was 'very averse' to alcohol and ganja ('I am a waterdrinker myself'), but knew among her tenants 'lots of people who take opium in small quantities; I cannot say that I know of a single man in our estate who takes it to excess'.[119] She testified from a desire to protect the livelihoods of her tenants. 'Yesterday, coming along, a man came flying over the Embankment to me, and said, "*Dohai!* Miss Saheb, I beg of you, do all you can not to have the poppy prohibited, because we cannot possibly live if it is stopped." '[120] By contrast some of the anti-opium testimony seemed unsympathetic. The American Methodist missionary in charge of Bareilly Theological Seminary excluded opium-smokers from his congregation: 'We would seek to break off the habit, and if they were irrevocable, we would cut them off.' He denounced opium as 'a moral evil' leading to 'mendacity', although his use of the opium habit as his church's 'test of membership' must have contributed to the lies.[121]

Testimony was specific to the Indian Empire. 'The healthiest people I knew, the best people, the wholesomest people, and those you trusted most in their work, were always the opium-eaters: invariably'. This was the testimony of Sir George Birdwood, but it was confined to India, where he had been a professor of materia medica in Bombay. 'Nothing can be more hurtful', Birdwood added, 'than the morphia habit now so prevalent in America.'[122] Diverting attention from opium shops, official testimony focused on the Rajputs and Sikhs. Strachey 'often thought that the best practical answer to those who enveigh against the use of opium would be . . . to bring one of our crack opium-drinking Sikh regiments to London, and exhibit them in Hyde Park. There is no more vigorous, manly, handsome race to be found, not only in India, but in the world. They are the flower of our Indian army, and one of the bulwarks of our Empire, and yet the use of opium among them is almost universal.'[123] Henry Waterfield (1840–1901), who had served in India since the mutiny of 1857 and ultimately reached the rank of major general, testified that 80 per cent of Sikh soldiers were 'occasional takers' of opium, 15 per cent took it habitually and half of 1 per cent excessively.[124] Another highly experienced officer, William Biscoe (1841–1920), declared that 60 per cent of opium-eaters in his Sikh regiment 'took it and left it off as occasion required'. From the regimental point of view, 'it was not considered a defect in a man if he took opium occasionally'. It was 'not a social vice at all' among his Sikhs. Regimental arrangements were made to provide men with opium when it was not available in bazaars: 'when we marched from Kandahar to Kelat, where there were no supplies at all, we had to look about us and get some for the men'.[125]

Cannabis drugs were also ubiquitous in British India, and like opium yielded government revenues. Ganja was smoked by labourers exposed to extremes of sun or wet, cartmen, porters, masons, palki-bearers, sanyasis, jogis, fakirs, mendicants, up-country darwans, rajputs acting as athletes and Brahmins worshipping Kali. During the 1880s these practices began to be contentious. In the Bengal Excise Report for 1883–4 Trevor Grant (1837–1924) condemned the 'rapid increase in the use of

ganja as altogether lamentable. It is the only exciseable article in favour
of which nothing can be said. It seems to have *absolutely no virtue*, and
to do harm the very first time it is used. In shorter time than any other
intoxicant, it establishes a craving habit, and is more irresistible than
that created by any other.'[126] Attempts to regulate the growth of
cannabis plants were unsuccessful. Indian hemp drugs were particularly
obnoxious to Christian missionaries. 'What with liquor and opium and
hemp drugs of various kinds, all licensed by Government, it does seem
as if the population was terribly exposed to degrading influences,'
declared a Calcutta missionary.[127] In response to missionary pressure,
the Indian government in October 1893 appointed a Commission to
inquire into the consumption and control of hemp drugs in India.
Again the evidence is an impressive array of both expert opinion and
amateur prejudice. The President of the Commission was Sir William
Mackworth Young (1840–1924), then Financial Commissioner of the
Punjab. This distinguished Anglo-Indian administrator was a sage, con-
ciliatory, terse man, and a strong supporter of missionary work in the
subcontinent.

Young's Commission report finding 'general ignorance' about the
effects of hemp drugs among both European and Indian witnesses.[128]
Although 'dogmatic statements' were made about the drug, these were
often based on minimal or unreliable evidence. 'This ignorance of the
effects of hemp drugs on the part of some able, intelligent and benevolent men' indicated to the committee 'that the injury caused by the
drugs is comparatively trifling. It must have attracted more attention
had evil effects been at all common.'[129] The Commission accepted 'the
strictly medicinal use of hemp drugs in the alleviation of human suffering and disease'. It felt that medical usage 'can hardly be separated by
a hard-and-fast line' from the 'popular use of the drugs by the ordinary
consumer'.[130] Balancing the evidence, the Commission concluded,

> there is a very large amount of moderate consumption of all these drugs,
> the evil effects of which are inappreciable, even if this moderate con-
> sumption is not quite harmless . . . that which is moderate and harmless
> to one man may be too much for another. And the moderate habit may
> undoubtedly develop into excess in some cases where excess might not
> have been looked for. It is so with all intoxicants; but moderation and
> excess ought to be distinguished. And on the whole the weight of the

evidence is to the effect that moderation in the use of hemp drugs is not injurious.[131]

They cited with approval testimony from West Punjab that 'all classes' would resent the British prohibiting the use in India of hemp drugs, 'which they have been using from time immemorial, and which is also religiously respected', if no action was taken against the preferred drug of the British, alcohol.[132] The Commission rejected as spurious the widespread belief that the hemp drugs were filling the Indian lunatic asylums. They concluded that it was unnecessary and inexpedient to prohibit the cultivation of the hemp plant, or the manufacture, sale and use of the drugs made from it. Instead they recommended a policy of harm minimisation aimed at suppressing the excessive use and restraining the moderate use of the drugs. This would entail reforming taxation of the drug, prohibiting cultivation except under licence, centralising cultivation, and limiting the number of shops and the extent of legal possession.[133] In summary, Young's Commission, like Brassey's, collectively disbelieved that governments could *eliminate* intemperance by drastic or ambitious measures; they realised that the best hope of *reducing* drug-taking lay in the introduction of finely tuned, understated, localised measures aimed at containment or minor diminishing of consumption. They scorned the idea that drugs policy should be an affair of political gestures intended to impress the domestic electorate.

Young and his colleagues had the benefit of the highest expert testimony. The botanist Sir David Prain (1857–1944), Curator of the Calcutta Herbarium, testified that he had been unable to find a single instance of evil effects arising from the use of the three products of Indian hemp. This was contrary to his 'preconceived idea, derived from copious assertion'.[134] Similar evidence was given by Lieutenant-Colonel Alexander Crombie (1845–1906), who had been a professor at Calcutta Medical College and Surgeon Superintendent of the hospital there. Crombie judged that 'alcohol is more harmful in all respects' than hemp despite the fact that 'complete oblivion can be produced by hemp'.[135] He cited the example of his own servant, 'who takes ganja or bhang in excess, but is always at his post and capable of doing his duty', whereas if he took alcohol 'to the same extent he would be useless'. Crombie compared ganja with opium. 'Like ganja, opium is smoked in company, and it is therefore an incentive to idleness, dissipation, and bad company, with all its results.' The habit of smoking opium took firmer hold than that of ganja, and by comparison was ruinously expensive. 'The opium-eater is as a rule a respectable, well-doing member of society, who takes his opium pills before leaving his house in the morning, goes about his business, and returns without any apparent effect from the drug. I think there is a respectable use of ganja corresponding to this—the moderate use.'[136] It was estimated that 80 per cent of Hindustanis were habitual consumers, of whom 10 per cent drank to excess and the rest moderately. A beverage of *bhang* and sherbert was essential at the celebration of Hindu festivals and marriage ceremonies. The drink, which signified success and safety from mishap, was offered to all the family and every guest. Small children had drops smeared on the temple by the tip of the finger. On such occasions, 'some people, chiefly males, indulge to excess; but it does no harm to them beyond promoting a little merriment or hilarity and producing protracted sleep'.[137]

Many witnesses distinguished between Indians who took drugs to improve their productivity, and those who took the 'depraved course' of using drugs for pleasure. Although the use of narcotics by factory workers had been a source of anxiety in the industrialising Western economies from the 1820s, it was not thought undesirable for outdoor labourers in industrially undeveloped regions to drug themselves. British officialdom in India recognised the necessity for drugs to help some workers to cope with their jobs. Typical testimony came from Edward Vesey Westmacott (1839–1911), a senior official in Bengal. 'It would be a wicked thing to deprive hardworking men, much exposed to weather, on the mud soil, of their stimulant,' he testified, but 'among the more effeminate classes, the Babus, a man, and especially a young man, who takes to ganja would be looked on as going to the devil'.[138] There were class demarcations too. Philip Nolan (d. 1902) was a Commissioner in Bengal, where drinking *bhang* on festive occasions was 'an honoured custom.' In his district

> ganja-smoking is despised by the well-to-do, because its consumption is confined to the poor who can afford no other indulgence, just as drinking gin in a public-house is looked down on by gentlemen who take champagne and liquors in clubs. But the sentiment is stronger here, for in this land of caste, more than any other, the well-to-do feel a repul-

sion for any food or stimulant used exclusively by those beneath them in the social scale. Opium is certainly more injurious than ganja, and yet its use excites no such aversion, as it is taken by the rich.[139]

Sir Edward Henry (1850–1931), then Inspector General of Police in Bengal, and afterwards Commissioner of Police for London, consulted the opinions of his officers before testifying on the effects of hemp drugs. Although some 'petty thefts' were committed in order to pay for the drug, overall there was 'no established connection in the way of cause and effect between hemp drugs and professional crime'.[140] The magistrate at Bogra, Alfred Edgar Harward (1865–1927), agreed. The Indian criminal underworld he described as town dwellers lacking social ties and of low origin. They all used intoxicants in some form, and became habitual ganja smokers, often to excess. 'Men of this class are criminals first, and ganja-smokers afterwards'. Those individuals who spurned their 'respectable families' and took to crime often smoked ganja, but 'the habit is generally the effect and not the cause of their fall'.[141]

The Lieutenant-Governor of Bengal, Sir Charles Elliott (1835–1911), had declared in 1892 that it was as 'reasonable to suppose that excessive ganja smoking may be due to insanity, as that insanity may be due to excessive ganja smoking'. One prohibitionist missionary was outraged by this 'fanciful witticism' being used 'at this crisis for minimising the evils done by a dangerous drug'.[142] He did not recognise a serious point. As Lieutenant-Colonel Edward Bovill (d. 1908), superintendent of the Patna asylum observed, 'persons whose minds are becoming diseased . . . seek . . . sleep, relief from pain or excitement, or for alleviation from trouble, in the use of hemp drugs, as they do in other countries in the use of alcohol'.[143] Young's report concluded after minute enquiries into asylum admissions in British India 'that the usual mode of differentiating between hemp drug insanity and ordinary mania was in the highest degree uncertain, and therefore fallacious'.[144] Even the Edinburgh alienist Thomas Clouston, with his emphasis on self-restraint, accepted the Commission's conclusion that 'hemp drugs cause insanity more rarely than has been supposed, and the resultant insanity is usually of a temporary character and of shorter duration than that due to other causes'.[145] The distinction between the elated state of cannabis intoxication, and the alarming hallucinations, fear of neighbours, restlessness, insomnia and incoherence of cannabis maniacs, was summarised by Alexander Crombie, who had superintended a lunatic asylum in India.

> Acute ganja intoxication is marked by the extreme vehemence of the mania. The maniac is excited in every fibre. His aspect is infuriated, his eye glares and is tense and glistening, while at the same time the conjunctiva is red and injected. He shouts, vociferates, sings, walks quickly up and down or round his cell, and shakes the door out of its fastenings. If at liberty, he is violent and aggressive and may run *amok* ... Most cases entirely recover, and those in which the mania was caused by a single debauch in a person unaccustomed to its use almost invariably do so .. . The insanity produced by the long-continued immoderate use of ganja has also features of its own. The patients are hilarious, attitudinise, and are full of sense of well-being; they as a rule are good-natured and trustworthy, and recover in a large proportion of cases under confinement and deprivation of the drug. These cases characterise Indian asylums by the large number of happy amusing lunatics they contain.[146]

Missionaries loathed cannabis for its lascivious influence. 'Moderate use has an aphrodisiacal effect, which must be very harmful,' one of them testified. 'Many youths and young men and even boys are tempted into this evil habit of ganja smoking just to encourage themselves in the excessive indulgence of sexual vices, and no doubt a very large amount of impotence is the result.'[147] He would have recoiled from Oscar Wilde's account of his visit to Algiers in 1895 with his lover Lord Alfred Douglas (1870–1945). 'Bosie and I have taken to haschish: it is quite exquisite: three puffs of smoke and then peace and love'. For them, love meant sex with beautiful youths.[148]

The Commission assessed the desirability of suppressing Indian hemp drugs. The evidence that it received about the probable adulteration or substitution of alternative drugs was shrewd. Henry Clissold Williams (1848–1927), formerly inspector of police and jails in Assam, disliked the use of ganja, but felt that if the drug was criminalised, 'the majority of its consumers would infallibly turn to something else'.[149] An Indian witness agreed that ganja-smokers would substitute other indigenous plants, such as datura, which the Commission understandably thought more deleterious.[150] 'Prohibition', in the opinion of E.V.

Westmacott, 'would require an army of detectives to enforce . . . discontent among consumers would be enormous, as . . . the illicit article cultivated and prepared secretly would be most inferior.'[151]

The temperance movement gave vociferous evidence to the committee but was not heard sympathetically. The most implacable opponents of hemp drugs were those pledged against all intoxicants. Major-General Montague Millett (1839–1901), a teetotaller who served in the Punjab Police Department for thirty years, was an extremist who was convinced by recent legislative experiments in the USA that 'people are happier and more moral' under absolute prohibition. 'The State has but to be boldly despotic . . . to crush out evil practices to strengthen its rule; it will suffer by fostering evils; it will never suffer by fostering good.' He urged the dismissal of all government employees addicted to drugs as well as confiscation of drugs which then 'should be publicly destroyed by fire in the presence of the community'.[152] Prohibitionists like Millett were prototypes of the twentieth-century American warriors against drugs: their histrionic extremism, ambitious aims and self-confident morality were recognised by both the Brassey and Young commissions as inexpedient, ineffective and counterproductive.

Both the Brassey and Young reports offered intelligent alternatives to Prohibition: they provide honourable models for twenty-first-century policy-makers. It is true, though, that they were studies centred on underdeveloped societies, and by the 1890s distinctly important new trends were emerging in the Western world. There was increasing intellectual curiosity about the consumption of psychoactive substances. This was exemplified by the experimental use—by Louis Lewin in Germany, Weir Mitchell in the USA and various British literary figures associated with Havelock Ellis—of peyote, the small, spineless cactus found in the deserts of Mexico and Texas which contains the vision-producing alkaloid known as mescal.[153] Mitchell and Ellis reported their hallucinations with the puritan's anxiety to justify his pleasures with a veneer of educational improvement. Their drug use was secondary to another significant Western drug trend at the end of the nineteenth century. There was an emergent tendency (first noticed in a few communities of the western states of America during the late 1870s) to use opium-smoking or cocaine to defy parental or other authorities, and to disrupt communities—in short, to play at being vicious. 'Nowadays', Allbutt wrote in 1897, 'there is a good deal of such naughtiness in this world.' He identified a new 'troop' mustering for the twentieth century 'who scent intoxicants from afar with retriever-like instinct, and, curious in their sensations, play in and out with all kinds of them'. Whether these 'neurotics' used morphine, alcohol, chloral or cocaine had little importance: 'The toxication with its hours of excitement and repose must be had at any price, and every reform is followed by a relapse.'[154] Allbutt, who had been so prescient about the dangers of hypodermic injections of morphine, was equally shrewd about the new character brand of drug addicts: inquisitive, sensation-seeking delinquents with blunted consciences and perhaps a certain staginess in acting out their own specialised vice. It was his intimation that in the context of drug habits, the twentieth century would belong to the naughty.

SEVEN

The Dawn of Prohibition

They that endeavour to abolish vice, destroy also virtue; for contraries,
though they destroy one another, yet are the life of one another.
—SIR THOMAS BROWNE

When the imagination is continually led to the brink of vice
by a system of terror and denunciations, people fling themselves
over the precipice from the mere dread of falling.
—WILLIAM HAZLITT

I N 1911 A geography teacher in a mining district of Derbyshire noticed that most of his class were dozing or asleep. Swishing his cane through the air, he demanded an explanation from one of the pupils. 'Percy Toplis brought in a bottle of laudanum, sir, and passed it round the class, sir,' he was told. When, rather than submit to a beating, the miscreant bolted from the room, the schoolmaster called after him, 'You'll end your days on the gallows, Percy Toplis.'[1] In fact the fugitive died less than ten years later in the dust of a country lane. After a career that sped from imprisonment for travelling on a railway without a ticket to confidence trickery, mutiny and murder, Percy Toplis (1896–1920) was ambushed and shot dead by English policemen. Nevertheless, that scene at South Normanton Elementary School was a pioneering episode in the history of juvenile delinquency and drugs. An analysis in 1916 of 147 addicts treated at Philadelphia General Hospital found one patient who began sniffing cocaine at the age of sixteen and five at seventeen; one patient who first used heroin at sixteen and five at seventeen; and the first use of morphine by one fifteen-year-old and one seventeen-year-old. Such 'social dissipation' grew more common.[2] There were reports from New Orleans in 1926 and from Chicago shortly afterwards of 'marihuana cigarettes sold to school pupils and other youthful thrill-seekers'.[3] By 1926 the cocaine habit among waifs and strays was 'appalling' in Moscow, where a special clinic for boy addicts was opened.[4] When André Gide visited Zurich in 1927, he noticed 'many opium smokers and cocaine addicts'. A Swiss journalist explained to him that they 'began to inject themselves during their final year at the Gymnasium . . . when aged sixteen or seventeen. He personally knows someone whom the professors caught using a syringe in a final examination. Cornered, he confessed he had got his habit in class. "Do you think anyone could endure the dullness of X's teaching without shooting up?" he added with a smile.'[5]

The consumption of drugs became a rite of passage for some young people. It marked a phase through which many emerged unscathed on their way to maturity. At a strained dinner party in London early in the First World War, the society beauty Lady Diana Manners (1892–1986) abruptly announced, 'I must be unconscious tonight.' A taxi was sent to a pharmacy, and soon returned with chloroform. 'Jolly old chlorers,' she exclaimed when the packet arrived. Later she used morphine to stupefy her feelings about friends who had been killed or were away fighting. In 1915 she described to the Prime Minister's son Raymond Asquith (1878–1916) how she had recently lain with his wife Katharine Asquith (1885–1976) 'in ecstatic stillness through too short a night, drugged in very deed by my hand with morphia. O, the grave difficulty of the actual injection, the sterilizing in the dark and silence and the conflict of my hand and wish when it came to piercing our flesh. It was a grand night, and strange to feel so utterly self-sufficient— more like a Chinaman, or God before he made the world or his son and was content with, or callous to, the chaos.' Some months later her fiancé Duff Cooper (1890–1954), who afterwards became a British cabinet minister, found her 'looking very bad, obviously suffering from a debauch of morphine. She at first denied but at length confessed. I told her how ugly it made her look. Her fear of ugliness is, I think, the best preventive.'[6] Toplis, Cooper and the miscreants in Chicago, Zurich and Moscow used drugs partly to cope with the social and emotional stresses of growing up, and partly to defy authority and make mischief. The inducements to misconduct set up by prohibition—the fostering of vice when virtue is pursued to extremes—furnish the great conundrum of drugs policy.

New substances continually became available for teenage rascals to find fashionable. The English chemist C. R. Alder Wright had in 1874 cooked some morphine with acetic anhydride and obtained a white crystalline powder. This substance, which became known as diacetylmorphine, received little attention for over twenty years, although tests were to prove that it was up to eight times more powerful as an analgesic than morphine. Then Heinrich Dreser, chief pharmacologist of the German pharmaceutical company Bayer, tested diacetylmorphine on sixty hospital patients. If taken orally, as Dreser announced in 1898, it was effective in treating coughs, catarrh, bronchitis, emphysema, tuberculosis and asthma by sedating the air passages. Bayer forthwith began marketing diacetylmorphine under the trade name of 'heroin' (probably derived from the German word *heroisch*, meaning powerful). Patients relished the drug: 'Doctor, that powder you gave me, it worked so well, I felt relief right away when I took it.'[7] Bayer, which launched a new analgesic under the trade name of aspirin in 1899, stressed heroin's function as a cough suppressant and did not promote it as an analgesic. Dreser's report was published in Germany in the autumn of 1898, summarised in the *Journal of the American Medical Association* in November 1898 and soon afterwards by the *Lancet*.

Heroin did not become a baneful substance as quickly as ether, chloral or cocaine. Its medical use never aroused the level of addiction previously associated with physicians' hypodermic injections of morphine. This was partly because after their recent experiences, doctors were finally becoming chary in their use of new medicinal substances. Indeed they were more restrained in prescribing opiates. In 1912 a leading London hospital treated annually 8000 in-patients and 130,000 out-patients with 6 kilograms of opium and 100 grams of morphine; twenty years earlier the equivalent figures had been 10 kilograms and 500 grams.[8] There is also evidence that the Pharmacy Act (even before it was reformed in 1908) was being administered more tightly. By the turn of the century deaths from narcotics in Britain (mainly accidental overdoses) were running at just over two per million of the population compared with the nineteenth-century highpoint of six per million. But heroin, decisively, was never regarded as a panacea, even by its manufacturers, and was prescribed by physicians for the limited number of respiratory diseases listed by Dreser as well as whooping cough, laryngitis and hay fever.[9] The medical profession seldom used it either to subdue pain or treat non-respiratory illnesses. Moreover, it was generally administered orally by physicians in the form of tablets, pills, pastilles or glycerine solution. Injections were rare. The small amounts of heroin administered orally to patients with stubborn coughs would not so easily have aroused a habit as injected morphine.

Admittedly the drug's commercial launch was tinged with hopes that might have proved destructive of patients. Dreser presented heroin as non-habit forming.[10] 'Heroïn is said to be free from other disagreeable secondary effects of morphine, so that it may be administered . . . in comparatively large doses,' the Lancet reported when introducing it to British physicians in December 1898.[11] A few months later the Berlin physician Albert Eulenberg suggested that it might be substituted for morphine to wean patients from their addiction. But there was not the rash optimism that had surrounded cocaine or chloral. The Lancet called for 'a careful clinical trial', and as early as 1899 the Philadelphia neurologist Horatio Wood (1841–1920) urged caution. In 1901 Oscar Jennings (1851–1914), the Parisian who had devised a withdrawal treatment for morphine habitués, advised against 'heroin which is largely vaunted now as the treatment of the morphia habit par excellence. The craving following its use is infinitely more unmanageable than is that of morphine and in two cases treated by me recently the doses were rapidly increased and the patient became violent when it was attempted to suppress it. It is only second to cocaine as a drug to be avoided.'[12] Despite such warnings, cases of therapeutically induced addiction occurred. A patient from Cleveland, Ohio, undergoing treatment for laryngitis asked his physician not to prescribe any medicine containing opium, 'because he had formerly been a slave to that drug'. The physician replied: 'I will give you some heroin; there is no danger of habit from that.'[13] A Frenchwoman described in 1909 how two years earlier she had been prescribed heroin by a physician who undertook to cure her morphine habit contracted under treatment for haemorrhoids. His method 'made me fall from morphine into heroin, that is to say he put me into servitude to the one so as to cure me of the other, without thinking of how I would then give up this new poison'.[14]

Such disasters were not surprising given the uneven quality of teaching to medical students. 'A Clinical Lecture on the Opium Habit and Morphinism' delivered in 1908 to the London School of Clinical Medicine by Sir Dyce Duckworth (1840–1928) of St Bartholomew's Hospital (and subsequently published in the *Lancet*) was a complacent muddle of misinformation.[15] Given the deficiency of such teaching, it is not surprising that Oscar Jennings in 1909 stated that 'medical addicts' accounted for 75 per cent of his practice, 'that one medical man out of four is a drug *habitué*, usually a morphinist' and that 20 per cent of medical deaths were drug related.[16] Arthur Gamgee described Duckworth's endorsement of attempting to cure morphinism by the sudden total withdrawal of the drug as 'a violent and positively cruel system which is marked by the almost invariable relapse of the patient'. A systematically planned reduction of the morphine, discussed with the patient, was more likely to succeed. Gamgee emphasised a rule for morphine that he thought was not generally known and should never be forgotten: 'never to give morphine for a longer period than 21 consecutive days', for otherwise morphine craving was certain to be engendered. In the rare cases where the administration of morphine up to 'the 21 days' danger limit' was indispensable, the course should be interrupted, even at the cost of increased pain, and small doses of veronal or chloral substituted.[17] In truth, ten days or at most a fortnight would have been a safer maximum length of treatment.

Opiates, of course, were not the only misused drugs. American consumption of cocaine and cannabis resulted during the opening decades of the twentieth century in restrictive legislation, which soon acquired worldwide ramifications. Both drugs were stigmatised in the USA by their association with poor labourers drawn from racial minorities. During the late 1880s black stevedores at New Orleans began taking cocaine to help them endure their strenuous work in great climatic extremes. It is unclear if they began this practice on their own initiative, or were introduced to it by waterfront foremen as a way of sustaining their productivity. They usually sniffed the drug as the fastest way to introduce it into the bloodstream. Sniffing was cheaper than buying needles, and smaller amounts were needed to get a hit from inhalation than from injection. This method of administration immediately distinguished labourers from the physicians, lawyers and middle-class users, who at this time were predominantly injectors.[18] Jobs on the waterfront were seasonal: the roustabouts at other times of the year worked as agricultural labourers on southern cotton plantations or

lived in construction camps, while they built levees, railways and other
public works. Employers soon recognised cocaine as a means of
improving productivity and controlling workers: they reportedly supplied it to labourers in southern construction camps. A medical journal in 1902 reported one big planter issuing regular rations of cocaine
instead of the traditional whisky rations to his workforce. Supposedly
'on many Yazoo plantations this year the negroes refused to work unless
they could be assured that there was some place in the neighborhood
where they could get cocaine'. Planters complied because it improved
productivity. Elsewhere, by 1894, cocaine was being supplied at the
company stores of isolated Colorado mining camps: 'The workers, once
addicted, cannot think of going away from their source of supply.'[19]

The fantasy of cocainised blacks from plantations and construction
sites going on sexual rampages among white women soon raised a
racist panic. A writer in the *Medical Record*, for example, warned that
'hitherto inoffensive, law-abiding negroes' were transformed by
cocaine into 'a constant menace' whose 'sexual desires are increased and
perverted'.[20] Although cocaine-sniffing was also popular in the white
criminal *demi-monde*, among prostitutes, their clients and pimps as well
as gamblers and other types of urban hoodlums, the drug was unduly
identified in the USA with black men. 'One of the worst features of
the drug habit in this country is the spread of cocaine abuse to even
higher ranks of society than the criminal, and to all but the highest
classes of negroes throughout the country,' wrote a leading US anti-
narcotics campaigner in 1910.[21] In consequence New York State, for
example, enacted four laws between 1907 and 1913 the effect of which
was to prohibit the distribution of cocaine. Such measures did not succeed in suppressing the drug's illicit use. As Joseph Spillane has shown,
the sale of cocaine by druggists was subject to strict social sanctions by
1900—well before official regulations and prohibitions.

> Countless individual druggists made the critical decision whether to sell
> cocaine in limited ways or at all. This decision was not always based sim-
> ply, or equitably, on the known dangers of cocaine; druggists claimed the
> right to refuse cocaine sales on the basis of the consumers' social status
> or race as well. The cumulative effect of these individual decisions was
> to close equal access to the legal supply of cocaine. This, in turn, became
> a powerful factor in the creation of the shadow market.[22]

The association of cocaine with black Americans was ineradicable. Caleb Saleeby (1878–1940), the temperance campaigner and eugenicist who was Britain's first medical broadcaster, for example, warned newspaper readers in 1916 of 'a very marked increase in London of that disastrous and degrading habit . . . hitherto associated principally with the American negro'.[23] This association was perpetuated under medical authority. 'The American negro is, seemingly, a willing addict,' Thomas Blair (1867–1953), Chief of the Bureau of Drug Control of Pennsylvania Department of Health, claimed in 1919. 'The negro labor camps in the South simply breed addicts . . . The men work about four days in the week and "celebrate" the rest of the time, usually by taking a trip to another camp, where high carnival is held—carnival which involves the use of considerable cocaine or other narcotics when they can be obtained. The supply is usually irregular, and hence there is more of drug debauchery than of regular addiction.' However 'the participants become regular addicts if they leave the camp' and settle in 'slum districts of the northern cities'.[24] The recruitment of some of these labouring poor as soldiers or sailors prompted articles by a naval surgeon about the importance of eliminating cocaine *habitués* from the US armed services published in 1910–12.[25]

During 1871–2 the defiantly disturbed adolescent Arthur Rimbaud (1854–91), who was contemplating a career as an urban terrorist, began smoking hashish in Paris, and commemorated the experience in his prose poem 'Matinée d'ivresse'.[26] A decade later young Englishmen at university experimented with eating cannabis as a way of distorting their visual and auditory senses.[27] Such consumption was neither illegal nor illicit; it attracted little attention. There were different responses, however, when early in the twentieth century Mexicans brought the practice of growing and smoking marijuana across the Rio Grande into Texas and New Mexico, and when West Indians similarly introduced these habits on the Gulf Coast. Among Mexicans the drug was identified with the poorest class of labourers; the Mexican professional classes disdained its smokers in rather the way that *coqueros* were despised by more educated citizens in Latin America in the mid-nineteenth century. There was heavy migration of such labourers to the USA around 1900. The plant was cultivated in the vicinity of Mexico City, and supplies were sent to Laredo, which had railway connections with Mexico

City, El Paso, San Antonio and sundry border towns. Within a decade importers were distributing marijuana to druggists (cannabis was listed in the US Pharmacopoeia as a recognised medicine from 1850 until 1942) as well as retailers, mostly grocers, who advertised openly. In addition to these counter sales there was a flourishing mail-order business: one druggist at Floresville, Texas, supplied customers in Texas, Arizona, New Mexico, Kansas and Colorado. Pharmaceutical firms offered marijuana as a herbal remedy and as a tincture, although few medical practitioners prescribed or recommended it. Smoking the drug was a traditional way for Mexicans with gruelling jobs and poor prospects to cheer themselves, but it often made the smokers loud, obstreperous and disorderly. There were fights, and confrontations with the police, who reported that like Chinese opium-smoking a generation earlier, the smoking of this drug was spreading from the Mexicans to white prostitutes, pimps and hoodlums and to blacks. The more extreme anecdotes of drug-crazed violence are unsubstantiated, and resemble the more dramatic police reports that the Indian Hemp Drugs Commission of the 1890s had dismissed after investigation.

Reactions to the use of cocaine and cannabis in the USA were inseparable from American responses to opium-smoking in the Far East. Together these instigated great changes in policies towards drugs in the twentieth century: American drugs prohibition eventually culminated in the outbreak of the global War on Drugs. The annexation of the Philippine Islands by the USA in 1898 was a crucial event in this process. Many Americans felt racial contempt for the vanquished: 'What a thieving, treacherous, worthless bunch of scoundrels these Filipinos are,' an army medical officer declared in 1902. 'You can't treat them the way you do civilized folks.'[28] Many of the 70,000 Chinese inhabitants of the islands smoked opium. The Spanish colonial rulers of the Philippines had operated a lucrative opium monopoly: contracts to sell opium (obtained mainly from Turkey, Persia, Indo-China and China) were auctioned to the highest bidders, who were, however, forbidden to sell to the majority Filipino population. The opium-contractors were mostly, but not exclusively, Chinese: the operators of the 'dens' were entirely Chinese. Rich Chinese, who were too fastidious to smoke in the company of labourers, were permitted by Spanish officials to establish more luxurious and exclusive meeting places, and in Manila a few private houses and workplaces were authorised to be used for smoking. This system raised about US $600,000 annually and had deterred Filipinos from contracting the opium-smoking habit.[29] The new American rulers of the Philippines swiftly repudiated these arrangements. The opium 'farm' monopolies were abolished 'as repugnant to American practice and theory of government';[30] opium shops and smoking were prohibited. At one level this policy was an honest effort to combat a real evil, but it occurred in the context of American antagonism to Chinese settlement in the USA and its possessions. Although Chinese migrants were recognised as industrious and orderly, there was a feeling that they should be restricted both numerically and culturally. As the US diplomat Charles Denby (1830–1904), a member of the presidential Philippine Commission, declared in 1899, 'wherever the Chinese go in the world they supplant everyone else. You go to Singapore and you find twenty or thirty thousand there; you go to Colombo and you find the same thing. They undersell everybody and they work cheaper than any other person, and after they have made a certain amount of money, they return to China.'[31]

American suppression of the traditional Spanish policy towards Chinese opium-smoking in the Philippines resulted in an immediate and marked increase in opium consumption, especially among Filipinos. This was only partly attributable to a cholera epidemic of 1902 during which opiates were administered medicinally. The administration of William Taft (1857–1930), Governor of the Philippines and afterwards twenty-seventh President of the USA, soon became convinced that the contract system should be restored. Colonial administrators of all nations believed that such systems provided the surest means of regulating and containing opium-smoking, as the Governor of Hong Kong, Sir Matthew Nathan (1862–1939), explained to an Anglican missionary in 1907:

> the existing system under which the sole privilege of preparing Opium for smoking is farmed out to one person or syndicate of persons, is the surest way to confine the smoking of Opium within the narrowest limits, for the reason that under this system the monopolist is able to charge a very high price for prepared Opium, and, being a Chinese assisted by a large and interested body of his fellow countrymen, is able to prevent the illicit preparation within the Colony, and the smuggling into it whether in the raw or prepared state, of Opium which could and would be sold at a much lower figure than he charges.[32]

However Taft's proposal to restore the contract system was strenuously resisted by American missionaries such as Homer Clyde Stuntz (1858–1924), the Methodist Bishop of Manila, and Charles Henry Brent (1862–1929), Episcopalian Bishop of the Philippines.

Brent ranks among the most influential figures in twentieth-century drugs policy. An American official in the Philippines hailed him in 1912 as 'one of the noblest and most saintly characters that ever lived'.[33] Theodore Roosevelt (1858–1919) admired his 'combination of serene and lofty spirituality, of broad-minded charity and of sincere desire to do good'.[34] A Canadian by birth, Brent went to the Philippines in 1901 'solely because the Church bade me, against my taste and with a repulsion for work in a Latin country'.[35] Time-wasting, luxury and self-centredness revolted Brent: the prohibition of habit-forming drugs he accordingly regarded as central to the Christian civilising mission of *pax Americana*. A memorandum of 1904 conveys the tenets of his faith, which proved crucial in shaping American attempts to suppress the international traffic and use of drugs. The Philippines, he hoped, would come to uphold American values in a backward, undisciplined region of the world. But 'the worthlessness of the . . . degenerate, criminal and immoral' Americans in the Philippines pained him. The US occupation of the Philippines had attracted 'the adventurer, the irresponsible weakling, the human bird of prey' who had previously opened up the American Wild West. 'The round of unwholesome pleasure-seeking . . . is the undoing of many in Manila,' he lamented. 'Lives of promise have been wrecked . . . by the hitherto untried and cruel temptations of the Orient.' The weakness of Oriental character was much to blame. 'The constitutional fault of the Filipinos, a fault common to all Orientals, is sensuality, which in this case finds vent in laziness, concubinage and gaming,' Brent reported. As to Chinese opium-smoking, 'Unless uncompromising measures are adopted by the government it will only be a matter of time before the Filipinos are submerged in the most horrible vice of the Orient.'[36] Brent's constructive, affectionate and staunch character was evident in his anguished attentions to his brother Willoughby, who was an overworked country doctor on the harsh Atlantic coast of Nova Scotia until his death in 1916.[37] This brother was a drunkard, as Brent confided in 1910 shortly before taking him away for detoxification:

Sin that has a physical basis ought to have physical treatment ... frequently when men have broken away from the abuse of alcohol & choose their company from among violent opponents to intoxicants they remain steadfast. If a compact, unselfish Christian community could receive men struggling to regain their manhood the majority would never fall again. Society is too selfish, too inconsiderate to give up its pleasant things for the sake of the weak ...After the treatment for his body I am going to keep him in cheerful, hopeful surroundings.[38]

In 1902 Brent orchestrated the outcry that obliged the Washington administration to instruct Taft to withdraw the proposal to restore the Spanish system of opium supply in the Philippines. Instead, in 1903, Taft appointed the Philippines Opium Committee to investigate the problem. Brent was the driving force of this committee: its other two members were a Filipino physician and the US commissioner of public health in the Philippines. In the course of five months they visited Shanghai, Singapore, Burma, Java, Formosa and (for the longest stage of their tour) Japan. Brent was determined to negate the influence of 'the official mind of Great Britain in the Orient' as represented by Brassey's royal commission.[39] After his own committee reported in 1904, the importation and sale of opiates into the Philippines (except for medicinal purposes) was banned with effect from 1908. Brent was, however, disappointed by the sequel. Publicly he declared (in 1913): 'What the Americans have done is to get the Filipinos out of bed. They are now instructing them how to dress themselves'.[40] Privately, so far as opium was concerned, he admitted that his hopes had been confounded. 'We are suffering from constant smuggling from and through Borneo,' he conceded in 1912.[41] The vice squad of the Manila police was until 1921 in the charge of Ray Conley, a former US soldier, who relished his pursuit of gamblers and opium-dealers. 'The matching of his Western wits against the wits of the massed Orientals, lured him. The love of his life was to catch some local politico red-handed. And when he was about to launch some particularly difficult or spectacular raid, he was very likely to send a hint to the American newspaper men.'[42] Despite the publicity surrounding this militant policing, the reality was that, as an American authority concluded in 1927, 'prohibition of opium smoking in the Philippines does not in fact prohibit'. The USA was shy of releasing its Philippine opium statistics, which were repeatedly sought by League of Nations delegates during the 1920s, and evinced 'unwillingness to face the facts on the non-functioning of prohibition in the Philippines'. The truth was that twenty years after prohibition, smuggled opium was 'coming into the Islands in such quantities as to make opium procurable freely at very low prices'.[43]

These measures in the Philippines were not unique. Legislation had earlier been introduced in the USA, Australia and New Zealand against opium-smoking as part of policies to contain Chinese immigrants. In 1905, shortly after the report of the Philippines Opium Commission, an ordinance was enacted in the Transvaal prohibiting anyone except registered medical practitioners and druggists from importing or possessing opium; infractions were subject to a fine of £500 or six months' imprisonment. This measure was directed at the Chinese contract workers in the Witwatersrand mining district. Sir Lionel Phillips (1855–1936), a leading South African gold-mining director, opined in 1905 that 'while a great many Chinamen indulge in a few whiffs of opium . . . it is only in the most exceptional cases that they have evinced any sign of losing their self-control'.[44] However, there was at this time mounting anxiety at the number of contracted Chinese labourers who absconded from their work in the mines (chiefly because they had borrowed large sums to cover gambling debts that they could not repay). Under local laws, deserting coolies who left the gold-mining district became outlaws, and perforce entered the underworld of opium-trafficking or thieving. White people accordingly were 'frightened' by the threat of 'marauding' coolies.[45] The Transvaal authorities regarded opium-smoking as a symptom of insubordination rather than as grave criminality. Discipline on ships transporting Chinese labourers to the mines in 1904 reflected the prevalent view that opium-smokers were uneducated and irresponsible men who had to be disciplined like recalcitrant schoolboys. Gambling, fights, thieving, opium-smoking or possession of opium-smoking appliances and violation of sanitary regulations were the principal offences. Punishments included deprivation of food, a spare diet, being tied or locked up for a period, or a number of strokes with the bamboo.[46] These anti-opium measures in southern Africa had no international repercussions, but Brent's example in the Philippines was soon rousing campaigners around the world.

In Britain the Liberal politician Theodore Taylor (1850–1952) instigated a momentous change when in 1906 the House of Commons (lately elected with a large Liberal majority) resolved 'that the Indo-Chinese opium trade is morally indefensible', and requested the new Campbell-Bannerman government to take steps 'for bringing it to a speedy close'. Taylor was impressed by the recent decision 'that there should be strict prohibition in the Philippines after 1908'. Like Brent, he extolled the moral example of the Japanese. 'If ever there was a nation that had astonished the world by its *morale*, health, strength, and vigour, it was Japan'. Taylor cited the Philippine Opium Commission's report ('the Japanese to a man fear opium as we fear the cobra or the rattlesnake') before concluding that 'the Chinese curse had been to the Japanese a warning'.[47] In reality, as will be shown later, Japan saw the Chinese curse as a marketing opportunity, although their own domestic opium-smokers were liable to three years imprisonment with hard labour and those selling opium seven years. Answering Taylor's speech, John Morley (1838–1923), Secretary of State for India, distinguished the attitudes to this question of 'philanthropists' and (using a concept of Brent's) 'the official mind'. The previous Liberal government of the mid-1890s, in its reception of the Brassey report, had 'somehow or other failed to satisfy public opinion in this country'. Morley admired the enquiry in the Philippines because it 'did not take the medical evidence as conclusive', but took a broader view: 'The United States so recognised the use of opium as an evil, for which no financial gain could compensate, that she would not allow her citizens to encourage it even passively.'[48] A few years later it was a wonder to Sir Frank Swettenham (1850–1946), who spent his career as a colonial official in the Malay States, that the Brassey report, 'made after very full and extended enquiries in the East', was so forgotten.[49] The strenuous insistence by anti-opium campaigners that the Commission had been a bigoted, partisan or corrupt body prevailed. Brent dismissed Brassey's report as 'whitewash',[50] and English prohibitionists asserted that its evidence 'was invalidated by the fact that it was got together by a powerful alien Government' financed by opium revenues.[51] It was a short step for American anti-imperialists to depict the British Empire in India as 'debauching the world' and as 'the greatest purveyor in the world of habit-forming drugs'.[52] The truth is that the majority reports tendered by both the Brassey and Young commissions made a more realistic appraisal of opium and cannabis than the prohibitionists, but that after 1906 expertise was discounted by politicians as an inferior factor to popular feeling. In little more than a decade, the destructive effects of populism were all too evident. As that shrewd observer of the European and American drug scenes, Aleister Crowley, wrote in 1922, 'Nobody in England—or America for that matter—seems to have the remotest idea of the enormity of public ignorance. Compulsory education has made every noodle the peer of the greatest knowers and thinkers—in his own estimation. The really educated classes have lost their prestige. The public imagines itself entitled to pronounce with authority on questions which the experts hold most debatable.'[53]

Brent had doubted that the Chinese would suppress opium-smoking without foreign intervention. However, in September 1906 the Chinese central government issued an edict providing for the progressive suppression of the opium trade over the next decade. In the following year Britain agreed that the Indo-Chinese opium traffic would fall from 61,900 chests in 1908 to zero in ten annual reductions. 'I am no opium faddist,' announced the Viceroy of India in 1907. 'I quite admit the hardship a proscription of opium would entail on those who use it in moderation . . . but there is no doubt throughout the civilised world a feeling of disgust at the demoralising effect of the opium habit in excess.'[54] Government policy was explained by Morley to the Archbishop of Canterbury in 1908: 'We *must* come into line with the best opinion in the United States; in Japan; and in China, where the force of the anti-opium movement is proving a marked surprise to people who represented that movement as insincere, and little more than a dodge of the Chinese officials.'[55] The Chinese National Assembly met for the first time in 1910, and gave priority to the stricter enforcement of anti-opium laws. The Revolution of 1911 established a republican government. The anti-opium movement became 'a national crusade, enlisting every Chinese reformer and patriot', Taylor wrote in 1913.[56] As an English delegate to the League of Nations noted of this phase of Chinese opium policy, 'people found with a patch of poppy cultivation were apt, not only to have their crop destroyed, but to be executed'.[57] Reports of suppression often proved bogus. A 'bumper' crop was yielded in the province of Szechuan in 1912 only months after the reported elimination of poppy cultivation there. Such episodes, according to the *North China Daily News*, demonstrated 'the virtual inability of the capital to control the provinces, and of the provincial governors to control the farmers'.[58]

Brent's work stimulated US attempts to enforce a global policy of drug prohibition. At the instigation of President Theodore Roosevelt, an international Opium Commission was convened in Shanghai in 1909. Brent was senior US delegate at Shanghai, and chaired its successor conference at The Hague in 1911–12; both events were inseparably intertwined with domestic drug policies in the USA. To enable the American delegates to speak at Shanghai from a position of irreproachable rectitude, Congress hurriedly passed the Smoking Opium Exclusion Act of 1909 prohibiting the importation and use of opium in the USA for non-medicinal purposes (following the model of Brent's Philippines laws). Representatives from Austria, Britain, China, France, Germany, Italy, Japan, the Netherlands, Persia, Portugal, Russia, Siam and the USA attended the Shanghai conference to discuss Far Eastern opiate consumption, and support Chinese measures to suppress opium-smoking. 'Our desire is to give the Orient civilization,' Brent preached in Shanghai cathedral. 'Civilization is dependent for its very existence upon character, and . . . character . . . is dependent upon Christianity.' He decried materialism, sensuality and weakening parental authority. 'Prosperity without character is a deadly curse. Today the children of the prosperous are frequently moral failures because indulgent parents put material safeguards around them so as to rob them of robustness, instead of flinging them bravely out into that wholesome hardness and moral discipline that creates stamina and strength.'[59]

The Shanghai delegates called on governments to work 'for the gradual suppression of . . . opium-smoking in their own territories and possessions', and to prohibit or stringently regulate the manufacture, distribution and non-medicinal use of opium and its derivatives. This was the first diplomatic recognition of the need for international cooperation to prevent drug-trafficking, especially by way of control at the source. The recognition at Shanghai that drugs other than opium for smoking required scrutiny showed, in the words of the Liberal MP and surgeon Sir William Collins (1859–1946), 'that the problem was rapidly passing out of the limitations of the "Far East" . . . and was becoming a question of world-wide importance'.[60] Brent considered the Shanghai meeting 'a moderate success.' While recognising that controls on the manufacture and distribution of morphine came 'too late for awful havoc is already being worked by its abuse', he predicted that 'happily the recent discovery of heroin promises to distract attention from a most insidious to an apparently safe derivative of opium'.[61]

After the Shanghai resolutions the next stage of drugs international-ism was The Hague Conference of 1911–12 (chaired by Brent). The invitations to this conference were issued by the President of the USA, and made no mention of the abuse of manufactured drugs. However, the agenda was modified on the representations of several European powers to include the traffic in morphine and cocaine as well as opium-smoking. This modification was important to the British gov-ernment: its Liberal ministers were keen to demonstrate their ethical values to public opinion; their officials were concerned at the increased smuggling in the Far East of morphine and cocaine, and anxious to divert discussion from Indian opium. The International Opium Con-vention, which was signed by twelve contracting powers at The Hague on 23 January 1912, resolved that the use of opiates and cocaine should be confined to medicinal purposes, and committed its signatories to 'the gradual suppression of the abuse of opium, morphine, cocaine, as also of the drugs prepared or derived from these substances which give rise or might give rise to similar abuses'.[62] Serbia and Turkey having signalled their intention not to sign, Germany declined to adhere to a convention that might restrict the business of its cocaine-manufacturers and thus provide opportunities for cocaine-makers in other countries. The Board of Trade in London were equally keen to ensure that 'we should not find ourselves bound to carry out a course of action whilst Germany can evade her obligations'.[63] As a result it was agreed that The Hague Convention would not become operative until thirty-five nations had ratified it. The signatories pledged themselves to the grad-ual suppression of opium-smoking in their territories, to reduce pro-gressively opium exports to China to zero in 1917 and to prohibit worldwide opium imports and exports (if not 'immediately' then 'as soon as possible'). The summary of the Convention by Sir William Collins, who was one of the British delegates, stressed the dichotomy between expert and public opinion set up by Brent:

> The 'official-minded' distinction, sometimes attempted, between the evils of opium-smoking on the one hand and the benefits of opium-eating on the other, or between the relatively harmless effects of opium on the one hand and the perniciousness of morphine and cocaine on the other,

can no longer be sustained. That these drugs whose use leads to repetition and at last to habituation, when so used give rise to volitional palsy, moral degradation, vice and crime, is a fact now authoritatively and internationally recognised. It has further been agreed that the consequences of the trade in, and the illicit use of, the drugs in question is such that civilised Powers should do what they can to put a stop to so flagrant an abuse.[64]

Such dogmatism brought a new attitude to drug-users. Throughout the nineteenth century European drug *habitués* had been stigmatised as unproductive, dishonest or lacking in self-control, but they were not represented as criminals. The associations of opium-smoking and later cocaine with the American underworld were, however, changing European representations of the addict by this period. Some European policy-makers were drawn towards the American conceptualisation of addiction as crime, and moreover saw this subspecies of criminal as a pollutant. At The Hague Conference, Collins recorded, there had been 'a disposition in some quarters to regard the morphinist and the cocainist merely as invalids and objects of pity, but . . . many of them are social pests of the most dangerous kind. Bankrupt of moral sense and will power, they are lying and deceitful, prodigal of time, plausible to a degree, backbiting and contentious, prone to vice and apt for crime.'[65] In addition to the rhetoric of criminality, addicts (rather than addiction) were soon being represented as a contagious disease. Typically, in 1919, a physician with the US Navy characterised addicts 'as a focus of infection who through contact with susceptible individuals serve to spread the habit'.[66] Oscar Jennings protested in 1909 against such miserably tendentious representations:

It is as a rule assumed that the *habitué* is necessarily a drug fiend, a cheat and a liar. His word is not believed, his self-respect, already lessened, is still further depressed by this attitude, and suspicion can but excite hostility . . . the incomprehension of the subject shown by some directors of sanatoriums has sometimes been phenomenal. That many morphia-takers are narcomaniacs is undeniable, but there are others whose self-control, in restricting themselves to the minimum of morphia necessary to comfort, is infinitely greater than that of an ordinary so-called moderate drinker. Between the two extremes there are many gradations of

mentality, but in nearly every case mutual confidence (on the doctor's
part, from the conviction of his ability to help) should be the keynote
of management.[67]

Despite the accuracy of Jennings's protest, exclusive identities were
being constructed for drug-users. These were chiefly devised from
American reactions to cocaine and cannabis as well as opiates.

American physicians, like their European colleagues, had learnt from
their experience of drug cravings in the nineteenth century. Politicians
in the USA had not, and took powers to control the physicians. Legislative measures against drug addiction began auspiciously, but were
soon carried away by puritanical zeal into a policy that was idealistic,
punitive and unforgiving. Its rigidities were counterproductive. The
prohibition movement was historically linked to the abolitionist cause,
and its propagandists often stressed that both groups were working to
free the enslaved. Prohibition continued to be associated with other
progressive causes, especially those requiring legal interventions by state
or federal governments. Poisonous substances provided an issue on
which prohibitionists, social reformers and proponents of federal intervention combined with enduring results. Purification, and the protection
of children, were emotive and irresistible issues. Initially 'muck-raking'
journalists investigated the concoctions, irresponsible advertising and
aggressive marketing practices of patent medicine-makers. They
reported that many popular substances contained opiates, cocaine, or
other poisonous substances. Ryno's Hay Fever and Catarrh remedy had
a cocaine content of 99.9 per cent. More typically, Birney's Catarrh
Cure had a cocaine content of 5 per cent: this was so well known that
a hotel in New York City favoured by cocaine sniffers ('Birney blow-
ers') had a decorative tree in its backroom, 'fancifully bedecked with
tiny discarded black rubber hoses' that had been used for squirting
cocaine solutions into nostrils.[68] As a result of the muck-rakers' revelations, American politicians targeted patent medicine-makers with regulations intended to prevent the exploitation of the poor and gullible,
and to forestall the inculcation of drug habits among children. The Pure
Food and Drug Act of 1906 required the labelling of all preparations
containing significant levels of opiates, charged the Bureau of Chemistry with the duty of investigating adulteration and misbranding of
food and drugs, and cut consumption of the more odious proprietary

products. The Act was not however immediately effective. Catarrh powders containing cocaine were available in many drugstores: coca leaf imports into the USA in 1907 were twentyfold higher than in 1900. A Chicago clergyman described in 1909 watching local boys sniffing outside his rectory, and in the morning finding his lawn strewn with empty vials of Gray's Catarrh Powder, which contained eight grains of cocaine.[69]

Meanwhile an earnest intriguer was at work. Hamilton Kemp Wright (1867–1917) was an ambitious physician who had settled in Washington DC after marrying Elizabeth Washburne (1875–1952), whose father and uncles were Republican congressmen. Wright was recruited in 1908 to undertake research preparatory to the Shanghai Conference, and established himself, to his own satisfaction at least, as an expert on China. He was an instigator of the Smoking Opium Exclusion Act that was hustled into being to raise the moral tone of American interventions at Shanghai in 1909. He was an American delegate there, and wrote a report on the proceedings for Congress. Confident of the righteousness of his cause, this report raised sensational racist alarms about the cocaine debauches of southern blacks, and inflated statistics on drug consumption. 'I painted in middle tone the conditions in the United States, as I wished to avoid all exaggeration,' he claimed mendaciously to the Archbishop of Canterbury in a letter that claimed that morphine addiction was a greater problem in some states of the union than opium-smoking in China.[70] In 1910 Wright induced a Vermont representative, David Foster (1857–1912), chairman of the House Committee on Foreign Affairs, to sponsor a bill controlling opiates, cocaine, chloral and cannabis (which failed in 1911). Wright led the American delegation to The Hague Conference where he was so refractory that Brent afterwards suggested that he should retire. His efforts to override the agreed agenda smacked of 'impudence' to the British.[71] As their ambassador in Washington commented, Wright had 'the eagerness of the specialist who has been placed in charge' in pursuing his mission to protect 'the interests of humanity at large'.[72] Wright next interested Francis Burton Harrison (1873–1957), a Democrat from New York, in reviving a version of the Foster Bill. With the minimum of press comment, or of public discussion by any professional group other than druggists, the Harrison Act passed in December 1914 and came into effect on 1 March 1915. (Wright's widow continued his work, and served as American assessor of the League of Nations advisory committee on opium until 1925: the British characterised her as 'incompetent, prejudiced, ignorant, and so constituted temperamentally as to afford a ready means of making mischief'.)[73]

The Harrison Act remained the foundation of federal controls on narcotics until 1970. It required registration and payment of an occupational tax by all those who imported, produced, dealt in, sold or gave away opium and coca leaves and their derivatives. All registered handlers were required to file returns detailing their use of the drugs and to record transfers on special forms. It became unlawful for anyone to buy, sell, dispense or distribute any of these drugs without an official written order form prepared by the recipient. Possession of these drugs without a prescription was taken as presumptive evidence of violation of the Harrison Act.[74] In the previous few years, it had become almost mandatory to affirm that drug consumers were criminals or degenerates who were enslaved to their habits; that they threatened social order both in cities and the South, impeded business and retarded productivity. 'The anti-narcotic propagandist has over-stated his case,' declared Thomas Blair of the Pennsylvania Bureau of Drug Control in 1919. 'Virtually there is no opposition, as there is in the matter of [alcohol] prohibition; but there is inertia on one hand and more or less hysteria on the other. The propagandist has had things largely his own way.'[75] This imbalance resulted in a series of poor decisions. In addition to the Harrison Act, habit-forming drugs were brought under state restrictions. Few US states in 1900 confined the availability of opiates and cocaine to prescriptions, but by 1912 every state except Delaware had laws controlling them. In 1912 prescriptions were required to obtain cocaine in forty-five states, opiates in thirty-three states and chloral in fifteen states. Some dozen states prohibited physicians from dispensing maintenance prescriptions to people with drug cravings. Nor were state efforts at comprehensive drug regulation or prohibition limited to cocaine and opiates. El Paso in 1914 passed an ordinance prohibiting possession and sale of cannabis. Although there were no known cases of recreational cannabis use in New England, sale of the drug without medical prescription was among the prohibitions in drug regulatory laws in the states of Maine (1913), Massachusetts (1914), Vermont (1915) and Rhode Island (1918).

Around 1900, in the USA, morphine had apparently supplanted opium-smoking as the most prevalent illicit drug habit. But after 1910 heroin came to the fore. Indeed the rise of heroin addiction in the USA is attributable to legislative measures directed against illicit or recreational drug use. The drug was not a problem until the inaugural campaign of the twentieth century American War on Drugs. 'It is a notorious fact', warned Congressman Joseph Holt Gaines (1864–1951) of West Virginia in a debate on the Smoking Opium Exclusion Act of 1909, 'that those who are addicted to the opium habit will secure the drug in some [alternative] form . . . if they are prevented from getting it in the form in which it is preferred.'[76] An example of multiple drug substitutions was described by a San Francisco woman:

> I started on the pipe—smoking opium. It was great fun at first, and then one morning I woke up and realised that it was no longer play—that it was a habit. Then the law knocked over smoking and I took to heroin. I sniffed it and in 3 minutes had the 'kick' that opium took 2 to 3 hours to give me. A lot of us didn't know really what heroin . . . was, until after it was too late. And then the reaction was terrible. It takes your memory you know. After a while you can't think. I got scared and quit and took up cocaine and morphine. I guess that's just as bad.[77]

As early as 1912 Dr John Phillips (1879–1929) of Cleveland, Ohio, reported that 'heroin is being extensively used by means of "snuffing" in the tenderloin districts of large cities'. A patient aged twenty-one, who had changed from morphine to heroin because 'it was easier to obtain', claimed 'at least twenty of his associates, many of whom work at soda-water fountains in drug stores, use this drug'. Another of Phillips's patients came from Toledo, the Lake Erie port, where heroin was used 'extensively' by both sexes.[78]

According to Joseph McIver (1887–1940) and George Price (d. 1953), physicians who treated addicts in Philadelphia, following the Opium Exclusion Act of 1909, 'crude opium naturally became very expensive and could only be obtained in small quantities by those who could afford it at all'. As a result 'the pioneers' began substituting heroin for opium-smoking. Then, around 1912, 'the dissipated and vicious' began using heroin as 'a social diversion.' By 1913 heroin was 'spreading among the *habitués* of the "tenderloin" at a terrific rate. No other

drug has ever claimed half so many victims in such a short time.'
McIver and Price believed that this growth was mainly attributable to
price and availability; but noted as a subsidiary influence that many
addicts 'stated that while heroin did not stimulate their sexual desire,
they would take it because it enabled them to prolong the sexual act'.[79]
Pearce Bailey (1865–1922), the New York psychiatrist and sometime
professor of neurology at Columbia University, concurred with McIver
and Price.[80] Dr Walter Conley (1869–1946) gave a convincing summary in 1924 of the heroin addicts whom he had treated in New York
City.

> Heroin users are not secretive as are morphine addicts; they get together
> in crowds and gangs. One boy will begin to take it, and through his
> influence there will be ten or twelve boys taking it . . . our trouble in
> heroin addiction is that the boys buy it on the street from pedlers; they
> do not get it from the physician . . . We have had 4,000 cases of boys in
> the Metropolitan Hospital, some repeaters, and they all give the same
> history . . . They are in gangs, they are full of braggadocio, they commit
> crime while in this condition, and they do many other things that the
> ordinary morphine addict would not do, because the latter are secretive,
> remain by themselves, and do not allow others to see them take the
> drug. The heroin addict wants other people to know that he takes
> the drug.

Conley understood that it was exciting to become addicted to heroin.
He asked one patient why he had undergone five withdrawal cures
only to resume his habit. The boy replied: 'I take the treatment to get
off the drug in order to have the sensation of beginning again.'[81] For
these youths, the thrill of heroin was like the excitement of being a spy
caught far behind the lines in enemy country. In order to survive, they
had constantly to scrutinise people and situations with covert attention,
seeking signs that would help or ruin them. They were simultaneously
reduced to the pursuit of a simple, brutal need to survive, and involved
in a shadowy plot, with ramifications that would seem cryptic and
senseless to the uninitiated.

Restrictions on the supply of cocaine as well as opium for smoking
diverted users towards heroin. When cocaine prices rose, its users in
American cities sought alternatives, and found heroin cheap and (as a

drug that could also be sniffed) alluring. Moreover, heroin tranquillised people in whom enforced cocaine abstinence aroused anxiety and depression. Before the Harrison Act, most cocaine-users confined themselves to the one drug. But by 1924 only seven out of a sample of 150 addicts studied by Lawrence Kolb (1881–1972) used cocaine exclusively. As Kolb explained, 'The person who starts with cocaine today either discontinues it after a short time, which is not difficult to do, or takes so much that the symptoms of anxiety it brings on him, impel him to resort to morphine or heroin for relief. He quickly becomes addicted to one of these drugs.'[82] The proliferation of substitute drug habits among addicts who found the supply of their preferred substance was disrupted or severed became an international phenomenon. Herbert L. May (1877–1966) undertook a *Survey of Opium Smoking Conditions in the Far East* for the Foreign Policy Association of the USA, and was a US representative on League of Nations drug committees during the 1930s. After touring the Far East, he concluded in 1927 that if an opium-smoker was 'inhibited' from his habit he became 'a potential user' of manufactured drugs such as morphine and heroin, 'and that restrictions upon [opium-smoking] addiction lead to increase of "[manufactured] drug" addiction'.[83] Such substitutions were used, astonishingly, to justify extending drug prohibitions rather than hesitating before introducing them. When in 1914 the Board of Health of New York City added cannabis to its list of prohibited drugs, the *New York Times* praised this initiative against what it misleadingly reported as a 'narcotic' with 'practically the same effect as morphine and cocaine'. It editorialised that the measure was 'only common sense' for, although 'devotees of hashish are now hardly numerous enough to count here . . . they are likely to increase as other narcotics become harder to obtain'.[84]

The USA was not unique in experiencing a mushrooming of drug habits. In Berlin and Hamburg during the first decade of the twentieth century there were shops offering discount injections of morphine for people with 'delicate nerves'. Five or ten marks were charged for the first injection; the second was half price. Partly in response to such activities, the Reichstag in 1910 sought stricter controls over the supply and illicit use of morphine and cocaine. Dr Louis Merck (1854–1913), on behalf of his own pharmaceutical company and four other German cocaine-manufacturers, resisted these proposals, which were given added momentum by The Hague Conference. Cocaine was chiefly used illicitly in capital cities and ports. Paris physicians in 1913 lamented that although the drug was ostensibly unobtainable in France without medical certification, 'in spite of this a great deal is sold in the Montmartre quarter', where in certain cafés, 'after a certain hour of the night, it is sold almost openly'. Many Parisian users belonged 'to the *demi-mondaine* class'.[85] One such woman was Mathilde Fossey, better known under the stage name of Geneviève Lantelme (1887–1911). At fourteen she was one of the lures at her mother's brothel, but soon became an acclaimed Paris actress. Theatregoers savoured her reputation for enjoying the bodies of men and women with equal pleasure: her languid slouch was imitated by other Parisian vamps. Lantelme's notoriety reached its shrillest heights in the mystery of her death. Having come under the protection of a vulgar and violent Anglo-Levantine coprophiliac, Alfred Edwards (1856–1914), founder of *Le Matin* and owner of the Théâtre de Paris, she drowned after falling from his yacht. Probably she died accidentally while intoxicated by cocaine: although Edwards's enemies suggested that he threw her overboard when she declined to gratify his perversion.[86]

Cocaine apparently began to be taken as a social drug in London around the time of Lantelme's death in 1911. Perhaps significantly, the earliest dating involves an American actress. The thriller writer Edgar Wallace (1875–1932) recalled in 1922 that he was first shown cocaine eleven years earlier by a chorus-girl from an American troupe performing in London.[87] Sir Edward Henry, chief of the Metropolitan Police, stated that his force was not aware of a cocaine problem until late in 1915. The London *Evening Standard* in January 1916 reported cocaine-sniffing among nightclub *habitués*: 'In the ladies' cloakroom of a certain establishment two bucketsful of thrown away small circular cardboard boxes were discovered by the cleaners the other day—discarded cocaine boxes.'[88] Shortly afterwards two policemen from Liège, who were exiled from Belgium during the German occupation, sent information on cocaine-dealing to Vine Street police station. They drew police attention to a sandwich shop at 89, Shaftesbury Avenue, and gave the names of 'Jewish boys' and other men who were selling cocaine to women. The shop, which was accordingly put under surveillance, 'was patronised chiefly by prostitutes and Continental undesirables, but we saw nothing to justify Police action', the detective inspector at Vine Street reported. 'We interviewed several prostitutes and were astonished at the manner in which this dangerous habit had developed among that class of persons, also amongst soldiers'. Detective Inspector Francis Carlin judged that cocaine had 'a very dangerous effect upon the brain of any person who indulged in its use' because it 'ultimately results in the total loss of will power'.[89]

Cocaine's reduction of self-control was part of its attraction for sex workers and their clients. The divisional police surgeon at Vine Street reported in 1916 that most users were prostitutes or Canadian soldiers; the majority were 'snuffing it up the nose', but a few took it intravenously.[90] A sergeant from the Canadian Military Police, who worked undercover in Soho during 1916, testified that the chief supply came from chemists' assistants in west central London. In the USA, at least, heroin as well as cocaine was associated with prostitution. The physician of the American Thread Company of Holyoke, Massachusetts, encountered three young male heroin-users during 1919. 'All gave the same history of the beginning of this habit, although it was contracted in very different sections of the country—one in Boston, one in Hog Island Shipyards, and the third at Charleston'. Each youth had first received heroin from prostitutes in whose company they had been. 'They had been drinking very heavily the night before, and were given this drug to brace them up so they could report for [military] duty in the morning.' They continued using heroin to cover hangovers until they were addicted.[91] Such anecdotes confirmed the impression of Blair that 'drinking leads to venereal excess and that to drug habituation'.[92] A delegate to the League of Nations similarly noted in 1925 'the hidden link which exists between the stimulation of vices and passions and their satisfaction; the connection between those who sell drink and drugs and those who sell women'.[93]

British hostility to cocaine increased after the declaration of war. Forgetful of the importance of the Dutch in the cocaine business, the *British Medical Journal* in 1916 noted that 'the production of cocaine was almost entirely in German hands' before the hostilities, and that most illicit suppliers were still 'foreigners'.[94] The Vine Street policeman's remark that drugs sapped will power chimed with the alarm of the military authorities about a vitiated war effort. They became alarmed that the drug traffic could be used to undermine British fighting power and military discipline. 'I am told that this evil practice is exceedingly rife at the present time,' Sir Francis Lloyd (1853–1926), who was the general in command of the London district, declared of cocaine. 'It is doing an immense amount of harm, I am told. They say that it is so ingrained that once you take it . . . you will not give it up.' His information was that cocaine was being used as 'an aphrodisiac'.[95] Some prostitutes sold cocaine to 300 or 400 of the 250,000 Canadian soldiers who were passing through Britain on their way to the Western Front. Canadian military pay was five times greater than that of English soldiers, which made them 'a natural mark' for prostitutes, as Brent lamented in June 1916. Canadians were 'in a state of indignation . . . amounting almost to revolt' over the corruption of their young men.[96] Moreover, some officers suspected that 'the unhappy young Canadian lieutenant', Georges Coudere (1893–1916), who bludgeoned to death a canteen sergeant, had used cocaine.[97] His accomplice testified that 'he looked like as if he was doping himself', but the truth was probably that he was mentally ill: he was nicknamed '*fou Coudere*' ('mad Coudere') and as the Lord Chief Justice said, was 'a very peculiar person'.[98]

In response to these anxieties an Army Council order of 11 May 1916 decreed that soldiers in Britain would require a medical prescription to obtain barbiturates, benzamines, chloral, coca, cocaine, codeine, diacetylmorphine, Indian hemp, opium, morphine, sulphonal and any preparations or derivatives associated with these drugs. Shortly afterwards the Vine Street policemen secured a conviction against one of the dealers who had been denounced by the Belgian exiles. The police apparently exacerbated alarm by telling journalists that cocaine 'is driving hundreds of women mad', which resulted in the *Daily Chronicle* blaring on 19 July that 'the use of cocaine has become in six months a veritable mania, an obsession only too terribly common among the women who haunt the West End at night. Unhappily, too, this vicious craze has spread among soldiers.' The same newspaper stated that cocaine was being 'sold at a profit of 1,000 per cent'.[99] Stories circulated alleging that prostitutes were using cocaine to drug, stupefy and rob their johns. 'The drug not only enslaves and ruins the whole constitution of its victim, being far more deadly than either opium or alcohol; but it directly promotes the committing of crime.'[100] This storm led Malcolm Delevingne (1868–1950) of the Home Office to minute on 22 July that morphine 'is not nearly so serious or so urgent' as cocaine.[101]

Delevingne was Britain's equivalent of Bishop Brent. He had been involved in drug policy since becoming Assistant Under Secretary of State in 1913, and after 1916 emerged as the driving force in regulating and policing dangerous substances. His promotion to Deputy Permanent Under Secretary in 1922 vested him with international importance until his retirement ten years later. In the House of Lords in 1925 he was described as having 'done more . . . than any living man to carry forward the struggle against the illegitimate use of these drugs'.[102] The Chairman of the Central Opium Board of the League of Nations admired Delevingne's 'modest, selfless and righteous life' together with his 'minute knowledge of all the ramifications of this complicated and difficult subject'. Another colleague, associated with Delevingne's chairmanship of Dr Barnardo's Homes for orphans and abandoned children, testified to his 'burning desire to help his fellow men'. Delevingne 'always sensed where improvements were needed'. His 'strong religious faith . . . was the mainspring of his life and the guiding force in all he did'.[103] Drug addiction 'in the countries of the West' Delevingne regarded as 'largely an outcome of the stress and strain of modern life'.[104] He was autocratic, and won only grudging admiration from diplomatist colleagues. 'Sir M. Delevingne can see the world only in terms of narcotics', noted Lord Strang (1893–1978) in 1925; and again a year later, 'an accurate appreciation of the value of evidence is not Sir M. Delevingne's strong point'.[105] William Cavendish-Bentinck (1897–1990), afterwards last Duke of Portland, mistrusted 'his zeal to see the world a nice clean place for all races' which resembled that of 'the anti-opium American enthusiasts who prowl around Geneva'.[106] On certain subjects, according to Lord Dalton (1887–1962), 'Delavigne [sic] is not only wrong, but simple minded'.[107]

Delevingne's strategy against illicit drugs was strengthened by the imposition of stricter controls on cocaine and opium under Regulation 40B of the Defence of the Realm Act (DORA) of 28 July 1916. This regulation was made at the request of the police commissioner, Sir Edward Henry, who had written a week earlier, with exaggeration, that the 'evil' of cocaine was 'rapidly assuming huge dimensions'.[108] Henry's information was largely second-hand: 'As far as I can learn from reading it is the most baneful drug known.'[109] DORA had been introduced on the outbreak of war in 1914, and its regulations enabled the government to quell or quash anything that might jeopardise the prospects of British victory or assist the enemy. Munitions output was in its clutches; earlier restrictions on the supply of alcohol were intended to keep factory workers sober and productive. Regulation 40B suspended the more complicated minutiae of the Pharmacy Acts regulating the retail trade; the supply of dangerous drugs to troops became a criminal offence as did their possession by a civilian without medical prescription. It prohibited the import of cocaine and opiates except under licence, their possession without authorisation, and their supply by a pharmacist except under medical prescription. The *Lancet* regarded these rules as 'less stringent than those after which they are fashioned, namely the ... Harrison law', but predicted that 'in future the cocaine *habitué* will be dependent for his supplies of the drug on clandestine sources', and consequently 'will soon be an almost extinct type in this country'.[110] As Delevingne explained, Regulation 40B 'was not based on an assumed prevalence among the general population. It was an emergency measure based on the known evil existing among, at any rate, a section of the troops. The evil was believed to be a spreading evil. It could only be stopped by a *general* restriction'. The existence of 'a general evil ... recognised by almost all civilised countries at the Hague Conference ... was a support of the Regulation, but not its ground'.[111]

Drugs were feared as a technique of foreign subversion. During 1917 the English author Beverley Nichols (1898–1983) was sent by the War Office to act as an *agent provocateur* of pacifists and defeatists at the Café Royal in Regent Street. His effeminacy aroused the hostility of vice policemen, who raided his rooms to search for drugs and question his landlady about male visitors.[112] Devotees of drugs and sodomy both connoted threatening weirdness: they formed coteries held together by bonds of mutual vice; they were ruled by instinct rather than discipline; they indulged in luxuries that were thought to sap the war effort. The identification of drugs with unorthodox sexual tastes continued into peacetime. Professor Victor Balthazard (b. 1872) of Belgium in 1923, Hans W. Maier of Zürich Psychiatric Clinic in 1926 and Dutch physicians in 1929 identified cocaine with homosexuality or the stimulation of latent bisexuality.[113] According to Sir William Willcox (1870–1941), Medical Adviser to the Home Office, in 1924, cocaine was 'an important factor in the causation of unnatural sexual vice'.[114] Delevingne said 'that drug addicts—at any rate those of the vicious type—seek to make converts (or perverts) of others, and it is common ... in ... most

Western countries to find . . . coteries of persons—usually of a degenerate type—where the practice prevails'.[115]

British interest in cocaine and sex was intensified by Florence Stewart, better known by her stage name of Billie Carleton (1896–1918).[116] 'Oh, la, la, what a knockout!' wrote an American airman who met her in May 1918. 'How that woman can dance! . . . She has a gorgeous flat and there was a supper waiting for us when we got there and a maid to serve it. She slipped on a *negligée* and looked like a million dollars.'[117] A few months later Carleton was dead. In November she took some cocaine so as to enjoy a ball at the Royal Albert Hall, and afterwards probably succumbed to an overdose of a soporific called veronal. What one MP described as 'a tremendous hullabaloo to get hold of the man who had distributed the cocaine' inspired a flurry of novels and plays on the subject.[118] *The Parts Men Play* (1920), a novel by the Canadian journalist Sir Beverley Baxter (1891–1964), featured a young woman who 'took to opium cigarettes, and then to heroin' and finally 'disappeared one night'.[119] Arthur Sarsfield Ward (1886–1959), writing under the pseudonym of Sax Rohmer, wrote a novel after the Carleton case entitled *Dope, A Story of Chinatown and the Drug Traffic* (1920). Its central character is an actress, who begins by taking cocaine for stage nerves, then veronal for the cocaine-induced insomnia, and finally takes to opium-smoking after being corrupted by bad company. 'It's bad enough for the heathens, but for an Englishwoman to dope herself is downright unChristian and beastly,' declares Inspector Kerry of New Scotland Yard.[120] The villainess of the story is Mrs Sin, formerly 'a variety artiste known as La Belle Lola, a Cuban-Jewess', but now 'one of the night-club birds—a sort of mysterious fungus, sir, flowering in the dark and fattening on gilded fools', in Kerry's phrase.[121] Having murdered a baronet with a stiletto, she is herself strangled in Limehouse by her Chinese husband with his own 'pig-tail'.[122] Rohmer reinforced the association of drugs with sexual unconventionality. One of his characters is marked as a 'dope fiend' by her exclamation: 'I could die for a man who lashed me with leather thongs. Englishmen are so ridiculously gentle to women.'[123] When a Soho vice den is raided in this book, all the *habitués* are in evening dress except 'a masculine-looking lady who had apparently come straight off a golf course, and who was later proved to be a well-known advocate of women's rights'.[124]

Rohmer and others loathed the destruction of class distinctions in the *milieu* where drugs get taken. He depicted a Soho nightclub containing 'women entitled to wear coronets dancing with men entitled to wear the broad arrow, and men whose forefathers had signed Magna Carta dancing with chorus girls'.[125] The heroine in another 'dope' novel, *The Laughter of Fools* (1920) by Lady Dorothy Mills (1889–1959), lives with her uncle, a Suffolk baronet, with all the *appanages* of a county family, yet 'would rather serve behind a bar than live here'.[126] She ends up in Chelsea, taking drugs. The reactions of British censors in 1923–5 to *The Vortex* by Noël Coward (1899–1973) show similar sensitivities. The central figures of this play are an upper-middle-class addict and his adulterous mother. The significance of *The Vortex* in narcotics history is that it is the earliest text to blame addiction on bad parenting, and to exonerate addicts' egotistical demands by presenting them as the result of childhood emotional deprivation: 'You're not going to be beautiful and successful ever again—you're going to be my mother for once—it's about time I had one to help me,' the young man insists as part of the compact by which he abstains from drugs.[127] The upper-class officials charged with administering stage censorship were not squeamish about theatrical allusions to drugs, but loathed the depiction of *déclassé* or discreditable members of the governing classes. 'This picture of a frivolous and degenerate set of people gives a wholly false impression of Society life,' wrote the Earl of Cromer (1877–1953), who as Lord Chamberlain controlled theatrical censorship. 'I should be inclined to ban this play entirely.'[128]

Although Sir William Collins extolled 'the magical achievements' of DORA, there was one loophole in 40B.[129] In many areas of Britain the poor received dental treatment from individuals with incomplete or non-existent professional qualifications; some Welsh counties had as few as one qualified dentist. These unqualified practitioners were not all inept or disreputable, and were entitled to use cocaine as an anaesthetic. Sir Edward Henry deplored this situation because he believed it was 'tremendously in the interests of the working-class that no facilities for acquiring a baneful habit should be permitted'.[130] Consequently, in November 1916, a parliamentary committee was appointed to investigate the use of cocaine in dentistry. Its chairman was a former Cabinet Minister, Sir Charles Hobhouse (1862–1941), and its members included a future prime minister, Stanley Baldwin (1867–1947). They heard evidence from Henry, Sir Francis Lloyd, Delevingne, the Canadian military policeman who had worked undercover in Soho, physicians, dentists and other interested parties. As part of the enquiry, chief constables of major provincial centres were asked to report on drug problems in their districts. Their replies indicated that police were unaware of appreciable cocaine use. One chief constable mentioned lavish consumption of throat pastilles containing small amounts of cocaine, but the only significant report came from Southampton. Although there was 'no demand' for cocaine by soldiers or civilians there, 'Lascar seamen on His Majesty's Troopships' occasionally sought the drug. 'Two women of ladylike appearance have also recently applied for a supply.'[131] The Committee on Cocaine in Dentistry was the first enquiry into the drug in Britain: it concluded that there was no evidence 'to show that there is any serious or, perhaps, even noticeable prevalence of the cocaine habit amongst the civilian or military population of Great Britain'.[132]

The fact that cocaine was little used in Britain for another sixty years reflected the easier availability from the 1930s of another type of stimulant, amphetamines. In Europe and the USA, the low level of recreational cocaine use was a matter of fashion: it had little to do with the criminal laws, or prison sentences, that became such a pronounced part of drug policy after 1920. It is easier to make things illegal than to change human nature. The outburst of twentieth-century legislating on the use of drugs modified the way people behaved: but it could not stop drug use.

EIGHT

Law-breaking

Opiate. An unlocked door in the prison of Identity. It leads into the jail yard.
—AMBROSE BIERCE

Dope, *Oliver said to himself, was the worst possible thing.* Dope *was the
very denial of courage, of determination to face the facts, a betrayal of responsibility.*
Dope *was a cowardly means of escape, of hiding one's head like an ostrich, and
choosing not to know, or to act or to think. And yet in close association with that
miserable* dope*, appeared this strange serenity, this cool challenge to the world,
this smiling and beautiful death in life, or life in accepted death.*
—GEORGE SANTAYANA

'ONE HEARS NOWADAYS', the American critic Edmund
Wilson (1895–1972) wrote in 1927, 'less often of people
going on *sprees, toots, jags, bats, brannigans,* or *benders.*' These
terms, all suggesting 'not merely extreme drunkenness, but also an
exceptional occurrence, a breaking away by the drinker from the
conditions of his normal life', were less prevalent because under Prohibition 'this kind of fierce protracted drinking has now become a
universal . . . feature of social life'.[1] Alcohol prohibition made the
Americans a nation of law-breakers with such evidently disastrous
consequences that the Volstead Act was repealed in 1933. Drugs prohibition was also a godsend to criminal organisations; but drug-users
were stigmatised as criminals, and subjected to criminal sanctions,
much more fiercely than citizens who crept into speak-easies to gulp
bootlegged booze. It was not only in the USA that drug-users were
made into law-breakers in the 1920s. This was a European phenomenon, too. At the end of the First World War, the ratification of the
International Opium Convention of 1912 was made one of the con-

ditions of peace by the victorious powers. Article 295 of the Versailles Peace Treaty of 1919 bound the contracting powers to bring the Convention into force, and to enact the necessary legislation without delay.

The death of the actress Billie Carleton prompted Sir Basil Thomson (1861–1939), Director of Intelligence at Scotland Yard, to recommend to the Home Office in February 1919 'enacting permanent legislation to take the place of Regulation 40B' so as to counter 'the undoubted growth of the drug habit, both in America and in this country'.[2] Accordingly, and in fulfilment of Article 295 of the peace treaty, the relevant war regulations were in 1920 transformed into the Dangerous Drugs Act. This legislation passed after a cursory debate involving only six MPs. The only note of dissent came from a Scottish physician, Walter Elliot (1888–1958), who warned against following the moral absolutism behind the Harrison Act and those 'barbarians of the West', American prohibitionists. 'In their treatment of people who disagree with their social theories, there are none more violent or ill-judged than the people of the United States.'[4] The Dangerous Drugs Act of 1920 limited the manufacture, sale, possession and distribution of opiates and cocaine to authorised persons. It required that the movements of drugs, from manufacturer to supplier to consumer, should be documented in registers available for official inspection. The control of imports and exports of opiates and cocaine was also brought under the regulation of the Home Office.

At the time of the Hague Conference no British government department had been keen to administer any laws more restrictive than the Pharmacy Act of 1908; but Delevingne's zeal changed this lukewarm attitude. He wrested control of drug policy from the newly founded Ministry of Health in 1919 by insisting that it was 'very largely a police matter'.[5] During the next few years he tried to push Britain towards the penal drug policies that were being enforced in the United States. By 1926 the Colonial Office were 'on the verge of revolt against what they regard as the usurpation by the Home Office of a kind of general supervision in narcotics questions'.[6] Several of Delevingne's initiatives seemed constructive. In 1922, for example, the Home Office issued new regulations directed at physicians addicted to cocaine and morphine, and obliging doctors to preserve for two years all prescriptions and related records.[7] The Dangerous Drugs and Poisons (Amendment) Act of 1923 plugged some gaps in the earlier Act, and amended the Pharmacy Act. The results were pleasing.

During 1921–3 there were between 200 and 300 prosecutions annually under the Dangerous Drugs Act; thereafter never more than a hundred. Opium cases fell from an average of 148 a year in 1921–3 to an average of thirty-six a year in 1927–9. Cocaine cases fell from a yearly average of sixty-five in 1921–3 to a yearly average of five in 1927–9. Comparable morphine averages dropped from thirty-two to seventeen.[8] The largest number of defendants were older morphine-users (who had become addicted through medical treatment and did not consume drugs for pleasure) followed by Chinese opium-smokers and a small number of people who resorted to cocaine for glee. Those in the first category were solitary individuals remote from any subculture; but the Chinese smokers were more sociable, and a few of them supplied the younger delinquents. Kate Meyrick (1875–1933), the Soho nightclub owner, first encountered the trafficker 'Brilliant' Chang in 1921 when he began entertaining her hostesses at his Regent Street restaurant. 'His snake-like eyes and powerful personality used to fascinate nearly all the women he met,' she wrote. She soon noticed 'that whenever my girls came back from these little excursions to Chang's place they showed signs of some queer nervous excitement'. Having deduced that he was supplying them with drugs, she forbade further contact. Those hostesses who continued 'secret visits' to Chang were banned from the club: the 'dope-peddler' working for Chang, whom she detected 'plying his loathsome trade' in her club, was 'flung in the street'.[9]

Under the Dangerous Drugs Act it was easy to identify, rebuke or prosecute physicians who were too lavish in their prescriptions of cocaine or opiates. Dr C. with a practice in the Tottenham Court Road area was discovered in 1919 prescribing 'cocaine to men more or less in the underworld'. He claimed to be using cocaine as an anaesthetic in venereal disease treatment. In 1922 one chemist estimated that Dr C. had over 300 addict patients. As the Home Office stated in 1924, 'he is prepared to give prescriptions for dangerous drugs to practically any person who asks for them'.[10] It is not clear what steps were taken against Dr C. However, Dr Joseph Hirschmann (1895–1977) of Maida Vale, who began prescribing large amounts to morphine addicts in the mid-1930s, was convicted on a technical record-keeping offence in 1936, and stripped of his authority to possess and supply dangerous drugs. He subsequently retreated to obscurity in Shropshire. Dr Gerald Quinlan (1900–1976) of Westminster, who succeeded Hirschman as an objectionably lavish prescriber to addicts, amended his ways in 1942 after concerted pressure from the General Medical Council and Home Office.[11] Plausible drug-users could dupe doctors. An Englishman wrote in 1924 of his brother-in-law who had become dependent on morphine as the result of hospital treatment for war wounds. 'Possessed of an engaging personality and charming address, my friend can, as he himself admits, rely upon getting more or less of the drug from three out of five medical practitioners whom he approaches.' The writer had been sharing a room with his brother-in-law in a futile attempt to stop him getting the drug; gullible physicians made it impossible. 'Restraint—forcible restraint—and that alone can save my friend from degradation unspeakable or the merciful oblivion of a suicide's grave.'[12]

Few Europeans doubted the necessity for giving maintenance prescriptions to people with drug cravings. The English physiologist Arthur Gamgee had written in 1908 that 'A medical man has no right to inflict untold suffering on a patient on the ground (which experience has proved to be absolutely fallacious) that the great suffering endured will act as a deterrent against further lapses.' The physician's duty was 'not only to heal the sick, but to alleviate pain, and in no sense to employ a punitive method of treatment'.[13] However, punishments were enforced as official American practice. It is unclear whether Congress, in passing the Harrison Act, intended to suppress maintenance prescriptions. In the first four months of the Act 257 physicians and forty dentists were prosecuted under its provisions: some, no doubt, supplying users cynically, and others knowingly providing maintenance prescriptions. Blair's Philadelphia survey of 1919 found that the 'class of debased physician who make a business of catering to drug addiction' clustered

in the vice districts, in the sections where the wealthy reside, and in the industrial communities where no industrial medical service is furnished . . . Like the abortionist, they are there because there is a demand for them—a demand too often the result of the fact that incompetent physicians have started a large number of drug addicts, refuse to prescribe after the addiction becomes confirmed, and leave the victims of poor therapeutics to resort to the man who makes a business of supplying them with drugs.[14]

In March 1919 the Supreme Court held, in *Webb et al. versus the United States*, that a physician must not provide opiates for the sole purpose of maintaining an addict. Physicians who treated addicts were raided by Treasury agents, and prosecuted as drug-peddlers. The intention and the effect were to cut addicts off from legitimate medical supplies. Realising that this might drive some users to crime, and encourage organised illicit suppliers, several municipal authorities established dispensaries to serve as legal sources of supply. Willis Abbot (1863–1934), editor of the *Christian Science Monitor*, saw at this time 'queues of drug addicts, men and women in different lines, extending for two blocks from the doors of a public dispensary in New York, awaiting their allowance of the drug thus officially dispensed to registered victims'.[15] However, the Narcotics Division of the Prohibition Unit opposed such clinics. This Unit had been formed under the Bureau of Internal Revenue to administer the Volstead Act of 1919 and the Eighteenth Amendment prohibiting the sale (but not possession) of alcohol. From early 1920 the Unit had a separate Narcotics Division under the direction of a former pharmacist, Colonel Levi Nutt (d. 1938). Nutt's agents embarked on a robust campaign of intimidation against both individual physicians and dispensaries such as New York's Worth Street Clinic. The narcotics agents (soon known as 'narcs') used the courts to pressurise physicians to have nothing to do with drug-users. This suppressed both unscrupulous, profiteering doctors and colleagues whose motives were irreproachable in issuing maintenance prescriptions. In New York City the number of physicians prescribing opiates fell from sixty-five in May 1919 to four in November 1920.

Though many physicians resented the Prohibition Unit's tactics, others approved. Dr Alexander Lambert (1861–1939), President of the American Medical Association in 1919, whose drastic morphine withdrawal cure involving belladonna and hyoscyamin was popular at this time, believed that 'ambulatory self-reduction in the majority of patients is a dishonest and useless method doomed to failure. It is the method under which the trafficking and disreputable physician cloaks his practice.'[16] Similarly a physician who treated addicts at Philadelphia General Hospital opined that 'The private physician who endeavours to treat a patient by withdrawal while the patient is about his work is either a super-physician, or a Simple Simon, or else he is illegally evading the law.'[17] The Prohibition Unit also rallied the courts and exerted other pressure against municipal dispensaries and clinics. Its policy was endorsed by a short but influential leaflet, inspired by the report of a small committee of the American Medical Association, which the Unit issued in 1921. Addicts should be confined during treatment, this leaflet advised; and although it had no legal status, it was used to enforce the closure of clinics, which were effectively suppressed by the end of 1921. 'Many observers have remarked that on this single, almost forgotten leaflet', a commentator wrote thirty years later, 'the narcotics crime picture which we see today, in fact much of the narcotics evil is based.' The clinic's suppression forced patients to become small-time suppliers to protect their supplies: 'In order to sell enough dope to earn the cost of their own they made addicts out of the easiest marks— young, ignorant, frustrated kids. The single bureaucratic step, unauthorised by Congress, destroyed all honest attempts, other than forced hospitalization, to treat addiction as a medical problem instead of a crime.'[18] The punitive rigidity of US addiction treatment was increased by a Supreme Court ruling of 1922 that physicians must not prescribe for an addict even in diminishing amounts as part of a withdrawal cure. The Jones-Miller Narcotic Drugs Import and Export Act of 1922 further institutionalised and restricted drug supplies. The Porter Act of 1924 prohibited the manufacture and medical use of heroin.

The effect was calamitous. For the year ending June 1923, there were 4194 convictions under internal revenue narcotics laws for which sentences aggregating 4692 years and fines amounting to $291,690 were imposed.[19] People with drug cravings were cut off from medical support, and were forced to obtain their supplies from illicit sources. By 1923, 717 out of 1482 prisoners in the federal penitentiary at Leavenworth, Kansas, were incarcerated for drugs offences. Excluding measures dating from the 1880s against opium-smoking, in 1914, when the Harrison Act was passed, only six US states had criminalised the possession of regulated drugs. By 1931, thirty-six states prohibited possession of cocaine, thirty-five prohibited possession of opiates, and eight prohibited possession of hypodermic syringes. Criminal penalties were also made more severe at state level in the aftermath of the Harrison Act. The Federal Narcotics Control Board was authorised in 1922 to determine how much opium, cocaine and their derivatives were needed for medical purposes and to set import quotas accordingly. Possession without a prescription was made presumptive evidence of holding illegally imported drugs; by this device possession became a federal crime too. All habitual drug users were thus herded into a corral of criminality, and branded as vicious. Addiction not only became a crime, but law enforcement ensured that virtually all addicts had to behave like criminals. 'The medical profession', a British diplomat reported from Washington DC in 1924, 'recognises addiction as a specific disease and a large proportion of the victims as innocent sufferers; on the other hand, the police authorities, in the person of the [New York] Commissioner of Correction, regard the phenomenon as a wilful vice which must be dealt with by penal measures.'[20]

This situation created an opportunity for men like Arnold Rothstein (1882–1928). Rothstein was a phenomenal gambler who won $825,000 at the race track in a single day, and provided the model for Jay Gatsby's friend Meyer Wolfsheim, 'the man who fixed the World Series back in 1919'. He made a fortune in gambling rackets, a second fortune smuggling whisky in the early days of Prohibition, and backed such notorious New York speak-easies as the Cotton Club. He invested his profits in real estate, stocks and bonds, and was a pioneer among American criminals in the techniques of money-laundering. One of his underlings was Charles ('Lucky') Luciano (1897–1962), who had first been arrested in 1916 for peddling heroin on the streets. Like other gamblers, Rothstein smoked opium when young. He saw the Jones-Miller and Porter Acts of 1922–4 as providential. From about 1925, drawing on the profits of his criminal connections, he sent minions to Europe to buy opiates and cocaine, and used his contacts with big criminal gangs throughout the USA to distribute drugs. His influence at Tammany Hall protected these operations, and Rothstein was soon the leading US trafficker. Seizure figures indicate the increasing traffic, although most of Rothstein's contraband got through. During the twelve months to June 1926, US customs confiscated about 204 kilograms of opium, 19 kilograms of morphine, 1.6 kilograms of heroin and 4.5 kilograms of cocaine. The comparable figures for the year to June 1928 were 1070 kilograms of opium, 41 kilograms of morphine, 12 kilograms of heroin and 13 kilograms of cocaine. One New York journalist described the pandemonium of Rothstein's office life with its perpetually ringing telephone. 'He was constantly barking out instructions on buying real estate and selling it, buying and selling stocks, placing bets on horses, lending or calling in money and paying or demanding pay for gambling debts.' Rothstein despised people. 'The majority of the human race are . . . dumbbells,' he said. 'I never played with a man I wasn't sure I couldn't beat.'[21]

The large-scale activities of Rothstein's criminal organisation were not comparable to the petty crimes to which US addicts were driven in order to secure opiates. Nevertheless, the addicts' Prohibition-induced crimes accentuated the myth that opiates had some inherent sinister power to transform good citizens into offenders. One example of this vehement American opinion was the report of a special committee appointed in 1923 by the Governor of New York State. In the paraphrase of the *Journal of the American Medical Association*,

> the majority of narcotic *habitués* are criminals, with criminal records in the courts. In fact, narcoticism is so involved with criminality that to relax police vigilance over the one is to enhance the other. All drug addicts should, therefore, undergo institutional confinement, the criminal addict in penal institutions and the non-criminal addict in state-licensed and supervised public or private institutions. It is the sense of the committee that the criminal addict was a criminal prior to his addiction, or was arrested in some criminal act. When a criminal addict is confined in a penal institution, he should be placed under medical treatment.[22]

A report of 1919 from the Treasury Department entitled *Traffic in Narcotic Drugs* estimated that there were one million drug-users in the USA (300,000 in New York alone). These figures were inflated in the ruthless manner of Hamilton Wright. In the most reliable US study, published in 1924, Laurence Kolb and Andrew Du Mez (1865–1948) estimated the number of American addicts at a maximum of 150,000: they suggested the figure had been falling since 1900, for which date they estimated 264,000 addicts. This improvement was attributable to the increased chariness of physicians in prescribing habit-forming substances, and to the impact of the Food & Drug Act, the Harrison Act and other measures that were 'preventing innocent, normal people from being addicted' by careless medical treatment. Instead the USA was confronted by a new 'delinquent kind of addict'.[23] Kolb concluded from studying the cases of 230 addicts that most were abnormal in that they experienced enhanced pleasure when using drugs whereas most people experienced only relief of pain. 'Addiction is becoming more and more a vicious practice of unstable people, who, by their nature, have abnormal cravings which compel them to take much larger doses than those which were taken by the average normal person who so often innocently fell a victim to narcotics some years ago.'[24] Kolb's belief in addiction as a personality disorder was contested by physicians who believed that addiction was a drug-induced pathology that could afflict anyone, and was seldom articulated between 1930 and the 1960s.

Some commentators coupled drugs with venereal diseases as 'another secret menace which [we] must ferret out and destroy'. Both resulted from illicit pleasures taken with corrupt companions: those involved could be construed as pollutants poisoning the innocent, including the unborn. The medical director of the Firestone Tire and Rubber Company at Akron, Ohio, for example, reported in 1919 that he had 'been able to isolate and eliminate' two men and one woman 'drug users' in the past year.[25] Isolation and quarantine became fashionable measures. Typically, under legislation enacted in 1923 in the state of Washington, the board of health was empowered to determine whether 'the quarantine or isolation of persons habitually using narcotic drugs is necessary; and if it so determines, the officers named above may then isolate or quarantine such persons'.[26] These draconian powers were enacted despite the fact, as Thomas Blair acknowledged, that 'drug tippling may never become drug addiction . . . in many people'.[27]

The American desire to enforce world prohibition on heroin aroused prolonged controversy. As early as 1920 the Treasury Department supported a bill to eliminate heroin from the US by forbidding its importation. This proposal enraged physicians such as Hobart Hare (1862–1931), a Professor at Jefferson Medical College in Pennsylvania and editor of the *Therapeutic Gazette*. 'A large number of people are being deprived of relief from [heroin] by the crusade that is being made to save a whole lot of "rotters" who would be better off if they were dead . . . the very fact that it is abused by the degenerate is a sign that it has the power for good when prescribed by the physician for the patient who really needs it.'[28] Few American physicians felt free to speak out like Hare; heroin was finally outlawed in the USA in 1924. However, European physicians resisted US politicians who campaigned for the world prohibition of heroin in medical use. The English pharmacologist Professor Walter Dixon (1870–1931), who was a League of

Nations adviser on addiction, complained in 1923 that London officials 'do not seem to have learnt anything from the experience of our American brethren'. The Harrison Act had 'signally failed' to contain levels of addiction in the USA. 'The main reason for this is . . . that the law takes no account of the causes of addiction; the drugger is regarded as a criminal, just as the insane were in medieval times. Everything can be obtained if the price is commensurate with the risk, with the result that smuggling is rampant from end to end of America.' Dixon rejected penal policies and urged that 'our only hope of stamping out the drug addict is through the doctors, that legislation above the doctors' heads is likely to prove our undoing and that we can no more stamp out addiction by prohibition than we can stamp out insanity'.[29] Drug-users were equally scornful. 'It ought to be obvious', Crowley asserted, 'that if England reverted to pre-war conditions, when any responsible person (by signing his name in a book) could buy drugs at a fair profit on cost price'—cocaine say at 16 shillings and heroin at 20 shillings instead of as many pounds—'the whole underground traffic would disappear like a bad dream.' He admitted that such a policy might result in the fatal overdoses of 'a few score wasters too stupid to know when to stop', but this should not be inconceivable so soon 'after the war in which we sent our sturdiest sons as sheep to the slaughter'.[30]

These policy questions, and other related issues, needed careful scrutiny. Delevingne and the Home Office therefore welcomed the appointment in 1924 by the Ministry of Health of a Departmental Committee on Morphine and Heroin Addiction. The chairman of this committee (which reported in 1926) was the President of the Royal College of Physicians, Sir Humphry Rolleston (1862–1944), 'a very learned, kind-hearted, considerate man of untiring energy'.[31] All its members (including Dixon) were distinguished physicians. The committee held twenty-three meetings, and interviewed thirty-five witnesses, of whom twenty-four were physicians. No known addicts testified. One cogent and persuasive witness, Dr Frederick Hogg (1859–1937), had been the attentive superintendent of the Dalrymple House Retreat at Rickmansworth since 1899. Over twenty-five years he had treated 1300 male inebriates, including a hundred users of morphine or opium, sixteen combining morphine and cocaine, eight of heroin, twenty-six of cocaine and various veronal, chloral and sulphonal cases. The addicts included forty-four medical men, seven students of medicine or chemistry, four dentists and three chemists. Hogg stressed that the 'sudden withdrawal' cure prevalent in the USA was 'barbarous and inhumane'. It was 'adopted by some to save themselves trouble or because they are quite indifferent to the feelings of their patient'.[32] Another witness, the psychologist and neurologist Sir Maurice Craig (1866–1935), commented that 'the chief danger' of the Harrison Law 'was that attention was apt to be concentrated on the drug itself rather than upon the patient—upon the legal aspect rather than upon the medical aspect'.[33]

The Rolleston Report concluded that morphine and heroin addiction were rare in Britain, and had become less prevalent since 1920, as the result of drugs becoming harder to obtain except by medical prescription. Morphine addiction was much the commoner, but heroin addiction the more incorrigible. The committee preferred to define addiction not as vice, or in other pejorative terms, but as 'the use of the drug for a sufficient time to produce the constitutional condition that is manifested in the overpowering craving and the recurrence of withdrawal symptoms when use is discontinued'.[34] Partly as a result of this less puritanical approach, Rolleston's committee accepted as legitimate the administration of morphine or heroin to addicts for an indefinitely prolonged period, with the proviso that one or two consultants must approve such continuous administration. Similarly, contrary to the methods imposed on physicians in the USA after 1920, the committee tended against abrupt withdrawal cures, except in certain specialist institutions; gradual withdrawal was the only practicable method of treatment under the conditions of private practice. Institutional treatment afforded the best hope of cure, under both gradual and abrupt withdrawals, and indeed was essential in cases of rapid withdrawal. A lasting cure could not be claimed until the patient had been clean for three years. Few witnesses claimed more than 15 to 20 per cent success in cures. The committee rejected a complete ban on heroin, as had recently been enforced in the USA; even Willcox accepted that heroin had therapeutic properties not possessed by any other drug. Similarly, after being consulted in the case of a painter of miniatures and retoucher of photographs who had been taking morphine for forty years, Willcox conceded that some cases could only be treated by indefinite maintenance prescriptions. Overall the committee were emphatic that the prevention and control of addiction should 'rest mainly in the hands of the medical profession, since, in the main, it is through them alone that the drug can be obtained'.[35] This assertion of medical supremacy was welcomed by British officialdom. Delevingne praised Rolleston's report as 'of great service' to the Home Office.[36]

The high proportion of medical men who were addicts must have influenced the committee's determination to avoid the Harrison Act's punitive approach. It seems that the British injectable drug use considered by the committee was subcutaneous or intramuscular—that is, injected under the skin or into muscles—rather than intravenous. The steady spread of intravenous use of opiates, especially heroin, by delinquent young men in the US since the imposition of the Harrison Act was apparently not evident in Britain in 1926. It seems intravenous use of heroin in Britain only became common around 1950. It is questionable whether the committee would have dared make such recommendations if Britain's problem had been graver. Sir Maurice Craig had encountered thirty-five cases of addiction during thirty-three years; his colleagues confirmed having 'very, very few' such cases, and he found it 'difficult to reconcile statements in the Press with my experience'.[37] Another witness, Sir Farquhar Buzzard (1871–1945), had treated fewer than thirty cases in his career, and felt that 'The evil of addiction, especially in respect of Heroin and Morphine, was not sufficiently prevalent to justify any further restrictions.'[38] These were distinguished London physicians, with prosperous patients, but a medical witness who treated poorer cases in a northern industrial city reported 'very little addiction in Sheffield', where the impact of recent regulations meant that a few individuals were substituting chlorodyne 'to gratify their craving for Morphine'.[39] The forensic psychiatrist Sir Norwood East (1872–1953), who worked for the Prison Commission, testified that thirty-six men remanded at Brixton Prison between June 1921 and April 1924 had been drug-traffickers (including fifteen Orientals) and twelve were stated to be addicts, of whom he decided only eight cases were genuine. It is doubtful that the Home Office would have submitted to the Rolleston credo if British cities had suffered the levels of intravenous street addiction known in New York, Chicago or Philadelphia.

The American editor Willis Abbot in 1925 found it is 'hard to accept as truthful' the 'mass of information' alleging 'the spread of the drug evil among children . . . who are enslaved and made to peddle the drug to others to get their own supplies'. These scare stories had instilled 'in the American mind a feeling that narcotic drugs have taken the malign position once held by whiskey, and that they must be banned from the United States'.[40] Aleister Crowley similarly deplored the 'nauseating publicity' in British and American newspapers. 'Indulgence in drugs is described with an unholy leer; it is connected lewdly with sexual aberrations; and the reprobation with which the writers smear their nastiness is obviously hypocrisy of the most oily and venal type. The object is to sell the paper by making people's flesh creep.'[41] Such publicity was not a deterrent. On the contrary, 'The infernal suggestions of the Press, and the vile venality of the villains attracted to the traffic by the immense profits, are deliberately creating new addicts every day of people who would no more think of indulging in narcotics than a cat in a cold bath.'[42] Self-promoting publicists were as deplorable in their influence as opportunistic anti-drugs journalists. 'Exaggeration is the weapon of the crank,' as an English visitor to the States noted in 1925, and particularly beloved of prohibitionists.[43]

Richmond P. Hobson (1870–1937) was a peculiarly objectionable crank. His early career was sketched in 1924 by Sir Arthur Willert (1882–1973), who had been *The Times*'s correspondent in Washington: 'He did something very gallant in Manila harbour, I think; came home as a national hero; but unfortunately allowed himself to be kissed in railway stations and other public places by female admirers. That finished him and since then [he] has been an unregarded though pushing member of the Democratic Party.'[44] As a congressman in 1907–15, Hobson was a leading American naval supremacist. He was the first to introduce in Congress an amendment for total prohibition of alcohol, and advocated nationwide and global prohibition. He organised and presided over the International Narcotics Education Association in 1923, and in the following year sent a lurid memorandum, 'Menace of Narcotics Shadows the World', to King George V (1865–1936):

There are probably five times as many narcotic drug addicts as there ever were slaves at one time, and the bondage is far more abject and far more dangerous. These addict slaves, driven by the lash of a terrific craving, resorting to organised theft and robbery, are immensely profitable to their masters—the traffic—involving gigantic financial interests with a constant urge of expansion . . . America is assailed by Opium with Asia as a base, by Cocaine with South America as a base, by Heroin and Synthetic Drugs with Europe as a base. This deadly drug warfare, that from three sides is striking at our citizens, our homes, our institutions, the very germ plasm of our people, is more destructive and biologically more dangerous for our future than would be united warfare against us from these continents.[45]

Hobson's broadcasts and published writings—articles such as 'One Million American Victims of Drug Habit' for the *New York Times* (9 November 1924) or his books *Narcotic Peril* (1925), *The Modern Pirates—Exterminate Them* (1931) and *Drug Addiction: a Malignant Racial Cancer* (1933)—were bombastic and inaccurate.

As part of such propaganda, traditional forms of drug consumption were attacked. The Gandy bill introduced in 1921 aimed to prohibit the use of peyote among the Indian tribes in such states as Texas, Arizona and California. But peyote was insignificant compared with the rising US consumption of marijuana following the Eighteenth Amendment coming into effect in January 1920. Alcohol prohibition was the mainspring of the marijuana boom. As alcohol became harder to obtain, more expensive, and often of inferior quality, 'tea-pads' started to open: they resembled 'speak-easies', except that they provided marijuana at low prices rather than overpriced bootlegged booze. It was estimated that there were 500 'tea-pads' in New York City by the 1930s. As one scholar concluded in 1972, 'It was a change in the laws rather than a change in human nature that stimulated the large-scale marketing of marijuana for recreational use in the United States.'[46] Federal legislation aside, marijuana was included in Texas legislation of 1919 restricting narcotics except for medicinal purposes, and in 1923 the Texas state legislature prohibited possession of narcotics, including marijuana, with intent to sell. New Mexico in 1923 also prohibited the cultivation, importation or sale of cannabis, and following the federal Narcotic Drugs Import and Export Act of the previous year, treated possession of the drug as evidence of illegal importation. Journalists' coverage of these far-reaching laws was exiguous: two tersely factual sentences reporting the existence of the Texas bill in a newspaper of the state capital; one paragraph in the Sante Fé *New Mexican*; and nothing else.

The effects of alcohol prohibition on the demand for marijuana were compounded by the half million Mexicans who migrated to work as labourers in the USA between 1915 and 1930. Two-thirds settled in Texas while the others dispersed in the states west of the Mississippi river. State laws were accordingly passed against marijuana in California and Utah (1915), Colorado (1917), Texas (1919), Iowa (1921), New Mexico, Arkansas, Nevada, Oregon and Washington (1923), Idaho, Kansas, Montana and Nebraska (1927), Wyoming (1929), South Dakota (1931), and North Dakota and Oklahoma (1933). Minimal public discussion attended these laws, which were partly motivated by antagonism against Mexicans (comparable to the earlier hostility to Chinese immigrant mine-workers). The levels of debate in the legislatures are conveyed by the report in the *Montana Standard* (27 January 1929) of a new and tighter law prohibiting the use, sale or possession of the drug.

> There was fun in the House Health Committee during the week when the Marihuana bill came up for consideration. Marihuana is Mexican opium, a plant used by Mexicans and cultivated for sale by Indians. 'When some beet field peon takes a few rares of this stuff', explained Dr. Fred Ulsher of Mineral County, 'he thinks he has just been elected president of Mexico so he starts to execute all his political enemies. I understand that over in Butte where the Mexicans often go for the winter they stage imaginary bullfights in the "Bower of Roses" or put on tournaments for the favor of "Spanish Rose" after a couple of whiffs of Marihuana. The Silver Bow and Yellowstone delegations both deplore these international complications'. Everyone laughed and the bill was recommended for passage.[47]

During the 1920s Mexican labourers went to work in the steel mills, construction gangs and industries of Chicago, Kansas City, Cleveland, Detroit, St Louis and other such cities. The estimated 30,000 Mexicans in Chicago by 1930 were resented by families of European origin, and suffered from racial aggression in mixed neighbourhoods. Police conduct towards these Mexicans was discriminatory, and indeed often violent or unlawful. The poor, ill-educated and politically supine Mexican community presented a tempting target for officials who wanted to be seen enforcing prohibitionist laws but did not wish to offend politically influential constituencies with raids. By the late 1920s there were widely reported crackdowns against Mexicans' marijuana habits. Although there was no legislation in Illinois against the possession or sale of the drug, there were revenue statutes against cigarette substitutes on which tax had not been paid. There were raids and arrests in 1929 accompanied by rhetoric about the protection of school pupils.

Whereas the Mexican marijuana habit remained largely confined among migrant labourers, the habit was introduced by Caribbean sailors and immigrants to the local population in US ports on the Gulf of Mexico, notably Houston, Galveston and above all New Orleans. Marijuana was available at local pharmacies in Texas until 1919 and in Louisiana until 1924. Druggists in those states were therefore an important source. In Galveston in 1917 one druggist identified his marijuana customers as 'Mexicans, a low class of whites, and East Indians coming off the boats' while another druggist defined them as 'Mexicans, Negroes, and chauffeurs, and a low class of whites such as those addicted to the use of habit-forming drugs, and hangers-on of the underworld'.[48] The users around El Paso and the border towns had not caused much anxiety, but the characterisation of smokers in port towns as hoodlums was more disturbing. A campaign by New Orleans journalists in 1926 transformed public perceptions of the drug. Their reports of its effects were lurid and exploitative. Rather than focusing on street users, they raised alarm over pushers lurking near schools to entice hundreds of pupils into the marijuana habit. The Women's Christian Temperance Union identified the soft-drink stands that had mushroomed on the streets of New Orleans since Prohibition as loci where the drug could be bought. In response to this agitation, which resembled the reasons given for the earliest town ordinances against opium-smoking in Nevada in the 1870s, there were over 150 arrests in 1926. Elsewhere, the steel magnate Senator Lawrence Phipps (1862–1958), contended that the use of marijuana increased in Colorado after 1926. He linked it with peyote, and urged federal prohibition rather than recognising the role of alcohol prohibition in arousing the drug's use. Phipps's calls for federal action were supported by the New Orleans anti-marijuana coalition. This combination proved important in the federal criminalisation of the drug in 1937.

The British response to cannabis in this period was far less militant. There was no widely held belief among officials in the need for cannabis prohibition, despite a brief press agitation; the change in the law occurred (without informed discussion) as the result of a diplomatic initiative launched by the Egyptian Ministry of the Interior. The Home Office file opens in August 1922 when the Chief Constable of the north-eastern port of South Shields sent the Home Office a pipe found in the coalhouse of A. Hamed, an Egyptian coffee house-keeper, of 5 Tiny Street, South Shields. His police officers suspected that Hamed supplied opium to Indian sailors, 'but he asserts that the substance was hasheesh'. The Chief Constable enquired if hashish fell within the scope of the DD Acts and was told that it did not. Analysis confirmed that Hamed's substance was cannabis.[49] The Home Office did not overreact to this incident. The sale of 'Hashish or "Bhang"' was 'controlled in India, British North Borneo, and South Africa, and totally prohibited in the Straits Settlements and Ceylon', wrote an official, but 'has not been investigated in this country'.[50] Next, in the summer of 1923, ten tons of cannabis resin (shipped from Bombay) was detained in the Seychelles. The cargo, which was eventually allowed to proceed to Djibouti, the French Somalian port, first brought to the attention of the European authorities a debonair Frenchman named de Monfreid, who became notorious as a drug-smuggler. The Home Officer's medical adviser, Sir William Willcox, had suggested that 'the restrictions on the traffic in opium and other drugs will create a demand for Indian Hemp', but to Delevingne it still seemed in 1923 as if 'there is no serious international traffic in it'.[51]

Shortly afterwards, in the news doldrums of August 1923, London journalists saw a chance for a few days of indignant scarifying. An Italian named Thomas Garza (b. 1891) and a Sudanese named Idris Abdullah (b. 1882) were arrested in Old Compton Street, Soho, and accused of offering to supply raw opium. In fact the brown substance in their possession was hashish, which was not covered by the DDA and therefore legal to possess. Abdullah was accordingly discharged although Garza continued to be held on remand.[52] On 20 August the first newspaper reports appeared: under such headlines as 'MADDENING "DOPE" FOR THE ASKING', for example, the *Daily Chronicle* announced 'a serious growth in the traffic of hashish, a deadly Eastern drug which induces madness'. A *Daily Mail* report of 23 August blazoned 'HASHISH PERIL' attributed views and intentions to the Home Office (on the basis of a purported interview) that provoked its official to write 'Liar!' in the margin of the newspaper cutting. Other headlines proclaimed 'THE NEW DOPE PERIL' and demanded 'PENALTIES TO STOP TRAFFIC IN A HORRIBLE DRUG'. Even Delevingne despised this 'little excitement' as the work of journalists 'having nothing better to do'.[53] One of his subordinates summarised the current position on Indian hemp. 'Its greatest use in England', he wrote, 'is for the manufacture of corn plaster'. The Metropolitan Police had recommended the inclusion of Indian hemp in the original DDA, 'but upon no evidence that it was being generally consumed in this country for vicious purposes . . . it is used by a few Egyptians, and is occasionally taken as an experiment by persons interested in oriental vices'. Internationally 'excessive indulgence in the drug is very rare, but leads to general ill-health and occasional insanity'. The 'only result' of prohibiting the drug in Egypt had been 'an increase of price to its consumers'.[54]

Following the Garza case of 1923, the Metropolitan Commissioner of Police repeated his request for hashish to be included in the DDA, a CID officer advising 'that it has practically the same effect as cocaine and morphine upon its victims'.[55] The Home Office reaction was dismissive. 'No sort of evidence is adduced that there is any real evidence of the hashish habit, or that the habit if acquired has any results subversive of public morality.' Its official scorned the prosecutor's 'entirely unsupported inference that as the accused were coffee-servers in West End Restaurants they were probably serving hashish to their (white) customers with the coffee!'[56] When a Parliamentary Question about hashish was asked in the House of Commons in February 1924, the Home Office had not shifted. 'The existing situation in this country does not at present call for the inclusion of Haschish in the DDA'. As the drug's consumption was 'confined to Arab, Greek and Lascar seamen, it is doubtful whether restrictions would diminish the vice amongst them, who could always smuggle in'. The Home Office however foresaw that 'the prevalence of the vice in Egypt' might result in 'international regulation of the drug'.[57]

A month later the Egyptian Ministry of the Interior concluded that as it was 'practically impossible to keep hashish out of Egypt', the best solution was that 'The League of Nations should consider hashish traffic as an international affair and should try to persuade its members to make dealing in or consuming the drug a crime punishable by severe

penalties.'[58] Consequently, at the Geneva Conference on Opium of
1924–5, Egypt's delegate proposed bringing hashish within the Hague
Convention of 1912. His memorandum circulated in support of this
proposal was exaggerated. It described hashish as 'a dangerous narcotic
. . . more harmful than opium', and stated that 'about 70% of insane
people in lunatic asylums in Egypt are haschiche [sic] eaters or smokers'.[59] The leader of the US delegation supported this initiative. 'We are
asking them to help us to destroy the vice of opium, and coca leaves
and their derivatives,' he declared of the Egyptian and Turkish governments. 'This is a good time to practice a little reciprocity. They have
their troubles and we have ours.'[60] As a result of this Egyptian initiative,
the contracting powers agreed from 1925 to prohibit the import or
export of cannabis except for certified medical and scientific purposes,
and to regulate its sale and use. In Britain the drug was rescheduled as
a poison, with effect from April 1925.[61] A few months later the Dangerous Drugs Act of 1925 enabled Britain to meet the September
deadline for the ratification of the Geneva Convention. It should be
stressed that the House of Commons debate on this bill (on 5 August
1925) lasted less than five minutes: Indian hemp, or cannabis, was not
mentioned once (although there was a brief reference to coca leaves,
which were also included in this new legislation).[62] The House of
Lords debate was more informative. Viscount Cecil of Chelwood
(1864–1958), for the government, presented the bill as 'not . . . contentious' in its contents, and a necessary preliminary to ratification of
the Geneva Convention. His remarks were confined to technicalities,
except when he invoked the protection of children: in other countries
peddlers of 'heroin, morphine, cocaine and the like . . . have been found
pushing their pernicious wares even in the schools of the country and
leading the unhappy children—for they are little more than that—into
vice before they know what vice really means'.[63] (This emotive assertion was a reference to the reports of cannabis being used by pupils in
the USA; but it was misleading to group cannabis with the traffic in
heroin and cocaine.) The only other speaker of substance in the brief
Lords debate was the distinguished lawyer Viscount Haldane
(1856–1928), who found it 'impossible to form any judgement on the
details of the Bill', and urged that it 'be taken by the House to a large
extent on trust'. It was on this casual basis that the criminalisation of
cannabis in Britain was nodded through.

The use of Indian hemp in inter-war Britain was negligible compared with the demand for habit-forming new sleeping draughts derived from barbituric acids. The most notable of these was diethylmalonyl, which was discovered in 1902 by the German chemist Emil Fischer (1852–1919) and the physician and physiologist Baron Josef von Mering (1849–1908). Their discovery was first marketed by the German companies of Merck and Bayer under the trade name of Veronal in 1903. It immediately joined the older established hypnotics such as chloral and sulphonal as substances abused by distressed people. As early as December 1903 a physician in Bayswater, London was called to a nineteen-year-old woman who since returning from honeymoon had suffered several hysterical attacks, and was now inexplicably comatose. A box of Veronal cachets was found secreted in her room. She recovered when this was confiscated, but soon relapsed after hiding another bottle under the mattress. She implored and threatened the doctor for more of the drug. Shortly afterwards, the same physician encountered two instances of 'suicidal mania' involving Veronal.[64] A few years later 'the insidious drug notorious under its trade name of Veronal' was featuring in popular novels.[65] The Bayswater abuser, and the case of a depressed Jersey woman who took a suicidal overdose of sulphonal,[66] roused a Scottish physician to a ringing denunciation in 1903: 'All hypnotics are dangerous, and medical men cannot be too careful in prescribing them for their patients, and no druggist should repeat such prescriptions unless with the consent of the prescriber'. He warned that the prescription of 'trumpery' substances like Veronal, produced by manufacturing chemists, rather than powders, pills and cachets personally compounded by physicians, enabled patients to dose themselves, and increased the possibilities of mischief.[67]

The mortality statistics for England and Wales reported one accidental death from Veronal in 1906 and another in 1907; these figures rose to eleven accidental deaths and two suicides in 1909, and twelve accidents and three suicides in 1910.[68] 'Chloral, sulphonal, trional, veronal, paraldehyde', Clouston remonstrated in 1909, were 'sedatives that some of our people have got into the evil habit of using without sufficient medical reasons'.[69] In 1913 Veronal's German manufacturers, Bayer, cautioned against exceeding therapeutic doses, but many insomniacs had difficulty in abstaining from their soporifics, and consumed undesirable amounts. The sociologist Max Weber (1864–1920) overworked so ferociously as a Professor at Heidelberg that he came to reply upon barbiturates for both sleep and sedation. In 1913 and 1914 he went on rest cures at Lake Maggiore in Italy to break his habit, and suffered all the frustrations of an insomniac: 'The night was as usual, I lie thirteen hours in bed, sleep seven with breaks.'[70] Barbiturates were often used in conjunction with other substances. Virginia Woolf (1880–1941) attempted suicide with Veronal in 1913, extolled 'that mighty Prince with the moth's eyes and the feathered feet, one of whose names is Chloral' and suffered hallucinations apparently as the result of being prescribed hyoscyamine.[71] Marcel Proust 'half-destroyed' his memory 'by incessant medications', and confessed in 1913 to 'the abuse of veronal'.[72] He indulged in polydrug abuse: 'hasn't slept for a quarter of an hour for two days despite dial [a barbiturate for insomniacs], veronal, pantypon [an opiate extract]', he wrote of himself on one occasion.[73] He suffered an overdose—what he called 'a terrible poisoning'—in 1921, and ruined his health by these eccentricities.[74]

The English journalist and politician Charles Masterman (1873–1927) was a similarly self-destructive insomniac. He contracted the paraldehyde habit in an unavailing effort to conquer crippling insomnia after his reluctant resignation from the Cabinet in 1915. He confided in 1918 that 'he hadn't had a happy day for 19/20 years, and that the only thing that really bucked him up was winning an election' (he lost many more than he won).[75] In a letter of 1920 written from their holiday bungalow he beseeched his wife: '*Perald*, *Perald*, *Perald*, I have absolutely run out. Please send by train *immediately* you receive this, a bottle; and send down by post 3 or 4 more ... I must have some tomorrow. Nights are torture with neuralgia—meals of aspirin.' On Boxing Day of the same year he reproached her bitterly: 'You haven't sent down *Perald* you must by special train directly you receive this as I am run out. I oughtn't to be forced to these desperate plans.' By the early 1920s Masterman was consuming at least a bottle daily of this foul-smelling soporific, together with copious amounts of wine, sedatives such as bromide and valerian, and supposed stimulants such as strychnine and cocaine (ostensibly for hay fever). 'I really do get afraid of your killing yourself with this stuff,' his wife wrote in 1923. These self-medications, especially the paraldehyde, aggravated Masterman's depressions, which in turn hastened his death.[76]

Some sleeping-draught fatalities attracted considerable publicity. In the 'St. John's Wood Veronal Poisoning Case' of 1917 the English novelist Dame Ivy Compton-Burnett (1884–1969) found two of her younger sisters, Stephanie Primrose (aged eighteen) and Katherine (aged twenty-two) dead in bed together. 'Baby' and 'Topsy' had said that they were going away together for a holiday, but not hearing from them, Ivy and their housekeeper sixteen days later broke into the locked bedroom of the house that they shared with the pianist Dame Myra Hess (1890–1965). They had poisoned themselves with Veronal. A chemist deposed that his firm had supplied the Compton-Burnetts with four or five bottles during the previous six months, and had 'advised . . . that it was dangerous to take too much'.[77] Family life for the sisters had long seethed with aggression, possessiveness, nerve storms and spite, with Ivy recently replacing her mother as chief bully and tyrant. It is likely that the sisters killed themselves on Christmas Day in a furious grief at the desolation of their girlhoods; an open verdict was recorded. A month later, in January 1918, General Sir Beauchamp Duff (1855–1918) was found dead in bed at his club in St James's Square. Duff had been relieved as Commander-in-Chief of the Indian Army in 1916 after that army's advance on Baghdad had ended in the disastrous surrender at Kut.[78] Afterwards he became anxious, depressed and sleepless, but his son successfully quelled suggestions of suicide. 'Medical evidence showed that while Sir Beauchamp may have taken veronal recently in excess of the usual amount to induce sleep, he had not taken very large doses of the drug, which had extremely variable effects on certain people.'[79] Some doctors seemed almost insouciant about such fatalities. One of the cherished anecdotes of the royal physician Lord Horder (1871–1955) concerned an insomniac nobleman:

> Once I prescribed a change of sleeping draughts for a very old peer, telling him that with this new draught he might well wake up for a bit in the middle of the night; then he should take another dose and shortly he would fall asleep again. This duly occurred on the first night, and he got his nurse to measure him his second dose; as he dozed off again he turned comfortably on his side murmuring, 'I think this new stuff of Horder's is going to make a big difference to me.'
> He never woke again.[80]

Just as insurance companies in the 1820s had discriminated against opium-eaters, so the Yorkshire Insurance Company refused to pay when a Newcastle estate agent, Robert Smith (1870–1917), died of an accidental Veronal overdose a few months after insuring his life for £1000. The company resisted the claim on the ground that he had not disclosed on the proposal form that he had been taking the drug since 1911. One of the medical witnesses, Sir Farquhar Buzzard, testified that 'irritability, excitability and nervous prostration were characteristics of persons who took veronal. He would refuse a person for insurance purposes on the ground alone that he took veronal, largely because of the risk of an overdose—a very common incident.'[81] Business colleagues testified that Smith 'was a fine-looking, energetic, and clear-eyed man' who 'dressed smartly', although his partner admitted that two months before his death, 'his eyes were sunken and they had a glazed appearance. He asked Mr. Smith what was the matter, and he replied: "It is the drug." '[82] The death of Billie Carleton in November 1918 was probably caused by Veronal, although the newspapers made her name synonymous with cocaine. A month later the death by Veronal poisoning of Mary Elvira Boshell (1896–1918), a voluntary wartime nurse from a prosperous background, was widely publicised, though with less sensational overtones. Grieving for a fiancé who had been killed in action, she 'worked herself to death on the battlefield, and was suffering from shell-shock and internal strain', which led her to inject morphine and dose herself with Veronal obtained by a tampered-with medical prescription.[83]

The Home Office opened a file of newspaper cuttings on the Compton-Burnett, Duff, Smith, and Boshell cases, but took no action until 1923 when an MP, Sir John Ganzoni (1882–1958), afterwards Lord Belstead, suggested to the Home Secretary listing Veronal under the Dangerous Drugs Act. In justification he enclosed a short, scrappy note written by a prominent East Anglian doctor. According to this,

> More deaths have resulted from Veronal, taken in either an accidental overdose, or with suicidal intent, than from all other drugs put together, during the past 20 years . . . The 'Veronal habit' is not uncommon, it is easily acquired and it is far more dangerous to life than the Opium or Morphia habit, because in the case of Opium or Morphine, tolerance of the drug is quickly established, so that the habitual user cannot poison

himself unless he takes a very large dose, and accidents are not likely to happen. But with Veronal tolerance is only established to a very slight degree.[84]

The earliest Home Office reaction to Ganzoni's suggestion was that soporifics such as Veronal, chloral, paraldehyde and sulphonal acted 'without the phantastic dreams which are part of the attraction of opium', and were therefore not significantly 'insidious and attractive on account of superficial pleasurable sensations which they produce'.[85] However, the Home Officer's Medical Adviser, Sir William Willcox, who had trained as a chemist and only later qualified in medicine, had published an authoritative paper on veronal in 1913.[86] Willcox had commanded a high reputation since 1910, when his brilliant identification of hyoscine in the corroded remains of Belle Elmore clinched the murder conviction of her husband, Crippen.[87] He was temperamentally unsympathetic to those who yearned for deep sleep. ' "Wilks" was a prodigious worker,' recalled an admirer: 'an hour after midnight was the best time to catch him on the phone, but he was to be seen riding in the Park before breakfast'. His attitude to Veronal confirmed the same friend's tribute: 'slow to form opinions he stuck to them when reached with the tenacity of honest conviction'.[88] Willcox told Delevingne that 'the Veronal habit causes a complete disorganisation of the moral sense, just as is the case with the morphia and cocaine habits', whereupon Delevingne espoused the cause of its regulation.[89] Ganzoni's suggestion was challenged, however, by the Home Office's most senior official, Sir John Anderson (1882–1958), afterwards Viscount Waverley. 'Is there any evidence that it has caught on?' Anderson enquired in 1924. 'If not, is there not a danger that by bringing it partly within the scope of the D.D. Acts, we may only advertise it?'[90]

Willcox nudged his scheme forward, although barbiturate controls proved more controversial than Indian hemp prohibition. At a Home Office conference of 1924, he described 'the characteristics of Veronal addiction' as 'a mental condition similar to G.P.I. [tertiary syphilis], ataxic gait, tremors, hallucinations and suppression of the moral sense'. He insisted that 'continual veronal-taking' caused 'great depression', although other physicians present suggested that it was existent depressives who often turned to soporifics to treat their insomnia. There was no demur from Willcox's view that the 'sulphonal and chloral habits were now almost unknown'. A further conference was convened at the Home Office in 1925. A survey of 291 British physicians that year found seventeen reported cases of Veronal addiction, and ten cases of accidental or deliberate overdoses (of which about half were fatal). Willcox accepted that barbiturates 'did not create a craving as intense as the existing dangerous drugs', and that three or four weeks' abstinence brought recovery. But like Ganzoni, he thought the margin between safe and fatal doses was dangerously narrow, and asserted 'that a veronal addict would stick at very little to obtain the drug if his normal supply was cut off'.[91] For Willcox restrictions on barbiturates were an 'urgent' need.[92] Both the British Medical Association and the Pharmaceutical Society, representing pharmacists, resisted Willcox's initiative.[93] He did not launch a similar initiative against aspirin: the difference seems to have been that he did not consider aspirin-eaters were vicious, and that barbiturates, in a Home Office phrase of 1934, were among the drugs with 'news value'.[94]

Nevertheless barbiturates were restricted under the Dangerous Drugs Act in 1926.[95] Henceforth their supply by retailers was confined to medical practitioners, individuals with a medical prescription, hospitals, public institutions and individuals authorised by the Home Secretary. Barbiturates were not to be supplied more than once on the same prescription, unless the physician had filled out his prescription with not more than three repeats. Chemists could only legally supply barbiturates to individuals personally known to them, or introduced by known persons, after entering each transaction in their Poisons Register. Most chemists resented these formalities, and in 1934 a stunt journalist took only half an hour to buy from eight Central London chemists, without a doctor's prescription, 'enough of these poisons to kill seven persons'.[96] Barbiturates were supplied lavishly under medical prescription. Their use increased after a German physician's recommendation of them in 1926 as a preventive of travel sickness.[97] Within a few years, as F. Scott Fitzgerald (1896–1940) recounted, the stewardess on a civil airliner flying across the United States in rough weather might routinely ask a passenger, 'Dear, do you want an aspirin? . . .—or nembutal?'[98]

Drug regulations and laws were developing throughout Europe, but the mainsprings of action were not European. The sordid death in 1928 of the New York gangster Arnold Rothstein had loud repercussions on the world. He left documents incriminating members of the New York City administration, and other highly placed individuals; a Grand Jury investigation elicited that he had employed Levi Nutt's son as an attorney and his son-in-law as an accountant to negotiate his tax assessments with the US Treasury in Washington DC. The Grand Jury uncovered evidence that Nutt was responsible for inflating the figures for narcotics seizures in New York, where federal narcotics agents were arresting small dealers but letting off the bigger criminals. The presumption of collusion between narcs and racketeers resulted in March 1930 in the replacement of Nutt as head of the Narcotics Division by Harry Anslinger (1892–1975). Anslinger, who was of Swiss extraction, had been reared in small-town Pennsylvania. As a teenager he was (reportedly) shocked when the best pool player in town died of opium-smoking. His linguistic skills helped him to a job in the consular service, where his success in reducing rum-running from the Bahamas led to his appointment as Chief of the Foreign Control Division of the Prohibition Bureau. In June 1930 Congress abolished the Federal Narcotics Control Board, and transferred its responsibilities, together with those of the narcotics division of the Bureau of Prohibition, to a new Federal Bureau of Narcotics under the aegis of the Treasury Department. A distinguished admiral had already been nominated as the bureau's Commissioner, but Anslinger manoeuvred with such agility that in September 1930 he was given charge of the new organisation. The pursuit of oblivion, together with the pursuit of euphoria, changed for ever. But first we must examine the impact of American prohibition on the rest of the planet.

NINE

Trafficking

Idealism is a kind of sulking.
—PAUL VALÉRY

There are a few other vices besides drugs, but none of them is as decisive.
—PIERRE DRIEU LA ROCHELLE

AMERICAN IDEALISM STARTED the international campaign against drugs at the Shanghai and Hague conferences: in doing so, it also started a new form of capitalist enterprise. The USA and several European powers tightened their regulations after 1912, partly to satisfy treaty obligations, but also to restrict wartime drug use. Nevertheless, at the time of the Armistice in 1918, 'the supply of drugs for purposes of abuse', as Delevingne wrote, 'was in most countries not actually illegal'.[1] Post-war supervision of international drug regulations was allotted to the League of Nations, which after 1921 obtained increasingly strict controls. These controls created new opportunities to make money, and the increasingly strict regulatory system created new networks of international traffickers. Smugglers exploited the possibilities wherever regulations to restrict or suppress the import of drugs operated. Contraband drugs had been shipped into China in earlier centuries; but the drug prohibitionist policies sponsored by the Americans, and supported by other European powers, resulted in a global eruption of crime. 'Smuggling of dangerous drugs on a large scale is being carried out in many parts of the world,' Delevingne declared in 1926.[2] The 1920s thus provided prototypes for the global drug rackets of the rest of the century. It was a crucially instructive period. The cruel and enormously lucrative Colombian cocaine gangs of the 1980s, and the irrepressible illicit traffic of the early twenty-first century, had their antecedents in the 1920s. Initially illicit drug supplies seeped out from major commercial pharmaceutical companies, but by the 1930s clandestine laboratories had replaced them. Some individuals involved in the early supply were reputable businessmen; others were mischievous rebels who enjoyed transgression; but they were united in their determination to exploit the new market opportunities.

This account of the early history of trafficking begins with a great Swiss commercial dynasty. In 1894 Fritz Hoffmann (1868–1920), the difficult son of a successful Basle merchant, married another prosperous businessman's daughter, Adèle La Roche, and opened a small drugs laboratory that became known as Hoffmann-La Roche. He determined to produce quality pharmaceuticals stamped with a recognisable brand name for mass distribution in Europe and the US. A cough syrup laced with the delicious tang of orange was strenuously marketed, and yielded considerable profits. However, the loss of the Russian market after the 1917 revolution almost bankrupted the business, which was reconstructed as a joint stock company in 1919. During the next difficult years Hoffmann-La Roche needed to exploit every commercial opportunity. By 1925 the British government was so provoked by the company's supply of opiates to the Far East that Hoffmann-La Roche products were banned throughout the British Empire. This embargo was lifted when the Swiss government introduced a system of export controls in 1926. Delevingne disliked raising the embargo and itched for its restoration after the League of Nations alleged that 'large' amounts of narcotics seized by police in the free port of Hamburg 'came exclusively' from Hoffmann-La Roche.[3] In 1927 he told the Foreign Office that the firm's Paris branch had supplied 760 kilograms to an old customer, Strykowski, a Pole who had been convicted at Hamburg in 1925 of drug-smuggling. The Home Office alleged that Hoffmann-La Roche, and other Swiss businesses, were 'still supplying drugs to the illicit traffic', and urged that the embargo should be re-imposed.[4]

Hoffmann-La Roche's business became less objectionable during the 1930s. In 1934 Maja Hoffmann-Stehlin (d. 1989), widow of Fritz Hoffmann's son Emanuel, married Paul Sacher (1906–99), the son of a Basle forwarding agent and a seamstress. Having asked for a violin as his sixth birthday present after hearing Bach's *Passions* played in the cathedral, Sacher studied music in the local Conservatoire and founded the Basle Chamber Orchestra when he was twenty. Artistic interests drew Maja Hoffmann to him: she was a sculptor who became the patron of the French cubist Georges Braque (1882–1963), of Paul Klee (1879–1940) and of Marc Chagall (1887–1985). Sacher joined the board of Hoffmann-La Roche in 1936, and served as a director for sixty years. He became a dominant force in its activities after recovering the majority of the voting shares in a carefully executed *coup* during the mid-1940s. He was secretive but loved worming out the secrets of others. Seventy years after first mounting the podium, he held his farewell concert at the age of ninety with his friend Mstislav Rostropovich (b. 1927) as soloist. Other friends include Béla Bartók (1881–1945), Igor Stravinsky (1882–1971) and Pierre Boulez (b. 1925). Once listed as the third richest man in the world after Bill Gates and Warren Buffett, Sacher lavished money on expanding the repertoire, musical education and shrewd patronage.[5] His stepson Lukas Hoffmann (b. 1923) was a comparable ecological benefactor who established a major bird sanctuary in the Camargue. The Sachers used their money magnificently, but American officials mistrusted the source of the profits that paid for the cubist pictures, symphonies and endangered flamingos. 'Profits substantial will always be made / By Switzerland engaged in the drug making trade,' a member of the Federal Bureau of Narcotics versified. 'Hoffmann-La Roche will win in the end.'[6]

The Sachers kept their hands clean; those of other traffickers were sullied. The Frenchman Henry de Monfreid (1879–1974) also had an artistic background: he was the son of an American art-dealer who befriended Gauguin and also knew Verlaine and Toulouse-Lautrec. He settled at Djibouti in 1911 as a clerk for the merchant who had employed Rimbaud twenty-five years earlier, but soon repudiated the *petit bourgeois* morality of his compatriots. He decided that most Europeans 'live too artificial a life, run into the social mould, like one brick out of thousands for building a wall. As soon as a man resumes his individuality, as soon as he faces life as a free man, when he uses his will-power to stimulate his fighting instincts, he develops like a plant in fertile soil.'[7] He consorted with Danakil tribesmen, whose language he learned, discarded his job, became a Muslim, fished for pearls, ran guns into Abyssinia and romanticised criminals. 'It is only in the hell of a convict prison, when men have given up all hope of being able to exploit, enslave and oppress others for their own enrichment, that their thoughts turn to brotherhood.'[8] Around 1920 he began smuggling hashish. At first he 'didn't even know exactly what hashish was', he wrote. 'I knew only two things—that it was grown in Greece, and sold very dear in Egypt'.[9] He obtained his first consignment at Piraeus—using a priest as intermediary—and smuggled it via Djibouti and Suez. He realised the underworld he was entering. 'I should have to struggle now against cowardice, cupidity, trickery: a crooked fight.'The personal risk was high. 'If I failed it meant ruin. Goodbye to the sea and open air, goodbye to the life of freedom I so loved. I should be obliged to accept the slavery of some dreary job and become a domestic animal.'[10]

At this time the Egyptian labouring poor were smoking 20 to 25 tons of hashish annually. 'The young gentlemen with the fez think it is too vulgar a drug and prefer cocaine, a poison making great strides in this country,' de Monfreid was told by a Greek member of the gang he supplied on his first run.[11] He soon realised that he could bring pure resin (*charas*) from India without officials regarding it as contraband. It was his shipment of 10 tons from Bombay to Djibouti that first alerted the Home Office in 1923 to the beginnings of an international traffic in hemp drugs. As the world powers moved to prohibit drugs, he saw his chance to use Abyssinia as an entrepôt, both for the transit of drugs to Arabia, Egypt and the Sudan, and also for the purpose of 'breaking the scent' of those trafficked from Europe. An informant described him in 1927: 'about 45 years of age, height about 5' 8", slight build, long dark hair, artistic disposition with distinct ability as a watercolour painter and pianist, speaks some English. His wife is a tall, sturdy German with bobbed hair and an excellent knowledge of English.'[12] At Dire Dawa in the 1920s he ran the flour mill, macaroni factory and electric light system; he grew hashish in the surrounding province of Harar, exporting it through Djibouti in boxes of macaroni and flour. He also ordered morphine and cocaine under licence from Merck, which he sold on to traffickers, until in 1927, following pressure from the British government, instigated by Delevingne, the German Ministry of the Interior instructed that no further export licences should be issued to de Monfreid.[13] His activities were notorious, but as the British Minister in Addis Ababa lamented, his 'skilful arrangements and friends in official positions make it extremely difficult to bring his offences home to him.'[14] Finally, in 1933, he was expelled from Abyssinia. During his enforced retirement from lawlessness he wrote his elegant *La Croisière du Hachich* (1935) (published in England under the title *Hashish*), which is a first-rate source on trafficking. As an active supporter of Mussolini's colonial expansion, he was able to return to Abyssinia following the Italian annexation in 1936. His contempt for the European authorities was ineradicable. Describing the chaotic opening ceremony of Place Rimbaud in Djibouti in 1938, he asked with relish, 'Who can say that this wasn't the ghost of Rimbaud whistling like a wind of misrule among those official puppets who serve the mountebanks of international politics?'[15] After British forces restored Emperor Haile Selassie I (1892–1975) to power in 1941, de Monfreid was deported to Kenya along with Italian prisoners of war, and imprisoned. In 1947 he retired to France, settling at Indre-en-Berry, where he was detected cultivating a field of opium poppies. Among many other writings he published a sequence of eight novels entitled collectively *L'envers de l'aventure* (*The Other Side of Adventure*) (1953–64).

Companies like Hoffmann-La Roche and traffickers such as de Monfreid were representative types of suppliers during the 1920s. According to the prohibitionists the new drugs crisis of the twentieth century was the responsibility of these men. 'Drug addiction is, at the bottom, a matter of drug supply,' Delevingne declared in 1934. He regarded regulation of the retail sale of drugs together with the suppression of trafficking as the two effective ways to control supplies. With retailers controlled under the Dangerous Drugs Acts, 'traffickers' remained 'the most potent cause' of addiction. In furtherance of the ideal of total world suppression of non-medicinal drug use, the authorities initiated enforcement policies that proved counterproductive. Delevingne knew that traffickers flourished because there were big profits in illicit drugs:

The imperative nature of the craving, once induced, makes its victims prepared to pay anything and to sacrifice anything in order to obtain the

drugs, and the profits to be derived from large-scale trafficking are consequently great. As with slave trading or liquor running, the prospect of
such profits has been an enormous stimulus, and numerous organisations
with large financial resources, employing many agents and working
through many channels, have been unmasked and broken up during the
last dozen years.

Despite this knowledge, it was unthinkable for Delevingne to take the
money out of illicit drugs by abandoning the policy of prohibition. He
wanted the total extirpation of 'this soul and body destroying habit'.
When he cited conditions in China, Egypt and the USA to demonstrate 'the enormous harm that has been done', he meant the harm
inflicted by traffickers. He did not acknowledge that their profits
resulted from prohibition.[16]

The First World War, like the Prussian wars of 1866 and 1870, raised
European drug consumption. Shortly before her fatal veronal overdose
in 1918, Mary Boshell explained the origins of her morphine habit:
'The work she had to do as a nurse in France was so terribly hard that
the doctors used to give them drugs to keep them up; otherwise they
could not have done the work.'[17] The emotional intensity and physical
atrocities of battlefields and hospitals aggravated drug habits. An Englishman in 1924 described his soldier brother-in-law who had become
addicted to morphine after being treated for wounds received in trench
warfare: 'My poor friend is only one of thousands who today by their
maniacal ravening are fostering a traffic the ultimate fruits of which are
too hideous to contemplate.'[18] It was not only wounds that aroused
addictions. War also induced emotional splitting, Lady Dorothy Mills
suggested. 'It's curious, the psychological effect the war has had on
people. Half of them are being unbelievably good, working like galley-
slaves, wearing old clothes, going by bus; and the other half are going
on a bigger tear than they have ever done in their lives before.'[19]

The disturbance of post-war conditions both stimulated and facilitated drug-trafficking. 'An unexpected result of the World War is the
spread over Europe of the abuse of narcotics,' a Belgian medical correspondent reported in 1923. 'Before the war this was almost unknown
in Belgium, but at present more persons are engaged in illicit traffic in
drugs than ever before, and the number of drug addicts is constantly
increasing. Some persons attribute the situation to the large number of

foreigners in the country—diplomats, journalists, spies, officers'.[20] Herluf Zahle (1873–1941), who led the Danish delegation to the League conference on opium of 1924–5, urged fellow delegates to 'protect' the young 'against a peril . . . not unconnected with the economic and resultant disturbances resulting from the terrible disaster of 1914'.[21] Refugees and the dispossessed needed drugs to cope with what the war had done to their lives. One thinks of Aleksey Lvovich Luzhin, the broken *bourgeois* from St Petersburg in a story of 1924 by the Russian author and lepidopterist Vladimir Nabokov (1899–1977), who was himself exiled from St Petersburg and then living in Berlin. ('We don't print anecdotes about cocainists,' said the editor of the first magazine to which Nabokov submitted this early tale.) Luzhin has had no news of his wife since fleeing from the Soviet Union five years earlier in 1919. After toiling as a farm labourer in Turkey, a messenger in Vienna and a housepainter, he fetches up as a waiter in the international dining car of the Berlin–Paris express train. His grief and anxiety are unbearable without cocaine, and he always carries a

> little vial in his breast pocket. He kept licking his lips and sniffling. The vial contained a crystalline powder and bore the brand name Kramm. He was distributing knives and forks and inserting sealed bottles into rings on the table, when suddenly he could stand it no longer . . . He locked himself in the toilet. Carefully calculating the jolts of the train, he poured a small mound of powder on his thumbnail; greedily applied it to one nostril, then to the other, inhaled; with a flip of his tongue licked the sparkling dust off his nail; blinked hard a couple of times from the rubbery bitterness, and left the toilet, boozy and buoyant, his head filling with icy delicious air.[22]

Although the outbreak of war in 1914 delayed the ratification of the Hague Convention, several European powers nevertheless tightened their drug controls in this period. Britain's DORA and Dangerous Drugs Act had Continental counterparts. Under new Spanish regulations of 1916, for example, the sale of *medicamentos* was confined to prescriptions supplied at pharmacies, with stricter regulations covering ether, cocaine and morphine.[23] Enforcement was tightened, too. The French physicians Maurice Courtois-Suffit (b. 1861) and René Giroux reported fifty-three prosecutions in France for the illegal possession of cocaine in 1916 and 212 prosecutions in 1921.[24] Under a French law enacted in 1922 all persons found guilty of having 'facilitated' the use of toxic drugs, whether by providing premises for consumption or as suppliers, were liable to between five and ten years' imprisonment.[25]

It was 'due primarily to the crusading, generous and cocksure America of the pre-depression era, to the America of the "Noble Experiment" of Prohibition' (to quote a French observer) that the enforcement of the Hague agreements was referred, under the Versailles treaty, to the League of Nations.[26] The Social Questions and Opium Traffic Section was established in 1919 under Dame Rachel Crowdy (1884–1964), a formidable young English administrator who had been Principal Commandant of nursing volunteers in France and Belgium during the war. In 1920 the League appointed an Advisory Committee on Opium and other Dangerous Drugs. The Netherlands, Britain, France, India, Japan, China, Siam and Portugal had permanent representation on this committee. League officials and advisers worked to obtain the ratification of the Hague Convention by additional nations: the Hague Convention of 1912 had twelve original signatories; by 1921 thirty-eight states had become parties; and by 1934, fifty-six. The League also coaxed and cajoled member states into the adoption of a certificate system whereby no government would allow the export of dangerous drugs from its territories except on production by the exporter of a licence from the importing country, certifying that the drugs were required. There was some insincerity among its member states. As a British diplomat minuted in 1926, 'the Japanese Government have not the drug traffic really at heart, at least up to the H[ome] O[ffice] standards— but then few Governments have, except the American, whose zeal is sometimes embarrassing. Perhaps the Japanese consider their participation in Opium Advisory Committees . . . as part of the proof of their being "grown up" rather than as a burning moral question.'[27] The isolationist US had declined to join the League, but from 1923 US observers attended and intervened in the Advisory Committee sessions. This anomalous situation was recognised as a sign of American ascendancy. Writing of European decadence in 1926, the French poet Paul Valéry (1871–1945) predicted: 'Europe will be punished for her policy. She will be deprived of wine, beer, and liquors. And other things . . . Europe aspires to be governed by an American committee.

Her entire policy is aimed toward that end. Not knowing how to shake off our history, we shall be delivered from it by happy peoples, who have none or next to none. It is the happy peoples who will impose their good fortune upon us.'[28]

Although Bishop Brent attended League meetings on behalf of the USA, the most important American in international drugs policy of the 1920s was Stephen Porter (1869–1930), a lawyer who had served as a Republican congressman from Pennsylvania since 1910. Porter was Chairman of the House Foreign Affairs Committee from 1919 until his death, and highly sympathetic to Chinese aspirations. Otherwise he was an isolationist who mistrusted the League of Nations as a superstate. The British Embassy in Washington reported that Porter 'is supposed to hold very anti-British sentiments, particularly in regard to the restriction of opium growing, in which he takes a deep and almost fanatical interest'.[29] Like many prohibitionists he likened his cause to that of Lincoln and the abolitionists. 'We were cursed in America for over a century and a half by a form of human slavery,' he declared at Geneva in 1925. 'It took a great war that almost destroyed our Republic to suppress it. Opium is only another form of slavery.'[30] Viscount Cecil of Chelwood (1864–1958), who negotiated with Porter as leader of the US delegation to the Opium Conference of 1924–5, found him 'a typical American Congressman, perpetually on his guard against the wiles of European Diplomacy'.[31] Porter's attitude even to Delevingne was 'distinctly cool'.[32] The Dutch delegation equally disliked the congressman. 'Mr Porter never took the pains to explain his own point of view or even to reply to the arguments of his opponents.'[33]

The first phase of the Opium Conference, which opened at Geneva on 17 November 1924, was concerned exclusively with opium-smoking; it was confined to Far Eastern nations and powers with Far Eastern colonies in which such smoking was permitted. The second phase, which opened on 19 January 1925, was reserved for derivatives of opium and coca (especially heroin and cocaine). Many of the thirty-six national delegations were keen to impress newspaper readers back home with their ideals. Yet the majority of participants held that total suppression could not be enforced while illicit supplies remained uncontrolled. Instead they resolved that the system of 'farming out' the supply of opium to private (usually Chinese) contractors should end, and that government monopolies together with registration of licensed smokers should be imposed to regulate opium consumption more strictly. Lord Cecil of Chelwood officially declared that opium-smoking in British Far Eastern territories would be abolished within fifteen years of the date on which Chinese measures to suppress opium cultivation were effective enough to remove the danger of opium-smuggling from China.

In January 1925, at the resumed conference on manufactured drugs, from the remit of which opium-smoking was excluded, Porter proposed a requirement that nations in which opium-smoking was still permitted should reduce their non-medicinal imports in annual instalments to achieve complete suppression in ten years. This disruption was resisted by the European powers. 'The American authorities have taken up this attitude', the *New Statesman* suggested, 'partly because of their ignorance of the facts, partly because of their puritan tradition—which excuses and even exalts such ignorance—and partly because they want to find some scapegoat for their own failure to prevent the rapidly increasing use in the United States of derivatives of Chinese opium.' Their posture was baffling. Perhaps they were 'playing to the gallery of puritan sentiment in America . . . but probably they really do not know that there is a difference between Chinese opium and Indian opium, and between the chewing of opium and the injection of heroin'.[34] This view was universal among European delegates. The Netherlands' senior representative at Geneva in 1925 described the American position as 'destructive idealism'. Dutch officialdom thought that US government attitudes were inappropriate given the drug habits of their own citizens. 'Only by raising the moral level of the population can the American people rid itself of this deep-seated evil,' the Netherlands' Ministry of Labour commented in 1926.[35] The US proposals for world prohibition of heroin and for strict control of the cultivation of coca leaves were also rejected. (The Bolivian delegate successfully argued that the habit of chewing coca leaves 'has neither the contagiousness nor the attraction which characterises all vices'.)[36] Porter led the US delegation in a walk-out on 6 February when he could not prevail over the Europeans' pragmatic scepticism.[37] Next day the Chinese delegation also decamped. After the Americans' departure, there was a virulently anti-British reaction among US journalists, who attributed Porter's defeat to imperialist greed for drug profits. In fact Indian opium was not strong enough to be used for American heroin, which was manufactured from smuggled Persian, Turkish and Chinese opium or supplied in manufactured form from Japan, Switzerland and Germany. As Lord Olivier (1859–1943), a recent Secretary of State for India, observed in 1925, Indian opium was a bugbear with 'politicians hostile to the League of Nations and to Great Britain for the purpose of demonstrating the futility of the League and the bad faith of this country'.[38] American newspapers, commented a British diplomat, 'slurred over the facts about all the smaller countries', such as Bolivian coca production or Serbian poppy cultivation, 'in order to concentrate their attack on us'.[39]

Despite this disruption, the conference produced a Convention committing the contracting powers to control the manufacture, sale and transport of dangerous drugs, and to report annually the quantities manufactured, consumed and held in stock, together with quarterly reports on imports and exports. Governments thus accepted responsibility for the legitimacy of their import and export trade, and established the means for detecting the diversion in transit of drugs by a system of compulsory import certificates and export authorisations. A Permanent Central Board was established at the League to supervise the necessary statistical controls. The Danish President of the proceedings described it as 'the most difficult Conference in the history of the League of Nations'. It was the longest and most complicated hitherto. Over two million sheets of paper were roneoed and distributed for nearly seventy days of sessions. 'The drugs question', he declared, 'is now caught in the day-to-day machinery of the League of Nations. It cannot escape.'[40] The Convention became operative in 1928, and by 1932, according to League statistics, the amounts manufactured by licensed pharmaceutical factories for the first time approximated to the amounts required for legitimate use. Western European factories ceased to be the chief producers of drugs for the illicit traffic. The quantity of licit morphine manufactured in the world fell from 46,106 kilograms in 1928 to 25,656 in 1932; heroin from 7810 kilograms in 1928 to 1315 kilograms in 1932; and cocaine from 7200 kilograms in 1928 to 3973 kilograms in 1932.[41]

The US withdrawal, and Porter's subsequent block of American participation in the League's narcotics policy-making, deprived his country of a position that many of its citizens felt it had established in drugs policy since 1909: hegemony. This dismayed such compatriots as

Colonel Arthur Woods (1870–1942), the former Police Commissioner of New York who succeeded Elizabeth Wright as American assessor on the Opium Advisory Committee. Woods judged that undue emphasis had been laid on opium-smoking, opium-eating and coca-chewing. These practices 'might or might not be deleterious, but were confined, in fact, to Indians, Chinese and Bolivians respectively, and consequently did not raise any question of international importance'.[42] The American journalist and social worker John Palmer Gavit (1868–1954), who also regretted Porter's walk-out, welcomed in 1927 a chance 'to restore . . . Uncle Sam to the place where he belongs, in the leadership of the war against narcotics'. Like Woods he thought this chance lay in accepting 'that opium-smoking is a relatively small and negligible affair as compared with the overwhelming tide of manufactured drugs which is flooding the world, including China and India, out of the pharmaceutical laboratories of the western countries, more particularly Germany and Switzerland'.[43] The British, however, judged in 1927 that 'so long as Porter dictates the Opium policy of the U.S. Government we are not likely to get a change for the better'.[44] The US boycott of Geneva was enforced until Porter's death in 1930.

Some European powers were reluctant to enforce the import and export regulations to which they were committed. The French were remiss until the intervention of Aristide Briand (1862–1932), winner of the Nobel peace prize in 1926.[45] Briand held the portfolio of foreign affairs during a crucial phase of 1925, and again from 1926 until 1932. According to the story that Delevingne heard at Geneva, 'Briand, who then represented France on the League, when he became aware of what was happening in France, declared emphatically to the authorities at Paris that it "had got to stop".' France, which had been 'very slow to move' on drugs controls, became energised in the late 1920s.[46] Switzerland, too, was tardy in fulfilling its international commitments. The influence of investors in the Swiss pharmaceuticals sector was blamed for delays in ratifying the Hague Convention. As a British diplomat wrote in 1925:

> I once lived in Switzerland as a Swiss among the Swiss (in so far as it is humanly possible to live as a Swiss) and . . . my impression was that the great fault of Swiss public life—counter-balanced, as I know, by many virtues—is the politico-economic corruption, on the American plan,

which seems to run right through it. The big 'interests' (in the American sense) have so much power over the Government, and this is so notorious, that it is not surprising that people outside Switzerland are very suspicious of Swiss intentions in matters which may affect the pockets of those 'interests'.[47]

The European nation that most firmly resisted American prohibition was the kingdom of the Netherlands. Dutch society was confident and united in the 1920s: the country had not fought in the World War, and maintained high levels of social and economic equilibrium afterwards. The Dutch Opium Act of 1919 (passed in accordance with the Hague resolutions) outlawed the production and trade in patent medicines containing opium and cocaine. But the Dutch authorities were unimpressed by both the absolutist beliefs and tactics of American prohibitionists. Professor Westel Willoughby (1867–1945), who advised the Chinese delegation at the Conference of 1924–5, thought that remarks of the Dutch representative at Geneva were 'tinged with bitterness' when he spoke of 'American idealism' and the US determination 'to impose its will' on other nations' drug policies.[48] After the Dutch criminalised possession of opium and cocaine in 1928, to comply with the Geneva resolutions, their police did not pursue users, and tolerated small-scale dealing. Dutch drug laws were not seen as penal legislation but as a means to regulate the production and distribution of substances. Just before the Netherlands government imposed a certificate system for drug imports and exports in 1928, one million kilograms of coca leaves were dispatched from Amsterdam's warehouses: nevertheless in 1931 they still held enough stocks to supply European cocaine needs for five years. In the inter-war period cocaine-sniffing was supposed to be prevalent among prostitutes and seamen, especially in Rotterdam (which contained the largest Chinese community in Europe). There was both smuggling by sailors and illicit supply by pharmacists. Users were not put through the punitive withdrawal cures favoured in the USA. Physicians in the Netherlands enjoyed considerable social prestige, and their right to determine the treatment of their patients was recognised as inviolable.

The belief of many Geneva experts that governments must control manufacturing was accentuated by several scandals after the 1925 Convention. During eighteen months of 1927–8 a Dutch company called the Chemische Fabriek Naarden, which was licensed by its government to manufacture and trade in drugs, was able, through defects in the control system of the Netherlands, to export under misleading descriptions 3000 kilograms of heroin, 950 kilograms of morphine and 90 kilograms of cocaine (mainly for the Far East). Its malpractice was revealed when 60 kilograms of heroin (concealed in a box shipped from Antwerp in Belgium destined for China) was discovered when the ship passed *en route* through the port of Rotterdam. After investigation, the Dutch authorities concluded that Naarden had not breached any Dutch laws, although it had ducked and dived under numerous regulations. The Naarden scandal had a French counterpart. 'The Factory of Roesler & Fils' was described in 1927 by an agent of the Cairo City Police as 'one of the most dangerous firms' exporting clandestinely to China and Egypt, in the latter case either directly or via Greece and Constantinople.[49] The factory was situated at Mulhouse, in eastern France, only twenty-one miles from Basle. During 1926 Roesler legally supplied 200 kilograms of heroin worth 2 million francs to a Pole resident in Vienna, Josef Raskine, 'who appears to be the worst type of adventurer and probably in Soviet pay'. Raskine persuaded Ghulam Nabei, Afghan Minister in Paris, to ship the heroin from Marseille to Constantinople, and thence to India, in diplomatic baggage. The Marseille customs authorities became suspicious, and the Afghan sent the heroin to Belgium, from whence it was reconsigned by the Gare du Nord in Paris. When difficulties were made about handing over the case to the Afghan envoy's dragoman, the Minister sharply left for Moscow.[50] The League regulators established that in three and a half years to June 1929, Roesler exported 6414 kilograms of heroin and 943 kilograms of morphine. Other major European manufacturers supplied the illicit traffickers more discreetly. One ruse was to convert morphine into 'esters' such as benzoyl morphine, which were not forbidden under any diplomatic conventions, and later to reconvert the esters into addictive substances.[51] The League, in a careful estimate, stated that between 1925 and 1930, 72 tons of legally manufactured morphine escaped into the illicit traffic.

The Naarden and Roesler cases, together with continuing suspicions about Swiss malpractice, determined League experts to limit drug supplies by imposing maximum levels of licit production for each manufacturing nation. Initially France and the Netherlands resisted such schemes so as to protect their pharmaceutical manufacturers. At the Geneva Conference on the Manufacture of Narcotic Drugs of 1931 there was opposition from the leading trafficking nation, Japan, supported by two governments protecting their poppy-cultivators, Turkey and Yugoslavia. Finally, despite serious national divergence, the Limitation Convention of 1931 introduced a quota system. Each signatory country was required to furnish annual advance estimates of the drugs needed for medical and scientific purposes. These estimates were scrutinised by a supervisory body of four government experts, who determined the maximum amounts to be imported or manufactured in any year by each country and issued an annual statement of estimated world requirements of dangerous drugs. By 1934 all manufacturing countries except Yugoslavia had ratified the Convention. Restrictions were also placed on codeine (chemically derived from morphine) and other recently discovered synthetic opiates, which by the late 1920s were being trafficked. Despite these achievements, the 1931 Conference results seemed 'very meagre' to Delevingne.[52]

The traffic in drugs had in the recent past been only a localised problem, but was swiftly being turned by market forces into a world problem. This was reflected in the fact that whereas Levi Nutt of the US Narcotics Division had never organised undercover overseas work, Anslinger as the first Commissioner of Narcotics started an international intelligence network in 1930. US narcotics agents were stationed in Paris, and had regular contacts with European policemen. These new arrangements soon resulted in the destruction of an international gang. In April 1931 a Russian-Greek named David Gourevidis (b. 1899) quarrelled with Anasthasios Eliopoulos (b. 1897), a Greek describing himself as a *banquier*, in whose Paris apartment he was living. Gourevidis denounced Eliopoulos and his two brothers, who belonged to a Piraeus trading family, to the French authorities for drug-trafficking on a huge scale since 1927. The eldest, Elie Eliopoulos (b. 1893), who sometimes used the alias of Eric Elliott, also lived sumptuously in Paris. The US narcs were swift to join the investigation, forwarded crucial information to the British, Dutch and other governments, and as a result Elie Eliopoulos was expelled from France. In a related move, a New Yorker named August ('Little Augi') Del Gracio (b. 1895) was detained when the Simplon Express reached Berlin from Istanbul in

November 1931. He was carrying papers revealing further ramifications of the network. Sir Thomas Russell (1879–1954) of the Central Narcotics Intelligence Bureau in Egypt thought that most European traffickers were of low calibre.

> From all that I was told by American police and narcotics officers, when over there in 1923 and subsequently, it is clear that gang discipline in the States was extremely severe and spilling the beans or any disloyalty by a member of a gang brought quick retribution by knife or gun. The Levantine drug smugglers, on the contrary, were a low class crowd with little toughness or discipline among them. Double-crossers or squealers for the most part, they soon viewed each other with so much mutual mistrust that the business became seriously affected.[53]

Traffickers were helpless without the cultivators of coca leaves and opium poppies. The world's cocaine came from the coca of Latin America and the Dutch East Indies. In 1900 Peru was the world's largest exporter of raw coca (supplying about one million kilograms annually). It was also the world's leading cocaine producer supplying 10 metric tons of cocaine (mainly to France, Germany and the USA) in 1905. A modernising landowner in the Huánuco region, Don Augusto Durand, hoped that licit cocaine production would remedy Peruvian economic retardation. He rationalised coca-growing, built a laboratory for the extraction of crude cocaine and recruited Croatian immigrant staff. In addition to his own operations, Durand was the intermediary in 1917 when the agents of a Japanese company, Hoshi Pharmaceuticals, bought nearly 3000 square kilometres with the intention of growing coca and supplying cocaine. This initiative, however, faltered after the collapse of Hoshi Pharmaceuticals in a Japanese scandal of 1921. It proved increasingly difficult for Peruvian production to compete internationally with Dutch exports from colonial Java; Peruvian producers also suffered as the USA restricted and then forbade coca imports. By the time of Durand's murder in 1923, Andean coca production was reverting to its traditional market of Indian locals.[54] Other Latin American countries produced coca. Bolivia exported 388,170 kilograms of coca in 1925, mainly to Germany. The British envoy in La Paz reported after conferring on coca with his US counterpart in 1926:

In the mines and on railway and road construction the Indians knock
off twice during the day for an hour to roll their coca, and it might
almost be said that this plant is one of their permanent staple foods . . .
Coca is a mild intoxicant that stimulates the consumer and enables him
to support great fatigue, but there is little question that its effects
in the long run must be deleterious, if not bodily at any rate mentally.
Physically the Indian is sturdily built and does not appear to have
deteriorated, but mentally the majority appear to be below the average
intelligence of an animal, say an ape, to which they have a strong like-
ness in their features, in fact the Bolivian Indian is the nearest approach
to the Darwinian theory of the missing link that can be found, and I am
inclined to attribute their mental torpitude to generations of coca
chewing.[55]

Although coca continued to be chewed in Argentina, Chile prohibited
its import in 1926.

More systematically than the Bolivians, Dutch colonists during the
1890s experimentally planted some 500 acres in Java with coca with
which to supply German manufacturers. In 1900 the Nederlandsche
Cocainefabriek (Dutch Cocaine Factory) was opened in Amsterdam,
and became by 1910 the world's largest single cocaine-manufacturer:
Amsterdam supplanted Hamburg as the world's coca trade centre. During the war leading European cocaine-manufacturers cut prices in successful attempts to increase demand, but in peacetime cocaine prices
plummeted as the result of overproduction. The European Convention
of Cocaine Producers signed in 1924 by Nederlandsche Cocainefabriek, Hoffmann-La Roche and the Germans C. F. Boehringer Söhne
and Merck was intended to stabilise prices. Cocaine-producing companies in Britain, France and Germany declined to join the cartel. They
apparently balked at the likely purpose of the cartel's output: as the
medical use of cocaine fell in the 1920s, so increasingly the cartel's production was used for mischief.[56]

The cultivation of poppies was more geographically dispersed than
coca. This was more than ever the case after the Viceroy of India
announced in February 1926 that his government would reduce pro-
gressively the export of Indian non-medicinal opium in ten annual
instalments: such exports would cease altogether in 1937. This decision
was partly reached under Home Office pressure: Delevingne resented

the export of Indian opium to French Indo-China because officials there were not 'above-board' in their drug dealings.[57] Already a quarter of Persian exports and one-twelfth of state revenue rested on poppy cultivation; but as Indian opium exports fell, demand rose for alternate supplies from Persia. European attitudes to Persian opium cultivation were generally complaisant. In 1913 the colonial administrator Sir Arnold Wilson (1884–1940) visited a sultan in Luristan. 'He was a man of middle age, a thorough and heavy opium smoker, was a clear thinker, a good talker and a man who knew how to command obedience. We took coffee, tea and light refreshments in proper order, and discussed in conventional terms the prevailing disorder, the price of wood and . . . the relative virtues of the Mauser and Lee Enfield rifles.'[58] During the 1920s, as resident director in Tehran of the Anglo-Persian Oil Company, Wilson defended opium usage. He considered that 'the existence in Western countries of a few weak-minded drug addicts is a poor excuse for undermining by harassing legislation . . . the Persian race'.[59] Persia became increasingly important as a supplier of opium for Far Eastern consumption. A key figure in this traffic was Hassan Nemazi (b. 1860?), a British subject of Indian origin, who lived successively in Hong Kong, Bombay and Shiraz.

Nemazi's 'Opium Ring' controlled Persian opium sales to the Far East.[60] Even before the Viceroy's declaration, the opium exported from the Persian port of Bushire was worth £664,340 in 1922–3 and £1,246,433 in 1923–4. Nearly half of these exports were declared for Russia, from whence the opium was dispersed through the Far East.[61] During the 1930s, until the outbreak of war, there were large shipments from Bushire to Japan, where the opium was manufactured as heroin.

The Viceregal declaration of 1926 created a great marketing opportunity for illicit Chinese opium supplies as well. It became harder to regulate official programmes to reduce habitual opium-smoking. 'India's impulsive gesture, which earned such easy applause at Geneva', complained the financial adviser to the Siam government, Sir Edward Cook (1881–1955), in 1927, 'is making more difficult the task of those governments of opium-smoking countries which are genuinely trying to bring the habit under effective control.' Illicit opium, mainly from China, 'is pouring into Siam, partly by sea and partly from the north', Cook reported, and 'sells vastly cheaper than licit opium'. This traffic had forced Siam to postpone its scheme to register opium-users and ration their supplies, and was corrupting officials.[62] Further repercussions of the Viceroy's announcement were summarised by a diplomatic observer in 1927: 'Hong Kong, being next door to China, is flooded with illicit opium, which it would need a huge and costly preventive service to exclude even partially ... the smuggling of illicit opium [has] ... attained outrageous proportions. As smuggling grew, convictions grew, until the gaols were filled with "artificial criminals".'[63] The deterioration in ten years was marked. 'Hong Kong is the centre of a highly organised international traffic in raw and prepared opium,' Lord Talbot de Malahide (1912–73) reported in 1937. 'The opium situation in Hong Kong is appalling. On the one hand no raw opium is grown there, nor does the government manufacture any prepared opium. Although there is a government monopoly on the sale of prepared opium, there are only 1,194 licensed smokers and no licensed smoking establishments. On the other hand it is estimated that there are nearly 3,000 illicit divans, in about half of which heroin pills are smoked.' Divans, or 'dens', had been prohibited since 1910 in Hong Kong. Among a population of about one million (98 per cent Chinese), there were an estimated 24,000 heroin-users and 40,000 opium-smokers. In 1936 3,600,000 heroin pills had been seized alone. The prisons could not cope.[64]

Apart from Persia and China, other sources of opium were developed after the Viceroy's pronouncement in 1926. Drug-traffickers centred their onslaught on the Balkans: Serbia, Turkey and Bulgaria successively enjoyed a vogue in poppy cultivation. The 1924 opium output from South Serbia (in what was then called the kingdom of the Serbs, Croats and Slovenes) was about 38,400 kilograms; that for 1925 nearly double. Serbian poppies had a 13 per cent morphine content, compared with 9 per cent in Asian opium, which made them highly desirable to traffickers. Poppies were a popular crop with peasants because harvesting occurred when they were least busy with other agricultural work. Moreover, harvesting was suitable for women and children, returns were quick, and if the crop was wiped out by a hard winter, it was possible to recoup with a spring sowing.[65] The Serbian poppy crop was sold to French and Salonikan merchants. Around 1924–5 a French company, Comptoir Central des Alcaloides (whose moving spirit was a Belgian named Paul Mechelaere), bought land in south Serbia for poppy cultivation.[66] Eventually (Yugoslavia having delayed its ratification of the 1931 Limitation Convention) a factory at Hrast-nik began exporting in 1932.

European and Japanese traffickers also betook themselves to Turkey (which was not a signatory of the Limitation Treaty), where abundant supplies of raw opium were freely available. A Japanese-financed factory established at Constantinople was producing ten kilograms of heroin daily in 1927. This was up to ten times the amount legally produced in Britain.[67] The Turkish Chamber of Commerce urged in 1929 'that the gradual suppression of poppy-growing in India, gives Turkey the opportunity of making her opium supreme in the European markets'.[68] A Turkish official admitted that in the first six months of 1930 over 2 tons of morphine and over 4 tons of heroin had been exported, almost wholly to European destinations, without authorisation from the governments of the importing states (as required by League regulations). By the early 1930s there were three factories at Istanbul each capable of producing up to 2000 kilograms of heroin monthly. In addition to the Japanese outfit, two French operations had transferred there. Much of the 251 tons of Turkish opium imported into France in 1928 had been destined for two factories near Paris working preponderantly for traffickers. One of these factories belonged to Paul Mechelaere's Comptoir Central des Alcaloides. The other manufacturer was the Société Industrielle de Chimie Organique (known as 'Sido') controlled by Georges Devineau. They freed suppliers of narcotics to the USA, Egypt and the Far East from relying exclusively on 'leakages' from such factories as those at Naarden and Mulhouse. In 1930, after the withdrawal of Devineau's licence by the French government, he set up an alternative factory at Kusdundjuk, a northern suburb of Istanbul on the Asiatic coast of the Bosphorus. Shortly afterwards Mechelaere set up the Etkin factory at Eyub on the Golden Horn. He collaborated with Eli Abuisak (b. 1899), a Turk who had trafficked on Italian vessels of the Lloyd Triestino line. To protect them from blackmail by Turkish customs officials and shipping companies' employees, the Frenchmen hired strong-arm protection from a Corsican, Paul Venture, alias Carbone, who was a gang-leader in Marseille.

There were arrests in 1931 following a spirited denunciation at Geneva by Russell, the English chief of Egypt's Central Narcotics Intelligence Bureau, of the French factories in Turkey, and strenuous representations by him during an official visit to Ankara and Istanbul.

The US Ambassador, Joseph Grew (1880–1965), was informed in 1931 that the Turkish government 'had decided immediately to seal up these factories providing opium derivatives as well as all stocks of the manufactured product now on hand.'[69] Henceforth exports from those factories were prohibited without documentary proof of destination and government permits. The League was asked to list foreign traffickers operating in Turkey: as a result both Devineau and Mechelaere were deported in October 1931. The diplomatic pressure was maintained by Grew's successor as Ambassador, General Charles Sherrill (1867–1936). He convinced the Turkish ruler, Mustapha Kemal Atatürk (1881–1938), 'that not only was Istanbul becoming a menace to the health of the world but also that local addiction was spreading among the officer class of his own army'.[70] As a result the illicit traffic was targeted under a programme enacted in 1932. However, twenty years later Anslinger declared of Turkey, 'There is uncontrolled production of opium, and no control of distribution. Almost every shop in the opium growing centers sells opium. There are many clandestine heroin laboratories.'[71]

In neighbouring Bulgaria, the area under poppy cultivation rose steadily during the early 1930s. Bulgarian opium output increased from 800 kilogams in 1932 to 5000 kilograms in 1933. The first factory for manufacturing opium drugs opened near Sofia in 1932, and within a few months four other rival factories were built. In addition, there were at least four clandestine establishments.[72] The Bulgarian heroin factories centred on Sofia could satisfy over twice the world's legitimate needs. However, after two years' delays, Bulgaria adhered in 1933 to the Limitation Convention, and introduced licensing and regulations that cut opium profits. A member of the FBN travelled from Washington DC to Sofia in 1934, and increased pressure on the Bulgarian government.[73] When the last Bulgarian factory closed in 1938, the League could finally claim to control licit European production of opiates. As Dame Rachel Crowdy concluded, 'It was international control and not prohibition which lessened the international traffic.'[74]

Japan and Taiwan (which became the first Japanese colony in 1895) were also important sources of manufactured drugs.[75] Taiwan's Chinese population had entrenched opium habits, which the conquerors viewed with apprehension as likely to corrupt the rest of the empire. However the politician Gotõ Shimpei (d. 1929), who had trained in

Western medicine and studied in Germany, successfully recommended the legalisation of opium in Taiwan accompanied by a registration system for addicts and licensed opium shops. Gotõ devised a colonial system for Taiwan and later Manchuria in which opium monopoly revenues contributed to the costs of military occupation. He also encouraged the career of a peasant from Osaka, Nitanosa Otozõ (b. 1875), who was licensed to cultivate opium poppies in the home islands and became known in the 1930s as the Opium King. Private entrepreneurs, notably Hoshi Hajime (b. 1880), became involved in these initiatives. Hoshi had studied politics at Columbia University in the 1890s and translated Herbert Hoover's *American Individualism* (1922) into Japanese. As an admirer of the 'American Way' he included a canteen and ice-cream parlour in his seven-storey headquarters of concrete and glass. Around 1910, determined to oust German firms from their supremacy in the Japanese patent medicines business, he launched Hoshi Pharmaceutical Company. Next, he determined to supplant the Germans in the Japanese morphine business. He befriended both Gotõ and Nitanosa, and made a fortune from a state morphine franchise until a smuggling scandal in 1921. With the destruction of Hoshi Pharmaceuticals' influence, smaller producers began making heroin and morphine (mainly for supply to China). Hoshi and other Japanese heroin manufacturers used *rõnin* (soldiers of fortune) as distributors. Many of them had close contacts with the Japanese military. The Japanese clandestine traffic became notorious. The American expert Herbert May reported in 1927, 'That Japan can regulate her manufacture if she will is abundantly evidenced by her ability to keep her own people comparatively free from the evil and to control smuggling into the country where it is her interest to do so.'[76] It was Japanese policy to keep the price of opium for licensed Formosan smokers 'very low', as their delegate explained at Geneva in 1924: 'Smokers could thus obtain what they needed . . . and smuggling was discouraged because it was not profitable . . . Too high a price meant the smuggling of opium and its illicit smoking. This contention was proved by facts. In Hongkong, for example, the price of opium was four times higher than in Formosa, and the smuggling which went on in that port was on a very large scale.'[77]

A reactionary Japanese colonel named Yashimoto, who controlled the superpatriotic Cherry Blossom Society, subsequently conspired to use drug-dealing profits to fund a secret and deadly plot. In September

1931, at the instigation of staff officers of Japan's Kwangtung army, a small explosion occurred on the Japanese-run South Manchurian Railway, just north of Mukden. This incident became the pretext for Japan's seizure of Manchuria from China, which in turn was the prelude to the establishment of the puppet state of Manchukuo. Under Japanese army protection, drug-traffickers swiftly infiltrated North China. In 1934 Nitanosa Otozõ, the old Opium King from Osaka, surveyed the new Japanese dependency for suitable areas for poppy cultivation, and recommended the Antung region of Fukien province. After 1936, a protégé of Nitanosa supervised further poppy plantations in Jehol and Mongolia. The Manchukuo government opium monopoly developed illicit manufacture and trade as a matter both of profit and racial strategy. 'The use of narcotics is unworthy of a superior race like the Japanese,' the Kwangtung army handbook told Japanese soldiers. 'Only inferior races, races that are decadent like the Chinese, Europeans, and the East Indians, are addicted to the use of narcotics. This is why they are destined to become our servants and eventually disappear.'[78] This policy degraded the people of Manchuria, and was extended to other Japanese centres of power in China. In the late 1930s a European visitor to the Japanese concession in the treaty port of Tientsin saw a typical transaction at one of the 'while you wait' narcotic dispensaries, a sort of counter opening on to the street. An addict ordered his drug from the attendant within, rolled up his sleeve, thrust his bared arm in after the money, received his shot, and went on his way.[79] As Sir Thomas Russell wrote shortly after the Second World War,

by 1939 we had seen the Drug Barons chased from Switzerland and France, then from Turkey, the foreign settlements of China, and lastly from Bulgaria. One country only was left to them and there, I hope and believe, they met with bigger rogues than themselves. Japanese-occupied China soon became, and continued to be, the only country of the world where the increase of drug addiction was a studied government policy. Year after year at Geneva we had to listen to the specious talk of the Japanese delegate: year after year the American delegation and the C.N.I.B. gave chapter and verse showing the state of things in Manchukuo and China north of the wall, but to no effect. Japan had decided upon heroin addiction as a weapon of aggression and deliberately converted the territories she conquered from China into one huge opium farm and heroin den.[80]

The Colonial Office in London, and its administrators in the East, disliked both League policy and Home Office assertiveness. Their criticisms, which amounted to a rejection of the American model of punitive drug laws, were neither cynical nor irresponsible. They were convinced that prohibition was impossible to enforce, stimulated corruption and created a new criminal underclass. The Colonial Secretary, Leopold Amery (1873–1955), declared in 1927 that the administrations in Malaya and Hong Kong felt 'much anxiety at the multiplication of punishable offences' intended to repress opium-smoking. Eastern opium-smoking had 'little or no connection' with the heroin problem in Europe and the US, 'save in so far as the suppression of opium encourages and increases the demand of Orientals for these far more dangerous drugs'. The results of imposing the Geneva policy would be 'the crowding of the gaols, the banishment of numerous persons who are in no other way a danger to the Colony, the nourishment of a parasitic class of informers, the prevalence of blackmail, the corruption of Government servants and the evils attendant on the inevitable system of payment of rewards to informers'. This combination would be 'disastrous'.[81]

Before the First World War British colonies in the Far East had ceased farming out their opium monopoly to Chinese syndicates and substituted a government monopoly of preparation and distribution. During the 1920s these colonies still depended financially on opium. In 1925, 37 per cent of tax revenue in the Straits Settlements (now Malaysia) came from opium; 24 per cent in North Borneo; and 21 per cent in Brunei. Nevertheless, by 1925 as much illicit opium (mainly Chinese) was consumed as government opium. In the Straits Settlements a rationing system was introduced in 1920 whereby opium supplies to retailers were reduced by 10 per cent of average monthly sales of the previous year. This experiment caused such hoarding, profiteering and rowdiness that it was abandoned after a few months. A new initiative of licensed opium shops, registration and rationing was introduced in 1926. Sir Laurence Guillemard (1862–1951), Governor of the Straits Settlements, reported from Singapore in 1927: 'There is not, in Malaya, any "opium evil" calling for drastic or hasty remedy. The consumption of it does little harm and some good. Of course there are cases of excess, just as you have cases of delirium tremens in England; but they do not lead to crime or lunacy. The smoker simply atrophies and goes quietly out'. Given the length of the coastline, 'the whole British fleet could hardly hope to stop smuggling'. Prohibition was bad policy anyway. 'Severe restrictions on opium . . . would convert over a million peaceful Chinese, on whose labour depends the prosperity of this most important colony, into bolsheviks.' Restrictions would also stimulate alcohol-related crime. 'Even the better class Chinese drink far too much out here, and with the lower classes drink is at the bottom of most of our crime and disturbances.'[82]

The policeman Herbert Robinson (b. 1896) described corruption in Burma. Habitual smokers there were licensed to buy a fixed monthly amount from government shops. New licences were hard to obtain; the intention was that as registered smokers died off, there would be no further registration, and eventually total prohibition. But opium bought from government shops was resold to the black market, and smoked by unregistered users with police complicity. If the proprietor of an opium shop stinted in his bribery, the police would raid his premises, and confiscate the opium pipes should unlicensed smokers be discovered. As Robinson explained, older opium pipes were valued for thick accretions of residue inside the tube. If old pipes were taken in a raid, the proprietor would hasten to the police station, pay his arrears, and collect the bundle of pipes. For show, he would bring an equivalent number of new, valueless pipes, which were publicly burned. In 1924 Robinson was smoking in an opium shop called the House of the Deer when it was raided. 'An amazing thing happened. All those quiet and apparently comatose smokers in the adjacent room rose from their platform, padded swiftly through the room in which I was lying and so out into the night. I heard the splintering of wood and, looking out through the door leading to the courtyard, saw that the bamboo fence was no longer there. It had fallen flat before that stampede of startled humanity.' He then saw a smiling policeman standing in the room waiting for his bribe. 'What amazed me more than the complacency of the police was the panic of the opium-smokers,' Robinson wrote. They were unlicensed: 'Had they been caught and detained their source of supply would be automatically cut off', so 'it was not terror of the police that had lent wings to their feet but something far more terrible'.[83] Corruption was not peculiar to the Far East. De Monfreid recounted in detail the techniques by which Middle Eastern customs officers and coastguards enriched themselves from contraband drugs.[84]

The post-war international regulatory system ensured that the boldest traffickers made the biggest fortunes. As a type they never sheathed their claws when raking in wealth. 'Prohibition will always have the effects of prohibition whatever it may forbid the public to do,' a Greek merchant from Constantinople who became a trafficker around 1920 mused. 'The law will not kill the demand and the same class of adventurous men, not saints perhaps but men who can take a risk, will be found to supply the customers with what they want and are ready to pay for.'[85] World events as well as prohibition policies favoured their special brand of enterprise. The European War had been pursued to the extreme enfeeblement of its contestants, whose resources were consumed in the firing lines. It destroyed the imperial regimes of the Romanovs, Hapsburgs and Hohenzollerns, and the resultant instability created new opportunities for dealing in contraband drugs.

Trafficking by both Soviet officials and exiled White Russians in the Far East was a consequence of the disintegration of the Romanov Empire. The population of Harbin, the chief city of Heilungkiang (Heilongjiang) province in central Manchuria and strategic centre of the Manchurian railway system, rose from about 40,000 inhabitants in 1911 to 332,000 twenty years later. Five railways converged on the city, and the refugees who had been sluiced out of Russia after the revolution of 1917 soon recognised that it was a perfect entrepôt for trafficking. Moreover, the British Consul at Harbin reported in 1927, 'Soviet officials arriving from Russia carry a large quantity of various drugs, as also do officials of the Chinese Eastern Railway Company who travel in service cars.' Drugs were secreted in hidden panels, or under firewood for heating carriages in winter, and were also smuggled through the free port of Dairen (Ta-lien).

> Russian women, especially Jewesses, are largely employed in moving the goods from place to place; they are well paid and receive commissions on the amounts carried . . . The white Russian soldiers recruited for General Chang Tsung-chang . . . travel on military passports and thus evade Customs examination. Although their meagre pay is always months in arrears, they are noted for their lavish expenditure in the

night clubs of Harbin . . . The retail trade is mostly carried on by Japanese medicine shops . . . The Central Hotel at Dairen is a den of smugglers. It is owned by a Russian Jew named Lerner who is a go-between for sellers and buyers of narcotics and gets a commission on the deals which he puts through. His agent in Harbin is another Jew named Stavitsky, a former proprietor of the hotel who was deported by the Japanese in 1921 after several convictions for trafficking in drugs. The wealthier dealers have rooms at the Yamato Hotel, whence they direct the movements of the traffic. There are also a number of small hotels run by Russian Jews at Changchun in the South Manchuria Railway area which are used as meeting places for the traffickers and the Chinese Eastern Railway Company's conductors and car-tenders, where goods are entrusted to the latter for safe delivery to Harbin.

The Russian-born police chief, according to the British consul, derived 'a good income from watching and catching small traffickers of drugs; he mercilessly bleeds his victims and makes them pay up large sums as hush money'. A shoe store proprietor amassed a fortune from handling Persian opium, which reached Harbin from Russia. After diversifying into morphine and cocaine, he was in 1926 kidnapped and ransomed.[86] When Dairen became riskier for traffickers, shipments were diverted instead through Newchang (Ying-k'ou), a city port in Liaoning province. Korean communists, according to a British consul, supplemented their funds by smuggling opium grown near Vladivostok. As the German authorities became stricter in examining exports to the Far East, France became an increasing source of drugs.[87] During 1928 a Russo-Japanese drugs combine began operations in Harbin after ensuring that the Japanese wharf police, the Chinese Maritime Customs at Dairen and the Harbin police were all 'squared'.[88]

The Hapsburg Empire, like the Romanov, was destroyed by war mobilisation. Its capital, Vienna, suffered perhaps more than any other great city in the aftermath of the disaster that ended in November 1918. Vienna was transformed from the centre of a proud empire into the capital of an impoverished state with six million inhabitants. 'Austria', wrote an English visitor in 1921, 'is like a crab that has shed its shell.'[89] The currency of the truncated state was traumatically devalued in 1922. The fugitives from the eastern ghettos of Galicia and the Ukraine, who had settled in Vienna, were well adapted by their former hardships to surviving these troubles. According to the French financier Baron Harry d'Erlanger, these manipulators, with their 'smattering of two or three languages and a superficial knowledge of how to dodge in and out of the clumsy paragraphs of a code of laws', found drug-trafficking a 'glorious opportunity'.[90] A police raid in 1924 unearthed proof that one dealer alone had supplied 501 kilograms of morphine to Hungary, a quantity sufficient to anaesthetise all Central Europe. Although Austria's annual medical requirements for morphine were about 60 kilograms, licensed apothecaries and wholesalers had received 210 kilograms, which suggested that 150 kilograms had either been 'snuffed' in Austria or re-exported. The Vienna police knew of 200 cocaine-users in their city.[91]

The wreck of the Hohenzollern Empire was as destructive as the fall of the Hapsburgs. Germany, like Austria, endured a terrible post-war inflation accompanied by material suffering and ethical decline. Pharmaceutical companies such as Merck had productive capacities that outstripped domestic demand. Consequently, the smuggling of dangerous drugs from German factories was a major problem during the Weimar Republic. As Delevingne wrote in 1926, 'Germany is very far from having clean hands in the matter of illicit traffic in drugs; but the use of forged labels on an extensive scale (many of them appear to emanate from Japanese sources) gives the German government and manufacturers a means of defence.'[92] The New York trafficker Ike Berman boasted in 1931 about his work for Arnold Rothstein a few years earlier: 'We used to bring back a million dollars of junk from Merck's factory in Berlin,' he crowed. 'I once went there with a hundred thousand dollars of Rothstein's dough and sixty thousand of my own, and went to the main connection of the factory.'[93] It was satisfying to Anslinger 'that the Nazi regime bore down heavily on the addict, and had the situation pretty well in hand'.[94]

In 1926 an English member of the League's Advisory Committee, reported that 'vast fortunes' were being made from smuggling Swiss morphine into the US in electric bulbs, the stuffing of chairs, chocolates and toilet preparations.[95] The Swiss exported 95 per cent of their production of morphine and cocaine during the 1920s. One of the shadier participants in this trade was a US citizen, J. Willickes Macdonald. In 1919 Macdonald was based at The Hague, from whence he shipped drugs to the Far East via the free port of Copenhagen. Relocating at Freiberg, he supplied arms as well as drugs. After German government investigations, Macdonald settled near Basle in 1924.[96] He 'smuggled to Hong Kong and Shanghai in a series of consignments disguised as Sulphide of Soda and Carbolic Acid, drugs manufactured by Hoffmann-LaRoche', sometimes 'packing them upon the premises of that firm'.[97] His activities persisted for several years. 'We have just received word from one of our agents', Delevingne informed the Foreign Office in 1926, that 'Macdonald, the notorious drug smuggler . . . is at present making arrangements for the despatch of a quantity of opium and morphine to the Far East. The drugs will probably be concealed in consignments of Calcium Lactate and clocks.'[98] Despite regulations imposed by the Swiss government in 1926, it remained easy to obtain morphine in Switzerland. During the 1930s the couturier Gabrielle ('Coco') Chanel (1883–1971) and the flamboyant patron of avant-garde art and music Misia Sert (1872–1950) used to travel from Paris to Switzerland regularly to get morphine. For Chanel the drug was a 'useful sedative' while Sert craved the oblivion of forgetfulness. As they looked chic and calm in their train compartment, their vice remained a secret.[99]

The Allied occupation of Germany facilitated the contraband drug trade. 'French and allied soldiers became traffickers, tempted by the immense profits that the Germans held out to them,' the physicians Courtois-Suffit and Giroux reported in 1921. Stricter vigilance by the Parisian police meant that cocaine-traffickers moved south to the ports of Marseille and Toulon, the coastal holiday resorts of Nice, Monte Carlo and Biarritz, as well as into the Alsace-Lorraine border region. 'It is not rare to see members of the *demi-monde*, reduced to a state of frenzy, exchange their jewels and furs for the powder that inebriates.'[100] Employees like Nabokov's Luzhin on the express trains of the Compagnie Internationale des Wagons-Lits and troops from the French occupation of the Rhine were couriers. One kilogram of cocaine (colloquially called *poudre folle* or *respirette*) was then selling in France for 1300 francs (US $106); one gram for 20 or 30 francs (25 francs was the equivalent of £1). A profit of 20,000 francs could be made on every kilogram. As to the drugs exported from France, US narcotics agents discovered that in the first eight months of 1931, Eliopoulos's organisation received £250,000 (the equivalent in 2000 values of £4–5 million) from a Greek based in the French Concession at Tientsin.[101] Illicit drugs for domestic users were secreted in counterfeit wristwatches, medallions or double-bottomed powder cases. Some dealers sold tangerines with a supply of cocaine; others supplied artificial flowers containing within their petals a tiny pouch enclosing the drug. Drop points might be a drinking fountain, the seat of a parked taxi or lavatory compartments.[102]

The Third Republic's attitude to its citizens' drug habits could seem complaisant to Anglo-Saxons, but might as easily be called realistic. Policing and regulations were not fanatical, although the existence of an estimated 80,000 French regular drug-users (mainly cocaine and morphine) encouraged opportunistic journalists to indulge in ritual vilification on occasions. The case of Lazare (nicknamed 'Siber' or 'Lola') Kessel (1900–1920) is instructive. He was a brilliant young actor of Russian-Jewish origin whose family settled in France after the 1917 Revolution. He was 'an exquisite being', recalled a friend. 'To live, he often said, to live in order to pursue a desire and not attain it—what's the use?' In 1920, having just won first prize in competitions held by the Musical Conservatory, he shot himself in a Left Bank hotel. 'His suicide became the symbol of all that was morbid and vitiated in the spirit of his generation,' according to a recent account. 'The right-wing press picked up the story of Lola's suicide and, in a series of editorials that made up for in viciousness what they lacked in evidence, attacked his character. Lola was accused of winning his prize high on cocaine, of using morphine, of alcoholism, homosexuality, and a degenerate aestheticism. "Everything that's against nature pleases these young neurotics," wrote *La France du Nord*. "We shouldn't send them to the Odéon, but to a mental hospital." '[103] Lazare's elder brother was the political reporter and adventure novelist Joseph Kessel (1898–1979). 'Jef' had an omnivorous appetite for drugs, sex, bondage, gambling and other kinds of extreme excitement. The youngest brother Georges Kessel was nicknamed 'Smoke'. As editor of a crime magazine, *Détective*, he embezzled a fortune to cover his debts to bookmakers and cocaine-dealers. When he crashed his car in 1931 after partying on cocaine, his leg had to be amputated, and during post-operative treatment he became dependent on morphine. The celebrity of these unfortunate men was tied to drugs, which from the 1920s were an increasing preoccupation of journalists seeking stories of unbridled hedonism and its satisfying punishment.

Tamara de Lempicka (c. 1895–1980) was another Russian exiled after the revolution of 1917 who settled in Paris, where she prospered as a portrait-painter. She smoked three packs of cigarettes daily, used valerian as a sedative and gin to deaden her feelings. Her evenings were spent at smart parties, but as her biographer describes, she preferred rough trade.

> Her sexual drive stoked by a near constant supply of cocaine, she would make forays to the hastily constructed dirt-floored lean-tos that dotted the Seine's banks. Here shabby clubs harbored heavy drug use and rough sex among a rough assortment of types, including sailors, a few college students, male and female, and one or two upper-class society women . . . Tamara refused to kiss or be kissed during such episodes. Her favorite sexual activity was to be caressed over her very colorful, very excitable nipples and genitals by a beautiful young woman, while she performed similar activities on the most handsome sailor in the group. After such nocturnal stimulations, she returned home full of confidence and insight—and cocaine—and in a near frenzy painted until six or seven A.M. After several hours of sleep . . . she resumed her daily routine of art classes and café socializing, before preparing to begin her night life anew.[104]

During nights spent in Montmartre cabarets during 1925, the London nightclub owner Kate Meyrick realised that 'the drug evil' had 'a deadly hold upon the *demi-monde* there . . . cocaine and other forms of "dope" were peddled almost without concealment. Over and over again I saw it changing hands.' In her experience drugs were more destructive of women: she knew several men who 'had taken cocaine or other drugs for years, yet in many cases it did not appear to have affected them greatly'.[105]

A sense of the Paris drugs scene is given in *Le Feu Follet* (*Will o' the Wisp*) (1931), the heroin novel of Pierre Drieu la Rochelle (1893–1945), which in 1963 was adapted into a film directed by Louis Malle (1932–95). The novel charts the self-destruction of a user, Alain, who is susceptible to bad company. 'Always he found himself back with the same group of idlers. They began to do drugs because they have nothing else to do and continue because they cannot do anything else.' Even when Alain is detoxified in a clinic, heroin controls him. 'Drugs had changed the colour of his life, and when they seemed to be gone, this colour persisted. All that drugs had left to him of life was now impregnated with drugs, and led him back to drugs.'[106] His fellow users are wheedling, spiteful and deceitful. The French courtesan Liane de Pougy (1869–1950), Princess Georges Ghika, glimpsed this way of life when in 1931 she visited opium-addicted Jean Cocteau (1889–1963) in 'a foul slum' at Toulon. Cocteau's *petit ami* Liou 'opened the door of a sordid room, letting out a strong whiff of the drug ... Jean was lying on the floor, covered with a disgusting bedspread, behind a horrid filthy bed. His voice was deathly, dull, dry, hoarse . . . He had a three-day beard and his clothes were in disorder, dirty and crumpled ... "O poor Jean, poor Jean," I said, obsessed by that painful image of decay.'

The singer Félix Mayol (1872–1941) had recently told the princess that Cocteau '*wears badly*'. Mayol 'with those words ... was trying to say it all'.[107] Cocteau's friend Misia Sert also wore badly. Of Polish-Russian origin, she befriended Mallarmé, Toulouse-Lautrec, Renoir, Bonnard, Vuillard, Ravel, Poulenc, Satie and Stravinsky. She pestered Debussy on his deathbed, was a witness at Picasso's wedding and devised the idea of L'Eau de Chanel from a concoction of Empress Eugénie. Marcel Proust made her the model for Princess Yourbeletieff in *À la Recherche du Temps Perdu*. Her third husband was the Catalan interior decorator, José-Maria Sert y Badia (1876–1945), who used cocaine, as did her friend Diaghilev; so in time did she. When Sert became infatuated with a young princess, and their marriage disintegrated in the late 1920s, she took to morphine. Her privileges, she assumed, would protect her from public exposure. She disdained to hide her habit: while talking at parties, or out shopping, she would yield to her craving, and jab a needle through her skirt. By 1939 her health was broken. When her name was found on a dealer's list, she spent twenty-four hours incarcerated in a filthy cell. This humiliation pitched her into a final downward spiral. Broken in spirit, more dependent than ever on morphine, she trembled when unexpected callers came to her door. She neglected food and clothes. The English art historian John Richardson (b. 1924) visited her in 1947 'in her ornate apartment on the Rue de Rivoli—all mulberry-coloured velvet and rock crystal, dud El Grecos and bits of good Boulle'. He found her 'overwhelmingly awful' in old age, 'addicted to morphine, which she obtained through her morphinomane attendant, a heavily made-up waif of a man called Boulos Ristelhueber. The two of them seemed to have moved, ahead of time, into one of hell's grander suites.'[108]

De Monfreid wrote that 'For love of smuggling the Greeks are the first nation in the world'.[109] The Eliopoulos Paris-Greek group did not have to use conjuring tricks in their trafficking, but trusted for safe delivery to generous bribery.[110] European traffickers of the 1920s were defeated as much by their own parasitic followers as by police work, according to Russell.

> As the big dope gangs prospered, others wished to enter the business and share the profits, but it was not too easy without big capital. The smaller groups, like fish attracted by the smell, swam about near the dope factories of Europe to pick up what information they could and soon developed a good system of blackmailing the big fish. Sometimes, they would demand cash for their silence or sometimes a proportion of drugs for their own trafficking, but the cost of this racket grew and was a contributory cause to the eventual break-up of the big gangs.[111]

Elsewhere, in Latin America, trafficking developed in response to US prohibition. Chile, reported the British consul at Valparaiso in 1926, had become 'the centre of an extensive organisation for the distribution of Opium throughout America.' Traffickers based at Valparaiso 'live on an extravagant footing from their earnings. These men do a very large business through crews of ships plying between the United States of America and Chile'. When US naval ships had recently visited the port, large amounts of opiates were sold to seamen. Traffickers asked at least $1000 for each kilogram of opium.[112] The arrest at La Paz in 1926 of Samuel Kong, a Chinese gangster who trafficked in opium in the Argentine, Chile and Peru, only briefly disrupted the traffic.[113]

A scam in Central America showed that the League's supervisory system of certificates was not inviolable. During 1933 France and Germany allowed the export to Honduras of 76 kilograms of morphine, although the country had a population under one million and (according to official estimates) legitimate needs of only one kilogram. The French and German authorities were bamboozled by import certificates, which the Honduras government later declared to be false, 'but it should have been obvious that such large consignments could not have been wanted for any legitimate purpose', as Delevingne expostulated.

'How the very competent officials in charge at Paris and Berlin allowed the consignments to pass is beyond my comprehension.'[114] This was at a time when there was much Honduran civil unrest, including abortive revolutions against the dictatorship of General Tiburcio Carías Andino (1872–1969). Honduras was doubtless the 'Central American country' mentioned by Anslinger that imported 'a supply of narcotic drugs sufficient for one hundred years'. US investigators established 'that narcotics were leaving that country and were being smuggled into the United States in exchange for arms and ammunition which were being sent for use in a revolution. When the Director of Health of the country then refused to issue licenses for the release of narcotics, he was assassinated.'[115]

Diplomatic passports were used to protect drug couriers. Carlos Fernandez Bacula, successively Peruvian Consul at Vienna and Oslo, was able to pass his luggage through customs unopened, and on six trips took a ton and a half of heroin into the USA through Miami, Montreal and other points of entry. In August 1928 for a fee equivalent to £750 he took 150 kilograms of heroin manufactured by Röesler to New York. There he handed the drugs to Wilhelm Kofler, who had been sent from Vienna to meet him. 'On the very next day Kofler's body was found by the police; his wrists had been slashed open with a razor and he had been left to bleed to death.' The heroin has vanished. A New York mobster named Jack ('Legs') Diamond (d. 1931) was suspected of organising this interception and murder (Diamond was similarly suspected of killing his boss Rothstein three months later).[116] There were also State Department allegations of Soviet involvement in trafficking.[117] In response to these trends, a League of Nations Convention for the Suppression of the Illicit Traffic in Dangerous Drugs was signed in 1936. It stipulated that drug offences should be included as extradition crimes in future treaties negotiated between the contracting powers. In countries where extradition was not recognised, the powers undertook to prosecute nationals who returned home after committing drug offences abroad. A central office to supervise the prosecution of international traffickers was established. This Convention, which came into force in 1939, had been ratified by nineteen countries in 1952. However, the United States refused to sign because the Convention only covered manufactured drugs, and excluded trade in and distribution of raw drugs and opium-smoking. Anslinger inexplicably claimed that 'the Convention would weaken . . . the efforts of the American government to prevent and punish narcotics offences.'[118]

Child drug-users began attracting attention during the 1920s. The diplomat Sir Robert Hodgson (1874–1956) reported from Moscow in 1926 on 'the prevalence of the cocaine habit among the waifs and strays of the Soviet Union'. There were 50,000 waifs in Moscow and its outskirts. He cited Soviet newspaper reports that from 50 to 80 per cent of homeless children sniffed cocaine: between 3 and 5 grams daily, at 5 roubles per gram, cost up to £2. 10s. The 'child cocainists', according to a Muscovite newspaper, lived 'by begging, singing in the tram cars . . . but their fundamental trade is stealing. There are murderers amongst them. One can hear them say: "When one has 'sniffed' one does not feel blows. I always 'sniff' before going to work; it gives me courage." '[119] The director of Moscow's anti-narcotics and anti-alcohol campaign took Sir Bertrand Jerram (1891–1971) on a tour of the clinic for child drug-users in 1926. Jerram's findings were summarised by a colleague among the British government representatives in Soviet Russia:

> During the first few months the whole personnel had had to be changed several times owing to their maltreatment by the children. The building has been sacked and the children had escaped on several occasions, and it was finally decided to start with only five children, and after they had been tamed, to introduce another five and so on until the full complement of twenty-five was reached—a manoeuvre which proved successful. Children usually reach the dispensary upon being arrested on some charge or other. All are dextrous pickpockets or exponents of other anti-social habits. Only boys are admitted; the oldest inmate was aged fourteen years. Mr. Jerram was provided by the doctors and attendants with revolting pathological and sexual details regarding individual urchins of nine or ten . . . The doctor could only state that they are mostly of proletarian origin and that the 'Russian proletariat is horribly poor'; he admitted that no such evil existed in the old days . . . The children in the dispensary appeared well cared for . . . One had rather the impression that each was a specimen rather than a human being, but this attitude towards one's fellow man is common enough in Soviet life.[120]

Elsewhere, children were born addicted, too. An English missionary at Kernan in Persia in the mid-1920s saw 'an infant of 3 or 4 months in a state of collapse, as she thought, from some serious illness. The child was livid in colour, and looked as if it could not survive more than a few hours. Just then the mother came up with her opium pipe and puffed smoke into the infant's face which at once revived it. If the child survived, there was literally an opium addict from birth.'[121]

These stories were ghastly; but worse degradation was found in Egypt, where heroin became the drug of choice during the 1920s. Egyptians went 'one better than the riff-raff with their hashish or the sensation-snobs with their cocaine; they had taken with idiotic unanimity to the worst and most virulent of modern chemical poisons', as Baron Harry d'Erlanger wrote.[122] This Egyptian disaster ran counter to experiences elsewhere in the Middle East. Henry Law (1883–1964) of the Foreign Department of the Indian government, studying opium habits *en poste* at Kernan in 1925, saw 'faint signs that the habit is beginning, just beginning, to lose ground here. It is now considered not altogether good form to be seen smoking opium in a public restaurant; and those who chose to have a quiet pipe after their cup of tea do so at the back of the shop in modest privacy. The opium pipe is still an essential part of the household furniture, always kept at hand for the guest who may need it. But now it is often kept out of sight in case those should see it who disapprove.' These changing attitudes followed the Tehran government's disapproval of the habit.[123] But in Egypt official anti-drugs propaganda had less effect on feelings or behaviour. The case of Egypt deserves special scrutiny.

Contemporaries attributed Egypt's problems to its cosmopolitan population, notably 'Levantines', a term denoting Christians from Syria or Europeans from Levantine provinces of the former Ottoman Empire.[124] Many inhabitants of Egypt were the 'protected subjects' of European powers: individuals born in Tunis or Tripoli were classed as French or Italian; Cypriots and Maltese were British citizens; many residents in Alexandria came under Greek consular protection. This was crucial because all Egyptian civil cases involving European nationals, and cases in which foreigners were accused of misdemeanours, were tried in the Mixed Courts, which had been established in 1876. These were Egyptian law courts in which the majority of judges were nominated by the foreign powers from among their own citizens. Europeans tried for misdemeanours in the Mixed Courts were subject to derisory penalties. All criminal charges against foreigners were tried by a Consular Court of the nation to which they were subjects; there were wide variations in the conduct of these courts, and their attitudes to drug trafficking. Sir Thomas Russell, who was a policemen in Egypt for over forty years, opined that 'had it not been for the protection that the foreign traffickers derived from them, the narcotic problem in Egypt would never have reached the magnitude it did'.[125]

The story of Egyptian drugs policing in this period is epitomised by Russell Pasha. He was a cousin of the Dukes of Bedford, and entered the Egyptian government service as one of the Alexandria coastguards in 1902. Later, as Inspector of the Ministry of the Interior, he visited every police post in Egypt except two: one high up the Nile and the other on the western desert frontier. He was appointed assistant commandant of the Alexandria police in 1911 and promoted to commandant of the Cairo police in 1917. 'Tall and commanding, a sportsman, a dandy, a horseman who made history by riding his camel over fences, as much at ease in his wife's salon as in any desert company, ready for any discomfort on an ibex trail but a *bon viveur* in town, finding humour in everything and friends everywhere, Russell was a legend,' according to a contemporary.[126] He understood men's motives but was never blasé. In the first phase of his command of the Cairo police, he was preoccupied with political riots and assassinations, but never lost sight of the traffickers.

It was in 1916 that cocaine began to make its first appearance in Cairo, to be followed later by the pleasanter and more potent heroin, but there was little we could do at that time when trafficking or possession was a mere contravention with a maximum penalty of £E1 [£1 and sixpence sterling] or a week's imprisonment. The pioneer of the sale of heroin in Egypt [in about 1920] was a Cairo chemist [a Greek subject], who soon had a nightly queue of high-life carriages waiting outside his pharmacy. I twice entered his shop and while buying some medicine or other, watched the fashionable drug being handed over the counter to the gilded youths of the town. At this time the inspection of chemists' shops was outside police competence and repeated failures by the Public Health authorities to convict this popular chemist began to arouse my suspicions. It was not long before others coveted these profits, and the

A Voyage into Eternity (1830s). *Wellcome Library, London.*

ng Room at East India Company's opium factory at Patna (1850). *Wellcome Library, London.*

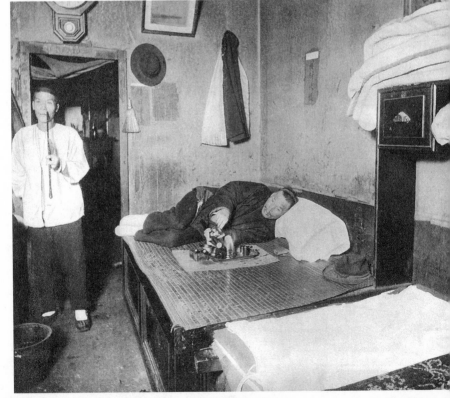

COCAINE
TOOTHACHE DROPS
Instantaneous Cure!
PRICE 15 CENTS.
Prepared by the
LLOYD MANUFACTURING CO.
219 HUDSON AVE., ALBANY, N. Y.
For sale by all Druggists.
(Registered March 1885.)   See other side.

Advertisement for cocaine, which was widely prescribed for medicinal purposes in the latter part of the 19th century. *National Library of Medicine.*

posite page above Mixing and *ing* opium at Calcutta (1900). *llcome Library, London.*

posite page below Opium den in *Francisco* (early 20th century). *llcome Library, London.*

Below Turkish opium fields (1930).

Above Harry Anslinger of the
Federal Bureau of Narcotics with
some intercepted contraband.
Pennsylvania State University.

Right Anti-drugs leaflet (1930s).

Beware! Young and Old—People
All Walks of Life!

This ■ may be handed you
by the friendly stranger. It contains the Killer Dr
"Marihuana"—a powerful narcotic in which lur
Murder! Insanity! Death!

WARNING!
Dope peddlers are shrewd! They ma
put some of this drug in the
in the or in the tobacco cigarett

Address: THE INTER-STATE NARCOTIC ASSOCIATIO
53 W. Jackson Blvd.
Chicago, Illinois, U.S.A

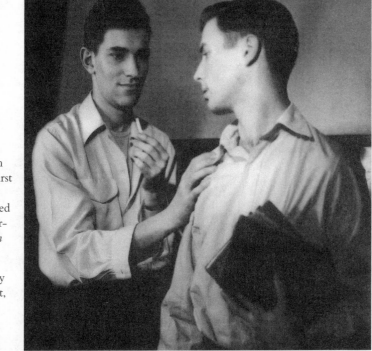

Brenda Dean
(centre), the first
h celebrity
t, photographed
a court appear-
(1933). *Hulton*
e.

H – the Story
eenage Addict,
nerican anti-
film (1950s).
n Archive.

Left Dr John Petro. *Hulton Archive.*

Below The Isle of Wight pop festival (1970). *Magnum Photos.*

Opposite page above Cocaine (1980s). *PYMCA.*

Opposite page below
Children playing with crack
vials in Philadelphia (1980s).
Magnum Photos.

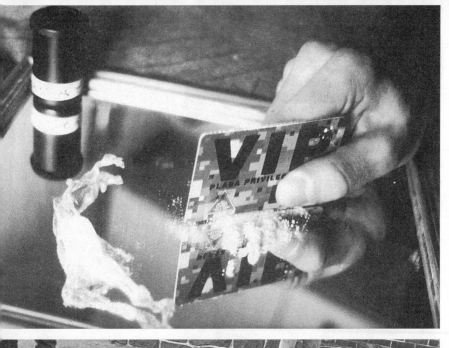

Two popular anti-drug posters from the 1980s, British (*top*) and American (*bottom*). *Advertising Archive and the National Library of Medicine.*

numbers of purveyors and addicts continually increased. Prices in those days were comparatively low, a shot only cost a few shillings, and the trade, wise in its generation, kept the price down until the vice had spread and caught large numbers of the population in its grip. We even had instances of contractors paying their labourers in heroin.[127]

In 1925 new narcotics decrees in Egypt made both trafficking and possession criminal offences. Field-Marshal Viscount Allenby (1861–1936), the High Commissioner for Egypt, reported that in ten years to 1925, 'the drug habit has taken a firm hold upon Egypt, not only in Cairo and Alexandria, where it has thoroughly permeated every class of Europeans, Egyptians and Levantines, but also in the provinces'.[128] As a result of the 1925 decree, prices for heroin and cocaine more than doubled in a year. Convictions rose by an average monthly increase of 333 in the first nine months. In consequence, Cairo Central Prison was 25 per cent above its statutory capacity owing to narcotics convictions. During 1926 the cultivation of the opium poppy was prohibited by decree, and 334 European traffickers were expelled from Egypt. Russell reported then that it was 'twice as difficult to-day to buy illicit narcotics as it was a year ago, but this is because the actual vendors and peddlers who were formerly well-known and easily accessible to the public are either in gaol or too frightened to carry on. But the big smugglers back of the trade are still untouched and ever on the look out for new agents.'[129]

Possibly this crackdown on opiates and cocaine caused an upsurge in the use of heroin (just as had happened in the USA after the passage of the Opium Exclusion Act of 1909). Perhaps, however, the dealers were just becoming more aggressive. Whatever the causes, around 1928 Russell realised there was a new problem in Cairo's slums: 'For the first time we heard of the method of intravenous injection of heroin and soon came across its victims.'[130] Until then heroin had either been sniffed or injected subcutaneously. Qasr El Aini Hospital reported the deaths of nine intravenous heroin-users from malignant malaria contracted by sharing contaminated needles. Interrogation of patients elicited that they had all been injected at the El Zahâr quarter, a wild tract of land containing filthy, fetid-smelling huts occupied by men who were paid by the heroin-suppliers to inject addicts. The injectors prepared the heroin in dirty tin syringes, which were heated by a match to assist dissolution.[131] Russell himself cross-examined many of the 'pitiful creatures' who were 'netted' by the CNIB visiting El Zahâr. 'They were from every class, working men, sons of small shopkeepers, cabmen, artisans, clerks from Government offices and even sons of well-to-do citizens.' A minority were strong enough to earn a pittance as labourers, 'but the rest existed by begging or stealing and satisfied what little desire for food they still had by scavenging the rubbish bins, in competition with the cats and kites.'[132]

By 1929 the Egyptian Prime Minister was alarmed at the deteriorating situation. 'The peaceful, happy villages of my inspector days were being rotted with dope,' Russell wrote. 'Had the damage been confined to the upper and educated classes of the cities I don't think that I should have been so stirred but when I . . . calculated that out of a total population of fourteen million possibly half a million were now slaves to the drug habit, and they the backbone of the land, I realized that here was a job worth doing.'[133] As a result of prime-ministerial discussions, the Egyptian government established the Central Narcotics Intelligence Bureau under his charge. Thereafter Russell collaborated closely with Delevingne, 'sending him confidential copies of our seizure reports and taking his advice as to the handling of complicated international cases'.[134] He put little effort into 'the irritating and purposeless chase of dealers in Egypt when the stuff comes pouring in from overseas'. As heroin and morphine were his priority, he made 'an unholy pact' with one trafficker 'that if he would stop dealing in heroin, we would ignore his black activities [in hashish and opium for smoking] in return for definite and productive information about the importers of cocaine and heroin'.[135]

It was doubtless through this informant that the CNIB made its first important arrest of an Armenian named Thomas Zakarian, who sold heroin from his carpet shop. His suppliers were two brothers Zahnwel and Ajzyk Zellinger, young Polish refugees based in Vienna, whose source was 'a private factory at Altstatten near Zurich belonging to a Dr Hefti, a talented chemist whose ingenuity had enabled him to elaborate a preparation known as Dionyl'. This substance was almost indistinguishable from heroin, 'yet it was chemically just sufficiently different to enable it to be manufactured and sold without infringing the Swiss anti-narcotic laws as they then stood'. Between October 1928 and February 1929 the Zellingers bought 300 kilograms of Hefti's Dionyl;

they also obtained heroin for Zakarian from Röesler of Mulhouse.[136] The CNIB soon discovered that in addition to Zellinger's organisation, a second Viennese gang was sending 'passengers first-class and all expenses paid to Alexandria—sometimes via Trieste and sometimes via Genoa and Naples'. These couriers travelled with 'American wardrobe' trunks, specially manufactured in Vienna by a Pole named Moses Lieb Wiedler, with secret compartments holding up to 20 kilograms of heroin. Meanwhile, the arrest in 1929 of Elie Chaskes, a Palestinian who had been importing heroin, led to his denunciation of a gang led by Joshua Friedman, a Palestinian resident in Vienna. An investigation in Vienna by Themistocles Marcou, a Cretan officer of the Cairo City Police, collaborating with local policemen, resulted in the arrest of both gangs. Friedman was detained in Alexandria, and sentenced to five years' imprisonment, but the Austrian traffickers were only fined or imprisoned for a few days. One of the Viennese gangs was reckoned to have sent 500 kilograms of morphine derivatives to Egypt during four years; the importers paid about £E 40,000, and after adulteration, sold the heroin for about £E 1,000,000.[137]

Egypt's prison population in 1929 stood at 22,000, including 800 convicted for drug-dealing and 3500 for drug use. Including an estimated 1800 addicts convicted of other offences, Russell reckoned that drug prisoners counted for about 30 per cent of the prison population.[138] In October 1931 there were 4088 traffickers and 2882 users imprisoned; three years later the comparable figures were 2603 and 438. The crisis seemed to have been alleviated. Russell's hopes in the early 1930s to establish withdrawal treatment centres for 'what is really a mental and not a criminal condition' were frustrated for lack of government funding.[139] Egyptian addicts were desperate for cures. In one Delta village a man who had been bitten by a rabid dog was sent to the rabies hospital in Cairo. He found on leaving hospital that his craving for heroin had ceased. As Russell described, 'Other addicts in the village, in longing for a similar cure, consulted the village barber who, being an ingenious man, fitted up a dead dog's jaw with a steel spring and at decent intervals furnished his addict clients with the necessary lacerations to prove to the local government doctor that they had been bitten by a dog that must have been mad.' They were sent in turn to the rabies hospital where they each endured 'the painful treatment and returned to their village cured of their desire for drugs and justified in their implicit faith in the "mad dog hospital" '.[140]

The work of the CNIB was a credit to Russell before his retirement in 1946. His strategies required compromise, and never aimed at perfection; he knew that in public affairs there is no room for good intentions; he believed in progress and liberty, but had no faith in populism or the reformation of human nature. Institutional power he treated as necessary but fallible. These were desirable characteristics in an administrator charged with reducing or controlling drug consumption. Russell was not a prohibitionist after the American model. By contrast, the great overseas test case of US prohibition theories—China—makes a dismal story.

Around 1900 the Celestial Empire was producing an average of 20,430,000 kilograms of opium annually. The province of Shanxi had 150,000 acres under poppy cultivation; Chengtu (Chengdu), the provincial capital of Szechuan (Sichuan), boasted one opium shop for every sixty-seven of its 300,000 inhabitants. Despite the falling demand for imported opium, $40 million worth of opium entered the treaty port of Shanghai (with its autonomous foreign districts, the International Settlement and the French Concession) annually in the first decade of the twentieth century. Shanghai had over 1500 opium-smoking houses supplied by a guild of merchants known as the Swatow (Chaozhau) clique. They in turn obtained Persian and Indian opium from four related merchant houses licensed by Shanghai Municipal Council to supply opium: David Sassoon & Company; E. D. Sassoon; S. J. David; and Edward Ezra. During 1913 the Sassoons hiked prices by forming the Shanghai Opium Merchants Combine. This became the exclusive supplier of the Swatow clique, and arranged with Shanghai Municipal Council that only its opium could be sold or smoked in the International Settlement. Shortly before the legal traffic in opium ceased in March 1917 (under the decree of 1906 and Anglo-Chinese undertakings of 1907), the Combine sold 1578 chests for a total of over $13 million to the warlord Feng Kuo-chang (Feng Guozhang) (1859–1919). Although most of these stocks were burnt in 1919, this intervention in the opium market by a provincial warlord was ominous confirmation that the central government's policy was unravelling. Indeed the situation in the 1920s was graver because the successes of the anti-opium movement had aroused a new demand for opium derivatives; morphine, heroin and codeine were easier to transport and consume surreptitiously. Sales rose among peasants and labourers who could no longer obtain or afford opium for smoking. 'The net results', according to the sinologist Herbert Giles (1845–1935) in 1923, 'of Chinese and foreign efforts to deliver China from the greatly exaggerated curse of opium have been (1) to increase enormously the area of poppy growing in the various provinces . . . and (2) to flood the country with morphine, cocaine, heroin, etc., which are admittedly more deadly still'.[141] The Englishman in charge of Shanghai customs made a similar assessment in 1931:

> The morphine habit came to the country with the prohibition of opium. As long as people were free to have their pipes, the hypodermic needle was unknown; but when opium and the pipe were prohibited, people had recourse to the needle because supplies of morphine were easier to smuggle, there was not the same risk of detection as in smoking, and morphine was so much cheaper than smuggled opium. His impression was that the injection habit was taught first by Japanese doctors in Shanghai and Fukien.[142]

The Swatow clique preserved its monopoly as wholesalers after 1917. In alliance with warlords and a secret criminal confederation, originally organised by river boatmen, called the Green Gang (*qingbang*), it sought to monopolise the contraband opium traffic. The warlords protected the contraband opium outside Shanghai; the Green Gang inside. By 1920 there were an estimated 100,000 hoodlums (*liumang*) in the Shanghai underworld, organised in small bands, controlled by the Green Gang. The military governor and two Swatow wholesalers ran the new opium monopoly under the cover of a real estate business. In 1923 the Shanghai Municipal Council established its own anti-narcotics force, which raided the Swatow monopolists' warehouses with such success that in 1925 the gangs withdrew from the International Settlement and regrouped in the French Concession, where they stored their opium under police immunity. The monopoly netted $50 million Chinese in its first year in the French Concession. By the mid-1920s 20,000 chests of Persian, Turkish and Indian opium and 18,000 chests of Chinese opium were reportedly stored there annually. Overall the Shanghai drug traffic alone was estimated to yield $6 million a month to the militarists controlling the city. The high stakes pro-

voked a localised war, which erupted in September 1924, between rival
governors for control of the city's opium traffic. A hundred and twenty
thousand men were enlisted on both sides.

Some members of the old Combine continued in the business,
notably the Ezra brothers, who used their Dahloong Tea Company as
a front. During 1923 several dealers, including Nissim Ezra (b. 1880),
jointly bought a large amount of Turkish opium. The contraband was
consigned in a Japanese vessel from Constantinople to Vladivostok,
from whence it was to reach the Chinese market. The ship's captain,
however, made a separate deal with rival smugglers, and in February
1924 unloaded fifty chests of opium into a junk outside the Woosung
Forts. The stolen contraband was then secreted at 51, Canton Road in
one of the subterranean warehouses constructed for the purpose
beneath the French Concession and International Settlement. Nissim
Ezra informed the Shanghai Municipal Police who, after an exhaustive
search, discovered the opium squirrelled away in an elaborate underground warren with false walls, secret doors and labyrinthine tunnels.
This stolen cargo was worth an estimated $1,250,000 (£156,666 at
1924 values).[143] In the ensuing scandal over Persian and Turkish opium
supplies to China, the League recommended that all ships heading for
the Far East should be searched in the Suez Canal. Japan, however,
stymied this proposal, which would have handicapped its own trafficking. Customs officials produced continuous counsels of despair. Sir
Francis Aglen (1869–1932), Inspector General of Chinese Maritime
Customs from 1911 until 1928, advised that a government opium
monopoly was the only way to control and gradually suppress the traffic.[144] His successor Sir Frederick Maze (1871–1959) told an Indian
customs official 'that, seeing the enormous profits in the traffic, the
amount of wealth and influence behind it, and the number and lawless
nature of those engaged in its actual operations, it is hopeless to try to
keep the narcotics out of any consuming country by means of preventive services and prosecutions'. Maze regarded heroin and morphine as
being incomparably a more serious menace for China than opium.[145]

'The policy of suppression', concluded the Peking correspondent of
The Times of London in 1924, 'has been entirely set at naught.' At least
11,000,000 kilograms of opium had been produced in China in 1923.
The provinces of Fukien, Kiangsi and Shensi were deriving taxes from
poppy cultivation worth annually upwards of $20 million Chinese

(about £2.5 million). In Kwangsi's provincial capital $1 million was annually collected in transit tax alone. As this journalist summarised it,

> The military commanders in nearly every province are paying their troops out of funds derived from the taxation of opium. In many provinces, the farmers are directly forced to grow opium, which is taken by the soldiers at a low price and sold for their benefit. In some places the land is taxed at a rate so high that the charges can be met only by cultivating a valuable crop like opium . . . In one district of Fukien, where the farmers drove away the soldiers sent to ensure the planting of poppy, the local general dispatched troops, who exterminated a whole village of men, women and children as an example to their neighbours . . . the country is covered with what are titled 'Suppression Bureaux' headed by 'Suppression Commissioners' whose sole duty is to promote the traffic and tax it to the utmost limit.[146]

Chinese officialdom was 'made up more and more of the very scum of the country, ex-bandits, ex-pimps, degenerates of every type', a resident complained in 1926. 'In their wake follow the professional politicians, irresponsible and ruthless. Together they farm disorder to their own enormous profit, and the Chinese people . . . sink into lower and lower stages of misery.'[147]

Huang Jinrong, who led the Chinese detective squad in Shanghai, was given an outright gift of $2 million Chinese and a share in the profits in return for protecting the city's opium entrepreneurs. It was his deputy Du Yuesheng (b. 1888), sitting at his side during his morning audiences for supplicants and secreting bribes in his suitcase, who transformed the Shanghai opium trade into the world's largest illicit cartel. Orphaned by the age of nine, Du went to live with an uncle, whose money he pilfered after squandering a small inheritance on gambling. Expelled from the household aged fifteen, he sold fruit on the Shanghai waterfront before becoming a runner in the numbers racket. In 1911 he joined the Eight Legged Mob, drug-smugglers run by a Chinese police superintendent. Soon afterwards, having been recruited as a police informant, he ingratiated himself with Huang Jinrong, partly by acting as the loans enforcer of Huang's wife. He was recommended to the Swatow merchants as an expert in protecting their opium from being hijacked in the docks, and soon controlled waterfront movements of opium. Until 1923 he remained a *daheng* (bigshot) who banked Huang's daily take and organised his own freelance opium heists. Du's opportunity for criminal greatness came after Huang became besotted with a young actress. One night in 1924, while Huang was listening to her performance from his private box, a warlord's son insulted her. Huang promptly had the young man beaten with ferocity. Two nights later Huang was seized at gunpoint by military policemen. Du convened a meeting of the ten major Shanghai opium wholesalers, ostensibly to raise his boss's ransom, and convinced them to invest millions of dollars in a bribe of Defence Commissioner He Fenglin to gain his support in imposing an opium monopoly over the entire city. The ten Swatow dealers and three Green Gang representatives then established the Three Prosperities Company (*Sanxin gongsi*), better known as the Big Company (*Da gongsi*). Du consolidated his position after the forces of the Kuomintang (literally National People's Party), which had been strengthened by Soviet aid and was led by Chiang Kai-shek (1887–1975), entered Shanghai in 1927.

After taking control of Shanghai, Chiang's administration established a government monopoly selling opium through a system of permits intended to control existing addicts and eliminate illicit drug-taking within three years. A British diplomatic assessment of 1928 attributed this target date to 'vanity' and 'inexperience': 'It was on much the same line that the American delegation seceded at the Geneva Conference.'[148] The opium cure institutes established in this period were worse than useless. 'The promised inspection and control by doctors proves to be a myth,' reported a British consul. 'The businessmen who manage these institutes . . . resort to every kind of artifice to get their customers to buy more opium or to turn those who have actually a taste for the drug into confirmed opium addicts.'[149] In a further sinister development, narcotics manufactured in Asia began to be substituted by users for those of European and Middle Eastern origin. As early as 1929 a secret morphine factory was discover at Chungking. Delevingne on a visit to Bangkok in 1931 was shown 'morphine made in a primitive manner in the wild interior beyond the Siamese frontiers'.[150] In the next few years factories were discovered at Shanghai, Tientsin and Dairen; crude morphine made in China was seized at Hong Kong, in Egypt and elsewhere. From the defeat of the Japanese in 1945 until the Communist take-over in 1949, Chiang Kai-shek's government in China resumed efforts (supported by the USA) to curb trafficking and addiction. There were many arrests of opium-takers and users, seizures of drugs and apparatus, and public bonfires of confiscated narcotics, beautifully wrought pipes and ornamental opium lamps. Yet the Nationalists, even with US backing, could not suppress trafficking and addiction. It took the tyranny of Mao Zedong (1893–1976), with its contempt for life and liberty, to curb Chinese opiate abuse.

In 1939 opium-smoking was still legal in the Dutch East Indies, British Malaya, Brunei, Formosa, Sarawak, Burma, India, Ceylon, British North Borneo, Hong Kong, French Indo-China, Thailand, Macao and Iran. Japanese forces invaded many of these territories during the Second World War. Congressman Walter Judd (1898–1994), a former medical missionary in China, urged that the elimination of the opium traffic and state monopolies should be incorporated into US war aims. After the USA entered the war in 1941, 'curtailment of the opium traffic' in the Far East 'became a matter of immediate concern to the United States in view of . . . the large number of young troops deployed in that area', as Anslinger wrote. The US authorities regarded the opium-smoker 'as a focus of infection for susceptible individuals' and anticipated from past experience a wartime rise in drug abuse. 'As long as opium addiction was permitted in the Far Eastern war theater, it was probable that troops would acquire addiction and that drug smuggling would continue from countries in the Far East to countries in the West,' Anslinger believed. It would be untrue to say that the War on Drugs mattered more to Washington than the war against the Japanese, but the influence of the drugs war on the strategy of the Pacific War was considerable. Beginning in January 1943, Anslinger held meetings in Washington with representatives of Britain, Canada, Australia, New Zealand, the Netherlands and China. He told the Dutch authorities in March 1943 that if they held to the intention to restore the state opium monopoly in the Dutch East Indies, no US troops would be sent to relieve those colonies from the Japanese invaders. He further stated that as soon as American forces reached the Dutch East Indies, all opium stocks would be confiscated, all opium shops would be closed and opium-smoking would be prohibited. The Dutch submitted to these terms. The US first obtained agreement on total prohibition of opium-smoking; then, in November 1943, the British and Dutch governments agreed to abolish the legal sale of opium in their Far Eastern territories. The French and Portuguese governments later issued similar announcements. Within a few years opium-smoking was illegal everywhere except in the independent kingdom of Thailand, where it was finally prohibited in 1959.[151]

The United Nations Economic and Social Council resolved in 1946 to establish a Commission on Narcotic Drugs to supersede the old League Advisory Committee on Opium and Dangerous Drugs. Fifteen governments were represented on this Commission: Britain, Canada, China, Egypt, France, India, Iran, Mexico, the Netherlands, Peru, Poland, Turkey, Soviet Russia, the USA and Yugoslavia. The Commission was vested with exceptional powers. It was the only United Nations body, other than the Security Council, General Assembly and International Court of Justice, able to adopt decisions binding on individual governments. It differed, too, from the League Advisory Committee in subtler ways. The United States, rather than boycotting the United Nations, dominated it, not least because it was located in New York rather than Geneva. The Commission on Narcotic Drugs was also based in New York until 1953; although far from a poodle of the Federal Bureau of Narcotics, it nevertheless accepted the agenda of American prohibitionists. The United States had recently been victorious in a world war waged with the unwavering object of obtaining unconditional surrender. So, as drug use accelerated after 1945, the Americans had a crude but self-confident response: they again demanded unconditional surrender.

TEN

The Age of Anxiety

'To be oneself', you say, is all-important. But is one's self really worth the effort?
—PAUL VALÉRY

To be happy is to be able to become aware of oneself without fright.
—WALTER BENJAMIN

'THERE IS A very real danger', said the physician Sir Bruce Bruce-Porter (1869–1948) in 1933, 'that the gin-palace is being replaced by the drug-palace.'[1] The shining modern emporia associated with Jesse Boot (1850–1931), whose prestige as a pharmacist was such that in 1929 he had been created Lord Trent, were catering to a startlingly expanded demand for pills and powders to treat insomnia, headaches and nervous ailments. Similarly a French visitor to the USA in 1935 pitied 'the many millions of unfortunate people who at present live on their nerves and pills'. He blamed the deplorable conditions prevalent in America on Prohibition.[2] Even after repeal, in the USA as in Britain, inebriety was more than ever socially unacceptable, especially for women. Pills, which had the veneer of being both scientific and hygienic, replaced alcohol as a support. 'There is to-day something in the make-up of the average British man and woman that makes them believe they can't be really healthy unless they're swallowing a pill or drinking medicine,' a psychiatrist said in 1955.[3] 'Drugs, like chewing gum, TV, oversize cars and crime, are part of the American

way of life,' noted Bruce Jackson, a Harvard fellow who in 1966 undertook research into drug habits for the President's Commission on Law
Enforcement. 'One result of all the drug propaganda and the appalling
faith in the efficacy of pills is a lot of people take a lot more pills than
they have any reason to. They think in terms of pills. And so do their
physicians.'[4]

People of every generation have needed chemicals to cope with life:
sobriety is not an easy state for human beings. People are resourceful in
obtaining drugs that help them cope. When sedatives were scarce in
London in 1943, for example, the choreographer Sir Frederick Ashton
(1904–88) doped himself with 'Calm Doggie', a canine tranquilliser to
prevent barking during air raids.[5] But the moral directives of journalists have made 'problems' out of some drugs and not others. Certain
types of consumer were stigmatised and stereotyped (particularly after
1950); others were not. Junkies in the 1950s and college kids in the
1960s were police targets and journalists' bugbears unlike the millions
of people dependent on commercial drugs. While recreational drug use
by young people was usually an experimental transitory phase, the
housewife stimulated by amphetamines and the businessman sedated
on Miltown were long-term habitual users who repudiated notions
that they had a drug problem.[6]

During the Geneva negotiations of 1931 the US representative
Herbert May established the principle that international regulations
should presume new narcotic substances as inherently addictive until it
was proven otherwise. Controls were imposed unless the substance
seemed non-addictive. Conversely non-narcotic new drugs, often collectively described as psychotropics, were regarded as non-addictive
until proven otherwise.[7] The distinction (held in the minds of both
Western authorities and consumers) between drugs which could be
treated as mere commodities and drugs associated with vice crystallised
around 1950 in new definitions prepared by an expert committee for
the United Nations Commission on Narcotics. 'Drug addiction',
according to this committee, 'is a state of periodic or chronic intoxication, detrimental to the individual and to society.' Its characteristics
included 'an overpowering desire or need (compulsion) to continue
taking the drug and to obtain it by any means; a tendency to increase
the dose; a psychic (psychological) and sometimes a physical dependence on the effects'. Addiction-producing drugs requiring strict global

regulation were distinguished from habit-forming drugs. 'A habit-forming drug is one which is or may be taken repeatedly without the production of all the characteristics outlined in the definition of addiction and which is not generally considered to be detrimental to the individual and to society.'[8] Spurious distinctions were made. The FBN pursued the illicit uses of opiates, marijuana and cocaine while leaving amphetamines and barbiturates within the Federal Drug Administration's jurisdiction.

The fashionable post-war habit-forming drugs were analgesics, amphetamines, barbiturates and finally benzodiazepines. 'This is the age of the all-powerful pill,' wrote *Daily Mirror* journalists Anthony Miles (b. 1930), Keith Waterhouse (b. 1929) and Ronald Bedford in 1955. 'Today you can take a pill to put you to sleep, wake you up, put on weight, take it off, pep you up, calm you down, boost your confidence, deaden pain.'[9] The decades after 1930 were characterised by Auden as the Age of Anxiety, and the *Daily Mirror*'s explanation of 'the drug craze' seemed to agree. 'Doctors will tell you the real answer is WORRY. Today that is the most common complaint in their consulting rooms.'[10] Physicians themselves succumbed to the spirit of the age. An English psychiatrist explained in 1956 that barbiturates were prescribed 'often to assuage the doctor's own anxiety' when confronted by plaintive patients. The National Health Service set up in 1948 was funded by tax contributions, and physicians found it hard to refuse patients who felt that as tax-payers they were entitled to NHS drugs by right.[11] General practitioners were paid according to the number of patients in their NHS practices. This made it hard, as a Newcastle physician regretted in 1962, to restrict prescriptions of substances like amphetamines. After requesting transfer to a doctor's list, the patient often produced a tablet and asked for a further supply. The doctor seldom refused for fear of losing a year's payment not only for the patient but in all probability for her family. Patients only had to change doctors to get all the barbiturates or amphetamines they desired.[12]

Anxiety was not unjustified in this period. The quarter-century after 1945 was darkened by memories of Hiroshima and Nagasaki, stockpiles of more powerful and destructive nuclear weapons and confrontations such as the Cuban Missile Crisis. The nuclear age engendered anxiety, and a sense of futility and mistrust of authority in some people.[13] 'Life has changed into a timeless succession of shocks, interspaced with empty, paralysed intervals,' the German philosopher Theodor Adorno (1903–69) wrote of this period. 'What is being enacted now ought to be entitled: "After Doomsday".'[14] The novelist Aldous Huxley (1894–1963), a pioneer of psychedelic drugs during the 1950s, dreaded the new weaponry: 'All this concentrated knowledge, genius, hard work and devotion, not to mention all those incalculable billions of dollars, poured forth in the service of vast collective paranoias—and meanwhile our three billion of mainly hungry people are to become six billions in less than forty years and, like parasites, are threatening to destroy their planetary host.'[15]

Back in 1911 the Irish writer Frank Harris had written a set of life rules for the twentieth century. 'The first commandment is: be your-self, never conform; be proud of yourself and wilful; for there is no-one in the world like you, and never has been, and your unlikeness to all others is the reason for your existence, and its solitary justification.'[16] This subjective and defiant individualism often degenerated into exis-tential angst, self-absorption and selfishness. It engendered (in the industrialised world, at least) creeds and cults averring that self-knowledge and self-fulfilment cured unhappiness and worry. The therapeutic cul-ture proved an infantilising influence: it repudiated the insight of the Italian author Cesare Pavese (1908–50) that 'one stops being a child only when one realises that telling one's trouble does not make it any better'.[17] As tokens of the therapeutic hegemony, the British Psycho-analytical Society had about 400 members in 2000 and the American Psychoanalytical Society about 3000 individual members. The British Association for Counselling had 16,173 individual and 954 organisa-tional members in 1999; the American Counseling Association had nearly 55,000 members. Self-absorption became legitimised, if not sacramental, during the twentieth century. 'Many of the pillheads are taking drugs not *only* to escape but also to have an experience that is entirely one's own,' Bruce Jackson suggested in 1966. 'There is no one else to be propitiated, there are no explanations or excuses needed for what happens inside one's own head when one is turned on.' Jackson asked one user why he took his 'voom-voom' pills, and was answered, 'Why smoke, drink, drive recklessly, sunbathe, fornicate, shoot tigers, climb mountains, gamble, lie, steal, cheat, kill, make war—and blame it all largely on our parents? Possibly to make oneself more acceptable to oneself.'[18]

In this secularised age people were disinclined to accept personal responsibility for their own discontents. 'In the Puritan morality that I remember', wrote T. S. Eliot (1888–1965) in 1937,

> it was tacitly assumed that if one was thrifty, enterprising, intelligent, practical and prudent in not violating social conventions, one ought to have a happy and 'successful' life. Failure was due to some weakness or perversity peculiar to the individual; but the decent man need have no nightmares. It is now rather more common to assume that all individual misery is the fault of 'society', and is remediable by alterations from without. Fundamentally the two philosophies, however different they may appear in operation, are the same.[19]

The puritanism of Eliot's Missouri boyhood provided the atmosphere in which young Americans—whether in the pursuit of oblivion or in defiance of social convention—took to opium-smoking or cocaine-sniffing. After 1945 the outlook in England (and other industrialised areas) that contributed to escalating drug consumption was one that blamed personal difficulties on externals ('they ought to do something about it') and expected to be given pills. As Alan Pryce-Jones (1908–2000) described his compatriots in 1958: 'The British behave like private soldiers in a decaying army: they complain.'[20] This phenomenon was not limited to Britain. Consumption of minor analgesics such as aspirin doubled in the USA between 1940 and 1948. A similar doubling occurred in Denmark during 1951–7 and in Australia during 1955–61.

Indeed analgesic misuse was an old Australasian problem. As early as 1907 one observer reported, 'What the drink habit is to men in Australia, the headache powder is among women.'[21] An Australian study of 1962 found that analgesics caused 20 per cent of renal failure in Australian patients requiring renal dialysis and transplantation; the comparable figures were 7 per cent in the USA, 5.5 per cent in Canada, and 3 per cent in continental Europe. Excessive consumption also caused gastric and intestinal problems. Another Australian survey of 1978 showed that 16 per cent of adult female and 10 per cent of adult male Queenslanders took analgesics daily. Less than one-fifth had medical reasons for their consumption. Consumers were often secretive or deceitful about their habits. From New Zealand the case of a man aged twenty-two was reported in 1963:

> A Southern Alps shepherd, he was rather naïve and immature. He treated his high level of anxiety and tension, which became unbearable under stress, with excessive quantities of aspirin daily. Aspirin can be bought at any country store, and served as an anodyne against his unsatisfactory marriage. He was able to keep working while under the influence of up to 240 grains a day ... on one occasion he fell off a horse in a semi-conscious state, while carrying a loaded rifle. On another day he was so doped with aspirin that he had to be taken away from the fire before he got his feet burnt.[22]

Heavy Swedish and Swiss consumption of analgesics had resulted by the early 1950s in a high incidence of kidney disease in both countries. In Sweden, during the influenza pandemic of 1918–19, a physician at Huskvarna named Hjorton had developed a powder containing phenacetin, phenazone and caffeine that became renowned in the district for its euphoric effects. Attractively wrapped packets of Hjorton's powder were given as gifts like flowers or chocolate in Huskvarna district; at parties people offered a powder as freely as a cigarette.[23] The death rate for renal failure in Huskvarna was thrice as high as in a nearby town where phenacetin consumption was one-tenth. In Switzerland thirty single doses of analgesic tablets or powders were sold per head of the population in 1955. Eighty per cent of regular users were women seeking 'relief from tension, in the same way as abusers in other countries may take to sedatives and hypnotics.'[24]

There was profuse advertising of analgesics. 'With the advances of science, our knowledge of pain—its causes and its cure—increases day by day,' announced a newspaper advertisement of 1955 for Phensic (a tablet combining aspirin and phenacetin). Phensic was recommended for headaches, nerve pains and neuralgia. The advertising copy ended, 'Always carry a packet of Phensic with you—and you can get rid of that headache wherever you may be.'[25] The invitation always to carry a packet of analgesics was intended to increase consumption. It succeeded. A survey of 1970 found that 9 per cent of the British population took analgesics weekly, and 2.8 per cent daily. Forty per cent of the English took analgesics for symptoms on which they had no pharmacological action, including insomnia. Consumption was most common among women, especially those aged 16–44. Advertising was even more pervasive in the United States.[26] Although phenacetin's withdrawal from common analgesics reduced new cases of renal disease in Sweden, Canada and Scotland, there was no downturn in Australia or Switzerland. Many manufacturers substituted paracetamol despite it being the major metabolite of phenacetin, while others increased aspirin dosage. The caffeine or codeine content of some analgesics was raised in order to maintain or increase consumption.

Analgesics were less controversial than amphetamines. Amphetamine (betaphenylisopropylamine) is an adrenaline-like chemical compound first described in 1910 by Sir Henry Dale (1875–1968) and George Barger (1878–1939). Its action and structure resemble ephedrine, which after 1924 was used to treat asthma. The American researcher Gordon Alles (b. 1901) first synthesised amphetamine in 1927 when seeking an economic substitute for ephedrine. Under the trade name of Benzedrine, Smith, Kline and French Laboratories of Philadelphia began selling amphetamine in 1932 as a decongestant nasal inhaler for asthmatics and people with hay-fever. It was soon recommended for treating narcolepsy,[27] epilepsy, Parkinsonism, seasickness, obesity and behaviour disorders of problem children. After analysing sixty-five cases, two New York physicians in 1937 warned against 'promiscuous use'. Some users felt depressed, irritable or anxious; others impulsive, aggressive, forgetful or boisterous.[28] The American Medical Association approved the sale of Smith, Kline and French's Benzedrine pills in 1937. Researchers at London's Maudsley psychiatric hospital reported that year a patient who had been purchasing Benzedrine at chemists' shops without medical supervision, and condemned its over-the-counter sale.[29] From 1939 Benzedrine was obtainable in Britain only by prescription of medical practitioners or the signing of the Poisons Register. Attempts were made to restrict its over-the-counter sales in the USA, too. Reacting to misuse of the pills, Smith, Kline and French reverted to supplying Benzedrine chiefly in nasal inhalers.

In addition to the original amphetamine (Benzedrine), there was also dexamphetamine (Dexedrine), which was twice as strong. A Japanese chemist named Ogata in 1919 developed methylamphetamine (Methedrine or Desoxyn), which was double the strength of Dexedrine. There was also phenmetrazine (Preludin). During the 1950s the Swiss pharmaceutical company Ciba began selling methylphenidate under the brand name of Ritalin. 'Amphetamines in general are prescribed readily and light-heartedly,' reported an Anglo-Australian physician Leslie G. Kiloh, who made a special study of amphetamine habituation in 1962. Kiloh quoted with dismay the Ministry of Health's annual report for 1954: 'The drugs of this group have the advantage of being relatively non-toxic, addiction to them is rare, and there are no serious ill-effects; they may therefore be given to out-patients without undue risk.' He was roused, too, by a US monograph on amphetamines that had recently concluded, 'As experience with the amphetamines has ripened they have become firmly established as versatile and helpful remedies given to millions of people and under such conditions as to offer remarkably low potential for causing harm.'[30]

Amphetamines had a high potential for harm. The phenomenon of amphetamine psychosis—with symptoms resembling schizophrenia—was reported from 1958 by psychiatrists, chiefly in male patients.[31] In addition to psychosis, the elation produced by amphetamines increased the possibility of habituation. The English poet W. H. Auden (1907–73) began taking Benzedrine daily after he settled in the USA in 1939 rather in the way that a later generation took vitamin pills at breakfast. He used amphetamines to accelerate his mind rather as a production engineer might use a chemical in a manufacturing process—'I'm a working machine,' he would say—and after a few years his functions faltered and misfired without the drug. 'SOS repeat SOS,' he wrote from Europe in 1952 to a friend in New York City. 'I must have left half my store of Bennies in Paris. Could you possibly find means to procure a hundred and air-mail them to me.'[32] The period when he came off the drug after 1957 coincides with arguably the dullest period of his poetic output.[33] The American writer Jack Kerouac (1922–69) recalled breaking open Benzedrine inhalers and immersing their contents in Coca-Cola or coffee.[34] 'Benny has made me see a lot,' he told the poet Alan Ginsberg (1926–97) in 1945. 'The process of intensifying awareness naturally leads to an overflow of old notions, and *voilà*, new material wells up like water following its proper level, and makes itself evident at the brim of consciousness.'[35] The drug, however, wrecked Kerouac's health. In December of that year he collapsed and was hospitalised with thrombophlebitis caused by taking too many Bennies. He continued, however, to use the drug to aid composition.

'I'm taking enormous doses of Benzedrine to write my novels i probably won't live long enough to enjoy money,' he confided in 1961.[36]

The Amphetamine drugs were cerebral stimulants. The Jungian psychotherapist Hugh Crichton-Miller (1877–1959) first began using Benzedrine (usually taken with glucose) in 1936 'for particular mental efforts, such as public speaking, and in a lesser way, to combat postprandial somnolence,' he reported in 1946.[37] The easy availability of Benzedrine diverted many people into amphetamine misuse who probably otherwise would have resorted to cocaine. 'Large doses cause prolonged sleeplessness with feelings of exhilaration,' according to the American writer William Burroughs (1914–97). 'The period of euphoria is followed by a horrible depression. The drug tends to increase anxiety. It causes indigestion and loss of appetite.'[38] Burroughs's friend the street hustler Herbert Huncke (1916–96) first heard of amphetamines from University of Chicago students around 1933. 'Someone would say, "Man, I have to cram for an exam and I'm exhausted"—and someone would know someone who was a nurse with knowledge of this new thing called Benzedrine—"Hey, why don't you get a few bennies?" (right away it was "bennies")—I'm guessing it started to spread like that, students in the know.' Huncke worked as an elevator boy at the Illinois Athletic Club on Michigan Avenue. 'A guy stepped into the elevator one night and asked me to buy him a bottle of pills—I think two dozen, 10 mg, for about 89 cents. This guy was considered a great athlete, and upper crust—I guess he figured I was only going to be there a short time, and that I wasn't likely going to squeal.' Huncke began taking Bennies in 'jazz joints' on the south side of Chicago. Some friends stopped using the drug because they found 'it killed the sex drive'. Others reported that 'once bennie kicked in, well . . . when you got going you could go on for hours and hours. We found that it *helped* the sex drive!'[39]

Amphetamine use had official endorsement. Early in 1940 a German pilot was shot down over England, and was found to be carrying sugar tablets containing a small amount of amphetamine. The Royal Air Force forthwith investigated whether the drug could be used to combat fatigue in bomber pilots, and whether it could enable airmen to fly at higher altitudes despite diminished oxygen levels. It was found to prevent sleep, but there was no evidence that it enabled a tired man to perform his work to a high capacity. 'Pilots as a class', reported an RAF medical officer, 'did not like being doped, and there was a rather well-marked feeling in the Air Force against improvements in performance being obtained by what seemed to the men to be rather "phoney" means.'[40] Nevertheless, during the Second World War over 72 million 'Energy Tablets' were supplied in Britain to the Admiralty, Ministry of War Transport, War Office and RAF, and a greater number to the US armed forces. US forces in the Korean War were also given amphetamines to enhance their physical endurance and courage. During 1966–9 the US Army used more amphetamines on its troops in Vietnam than the combined total of the British and American forces in the Second World War.

World leaders used amphetamines. Theodor Morell (1886–1948), a ship's doctor who had set up as a venereal quack before becoming personal physician to Adolf Hitler (1889–1945), fed the Führer at least 92 different drugs during the Second World War, notably strychnine and belladonna, as well as Methedrine, morphine, hypnotics and aphrodisiacs.[41] The British Prime Minister Anthony Eden (1897–1977) pepped himself with Benzedrine during the Suez crisis of 1956. The US President John F. Kennedy (1917–63) supposedly used Methedrine during his summit meeting in Vienna in 1961 with the Soviet Russian leader Nikita Khrushchev (1894–1971). A New York physician, Max Jacobson (b. 1900), supplied JFK with amphetamine shots. 'I worked with the Kennedys,' he once crowed. 'I travelled with the Kennedys. I treated the Kennedys. Jack Kennedy. Jacqueline Kennedy. They could never have made it without me.'[42]

The euphoric properties of amphetamines made people seem sparkling in company. A character in Fitzgerald's Hollywood novel, *The Last Tycoon* (written in 1939–40), for example took Benzedrine before going to a party.[43] Kerouac described an American soldier returning unexpectedly to his wife in New York.

> Harry Evans suddenly came clomping down the hall of her apartment in his Army boots, fresh from the German front, around September 1945, and was appalled to see us, six full-grown people, all high on Benny sprawled and sitting and cat-legged on that vast double-doublebed of 'scepticism' and 'decadence', discussing the nothingness of values, pale-faced, weak bodies, Gad the poor guy said: 'This is what I fought for?' His wife told him to come down from his 'character

heights' or some such. He divorced her awhile later. Of course we know the same thing was going on Paris and Berlin of the same month and year, now that we've read Günther Grass and Uwe Johnson and Sartre and even, of course, Auden and his *Age of Anxiety*.[44]

Two years later, in Belgrave Square, the Chicago-born Sir Henry 'Chips' Channon (1897–1958), who was an English MP, recorded hosting a dinner for the Queens of Spain and Romania. 'I "laced" the cocktails with Benzedrine, which I always find makes a party go.'[45] Benzedrine was *the* fashionable drug of the 1940s.

In some countries amphetamines swiftly drew the interest of criminals: a large illegal production of Methedrine began in Japan during the late 1940s, and by 1954 there were an estimated half a million users in Japan. Elsewhere amphetamines carried few stigmas until the mid-1950s. They were prescribed for post-natal depression and used on racing greyhounds; businessmen took them before conferences. During the early 1960s the college health services at the University of Texas at Austin routinely provided amphetamines at exam time, and speed was used even by the straightest students. The Brooklyn-born poet Diane di Prima (b. 1934) recalls, 'My aunt used to bring home bottles of Dexedrine from the hospital where she worked. She thought it was so wonderful that we wanted to write more and study more. Nobody knew there was anything wrong with it.'[46] Lord Segal (1902–85), an Oxford physician, reported as late as 1966 doctors in university towns prescribing amphetamines for students facing the prolonged ordeal of final examinations.[47]

By the late 1930s American truck-drivers were using amphetamines to keep alert on long journeys. Huncke remembered 'in the road-stops—in the rest room stalls—seeing "George the Bennie King was here", or things like that'.[48] In 1955 Kerouac hitched back from Mexico.

I'm standing by the side of the road at Santa Barbara cursing the motorists of America who really are NOT giving rides any more . . . screeeeeech stops a brand new 1955 Mercury Montclair persimmon colour . . . with blonde beautiful blonde in strapless white bathing suit at wheel and wearing little thin gold bracelet at sweet anklet, I run, jump in, she yawns, keeps yawning, wants to know if I can drive . . . she has been driving all the way from Fort Worth Texas without sleep I say 'O how would you like some Mexican Benzedrine?' . . . 'Crazy!' she yells, I whip out my Benzedrine, yanking out all my dirty underwear and unspeakable Mexican raggedy junks and give her, she takes Two, thankyou very much, we stop at coke station and she mumps out jumping, the sweetest little perfect everything you know, we swallow Bennies, by the time we've raced 100 miles an hour and once maybe 110 to Santa Ana in the Guadaloupe valley she's high, I'm high, we're talking and loving talk and driving and sweating and I can smell her sweet sweat and my own too and we move on up to the San Luis Obispo bump in the impossibly beautiful California dry blue-sky sundowns and she calls her Daddy bar-owner in San Fran to cable her money.[49]

They did not crash: Kerouac died of drink. Methylamphetamine was popular with truck-drivers (as well as night-shift workers): its reputation in the US as a redneck drug was accentuated in the 1960s when it was used and distributed by Hell's Angels motor-cycle gangs. As the drug can induce anxiety, paranoia, hallucinations and psychotic behaviour if taken in high doses, this was undesirable both for users and other motorists. (The drug is best known now in the US as 'crystal meth'.)

The US market in amphetamines provides a model of the workings of drug supply and demand. As Huncke recalled,

when amphetamine was first brought into the scene on a large scale, it was very inexpensive. When I first started to use, you could go into a drugstore and with a little bullshit you could buy an ounce of it for eight or ten dollars. So nobody thought anything at all of putting an ounce of it on the table for people to use as they wanted. When the druggists became aware of the fact that they had something going for them, they began to jack up the price a bit.

Then a sudden scarcity of amphetamines was engineered.

The shortage came about, of course, because people discovered they could make money selling the stuff—just like the junk scene. Suddenly, instead of being able to buy an ounce for ten, fifteen or twenty dollars, it was up to fifty and then a hundred dollars. When it reached that price, the guys who were using regularly naturally didn't have the money. A lot of them became thieves and muggers, though in the beginning they weren't.[50]

Then the Federal Bureau of Narcotics, 'who'd already ruined the pot scene, got on the ass of Benzedrine', partly because this resulted in 'a lot of payoffs down the line'.[51] The FBN was supported by an American Medical Association declaration in 1957 that amphetamines were 'by far the most dangerous drug existing today', potentially provoking 'violent, rapacious and criminal behaviour'.[52] Yet in 1958 eight billion pills and tablets were being legally manufactured in the US (the figure was 12 billion in 1971). By this period amphetamines were also being smuggled from Mexico to supply a clandestine market. People using illicitly obtained amphetamines began injecting. As the biographer of the singer Janis Joplin (1943–70) has summarised the situation, 'All over San Francisco and New York young kids were strung out from shooting speed, their jaws locked in a perpetual clench, their talk rapid-fire, and their nights unrelieved by sleep. Many turned to heroin to help them come down. "When people fall into smack or extreme use of meth[edrine] where they can't control it any more, they weren't exploring anything," says Diane di Prima. "That was seen as a lost place to be." '[53] Joplin, who began with amphetamines, fatally overdosed on heroin. Anti-drugs propagandists often insist that cannabis is a 'gateway' drug to heroin: more accurately, amphetamines in the 1950s served as 'gateway' drugs to heroin in the USA as in Europe from the mid-1960s.

The subversive popularity of writers like Kerouac, Ginsberg and John Clellon Holmes (1926–88) fuelled the FBN's hostility to amphetamines. It was Holmes in his novel *Go* (1952) with a phrase about 'this beat generation, this underground life' who provided journalists with an enduring sobriquet. The Beats were characterised by their 'inability to really believe in anything . . . and the craving for excess which it inspired', Holmes said. 'Everyone I know is kind of furtive, kind of beat. They all go along the street as if they were guilty of something, but didn't believe in guilt.'[54] The typical Beat, so Lady Caroline Blackwood (1931–96) noted in 1959 after a visit to California, 'in his rejection of the popular American concept that Success equates with Manhood, stresses a non-virility often mistaken for homosexuality.'[55] This ambivalence (emulated by the Mods in Britain) increased the likelihood that

men like Anslinger would label them as subversives and deviants. The
Beats' behaviour constituted a process of *becoming*—involving guilt, as
Holmes said, but also attitudinising—rather than anything fixed. They
scorned and reviled the self-assertion of American capitalism, yet they
advertised their own accumulation of experience—by drugs and other
means—as a way of asserting their own elite status. The Beats delved in
their unconscious, but unlike European Dadaists and surrealists
between the world wars, they relied on drugs to achieve their artistic
effects and often had a Peter Pan complex. Their extravagances of feeling and behaviour were a prolongation of adolescence.

Under the US Drug Abuse Control Act of 1965, passed despite
pharmaceutical manufacturers' opposition, both the retailing and prescribing of amphetamines were restricted, with Methedrine largely
withdrawn from legal use. The Bureau of Drug Abuse Control was
formed as an enforcement agency of the FDA. In the winter of 1965–6
Bruce Jackson went to a pill party in Chicago hosted by a painter who
had been awake for three days. There was a candy dish in the middle
of the coffee table filled with pills and capsules for guests to sample
after ritual consultation of their 'holy book'. This was the *Physicians'
Desk Reference* listing the effects of pharmaceuticals commercially available in the USA amidst enticing colour photographs of tablets and capsules. The party-goers relished sharing proscribed materials in a closed
community, loved the exegesis of colours, trade names and optimum
dosages, and savoured the arcane arts of sawing and grinding capsules.
They did not have the orgy that so often featured in FBN propaganda.
There was no flirting, wisecracking or sexual hustling that would have
been a correlative of other parties with mixed guests. No one was loud,
giggly or uncontrolled. Among these Chicago pill-heads, the most
common way of acquiring amphetamines was by medical prescription.
All a heavy user needed was to visit several physicians and extract refill-
able prescriptions from each. Few doctors recognised that individuals
needing amphetamines often had the kind of personality that easily
became dependent on them. In addition the pill-heads had the Source,
the generic name for suppliers of these drugs. They were seldom criminals but usually professional people with access to large quantities of
pills; often they gave them away. As the result of recent legislation
requiring physicians and pharmacists to maintain detailed records on
amphetamine prescriptions, the black-market price of Dexamyl rose

from 15 cents to 20 cents a capsule, when it was obtainable at all. Jackson concluded, 'It would be unfortunate if the price should be driven up so high that it would become profitable for criminal organizations to involve themselves with the traffic, as was the case with opiates in the 1940s and 1950s and alcohol in the 1920s.'[56]

Sir Adolphe Abrahams (1883–1967), formerly medical officer to Olympic athletics teams, resented allegations about amphetamine use by athletes 'as unfounded, unsubstantiated, ridiculous, and crazy'.[57] Such disavowals were unconvincing. The US National Football League, for example, did not prohibit amphetamine use by players until 1971, and the practice continued afterwards.[58] Other sports had a long history of drug use. Nineteenth-century competitive cyclists had used strychnine, coca, cocaine and morphine. The death of an Englishman named Linton in the Bordeaux–Paris race of 1896 had been attributed to drugs. After 1945 amphetamines became ubiquitous in cycling: their explosive effects resulted in them being known as *la bombe* in French, la bomba in Italian and atoom in Dutch. Their use was not widely prohibited by European sporting authorities. The Italian champion Fausto Coppi (1919–60) was asked during the late 1950s by a French radio interviewer if all competitive cyclists used amphetamines. ' "Yes", he replied, "and those who claim the opposite aren't worth talking to about cycling." "So did you take *la bomba*?" the interviewer continued. "Yes, whenever it was necessary." "And when was it necessary?" "Practically all the time." ' Jacques Anquetil (1934–87), a Norman who won the Tour de France race on five occasions, told a sporting journalist in 1967, 'You'd have to be an imbecile or a hypocrite to imagine that a professional cyclist who rides 235 days a year can hold himself together without stimulants.' (One exception was Coppi's rival Gino Bartali (1914–2000), who won the Tour de France in 1938 and 1948: 'I didn't need drugs: faith in the Madonna kept me from feeling fatigue and pain.')[59] During one Tour de France the English cyclist Tom Simpson (1937–67) died of heart failure while peddling up Mont Ventoux in Vaucluse. He had taken amphetamine and methylamphetamine (and perhaps drunk pastis in the nearby town of Bédoin) before his collapse. The drugs left him with so little sense that he had passed beyond the limits of his strength, and was dying of exhaustion, that his final words were a plea to be put back on his bike. He was carrying the drugs on him when he died.[60]

Amphetamine abuse was not confined to young men. Anne-Marie, a young English fashion student of the early 1960s, became deluded that she was about to marry, and showed symptoms indistinguishable from schizophrenia. Her psychiatrist discovered that she had secretly been obtaining amphetamines from a Harley Street doctor to help keep slim. When the psychiatrist telephoned this doctor to warn of the adverse reaction, he reacted angrily. 'Mind your own f— business,' he shouted. 'Keep away from my patients.' The physician had behaved unethically, both in seeing Anne-Marie without her general practitioner's knowledge, and in prescribing such large quantities. She recovered, resumed visiting Harley Street, and relapsed.[61] During the 1970s and 1980s a Harley Street psychiatrist, Robert Newton (1904–85), former psychiatric advisor to the Official Solicitor and Medical Director of the Child Guidance Clinic at Paddington, used to give women, including slim women, amphetamines to lose weight; memorably he injected his more attractive patients through their tights.[62] 'The "pseudo-therapeutic" drug abuser', a British expert recalled in 1970, was typically 'middle-aged fairly obese women who had been advised by acquaintances to start amphetamines . . . for slimming, and who soon experienced a heightened feeling of energy and uplift, and went on taking such drugs without a doctor's prescription or beyond the dose and length of time prescribed.'[63] The American film actress Judy Garland (1922–69) used amphetamines to slim, then needed barbiturates to sleep, and entered a miserable cycle which terminated in her suicide.

In Britain amphetamines were placed on Schedule 4 of the Poison Rules in 1957. This did not reduce their licit consumption. Kiloh reported in 1962 that the equivalent of 200,000 tablets were prescribed monthly to a population of 269,389 in Newcastle-upon-Tyne. Eighty-five per cent of the patients prescribed amphetamines were women, with a peak incidence aged 36–45 years. 'The reasons given by these patients for taking amphetamines are relatively few. Depression, fatigue, obesity, and, surprisingly, anxiety are the most common; less frequently the patient may admit that the drug is taken . . . to "pep up".' Men patients occasionally reported using these drugs 'to delay ejaculation'.[64] The regulations of 1957 aroused a vigorous amphetamine black market among the (mainly working-class) women of Newcastle. There was no organised illicit sales network, but many small-scale suppliers obtained tablets from their doctors and resold them profitably. One patient paid a neighbour, who was known locally as a supplier of Drinamyl, 14 shillings for fifty tablets. Another bought her tablets at three-pence each from a fellow factory worker. Many patients received their first tablet from a friend when feeling tired or miserable, and the reviving effect caused them to seek out their doctors, often clutching a tablet, to request a further supply. Several Newcastle women first received amphetamines from their hairdresser after complaining of depression or more commonly following a panic attack under a hair-drier. Many Newcastle women obtained amphetamines by ruses. To satisfy their increasing desire for the drug, they claimed to have lost their prescription, or that baby had thrown it on the fire, or that it had been left in the pocket of an apron put in the wash. It was common to obtain multiple prescriptions for various members of a family: in one Newcastle case a patient, together with her mother, mother-in-law, and eldest daughter received regular prescriptions for Drinamyl (an amphetamine-barbiturate mixture marketed by Smith, Kline and French from 1951). The patient collected them without her relations knowing of her activities. Another patient registered with fifteen different doctors from whom she obtained Drinamyl.[65]

Barbiturates were another fashionable group of drugs in this epoch. A total of 367,000 kilograms of barbiturates were produced in the USA in 1946 and 296,000 kilograms sold. These figures were equivalent to 5 million Americans taking a sleeping tablet daily for a year. By 1948 enough barbiturate was sold in the USA to provide every man, woman and child with 30 grains a year. In Britain during 1946 32,500 kilo-grams of barbiturates were sold, rising to over 40,000 kilograms in 1951. Barbiturates, for the British, reported the *Daily Mirror* in 1955, were 'as much a part of the daily routine for thousands as cleaning their teeth'.[66] The drugs were associated with unhappy and self-destructive women. From 1943 the British female suicide rate from barbiturates exceeded the male, with highest suicide rates by barbiturate poisoning being among women aged 45–64, who had been prescribed them for menopause, anxiety, insomnia and such like. During 1949 in Britain 2800 cases of barbiturate poisoning were treated in hospital; by 1954 there were over 6000 cases of barbiturate poisoning and over 500 deaths, twelve times as many as the forty deaths in 1938. Eight thousand people were admitted to hospital in England and Wales during 1960 following barbiturate overdoses. The probable total annual figure of overdoses was 10,000. The Scottish rate of accidental poisoning death—forty-nine per million in 1960—was the highest in the world (England was thirty per million). The highest English incidence of barbiturate poisoning was in the adjacent north London suburbs of Hampstead and Highgate.

Users taking barbiturates for more than four to six weeks develop tolerance, or become depressed, anxious and sleepless if the drug is stopped. Many users hoarded tablets: their behaviour resembled alcoholics hiding bottles in their house. As it was, 10 per cent of drugs prescribed in Britain in 1956 contained barbiturates; the cost to the NHS of barbiturates used in home treatment was £1,570,000 that year. Seven hundred and fifty million tablets of sedatives were taken annually in Britain by 1957. Fifteen per cent of NHS prescriptions in 1957 were for barbiturates, and 50 per cent in some medical practices, where general practitioners were spending 'up to half their time on the relief of mental symptoms'.[67] The physician in charge of a Barbiturate Poisoning Unit in Essex reported in 1957 that 'these drugs are misused on a vast scale'. It was difficult to deter or prevent such misuse: 'If the patient wishes to accumulate a supply of drugs she will'. The 'carelessness' of adults who leave these drugs 'within reach of young children' demonstrated the prevalent 'lack of appreciation of social and familial responsibilities'.[68] By the early 1960s there were an average of five prescriptions per head per year for persons on English doctors' lists. Of these 2 per cent per head per year were for sedatives and tranquillisers. Over nine *billion* barbiturates were manufactured globally in 1965.[69]

Barbiturates were used for murder and suicide. In 1956 the death by barbiturates overdose of an Eastbourne widow led to the arrest of her physician John Bodkin Adams (1899–1983), who was acquitted of murder in the following year. His trial highlighted his profuse administration of heroin, paraldehyde and other lethal substances to elderly women by whose wills he was to benefit.[70] Barbiturates were a fashionable method of self-immolation and suicidal gestures. 'Because his life was in such an unholy mess', Keith Waterhouse wrote in 1955, Mr A. was 'committing temporary suicide every night' by taking large doses of sleeping pills.[71] People who had no suicidal intentions were comforted by the possession of fatal quantities of barbiturates; they felt empowered at times of emotional disablement. When the marriage of the American actress Shelley Winters (b. 1922) fell apart in 1954, she went to a pharmacy in Rome and bought a hundred Seconal suppos- itories. 'I asked the Italian pharmacist, "How come you don't need a prescription for these dangerous sleeping things?" The man fixed me with a fishy eye and said in English, "Signora Gassman, in the whole history of Italian medicine, no-one—but no-one—has ever committed suicide in this fashion." '[72] The American poet Anne Sexton (1928–74) depended on Nembutal, which she dubbed her 'kill-me' pills from the time of her first deliberate overdose in 1956. She often referred to them in sessions with her psychotherapist. 'Can you be addicted in a calm way that doesn't hurt anyone?' she asked in 1961. In another session she insisted, 'There's a difference between taking something that will kill you and something that will kill you momentarily.' Barbiturates turned her into Sleeping Beauty every night. 'I ought to stop taking these pills, but I'd be in a state of panic. It's not that I'm killing myself, but that I'm controlling myself,' she rationalised in 1963.[73] In her poem 'The Addict' (1966) she gave an eloquent account of her dependence.[74] Her suicide did not involve 'kill-me' pills: instead she turned on the ignition of her red Cougar, sealed in the garage, and died listening to the car radio.

When the economist John Kenneth Galbraith (b. 1908), then US Ambassador to India, wired to the White House physician for barbitu- rates in 1962, he received an answer 'from the President, saying, "Lay off that stuff" '.[75] The drugs' reputation was no longer untarnished. Yet the demand for socially acceptable sedatives in industrialised nations was immense. After 1960, when the clinical effectiveness of chlor- diazepoxide was established, barbiturates were gradually supplanted by a new group of drugs, the benzodiazepines. Chlordiazepoxide was fol- lowed by the even more successful Diazepam. Twenty-five types of benzodiazepines were available within twenty years. By the early 1980s these were the most widely used of all prescribed drugs in Britain. They replaced barbiturates because they were more effective in alleviating anxiety, had fewer and less severe side effects, were safer in overdoses, and interacted less with other drugs. Pharmaceutical companies domi- nated the supply of information about these new substances, and devised aggressive marketing strategies. According to an estimate of 1981, 10 per cent of adult British males and 20 per cent of adult females took tranquillisers or hypnotics, mainly benzodiazepines, at least once a year. Of these one-half to two-thirds took tranquillisers for at least a month at a time. Two per cent of adults, say 600,000 people, were taking tranquillisers every day or night of the year. Over 4 per cent of all prescriptions were for Diazepam. Patients to whom this drug was administered intravenously 'described a "rush" . . . with euphoria, flight of ideas, pressure of speech, enhanced self-confidence, pleasant relaxation and calmness, followed by increasing drowsiness'.[76] Benzo-diazepines, predictably, could arouse physical and psychological dependence, and were involved in polydrug abuse.

Drinamyl, the triangular-shaped blue tablets known as 'purple hearts' (a mixture of amphetamines and barbiturates), was energetically promoted by its manufacturer, Smith, Kline and French after 1951. Free samples were sent to physicians—it almost seemed 'at every post'—especially to young doctors who had recently qualified. There was lit-tle effort to restrict access to Drinamyl in pharmaceutical laboratories and hospital pharmacies. In many English hospitals, at night, the phar-macy was unattended, and physicians or nurses could get the key and fetch what they wanted without superintendence. Some doctors and nurses gave liberal quantities of Drinamyl to their friends without any sense of impropriety.[77] By the mid-1950s girl prostitutes working on Cable Street in Whitechapel used Drinamyl to keep awake on the job.[78] The drug was obtainable in Soho at from sixpence to ninepence by the early 1960s. Philip Connell (1921–98), an English psychiatrist who published a monograph on amphetamine psychosis in 1958, listed Drinamyl's effects as sleeplessness, restlessness, a dry mouth, dilated pupils, volubility, euphoria, overactivity (leading to motoring accidents or aggression), trembling, unsteady gait and reduced inhibitions. Worst of all was 'a severe mental disturbance in which delusions and halluci-nations may occur—particularly of a kind in which the individual feels that everyone is against him, there are gangs or police chasing him, and with hallucinations of animals, police cars, crowds etc., which are not, in fact, there at all. This is what the pill taker calls "the horrors". Dur-ing this mental disturbance the individual can be dangerous.' Accord-ing to Connell, who specialised in maladjusted adolescents, 'The large majority of people will either not wish to take these drugs or will try them for fun, and will not become addicted.' He judged, however, that 'an unstable person . . . as so many of our teenagers today seem to be, will be more likely to become habituated'.[79] A fellow psychiatrist, Dale Beckett, who was one of the most clear and independent thinkers on drug dependence in this period, agreed. 'Nearly all' teenagers matured out of amphetamine as they emerged from adolescence, he wrote in 1967. 'I think of it as a phase which one is very likely to pass through comparable to the phase in babyhood of eating beetles.'[80]

In 1962 the Home Office called a conference of chief constables and detective superintendents to discuss the increasing supply of cannabis, amphetamines and barbiturates. At this conference it was reported from Cardiff that the use of amphetamines, and Drinamyl (costing 5 shillings for three tablets), by young people 'presented a far more serious problem than heroin, cocaine or cannabis'. Birmingham's Detective Superintendent referred to a murder committed after 'a beatnik party' at which amphetamines were supposedly used. In Sheffield, said its Detective Superintendent, university students used amphetamines and gave them to friends before examinations, while 'many criminals' used amphetamines to heighten their reactions before committing crimes. The Detective Superintendent representing Bradford felt these drugs were too freely prescribed by doctors, and cited the case of a woman who had visited eight doctors in one evening and obtained a prescription from each. The Manchester police had evidence that barbiturates and amphetamines were sold by retail chemists without prescription and resold by patients who were prescribed more than necessary by their doctors.[81] The relationship between crime and drug use was usually parallel rather than causative. Rebellious adolescents who found their parents' homes uncongenial met similar youths in the district, and used Drinamyl together. 'They do not usually take their regular girlfriend to drug taking parties, and the seeking of sexual adventure plays an unimportant part in such parties,' two psychiatrists reported in 1965. 'Most have seen heroin and cocaine being sold and used, but very few have tried it and there is a widespread and healthy awareness of the dangers of these drugs.'[82] According to another expert observer, amphetamine users got 'in trouble for something which doesn't really mean a great deal to them. Even the regular pill swallower, at 50 a day, can stop without too much discomfort.'[83]

In February 1964, only months after becoming Prime Minister (and a day after a report on purple hearts in Soho was published in the *Evening Standard*), Sir Alec Douglas-Home (1903–95), wrote to his Home Secretary, Henry Brooke (1903–84) about recent newspaper reports 'about Purple Hearts and . . . obscene publications'. He asked if his government should act on 'these colourful topics?'[84] Brooke replied on 18 February explaining that purple hearts were 'an evil that ought to be stamped out'. The police currently were not empowered to prosecute for unauthorised possession, 'as they can under the Dangerous Drugs Act in the case of narcotic drugs', but a bill was being drafted to prove that the Conservatives 'mean what we say about helping the young of our country to grow up straight'.[85] Douglas-Home replied approving immediate legislative action. Brooke forthwith consulted police chiefs about legislation on amphetamines and barbiturates.[86] The Chief Constable of Kingston-upon-Hull's reply typified the provincial response. He had 'no evidence' of misuse, although 'occasionally rumours are heard' that Drinamyl was 'passed at parties and in cafes and coffee bars, but there is no evidence that this practice is widespread. No reports of the misuse of barbiturates have been received, but of course, if this class of drugs is a problem in other parts of the country, I would support any move to have them included in the proposed legislation.'[87] The Metropolitan Police Commissioner, Sir Joseph Simpson (1909–68), however favoured their inclusion: although barbiturates were less widely trafficked than amphetamines, Scotland Yard advised that forged or tampered barbiturate prescriptions for Sodium Amytal, Soneryl, Nembutal, Seconal and Tuinal were 'extensively used, mainly by women with neurotic tendencies'. This misuse 'could be very dangerous and could create a problem almost parallel to . . . amphetamines'.[88] Pharmaceutical companies opposed controls on barbiturates on the basis that they were not stimulants like amphetamines. Their lobbying quickly and easily prevailed.

The Drugs (Prevention of Misuse) Act accordingly limited controls to amphetamines. It was hurried through parliament so that it could come into force in the same month as the October general election: 'I am extremely keen to get this Bill,' Brooke minuted.[89] This 'hastily conceived restrictive legislation', as The Times called it, was considered in committee and scarcely debated in either House of Parliament.[90] The Economist identified the bill's contents with the commercial needs of pharmaceutical companies: its effects would be 'probably bad, because clumsy wording brings its sledgehammer penalties down with equal force upon silly children as upon the men who sell them drugs'.[91] The unlawful possession of amphetamines was made an offence; the penalties on summary conviction were a fine of up to

£200, or imprisonment up to six months, or both. The Act included no controls on the manufacture, distribution or record of sales, and did not prevent lavish prescribing by physicians, but allowed magistrates to issue search warrants on clubs and cafés. It gave the impression of an unbalanced piece of legislation aimed at young people and their haunts. Amphetamines were resolutely brought within the criminal justice system. For the rest of the twentieth century they remained the stimulant most commonly used illegally in Britain. Despite their association with overdoses, psychoses, accidents and (from the 1980s) HIV transmission, government policy focused on policing—suppressing their supply and arresting their users—rather than medically orientated harm-reduction strategies.

Journalists' spurious identification on the 1964 Act with Mods and Rockers made it seem all the more retaliatory. The confrontations between these groups of scooter and motorcycle-riders began on the dismal Easter bank holiday weekend of 1964 at a melancholy eastern seaside resort called Clacton. The disturbances there were chiefly a reaction against everything connoted by the deadly phrase 'family weekend'. If the phenomenon was indeed an attempt to conquer ennui, it may be significant that many Mods were accountancy trainees.[92] During the next few years the Clacton disturbances were followed by bank holiday weekend confrontations between Mods, Rockers and the police at other seaside towns. These events were exaggerated and distorted by journalists. One of the press allegations was that purple hearts—and the feelings of persecution they engendered—were contributing to the excitement of rival gangs. The Clacton fracas happened a few days before the Drugs (Prevention of Misuse) Act was debated by the House of Commons on 31 March, and Brooke's legislation was misleadingly depicted by some journalists as a direct response to Mods and Rockers. Not all newspapers were impressed. 'Emotion is never a sound basis for law-making—particularly by the Home Office,' *The Times* editorialised. It questioned 'how much of today's hooliganism is due to these pills' and whether Brooke's 'unjustified' legislative stunt 'will have any effect on the behaviour of these restless youngsters'.[93] *The Economist* similarly thought that bigots were contriving a bogus panic. 'The possession of a scooter and peculiar (if clean) clothes is beginning to be taken as a sign of moral iniquity,' it noted. Brooke's proposals reflected this prejudice by menacing with imprisonment 'for up to six months any young person found in authorised possession of some currently fashionable and normally non-addictive drug, much valued (even if mistakenly) by students for over-coming pre-examination nerves. But nobody gets emotional about drunks who, in Liverpool, really ripped out the interior of a pub. Unreasoning prejudice against a new and as yet unexamined product of affluence is a bad basis for social legislation.'[94]

The engineers of moral panic were not deterred. *The Daily Telegraph*, for example, claimed that on August bank holiday weekend of 1965, parents summoned to Margate police station were aghast to learn 'that their daughters had been sleeping around with youths carrying the recognised weekend kit, purple hearts and contraceptives'. In fact, as Kenneth Leech was almost alone to notice, 'to the Mods, clothes were the central feature of the world', and 'girls were not popular in the Mod world'. The Mods were not aggressive, and deliberately resisted 'the conventional picture of masculinity'. They were 'an implicitly . . . bisexual phenomenon'.[95] At a time when all homosexual acts were still criminal in Britain, and national leaders fulminated against homosexuality for vitiating British manhood, the hostility to Mods is understandable.

There was no evidence in 1964 of extensive drug use at Clacton or other resorts where Mods and Rockers congregated. Amphetamines, or any other drugs, do not feature in the most detailed survey of the Whit Monday clash at Margate in 1964, which significantly concluded that the influence of young people's own age group now surpassed that of parental discipline.[96] The leading study of Mods and Rockers identified 'a rapid increase in the amount of drug usage in seaside towns' during the three years *after* the 1964 Act.[97] Some of this increase was attributable to 'My Generation', a song written by Pete Townshend (b. 1945) of The Who and issued in 1965. 'My Generation', sung in mimicry of the stuttering associated with amphetamine overdose, and containing the refrain 'I hope I die before I get old', became the Mods' anthem. A drug's consumption often rises after it has been prohibited or controlled. Perhaps, when a drug is prohibited, the number of occasional social users who move into heavy use is higher, because users of proscribed substances will be more disposed both to deviant behaviour and the personality disorders associated with addiction. This renews what ought to be a basic question about the practical politics of drug legislation: does misconduct lead to the imposition of controls, or do such controls provoke defiance? Certainly, if a good law is one that reduces misconduct while bad law results in increasing infractions, then the Drugs (Prevention of Misuse Act) of 1964 was, as *The Economist* stated, 'singularly ill-considered'.[98] (Under the Act, there were 958 convictions in the fourteen months to December 1965, and 1121 in 1966.)

Drinamyl consumption was heavy in vulnerable London sexual sub-cultures. Kenneth Leech (b. 1939), a redoubtable clergyman who was Secretary of the Soho Drugs Group in 1967–71, witnessed high-dose amphetamine use by sexually ambivalent youths congregating in small, all-night coffee bars in northern Soho. In this period, public houses were obliged to shut before eleven in the evening by long-established regulations intended to criminalise night-life except for a privileged few in private clubs. Leech worked around 1966–7 as a counsellor in a coffee bar off Wardour Street. Its customers

> were either homosexual or experimenting with homosexuality. The average age was about 18–19. There were at this time only a few het-erosexual girls, and a large number of 'chickens', that is, very young, pretty boys who were acquired and used by the older ones. Promiscuity was normal, and relationships changed very rapidly. The kids were always 'falling in love', acquiring new 'affairs' (which lasted for a whole week!), and having endless dramas. Clothes and money were often cru-cial in the creation of new affairs. The period was really the screaming peak of the young homosexual clothing industry, and frequently I got the impression that it was more a matter of falling in love with a boy's clothes than with him as a person. The atmosphere in the club . . . was superficially light-hearted, girlish and hysterical. Most conversations were about sexual exploits, and were a combination of fact and fantasy, where the borderlines between the two became very blurred. . . . Use of amphetamines by kids in the club was closely related to the confusion about sexual identity. There was as much boasting about the number of pills consumed as about the number of sexual acts . . . the amphetamine highs were more pleasurable than sex to many of the youngsters, or at least it was only when they were 'blocked' that they could act out their homosexual role. The maintenance of a 'camp' image was essential to the life-style of the club, and amphetamine use helped to create the artifi-cial security in which this was possible.[99]

Later he encountered in north Soho a group of lesbian Methedrine injectors united by the needle, sexual relationships and the subcultural life both of Soho and prison. Their love affairs were generally more enduring, and their break-ups more tragic, than among the youths. Leech found 'these girls tremendously kind and warm, but intensely jealous and possessive'.[100]

The heyday of the Soho club fashion for amphetamines was in 1963–4, but this scene was never as vigorous as the 'speed freak' extremism in San Francisco and other American cities. The more prevalent fashions among British young people were for cannabis and after 1966 for LSD. However, late in 1967 and during 1968 a deplorable new phenomenon erupted among London's needle-users. Methylamphetamine began to circulate widely, usually in the form of Methedrine ampoules. Anticipating changes in the law enacted in 1967, a Soho doctor began substituting Methedrine for cocaine as a stimulant to be used with heroin. Heroin addicts began injecting Methedrine instead of cocaine, and perhaps more ominously, amphetamine-users progressed from oral to intravenous use of the drug. As Kenneth Leech insisted, 'It was the spread of Methedrine ampoules which provided the bridge between the needle culture and the kids in the clubs. It was Methedrine that played the "escalation" role which is often, wrongly, attributed to cannabis. It was Methedrine that made the process of "fixing" an integral part of the West End drug culture. The West End was not the same after Methedrine: it was more destructive, more hopeless, more needle-centred.'[101] In response, pharmacists voluntarily withdrew Methedrine in November 1968, while the drugs advisory charity Release issued highly effective advertising with the slogan, 'Speed kills'. As a result of these restrictions, and of the diminishing supplies of heroin, users began injecting the contents of Tuinal and Nembutal barbiturate capsules. Barbiturates made many young people more irritable and aggressive than heroin.

The fashion for amphetamines became more entrenched in the provinces. A Balsall Heath physician signed orders for 43,000 Drinamyl tablets between March 1968 and November 1969. When challenged by the authorities, he claimed that he had consumed them himself, to alleviate depression; in fact he supplied Birmingham prostitutes, whose ponces resold on the black market. The General Medical Council in 1970 suspended him for ten months.[102] A doctor practising in St John's

Wood was struck off the Medical Register in 1970 for lavish prescriptions of Drinamyl to youths from as far away as Worthing, Welwyn, Reading, Romford, Bognor, Basingstoke, Southend, Portsmouth, Loughborough and Edinburgh. He charged five guineas per prescription, and allegedly earned about £6000 annually on Drinamyl fees alone.[103]

Amphetamines and barbiturates were far from the only therapeutic substances that were habit-forming. The 1950s saw the dawn of what David Healy, in his matchless study, has entitled *The Anti-Depressant Era*. The earliest impetus for this came from French drug discoveries. It had been recognised by the 1930s that a hormone called histamine was important in allergies, and researchers at the Pasteur Institute in Paris started seeking antihistamine agents. In 1939 the Institute began collaborating with the French pharmaceutical company, Rhône-Poulenc, and from 1942 the company began marketing such dimethylamines as phenbenzamine (Antergan) and diphenhydramine (Benadryl) as treatment for allergies. These substances were found to have sedative effects, and in 1943 French psychiatrists began to use them in managing schizophrenia and manic depression. Rhône-Poulenc researchers subsequently produced promethazine, which was initially marketed under the trade name of Phenergan as an aid against allergies and travel sickness before being introduced into anaesthesia in 1949. In the early 1950s the company's researchers tested a range of phenothiazines, of which chlorpromazine seemed especially promising. After a trial in 1952 on French psychiatric patients, chlorpromazine was recognised as a breakthrough. Indeed under the trade names of Thorazine and Largactil it was the first anti-psychotic drug, and the most important advance in psychopharmacology (a term revived in 1957). In 1954 Smith, Kline and French introduced the drug to the USA, where it soon had such sales to asylums that the company's estimated profits on the drug in 1955 were $75 million.

Psychopharmacology became a major new research area promising large profits. The Swiss pharmaceutical company Geigy (founded as a dye company at Basle in 1859) began investigating a compound named iminodibenzyl, which had first been synthesised in 1898. Roland Kuhn (b. 1912) of Münsterlingen Hospital near Konstanz reported in 1957 that the drug was a powerful anti-depressant. This was at a time when there was a widespread doubt that an anti-depressant compound could exist. When he presented his findings to a session of about a dozen people at the World Congress of Psychiatry in Zurich, his audience did not notice that he had said anything significant. He delivered a similar paper in 1958 at the Galesburg State Hospital in Illinois. Again this passed unnoticed until it was published.[104] Imipramine, Kuhn found, was an anti-depressant that did not arouse euphoria. Geigy were slow to act on his findings until a powerful shareholder, one of whose family was depressed, took home some imipramine, which swiftly cured her. This investor urged the launch of the drug, which was first marketed in Switzerland under the proprietary name of Tofranil in November 1957, and appeared elsewhere in Europe in 1958.

There were other crucial advances. The alkali metal lithium had first been isolated in 1817 by the Swede Johan August Arfwedson (1792–1841), and was recommended in 1859 for the treatment of gout by Sir Alfred Garrod (1819–1907). Its association with cardiac failure led to it being banned by the US Federal Drug Administration in 1949. However, in the same year the Australian researcher John Cade (1912–80) began investigating lithium, and found that it tranquillised manic patients. It was soon an important resource in psychopharmacology treating manic depression (bipolar affective disorder). The Swiss company Ciba in 1952–3 investigated *Rauwolfia serpentina*, a plant root used to treat hypertension and insanity in India, and from it isolated an active salt. The company named this 'reserpine'. The psychiatrist Nathan Kline (b. 1923) commended reserpine's anti-depressant powers to the American Psychiatric Association. As a result of lobbying by Kline and others, Congress passed the Mental Health Study Act of 1955 whereby two million dollars a year was allocated for psychopharmacological research. An American researcher employed by Ciba coined the word 'tranquiliser' to describe reserpine's effects. Also in the USA Wallace Laboratories in 1955 began marketing the sedative meprobamate under the brand names of Miltown and Equanil. 'America is passing from one age to another—from the Benzedrine Age to the Equanil,' the travel journalist Lord Kinross (1904–76) wrote after his 1956 tour of the US. 'Today the nation-wide slogan is RELAX!' He even saw it written up in offices. Relaxation was guaranteed by those 'blessed tranquillising pills of Miltown and Equanil, promising, in the words of *Life* magazine, "calming down the raging personality or lifting up those who remain inordinately depressed" '.[105] Meprobamate was marketed for psychiatric out-patients as well as stressed business-men; it became one of the most profitable commercial drugs before being deleted from the US Pharmacopoeia.[106] By 1961 Americans were spending $75 million a year 'on the Miltown-type of . . . don't-give-a-damn pills'. When swished in gin they were known as 'Miltini'.[107]

The success of meprobamate encouraged Hoffmann-La Roche to investigate other sedatives. In 1957 its researchers discovered a powerful sedative called Librium; it was patented in 1959 and swiftly approved by US regulators. Some of the early tests of Librium were conducted on leopards, lions and tigers at San Diego Zoo. After a promotional film showing the dramatic effects of the drug on these savage beasts was shown, one English newspaper ran the story under the headline: 'The Drug That Tames Tigers—What will it do for Nervous Women?'[108] Librium was the first of the class of drugs called benzodiazepines; Hoffmann-La Roche soon identified another benzodiazepine with five times the strength of Librium. In 1963 it was marketed as Valium. Hoffmann-La Roche became the world's most successful pharmaceutical company as a result of its marketing of Librium and Valium. Librium was the most prescribed drug in the US with sales worth $59 million by 1965. US sales of Valium rose from a value of $27 million in 1963 to $200 million in 1970. Hoffmann-La Roche's global sales of $840 million in 1970 far exceeded those of rival companies.

Other habit-forming drugs of this period included methylpentnol, which was introduced by Margolin in the USA in 1951 as a short-acting hypnotic for use in dentistry, childbirth and on children who were apprehensive visiting doctors. Proprietary brands were marketed in Britain in capsules and elixirs under the trade names Parafynol, Dormison and Oblivon. Oblivon was known as 'the confidence pill' because it was advertised to help with such emergencies as public speaking, job interviews, asking for pay rises and visiting the dentist.[109] There were reports of brides using Oblivon to gain confidence as they walked down the aisle to marry and of dogs being dosed with it on Fireworks Night. 'So many of my patients suffer from a lack of self-confidence,' a Surrey physician explained. 'Instead of facing their problems, reorganising their lives, they just beg for something to shield them from reality. I try to give them advice, but I can't leave my surgery to sort out their domestic problems. All I can do is give them a drug.'[110] As many as a million of these sea-blue capsules (costing fourpence each) were sold weekly until August 1955, when the supply of Oblivon in Britain was restricted to medical prescription.

Such drugs were intended to improve the lives of people who were finding it difficult to function, or to maintain stability in their behaviour. Users of anti-depressants and sedatives might be pitied, teased or despised; their habits were often thought to be evidence of a cultural malaise. But although these prescription drugs were sometimes misused, and despite their users often seeming emotionally importunate or socially disruptive, they were not the targets of hostility, ostracism or criminal sanctions.

It was different with another breakthrough of Swiss psychopharmacology. The fungus called ergot grows on rye and other grasses, and for centuries had been used in childbirth (it can prevent haemorrhages). In 1918 the Swiss chemist Arthur Stoll (b. 1887) isolated the alkaloid ergot, and his protégé Albert Hofmann (b. 1906) continued investigating the medical possibilities of compounds related to ergot in the laboratories of the Swiss pharmaceutical company, Sandoz of Basle. In 1943 Hofmann experienced vivid hallucinations after accidentally ingesting a small quantity of one of ergot's analogues, lysergic acid diethylamide. He repeated the experience on himself and volunteers. The first report on the mental effects of this substance, which soon became known as LSD, was published in 1947. Sandoz officials believed the drug could help psychiatric workers to investigate schizophrenia, and in 1949 supplied a sample to an American psychiatrist, who ran a trial in Los Angeles. Other American psychiatrists recommended its use in psychotherapy, in 1953 Dr Ronald Sandison opened a clinic therapeutically administering LSD in England, and it was used on Swiss psychiatric out-patients.[111]

In 1951 Sandison gave some Sandoz LSD to Alfred M. Hubbard (1901–82), a former US intelligence officer who had become a millionaire in the Canadian uranium business. In 1953 Hubbard was also given mescaline by an English psychiatrist, Humphrey Osmond, who had reported in 1952 on the possibilities of using the drug to treat schizophrenia. It was Osmond who coined the word 'psychedelic' (meaning 'mind-manifesting') in 1956. Hubbard was one of those optimistic millionaires who felt that the American business genius for universal simplification could find a swift answer for everything, including the profoundest religious mysteries. He began organising LSD group sessions in Vancouver, 'raising buried guilts and traumas and permitting people to get on better terms with themselves', according to Aldous Huxley, who was given his first LSD experience by Hubbard in 1955. Huxley, who lived in California, had previously experimented with mescaline: his descriptions and analysis of his hallucinogenic experiences, in *The Doors of Perception* (1954) and *Heaven and Hell* (1956), were highly influential. University of Texas students who had read Huxley found that peyote was legally procurable from Hudson's Cactus Garden in Austin during the early 1960s. Because the supply was legal, it was also cheap: 'In their crowd, drugs were about altering consciousness, not just getting fucked up, although this distinction doubtless meant more to some than to others.'[112]

Hubbard, who ordered forty-three cases of LSD from Sandoz in 1955, became a proselytiser for its mystical and therapeutic properties.[113] Many public figures interested in delving into their unconscious tried LSD in this decade. The drug was appreciated by such diverse figures as the film star Cary Grant (1904–86), the writer Anaïs Nin (1903–77) and *Time-Life* proprietor Henry Luce (1898–1967). In 1958 Hubbard financed a private clinic in Canada administering LSD therapy. Its session room was furnished with a couch, stereo music system and altar with burning candles, and decorated with a crucifix, a statue of the Blessed Virgin Mary and Dalí pictures. Typically, when a subject of LSD therapy broke into convulsive sobs near the end of his trip, Hubbard commented: 'This is all repressed material coming out; this is what we bury to become men.'[114] Thousands of people took LSD as a form of therapeutic self-exploration: some, such as Thelma Moss (1919–97), like Renaissance voyagers, published their accounts: 'I travelled deep into the buried regions of the mind. I discovered that in addition to being, consciously, a loving mother and a respectable citizen, I was, unconsciously, a murderess, a pervert, a cannibal, a sadist and a masochist.'[115]

Anslinger had sat on a wartime committee superintending pharmaceutical research for substances that would be useful in interrogation, brainwashing, debriefing agents or disorientating enemies. Cannabis, cocaine, ether, Benzedrine and opiates were tested inconclusively (with or without consent) on CIA officers, convicted criminals and others. In 1951 the Central Intelligence Agency (CIA) became enthused with the possibilities of LSD. Its Director Allen Dulles (1893–1969) in 1953 authorised a secret research programme, code-named MK-ULTRA, into mind control drugs: Sandoz supplied the LSD for MK-ULTRA in the same year. Among other trials, massive doses were given for as long as seventy-five consecutive days to inmates (mostly black) at Lexington prison-hospital for addicts. Much of this research was amateur, unsavoury and scandalous. MK-ULTRA recruited an FBN agent who lured unwitting civilians to safe houses in New York and San Francisco, administered LSD to them and spied on their reactions with surveillance equipment. He often arranged for his subjects to perform sexually, and watched through two-way mirrors as he drank Martinis. His work continued until 1963. 'It was fun, fun, fun,' he bragged. 'Where else could a red-blooded American boy lie, kill, cheat, steal, rape and pillage with the sanction and blessing of the All-Highest?'[116]

Huxley recommended a non-confrontational strategy of LSD research: 'Go about your business quietly, don't break the taboos or criticize the locally accepted dogmas. Be polite and friendly—and get on with the job.'[117] This discreet procedure was anathema to the noisy populists who began promoting LSD after 1960. As a result LSD ceased in 1962 to be regarded as a useful tool in psychiatry, and rapidly became the subject of high political controversy. In that year (under legislation primarily directed at amphetamines) it was classified as an 'experimental drug' in the USA, which meant that with effect from June 1963 all research had to be approved by the FDA in Washington. The FDA moved swiftly to terminate LSD research; the last authorised programme in the USA ended in 1975. The drug was also effectively removed from therapeutic use by psychiatrists. In the aftermath of Congress passing this federal law, LSD first appeared on the streets in American cities during 1963 (doses were dropped on sugar cubes); the drug began leaking from the Sandoz factory in New Jersey to Greenwich Village as soon as its non-scientific use was prohibited. LSD became illegal in the USA in 1966. The American example was followed in Europe.

Three individuals share responsibility for transforming perceptions of LSD: the novelist Ken Kesey (b. 1935), Allen Ginsberg, and the renegade psychiatrist Timothy Leary (1920–96). Kesey was one of those on whom LSD was tested under MK-ULTRA. He had dropped out of Stanford University, and was living as a Beat near the campus when he volunteered to participate in drug tests at nearby Menlo Park Veterans' Hospital. His motive was the fee, but LSD proved revelatory. Kesey, who had worked as an orderly at a psychiatric hospital, claimed that the idea of the mute, schizophrenic narrator of his novel about asylum life, *One Flew Over the Cuckoo's Nest* (1962), came to him on an acid trip. He began holding parties of self-exploration at which the guests ate venison chili laced with LSD. His psychedelic adventures of 1964 touring the States with his gang of exuberant, flamboyantly dressed 'Merry Pranksters' on a psychedelically decorated touring bus were publicised by Tom Wolfe (b. 1931) in *The Electric Kool-Aid Acid Test* (1968). Kesey and his 'Merry Pranksters' subsequently settled in a rural commune at which they introduced Hell's Angels to 'acid', and outraged their neighbours. Their intention was to defy and irritate suburban society.

Allen Ginsberg first took LSD in a trial conducted at the Mental Research Institute in Palo Alto, California, in 1959. He volunteered for the trial as part of a long personal quest. In 1948, while masturbating in East Harlem over a copy of *Songs of Innocence and Songs of Experience*, he had heard the voice of William Blake (1757–1827), and experienced ecstatic visions. When he crawled out onto the fire escape, and called to the women in the adjacent apartment, 'I've seen God,' they slammed the window shut. He was not deterred. Instead he vowed to widen his consciousness and began a systematic exploration of his mind by the use of strong drugs, including heroin, mescaline, peyote and psilocybin. He often hallucinated a monstrous serpent, representing death, but despite the panic that his visions aroused, he felt obliged to take mind-expanding drugs. After consulting Indian gurus, Ginsberg cast off his obsession with enlarging his consciousness. Afterwards he reflected, 'The remarkable thing is that I stupefied myself from 1948 to 1963. A long time—that's fifteen years preoccupied with one single thought.'[118]

His friend Leary, in early manhood, had been expelled from the US military academy at West Point for drinking and from the University of Alabama after being found in the girls' dormitory. He became a clinical psychologist in California and seemed on a steadier course until his wife gassed herself in their garage on his thirty-fifth birthday. Shortly after his appointment in 1960 to the Department of Social Relations at Harvard University, he sampled psilocybin (magic mushrooms) while in Mexico, and experienced what he claimed was a mystical revelation. He began controlled trials of psilocybin on 175 people and supplied the drug to the poet Charles Olson (1910–70) and then to Ginsberg. Wandering through Leary's house, naked except for his chunky spectacles, Ginsberg announced, 'I'm the Messiah. I've come to preach love to the world. We're going to walk through the streets and teach people to stop hating.' He wanted to telephone Khrushchev and Kennedy, but settled for Kerouac instead. 'The revolution is beginning,' he shouted down the line at Kerouac. 'Gather all the dark angels of light at once. It's time to seize power over the universe and become the next consciousness!'[119] In the next few months Ginsberg and Leary gave psilocybin to the painters Willem de Kooning (1904–97) and Franz Kline (1910–62), the jazz musician Dizzy Gillespie (1917–93), Thelonius Monk (1917–82), who epitomised bebop culture, and the poet Robert Lowell (1917–77). Anxious about the eccentricity of Leary's psilocybin research, the Harvard authorities suppressed it in 1962. He was induced thereupon to revert to experimentation with LSD by an Englishman who had a mayonnaise jar full of it.

Hubbard's approach to LSD was exclusive: Huxley's attitude was that of a member of a hereditary intellectual aristocracy. As the latter wrote to Humphrey Osmond in 1959, 'We met two Beverly Hills psychiatrists the other day, who specialize in LSD therapy at $100 a shot—and really, I seldom met people of lower sensitivity, more vulgar mind! To think of people made vulnerable by LSD being exposed to such people is profoundly disturbing.'[120] Ginsberg, however, encouraged Leary to take a democratic approach to the publicity and supply of mind-altering substances. Like Kesey they became brash populists. Leary claimed that everyone had a right to manage his or her nervous system, and started a psychedelic academy called the Freedom Center on the Mexican coast. One night in 1962, when 'all heads' had 'turned on', Leary 'looked out with a kind of glazed look in his eyes and said, "We're going to have to write a bible about this"'.[121] When the occupants of the Center were deported from Mexico, after pressure from the US authorities, in 1963 (the same year that Harvard University dismissed Leary), he became a major figure of the counterculture expounding the virtue of mystical development through psychedelic drugs. Newspapers seldom mentioned LSD until 1962, and then only in references to its psychiatric use. The change came in 1963, when the pathological opportunism of journalists found a new subject for sensationalism. Within a few years these were typical headlines mixing real tragedies with a persistent strain of prurience:

> MYSTERY OF NUDE COED'S FATAL PLUNGE
> NAKED IN A ROSE BUSH
> HER SON'S TRAGIC TRIP
> STRIP-TEASING HIPPIE GOES WILD IN LAKESPUR
>   ON LSD
> NIGHTMARE DRUG PERIL GROWS
> HOME DRUG LAB RAIDED IN BRONX
> BOBBY BAKER KIN IN TREE NUDE

Scare stories escalated. A series of syndicated American newspaper articles in 1967 began by warning, 'LSD may cause cancer in drug users—and deformity and death in their children.' The articles were advertised on Chicago radio by an announcer who said that acid-heads thought LSD was harmless: 'Well, they're wrong—*dead wrong*. People who take LSD eventually get cancer.'[122]

'Tune in, turn on, drop out' was Leary's slogan. In 1967 he founded the League of Spiritual Discovery as a psychedelic quasi-religion using LSD as its sacrament. 'The instruments of systematic religion are chemicals,' he wrote in *The Politics of Ecstasy* (1970). 'Drugs are the religion of the twenty-first century.'[123] He politicised the human nervous system: 'Congress shall make no law abridging the individual's right to seek an expanded consciousness.'[124] When Sandoz declined to supply him with LSD and psilocybin, black-marketeers quickly obliged. Leary became a colossal bugbear to the US authorities. A community of psychedelic experimenters established by him in New York State was raided under the direction of a local district attorney and former FBI agent, Gordon Liddy (b. 1930), afterwards notorious in the Watergate conspiracy. Sexual licence as well as drugs distressed the neighbours: 'The panties are dropping faster than the LSD,' it was said.[125] Leary was denounced by President Richard Nixon (1913–94) as 'the most dangerous man in America',[126] and jailed in 1970 for possession of a small amount of cannabis. He escaped from prison with the aid of an underground revolutionary group, the Weathermen, and fled to Algeria, where he lived with the Black Panthers, an exiled group of black activists of whom Eldridge Cleaver (1935–1998) was the best known. After other adventures, Leary was extradited to the USA in 1973, sentenced to twenty-five years imprisonment, and paroled in 1976. Following his death of prostate cancer, his ashes were put in a rocket and fired from the Canary Islands into outer space.

What Leary called 'consciousness expansion' could as plausibly be called a hallucination. When he and his followers spoke of the 'transcendence' of the ego produced by psychedelic drugs, the authorities could just as well speak of 'psychotic reactions'.[127] According to one reliable estimate, 2 per cent of those who took LSD 'freaked', and of that 2 per cent one-third became psychotic: seven of every thousand people who took the drug, in other words, had a breakdown. Following Anslinger's example with cannabis, the authorities spread grotesque exaggerations of the dangers of the drug. One fabrication, which entered national mythology, was of the youth, or group of young people, tripping on LSD who gazed at the sun until its rays blinded them. 'Only when you sensationalise a subject matter do you get a reform,' declared Senator Abraham Ribicoff (b. 1910) of Connecticut in justification of these distortions during Congressional hearings on the subject. 'Only when the press and television comes in and gives it a real play . . . as something that affects all the country, do you get action.'[128] The American authorities' mixture of lurid propaganda and heavy policing was a weak deterrent. Teasing people who pompously claimed transcendent experience would have been more effective. As it was, millions of young Americans tried LSD.

San Francisco's Beats started to leave North Beach in 1960 as the result of police harassment, rising rents and throngs of voyeuristic tourists. They relocated in the Haight-Ashbury district where, by 1962, there was a small, discreet colony of Beats, dressed in black, looking anxious and talking of futility and guilt. The Beats, who had been nicknamed 'beatniks' by hostile journalists wanting to evoke associations with Soviet Russia's 'sputnik' rockets, were superseded in 1964 by parti-coloured optimists talking endlessly of love. By a similarly McCarthyite process, the Beats' word 'hipster', meaning someone in the know, was reduced by the press around 1965 into the pejorative 'hippie'. Haight-Ashbury, in its hippie phase, was a sanctuary from American corporate aggression; it promised a therapeutic passivity based on the pleasures and self-discovery involved in drugs and fornication. Hedonism was meant to cure guilt and anxiety. 'This lad is certainly a nonconformist,' declared the head of the Narcotics Division of

Los Angeles Police brandishing before Congress a photograph snapped during a subversive Acid Test held by Kesey and his 'Merry Pranksters' in Haight-Ashbury. 'He is presently under the influence of LSD . . . the nonconformist signs on the back of his jacket together with his [painted] face would certainly indicate the young lad was a nonconformist with our society.'[129] Drug use, declared Jerry Rubin (1938–94), founder of the Youth International Party (Yippies), 'signifies the total end of the Protestant ethic: screw work, we want to know ourselves.' Hippies and Yippies rejected 'American society's sick notion of work, success, reward, and status.'[130]

Haight-Ashbury was the scene of a psychedelic festival, the Love Pageant, held in October 1966 on the day that LSD became illegal in California. Its sequel, the Human Be-In of January 1967, received huge publicity from journalists who knew that stories of sex and drugs sold newspapers. This Human Be-In marked the end of the idealistic phase in Haight-Ashbury. 'Up till then, people came because they were full to overflowing and were sharing their fullness,' recalls one participant. 'After that it was the empties who came, wanting to be filled.'[131] There were many 'bad trips' because of the crude way that LSD was being taken. The Haight-Ashbury Free Clinic was set up as a 'calm centre': about 10,000 patients were seen from July to September 1967 during the Summer of Love. In the first half of 1967 the predominant drugs in Haight-Ashbury were marijuana and LSD. But by that summer worldwide publicity about the San Francisco scene was drawing misfits, renegades and criminals; a proportion of the newcomers were intravenous amphetamine-users ('speed freaks'), and comparable neither in habits nor ideals to the hippies. Life in Haight-Ashbury deteriorated into squalor, crime, sexual exploitation and disease. Its prototypical street people included the drug-dealer Superspade, who sported a button reading 'Superspade, faster than a speeding mind', until he was shot in the back of the head. The hippies drifted away to communes elsewhere. Haight-Ashbury became a centre of horrific polydrug abuse. David E. Smith (b. 1939), the admirable Medical Director of Haight-Ashbury Free Medical Clinic, summarised this disaster area in 1970.

Uneducated, and lacking any mystical or spiritual interest, many of these young people have travelled from across the country to find money, stimulation and easy sex in the Haight and to exploit the flower people they assume are still living there. Some have grown long hair and assimilated the hip jargon in the process, but they resemble true hippies in no real way. 'Street wise' and relatively aggressive in spite of the passive longings which prompt their drug abuse, they have little love for one another and no respect for the law or for themselves. Instead of beads and bright costumes, they wear leather jackets and coarse, heavy clothes. Instead of ornate buses, they drive beat-up motorcycles and hot rods. Although they smoke marijuana incessantly and drop acid on occasion, they generally dismiss these chemicals as child's play, and prefer to intoxicate themselves with opiates, barbiturates and amphetamines . . . most of the adolescents share a dreary, drug-based life-style. Few have any legal means of support, and since many are addicted to heroin, they must peddle chemicals, steal groceries and hustle change to stay alive . . . the possibility of being 'burned', raped or 'ripped off' is so omnipresent that most of the young people stay by themselves and try to numb their anxiety and depression under a toxic fog. By day they sit and slouch separately against the boarded-up storefronts in a drug-induced somnolence. At night they lock themselves indoors, inject heroin and plan what houses in the district they will subsequently rob.[132]

Hubbard, who had lost his fortune, loathed this degradation of his beloved drug, and became a special agent of the FDA involved in raiding clandestine laboratories.

When Lyndon Johnson (1908–73) delivered his State of the Union address in 1968, the greatest applause occurred after he had outlined proposals for suppressing LSD trafficking and other forms of crime. Under Johnson's initiative, the sale of LSD was classified as a felony in 1968, and possession became a misdemeanour. Psychedelic drugs were classified as Schedule I in 1970: officially they had no medical value. In Britain, the Drugs (Prevention of Misuse) Modification Order of 1966 for the first time made a criminal offence of possession of LSD. Lord Stonham (1903–71), the Home Office minister, spoke 'of the increasing menace of . . . LSD which can induce madness'.[133] He was horrified by 'the half-world of the young "hippies" in California. The half world!: it seems to me to be no world at all, and the difference appears to be between us and the inhabitants of Mars.' His government was 'much concerned . . . that such a phenomenon should not arise here'.[134] The Home Office, however, was powerless against the new drug fashion. When legal, LSD had chiefly been favoured by under-graduates of Oxford and Cambridge universities; after criminalisation, it became fashionable with other more dispersed groups as a social drug. The new law did not deter consumption, but the quality of the drug deteriorated greatly. 'Most of my acid appearances were nightmares, particularly in . . . the early '70s,' according to one acid-head. 'All that gummy, Disney, meaningless shit at the tail-end hours of tripping.'[135]

About eighty British physicians used LSD clinically or experimen-tally after Ronald Sandison in the early 1950s, but the practice became discouraged. The Scottish psychiatrist R. D. Laing (1927–89), whose book on schizophrenia *The Divided Self* (1960) achieved cult status, was forced to resign in 1965 as chairman of a psychotherapeutic clinic because of his continuing interest in psychedelic therapies. Around 1959 he had met one of the psychiatrists at Shenley mental hospital who were testing LSD on themselves and a few patients.[136] Subse-quently, Ginsberg introduced him to Leary. As Laing recalled,

> Leary had a very enthusiastic belief that everyone was completely crazy, that we were all going to blow ourselves up very, very soon, that we were all on a crash course, that everything had been tried—reason, politics, and wars—but nothing worked. Here was a drug that he thought altered people's minds, that once you tried it, nothing was the same again . . . He wanted it to be marketed . . . I didn't share his enthu-siasm for doing it that way because people were crazy enough without being driven even crazier. It was too abrupt to be given to people in general.[137]

Laing, who was appalled by a visit to Haight-Ashbury, came to deplore the 'incredible arrogance' of Leary and his associates considering them-selves 'some sort of world high command'.[138] He found LSD a helpful therapeutic agent, but warned the Home Office that it 'was going to fall into the hands of international criminal groups'.[139] His overtures were spurned. In 1976 his house was burgled, and after he called the police to investigate, they forced open a locked cabinet containing ninety-four ampoules of LSD: he was charged with unlawful possession of a Class A substance. He had acquired the drugs for therapeutic use before the passage of the Misuse of Drugs Act, and as the prosecution could not prove that the drugs had been acquired unlawfully, the case was dismissed in 1977, when he was awarded £500 in costs. Laing attributed this strange episode to his appearance as a defence witness in the criminal trial of a disgraced politician.[140] In 1977 he was visited by Detective Inspector Dick Lee, who led the investigation of 1974–7 into a conspiracy to manufacture LSD at a farm in Wales and supply it throughout Britain, which he later commemorated in his book *Operation Julie* (1978). Lee told Laing and another psychologist that they had been 'major suspects'.[141]

Under the Misuse of Drugs Act of 1971, LSD was classified in Britain as a Class A substance (together with heroin and other opiates) with possession liable to a maximum of seven years' imprisonment. In Finland, France, Germany, Greece, Ireland and Italy too LSD is classified in the top level of dangerous drugs. This legislative reaction was not commensurate with the character of the drug. In 1973 the final Report of the US National Commission on Marijuana and Drug Abuse concluded that LSD had 'a low dependence liability', that its use 'tends to be age-specific and transitory', and that consumers under its influence 'do not generally act in ways qualitatively different from their normal patterns of behaviour'.[142] The severity of LSD prohibition did not stop its supply; only fashion, in time, reduced the demand for it. Its users just became risible. In 1975 the French historian Michel Foucault (1926–84) visited Death Valley for 'a visionary quest' on LSD. 'The only thing I can compare this experience to in my life is sex with a stranger,' Foucault confided as he 'tripped' to the sound of Stockhausen's music. 'Contact with a strange body affords an experience of the truth similar to what I am experiencing.' LSD made him maudlin and even more self-absorbed. 'I am very happy,' he said, tears pouring down his cheeks. 'Tonight I have achieved a fresh perspective on myself'. He ranked his Death Valley experience together with his sado-masochistic forays in San Francisco as providing the critical revelations in his life. The arguments of his acclaimed, if overrated, *History of Sexuality* were influenced accordingly.[143] Foucault's pitiful naïveté recalls Alasdair MacIntyre's reaction in 1967 to claims advanced for psychedelic experience. 'The kind of intellectual work which authentically leads to new truths about the nature of things, that is workaday science and philosophy, is hard and often unrewarding and boring. But what is even more important is that learning truths about the nature of things no longer seems in any way concerned with learning *the* truth about the nature of things.'[144]

The vehement opposition of the US and European authorities to LSD, and their determination to discredit researchers interested in the therapeutic possibilities of the drug, made a glaring contrast with governments' attitudes to new psychotropic substances. Rather than laboratory raids and arrests, pharmaceutical companies were permitted to make critical interventions in the supply and control of drugs. Although the abuse of stimulants and depressants was entrenched by the 1930s, governments took serious measures only in the late 1950s to restrict the supply of amphetamines, and pharmaceutical companies successfully resisted measures against barbiturates and tranquillisers in the 1960s. International efforts at drug control had, since 1912, defined an addictive drug in terms of the effects produced by opiates or coca derivatives. The reactions of the central nervous system to the substances discovered in mid-century by French, Swiss and other researchers were so different that 'uppers' and 'downers' could not be incorporated into the dominant beliefs about addiction. When restrictions were introduced in the late 1960s by Western governments, many pharmaceutical companies began aggressive marketing in the less developed economies of Latin America, Asia and Africa. Regulations were either minimal or lightly enforced there. Thus middlemen in some Latin American states imported psychotropic substances legally from the US so as to smuggle them back for more lucrative street sales.[145] There was one positive result from this soaring consumption of pills and capsules. The prohibitive enforcement model that had developed since 1909, based on suppression of the supply and punishment of the user, began to be challenged as the misuse of medicines spread among non-marginal types. As the historian William McAllister has demonstrated, discussion of alternative approaches, based on medical, psychological and sociological expertise, became more respectable.[146] Officials began to think not just about the supply end of drug-trafficking, but about the causes of demand. The Opium Protocol signed in New York in 1953 placed a heavy emphasis on reducing cultivation and supply. The Single Convention on Narcotic Drugs of 1961 reduced this emphasis, to the displeasure of the US Commissioner of Narcotics.

Throughout this period the United Nations Commission on Narcotic Drugs had an inequitable approach to potentially harmful drugs. Narcotics were condemned, but pharmaceutical manufacturers, government officials, scientific researchers and physicians all preferred to view new psychotropic substances as benign. Despite earlier lessons with chloral and sulphonal, most regulators accepted pharmacological claims in the absence of long-term clinical experience. Because the new substances were not marketed as painkillers, and addiction had been conceptualised since 1909 in terms of opiates, it was widely assumed that psychotropics had little addictive potential.[147] As shown in chapter 8, the Home Office had recognised the problems surrounding barbiturates since the Compton-Burnett suicides of 1917. Despite this pedigree, Norman St John-Stevas (b. 1919), who was the second canniest Conservative politician of his generation on drugs, was rebuffed when in 1970 he urged that controls over barbiturates should be included in the Misuse of Drugs Bill. The Home Secretary, James Callaghan (b. 1912), replied that barbiturates were 'not a longstanding problem of any major proportions.' He claimed that Stevas did not appreciate 'the speed with which these [drug] fashions change', and (astonishingly) that problems with barbiturates had arisen 'only within the last few months'.[148] Prescriptions for barbiturates on the National Health Service were at that date standing at 15 million a year. During 1970 47,200,000 prescriptions for psychotropic drugs—sleeping draughts, appetite suppressants, tranquillisers and anti-depressants—were issued in England and Wales. Prescriptions for such drugs had risen by 19 per cent between 1966 and 1970, from 39.7 million to 47.2 million. The prescription of non-barbiturate hypnotics had risen by 145 per cent in that period, chiefly as the result of the introduction in 1965 of the prescription drugs Mandrax and Mogadon. There was a 220 per cent increase in the prescription of the minor tranquillisers Librium and Valium over the same period.

The political reaction against the new psychotropic substances began in the United States. The first medical witness before Senate hearings on the drugs industry in 1969 posed two questions: 'To what extent would Western culture be altered by the widespread use of tranquillisers? Would Yankee initiative disappear?'[149] It was not just that Librium and Valium were presented as sapping the aggression of the American Way. Critics who have been termed Pharmacological Calvinists condemned the escapism of their users. Feminists argued that masculine medical hierarchies were using Valium to sedate, control and suppress women. The sales and price techniques of pharmaceutical manufacturers were condemned: the British government in 1968–9 extracted refunds from Hoffmann-La Roche after allegations of excess profits. The company's reputation was compromised long before an industrial accident caused a major environmental disaster at its Seveso factory in Italy in 1975.

Shrewdly, when a draft treaty on psychotropic drugs emerged in 1968, Hoffmann-La Roche and other pharmaceutical multinationals recognised that this might be turned to their benefit. As few governments had the resources to scrutinise all newly marketed substances, the companies anticipated that a treaty would install a global regulatory system following FDA standards. This would assist corporations in obtaining government approval for their products and devising marketing strategies on a global basis: minimum barriers would exclude interlopers. In the period after 1968 pharmaceutical companies whittled down regulatory proposals to the minimum required to secure these goals.[150] Their tactics came to fruition at the conference on psychotropic substances convened by the United Nations at Vienna in 1971. The Austrian-born and Swiss-based lawyer Adolf Lande (b. 1905), who had drafted the treaty that was discussed at Vienna, attended the Conference (to some astonishment) as a member of the US delegation representing the Pharmaceutical Manufacturers' Association. This was only one example of the curious constitution of delegations. Senior executives in American companies attended as unofficial US observers. As McAllister recounts, two of the Swiss delegates were ultimately found to be employees of major pharmaceutical multinationals based in Switzerland. Hoffmann-La Roche's man worked tirelessly until he had obtained the object of removing some of the company's products from controls. After six Latin American countries unexpectedly supported weakening the treaty, the Conference secretariat noticed that the group's leader spoke clumsy Spanish. Investigation revealed that he, too, was a Hoffmann-La Roche employee.[151]

This international diplomacy was abstracted from users' reality. A major Leeds University survey in 1970 concluded that it was 'fruitless to speak of a "drug" addict since most of our everyday existence involves the use of some drug or another; a far better approach being to write of "heroin addiction" or "barbiturate poisoning" and to treat each drug abused as a specific problem in itself'.[152] According to the Leeds study, users of the 'soft' drug cannabis admired LSD users, to whom they applied the complimentary epithet 'heads'. However 'speed freaks' (Methedrine-users) and 'fixers' or 'mainliners' (intravenous hard drug-takers) were objects of 'suspicion and abhorrence'.[153] Once someone is labelled as a rule-breaker, all his or her acts are interpreted according to that status. Mods, supposedly with their purple hearts, and hippies with their fashionable drugs of preference were presented as archetypes of what not to be. Housewives were labelled as home-makers, not rule-breakers, so their drug habits were not sensationalised: indeed these women were often presented as examples of normality or ide-alised in the manner of a Norman Rockwell mom. 'The thousands of solitary amphetamine abusers', wrote Bruce Jackson in 1966, 'take drugs to *avoid* deviance—so they can be fashionably slim, or bright and alert and functional, or so they can muster the *quoi que* with which to face the tedium of housework or some other dull job—and the last thing they want is membership in a group defined solely by one clear form of rule-breaking.'[154] The former government minister William Deedes (b. 1913) was the best-informed and most constructive Con-servative on the subject of drugs in this period. Even he asserted in 1970, 'No-one can doubt that medical props for sleepless adults or hard-pressed housewives represent quite a different problem from that embodied in this cult for mood-changing, self-manifesting drugs, the hallucinogens.'[155] This spurious dichotomy was reflected in the Vienna Treaty of 1971 whereby hallucinogens were put under strict control while far weaker limitations were placed on highly lucrative stimulants and depressants.

Although the controls agreed at Vienna in 1971 have been tightened subsequently, the pharmaceutical companies' impact has been endur-ing. It is one measure of their continuing influence that the US *National Drug Control Strategy* published in 1989 did not mention bar-biturates, amphetamines, and comparable substances that are acquired both legally and illegally for misuse. When William Bennett (b. 1943), Director of the Office of National Drug Policy, claimed in the docu-ment 'that drugs represent the gravest present threat to our national well-being', he did not mean drugs manufactured by great US corpo-rations, but drugs whose consumers could be labelled as rule-breakers. This was despite the insistence elsewhere in the *National Drug Control Strategy* that the 'essence' of the problem was 'use itself' and that the millions of non-addicted users were '*highly* contagious'. The Report equally condemned 'experimental first use, casual use, regular use and addiction *alike*' (italics added); but excluded the stimulants and depressants that enrich corporate America and whose early history has been provided in this chapter.[156] Although the rhetorical overkill of the late twentieth-century US war on drugs was implacable, some interests were exempt from its targeting. After all, as a US president once said, the chief business of the American people is business.

ELEVEN

The First Drugs Czar

The law does not content itself with classifying and punishing crime. It invents crime.
—NORMAN DOUGLAS

Any one side of any jailhouse wall is never much different than any other side.
There are only the same old threadbare variations on the same age-old
warnings against the well-tried ancestral foes: whisky and women, sin
and cigarettes, marijuana and morphine, marked cards and capped
cocaine, dirty laughter and easy tears, engineered dice and casual disease,
bad luck and adultery, old age and shyster lawyers, quack doctors
and ambitious cops, crooked priests and honest burglars.
—NELSON ALGREN

HARRY ANSLINGER, COMMISSIONER of the Federal Bureau of Narcotics (FBN) from 1930 until 1962, was egotistical, authoritarian, energetic, brutal and unscrupulous. Wily rather than intelligent, he was suspicious of conspicuous intelligence in others. He was the first American to be dubbed a drug 'czar': the word is inapt, for it promises an absolutist's solution to a problem that is in fact chronic.[1] Subsequent US drug czars have perpetuated his strategies and rhetoric: William Bennett, who was appointed in 1989 to head the Bush presidency's National Office of Drug Control Policy, trusted the efficacy of criminal sanctions and prisons, but mistrusted treatment programmes. The Clinton drugs czar, General Barry McCaffrey (b. 1942), was equally confrontational. Anslinger's despotic influence was not only enduring but had global ramifications. Since 1909 American drug prohibition has impinged on underdeveloped countries as well as on the industrialised world. During the 1920s these strategies became integral to the anti-imperialist agenda of men like Congressman Porter. In the 1940s the drug prohibition crusade remained part of an increasingly interventionist US foreign policy, and after Anslinger's retirement, in the 1970s and 1980s, the internationalisation of presidential anti-drug wars became a neo-colonialist technique. Beginning around 1950, American illicit drug consumption began to rise sharply, and the behaviour of some young American drug delinquents began to be imitated by young Europeans. Increasingly the techniques of US drug prohibition, which had so exacerbated the country's domestic problems, were imposed in European states. In the 1960s, and again in the 1980s, anti-narcotics agents believed that American culture was so pervasive and penetrating that every US drug fashion would ensue in Europe. This assumption proved erroneous in the cases of crack cocaine and some designer drugs.

It may seem harsh to blame Anslinger for these misfortunes when he was the figurehead for beliefs held by most congressmen, editors and community leaders; but no figure was more representative of the twentieth-century war on drugs. 'Drug addiction is an evil,' he declared; for it to be 'rooted out and destroyed', it was only necessary for the USA to behave like 'a well-coached football team, crisp in its blocking, sharp in its tackling and well-drilled in all the fundamentals'.[2] His priority was the severing of supplies followed by the imprisonment of traffickers and isolation of users. 'You need stiff penalty laws [for dealers], and you need to commit the addict for treatment.' He never explained why harsher laws would work if existing penalties were ineffectual. Indeed he acknowledged, 'A [drug] peddler is an innate gambler: he will gamble on being caught, on how much a sentence he will get, and so on.'[3] No one can extirpate drug deals: transactions occur in the most improbable circumstances. In 1944 American junkie soldiers could score morphine on the Normandy beach-head after the D-Day invasion.[4]

For Anslinger the 1930s were a period of defensive improvisations at the FBN. Although Congress allotted $1.7 million to the Bureau in its first year of operation (1931–2), this budget was cut by $700,000 over the next three years as the Depression set in. No major traffickers were caught in 1934 because the Bureau could no longer bribe significant informants. In New York City, the centre of US trafficking, only petty dealers were being detained, which indicated that the 'narcs' there were as corrupt as under Nutt's direction. In 1935 Anslinger was hospitalised with nervous strain. While he was away the Bureau was in jeopardy of being submerged in a new Treasury enforcement agency. The Secretary of the Treasury, Henry Morgenthau (1891–1967), formally complained to Anslinger in 1936 that the Bureau was failing. He did not fasten on the fact that, as ever, opium-smokers were being diverted into heroin injection by official policies; only on the poor detection rate. Anslinger escaped being fired for ineptitude by his deftness in office politics and his sudden, aggressive support for a cause that he found to restore his reputation: a federal initiative against marijuana.

As we have seen, the smoking of marijuana had spread into American industrial cities following the prohibition of alcohol in 1920, and by 1937 was outlawed in every state under laws that allowed no distinction between addictive narcotics such as heroin, stimulants such as cocaine and hallucinogens such as marijuana. 'Marihuana was something new and adventuresome,' Anslinger recalled of the mid-1930s. 'The angle-wise mobsters were aiming their pitch straight at the most impressionable age group—America's fresh, post-depression crop of teenagers.'[5] He did not perceive that the success of the mobsters' pitch was largely attributable to the market conditions created by prohibitionist laws. When some politicians demanded federal legislation, Anslinger initially felt that his agents were overstretched coping with opiates without having to suppress a drug that could be easily grown in many states of the Union. Moreover, he accepted then that 'the marihuana addict' did not 'graduate into a heroin, an opium, or a cocaine user'; still less did 'a hardened narcotic user ... fall back on marihuana'.[6] On this point, if on no other, he was in agreement with William Burroughs, egregious author of *Junky*. Marijuana's 'ill effects' were 'grossly exaggerated' because 'people believe what they want to believe without regard to the facts'. Cannabis was 'not habit forming', although 'drug psychosis may result from prolonged and excessive use'.[7]

Characteristically, Anslinger began backing federal legislation against marijuana in a manner calculated to strengthen both his own position and that of the FBN. At a League of Nations conference of 1936 he urged its inclusion in future drug-control treaties. Back in Washington DC, he helped to prepare legislation on this topic. He did not regard the drug as a priority, but spoke in implacable language intended to signal that he was an uncompromising prohibitionist. Thus he assured the House of Representatives in 1937 that under the influence of marijuana 'some people will fly into a delirious rage and may commit violent crimes'.[8] In one lurid article, he produced the story of a marijuana 'addict' who turned his Florida home into 'a human slaughterhouse' by killing his parents, brothers and sister with an axe.[9] This and similar anecdotes were widely reproduced. He spoke on radio and addressed public forums; his agents lectured parents, educators and civic leaders. His pronouncements sounded authoritative even when they were avowedly speculative: 'How many murders, suicides, robberies, criminal assaults, hold-ups, burglaries and deeds of maniacal insanity it causes each year, especially among the young, can only be conjectured,' he declared in 1937.[10] His corrupt rhetoric, of course, incited rather than deterred consumption, and left many contemporary experts unimpressed. As the *JAMA* editorialised in 1937, the proposed federal control of cannabis hardly seemed justified by experience of the Harrison Act: 'After more than twenty years of federal effort and the expenditure of millions of dollars, the opium and cocaine habits are still widespread.'[11] The representative of the American Medical Association who opposed the bill before Congress was bullied and insulted.

In June the Marihuana Tax Bill was finally brought before the House of Representatives. Texas Congressman Sam Rayburn (1882–1961) assured his colleagues, 'This bill has an unanimous report from the committee and there is no controversy about it.' (A similar assurance had been offered in the House of Lords in 1925 when Indian hemp was casually prohibited in Britain.) When asked the bill's provisions, Rayburn added vaguely, 'It has something to do with something that is called marihuana. I believe it is a narcotic of some kind.'[12] Given the ignorance and laxity of the discussion, it is not surprising that after less than half an hour's debate, containing no medical or scientific data, the bill was passed on 14 June. It stated that anyone who grew, transported, prescribed or sold marijuana must register and pay taxes; failure to file was a federal offence, but as marijuana was illegal in every state, registration would make one liable to prosecution. The first conviction came seven days after the Act came into force in October 1937. Judge Foster Symes (1878–1951) of Denver sentenced a man aged fifty-eight to four years in Leavenworth Penitentiary and fined him $1000. 'I consider marihuana the worst of all narcotics—far worse than the use of morphine or cocaine,' Symes announced. 'Marihuana destroys life itself.'[13] The exaggerations of FBN agents were equally ferocious. They warned a journalist in New York in 1938 'that an overdose of marihuana generates savage and sadistic traits likely to reach a climax in axe and ice-pick murders'.[14]

Anslinger was proud of the fact that in the first five years after the 1937 Act, about 60,000 tons of marijuana were destroyed in the USA, and about 1000 persons arrested annually for violating the law. Opiates became increasingly unobtainable in the USA in the late 1930s, and receded even further during the Second World War, when smuggling was nearly impossible. He needed a substance to arouse sufficient public horror to justify the funding of his Bureau, which had so nearly been dismantled in 1935–6. Consequently, he predicted a profusion of marijuana-smoking among soldiers, and in 1944 set his agents to investigate 3000 marijuana cases in or near military camps. Despite his predictions, rather than because of his agents' vigilance, the crisis never eventuated. He resisted attempts to put marijuana in an accurate perspective among other drugs. Given the FBN's commitment to pursuing marijuana-users after 1937, he did not want the importance of this work discounted by experts. It was essential to the maintenance and expansion of his *imperium* to pursue all types of prohibited drugs and their users without distinction as to which substance was the most addictive, the most unhealthy or the most costly to society. This strategic need explains the Bureau's repeated references to marijuana as a narcotic, though it is nothing of the sort.

Accordingly Anslinger attacked the publication in 1942 of research by New York hospital physicians stating 'unqualifiedly that use of marihuana does not lead to physical, mental or moral degeneration and that no permanent deleterious effects from its continued use were observed'.[15] He alleged in *JAMA* that 'unsavoury persons engaged in the illicit marihuana trade will make use of the statement in pushing their dangerous traffic'. He deplored a collaborative medical report of 1942 in which the possibilities of therapeutic uses were hinted.[16] This research was undertaken as part of a project initiated in 1938 by Fiorello LaGuardia (1882–1947), Mayor of New York, who was sceptical about exaggerations surrounding Harlem tea-pads. A committee including psychiatrists, physicians, chemists, sociologists and officials finally reported in 1945. Their conclusions refuted, or at least challenged, every alarmist claim associated with the FBN since 1937. 'The obvious implication of the Committee's report', wrote an army physician, 'is that marihuana is essentially a harmless drug, used by inade-

quate persons as a means of obtaining a little fun out of life and is nothing to be alarmed about.'[17] The report is not faultless. While it accepted
that petty crimes were committed under the drug's influence, it under-
estimated the rowdiness that can be aroused in more brutish smokers
and the passivity of some long-term smokers. Anslinger succeeded in
curbing discussion of the LaGuardia report. The *JAMA* was induced to
recommend officials 'to disregard this unscientific, uncritical study, and
continue to regard marihuana as a menace':

> One investigator has described some tearful parents who brought their
> sixteen year old son to a physician after he had been detected in the act
> of smoking marihuana. A noticeable mental deterioration had been evi-
> dent for some time even to their lay minds. The boy said he had read an
> account of the LaGuardia Committee report and that this was his justi-
> fication for using marihuana. He read in *Down Beat*, a musical journal,
> an analysis of this report under the caption 'Light Up Gates, Report
> Finds "Tea" a Good Kick.'[18]

The influence of *Down Beat* is a pointer to the new importance of
musicians in drug fashions. Marijuana was used by such jazz musicians
as Louis Armstrong (1900–1971), Dizzie Gillespie, the drummer Gene
Krupa (1909–73), who was imprisoned for possession in 1943, and
Milton Mezzrow (1899–1972), who served seventeen months for possession in 1940–1 and subsequently celebrated the drug in his memoirs
Really the Blues (1946). Such 1930s songs as 'Sweet Marijuana Brown'
and 'That Funny Reefer Man' glamorised it. Fats Waller (1904–43)
wrote the words and music of 'Viper's Drag' (1934) which Nathaniel
West (1903–40) reproduced in his Hollywood novel, *The Day of the
Locust* (1939).[19] Young actors as well as young musicians discovered
reefers. When the film star Robert Mitchum (1917–97) was arrested on
a marijuana charge in 1948, and convicted in the following year, his
career was not destroyed. Anslinger deplored 'how the public reacts
respecting glamorous entertainment characters who have been
involved in the sordid details of a narcotics case. Is there a spontaneous
reaction which drives them out of show business as might have been
done a generation ago? Not at all. There seems to be some sort of public approval of these degenerate practices. The character is not ostra-
cized. Instead he or she immediately becomes a box-office headliner.'[20]

Richard Nixon similarly indicted 'the enemy' who 'permitted the drug plague to take root': 'When the casual user is a powerful movie director, a millionaire rock star, or an influential columnist, he is more dangerous than a hundred Brooklyn drug pushers'.[21]

Meanwhile, the heroin-pushers' business had been unwittingly helped in the mid-1940s by US government agencies. First, the Office of Strategic Studies installed Mafiosi bosses in political office after Sicily was captured from the Fascists in 1943. The results were negligible until 1946 when the US deported about 400 gangsters, including Anslinger's bugbear Luciano, who interested the Mafia in the possibilities of drug-trafficking: a form of business in which they had seldom previously participated. They began buying raw opium from Turkey, Lebanon and elsewhere, opened heroin laboratories in Sicily and from 1948 smuggled on a large scale to the USA and also Canada. The OSS's successor organisation, the Central Intelligence Agency, showed equal misjudgement in 1947 by supplying arms and money to Corsican gangs to attack and harass French trade unionists and communists. Marseille docks were a designated centre of this activity: consequently French Corsican gangs were soon a controlling force there. The seaport had been a great entrepôt for Turkish opium in the late 1920s, although this trafficking had gradually receded during the 1930s. By 1950 Marseille had revived as an international drugs centre. The Sicilian criminals agreed to let their French counterparts have the US heroin market on condition that they restricted their trafficking to the Italian-American gangs in the USA. The first raid on a Corsican-controlled heroin laboratory in Marseille (processing raw opium from Turkey) occurred in 1951. The Americans knew of five large laboratories there by 1953. Although the French authorities closed thirteen clandestine laboratories during 1950–70, many others continued operating. Four Corsican families—with the surnames of Venturi, Francisci, Guerini and Orsini—ran their own couriers and organisations. The French authorities were unhelpful to the FBN partly from the irritation that several European powers felt at the colonial ambitions of American drugs enforcement policy; partly as a result of police corruption in Marseille; and partly because French military intelligence officers were covertly raising funds by opium-trafficking in Indo-China. Anslinger never publicly denounced 'the French Connection', and until the Nixon presidency, the US government tolerated French trafficking as a necessary evil in the Cold War.

Corsican junk was popular with American and Canadian junkies. By 1960 the average cache of heroin smuggled into the US by the French Connection was ten times heavier than in 1950. Heroin's street price in New York was up to twenty times higher than the price of black-market heroin in London (£1 per grain), which meant that the French Connection concentrated on the lucrative market, and were never interested in supplying Britain. Probably about four tons of heroin was smuggled annually into the US from France alone, with smaller amounts from Asia and Mexico, although in 1963 the FBN gave the presidential Advisory Commission on Narcotics and Drug Abuse the inaccurate figure of $1^1/_2$ tons from all the world. As late as 1962 Anslinger's public denunciations were reserved for Red China and Cuba. When the FBN's leading agent in Europe pressed in 1963 for action against Turkish opium and the Corsican gangs, he was transferred from Rome to Kansas City. By 1969 the FBN estimated that up to 10 tons of heroin was being smuggled annually into the USA from Marseille. It was only under the Nixon presidency in 1969–70 that the US began to make serious diplomatic representations to the governments in Paris and Ankara rather than working through intermediate agencies such as Interpol. After a military coup in Turkey in 1971, the new regime agreed to American pressure to ban all opium-growing with effect from June 1972, and was rewarded with $37 million in aid. When the Connection was finally cut after over twenty years, Mexican heroin suppliers filled the vacuum.

Anslinger confided in the early 1960s that he had 'a *secret* book' on the Mafia. 'I gave a copy to Bob [Kennedy] but I couldn't to anyone else. No, I couldn't give it to Hoover, I just wouldn't risk it.'[22] He was obsessed with Luciano's contribution to the mushrooming supply of heroin to the USA after 1948. He exaggerated Luciano's importance, partly because it suited his taste to have scapegoats, but also because of the shoddy and meagre analysis by the FBN of its intelligence reports. The characterisations by journalists, Congressional enquiries and law enforcers of organised crime in the USA were often fit only for pulp magazines. In fact many Italian-American gang-leaders withdrew from drug-trafficking in fear that proposed federal laws would enable their prosecution for trafficking if their subordinates had handled drugs. Cuban criminals settling in South Florida after the CIA's failed

Bay of Pigs invasion of 1961 were quick to fill this void. They began smuggling heroin and cocaine into the US. Further bouts of Cuban immigration in 1965–72 and in 1980 brought new recruits to the Cuban gangs.

Anslinger opposed 'direct propaganda on drugs' because 'most young persons . . . acquired this evil habit not because of ignorance . . . but because they had learned too much'.[23] He deplored the success of *The Man With the Golden Arm*, a novel of 1949 by Nelson Algren (1909–81) about a junkie card-dealer from the Chicago slums. Frankie Machine, the protagonist of Algren's novel, eventually hangs himself; played by Frank Sinatra (1915–98) in the 1956 film version of Otto Preminger (1905–86), he renounces his habit. Another such film opposed by Anslinger was *Monkey on My Back* (1957) about a boxer who became therapeutically addicted to morphine while serving at Guadalcanal. 'No one would want to drench the American public with illustrations concerning the techniques of sexual perversion. Then why single out drug addiction?' He equally wished television programmers would 'stop building detective stories around drug addicts' because 'the facts are distorted . . . and the youngsters' curiosity improperly . . . aroused'.[24]

Algren knew what Anslinger would have rejected as a Commie slur: that social deprivation aggravates addiction. A pioneering study of the social ecology of opiate addiction in Chicago published in 1937 found the addicts clustered in areas of the inner city with cheap rented accommodation, delinquency, mental illness, suicide and prostitution.[25] The inhabitants of Frankie Machine's neighbourhood were dwarfed in 'the twisted ruins of their own tortured, useless, lightless and loveless lives'. They were not only dehumanised by poverty, ignorance and despair but riven with a guilt that was intrinsic to the American Way:

> the great, secret and special American guilt of owning nothing, nothing at all, in the one land where ownership and virtue are one. Guilt that lay crouched behind every billboard which gave each man his command-ments; for each man here had failed the billboards all down the line. No Ford in this one's future nor ever any place all his own. Had failed before the radio commercials, by the streetcar plugs and by the standards of every self-respecting magazine. With his own eyes he had seen the truer Americans mount the broad stone stairways to success surely and swiftly and unaided by others; he was always the one left alone.[26]

This point was made even more forcibly in Hal Ellson's novel *The Golden Spike* (1952) set in the Puerto Rican ghetto of New York. Anslinger's sense that class, urban deprivation and despair were factors in drug-taking was put to politically complacent ends. His statement in 1950 that narcotics including marijuana, were favoured by a criminal underclass, and that 'the average youth with an average environment' would never meet a dealer, served the political and economic status quo.[27] It was an assurance to the physicians whom he was addressing, and the Congressmen whom he so sedulously courted on Capitol Hill, that drugs were never going to threaten middle-class families. They were an inner-city vice. There was therefore no need to be fastidious: higher walls and stronger bars would solve the problem of addiction. It was no part of the solution to soften conditions for losers and sinners.

Young black men in the 1940s took heroin because they admired junkie bebop musicians like Charlie ('Bird') Parker (1920–55). Parker's example was destructive to the musicians who played with him and to hipsters who came to hear him. Jazz musicians hooked on heroin included the trumpeters Theodore ('Fats') Navarro (1923–50) and Chet Baker (1929–88), the saxophonists Wardell Gray (1921–1955), Art Pepper (1925–82), and Stan Getz (1927–91), and the pianist Tadd Dameron (1917–65), who was imprisoned for heroin possession in 1958–61. In a futile attempt to stop the example of these musicians influencing their audiences, many of them, like Baker, were stripped of their city licences to play in cabaret. The harassment of these musicians could be pitiless. When the singer Billie Holiday (1915–59) lay dying in hospital, New York police raided her hospital room, and confiscated her heroin together with her radio, record-player, flowers, chocolates and magazines. They snapped photographs of her *in extremis* as part of their effort to make her last days as miserable as possible. Such cruelty was part of the prohibitionist culture that excluded and stigmatised the addict, in Anslinger's words of 1960, as 'an immoral vicious social leper'. The Newport Jazz Festival in 1957 began funding a free clinic for addicted musicians. Charles Winick, the psychologist attached to the clinic, surveyed 357 New York jazz musicians (69 per cent of them white) and published a fascinating report that received scant attention. A summary published in England noted:

A surprising fact that emerged—and one in conflict with the generalised theory that once a heroin main-liner always a main-liner until the
early inevitable death—is that heroin use was concentrated in the 25–39
group, after which it tapered off to very little. Only two musicians over
40 were referred to as heroin addicts. Five respondents over 40, who had
been regular heroin users, had kicked in their late thirties—usually
without knowing the reason. One 43-year-old jazzman said: 'There
were just longer and longer periods between the times when I took a
shot. I guess you could say I diminuendoed out of it.' Winick's theory is
that musicians who start on heroin in their late teens 'as a response to
the problems of early adulthood, mature out of addiction . . . possibly
because the stresses and strains of life are becoming stabilised for them
and because the major challenges of adulthood have passed.'[28]

Winick's finding that insecurity of employment and stressful working conditions were common factors in the decision to use narcotics
supports the wider observation that young black Americans with little
interest in bebop or jazz were also getting hooked on heroin in this
period. In the early 1950s there was less distinction between marijuana
and heroin than at any other time: both drugs were used by young men
to cope with the stresses of leaving primitive rural communities to survive in equally deprived but more brutalised inner cities. The band-
leader Cab Calloway (1907–94) in his *Hepster's Dictionary* (1938)
defined 'hip' as meaning 'wise, sophisticated, anyone with boots on'.
This last phrase referred to wised-up southern blacks who left the cotton fields, got themselves a pair of shoes and moved to northern
cities.[29] Dizzie Gillespie, for example, migrated from small-town South
Carolina to Philadelphia in 1935.[30] Malcolm Little (1925–65) was a
country boy from Omaha who moved to the eastern cities, became
'hip' and for a time in Harlem during the 1940s dealt in reefers under
the nickname 'Detroit Red'. After imprisonment for theft, he converted to Islam and re-invented himself into the black Muslim leader,
Malcolm X. He then tried to discourage drug use in the black community by focusing on the suppliers: 'Malcolm would trace this business back until he showed the addict that narcotics is a multi-million
dollar business controlled by the white man.'[31]

The Oklahoma-born musician Ralph Ellison (1914–94), who came
to New York in the 1930s, published his classic novel about the black

predicament in a white-dominated society, *Invisible Man*, in 1952. The narrator's grandfather on his deathbed advises his family on how to treat the whites: 'Overcome 'em with yeses, undermine 'em with grins, agree 'em to death and destruction, let 'em swoller you until they vomit.' But the narrator's yeses—his academic successes—are rebuffed by white society; he is ignored. 'I am one of the most irresponsible beings that ever lived,' he crows. 'But to whom can I be responsible, and why should I be, when you refuse to see me? . . . Responsibility rests upon recognition, and recognition is a form of agreement.' Ellison's narrator stops smoking reefers 'not because they are illegal, but because . . . it inhibits action'. This urban reject muses that the white man, 'for his own personal safety', should recognise 'my "danger potential" '.[32] Many young blacks excluded from the American Dream used drugs to spite the white authorities as well as to handle the stresses of early adulthood in city slums. Statistics from the Lexington prison-hospital illustrate the trends. Of Lexington's 2943 admissions in 1947, 7.3 per cent were black; in 1950, 32.2 per cent of 4534 admissions were black. By 1957 44.7 per cent of admissions were black. The FBN estimated in 1958 that 59 per cent out of 42,266 narcotics-users were black.[33] There were nearly 45,000 heroin-users in the US by 1960.[34] These figures did not stop Anslinger writing in 1961: 'Addiction in the United States has declined every year and continues to decline.'[35]

He became more aggressively mendacious after 1950 because his policies were failing. He admitted that year to 'a disturbing revival in the heroin traffic . . . from Europe and the Near East . . . with a consequent rise in addiction among young "hoodlums" in several of the larger cities'.[36] Heroin became a 'badge' to people like jazz trumpeter Red Rodney (1927–94): 'It was the thing that made us different from the rest of the world. It was the thing that said, "We know. You don't know." It was the thing that gave us membership in a unique club, and for this membership we gave up everything else in the world. Every ambition. Every desire. Everything. It ruined most of the people.'[37]

Heroin-addicted Herbert Huncke came out of prison in 1953 to find

the drug scene by this time was flourishing. The pushers had come back onto the scene again after nearly disappearing at the end of the forties. There was a new attitude among the drug addicts now; it all seemed to be much more wide open. This coincided with the bepop scene, which followed swing. Bepop jazz clubs were getting to be the big thing, and when it was discovered that a lot of the jazz musicians were using, gradually the drug scene began to erupt all over the place . . . The funny thing was that the drug scene was no longer confined to just one neighborhood. It started to happen in all neighborhoods, much more so than previously when you'd cop, say, in Harlem. More and more people, different types, began to use—not only heroin and morphine but amphetamine too. When I came back to the scene after my second bit, in '59, it was even more obvious. It was the younger generation becoming more involved, a batch of new junkies were making their move.[38]

This 1950s' phenomenon of polydrug use by a new and diversified generation of users occurred in a few European cities such as London at the same time. It was the most decisive achievement of the Federal Bureau of Narcotics.

Confronted with the slippage in his policies, Anslinger borrowed tactics from the House Un-American Activities Committee. His Bureau, more than ever, 'hounds and reviles' addicts, it was reported in 1952.[39] He gathered support for his *imperium* by inciting—like Senator Joseph McCarthy (1909–57)—the paranoid fears of American citizens. He presented their society as under siege from enemies without and within. 'Today it is the Communists of Red China who are exploiting the poppy, who are financing and fostering aggressive warfare through depravity and human misery,' he declared in 1953. 'Drug addiction is a cold, calculated, ruthless, systematic plan to undermine.'[40] Exploiting the paranoid style of the era, he urged politicians to work for harsher criminal penalties against all those who would destroy the American way. As the *St Louis Medical Society Bulletin* observed in 1951, 'If spies, saboteurs, and other traitors to our country can be given life sentences, then those who would sabotage the children upon whom the nation's future depends should be given life sentences.'[41]

Anslinger repeatedly averred that drug-trafficking could be eliminated if the law provided for compulsory imprisonment of users. In 1950 his claims encouraged a congressman from Louisiana, Hale Boggs (1914–72), to introduce a bill with far-reaching implications not just for the US but for international drug policy. The Boggs bill introduced mandatory minimum sentences: two to five years for first offenders with cannabis, cocaine or opiates; second offenders, five to ten years; and third offenders, ten to twenty. It was intended to prevent judges from pronouncing suspended sentences, or probation, in cases of repeat offenders. Boggs opposed any legal distinction between possession and supply. Anslinger had been clear enough in 1937 that experience of marijuana smoking was not a primary 'cause' of heroin use. There was evidence enough thirteen years later to confirm this opinion. Nevertheless, during Congressional hearings on the Boggs bill, he testified that 'over 50 per cent' of heroin-users 'started on marihuana smoking . . . and graduated to heroin; they took to the needle when the thrill of marijuana was gone'.[42] Such claims were surely insincere and opportunistic.

As the risks were too high for any public figure to question the need for draconian drugs legislation, the Boggs Act passed into law in November 1951. It raised penalties relating to cannabis on the basis that it was a gateway to opiate abuse, and ensured that marijuana was linked by law and in the public mind with opiates. It helped that Americans almost invariably referred to marijuana as a narcotic, although it is in fact a hallucinogen. Its association with opiates was enforced outside the US, too, and within a few years was alarming ill-briefed European politicians despite much contrary evidence. In a 1961 survey of sixty Texas heroin-users convicted of drug or drug-related offences, only two (3.3. per cent) named marijuana as their first illicit drug used. Thirty-seven (61.6 per cent) reported amphetamines as the first drug used. Eight per cent (five men) first used barbiturates, 10 per cent (six men) first used solvents, and 10 per cent cough syrup.[43] Notwithstanding such data, Henry L. Giordano (b. 1914), Anslinger's successor as Narcotics Commissioner, in 1968 luridly denounced cannabis as 'a calling card' or gateway drug that led to heroin addiction.[44] Anslinger's invented figure of 'over 50 per cent' in 1951 quickly escalated to more bogus heights. Britain's shadow Home Secretary Quintin Hogg, Lord Hailsham (b. 1907) assured a television audience in 1967 'on reputable authority, that of existing heroin addicts, 95 per cent started on marijuana', and bullied those who disagreed with him.[45] Introducing the Misuse of Drugs Bill in 1970, the British Home Secretary Reginald Maudling (1917–79), averred 'that more than 90 per cent of those addicted to hard drugs started on cannabis', while acknowledging that 'younger members of the public do not find this story a convincing one'.[46]

In 1972 the US National Commission on Marijuana and Drug Abuse found that only 4 per cent of former cannabis-users had used heroin; a Department of Health and Human Services report of 1999 indicated that 72 million Americans had used marijuana, yet there was only one regular cocaine-user for every 120 people who had tried marijuana. These politicians never considered that cannabis, rather than pre-eminently introducing people to harder drugs, might filter off a number who might otherwise have turned directly to them. It is true, though, that buying marijuana from black-market dealers increases the buyer's opportunity to obtain other illicit drugs. There are indications that the differences between cannabis and heroin were not fully known by many English users in the early 1950s; but as cannabis became more widely used geographically and socially, its use was increasingly distanced from consumers of opiates. Similarly, after the fashion for intravenous use of amphetamines developed in England after 1967, their users were a very different subgroup from 'pot heads'. The majority of heroin-users may start on cannabis; but the number of cannabis-users who move on to heroin is minute.

Anslinger's lies were vigorous. '*Marihuana has no therapeutic value*, and its use is therefore *always* an abuse and a vice,' he typically insisted in 1953.

> While opium can be a blessing or a curse, depending on its use, marihuana is only and always a scourge which undermines its victims and degrades them mentally, morally, and physically . . . In the earliest stages of intoxication, the will power is destroyed and inhibitions and restraints are released; the moral barricades are broken down and often debauchery and sexuality results. Where mental instability is inherent, the behavior is generally violent. An egotist will enjoy delusions of grandeur, the timid individual will suffer anxiety, and the aggressive ones often will resort to acts of violence and crime. Dormant tendencies are released and while the subject may know what is happening, he has become powerless to prevent it. Constant use produces an incapacity for work and a disorientation . . . often leading to insanity after prolonged use.[47]

Such exaggeration meant that drug-users, and inquisitive young people, discounted all official advice on drugs, and relied for information on each other. John Clellon Holmes in 1952 depicted a party in New

York at which 'tea' was smoked. 'Go ahead, Christine, it's harmless, it's not really a drug at all,' a Beat tells a novice. People who used marijuana for pleasure had their 'kicks' enhanced by the prohibitionist culture. For the party's host, 'there was an illegal or surreptitious air about everything that thrilled him'.[48] FBN agents were no deterrent. Many middle-class Americans who remembered the marijuana lies of the 1940s and 1950s treated with fatal disdain warnings about the new fashion for cocaine in the 1970s—with disastrous consequences for American society in the 1980s. Ginsberg had predicted this in 1966: 'When the citizens of this country see that such an old-time, taken-for-granted, flag-waving, reactionary truism of police, press and law as the "reefer menace" is in fact a creepy hoax, a scarecrow, what will they begin to think?'[49] As it was, despite the strenuous efforts of the FBN after 1937, 10 per cent of the total US population had tried marijuana by the late 1960s. Its use became 'a badge of dissociation'.[50] Making the war against drugs so central to the American Way provoked young people into their use: 'Deny, I deny the tastes and habits of the age / I am its punk debauché,' proclaimed one defiant drug-user in 1959.[51]

American propaganda misinformation had global repercussions. Thus the World Health Organisation, which in 1948 was drawn into formulating international policy on drugs, reported in 1955 that 'Under the influence of cannabis, the danger of committing unpremeditated murder is very great; it can happen in cold blood, without any reason or motive, unexpectedly, without any preceding quarrel; often the murderer does not even know the victim, and kills simply for pleasure.'[52] Succumbing to such rhetoric, Lord Derwent (1901–86), who had been a Home Office minister, similarly declared in 1967 that 'marijuana ... on its own leads to incurable insanity'.[53] The truth is that although some of the drug's users became too feckless to work productively, contrary to Anslinger and Derwent, few went mad.

During the Second World War Anslinger had achieved global importance by his control over supplies of pharmaceuticals. The control provisions embodied in the Opium Protocol of 1953 represented another victory for him and other hardliners. He wanted to maintain the US hegemony both because he was a patriot and because this gratified his vanity. When the United Nations' Division of Narcotic Drugs moved its headquarters from New York to Geneva in 1955, he was angry at this blow both to his own influence and to American power. In revenge he boycotted the meeting in 1956 of the UN's Commission on Narcotic Drugs, and those from 1958, which were also held in Geneva. His powers so heavily depended on the goodwill of Washington politicians, and he was so wary of critics, that he was loath to travel far, or be away for long, from Capitol Hill. The terms of the 1953 Opium Protocol were so restrictive that a reaction set in. A further conference held at New York during 1961, from which Anslinger disassociated himself, relaxed the stringent controls on agricultural production that had been central to American strategy since Congressman Porter's heyday. Anslinger became convinced that this Convention threatened the survival of his Bureau, and during 1961–2 engaged in extraordinary clandestine international manoeuvres, which involved defeating the wishes of the State Department, in an attempt to discredit his opponents.

The failure of the Boggs Act to deter drug use strengthened rather than discouraged its supporters. In 1954, for example, President Dwight Eisenhower (1890–1969) called for 'a new war on narcotics addiction', which suggests that the Boggs war had failed, but without any re-evaluation of strategies. The professional classes began thinking more flexibly than the politicians. A resolution of the American Bar Association in 1955 urging Congress to re-examine the Harrison Act resulted in the appointment of a Senate subcommittee chaired by Price Daniel (1910–88) of Texas. The senator, who was a former newspaper editor, used the hearings to promote his reputation before a forthcoming gubernatorial election. During the course of the Senate hearings, Anslinger agreed with a questioner that 'the marijuana user has been responsible for many of our most . . . terrible crimes in this Nation, such as sex slayings'. Senator Daniel himself declared that marijuana 'leads to the heroin habit and then to the final destruction of the persons addicted'.[54] These hearings identified the involvement of criminal organisations in the supply of narcotics and marijuana, but never analysed the way in which prohibition made these drugs such attractive commodities for gangsters to supply. The subcommittee's reports issued in 1956 rejected maintenance prescribing by specialist clinics, alleged that addiction was responsible for 50 per cent of all urban crime and identified spreading addiction as part of the subversive strategy of Communist China. Few Americans dared to question the punitive tactics of the 1950s. Alden Stevens (1907–68) of the Association of American Indian Affairs seemed almost deviant for warning that the chief effect of 'tightened laws against sellers, providing stiffer sentences and heavier fines' was to push 'the price of drugs sharply upward'. Higher penalties were no deterrent. 'Just as long as two pounds of heroin can be bought for ten dollars and when cut can be sold for $80,000, it will be cut and sold.' Punitive policies stimulated organised crime at the supply end of the market: the demand for expensive illicit commodities became increasingly associated with random thieving: addicts needing $15 to $75 daily for heroin necessarily often resorted to robbery. 'It is not the drug itself that drives the addict to crime. It is the need for the drug.'[55]

The Daniel recommendations resulted in the acme of Anslinger's era, the Narcotic Control Act of 1956. Penalties were again hiked. They included the unprecedented provision in federal law of the power to make arrests without warrant on the belief that a drug law offence had been committed. The increasingly severe criminal sanctions adopted in federal law against individuals in possession of prohibited substances were comparable to the laws aimed against subversion in their witch-hunting of social demons. In this period some citizens could be prosecuted under state laws as narcotics violators even though the authorities had no proof of purchase or possession. Several states followed the federal example and also hiked the sentence for first offence possession of marijuana from five to fifteen years' hard labour. In Massachusetts a person arrested in the company of someone possessing marijuana, or in a place where it was held, was liable to five years' imprisonment. These savage criminal sanctions had no discernible deterrent effect. There were only 169 marijuana-related arrests under federal law in 1960, but this figure had risen to 7000 in 1965 and 50,000 in 1966.

When the Egyptian government persuaded the member states of the League of Nations to adopt cannabis prohibition in the late 1920s, the drug was scarcely known in Europe, and had hardly penetrated the awareness of such stalwart American anti-drug campaigners as Congressman Porter. As late as 1937, it was a little-used medicine in the United States, smoked by Mexican immigrants and other marginal urban groups as a way of coping with a hard life, and by the young people who frequented tea-pads. It was one of Anslinger's enduring accomplishments that a drug that few people had heard of in the mid-1930s, and fewer used, became so fashionable. An opinion poll of 1969 found that one-quarter of the American college population had tried marijuana at least once. A federal survey of 1971 found that one-third of American university students had tried the drug, and that one-seventh used it regularly.

Anslinger survived by bluster and obfuscation. The FBN, under his direction, did not collect statistics on US addiction. He preferred to manipulate the numbers to serve his changing needs: in some months he might wish to convince his Congressional allies that his policies were succeeding; at other times, that America was in crisis. His strategies were pursued in a fury of accumulated dishonesty. As one addiction expert commented in 1974,

> The difficulty in dealing with the truly outrageous lies promoted by the Bureau of Narcotics is that like countering the anti-semitism of the infamous tract *The Protocol of the Elders of Zion* and the anti-black tracts, anti-Irish ones, etc., the audience reading them *wanted to believe them.* Unraveling and then exposing the complex of myth, fantasy, distorted half truth, and outright lies is a tedious process and cannot have the 'sex appeal' or salesmanship of the lies themselves ... During the fifties even harsher penalties were enacted against addiction on both the Federal and State levels. This policy of getting tougher with addicts that flourished then was a further exemplification of the mythology of addiction and addicts and of the fears that were quite literally created by such sources as the Bureau of Narcotics.[56]

The American writer Benjamin DeMott (b. 1924) described the first drugs czar in the final phase of his career:

> Commissioner Anslinger, who has held his job for more than three decades, carries on a portion of his official business by telephone from a small, yellow-brick house in Hollidaysburg, Pennsylvania, where he also cares for his ailing wife. A heavily-built, square-faced man ... with a thick, pock-marked neck and a preference for iridescent suitings and pale blue ties decorated with Chinese pagodas, the Commissioner enjoys an excellent reputation on Capitol Hill and is well thought of by most police officials ... A visitor who sees him sitting in the coffee shop of the Capitol Hotel in Hollidaysburg, chatting gently at midday with the country lawyers (the town is a county seat), enjoying a noontime

martini on the rocks, served small-town style in a stem glass, or carefully putting pennies in the meter for his muted-tone Cadillac, is unlikely to read in his behavior signs of a world-devouring public official.[57]

Anslinger wanted his successor to be recruited from among the Seventh Day Adventists, 'the only people who have ever gone all out to help us'. His preferred Adventist was a Californian physician: 'He's a doc', said Anslinger, 'they can't say he's just a dumb-headed cop.'[58] The FBN was increasingly beset. The American Medical Association and the American Bar Association in 1961 published a joint report arguing strongly against the position that addiction must be regarded as a crime rather than a disease. The FBN deterred the Russell Sage Foundation, which had financed the research, from publishing it (apparently by threatening the Foundation's charitable status), but when it was issued by a university press, FBN spokesmen accused their AMA-ABA critics 'of stooping to the technique of the Hitler Big-lie'.[59]

Back in 1953 Anslinger had warned that treatment clinics 'dispensing narcotic drugs to drug addicts for the purpose of maintaining addiction' would 'elevate a most despicable trade . . . to . . . a time-honored profession; and drug addicts would multiply unrestrained, to the irrevocable impairment of the moral fiber and physical welfare of the American people'.[60] Ignoring the use of maintenance prescriptions throughout much of Europe, he alleged that 'rationing of addicts has been frowned upon by the signatories to the narcotics conventions, and the only place in the world where such a policy is now in force is in the Far East'.[61] He discounted 'altruists' who sought to palliate 'the innate viciousness of drug addiction . . . by classifying all drug addicts as sick persons . . . whom treatment will cure and rehabilitate'. Most users 'had unpleasant and troublesome tendencies before drug addiction was superimposed', he insisted. 'We're not dealing with something hospitalisation alone will cure but a dreaded scourge that penetrates infinitely deeper.' His recommended treatment: 'About ten days in the "shot room" to get off the drugs, four to six months of work under healthy conditions, after which it becomes a mental problem which the patient, now discharged, must overcome for himself.'[62] But enforced withdrawal cures did not work. From 75 to 90 per cent of inmates leaving Fort Worth and Lexington prison-hospitals relapsed: officials at these federal treatment centres claimed a success rate of 13.5 per cent, although one patient who had been treated at Lexington believed the accurate figure was closer to 3 per cent.[63] 'I have been off junk for six months,' William Burroughs wrote from Mexico in 1951. 'It is easier here precisely because junk is easy to come by. You can really decide whether you want it or not without all that U.S. pressure.' Burroughs 'couldn't get back on the junk even if I wanted to', he told Ginsberg at this time. 'If you kick of your own choice you can't go back'.[64]

The most effective onslaught on Anslinger's treatment theories was led by Marie Nyswander (1919–86), who had worked briefly during 1945 at Lexington. After settling in New York as a psychiatrist and psychoanalyst, she was, in the 1950s, one of only three private physicians in Manhattan with experience of drug-users. As the pressure increased, the other two withdrew from work that was both stressful and derogated by opinion-makers such as Anslinger. Her experiences—recounted in *The Drug Addict as a Patient* (1956)—convinced her that drug-users should not be treated as outcasts. As her willingness to treat addiction became known, she was inundated with patients. Meanwhile Professor Vincent P. Dole (b. 1913) of Rockefeller University had recognised, like Nyswander, that locking up users and enforcing abstinence, or offering rehabilitation and urging abstinence, usually resulted in relapse once the user returned to the street. In 1962 he met Nyswander, and agreed to run a research project on addiction using her patients.

The FBN tried in 1963 to intimidate them into abandoning their work, and when this failed, spread rumours about their probity, stole their records and spied on them. As heroin was prohibited in the USA, Nyswander and Dole (who married in 1965) investigated giving maintenance prescriptions of morphine, but found the results unsatisfactory; next, in 1964, they pioneered the use of a synthetic opiate, methadone, to treat heroin-users. Methadone was a morphine substitute devised by IG Farbenindustrie when Germany's opiate supplies were severed during the Second World War. Unlike heroin, it was not prohibited in the US, so Nyswander and Dole switched users from heroin to methadone by massive, fixed daily dosages (drunk dissolved in orange juice) that were then stabilised. Methadone blocked acute narcotic effects, abolished the craving and thus avoided abstinence sickness in most users: heroin accordingly could be progressively reduced and stopped within a few weeks. The cost of daily medication was 13 cents. In a seminal article of 1966 Dole and Nyswander reported their approach. The typical user oscillated between two extremes. 'When "high"—or euphoric—he is sedated, tranquilised, absorbed in himself, and lost to responsibilities. When "sick"—or abstinent—he is desperate in his need for narcotic drug, with symptoms of general malaise, nausea, lacrimation and perspiration, tremors, and cramps.' In both conditions he or she was unemployable, but if maintained on methadone, 'the patient is firmly buffered in the zone of normal function'.[65] They could learn trades, hold jobs and fulfil social duties. 'The main idea is that we're able to function properly on methadone—as human beings with responsibilities,' one of Nyswander's patients explained in 1968. As a journalist wrote approvingly, methadone-users 'are making the adjustment to square society'.[66] By 1970 20,000 New York users were on methadone maintenance. Congress approved the use of methadone in narcotic addiction treatment programmes during 1971–2. In 2000 there were some 150,000 methadone maintenance patients in the US, including 40,000 in New York State and about 20,000 in California.

The FBN opposed these maintenance programmes, as did physicians who argued that the replacement of heroin addiction with methadone addiction was no cure. In time prescribed methadone was diverted to dealers, who created a clandestine market (particularly in Washington DC); some black leaders 'believed methadone maintenance had been plotted to sedate ghetto protest'.[67] Dole, though, was convinced after thirty years' experience, that methadone maintenance treatment had helped thousands of patients who otherwise would have died or been imprisoned. 'For me the most educational experience of the past three decades was to learn that the traditional image of the narcotics addict (weak character, hedonistic, unreliable, depraved, dangerous) is totally false,' he wrote in 1994. 'This myth, believed by the majority of the medical profession and the general public, has distorted public policy for seventy years.' His experience of thousands of users from different cultures convinced him 'that the typical heroin addict is a gentle person, trapped in chemical slavery, pathetically grateful for understanding and effective treatment'. He deplored the way that discussions about maintenance programmes had 'been so muddled by conflicting political interests, by ideological posturing and by disinformation in media, that the public has remained confused and prejudiced, and so also are the politicians it votes into office'.[68] Many users *were* difficult or dishonest patients, but this sometimes resulted from the assumptions on which treatment was based. The polydrug users who made Haight-Ashbury such an obnoxious district of San Francisco after 1967 had a hard time. Dr David Smith of the Haight-Ashbury Free Medical Clinic criticised physicians at Park Emergency Hospital.

> Like many policemen, the public health representatives seem to look on young drug-abusers as sub-human. When adolescents come to Park Emergency for help, the doctors frequently assault them with sermons, report them to the police, or submit them to complicated and drawn-out referral procedures that only intensify their agony. The nurses sometimes tell prospective patients to take their problems elsewhere. The ambulance drivers simply 'forget' calls for emergency assistance. They and the other staff members apparently believe that the best way to stamp out sickness in the Haight is to let its younger residents destroy themselves.[69]

Anslinger's approach was to depict the drug-user as an arch-deviant who committed crimes, would not work, sought instant pleasurable gratifications, especially sexual ones. He did not denigrate heavy drinkers, or habitual consumers of tranquillisers and barbiturates, who depended on their preferred substance to cope with the strains of their job or marriage. He perpetuated the mentality that had become pronounced in Europe back in the 1820s: drug use that retarded productivity, or was related to pleasure rather than enhanced output, should be deplored; drug use intended to accommodate the needs of an industrial society could be exonerated. His approach appealed to journalists who wanted sensational, titillating material liable to affirm that pleasure brought nemesis. They relished presenting LSD and cannabis as leading to madness or degeneracy just as during the 1980s they insisted that homosexuality led to HIV. Such views were not confined to the USA. The philosopher and sociologist Alasdair MacIntyre (b. 1929) was one of those who signed an advertisement published in *The Times* on 24 July 1967 calling for the legalisation of cannabis. He was shocked by the violence of the reaction: 'Most of the hostility that I have met with comes from people who have never examined the facts at all. I suspect that what makes them dislike cannabis is not the belief that the effects of taking it are harmful, but rather a horrifying suspicion that here is a source of pure pleasure which is available for those who have not *earned it*, who do not *deserve it*. Pleasure has rarely gone down well with the English and pleasure for which there is practically no cost is the most abhorrent of all.'[70]

There had been a special extremism about US drug use since the 1880s; it was only after 1950 that some European drug habits converged with those of the USA. The details and causes of this process vary between nations: there is a pressing need for comparative case studies. The next chapter is an account of British experience offered in the hope that comparable histories will be written of Switzerland, Italy, France, the Netherlands and other European powers.

TWELVE

British Drug Scenes

*1956. Elvis: 'Hound Dog', 'Don't be Cruel'; the Teds lounging in pink day-glow socks
at the Boys Club, Mr. Fairclough his pebble glasses steaming up; the jukebox at the
Rendezvous coffee bar; Anthony Tucker applied to Eartha Kitt at Belle Vue Boxing
Stadium, the day the circus left town; Wilf, hash; Marion Hanson wearing the first
sack-dress when everybody pale-pink lips, fifties jive-skirts, nylon petticoats. Burton
Wood Air Base: American cars with fins; suicide blondes, one Yank and they're off.*
                        —OSSIE CLARK

Turn off your minds, relax and float downstream. This is not dying.
        —TIBETAN BOOK OF THE DEAD/THE BEATLES

THE THERAPEUTICALLY ADDICTED English opiate-users of the
1930s included the first addict to become—while still living—
a celebrity because of her drug problems. Brenda Dean Paul
(1907–59) was one of the Bright Young Things immortalised in the
early novels of Evelyn Waugh (1903–66). She was born in Knights-
bridge, her father was a baronet and her mother a Polish *pianiste* who
had been a child prodigy. From the age of seventeen Brenda Dean Paul
herself toured Paris, Tahiti and the USA as an actress: shortly before her
death she impressed Anthony Powell (1905–2000) in the title role of
Firbank's play *The Princess Zoubaroff*. It was her misfortune to come to
epitomise two aspects of drug addiction that intensified in the mid-
twentieth century. She became a woman celebrity addict, whose infractions were seen as a challenge to patriarchal authority and punished
accordingly. She first took an illicit substance—a pinch of cocaine—at
a studio party in Paris in the 1920s. 'The result was hardly what I
expected, no exhilaration was mine, no re-born vitality, just a feeling
that the top of my head had been suddenly and neatly decapitated like

that of a boiled egg.'[1] A little time later, after being jilted, she collapsed and was prescribed morphine in a Parisian clinic; on returning to London she suffered abstinence sickness. 'Painful cold sweats drenched me, so that I could hardly bear a sheet to touch me, and my body ached like one vast growing pain, my nose and eyes streaming as with hay-fever. But what was infinitely worse than the physical side, was the unbearable and deadly depression and fear.'[2] She tried a variety of cures. Soon she was receiving maintenance doses.

Then in 1931, having altered a morphine prescription and obtained heroin simultaneously from several physicians, she was convicted of seven infringements of the Dangerous Drugs Act. The Marlborough Street magistrate imposed a fine of £50, and bound her over for three years to reside wherever the court directed.[3] This meant that she was compelled to obtain permission before changing address. Her solicitor warned her that unless she stayed in a physician's household, she would be put in 'Holloway Prison Infirmary, as the authorities could not permit a person in my condition to roam about'.[4] Following examination by Sir William Willcox of the Home Office, she was committed to a nursing home; doubtless he consulted Delevingne about the controls imposed on her. She was forbidden 'to live near or with anyone of my own age', or 'near or with anyone belonging to the set I had known and mixed with in the past'. She was treated as a youthful insurgent who must be constantly supervised by an older person.[5] After several months she absconded to Paris, but could not obtain drugs there, and was soon hospitalised. The revelation that she was in France provoked frantic publicity:

My *fiancé* ... left London post haste, and his progress was announced over the wireless in the following way: 'Brenda's *fiancé* leaves for Croydon.' 'He has reached Croydon and boarded the airliner.' 'He is over the Channel.' 'He passes Étaples.' 'He is at Le Bourget.' 'He is in a car.' 'He reaches Paris.' 'HE IS AT THE HOSPITAL.' ... the unfortunate officials of the British Hertford Hospital were nearly driven off their heads replying to the enquiries. *The Star, Standard, Evening News, Daily Express, Daily Mail, Daily Herald, Daily Sketch, Daily Mirror* would be simultaneously calling: 'Can I speak to Brenda?' 'Would you please tell us about Brenda?' ... police had to keep back the crowd eager to catch a glimpse of the sensational English 'Miss'. I began to feel sick and faint and horrified.

When she moved to a hotel, 'reporters discovered where we were, and throughout the night the telephone kept ringing, reporters standing five deep in the passages'.[6]

She was arrested again in 1932 for unlawful possession of morphine, and was remanded for seven days in Holloway Prison by another magistrate, Morgan Griffiths-Jones (1876–1939). In September she was sentenced. 'You require discipline,' he told her. 'I am going to remand you for one month to see that you behave yourself properly and that you obey the doctor, and I am going to remand you month by month for six months; and if I have an unsatisfactory report I shall be satisfied that Holloway shall be the best place for you.'[7] She was committed to the care at the Norwood Sanatorium of a physician who 'did more to restore me morally and physically than any other person during the whole of that disheartening time'. She felt she had a chance there of a permanent cure, 'but the lamentable blunderings of the law . . . rendered all his skill and my efforts useless'.[8] Two days before she was due to reappear in court, she underwent emergency dentistry: both her physician and dentist certified that she was unfit to attend. Griffiths-Jones suspected a ruse. He was adamant that he would accept no excuses from this defiant young woman, whom he sentenced to six months' imprisonment. The sanatorium doctor volunteered to bring her to court on a stretcher to prove her condition, but Griffths-Jones was too indignant. A police physician was sent with two detectives to fetch her, but after examination, he refused to sanction her removal.[9] Despite appeals to the Home Office, Griffths-Jones's will was enforced.[10] She was taken to Holloway Prison, where the Governor admonished her. 'You are here for six months, and the sooner you realise the fact and pull yourself together the better for you, because I warn you that we don't stand for any tricks here; you are like one of the others, a convicted prisoner, and . . . you'll get no exceptional treatment.'[11]

The handling of Brenda Dean Paul was stubborn, punitive and foolish. As the Public Health Inspectorate in the Netherlands advised the Ministry of Justice in 1938,

> the fight against drug addiction must be handled in a totally different way and be looked upon from the human side. Do not pursue these

addicts, as it will drive them to the dealers, but offer these people help. Addicts are not criminals but wretches, the morally weak, most of whom did not become addicted through any fault of their own, and lack the power to suppress the inclination ... Along with measures taken to trace these people, a way must be found to give them a withdrawal program and by means to follow up, send them back into society, as has already been done with so many others ... State money will surely be spent more efficiently that way than on an expensive and elaborate control machinery used to chase doctors, druggists and patients, while not solving the problem itself.[12]

After a judicial appeal, Paul was released, despite 'the tide of public opinion dead against my liberation'.[13] Her life was ruined as much by notoriety as by drugs. She was harried by blazing, vindictive headlines: 'Drugs or madness and death'; 'Unless she receives ever-increasing doses of drugs, Brenda Dean Paul will go mad and die'; 'Society girl lives five weeks in Holloway without dope, but would die without it in luxury nursing home'.[14] Her behaviour became self-victimising. 'The disadvantage of having become a public legend at a very early age', as Auden wrote of Cocteau, is that 'notorious people nearly always begin soon to act their own role and become fakes'.[15] Despite her repeated infractions, she did not deserve and was not helped by harsh treatment. She served journalists' commercial need for sensationalism and *schadenfreunde*; she gratified the public appetite to see the beautiful and glamorous humiliated; her case drew all the puritans with their dismal mentality which skims over life's pleasures but fastens on misfortunes.

Opium prosecutions in Britain steadily fell from 184 in 1921 to six in 1938. Figures rose after the outbreak of war to 201 in 1941, reaching a peak of 256 in 1944. The rise was attributable to stricter police enforcement in Liverpool, an increase in the number of Chinese seamen in certain ports, and the diversion through British ports of the transit of illicit Far Eastern opium destined for the USA. Henry ('Bing') Spear (1928–95), who joined the Home Office's Dangerous Drugs Branch in 1952 and became its head in 1977, had unparalleled knowledge of British drug use. During the late 1930s there was in London, according to Spear, one 'very small circle of heroin addicts' whose three leaders often visited mainland Europe, 'where their addiction had been acquired', and brought back heroin for fellow users. After the arrest of one of this set in 1937 on his return from Paris with six grams of heroin, its activities, which had never been extensive, were curtailed. Most pre-war heroin users were of good social standing. They met at chemists and doctors' surgeries, but there was no real social connection between the different groups. Despite a certain amount of borrowing and lending of heroin within these coteries, there was no evidence of widespread selling of the drug.[16] In 1938 there were 519 known opiate addicts, 246 men and 273 women.

The 164 known male opiate addicts and 219 known female addicts of 1947 included eighty-two doctors, one dentist, one veterinary surgeon, three pharmacists and a substantial number who had become therapeutically addicted. There were twenty known cases of forged prescriptions: but most addicts obtained their supplies legitimately from doctors' prescriptions. Among the addict physicians was Dr William Hubert (1904–47), formerly psychotherapist at Wormwood Scrubs Prison (1934–9) and Broadmoor Criminal Lunatic Asylum (1945–6). In conjunction with Norwood East, Hubert had compiled a special report on crime for the Home Office submitted in 1938, but within a few years morphine was wrecking his career. Hubert was 'capable no doubt on a good day of being as able as any other man, but on a bad day liable to be absolutely appalling'. In January 1947 he and a younger woman were found unconscious at his flat in Chelsea, and two months later he was dead in its bathroom of barbiturate and chloral poisoning.[17]

Superficially the illicit drugs supply seemed under control in this period. Out of 129 prosecutions in 1949 for unlawful import of opium or Indian hemp, only four offenders were Europeans: two British; one Dutchman; one Belgian. Chinese seamen smuggled in small amounts of opium for their own use, or that of their compatriots in seaport towns, including London. Under the surface, however, the market in illicit drugs was changing, The late 1940s were a period of pervasive corruption in Britain. Profit-taking from the supply of illicit drugs began to escalate during a crime wave reflecting the strict government controls imposed on free markets. Peacetime rationing of food, clothes, petrol and raw materials, together with controls over the import and export of currency and commodities, persisted until the early 1950s. These 'austerity measures', as they were known, increased lawlessness at all levels of society rather in the manner of the US alcohol prohibition in the 1920s. People of every age and every class learnt how to connect with a Source, or score what they wanted on the streets. Barrow boys made small fortunes illicitly supplying otherwise law-abiding citizens. This was the heyday of the 'spiv' supplying the black market and of the 'wide boy' evading official controls. A distemper of dishonesty spread over Britain. In 1947 there were over 30,000 prosecutions for breaches of the regulations that rationed food and clothes. The restrictions on currency movements created a new type of crime: the number of currency prosecutions jumped from 322 in 1946 to 4583 in 1948. The loot (mainly pilfered cups and towels) stolen from British railway companies in 1948 amounted to almost £3 million. The crime wave was such that whereas 266,265 indictable offences were recorded in Britain in 1937 the figure was 522,684 in 1948.[18] Visiting the French Riviera in 1949, Nancy Mitford (1904–73) found Cannes full of English proletarians 'in Rolls Royces & luxury yachts—the black marketeers ... but real working class accents, not RAF'.[19] These events provided the social and economic background to the beginning of the British drug scene.

During the 1930s there had seldom been more than half a dozen cannabis prosecutions annually, with a peak of eighteen cases in 1938. The number of persons prosecuted in Britain for unlawful import or possession of cannabis rose from four in 1945, eleven in 1946, forty-nine in 1947, fifty-one in 1948, sixty-one in 1949, to eighty-six in 1950. According to Sir Norwood East in 1949, the Indian hemp traffic 'originates with the Indian, Arab or Negro seaman, and extends from the dock areas to the West of London'.[20] In the late 1940s the Cable Street district in Stepney, the social centre of the London docks, and Old Montague Street, a few blocks north in Whitechapel, were centres of Indian hemp supply. Merchant seamen from Sierra Leone, Gambia, Nigeria and Somalia, together with recent immigrants from British colonies in the West Indies, were associated with the drug, although one expert observer concluded in 1955 that 'as far as Stepney is concerned the drug scare has been greatly overworked'.[21] The English novelist Colin MacInnes (1914–76) conceded in 1956 that blacks together with Maltese, Cypriots and the British had contributed 'their quota of pimps, ponces, weed-pedlars and all-round hustlers'. But black men, 'when detected, pursued and punished, enjoy, from the Sunday press, a generous publicity withheld from . . . native entrepreneurs'. In their Caribbean and African countries of origin, hemp was readily available and smoking was considered a trivial offence. It was tried by youths there at the same age as Europeans experimented with tobacco. Immigrants to England accustomed to smoking hemp were reluctant to shake the habit off 'as the legal forms of intoxication here are both more expensive and often more inconvenient to obtain'. These hemp-smokers 'can't see what all the fuss is about and regard its prohibition with the same annoyance (and the same determination to evade the law) as would an English alcoholic the ban on spirits in Bombay'.[22] Cannabis was being smoked in and around Soho by 1947. Bernard Kops (b. 1926) was introduced to drugs in that year by a pianist friend who

> often walked up to a policeman with a stick of marijuana. 'Can you give me a light?' He would tell them it was an asthma cure . . . So I started smoking greengage, or charge, or tea, or stuff, or pot, or marijuana. We always called the same thing by so many names. It was also called Shit. 'Shit' because the boys who went onto the white stuff, the cocaine and heroin addicts, the main-liners, no longer got a kick from a reefer, consequently it was 'Shit'. These boys were always sure that I had to follow their path. Like religious maniacs they were. 'First it's benzedrine, then shit and then you'll pop. You'll see.'

Kops decided hemp 'was forbidden because the governments of the world wanted to suppress people, didn't want them to be happy, to know too much'.[23] He was an eye-witness when 'the beatnik scene started in Soho in 1950', and decided that the drug suicides whom he knew 'were merely people who couldn't face up to mediocrity'.[24]

British officials discovered this subculture, and realised that cannabis use was no longer confined to black men when, in 1950, a ship's steward was arrested at Southampton with the drug concealed in chocolate boxes. Under interrogation the steward stated that he had obtained the drug at 'Club Eleven' in London. The police raided this private dancing club on 15 April. There were over 250 people on the premises. Ten men were found in possession of hemp, and twenty-three packets of the drug, several hemp cigarettes, a packet of cocaine and an empty morphine ampoule were found on the club floor. Three of the offenders were US seamen, all but one were aged between twenty-two and twenty-nine and, contrary to previous British experience in hemp cases, only one man was black.[25] Following the Club Eleven raid, the Metropolitan Police investigated cannabis further. As a result, one evening in July 1950, about eighty policemen raided the Paramount Dance Hall on Tottenham Court Road, and searched its 500 occupants. 'The men were mainly coloured and the girls white,' as Detective Sergeant George Lyle of Scotland Yard reported.

> Eight coloured men were arrested for having Indian Hemp in their possession. Several of the coloured men were very excited and hysterical during the raid. One of these men bit two policemen and a civilian. At court he solemnly stated that he had bitten these persons because they had bitten him first. As these men were all quiet and docile when seen on subsequent occasions, we rightly or wrongly believed that they had been suffering from the effects of hemp smoking at the time of the raid. During the search 20 packets of hemp, several knives . . . were found on the floor. In the ladies' toilet a large number of contraceptives were found.

The police felt that with 'young girls' visiting 'Bebop dance halls in London' and consorting with 'negroes', 'hemp may sap their moral fibre' so that they prostitute themselves 'to pay for the drug'.[26]

These two raids reduced drastically the availability of cannabis in London. This had important consequences when, in May 1951, 3120 heroin tablets, 144 grams of morphine and 2 ounces of cocaine were stolen from the dispensary of a hospital in Kent. During September 1951 Lyle and his colleagues 'heard that a man named "Mark" was selling white drugs in the West End'. A young detective, Catherine Arnold, 'attired herself in the appropriate uniform of the "bebop" dancers, blue jeans and short hair cut, etc., and by certain methods found herself in Mark's circle of acquaintances and went with him to the low clubs and cafés.'[27] As a result of her investigations, 'Mark' (whose real name was Kevin Patrick Saunders) was arrested. He was found to be a former employee at the hospital who had been suspected at the time of the theft. The police identified fourteen people who they believed had bought drugs from him: only two were previously known as heroin addicts although some were known cannabis and/or cocaine-users.

Altogether the Home Office identified twenty-six heroin-users connected with Mark: ten of them were dead by 1967. Another thirty-six cases notified to the Home Office after 1954 had personal links traceable to Mark's earlier customers.[28] Most of the new users associated with Mark chose to maintain their addiction with illicit supplies although they could easily have obtained prescriptions from physicians. The reasons for this choice are important in explaining subsequent illicit drug use. Some believed that 'you don't get hooked as badly as when you're buying on the black'. Others refused to accept the fact of their drug dependence by registering with a doctor, or were scared of being notified to the authorities. In some cases, a desire to transgress the rules may have been responsible.[29] Mark also sold cocaine to his heroin customers. They used cocaine partly for its own sake and partly to counteract the drowsiness caused by heroin. The use of both drugs in combination—as 'speedballs'—was an English characteristic of the 1950s: the practice was less prevalent in the USA.

There were articles about Indian hemp in the *Daily Telegraph* (28 August 1951) and the *Evening Standard* (5 September 1951). The trial at the Old Bailey in November 1951 of a West African who had supplied Indian hemp to two adolescent girls from the provinces received considerable publicity, including another article in the *Daily Telegraph* (23 November) and others in the *Daily Express* (26–9 November). Such incidents heightened the interest in *Indian Hemp: A Social Menace* (1952), a treatise with an unusual background. Its author, Donald Johnson (1903–78), had worked as a physician in Croydon before taking the lease of a hotel in Oxfordshire. During the course of 1950 many of his staff went to work for his ex-manager in a rival pub 200 yards away. He had other worries, and reacted to the additional stress by becoming psychotic, as did his wife. They thought their customers were private enquiry agents, that their rooms were bugged, that postmen were stealing their letters for blackmail, and suffered other delusions of persecution. Johnson began having pornographic dreams: his wife started winking licentiously at men, and sitting in indecent positions. After their madness became palpable to their family and neighbours, the police were summoned, and they were committed to hospital as mentally ill. Johnson, during his first weeks in hospital, thought foreign gangsters or spies had kidnapped him. As he recovered, he came to suspect that this episode was the result of being poisoned with cannabis by a business rival or drugs gang.[30] This was the background to his book denouncing the drug; shortly after its publication he was elected as a Conservative MP. Neither the genesis nor the contents of Johnson's *Indian Hemp* inspire trust.

The events of 1950–52, Spear believed, 'provided the first signs of an emerging drug subculture in the United Kingdom'. Until Mark's intervention, 'there was little or no heroin circulating in the West End of London but his appearance coincided with the scarcity of cannabis'. As a result, many cannabis-smokers substituted heroin and cocaine.[31] Thus a boy (born in 1934) who had started smoking cannabis in bebop clubs at the age of sixteen became, in August 1952, the first teenager to be arrested for possession of cannabis, and in 1955 was notified to the Home Office as a heroin-user. In 1965 he died by inhalation of his own vomit. During the 1950s a West African immigrant named Frances Tucker, nicknamed the Queen of Indian hemp, organised a thriving traffic in cannabis from Gambia to Liverpool 8, Moss Side in Manchester and Cable Street in Whitechapel, where she was based. Her murder in the East End was unsolved by the police, whose drugs work at the time was flawed. In 1955 Colin MacInnes was visiting a squalid East End gambling house when the police raided it. In the police station he was beaten, and some days later charged with possessing a packet of cannabis and a rolled joint. 'It was suggested to me that a bribe might help to get the charge, if not dropped, not pressed, but . . . I refused.' A packet of cannabis together with a reefer was produced at his third appearance in the magistrates' court; he assumed that these came from impounded stocks. The usual sentence at this time for a first conviction of possessing cannabis was a fine from £15 to £25, unless dealing was proved; imprisonment was the usual punishment for a second offence. Unlike the ten other (mainly black) men who had been arrested with him, and were tried and convicted before magistrates, MacInnes was able to afford trial at the Sessions, where he was acquitted. 'The reason was simply that the police hadn't done their homework. So that when they were asked what I was supposed to have said, or where I was standing, or what I had on—simple questions of that kind . . . they contradicted themselves.'[32]

The emergence of a drug subculture among a small number of young English people around 1950 was social and emulative. The growing taste for half-baked psychoanalysis contributed to the idea that neuroses made people more interesting, original or mentally fertile. 'The age of the week-end Bohemian had arrived,' Kops recalled of the early 1950s.

> Most of the boys I knew, the would-be writers and the painters, had gone the way of all flesh, into the ground . . . They were the unable, the unadjustable, the nothings, the unmighty fallen . . . For the old-timers of Soho things got desperate. Some tried to fit into the new coffee-bar society, became characters, dispensing old anti-social tales to the newly lost. They held court, were lionized but remained pathetic. Most of them died alone somewhere, at night in a lousy room, and they were forgotten within days.[33]

Soho's coffee bars were England's equivalent of Hollywood's lights in their defiance of the prevalent drabness. 'One thing is certain, and that's that they'll make musicals one day about the glamour-studded 1950s,' thinks the teenage narrator of Colin MacInnes' *Absolute Beginners* (1959).[34] He enthuses about the Soho clubs where drugs are passed. 'The great thing about the jazz world, and all the kids that enter into it, is that no one, not a soul, cares what your class is, or what your race is, or what your income, or if you're a boy, or a girl, or bent, or versatile, or what you are . . . you meet all kinds of cats, on absolutely equal terms, who can clue you up in all kind of directions.'[35] In the USA, after 1945, heroin was associated with urban deprivation and racial discrimination, but not in Scotland until the late 1960s and England until the 1970s. The principal psychologist at the Salter Unit, a treatment centre for heroin addiction opened in 1965 at Cane Hill Hospital, Coulsdon, Surrey, judged in 1967 that

> it is in the majority of cases not human misery in the sense of slum conditions, deprivation, broken and delinquent homes, lack of educational opportunities and a general 'under-dog' atmosphere which produces the British heroin addict. These young men come from lower or upper middle class families. They have rarely committed offences apart from 'being found in possession' or having tampered with prescriptions. Some have a surprisingly stable background and more often than not they are not rejected by their families. They are mostly of above average to very superior intellectual capacity and the picture is rather one of wasted oppor-

tunity . . . the young addicts often have peculiarities of attire and manner. There appears to be a wish for attention and recognition . . . conformity, authority, the 'rat-race', bourgeois ambitions of cots, kids and two-downs-three-ups are despised; nothing can be done about it, we are born into this sad, rotten world without being asked whether we wanted to and can only achieve our own personal perception of existence. Here the influence of Sartre can be clearly traced.[36]

Kenneth Leech confirmed that 'until the end of the 1960s . . . the needle culture did not affect many working-class youths'.[37]

A large international bureaucracy continued trying to suppress young people's drug scenes. The League of Nations' responsibilities for drugs limitation having been taken over by the United Nations in 1946, the World Health Organisation in 1949 renewed the pre-war US initiative to prohibit worldwide the manufacture and use of heroin. Its proponents urged that such a ban would help suppress trafficking because all heroin discovered anywhere would be illegal. In 1953 there came a unanimous WHO recommendation that the production and import of heroin should be abolished throughout the world. In that year two British companies manufactured 109 kilograms of heroin, representing 69 per cent of the world's total licit output; 23 out of the total of 27 kilograms exported went to Canada (where there were an estimated 5000 heroin-users). In Britain the drug was used as a therapy for intractable cough and uterine inertia, and in managing intractable cancer. The UN in 1954 urged all governments to prohibit heroin's manufacture, import and export, save for scientific purposes. Although the British Medical Association swiftly passed a resolution against this proposal, a medical advisory committee consulted by the Minister of Health concurred with the British government's intention to adhere to UN policy. The Eden government shrank from defying the wishes of fifty-four other nations, and early in 1955 announced that it would not renew licences for the manufacture of heroin after December. Lord Elibank (1879–1962), who had been treated with heroin when ill, promptly launched a campaign against the ban. In May the distinguished physician Lord Horder publicly criticised the policy: 'Heroin addiction in Great Britain is practically unknown and it is difficult to see why administrative action . . . should be allowed to hinder the relief of suffering.'[38] After an unsatisfactory meeting with the Home Secretary in July, the BMA orchestrated a powerful chorus of protest.

The government's intention was confounded by Earl Jowitt (1885–1957), the former Lord Chancellor, who initiated a parliamentary debate on 13 December 1955. Jowitt urged that a ban on licit heroin production would increase the danger of illicit heroin manufacture, which was hitherto unknown in Britain. He noted that only eleven grams of illicit heroin had been seized in Britain in the six years 1946–51, but 28,870 grams in the year 1951 in the USA alone. He challenged the government's powers to ban heroin absolutely under the Dangerous Drugs Act of 1951. The fact that licit British heroin was exported to Canada had led to the oversimplified assumption that this heroin (rather than drugs smuggled via France and the USA) was feeding their 5000 users. The Canadian government, however, accepted that thefts from pharmacies and hospitals of legally imported British heroin contributed little to the abundant supply available on the Canadian black market.[39] Jowitt's intervention—particularly his challenge to the ban's legality—resulted in a decision to withdraw the proposal.

Several medical peers supported Jowitt. 'We in this country have been wonderfully successful in preventing addiction to habit-forming drugs,' said Lord Webb-Johnson (1880–1958). 'Do not let us follow along the path of prohibition—a bad and dangerous way.'[40] Lord Amulree (1900–1983) took a different tack. 'It is the first time that a Government have ever stepped in between a doctor and his patient over the treatment he should give his patient,' he protested. Although he seldom used heroin in hospital work, 'When I get one of these nasty coughs that are uncontrollable . . . I like my little drop of heroin: it works very well for me.'[41] However, other physician members of the House of Lords supported the ban. Lord Waverley, who as Delevingne's superior at the Home Office, had been involved in legislating against cannabis, opposed heroin prohibition on pragmatic grounds, but overall the resistance to prohibition owed something to anti-Americanism. Among the political and other classes, there was jealousy of American prosperity, and surliness at the toppling of Britain by the US as leader of the English-speaking world. 'It's a sure sign of total defeat to be an anti-Yank,' thought Colin MacInnes at this time; but many British institutions were decrepit, and their leaders demoralised and resentful.[42] At a private meeting of the Joint Home Affairs and Health Parliamentary Committee of the House of Commons in December 1955, the forthright Conservative backbencher Sir Robert Boothby (1900–1986) declared, 'We are pandering to US pressure.' This was perhaps why 'Newspapers [were] solidly against [the] ban.'[43] Specialist physicians attacked the ban with a similar anti-American twist. 'We have', warned Dr John Dent (1888–1962), the English expert who used apomorphine to withdraw addicts, 'the least black market in dangerous drugs in the world and America has the largest and if we follow their example and prohibit the manufacture of heroin for internal use in this country our black market will grow as theirs has done.' He saw prohibition as a gift to black marketeers.[44] According to his American patient William Burroughs, whom he successfully treated in 1956, 'Dent was the least paranoid of men, and he had the full warmth and goodwill . . . the English can offer.' He told Burroughs, 'What the American narcotics people are doing is bad,' censoring the word he really meant. 'He didn't want to use the word: Evil.'[45]

In the event the government's law officers confirmed that there was no legislative authority to ban manufacture.[46] The Cabinet Secretary, Lord Normanbrook (1902–67), proposed a compromise whereby the government did not suppress heroin manufacture, but prohibited (as it was already empowered to do) all British imports and exports of heroin.[47] Normanbrook's suggestion was adopted. Britain was not alone in continuing to use heroin. Albania, Belgium, France, Hungary, Italy, Kuwait, the Netherlands and Romania also persisted in its medical and scientific use. Austria had banned heroin from medical practice back in 1946 (probably under US pressure), but kept stocks of the drug. Canada had prohibited imports with effect from January 1955, but continued to use stocks, as did Denmark, Ecuador, Ireland, Portugal and Uruguay.

In 1957 Sir Adolphe Abrahams complacently declared in the *British Journal of Addiction* that of 'drug addiction there is no evidence whatever in this country and very little (and that unconvincing) in any part of the world'.[48] He was out of touch. There were disturbing new trends in the use and social milieu of heroin and cocaine dating back to 1951, trends moreover which had been recognised by the Home Office Drugs Branch as early as 1955. The system that had prevailed for over thirty years since the Rolleston report was unravelling. It had never been faultless. The lavish prescribing by Dr Joseph Hirschmann and Dr Gerald Quinlan during the 1930s was mentioned in chapter

8. Dr Marks Ripka (1903–76) of Finchley in the period to 1953 and Dr Joseph Rourke (1892–1960) of Kensington were knowingly prescribing heroin to patients who then supplied other users. One of Rourke's patients was a Nigerian musician called Broderick Walker (1928–55), who died of heroin poisoning in Maida Vale. Walker's career resembled that of a heroin-user from Lagos in MacInnes's novel about young blacks in London, *City of Spades* (1957). When challenged about his intravenous habits, he replies, 'I'm licensed now, Johnny—no trouble with the Law. I buy my allotment, but sell half of it. That's one of my ways to live.'[49] In 1962 the number of notified heroin addicts exceeded morphine addicts for the first time. The Drugs Branch, in a review of the previous twenty years submitted in 1968, concluded that the typical addict had changed from 'a middle aged housewife whose illness was treated, if not understood, with some measure of success by the family doctor' to someone in whom 'the known mores of pre-war suburbia were exchanged for those of a youthful minority subculture'.[50]

George, a patient of Max Glatt who became addicted in the mid-1950s, felt that the transformation of the London addict scene was evident by 1961. In addition to increasing publicity about police raids, young people were searching for novelties. Drugs seemed 'their best bet . . . of proving themselves'. For George the new users were 'just a drag . . . because they don't take drugs because of some need or some personal defect. It's just a case of pure exhibitionism with them . . . They go around with the long hair and dark glasses with a hypodermic sticking out of their top pocket kind of thing, and just advertising the fact that they're on drugs.' According to George, the *cachet* of being a registered addict was such that some youths hoodwinked doctors into registering them as addicts, and prescribing heroin, before they had even used the drug. George's reluctance to live in his own time, and yearning for an idealised past, were evident. He harked back to the 'comradeship' among addicts of the 1950s: 'One would help the other out without having to be necessarily his best friend. But today, I mean, you can go to the chemist, and you can stand there all night and be as sick as a dog, and nobody would offer to help you out.' After seven years of addiction, George found the rituals of heroin use worked better for him than the drug.

After an addict has been using stuff for quite some time, he no longer gets this so-called flash from the drug itself. His main kick is the actual making of the drug, the hitting of the vein, and watching this kind of flower-like—the blood hitting the water. This, to him, becomes something personal, so that when he goes into hospital and it's done cold and clinically, he gets nothing at all from it. I mean, the fix may be exactly the same amount, but the fact that he hasn't cooked it, hasn't hit the vein, he hasn't watched the blood coming out counteracts any kind of feeling of joy . . . This, to ordinary people, may sound kind of masochistic, but it's about the only kick a junkie gets unless he has a terrible lot [of drugs], unless he's addicted to some ridiculous [high] amount, which he wouldn't get from anyone. I get this intense pleasure of hitting, especially if there is a non-junkie, some middle-class person there.[51]

The orthodox explanation of Britain's developing heroin crisis is that the stability of the Rolleston system was spoilt by irresponsible prescriptions by some half-dozen physicians who created a crisis of heroin addiction. These 'junkies' doctors' were condemned for cupidity and arrogance, denounced in the *Daily Mail* and pilloried by consultant psychiatrists. The truth is that (with one exception) they performed no worse than the system that replaced them. The exception was Lady Frankau (1897–1967). As Isabella Robertson she had qualified in 1920, and subsequently was funded by the Medical Research Council to investigate gastric secretions in depressives and schizophrenics.[52] Afterwards she undertook research at the Maudsley psychiatric hospital and was assistant psychiatrist in the children's department of University College Hospital. As a young widow she remarried in 1935 a distinguished surgeon, Sir Claude Frankau (1882–1967), who outlived her by a month. Later she began treating alcoholics in her private practice at 32, Wimpole Street. In 1957, during a consultation about an alcoholic, a general practitioner named Patricia Stanwell suggested that 'she might like to try her hand with an addict'.[53] The two women began treating opiate addicts, and published a report on their work in the *Lancet* in 1960.[54] Initially Dr Stanwell did the prescribing. Their partnership broke up after Lady Frankau began issuing prescriptions with a generosity and gullibility that shocked Stanwell.

It is significant that several of Frankau's earliest patients were Nigerian. Apart from the intervention of 'Mark' in 1951, there was little cocaine in the illicit British drug scene until 1954, when a Nigerian heroin addict persuaded an inexperienced general practitioner to prescribe cocaine on the pretext that it would help him reduce his heroin consumption. Two other Nigerian heroin addicts subsequently persuaded physicians that they needed cocaine, and a substantial amount of this prescribed cocaine was sold illicitly.[55] Lady Frankau recognised that cocaine aroused a strong psychological dependency, and that it was difficult to reduce dosages, and yet popularised 'speedballs' (a combination of heroin and cocaine) among her patients, of whom she had seen over a hundred by June 1961. She warned, accurately, in 1961 that the young heroin and cocaine-user group (non-therapeutically addicted) was 'greater in number than is generally recognised', 'increasing fairly rapidly' and 'potentially dangerous'.[56] She treated just over 500 addicts between 1958 and 1964.

In view of her subsequent notoriety, it is worth scrutinising her treatment technique. Lady Frankau cited Marie Nyswander as an authority for her belief that 'those who are addicted to narcotic drugs are sick people; nearly all of them suffer from a psychoneurosis or are psychopathic personalities'. She stabilised her patients on the minimal dose of their drug that enabled them to work, and thus achieve security and self-respect. Then she began psychotherapy intended to help the patient 'to understand and readjust—and eventually to control—his faulty reaction to events'. Finally she instituted a progressive reduction of drug intake concluding (usually in a nursing home) with complete withdrawal by cutting the dose by about 50 per cent daily over five or six days. Despite the influence on her ideas of Nyswander's *The Drug Addict as a Patient*, she was critical of those she treated.

> Addicted patients are asocial, inadequate, immature and unstable. They are selfish and self-centred, without any interest in the welfare of others and only concerned with their own problems. Their major problem is the maintenance of the supply of drugs or the immediate gratification of their desire for drugs. They will resort to almost any means—however unreasonable or dangerous—to satisfy this insistent craving ... They lack self-discipline, will-power or ambition, and avoid responsibility. They have a low threshold for pain or any form of discomfort and are unable to tolerate criticism or to beat frustration. Their personal relationships tend to be confined to other members of the drug

addict's world and thus they become social outcasts and very lonely people.[57]

For Lady Frankau, a major difficulty during the final stage of withdrawal treatment was to convince the patient that injections must be given intramuscularly by the nurse: most were still attracted to 'the ritual and ceremonial of the intravenous route, which is so much part of narcotic addiction'.[58]

As Bing Spear noted drily, 'Lady Frankau clearly had a distinct advantage over the other doctors since, as she frequently asserted, she could always tell if one of her patients was lying.'[59] She was often misled about their drug history. She would ask patients if they had been on cocaine and they usually answered 'Yes'. Max Glatt noted in 1967, 'As there seemed to be a "kick" in store for them for the asking, they didn't see why they should say: "No".'[60] Keith Richards (b.1943) of the Rolling Stones has recalled: 'The bizarre thing in England was that if you registered as a heroin addict, whether you wanted it or not, you were forced to take the same amount in pure cocaine. On the firm belief that you'd be more useful as a member of society instead of lying about smacked out. That would bring you up, the perfect speedball . . . Junkies would sell off their cocaine and a bit of their smack. It was easy to get, the best stuff in the world. It was never cut, none of that lowlife thing'.[61] The number of cocaine addicts known to the Home Office rose from thirty in 1959 to 211 in 1964: almost all the new cocaine-users combined the drug with heroin.[62] Although Lady Frankau believed in time-consuming psychotherapy, she was brisk and self-confident in handing out scripts. One morning she had twenty-one patients scheduled to come for prescriptions between 10 a.m. and 11 a.m. Her lavish gullibility was so famous that one internationally celebrated jazz musician, who ran out of supplies in Paris, flew into London one morning in 1962, and left in the afternoon with heroin, cocaine and methadone prescribed by her.

She subsidised her addict work from her private psychiatric practice, and had the prescriptions of some of her more desperate patients charged to her account at the pharmacists John Bell & Croyden. She knew that most were borrowing, lending, buying and selling drugs, but wanted to provide stable conditions for the withdrawal treatment of those users sincerely wanting to stop. She assured patients 'that while they were being stabilized on drugs and freed from the degradation and humiliation of the black market, it was better to state that they had overstepped the amount than to produce tales of accidents'.[63] This led her into difficulties. According to Home Office records, in 1962, of the one million hypodermic tablets prescribed, she was responsible for 60 per cent. Lady Frankau on one occasion prescribed 900 tablets of heroin to one user and as soon as three days later prescribed for the same patient another 600 tablets to replace some lost in an accident. Further prescriptions for 720 and 840 tablets followed later for the same patient. There were other instances of single prescriptions for 1000 tablets being issued.[64] She gave scripts for as much as 70 grains daily to individuals: this was about fifty times more than most physicians would prescribe.[65] Lady Frankau continued working after being diagnosed with cancer of the oesophagus, and may have been too tired and ill to cope with hard choices; certainly the chemotherapy provided in such cases during the early 1960s was even more gruelling than today. There were pragmatic reasons for physicians to tolerate the lies of users trying to obtain extra drug supplies. The Addiction Unit that opened in 1964 at All Saints' Hospital in Birmingham found that the typical patient often tried to 'persuade us to give him more drugs, using such excuses as his syringe broke, or his drugs were stolen. We go along in this to a limited degree and thus he learns to trust us as an institution'.[66] Of sixty-six patients (75 per cent under the age of twenty-five) treated in the period to February 1967, the Unit thought that about 30 per cent stayed clean. But Lady Frankau's prescribing practices were on a calamitously larger scale.

This situation was complicated by the arrival in London from 1959 onwards of Canadians who had become addicted to heroin supplied from Marseille. Many consulted Lady Frankau.[67] She reported that her first ten Canadians

differed very little from certain of my British and American patients in that they were between 20 and 30 years of age, had a good cultural and social background, were anxious to be considered artistic, and were interested in jazz music, modern or abstract painting. Several of them had written articles or plays . . . The majority came from broken homes or had unsatisfactory parental relationships and were entirely undisciplined. All had a slight degree of resentment against authority and all had obtained drugs illegally on the black market, chiefly in London or Paris.

Starting around 1962, forty further Canadians from much less privileged backgrounds presented for treatment—mostly coming to her directly they reached London. She conceded that 'the few who had money belonged to the upper hierarchy of the drug peddling world' and that the majority had one time or another supplied drugs to finance their own addiction.[68] Some of these Canadians became suppliers to English youths by selling from the large and sometimes enormous surplus of their Frankau prescriptions.[69] Many of her Canadian patients complained that the pure heroin they received as registered addicts provided a disappointing 'hit'. She arranged for them to be supplied with adulterated heroin, such as they had bought on the Canadian black market, and also prescribed cocaine, which they had never used in Canada.

Meanwhile, in 1958, the government had convened an Interdepartmental Committee on Drug Addiction under the chairmanship of the neurologist Lord Brain (1895–1966). The Eden government's defeat three years earlier, when it had ignored the British Medical Association's opposition to heroin prohibition, made politicians and their officials reluctant to challenge medical prerogatives. The Brain committee was therefore exclusively composed of medical men, and set about its work with little reference to social trends or criminal laws. Astonishingly, no members of the esteemed and authoritative Drugs Branch Inspectorate of the Home Office testified to the committee. In consequence, after prolonged deliberations, the Brain committee knew less about the subject than the pharmacist of John Bell & Croyden, who exposed their ignorance at the memorable meeting of the Society for the Study of Addiction in 1961. Brain and his colleagues had reported in 1960 that, owing to public attitudes and 'the systematic enforcement of the Dangerous Drugs legislation', addiction was 'still very small and traffic in illicit supplies is almost negligible, cannabis excepted'. (The quality of their deliberations is indicated by their inference that cannabis was addictive.)[70] They stated, inaccurately, that in the past twenty years, there had been only two doctors who prescribed excessively, and 'in spite of widespread inquiry, no doctor is known to be following this practice at present'. They provided several case histories of stabilised addicts who were all middle-aged, therapeutically addicted users: these patients had little in common with Frankau's new group. Brain affirmed there was 'no cause to fear . . . any real increase' in addiction, and implicitly rejected the US model of punitive drug policy: 'Addiction should be regarded as an expression of mental disorder rather than a form of criminal behaviour'. Their report was 'a whitewash', thought Max Glatt, who treated addicts at Warlingham Park Hospital.[71] Bing Spear called it 'a classic of complacency and superficiality'.[72]

Addiction figures trebled in the next six years. Doctors were not obliged to notify the Home Office, which monitored figures by periodic inspections of pharmacists' records of dangerous drugs; official statistics, therefore, were certainly underestimates. The number of known opiate addicts rose from 454 in 1960 to 1349 in 1966. The number of heroin addicts rose from sixty-eight in 1959 to 899 in 1966. This was a thirteenfold increase. During the mid-1950s most addiction to opiates 'occurred among the middle-aged and was of therapeutic origin': as late as 1967 36 per cent of women addicted to opiates were aged over fifty.[73] There was a 300 per cent increase from one heroin addict aged under twenty in 1960 to about 300 in 1966.[74] The suicide rate among male heroin-users in this period was fifty times the national average. The thirty known users of cocaine in 1959 had risen to 211 by 1964 (all but three of whom also used heroin). In 1959 11 per cent of opiate addicts were aged under thirty-four; by 1961, this had risen to 40 per cent (mostly heroin and cocaine). The number of known addicts in England and Wales rose by about 300 per cent in the fifteen years from 1955. By 1970 the Home Office knew of 2240 heroin addicts, most of them polydrug users.

These figures have often been misread. British heroin production was 68 kilograms in 1959, 66 kilograms in 1960 and 69 in 1961; consumption increased from 45 kilograms in 1959 to 50 in 1964. If these figures were believed, 342 addicts in 1964 used only 5 kilograms more than 68 addicts five years earlier. This is improbable. The truth is that in the early 1960s there was not a sudden massive rise in the number of heroin addicts, but a gradual surfacing of addicts who had been using opiates for years. In justice to Lady Frankau, she had warned of this as early as 1961. It is important to reiterate emphatically that heroin misuse was already escalating in the 1950s because the myth that the 'permissive society' of the 1960s created a new drug problem is one of the most cherished assertions of drugs prohibitionists and the more punitive public moralists. The myth of 'permissiveness' had disastrous power over anti-drug policies during the Reagan–Bush and Thatcher–Major administrations of the 1980s and 1990s.

The facts in some ways counted for less than changing perceptions about illicit drug-users. The Alcoholic Unit at St Bernard's Hospital, Southall, for example, traditionally had seldom seen patients dependent on heroin or other narcotics: 'The more usual patient was a middle-aged person dependent on alcohol and barbiturates or, less frequently, on alcohol and amphetamines; but from May 1963 onwards the young heroin and cocaine addicts began to form the greater proportion of those dependent on drugs.'[75] Morton Hall, a Lincolnshire borstal, first received 'serious drug-takers as opposed to pill-swallowers' in 1965. These included two heroin-users and 'five or six who were regularly taking Indian hemp'. Whereas 'pep-pill users' had once been restricted to the London area, drugs now seemed 'commonplace in most large provincial cities'. Similarly 'the most marked and alarming feature' during 1965 in the Boys' Prison at Wormwood Scrubs was

the sudden surge of drug taking amongst boys. Whilst one cannot classify them as drug addicts, they are nevertheless persistent drug takers . . . The majority seen, have talked quite freely and openly about their drug taking; the sources of supply; the Clubs, Coffee Houses, Bowling Alleys, Youth Clubs . . . it has spread to all parts of the country, from North to South, but confined to the large cities . . . The majority . . . look upon the whole subject as just a way of life, which we as adults quite fail to understand. A more insidious method of obtaining drugs is beginning to creep into the London area, inasmuch that some boys are turning to male prostitution—allowing themselves to be used by older men for homosexual practices, and then blackmailing them in order to obtain money to buy drugs.

The physicians who had sat on the Rolleston Committee in the 1920s had been concerned—not discreditably—to protect their private patients and the significant number of their own professional colleagues who had drug problems: they heard scarcely any evidence of street addicts. Intravenous drug use seems not to have existed in 1926. But by the early 1960s the new intravenous drug trends that had begun around 1950 were involving young people who were from the borstal rather than the private patient classes. This seemed much more threatening to those in authority. Dale Beckett, the consultant psychiatrist at Cane Hill Hospital, believed that the attraction of drugs scenes to these young men could be explained by the principle of counterstimulation—the idea that a strong external stimulus reduces the intensity of internal nervous impulses.

> If a disturbed adolescent can put himself into a highly stimulating and unpredictable situation he will find his mental distress quietened. So he will go into the bright lights, the flashing neons, the crowds of people, the frenetic activity, the clanging pin tables. He may put himself in danger by delinquent acts, such as housebreaking, shoplifting, or robbery, for the excitement is stimulus enough to give him a degree of inner peace. The recurrent impulse to steal and drive away fast cars is well recognized. Horror films and horror comics may also be of help. The stimulus of hustling for heroin is of a high order.[76]

In 1965 convictions for offences against the DDA totalled 767, including 626 for cannabis. In 1966 the total was 1174, including 978 for cannabis. This represented an increase of 50 per cent in one year. Such reports aroused sensational fears of national decline. According to a Cambridgeshire physician in the *British Journal of Addiction* of 1965, 'THE SOFTENING TO WHICH A COMMUNITY MAY BE SUBJECTED HAS NO LIMITS UNLESS WE EMPLOY EVERY POSSIBLE METHOD TO PREVENT, CONTROL AND EVENTUALLY TO ABOLISH THIS TERRIBLE SPREAD OF DEPENDENCE ON DRUGS.'[77] America's example seemed even more appalling than ever. Viscount Amory (1899–1981), who had visited the US as a member of the Royal Commission on the Penal system, reported in 1966 that 'drug-taking by the young' was approaching 'a national calamity' there. He thought that drugs were such 'an insidious and deadly influence' that dealing should be treated 'as an offence second only in gravity to murder'.[78] These laments, and other moral hectoring, were addressed by adults to one another, and went unheeded by the young. Often the lamentations were wild or inaccurate. 'Drug-taking' was equated with 'drug addiction'; the properties of cannabis were misrepresented; 'the adolescent experimenter' was lumped together with the junkie.[79]

Discussions were heated by the insistent sexualising of drugs, which had characterised anti-drugs propagandists since the early American scares about opium dens and cocainised blacks. 'The handmaid of the cop mentality in the Narcotics Bureau is a whole complex of attitudes associated with Bible-Beltism,' Benjamin DeMott wrote in his shrewd profile of Anslinger. 'It is a well-established medical fact that addiction to heroin dulls sexual appetites—but Narcotic Bureau officials are strongly given to tales of sex and drug orgies.' Anslinger's last book, *The Murderers: the Story of the Narcotics Gangs* (1961), brims with senile prurience, including this account of a tea-pad: 'There were fifty people but it seemed like five hundred. It was like crazy, couples lying all over the place, a woman was screaming out in the hall, two fellows were trying to make love to the same girl and this girl was screaming and crying and not making any sense. Her clothes were mostly pulled off and she was snickering and blubbering and trying to push these two guys away.'[80] Drug users seemed to epitomise the deviant who scorned work, and revelled in reckless pleasures, especially licentious ones: they created a scene that thrilled prurient people, for it compelled attention even as it repelled. Thus a religious-minded volunteer working with London drug users described in 1968 how

> a youth took me back to his 'pad' which he was sharing with two other boys and three girls. We entered a room which was bare save for three mattresses, a gas ring and four syringes. They all sat holding each other's hands and as the evening progressed and the fixes began to wear off, they fell upon each other kissing and fondling the other's body; the sexual orgy that followed sickened me. Some drugs stimulate the sexual organs, and then it can be dangerous if not fatal.[81]

In Britain during the 1960s a series of laws were enacted to confront new (or newly perceived) problems. In addition to the Drug (Prevention of Misuse) Act of 1964, there was the Dangerous Drugs Act of 1964, which enabled Britain to ratify the Convention on Narcotic Drugs agreed at New York in 1961. The Indian High Commission had formally complained to British officials about official use of the archaic phrase 'Indian hemp', and in the 1964 DDA the substance was renamed 'cannabis'. Among other provisions, it became a criminal offence to permit premises to be used for smoking cannabis. The Dangerous Drugs Act of 1965, which imposed requirements for safe keeping and record-keeping of dangerous drugs, was followed by the Drugs (Prevention of Misuse) Modification Act of 1966, which for the first time made an offence of unlawful possession of LSD. The political stakes escalated in Britain after the Douglas-Home government's decision to use a legislative programme on drugs to improve its hopes of winning the 1964 general election. The situation was summarised by one authority a decade later: 'It is impossible to exaggerate the dominance of the American drug scene in our thinking then—its dominance and its alleged *closeness*: a new drug would be reported in San Francisco one day and within a week there'd be overdoses of that same drug rumoured in London. But this was largely anecdotal. Unsupported gossip. And yet one had the pressure of the American experience for years.'[82] During 1966 Nelson Rockefeller (1908–79) used crime problems associated with drug-users as a central tactic in his strenuous campaign for re-election as Governor of New York State. Drugs became a decisive electoral factor for the first time. Rockefeller's narrow victory was widely attributed to his bold rhetoric and his opponent's lack of extremism on the subject. However, the US Narcotic Addict Rehabilitation Act of 1966—the first blow against the Anslinger credo that all users were criminals—reflected the new realisation that junkies were not all confined in the ghetto. Middle-class young whites had started dying or being arrested. There were 670 fatal drug overdoses in New York City in 1967 (compared with fifty-seven in 1950). Juvenile arrests for drugs rose in USA by 800 per cent in 1960–67.

In Britain the legislative controls of the 1960s culminated in the Dangerous Drugs Act of 1967, which itself was fashioned by a second report from Lord Brain's committee. These medical men had been reconvened by the Douglas-Home government in July 1964 to report *exclusively* on physicians' prescription of addictive drugs. Their report had far-reaching consequences, although it is an inadequate, archaic and pompous document. 'Witnesses have told us', paragraph 40, for example, pronounced, 'that there are numerous clubs, many in the West End of London, enjoying a vogue among young people, who can find in them such diversions as modern music and all-night dancing. In such places it is known that some young people have indulged in stimulant drugs of the amphetamine type.' As a result of their narrow remit and exclusively medical background, the committee focused excessively on the problems of medical prescription: the word 'pusher' never appears in their stately and sonorous paragraphs. Their approach was insular: they published no comparative statistics between Britain, where the system was permissive, and the US, where it was repressive. They however veered towards the American tradition of quarantine and isolation by suggesting that 'some patients may have to remain indefinitely under the care of treatment centres'. Indeed, Brain's statistical interpretations were skewed. Paragraph 12 of the report referred to 'not more than six doctors' prescribing excessive amount of drugs. This was misleading. With the exception of one single prescription, Lady Frankau had signed every excessive script. It is hard to think that the implementation of Brain's recommendations for drastic inroads into clinical autonomy would have occurred if it had been known that there was only one errant physician: 'I think your problem can be summed up in two words, Lady Frankau,' as Brain acknowledged informally.[83] Moreover, it was generally understood that these imaginary doctors giving improper scripts to addicts were private doctors charging fees. In fact, all the other junkie doctors seeing addicts at this time were general practitioners working on the NHS. Lady Frankau, whatever her faults, was not motivated by money; but an idea arose that maintenance prescriptions were associated with corrupt private practitioners. This misinterpretation had serious consequences in the 1980s.

Brain's committee wanted to curb the increase in opiate addiction while continuing maintenance prescriptions. Spear and the Home Office Drugs Branch argued that this would be possible by minor adjustments to the rules for prescribing heroin. They wanted to protect the work of the better doctors and neutralise delinquent prescribers by limiting the number of addicted patients a general practitioner was allowed to treat, and by requiring second medical opinions from a consultant psychiatrist before settling the levels of doses. This, however, was at a time when both the status and total numbers of general practitioners were declining: the comment in 1966 of Brain's predecessor as President of the Royal College of Physicians that general practice medicine was for those who 'fall off the ladder' by failing to become specialists indicates the probable attitude of Brain's committee to the abilities of GPs.[84] Spear was not a physician, and the medical men deliberating with Brain preferred an alternative strategy proposed by the Irish-born psychiatrist Thomas Bewley (b. 1926). Bewley's precise, emollient and attractive manners were in time to win him high influence in the Department of Health. The Brain committee, too, found him convincing. Bewley was a qualified admirer of American methods. In a highly influential paper (published in 1965) he cited Lady Frankau's article in the *Lancet* before quoting a recent conclusion of the American Medical Association and the National Research Council: 'The maintenance of stable dosage levels in individuals addicted to narcotics is generally inadequate and medically unsound.' He made the astonishing assertion that 'The continuing reduction [sic] in the number of addicts in the United States is due more to the activities of the Federal Bureau of Narcotics than to better treatment.' He recommended compulsory notification of addicts and restrictions on prescribing drugs for addicts outside hospital. Describing 33 opiate-users whom he had treated at Tooting Bec Hospital, he noted that in the course of two years, several had brought drugs into the hospital, two had been arrested while in hospital, one had stolen £100 from the hospital shop, another tried to break into the hospital pharmacy, two took overdoses while in hospital and one committed suicide. 'Such behaviour is not tolerated outside a mental hospital. The provision of special treatment-units is therefore important. Mental hospitals are overcrowded and understaffed and cannot provide adequate follow-up or case-finding among contacts. Possibly the best solution would be a unit in a mental hospital, but with adequate staff, run preferably in conjunction with a teaching hospital.'[85]

Several comments can be made on these recommendations. First, it is debatable just how typical Bewley's delinquent patients were of the addict population in 1965. Tooting Bec Hospital was something of a backwater, with a reputation as a 'dumping ground' for recalcitrant alcoholics and the more unstabilised opiate addicts.[86] Drugs, certainly, were smuggled into most hospitals treating addicts, but the junkies at Tooting Bec seem to have been more disruptive, say, than those at Cane Hill Mental Hospital. Secondly, as a result of Brain following Bewley's proposals, 'the "psychiatrizing" of addiction treatment policy in the United Kingdom was assured' (to quote Spear).[87] Bewley's recommendation that new special units should be attached to teaching hospitals had the incidental result of raising the status of consultant psychiatrists treating addiction. In 1965 Bewley was still consultant psychiatrist at

Tooting Bec Hospital and at the Alcoholism Unit at Wandsworth Prison; but his career accelerated after he was appointed as a senior lecturer in addictive behaviour at a London teaching hospital, St George's. As a consultant in a teaching hospital he became an imposing figure in the medical hierarchy.

Under the influence of such arguments, the Brain committee in its report published in November 1965 proposed overturning the Rolleston system after forty years. It recommended the notification of addicts; the establishment of specialist treatment centres; restrictions on prescribing; and expert diagnostic advice. Physicians who offended against new prescription policy would be liable to disciplinary action by the General Medical Council. In the same week as the Brain report was published, Bewley contributed an authoritative analysis of statistics supplied by Spear on heroin addiction covering 1954–64. This concluded,

> The practice of prescribing drugs for maintenance of addicts worked successfully only when the majority of addicts became addicted from [medical] treatment. Treating other addicts this way makes it easier for new individuals to become addicted to these drugs. Liberal prescribing has no beneficial effect on the addict. The chief source of illicit heroin and cocaine in this country is the sale of drugs by addicts who have more than they need prescribed for them. It is essential to limit the prescribing of heroin for addicts. The argument that this might lead to the creation of a black market is irrelevant, as the present practice supplies drugs free for illicit sale and encourages spread of further addiction.[88]

Bewley represented the spirit of the new system.

After April 1968 a doctor needed to be licensed by the Home Office before prescribing heroin or cocaine to an addicted patient. The right of doctors to prescribe them to treat organic disease was not challenged. Several general practitioners with addiction expertise applied to the Home Office for licences, but none were granted. These powers were reserved for a few hospital physicians and for the consultant psychiatrists in charge of the clinics recommended by Bewley to the Brain committee. Yet it was always probable that many addicts would avoid centres, especially when attached to mental hospitals, and buy from other sources, as three voluntary workers warned in 1967. 'Attempts to "cure" addicts by authoritarian methods of compulsion are doomed to failure, and we regard with horror the mistrust developing between the addict and the authorities.'[89] General practitioners treating addiction were limited to prescribing methadone. Under the Brain committee's sequel, the Misuse of Drugs Act of 1967, the Home Office was empowered to summon to a tribunal any physician who was believed to be prescribing irresponsibly. This tribunal could remove the doctor's right to prescribe controlled drugs, although this procedure was only invoked three times in the next fifteen years. Nor did the Brain committee recommend that general practitioners, instead of the junkie doctors, should be encouraged to treat known drug-users—still numbering a thousand at this time. A critique of their report prepared by Dale Beckett's patients in the Salter Unit had previously warned that it would be 'a great mistake' to exclude the NHS junkie doctors from the prescription of heroin maintenance treatment.'We know these doctors. Their humanity is outstanding. We have heard a lot about the doctor–patient relationship, and here it really counts.'[90]

Some psychiatrists were determined to conquer new empires even though there were few experienced people to staff the clinics. When the legislation based on the Brain recommendations received its unopposed third reading in May 1967, the psychiatrist Philip Connell acknowledged that 'To set up many outpatient services staffed by people who have little basic knowledge or little basic interest in the problem of addiction may well be disastrous'. Yet this is what was done in many places. Connell was reluctant to let voluntary bodies, including the Church, assist because an 'ability to be reasonably objective is particularly important in the field of drug addiction, and the drug addict is often a past master at manipulating those who are emotionally involved.'[91] Only consultant psychologists, it seems, were proof against subjectivity. In fact 1967 was the foundation year of two important voluntary bodies, the Association for the Prevention of Addiction, and Release, both of which undertook valuable work. Connell specialised in treating maladjusted children and adolescents; he had published a monograph on amphetamine psychosis in 1958. Now he became a prominent and powerful member of official bodies. He served as Consultant Adviser on Drug Dependence to the Department of Health and Social Services in 1965–71 and 1981–6; as Chairman of the Institute for the Study of Drug Dependence, 1975–90; and was a member of the

Advisory Council on the Misuse of Drugs during 1982–8. Connell was Physician at the Maudsley Hospital from 1963 to 1986: this was at a time when there were bitter differences between those of its psychiatrists who believed in 'talk cures' and those who believed in electric shock, chemical or other interventions to treat depressed or disturbed patients. The consequent disputes sometimes degraded the patients, and felt shameful to younger doctors. Connell was not a pluralist. Like others who worked at the Maudsley in this period, his professional activities reflected a set of norms that were regarded as unitary in society. As late as the 1980s homosexuality was a major obstacle to Maudsley promotion or good references for jobs elsewhere: talented young physicians, in stable relationships with other men, understood the necessity of bringing an accommodating woman nurse as their companion to social functions.

Earlier generations of alienists, such as Sir Thomas Clouston, had regarded doctors as priests of the body with strong responsibility for guiding social policy. Connell comparably believed that successful psychologists should instruct, or intervene in, citizens' performance of their social and familial duties. In 1964, for example, he advocated 'far greater efforts in the field of child care [and] child psychiatry' so as to reduce 'the incidence of personality disorders which are the basis for so many of the tragedies of amphetamine misuse'. He wanted psychiatrists to have 'contact with families' beginning 'when the child or children are under five . . . to prevent the development of pathological parental attitudes such as gross overindulgence and spoiling, gross rejection and perfectionism, and inconsistencies of disciplining'. He desired large-scale, heavily funded social intervention—what he called 'prophylactic measures'—so that 'teenage and adult personality problems . . . could be aborted by early evaluation'.[92] This amounted to a national strategy of character-policing by consultant psychiatrists, no doubt under his guidance, and would have established his profession as central to society as a whole. Connell was not as mistrusted as he deserved. 'He had a justified conceit of himself and could be moderately bombastic and boastful,' his friend and colleague Thomas Bewley wrote. 'It was impossible to restrain him from speechifying at meetings and he enjoyed mingling with the great and the good . . . he loved power, committees and medical organisations.'[93] In the fifteen years after the second Brain Report, his tactics (and those of his allies) became entrenched orthodoxy, and were ruthlessly enforced.

Initially Connell's views were not sacrosanct. John Owens, a consultant psychiatrist who had in 1964 opened an addiction unit in Birmingham that served as a model for the new national clinic system, warned that 'the exclusively medical composition' of the Brain Committee had resulted in 'two fundamental errors' pervading the 1967 Act. These were 'the notion that narcotic addiction is exclusively a medical matter' and 'the implicit assumption that heroin addiction is an entity in itself . . . uncontaminated by other drug-taking.'[94] Beckett, whose experience and successes equalled Owens's, was equally doubtful about the new system. 'One of the first essentials in treating heroin addicts', he wrote in 1967, was establishing a 'one-to-one relationship' between the patient and his 'junkie doctor' which might help the patient to reassess his priorities. Beckett suggested that this might be achieved, at little cost to the taxpayer, if general practitioners, taking the advice of a specialist unit as to dosages, each took one heroin addict on to their lists. He regretted the decision to situate the treatment centres in teaching hospitals.

> In line with their traditional skills, the staffs will be medically orientated and not sociologically. To a great extent the nurses' attitudes to the addicts will be determined by their experience of physically ill patients who, by and large, are biddable and quite easily shepherded, and they are likely to be disgruntled by what they take to be the addicts' non-cooperation . . . Since it has been hostility and rejection which will have most deeply troubled the inadequate adolescent and led him into heroin addiction, it is all too likely that he will quit the centre to get heroin from people who understand him better (and this unfortunately will mean the black market).[95]

The proposal to restrict prescription to treatment clinics was intended to reduce the circulation of heroin; but in doing so, it put financial incentives into the business. 'If the recommendations are accepted there is a risk that illicit traffic in drugs will increase,' the Scottish addict writer Alexander Trocchi (1925–84) wrote after the Brain proposals were published. 'One would think that the point was self-evident. Gangsters will move in; prices will rise, and with prices, the crime rate; it will be in the interest of these unscrupulous men, when this happens, to "manure the field" for new customers.'[96] Similarly Beckett's patients in the Salter Unit warned that 'There is already in the wings, waiting its opportunity, the efficient and well-tried Mafia organisation, eager to exploit a situation in which heroin is difficult to obtain'. They expected heroin to begin being smuggled into Britain from the French Connection's clandestine laboratories. Organised criminals were monitoring 'the size of the pool of current addicts; its rate of increase; and the proportion of addicts who are or will be unable to get the heroin they need. When all three, taken in conjunction, reach a critical level, the trade can be put on a proper footing.'[97]

The period between the publication of the Brain Report in 1965 and the opening of the clinics in 1968 was crucially unfortunate. The closest parallel is to the disastrous phase after the judicial decision in *Webb versus the United States* (1919) when maintenance prescriptions were suppressed in the USA. It was in 1965–8 that the phrase 'junkie doctors' gained currency as a term of obloquy. In fact, junkie doctors undertook thankless work which was increasingly stigmatised and not conspicuously profitable. Dr Morris Browdy (1885–1970), a venereologist practising at 52, Shaftesbury Avenue, who took over several Frankau patients (one of whom tied him up), left an estate worth £428. Junkie doctors were often admirably dedicated physicians treating patients whom their colleagues rejected. Dr John Dent, who in 1956 withdrew William Burroughs from morphine in seven days, was a 'really great' man in his patient's opinion: 'would often come to see me at 2 A.M. and stay till 5 since he knew I couldn't sleep'. Burroughs admired British medical attitudes of the 1950s: 'They figure an addict has a right to junk like a diabetic to his insulin.'[98] Another man whose memory deserves honour was Dr Arthur Hawes (1894–1974), who described himself in 1966 as one of 'the small, diminishing and despairing band of "junkies" doctors'.[99] He had treated some 1000 addicts on the NHS since the 1950s in his Fitzroy Square surgery. Patients waited in the homely front room lined with the poetry of Ogden Nash. His formidable elderly sister, Una Stangroom (1901–74), who worked as his pharmacist on the premises, would feed waiting addicts with sandwiches. Hawes was eccentric and forgetful. His friend Ken Leech was never sure if Hawes 'was genuinely absent-minded or deliberately pretended he didn't know who people were in order to deflate their pomposity'. On one occasion the consultant psychiatrist David

Stafford-Clark (b. 1916) gave a lecture on addiction that seemed too impeccably polished and self-assured to be quite real. Hawes, who was due to speak next, pricked Stafford-Clark's bubble by referring to him throughout as 'Sir Stafford Cripps', the name of an unpopular dead politician.[100] Hawes knew of only one of his patients who remained clean after five years; he dismissed psychiatric treatment as '100 per cent a failure.' He was uncompromisingly realistic about both addicts and illicit supplies.[101] He accepted that doctors who prescribed for addicts inevitably supplied what was called 'the grey market' in which users resold part of their scripts for about £1 per grain.

> I may be one of these myself, although I do my best not to be. There is no other source of supply beyond an occasional and negligible robbery at a chemist's shop. To cut off the supply by prescription would be easy; it has been done in the United States where doctors are not allowed to prescribe for addicts, with the result that the provision of drugs has become a flourishing industry and drug addiction increases there yearly. So we arrive at the curious anomaly that if we are to keep big business off the black market trade in drugs, we need a number of over-credulous, over-sympathetic, over-prescribing doctors unless we want to run the serious risk of having thousands of addicts instead of the few hundred we have at present.[102]

Following the death of Lady Frankau at her house at Saffron Walden on 20 May 1967, her patients were bereft. Hawes in that month wrote to the Minister of Health urging him to open several temporary clinics in London as a matter of urgency. On 22 June the Ministry replied with a list of hospitals that it claimed provided out-patient treatment facilities for heroin-users, but warned against publicising them. Hawes contacted the listed hospitals, and received a stream of denials that they provided out-patient treatment.[103] A government spokeswoman in the House of Lords on 5 July stated that eleven out-patient clinics were operating in London, but this was untrue. 'I certainly got the impression in 1967', Kenneth Leech recalled later, 'that the attitude of the Ministry of Health was twofold. First, they condemned those wicked, over-prescribing doctors. But secondly, they hoped that these same doctors would continue to prop up the old system until the Ministry was ready with its new treatment centres, and would then gracefully withdraw. Lady Frankau's death took them by surprise, and it led to Dr. Hawes's unexpected revelations in the Press, and so brought the whole terrible business out into the open.'[104] The Minister of Health resented this publicity, and his Ministry made false claims about the availability of treatment, to the embarrassment of the Home Office Drugs Branch.[105] Beckett believed that the delays in opening the treatment centres were not the fault of the government but arose from the doubts of the hospital boards and doctors who would be required to run them. This hesitation reflected 'the moral obliquity with which narcotic addiction is viewed [which] tends to rub off onto a doctor who takes addicts on for maintenance'. He found that his involvement with addicts affected him in his social relations with other doctors ('the smut clung to one'), but not professionally.[106] Arthur Hawes confirmed in *The Times* of June 1967 that restrictions on prescribing by 'junkie doctors' was already attracting large-scale foreign traffickers to Britain. His patients had recently reported that heroin 'is now appearing on the black market in powder form, which has never been available before'. Hitherto the British had used heroin tablets (jacks) for injection. 'The little plastic bag seems to be replacing the tablet, and as powder is more easily adulterated than a tablet, the new regime is looked upon with disfavour by such addicts as I have asked. Unfortunately when, as in America, the big boys control the black market, then there will be little choice.' He warned the position was critical. 'The Ministry of Health does not seem to understand the implications of what they are doing. Nevertheless they soon will.'[107]

A convenient whipping-boy was discovered in the form of an elderly doctor with a funny surname, foreign antecedents and an epicene photogenic appearance. Dr John Petro (formerly Piotrkowski) (1905–81) was a Polish-born Cambridge graduate who had worked in a Hackney children's hospital, as a ship's surgeon and as a clap doctor in a Royal Navy hospital in Ceylon. Later he was a general practitioner with a disarmingly melodious and vibrant voice, and medical adviser to the Portland Cement Company (the Duke of Argyll thought him 'the most able diagnostician in London'). After being hit by a car in 1966 he was unable to continue his practice. His finances were drained by continual losses on fruit machines until ultimately he went bankrupt. He had little experience of drug-users until, following Lady Frankau's death, many of her patients consulted him. Some believe that the patients were diverted to him by Sir Claude Frankau, who had been his superior at St George's Hospital; junkies gossiped that he started prescribing after meeting some of her Canadian patients in the Golden Nugget Casino in Shaftesbury Avenue. He was discovered by the *Daily Mail* in July 1967 holding drugs clinics in the buffet of Baker Street underground station. After being banned by the buffet manager on 7 July, he moved his operations to a Bayswater hotel. Unwisely, he jotted the records of his prescriptions on the backs of cigarette packets and employed a Soho stripper as his receptionist. Consequently, in January 1968, leaving the set of an inquisitorial television programme fronted by Sir David Frost (b. 1939), he was arrested by an officer of the Drug Squad, and charged with failing to keep his Dangerous Drugs register.[108] He complained that he had been set up: 'I had two hours with Frost beforehand and everything was put down on paper, but it bore no relation to that bear-garden.'[109] Next month he was fined £1700. On the day of his court appearance a young ex-patient discussed him with Margaret Tripp: 'Course he gave us too much and got us hooked too fast but like everyone else we thought it could never happen to us and kept going back for more. Straights are funny about doctors. They think doctors are like God and have only to gaze into our eyes to tell if we are lying and what dose of drug we really need. I'm telling you God himself would have trouble knowing if some of these cats were lying.'[110]

After his conviction Petro continued prescribing to drug-users from Tramway Avenue, Stratford, East London. After being struck off the Medical Register in May 1968, but before his appeal had been heard, Spear went to watch him at work. 'He was in Piccadilly Underground station, opposite the ticket office, sitting with his back against the wall and legs stretched out in front of him writing prescriptions for a queue of addicts which stretched almost the whole way around the station. The most impressive parts of this whole operation were the speed at which he would write prescriptions and the orderliness of the queue. Any pretence that clinical judgement was being exercised had long been abandoned.'[111] From 1967 onwards Petro was as committed to the lifestyle of the street addict as any user: 'almost a beggar—conning his patients, scrounging cups of tea, sleeping on the floor at Centrepoint and at the Simon Community as well as in the rooms of addicts'.[112] For some years after 1968, Petro continued ministering in

Soho, dealing with abscesses and overdoses, and tendering advice. He was briefly imprisoned, as he could not afford to pay his fine. Margaret Tripp of St Clement's Hospital, who took over many of his patients, watched Petro in 1969 talking to intravenous barbiturate-users in Piccadilly. 'There was no doubting the genuineness of the affection of the addicts for him . . . He was both their doctor and one of them. Listening to them I realised for the first time how total was his addiction. His committal to the lifestyle was as great as any user in the clinic. He had reached the position where nothing else is as interesting and everything else seems less real in comparison.'[113]

Another tragic character was Dr Christopher Swan (b. 1936). He became obsessed with the drug underworld and in April 1968 set up the East London Addiction Centre in Shoreditch. The demand for his services became so intense that he gave blocks of signed prescriptions to his unqualified medical secretary, who filled them out and took the fees. To keep order in his waiting room, Swan hired an addict; when he discovered this person was selling drugs in a club, he paid a nightclub bouncer to attack him: the orderly was stabbed twice. While detained in Brixton Prison, Swan also tried to arrange the murder of his medical secretary to prevent him testifying. Sentenced to fifteen years' imprisonment,[114] he was afterwards confined in the Broadmoor asylum for the criminally insane. Tripp, who coped with some of the most immediate clinical consequences of Swan's arrest, was among the few people to sympathise with him. 'I had the same pressures on me in the outpatient clinic that Swan had in his surgery,' she said. 'He was an unfortunate and ill-used man, and when I first met him was by no means mad. He explained to me at great length and in great detail why the clinics were going to fail. At that stage, he began to see himself as the only one who understood the addicts, and as their saviour.'[115]

The Home Secretary, Roy Jenkins (b. 1920), recalled his strategy at this time. He visited the USA in 1967 and was 'forcibly' struck by the link 'between addiction and crime' there. He wanted the new system to protect physicians as well as addicts. 'We thought a chief objective had to be to institutionalise the care of addicts through the clinic setting, in which nobody would be acting alone but, instead, as part of a group with checks and supports.'[116] The system, as it operated, fell short of Jenkins's ideal. The more diligent physicians in the clinics remained isolated. Tripp recalled one evening in the early chaotic phase: 'Alone in the out-patients late at night, having said no and sent away two older aggressive men just out of prison who wanted speed right now . . . I fell into the light trance that follows extreme fatigue. It was a very pleasant feeling. It was easy to feel how junkie doctors felt eaten alive by the unending demands of their patients. It was also easy to see why they took their own drugs.'[117]

James Willis (b. 1928), the author of a valuable textbook *Drug Dependence* (1974) written for nurses and social workers, was a consultant in charge of one of the clinics opened in 1967, and thought they 'failed'. He had 'no misgivings about the maintenance prescription of injectable heroin', but among other consultants, 'the clinic experience changed into a race between colleagues to prescribe the least heroin'. Willis felt 'This race was engendered by a mixture of good and bad motives, the good motives having to do with a genuine wish to replace injectable drugs with oral drugs such as methadone, and the bad motives having to do with the innate tendency of many doctors to moralise to and about their fellow creatures.' This situation became 'near farce' when he was telephoned by a colleague from another clinic and asked to prescribe heroin, 'because he knew that I did, whereas he did not feel able to do so although he was licensed to do so'.[118] It is also notable that some of the funds allotted to teaching hospitals for drug dependence units were not spent on that purpose, but diverted by senior physicians and administrators to other causes.

Under the 1967 Act, a Standing Advisory Committee on Drug Dependence was established under the chairmanship of Sir Edward Wayne (1902–90). One of its most powerful figures was Philip Connell. Thomas Bewley was also appointed to the Standing Advisory Committee on its formation; he later sat on the Advisory Council on the Misuse of Drugs for twelve years from 1982, and was Consultant Adviser on Drug Dependence to the DHSS in the interregnum between Connell's two stints in that job. The Act also introduced powers to stop and search people and vehicles for drugs. Under the Metropolitan Police Act of 1839, the London police had been empowered to stop, search and detain any cart or carriage suspected of carrying stolen goods, and the Central Drugs Branch of the Metropolitan Police estimated that the majority of its arrests in 1966 were under this local act. In 1967 this power was expanded nationally. It followed the example of recent legislation providing police search powers to protect the eggs of rare wild birds from thieves. There was no difference between the power of search 'carried out at the foot of a fir tree in a Highland in Scotland than if it is done at the foot of Eros in the middle of Piccadilly', explained Lord Stonham of the Home Office. The 'drug trafficking . . . evil has spread widely', he said. 'It is not only around the cafés—or "caifs", as I think they are often called—clubs and dance halls of town and cities. Coastal resorts, even camping areas, are visited by . . . pushers, some of them sleeping rough, others delivering the goods well concealed in their vehicles.'[119] Provisions for the safe custody of drugs on the premises of retail pharmacists were strengthened, too. 'The flimsy doors leading to easily-forced drugs cupboards of a city's chemists shops are the main supply sources of a teenage drug traffic in Manchester,' the *Daily Mail* had reported in an exposé entitled 'The Pushers' in 1965. Their report followed an eighteen-year-old's fatal overdose on stolen morphine. 'The boy's degeneration into full-time junkie followed the now-familiar pattern. He left home 18 months ago after a row with his parents over his long hair and dress, started on purple hearts and moved on to marijuana. Finally he reached the hard narcotics.'[120] Stonham noted that in 1966 there were at least sixty cases of pharmacy burglaries in London, thirty-five in Manchester, twenty-five in Lancashire and fourteen in Liverpool. 'Well over half a million tablets were stolen. In some areas it has been quite clear that pharmacy-breaking has been a significant source of local drug abuse.'[121]

Critics of the new hegemony suffered for their dissent. After the publication of the Brain Report, in 1965, Peter Chapple (1920–75) formed an unofficial committee of doctors interested in addiction.[122] Believing that addiction units isolated from the community had drawbacks, in 1967, with the support of the Salvation Army, he started the National Addiction Research Institute (later renamed CURE) in Chelsea. He built a committed team treating about 200 polydrug-users annually, and published some notable research, but was not an easy man, and had poor relations with both Connell and Bewley. Officials at the Department of Health treated drugs clinics outside the NHS as suspect in this period, and CURE had to rely upon charitable support because government funds were refused until a few months before its closure became inevitable in 1975.[123]

The diversity of available treatment was further restricted by the closure of the Salter Unit at Cane Hill Hospital. During the early 1960s, when the number of its inmates was falling and its closure had been mooted, the hospital board and Regional Health Authority had decided that Cane Hill's survival would be promoted by treating addict in-patients. Beckett volunteered to run the Unit, which opened in 1965. He instituted 'a self-running unit, where the patients were the governing body. The doctors, the nurses had an in-put, but it was the patients mainly who had a say in how the place should be run, and it seemed to work well.' A weekly management meeting of addicts, nurses and a member of the nursing administration decided who should be admitted as an in-patient. The prospective patient would present his case, explaining why he wanted to be admitted and come off heroin. Several were disbelieved and rejected by the existing patients, including some who had only approached the Unit after being arrested.[124] Beckett's patients aged under twenty-one agreed to be sectioned under the Mental Health Act. As he described in 1966,

> I tell each potential patient all the bad points about the place. I make it clear to him that he is going to be locked up in a closed ward for about a month . . . I paint everything in the gloomiest possible colours, telling him he'll be detained legally for at least six months and maybe as long as a year. If he still wants to come in after that, I know he is serious, and that he's not going to waste our time or his own . . . We try to reorientate their outlook by having group discussions about their motivations—about the reasons, the impulses which led them to drugs in the first place.

Each newcomer accepted into the Unit was handed a pamphlet reading in part:

> This Unit has been set up with one object—to help you enjoy life again. Or begin to enjoy it, if you've never had a chance before.
>
> Now that you are here make yourself at home and listen to what everybody has to say. You will be here for some time yet; so settle in and find out what's what.
>
> The ones who have been off the stuff for some time are likely to be the friendliest because the others will still be a bit self-centred. You will find yourself working pretty hard, finding out what makes you tick and why you, especially, should have fallen into the trap. What did you miss?

Is it worth looking for? Why? These interesting things are going to be explored by you, backed up by the whole lot of us, and you will have to play your part in helping other junkies take their psyches to bits likewise. Exhausting, but rewarding . . .

From time to time some other poor bloke will be coming in for withdrawal of his drugs; so try to make it easy for him, remembering what you went through yourself. You know the kind of thing that will make it more difficult for him; so even if it makes you feel good, don't take advantage of him.[125]

Beckett developed an effective withdrawal method: 'Over 50% of my patients were able to get off heroin because of it.' His technique relied on using 'jacks', tablets of about 10 milligrams of heroin which were dissolved in water by the addict, nurse or physician before injecting. The amount of heroin given to a patient could be closely monitored and reduced. But around 1970 the authorities substituted freeze-dried heroin ampoules for jacks. The advantage of ampoules was that unlike jacks, it was not necessary to dissolve them in water: a significant minority of addicts used toilet water or other contaminated sources. However, ampoules could not be sliced up like tablets, which made the progressive reduction of doses harder to control. Beckett was reluctant to use methadone, finding 'it's really difficult to come off, far more addictive than heroin'. Meanwhile, in 1968, Cane Hill's hospital board and managers became 'very anxious lest the addicts should sell marijuana-cannabis on the corridors. There was no evidence of this happening, but eventually they decided to close the Unit.' Their deviousness in achieving closure, despite the Unit's success, is an early example of the ruthlessness that became characteristic of the administration of British addiction treatment during the 1980s. The Unit's two charge nurses were due, by rotation, to move to different wards, and the Management Committee stated that nobody would agree to replace them. A year later Beckett discovered this was untrue and that two charge nurses had wanted to work there. The truth is that the Unit's self-government seemed threatening to outsiders. Most nurses were supportive, but around 1967–8 'A nurse was appointed with the job, as I understand it, of reining in this democracy, of establishing an authoritarian unit.' He proved highly obstructive. The *coup de grâce* came around 1969 when this nurse attended a meeting of consultants, and gave a long list of faults that he claimed were found in the Unit. Beckett was worsted in this confrontation.[126] This was not the last occasion when British physicians with humane and successful techniques in treating addiction proved to have defective skills in the politicking of medical committees.

MacInnes warned in 1967 that 'Enforcement of narcotic prohibitions would involve a far larger narcotic vice squad than we have at present, largely operating in secret and in an extreme zone of criminal corruption.'[127] According to a reliable contemporary estimate, at least 20 per cent of FBN agents were corrupt, colluding with heroin-traffickers and supplying heroin themselves.[128] Bruce Jackson, who travelled the USA during 1966 investigating drug abuse and control for the President's Commission on Law Enforcement, worked the streets of New York, Houston and Los Angeles with the cops. 'Exiled from our American dream . . . the junkie and the cop find themselves bound to one another in one agonizing coil,' he wrote: 'people who bleed each other need each other'.[129] In Britain, in 1977, Commander Wallace Virgo (b. 1917), who controlled the Drugs Squad and the Obscene Publications Squad at Scotland Yard, together with his Chief Superintendent Alfred William ('Bill') Moody (b. 1925), were convicted of corruption. Other London detectives involved with the Drugs Squad were suspended, retired early or imprisoned.[130]

Most physicians in 1968 disliked maintenance prescriptions, but a Home Office licence to prescribe to addicts 'became, instantly, a mark of status among psychiatrists; some six hundred licences were issued, many to the same men who had said categorically that they couldn't conceive of giving an addict heroin.'[131] Glatt was among the licensed consultants:

Most of us were very averse to prescribe what we thought were killer drugs. But in the end when we were asked to man the new addiction centres, the arguments were that if we didn't prescribe, the black-market would take over. The aim was to take the prescribing of narcotics out of the hands of private and general practitioners and put it into the hands of the NHS doctors at specially licensed clinics. Whilst one hated doing what one was doing, one would participate, as it seemed the lesser evil. But it's quite wrong to say (as people do nowadays) that we thought at the time this was the *treatment* for drug addiction. It was just a kind of first

aid and one hoped, partly naively, but partly to give one's own conscience
a kind of alibi, that the new centres would not be just prescribing units.[132]

Glatt, and other consultants, evidently did not consider 'first aid' as a
stage of treatment. Ann Dally (b. 1926), who later treated drug-users in
her private psychiatric practice, was more critical than Glatt of the
clinic system:

> It was the beginning of a new kind of doctor, a psychiatrist specialising
> in 'drug abuse'. Other psychiatrists were thankful not to have to deal
> with addicts. Some of these drug dependency doctors were eager to
> extend their power and gain prestige, and some achieved powerful posi-
> tions. The new drug clinics needed to attract patients, and they pre-
> scribed liberally. In the process they even created new addicts . . . The
> clinic doctors realised that nothing was going to make their patients give
> up drugs quickly, and so they gave priority to stabilising their working
> and social lives.

Stabilised users were given maintenance doses, as under the Rolleston
system, while more recently addicted patients received diminishing
doses.

By 1970 pharmaceutical heroin was prescribed to only 10 per cent
of registered habitual users and methadone to 51 per cent; these figures
were 4.5 per cent and 67 per cent by 1975. This prescribing trend
increased the value of pharmaceutical heroin on the grey market, and
began a new black market in injectable methadone. Whereas Nyswander and Dole administered methadone orally, in orange juice or fizzy
drinks, 75 per cent of methadone prescribed in British clinics was for
mainlining rather then drinking. This was a measure of the inexperience of the consultant psychiatrists running certain clinics. (As another
example, a London psychiatrist in 1968 defined 'skinheads' as 'people
addicted to subcutaneous injections').[133] The justification for prescribing injectable methadone was that drug-users would be unwilling to
renounce needle rituals; but clinic prescribers were heedless that, as
drugs taken intravenously are absorbed faster than those taken orally, it
was likely that people using needles would inject more frequently to
maintain their hit. The role of needle-sharing in spreading such diseases
as hepatitis was also discounted. In short, the consultant psychiatrists

were confronted by all the same miserable difficulties as the junkie doctors, and collectively did not acquit themselves any better. As Ann Dally explained,

> Addicts exploited doctors and persuaded them to prescribe huge doses. People who worked in the clinics discovered that many addicts were neither responsible nor pleasant. Non-medical workers in the clinics resented the role of the doctor, who was the only one who could prescribe; they thought that non-prescribing methods of treatment should be given more prominence. Doctors in the clinics disliked having to write so many prescriptions and wished to delegate some of their work to their non-medical colleagues. Moralists gained influence, spreading the idea that addicts should be forced to give up their habits and behave like everyone else, and the uncritical acceptance of this idea enabled the chief consultants to extend their power.[134]

Compulsory notification of new cases began in February 1968; prescribing of heroin and cocaine by general practitioners ended in April. In that year the Home Office knew of 2294 heroin-users. Official statistics showing a decrease in known opiate-users from 2881 in 1969 to 2661 in 1970 represented the first fall since 1958. This did not indicate a fall in heroin consumption or in the number of users. It reflected the withholding of the drug in clinics, and the consequent resolve of some users to keep outside the clinic system and move into the black market. Other users preferred a self-image as outlaws moving in an illicit market to that of 'sick' people submitting to a clinical regime. Certainly, the first imported heroin reached London about six months after prescription by general practitioners to addicted patients was prohibited. Although a grey market in which addicts resold prescribed pharmaceutical heroin had long existed in London, it was not nearly as destructive to users or the community as the culture of illegality that developed rapidly after 1968. Seymour Collins (1906–70), the West London magistrate, 'said that drug addiction centres terrified him'.[135] He likened them to the eighteenth-century coffee houses where London merchants had foregathered to exchange market intelligence. Glatt recalled of the late 1960s, 'I felt guilty whatever I did at that time. When I prescribed the stuff I felt guilty prescribing killing drugs. And if I didn't prescribe to someone who came along and said, "I really need it,

I've got severe withdrawal symptoms and you only give me so little," well then again I felt bad. Nevertheless compared with the sometimes scandalous over-prescribing that had been going on before 1968, I still feel that at the time the Clinics were justified and for a time did quite well.'[136] Drug users were not supplied from the clinic, but a week's prescriptions would be sent directly to a pharmacist: the patient could only collect it in daily doses. This process often prevented addicts from working in conventional hours or having reliable earnings. To reduce drug-related crime, London drug-squad detectives wished clinics would 'open around the clock, providing drugs on the spot'.[137]

The year 1967 was crucial in the growth of the British drug scene.[138] In February that year the *News of the World*, which was being sued by Mick Jagger (b. 1943) of the Rolling Stones, tipped off the police to raid a house-party in Sussex hosted by Jagger's colleague, Keith Richards. No charges were made against the Canadian dealer who had supplied LSD and cannabis to the party, and was present during the raid, but Jagger, who possessed four amphetamine tablets bought legally in Italy, was prosecuted. Jagger's infraction was as mild as any drug case brought before the courts, yet he was given the excessive sentence of three months' imprisonment (overturned on appeal) after a show-trial described in *The Times* as 'a symbol of the conflict between the sound traditional values of Britain and the new hedonism'.[139] An example was made of the sole heroin-user caught in the raid, the self-destructive art dealer Robert Fraser (1937–86). He had progressed from smoking Indian hemp to snorting cocaine around 1965. As Sir Paul McCartney (b. 1942) has recalled, 'I felt very lucky because he introduced me to it a year before most people were doing it. That was '66, very early. I did a little with Robert, had my little phial, and the Beatles were warning me. I said, "Don't worry. Johnny Cash wrote a song about it." . . . the first couple of months were fine, but then I started to think, "No, this is not too wonderful. I'm not in love with this." So I got in and out of coke very quickly.'[140]Fraser also introduced his London set to LSD during the summer of 1966. Then he started using heroin. As a result of being found during the Stones raid with twenty-four jacks of heroin, Fraser was sentenced to six months; he reverted to old habits after his release. 'The bathroom was the most important place,' recalled a German actress who stayed in his flat during the late 1960s. 'First you'd shoot up, then you'd puke, then you'd feel great. For me, though, it always fizzled out, because next morning I had to go to work.'[141] Most friends introduced by Fraser to heroin decided that they preferred to live a less obsessed existence. 'Drugs really diminished Robert's personality,' according to Jim Dine (b. 1935), who had been one of the painters handled by Fraser. 'When he started to do heroin it was the end for him. He was never very interesting after that. The thing that killed Robert finally was his shallowness. He had the potential to be a profound human, but he couldn't get above style'. Dine's epitaph for Fraser was poignant: 'He was an amazing survivor, except he didn't survive.'[142]

The Rolling Stones case was followed by sensational press coverage of other prosecutions of pop stars. 'Drug abuse', the Home Office minister Lord Stonham lamented in 1967, 'sometimes starts by youngsters copying the unhappy example of a few of their "pop" idols.' He felt that 'The sensational publicity given to drug-taking by young people has not only created a false impression of the extent of this problem but has tended to intensify it.'[143] Popular music seemed saturated in drug allusions. Bob Dylan (b. 1941) with his song 'Rainy Day Woman' (1966) with its chorus 'everybody must get stoned' and the heroin allusion of his album title 'Blood on the Tracks' (1975); the Rolling Stones with 'Mother's Little Helper' (1966) and 'Connection' (1966); the Beatles' 'Lucy in the Sky with Diamonds' (1967) and 'With a Little Help From My Friends' (1967); Frank Zappa (1940–93) and the Mothers of Invention's 'Hungry Freaks, Daddy' (1966) and 'Help I'm a Rock' (1966); Jefferson Airplane's 'White Rabbit' (1968); Procol Harum's 'A Whiter Shade of Pale' (1967); and Velvet Underground's 'Heroin' are a few examples. Perhaps one child influenced by this publicity was a boy born in the year of Stonham's speech, Kurt Cobain (1967–94). As a singer in Nirvana, the most influential rock band of the 1990s, Cobain personified grunge music, and became a habitual heroin-user. After his death, his grieving mother said: 'Now he's gone and joined that stupid club. I told him not to join that stupid club.'[144] Everyone knew the club she meant: its members were the musicians who died young. The fatal overdoses included Brian Jones (1942–69) of the Rolling Stones, the guitarist Jimi Hendrix (1942–70), Janis Joplin, Jim Morrison (1943–71), the country rock musician Gram Parsons (1946–73), who played with the Byrds and the Fallen Angels, Keith Moon (1946–78) of The Who, and Sid Vicious (1957–79) of the Sex Pistols.[145]

The Reverend Kenneth Leech was a highly intelligent, tireless, unselfish and implacably honest observer of successive drug fashions. For him 1967 was not only the year of the junkie doctors and the Rolling Stones bust, but 'the "freaky" summer when Scott Mackenzie's "San Francisco" topped the hit parade, when Carnaby Street rang with bells and the word "hippy" came into common usage with the swift exploitation of the psychedelic movement by the very straight capitalists in the textile trade; and with the idealising of San Francisco as a paradise state, "gentle people with flowers in their hair", the upsurge of LSD use and the emergence of an acid culture'. John Petro, the doctor who had taken over Lady Frankau's patients, deplored cocaine, and transferred his patients from that drug to Methedrine ampoules. In anticipation of stricter regulations coming into force under the 1967 Act, Christopher Swan similarly began switching his addicts to Methedrine. One of them was prescribing the equivalent of 46 ampoules of Methedrine per patient daily.[146] This resulted in the proliferation of needle use around Soho. Moreover, once the new clinics opened in April 1968, their doctors understandably began reducing the doses of cocaine prescribed for heroin-users, and within a year had almost entirely stopped prescribing injectable cocaine. Until 1967, then, drug-users in London injected heroin and cocaine; but there was a swift transition to the use of Methedrine, with or without heroin, followed by the intravenous use of methadone and barbiturates. Injection, in other words, became more important to users than the substance used. Until then, there had been only superficial similarities between Haight-Ashbury and Soho. However, according to Leech, who was Secretary of the Soho Drugs Group (1967–71) and author of *A Practical Guide to the Drugs Scene* (1972), 'Those who took amphetamines in Soho, as in Haight-Ashbury, were more the very delinquent, emotionally disturbed type of youngster, and the arrival of Methedrine was the sacrament of the pill scene's coming of age.' He was convinced that Methedrine 'played the escalation role so often, wrongly, attributed to cannabis'.[147] The condition of London street addicts began to deteriorate after the winter of 1968–9. Treatment centres were fraught places in 1967–70 because of Methedrine. 'Streams of foul language from amphetamine-soaked scarecrows on the one hand, and gratuitous advice from ignorant well-meaning busybodies on the other, did little to boost the morale,' James Willis recalled. 'There was a superabundance of very disturbed patients taking large doses of heroin and methylamphetamine, and a significant percentage were individuals with major personality disorders often compounded by drug induced psychoses.'[148]

Following this Methedrine crisis, heroin smuggled from Hong Kong began in the winter of 1968–9 to be sold in the Gerrard Street area of Soho at about £1.50 per grain. This was a time when chemists from Hong Kong were opening heroin laboratories under the control of warlords in Burma, Laos and Thailand, who were themselves supported by the CIA as part of its Vietnam strategy. The Home Office believed that Hong Kong heroin was initially smuggled for the use of immigrant workers in Chinese restaurants, but that indigenous addicts soon began supplementing their clinic drugs with the Chinese heroin. Crucially this was the first time in British history that heroin-smuggling from abroad by organised criminals occurred in Britain (not forgetting the small amounts smuggled by addicts from Paris in the 1930s). This heroin found an expanding market among users who had either been deterred from attendance at clinics or, after 1979, found a new hostility in the clinics to maintenance prescriptions of methadone. The triads of Hong Kong dominated London's heroin black market during the 1970s; suppliers from Iran entered the market after 1979, and from Pakistan after 1980.

The West End drugs scene had changed in other ways during the critical year of 1967. The word went out, as a youth worker noted in 1969, that 'the West End's had it'. From 1967 'the action' moved to London's suburbs and surrounding new towns.[149] A serious heroin scene started at Welwyn Garden City in Hertfordshire during 1967. 'Frightful damage has been done by the notorious doctors Petro and Swan,' Lord Sandford (b. 1920) of the Institute for the Study of Drug Dependence declared in 1969. 'I live in a county the middle of which has been ravaged by the former.'[150] From 1967 the use of cannabis and amphetamines, and after 1969 of LSD, spread down through the classes, and into urban communities nationally. The spread of cannabis use had the benefit of distancing it from the more destructive world of heroin, Methedrine and intravenous barbiturate use. The use of cannabis, it seemed from a 1970 survey of 1093 Greater London schoolchildren (of whom only 5.4 per cent had taken drugs), was 'one more element in the behaviour of a lad who wants to grow up quick, who smokes cigarettes young and bluffs his way into the pub underage'.[151] There was no confusion, and little common ground, between users of cannabis and heroin, as there had been twenty years earlier. 'Being a junkie is a full-time occupation and has little to do with being alive,' Richard Neville (b. 1942), the Australian founder of the underground newspaper *Oz*, advised in 1970. 'It is one of the many ways to destroy yourself, if that's what you want.'[152] A survey of 200 drug-takers in Cheltenham (1970–72) found that

> while multiple drug use was commonplace, there was a general trend towards *de-escalation* after an initial period of experimentation with a wide range of drugs . . . most chose cannabis, with occasional use of hallucinogens, or other substances, such as cocaine and opium, which were available only occasionally . . . in general, the students and middle-class bohemians controlled their drugtaking so that it did not interfere with their careers or education. Only a single respondent in these two groups had ever injected drugs, and this had been purely experimental. The overwhelming majority of these two sub-groups were hostile to the notion of injecting drugs, which they regarded as a sign of sickness or folly. The low-status unemployed or manual workers had the most catholic taste in drug use and were observed to use the widest range of psychotropic substances, both legal and illegal. These individuals had the least commitment to conventional career goals and were more deeply involved in a drugtaking milieu.[153]

Traditionally opiate addicts had become addicted independently of each other, either accidentally in the course of treatment, or because as physicians or nurses, they had easy access to drugs. But by the end of the 1950s increasing numbers of opiate-users, and people combining heroin with cocaine, acquired their habits by personal contact. This was exemplified in a study of Crawley New Town, which had been designated in 1947 as a conurbation receiving London's overspill population. There were six new cases reported of Crawley inhabitants with intravenous heroin or methadone habits during 1962–4. Although this was doubtless an underestimate, so too were the escalating figures after 1965. There were five new cases in 1965, twenty-four in 1966 and thirty-two in 1967, falling away to four in 1969. New users were acquainted through school, truancy, clubs, minor delinquency and in a

few cases work. Small intimate groups were bonded together by their
interest in drugs. 'Initiation was on a convivial basis—drug users wishing their friends to enjoy the experience they had experienced, some
who were non-users wishing to experiment and satisfy a curiosity and
others not wanting to be different from their "mates".'[154] They bought
drugs for each other, which involved trusting each other with money
and protecting friends from arrest. Beckett treated several Crawley
patients. He learnt that when the place was built, as a new town, there
had been three dance halls for young people's evening entertainment.
But on police advice, local magistrates had closed one dance hall, and
then another. There was less than ever for local youths to do at night.
'One or two of them started to go up to London to score heroin, and
bring it back for people. Then drugs were used in this last dance hall,
so the police closed that down, and so there was nothing to do except
go up to London and buy heroin. Extraordinary! The police and magistrates did a lot of disservice to society.'[155]

Another sinister development was the association of heroin with
urban dereliction, unemployment and social disadvantage. This followed the pattern that had been noted in Chicago during the 1930s,
and in other American ghetto communities from the late 1940s. Some
of the earliest trends can be traced in Scotland, where by the 1970s
there was a major heroin problem that only received appropriate attention in the late 1980s after needle-sharing had resulted in the transmission of HIV. According to a report of 1972, Glasgow's 'drug scene'
began when a young man accustomed to using heroin and cocaine in
London found himself without drugs while visiting Glasgow in 1963,
and was admitted to hospital. A small, permanent drug community was
soon expanding by social contacts. A serious burglary in 1966 of a large
pharmacy resulted in the number of known intravenous drug-users in
Glasgow rising from five in 1965 to about twenty by 1967. Heroin and
morphine were used exclusively until the stolen supplies were
depleted. During 1967, users turned to intravenous barbiturate use, oral
hypnotics, LSD and cannabis. Some, at least, of the staff operating Glasgow's four new clinics opened in 1968 were relieved when addicts
shifted out of their area: 'Subsequent cells of addiction have not settled
for admission and have left for London.'[156]

Many clients at the Drug Addiction Treatment Centre, which
opened at Edinburgh Royal Hospital in 1968, were jobless. A report on

the centre's first hundred referrals, published in 1973, commented: 'Handicapped as so many of the drug takers were by a criminal record, no skills, no references, and (often) their "hippie" appearance, they stood little chance of a job other than casual labouring. Emigration was barred; they would not be acceptable in the Army; marriage and children on Social Security an unenviable prospect. In such circumstances, it is understandable that they sought pharmacological oblivion from their dimly realised despair.' The Edinburgh Centre refused to prescribe opiates as a way of 'discouraging addicts from flocking to the city.' The fact that there were only seventeen referrals to the Clinic from May 1971 to March 1972 was said to 'reflect the vigilance of the Edinburgh Drugs Squad; increased security precautions taken by chemists; and a less lenient attitude towards drug offenders on the part of the Courts'.[157] It is not clear whether this 'vigilance' included officers sitting in their police cars outside clinics to deter addicts from attendance, as happened during the 1980s; but certainly, these policies resulted in clinics losing touch with the local client population.

Scotland's experience indicated that social deprivation was becoming a significant cause of drug misuse, and that poverty and barbarous surroundings made such misuse more intractable. Overall, the Edinburgh and Glasgow clinic policies of the 1960s were myopic and narrow-minded. As intended, they only displaced the pain from their communities. In the early hours of a dismal wet London morning in 1969 Margaret Tripp watched IV barbiturate-users, 'loaded with barbs, abscesses and their internal conflicts', circling near the Eros statue in Piccadilly. 'They formed a small group, mainly Scots and Irish and all troubled with . . . a strange combination of uncontrolled aggression alternating with servility which makes equal loving relationships practically impossible. Separated from their friends and family, the Dilly was their end point, there was no where else for them to go.'[158]

These developments were politically invisible. More attention was given to a report of a subcommittee of the Advisory Committee on Drug Dependence submitted to the Home Secretary, James Callaghan, in 1968. Baroness Wootton of Abinger (1897–1988), a distinguished sociologist, chaired this subcommittee: its members (including Philip Connell, Thomas Bewley, Sir Edward Wayne, the psychiatrist Sir Aubrey Lewis [1900–1975] and a senior London magistrate) were equally elevated. Their report concluded 'that the adverse effects which the consumption of cannabis in even small amounts may produce in some people should not be dismissed as insignificant. We have no doubt that the wider use of cannabis should not be encouraged. On the other hand, we think that the dangers of its use as commonly accepted in the past and the risk of progressing to opiates have been overstated, and that the existing criminal sanctions intended to curb its use are unjustifiably severe.'[159] Seventeen per cent of young people on cannabis charges were receiving prison sentences at this time. In paragraph 29 the Wootton committee also posited that long-term consumption of cannabis in moderate doses has no harmful effects. These conclusions violated political orthodoxy, and were subject to a flood of invective suggesting that the committee's members, remote in their ivory towers, had been duped. Its temperate and careful research was headlined as 'CHARTER FOR JUNKIES' by the *Daily Telegraph* (9 January 1969). 'Foreign "dealers" flew into London the same morning the Wootton Report was published,' claimed the *News of the World* (12 January). 'In a matter of hours the capital became one of the easiest places in Europe to buy cannabis.' One *Daily Express* headline read 'RUSSIAN ROULETTE WITH A FULLY LOADED REVOLVER—THAT'S POT' (13 January 1969). The report was represented as demanding the immediate legalisation of cannabis, although it did nothing of the sort, and thus of facilitating the corruption of the young. Disgracefully, the Home Secretary, Callaghan, pretended to think that 'the Wootton Sub-Committee was over-influenced by this lobby' that favoured 'legalising pot'. The existence of these ideas was 'a shock to most people', and 'something that . . . public opinion should . . . combat, as I am.' He presented his rejection of the report as 'call[ing] a halt to the advancing tide of so-called permissiveness'.[160]

His refrain of plain man's anti-intellectualism was popular in the House of Commons. 'God save us from the rule of the clever fool,' prayed a Conservative MP debating the Wootton Report. 'No one with any common sense would give two thoughts to its recommendations,' which he dismissed as 'academic drivel'.[161] Callaghan had a cosy relationship on drugs with Quintin Hogg, his front bench shadow, who was impatient with a trivial matter such as accuracy. 'If the habit is vicious . . . do not let us have a semantic argument about whether they are drugs of addiction or dependence.' Hogg had discussed the subject with friends whose hunches he preferred to the expertise of Sir

Edward Wayne and Sir Aubrey Lewis: 'although they cannot always give figures which prove these facts' [*sic*], his friends associated cannabis 'with crime, violence and abnormality'. Hogg presented this unpleasant gossip as 'overwhelming' evidence proving 'the most appalling results of hashish addiction [*sic*].'[162] He was a loud patriot who justified legislation on the basis of treaty obligations and Britain's global status—what he portentously called 'the important issue of international comity'—and scorned any 'namby-pamby attitude'.[163] Given the failure of the policy about which there was such ostentatious unanimity, the politicians' smugness in 1969 was nauseating. 'It is really a most important day for the House of Commons when both Front Benches . . . can show to the people of the country that we at least march together,' Sir Patrick McNair-Wilson (b. 1929) gloated. He likened the Wootton Report to the threat of Nazi Germany: unless it was rejected, 'we may well go down in history as the great appeasers' by whose inaction 'social order in this country' was destroyed. His strategies were as empty as his clichés. 'The possession of cannabis and its use is a serious crime'; any youngster offered it should 'walk out of such a party and report the person who tried to corrupt him'.[164]

Around this time the father of a Welwyn Garden City user was explaining the drug fashions among the young. 'They are bored. What they need is a war to put fibre into their generation.'[165] This was not utterly fatuous: young people need to prove themselves by taking risks; if completely protected from danger or hard decisions they cannot mature; they may cope better with inner emotional distress if they are in an externally disturbing environment. Perhaps the Welwyn father half-sensed this. In any case, the US President, Richard Nixon, then waging war in Vietnam, was soon to oblige by launching another war: the War on Drugs.

THIRTEEN

Presidential Drugs Wars

Everything that's illegal is illegal because it makes more money
for more people that way.

—JACK GELBER

The only law the narcoterrorists don't break is the law of supply and demand.

—VIRGILIO BARCO VARGAS, PRESIDENT OF COLOMBIA

RICHARD NIXON, PRESIDENT of the United States from 1969 until driven to resignation in 1974 by his complicity in the Watergate conspiracy, was the first man in the White House to have direct, calamitous influence on drug policy. He did not want to understand: he wanted action for its own sake. 'The country should stop looking for root causes of crime and put its money instead into increasing the number of police,' he wrote in 1967. 'Immediate and decisive force must be the first response.'[1] His cures usually escalated his problems. Nixon was a chronic insomniac who indulged in binge drinking when stressed. He also acquired a clandestine drug habit from his friendship with the New York financier Jack Dreyfus (b. 1913). Dreyfus credited the anti-convulsant phenytoin (Dilantin) with curing his chronic depression in 1958, and spent a fortune promoting the drug, which had first been marketed in 1938. Nixon asked Dreyfus for some Dilantin in 1968. Dreyfus, expecting him soon to be elected president, thought, 'What the heck', and gave him a bottle containing 1000 pills. Dilantin's adverse effects include mental confusion, slurred speech,

420

diminished co-ordination, dizziness, insomnia, and nervousness. Nixon, who procured further supplies from Dreyfus, may have been mixing Dilantin, alcohol and sleeping pills during his final months in the White House. Nixon's admirer, the evangelist Billy Graham (b. 1918), regretted his drug use. 'He took all those sleeping pills, and through history, drugs and demons have gone together,' he said in 1979 in explanation of Nixon's downfall in the Watergate scandal.[2]

Nixon's outlook on drugs was bitter, rigid, triumphantly righteous and as irredeemably self-centred as only a paranoiac can be. He blamed them on his enemies.

> America's leadership class will be remembered for the role it played in helping lose two wars: the war in Vietnam and, at least so far, the war on drugs. The leadership class is made up of highly educated and influential people in the arts, the media, the academic community, the government bureaucracies, and even business. They are characterized by intellectual arrogance, an obsession with style, fashion, and class, and a permissive attitude on drugs. In Vietnam, they felt more comfortable criticizing the United States for trying to save South Vietnam than criticizing the Communists for trying to conquer it. In the drug war, they simply went over to the other side. For years, the enemy was them.[3]

Both as a puritan and as a man perennially frustrated with his circumstances, Nixon detested the hedonism and easy gratification of many young people. Healthy white adult males had a duty to work: 'drop outs' defied the core values of good Americans. The Woodstock peace-and-love music festival of 1969 brought out all the ferocious aggression in him. 'To erase the grim legacy of Woodstock, we need a total war against drugs. Total war means war on all fronts against an enemy with many faces.' He expected the drugs war would give him the stature of Abraham Lincoln: 'The war on drugs is our second civil war.' His instincts were undemocratic, and he hoped to justify his unscrupulousness by the greatness of the cause.[4]

Crucially the drugs produced by corporate America were exempt from Nixon's hatred. When he entered the White House, US pharmaceutical companies were manufacturing 8 billion amphetamine tablets annually; but he did not denounce them. Nor did he decry Methedrine use by motor-cycle gangs and other rednecks, despite the associated violence. After all, he depended upon Dilantin obtained without a doctor's prescription to cope with stress. It indicated Nixon's outlook that under the Controlled Substances Act of 1970—part of the Comprehensive Drug Abuse Prevention and Control Act that after fifty-six years superseded the Harrison Act—marijuana and heroin were classified as Schedule I drugs with the heaviest punitive panoply. By contrast, amphetamines (other than Methedrine) were initially Schedule III and barbiturates were Schedule V.

Towards the end of the Johnson administration, in 1968, after corruption scandals and other discreditable events, the FBN had been wound up, and its responsibilities transferred to a new Bureau of Narcotics and Dangerous Drugs (BNDD). In July 1969, seven months after taking office, Nixon announced a global campaign against drugs and their traffickers. The earliest manifestation of this new priority was Operation Intercept, launched in September 1969. Nixon ordered the closure of 2500 miles of the Mexican–US border. Over three weeks 418,161 individuals and 105,563 vehicles were searched. Reactions were overwhelmingly favourable, except among people with some grasp of the subject. One result of Operation Intercept was that the US developed into the world's leading marijuana-growing country. Increased US border vigilance drove small, independent Mexican suppliers out of business, and thus reserved the market for larger organised trafficking gangs commanding more sophisticated resources. Colombian marijuana production escalated, and smugglers were soon bringing larger amounts of their other illicit product, cocaine, into the US. As the Haight-Ashbury drug expert Dr David Smith commented, 'The government line is that the use of marijuana leads to more dangerous drugs. The fact is that the *lack* of marijuana leads to more dangerous drugs.'[5] Each time law enforcement is escalated, drug-trafficking has to escalate to survive. When the US government attacked the entrepreneurial organisations created by Operation Intercept with new laws and aggressive enforcement, it created a new adversary—the Colombian cartels. These cartels, with vast manpower and resources, flourished in the market environment created by the War on Drugs of the 1980s. They enforced their rules and terrorised their opponents with pitiless violence, they corrupted politicians and officials and they contaminated the international financial system with laundered money. After 1989 they replaced the Soviet bloc as the targeted adversary of US foreign policy, but remained unbeaten.[6]

Nixon renewed his War on Drugs in a television broadcast of 17 June 1971, predicting that drugs would destroy America. Heroin use by US troops in Vietnam particularly alarmed him. He misunderstood, however, what was happening. Men drafted into the US Army typically arrived in Vietnam at the age of nineteen: military regulations prohibited the sale of alcohol to soldiers aged under twenty-one. Scarcely any military leaders in world history have been so naïve as to expect a young conscript army to face battle conditions without the help of some intoxicant. With alcohol prohibited, the young men sought other salves. Arrests for marijuana offences among US troops in Vietnam increased by 2,553 per cent during 1965–7. When US military police drastically cut marijuana supplies in 1968, the drugs market quickly adapted. Many soldiers in Vietnam began using heroin, which was more compact and easier to conceal than pungent marijuana. By the early 1970s 80 per cent of US servicemen were offered heroin within a week of first reaching Vietnam. Because of the purity of heroin available in South-east Asia, US troops could get an effective hit by smoking the drug in cigarettes or by inhaling it ('chasing the dragon'). Intravenous heroin use was less prevalent. Although it was estimated in 1971 that over 10 per cent of enlisted men in Vietnam (at least 25,000 men) were using heroin, many were occasional users, who did not take it daily for long enough to become addicted. When the US authorities introduced mandatory drug urinalysis tests for all departing soldiers, the numbers testing positive for heroin fell from 10 per cent to under 2 per cent in six months. This would not have happened if the users were addicted. Indeed, of a sample of 495 soldiers who tested positive for opiates when leaving Vietnam in 1971, 95 per cent were found to be 'clean' when contacted a year later.[7] These experiences diverged from those of addiction clinics in the US and Europe: the fact that US servicemen had experimented with heroin as a result of alcohol and marijuana prohibition, voluntarily renounced its use and did not relapse undermined most assumptions of US drugs policy. Such nuances were lost on Nixon. Heroin use by American forces largely prompted his declaration of drugs as 'the number one domestic concern' in 1971. He claimed that heroin-users were responsible for $2 billion of property crime annually. This was another 'Tricky Dicky' lie. All property crimes during 1971, including hijackings, amounted to $1.3 billion.[8]

American strategic involvement in South-east Asia had aggravated the heroin problem. The CIA in the 1950s had supported anti-Communist Chinese Nationalists who had settled near the China–Burma border, and trafficked in opium from Shan province. Next the CIA supported Hmong tribesmen in Laos in their resistance to Communists near the North Vietnam frontier. The Hmong's main cash crop was opium for smoking; their warlords expanded the cultivated area under the pretext of funding anti-Communist activities. The CIA reportedly helped to transport this opium to laboratories in the 'Golden Triangle' where the borders of Burma, Laos and Thailand converge. Equipped with American aircraft, helicopters and boats, the Hmong began supplying high-grade heroin to South Vietnam. Many senior military officers and politicians in producing countries such as Thailand and consuming countries such as Vietnam participated in the traffic. The CIA protected the heroin business of its warlord allies while its operatives distributed heroin in Vietnam.[9] As in the Mediterranean during the late 1940s, covert CIA action resulted in increased levels of heroin trafficking. Just as Anslinger and the Daniel Committee had blamed 'Red China' rather than the 'French Connection' for supplying heroin to the US in the 1950s, so the US in the early 1970s blamed the Communists rather than the warlords for the rising drug trade in South-east Asia. After the US withdrawal from Vietnam in 1973, the Golden Triangle laboratories supplied about one-third of heroin smuggled into the US.

'The bureaucratic machine has a vested interest in playing cops and robbers,' Gore Vidal (b. 1925) noted in 1970. Both enforcement agencies and criminals 'want strong laws against the sale and use of drugs because if drugs are sold at cost there would be no money in it for anyone'. If drugs were cheaply available, 'addicts would not commit crimes to pay for the next fix', but 'if there was no money in it, the Bureau of Narcotics would wither away, something they are not about to do without a struggle'.[10] The institutional vested interests grew apace. In 1972 Nixon appointed the lawyer Myles Ambrose (b. 1926), Commissioner of US Customs, as his drug law enforcement consultant. The new unit headed by Ambrose, the Office of Drug Abuse and Law Enforcement (ODALE), conducted raids and became actively involved in fighting street dealers rather than high-level racketeers. Some suspect that Nixon hoped to use ODALE to defend himself against his enemies as the Watergate scandal unravelled. The BNDD was in 1973 merged with ODALE to form the Drug Enforcement Administration (DEA). The bureaucratic apparatus established by the Nixon and Reagan administrations also included the Office for National Narcotic Intelligence (1972), the Regional Information Sharing System (1980), the Organised Crime Drug Enforcement Task Force (1983), the National Narcotics Drug Policy Board (1984) and the Office of National Drug Control Policy (1988). These bodies had a vested interest in escalating the War on Drugs. The DEA had 1900 special agents in 1980, 2800 in 1989 and 3400 in 1998. The amount of federal money spent on drug control rose from $3 billion in 1986 to $8 billion in 1990 and $15 billion by 1997. In that year the DEA obtained its first billion-dollar budget. The federal government spent $1.7 billion on drug control along the US–Mexican frontier in 1998 alone; nearly 8000 agents were employed there. These figures exclude the expenditure of state bodies such as the Bureau of Narcotics Enforcement in California and on the soaring prison population. In the 1960s economists wrote of the military-industrial complex influencing US policy untowardly; but the complex of punitive organisations working on drugs is more formidable today. Media images of heavily armed police units storming crack houses or dealers' premises enforce the military associations, and make any dissent seem subversive or treacherous. These enforcement agencies have accelerated trends towards more structured operations in the illegal drug market.

In the Nixon era many American commentators regarded each illicit substance in isolation, which handicapped policy-making. Margaret Tripp, who worked with east London addicts before moving to Memphis, noticed a singularity in US policy during the early 1970s. In London, she knew, when clinics cut down on prescribing heroin, the users would begin substituting amphetamines, barbiturates or other drugs. But in Washington DC and elsewhere, when the heroin supply was reduced, and a 'terrible amphetamine problem' ensued, 'Nobody saw the slightest connection between the one and the other.'[11] Americans regarded British pragmatism as 'the epitome of amoral expediency': Nixon's Attorney-General stigmatised it in 1972 as 'surrender'.[12] Another legacy of Nixon's drugs war was that the Western world began to be afflicted by drug fashions—or at least drug publicity—following the cycle of American national and state elections every two years. Thus the heavy attention that was focused in the presidential election year of

1980 on Methedrine in Philadelphia (which was misleadingly dubbed the 'speed capital of the US') reflected the needs of two Republican Congressmen from prosperous districts near the city. In 1989, the promoters of the 'Ice' (smokable Methedrine) panic were Hawaiian legislators vying with each other on local drug issues, and the proliferating nationwide alarm derived from the impending contest for the state's US Senate seat. There was a similar story with Methcathinone, a laboratory-designed drug first synthesised in Germany in 1928. Some fifty years later it came to the attention of a University of Michigan student interning at the Parke, Davis pharmaceutical company, and was soon a cult drug on the Ann Arbor campus. It was nicknamed 'CAT' (also 'Jeff' or 'Goob'), and was usually snorted, although sometimes diluted in soft drinks. This localised drug habit was in 1993 transformed into a national concern largely by the activism of just one politician.[13]

The US National Household Survey on Drug Abuse was launched in 1971, and reported in 1972 that 7 per cent of the youngest age cohort surveyed (aged twelve to seventeen) had smoked marijuana in the last month, which suggests they were regular users. By 1974 the figure had doubled to 12 per cent, and by 1977 it was nearly 17 per cent. Among those aged eighteen to twenty-five, 27.8 per cent had smoked marijuana in the last month in the 1972 survey. By 1979 the figure was 35 per cent. Sixty per cent of those aged eighteen to twenty-five in 1979 had smoked marijuana at least once. The gradual raising of the minimum legal age for alcohol consumption to twenty-one throughout the states in the late 1970s and early 1980s both diminished young people's respect for prohibitionist laws and stimulated their demand for marijuana as a substitute (as had occurred with the New York tea-pads of the 1920s). As it grew harder to pretend that marijuana-smokers were deviants, drug-suppliers (who conveniently were often foreigners) and dealers (who were all heinous) replaced the users in the authorities' demonology. But the targeting by American police of marijuana-dealers rather than users only made sense if there was a clear-cut distinction between marijuana-users and sellers. However 44 per cent of 204 New York City marijuana-users surveyed in 1970 had sold the drug at least once. In the marijuana market friendships and sales interacted.[14] The desire to extenuate middle-class drug delinquency by devising harsher penalties for suppliers was also manifest in Europe although there too, as John Marks of Liverpool Drug

Dependency Clinic wrote, 'most addicts are also traders'.[15]

Legislators on Capitol Hill and in Europe began to distinguish between users and suppliers. This distinction was central to thinking in Britain when the Home Office, under James Callaghan, resolved to modernise the complicated set of laws and controls that had been established since 1920. The Misuse of Drugs Bill drafted by his officials in 1969–70 provided heavier penalties for trafficking and lighter penalties for possession. Journalists, however, successfully flustered Callaghan, as his colleague Richard Crossman (1907–74) recorded in 1970. Initially Callaghan proposed 'to have drugs reclassified into three sorts, hard drugs, drugs of secondary danger, such as purple hearts and cannabis, and drugs of tertiary danger'. The Cabinet agreed to this: penalties for possession of drugs in the second class were to be reduced, while trafficking penalties were increased. 'There was then an absolutely outrageous leak saying that Callaghan had been overruled and that the Government was going to go soft on drugs and make major concessions on cannabis.' As a general election was imminent, Callaghan decided to consult his Cabinet colleagues as to whether the original proposal should proceed. 'Partly in view of the leak and partly in view of public opinion, he now proposed to have no reduction at all in any penalties on cannabis,' Crossman reported. 'It became absolutely clear that the issue was really whether we should kowtow to public opinion or not'. Cabinet opinion divided entirely upon educational lines. 'Every member of the Cabinet who had been at University voted one way and everyone else voted the other.' The non-graduate ministers, 'all saying public opinion was too strong for us, were ... outvoted', but 'having lost this battle, however, Callaghan whipped in with another suggestion'. As a result the Cabinet gave him 'the major concession that we would make the maximum penalty for cannabis offences not the three years originally proposed but five'. Crossman stressed that no Cabinet ministers denied the principles of the reform. 'They simply said that the public wouldn't understand it and that we now couldn't afford to alienate people on this issue.'[16]

The three categories of controlled drugs were Class A (including opium, heroin, morphine, methadone, hallucinogens such as LSD, and Methedrine) for which the maximum penalty for unlawful possession was seven years' imprisonment, or a fine, or both. Class B included codeine, cannabis, and amphetamines. The maximum penalty for Class

B was five years' imprisonment, or a fine, or both. For Class C substances the maximum penalty was two years' imprisonment, or a fine, or both. It became an offence to be in any way knowingly concerned in the unlawful production or supply of a controlled drug; unlawful for the occupiers of premises to permit unlawful production or supply of controlled substances (including the preparation for smoking of either opium or cannabis); and an offence to possess a controlled drug (lawfully or not) with the intention of supplying it to another person. These offences carried maximum penalties of fourteen years' imprisonment (or a fine, or both) for Classes A and B, and five years' for Class C. The government was insistent that hallucinogenic drugs, including LSD and cannabis, had virtually no therapeutic uses: licences for their use were seldom issued, and strictly controlled. The Home Secretary was empowered to direct the withdrawal of a doctor's authority to possess or prescribe specified controlled drugs. The Misuse of Drugs Act came fully into force in July 1973.

In the US, after Nixon was deposed, there was a mild reaction against his War on Drugs as against so much else of his shoddy regime. The more pragmatic approach was evident in 1977 when President Jimmy Carter (b. 1924) advocated abolishing all federal criminal penalties for those possessing small quantities of marijuana. 'Penalties against possession of a drug should not be more damaging to an individual than the use of the drug itself,' he told Congress.[17] His administration was unique in having the courage and realism to acknowledge that drug use would not be suppressed by prohibitionism. His strategies were, however, wrecked when in 1978 his Special Assistant for Health Issues was forced to resign after mysteriously prescribing for his assistant a non-barbiturate hypnotic, methaqualone, which was marketed in the US as Quaalude and in Europe as Mandrax.

A more grievous development followed in 1979 when the Carter administration shipped arms to the mujaheddin guerillas resisting the Soviet occupation of Afghanistan. This was a mistake comparable to that made in Laos during the Vietnam War: the rebels raised money for arms by selling opium, with CIA complicity, and by 1980 60 per cent of heroin in the US originated in Afghanistan. The country remained at the end of the century the world's largest illicit opium-producer: the CIA estimated that 51,500 hectares were under cultivation in 1999 with potential production of 1670 metric tons. (The world's second

largest illicit producer in 1999 was Burma, with 89,500 hectares potentially producing about 1000 metric tons). The Afghan traffic led to a
proliferation of heroin refineries in neighbouring Pakistan, where there
was an appalling rise in addiction during the early 1980s. The number
of heroin users in the US had fallen from an estimated 500,000 in the
late 1960s to about 200,000 in the mid-1970s, but these figures rose
following the US–Soviet stand-off in Afghanistan. Gary Indiana (b.
1950), once a columnist on the *Village Voice*, has depicted the New York
heroin scene of the early 1980s.

> There were many people who found heroin addiction glamorous. The
> idea of being beautiful and damned was a perennial youthful myth in
> the downtown area. People went on smack when they had money and
> stayed on smack after all the money got used up, and then started rip-
> ping off their friends and families and usually became incredibly sick
> and horrible-looking and got these strange diseases like lupus or hepa-
> titis B and now . . . half the addicts in New York have HIV infection
> through needle-sharing, and of course the terrible thing is, the addict
> knows all this but can't do anything about it because it's the drug that
> makes the decisions.[18]

Although Nixon's War on Drugs abated after his resignation, the
drug enforcement bureaucracy grew into a massive instrument of
international intervention. The first permanent overseas FBN office,
which had been opened at Rome in 1951, had been followed by offices
in Paris (1960), Marseille (1961), Bangkok, Mexico City and Monterey
in 1962–3, and later in Hong Kong, Singapore, Korea and Manila. By
1993 the DEA had 293 agents in seventy-three foreign offices. In 2000
the DEA had 9132 employees, including 4561 special agents, and an
annual budget of $1,550 million. As Ethan Nadelmann, Director of a
New York drug policy foundation, the Lindesmith Center, has summarised, the DEA

> plays a unique role in international politics. As a transnational organiza-
> tion, it is a hybrid of a national police agency and an international law
> enforcement organization. It represents the interests of one nation and
> its agents abroad are responsible to the ambassador, yet it has a mandate
> and a mission effectively authorized by international conventions and

the United Nations . . . its principal role is one of liaison. But unlike virtually all other agencies except the CIA and the military's investigative
divisions, its agents are 'operational' in most of the countries where they
are stationed—they cultivate and pay informants, conduct undercover
operations, and become directly involved in the activities of their local
counterparts.[19]

The impact in Europe has been considerable since the 1960s. US drug
enforcement agents introduced to Europe a range of police techniques
that had been approved in the US courts since the Prohibition era of
the 1920s. These included controlled delivery of illegal drug consignments, 'buy and bust' tactics, undercover surveillance, and offers of
reduced charges or immunity from prosecution to turn arrested drug-
dealers into informants. The civil law tradition prevailing across much
of the European mainland was opposed to such techniques—unlike
British common law—and during the 1960s many European police
officers and judges regarded them as unacceptable except, perhaps, if
undertaken by intelligence services. Those European countries with a
history of authoritarian regimes spying on their citizens were particularly sensitive about the American practice of using *agents provocateurs*.
Nevertheless, by the 1980s, most of these investigative tactics, vigor-
ously demanded and incited by the DEA, were adopted by European
police charged with drug enforcement, although with differing commitment. Austria, Belgium and Germany followed the US model;
France and Italy were less responsive. European courts and legislatures
upheld these changes in investigative tactics.[20] The European powers
succumbed to the 'Americanisation' of their anti-drug enforcement
partly because DEA agents were seen as the experts. It was rarer for
European governments to argue, as several had done in the 1920s, that
if the US had such extreme problems, it might be wise to avoid the
failed solutions that they were exporting. Since the 1970s the Netherlands had led the movement towards public-health-centred policies.
Denmark has been lenient. Spain in 1983 revised its drug laws to distinguish sharply between hard and soft, and to decriminalise possession.
Germany has been the most punitive and Americanised in its tactics.
For much of this period the British have not tarried far behind the
Germans.

Overall, Latin America and the Caribbean have been of higher importance to the DEA than Europe. American prohibitionism has ensured that drug-related corruption is rife in Mexico, Bolivia, Colombia, Peru, Belize, Ecuador, Jamaica, the Bahamas and Central America. The violent and grasping character of dictators and gangsters makes them natural allies. One of the most flagrant alliances was in Bolivia, where in 1980 General Luis García Meza launched the 189th coup d'état in his nation's history at the behest of Santa Cruz gangsters. García Meza, who was allegedly paid $50 million by Bolivian traffickers, employed former Nazis to operate death squads. The Carter administration severed economic aid, and several members of the regime were indicted in the US as cocaine-traffickers, although none were brought to trial. García Meza's overthrow in 1981 did not eradicate cocaine-trafficking. During 1986 the Bolivian army, supported by US forces, struck against cocaine-suppliers in Operation Blast Furnace, seizing 27 tons of cocaine and destroying twenty-two laboratories. Unfortunately, these laboratories were empty, containing a few barrels of precursor chemicals, a few kilograms of processed drugs, but little else. No traffickers were arrested. Washington averred that Operation Blast Furnace disrupted Bolivian cocaine-trafficking, although US diplomats in La Paz conceded that the business soon revived.[21] Arguably the most notorious dictator allied with trans-national criminals was Manuel Noriega (b. 1938), who became a CIA operative around 1967 and commander of the Panamanian Defence Force in 1983. He had a long collaboration with Colombia's Medellín cartel, and supposedly received $1000 per kilogram of cocaine shipped through Panama en route for Florida or Los Angeles. The Bush administration urged Noriega to relinquish power in 1988, and after his refusal, launched Operation Just Cause in 1989. Twenty-four thousand soldiers were sent into Panama, Noriega was seized and sentenced after trial in the US to forty years for drug-trafficking, money-laundering and racketeering in 1992.[22] Panama remains, in 2000, a major centre of drug money-laundering, and an important link in cocaine shipments.

The Latin American police, often reflecting public opinion, 'don't look at the trafficker as just a crook', according to a DEA agent. 'Rather, they see him as a businessman who happens to deal in drugs, with certain contacts, interests and protectors.'[23] Nevertheless, the USA has developed increasingly powerful, streamlined and effective techniques to immobilise traffickers, including tighter extradition and mutual assistance treaties. Targeting of leading traffickers was begun by the Nixon administration. Auguste Ricorde (b. 1911), a former Marseille trafficker and Gestapo collaborator who settled in Paraguay, was estimated to have smuggled 5.5 tons of heroin into the US after 1967. Following his detention in 1972, the Paraguayan government initially insisted that he should serve his imprisonment there, but rescinded this policy after Washington declared that it would cut US aid unless Paraguay consented to extradition. Understandably extradition is seen as an imperialist tool in Third World countries that cannot afford to defy the US government. Since Nixon, criminal justice issues have been incorporated into high-level US diplomatic activity. 'No other government', according to Nadelmann, 'has acted so aggressively in collecting evidence from foreign jurisdictions, apprehending fugitives from abroad, indicting foreign officials to its own courts, targeting foreign government corruption and persuading foreign governments to change their criminal justice norms to better accord with its own.'[24]

This process has intensified since the end of the Cold War in 1989. The fight against drugs has replaced the fight against Communists as the principal moral imperative of US foreign policy. As a result, US policy-makers have promoted anti-drugs tactics that are neo-colonialist. The War on Drugs has been escalated to an unprecedented pitch, involving the use of armed forces, including the Green Berets, to attack the traffickers' strongholds in such countries as Peru and Colombia. These incursions were justified by opinions issued from the Justice Department's Office of Legal Counsel that US forces could arrest drug-dealers and other criminals overseas without the concurrence of the foreign governments concerned. Indeed, White House and State Department officials know that they jeopardise their positions if they seem lackadaisical in pursuing international law enforcement initiatives. The number of officials willing to resist such initiatives on pragmatic grounds has fallen as anti-Soviet objectives have lost their primacy in US foreign policy. Rather than reassess the failure of US prohibition policies, federal officials blame smaller countries with meagre resources for the problems in their inner cities and suburbs. Overseas governments have become increasingly wary of offending US Congress and American public opinion by appearing indifferent to these criminal justice concerns. The anti-drug warriors in the US and abroad have been increasingly characterised by the crude stridency usually associated with fundamentalist religions.

US policy has been most aggressive about cocaine. The drug was marginal throughout the world from the mid-1920s until the end of the 1960s. The FBN seldom seemed concerned about the drug; before 1939 cocaine had proportionately more *habitués* in Paris than the USA, while in Britain its popularity as a 'speedball' used in conjunction with heroin began in 1954. Probably the easy availability from the 1930s of amphetamines contributed to the disfavour with which cocaine was held in drug fashions. Certainly, the steady rise in cocaine use after 1969 coincided with the imposition of severer restrictions on the supply of amphetamines, and police raids on clandestine laboratories. But the late twentieth-century cocaine boom was chiefly the creation of the presidential drugs wars.

First, Nixon's Operation Intercept of 1969 diverted many marijuana-traffickers into the cocaine business. Next, when Augusto Pinochet (b. 1915) seized power in Chile in 1973, he conciliated Nixon's administration by handing over several drug-traffickers, including Chilean citizens, to the US government. This prompted other cocaine chemists and traffickers to shift operations to Colombia, and Chile lost its predominance as the leading South American source of illegal drugs. The Ford administration of 1974–7 focused enforcement tactics on heroin from Mexico just as the smuggling of cocaine from Colombia into Florida accelerated. Within a few years the Colombians had taken control of Peruvian and Bolivian cocaine production and of Chilean cocaine-refining. Hitherto most drugs had been smuggled into the US by ship or stashed in vehicles. The Colombians transformed smuggling into the US by hiring couriers to travel on commercial flights with a cache secreted in their clothes or luggage. The DEA estimated that by 1980 drug-trafficking through Florida was worth $7 billion a year. Cocaine sniffing became regarded as a pleasurable accoutrement of worldly success. Its paraphernalia was commercialised. The number of people with cocaine-related problems seeking admission to federally funded clinics climbed by 600 per cent from 1976 to 1981. In the early 1980s cocaine supplanted coffee as the primary earner of foreign exchange for Colombia. The wholesale price of cocaine fell from $60,000 to $10,000–$15,000 per kilogram in the USA during 1980–88.

Much of the US cocaine supply was routed through Mexico. Amado

Carillo Fuentes (c.1953–97), leader of the Juarez cartel, enjoyed intimate relations with Mexican politicians, officials and officers, and used sophisticated technology in his business. His organisation reportedly invested $20 to $30 million in each operation, and earned weekly profits running into tens of millions. He died after undergoing plastic surgery to disguise his appearance: probably he was murdered. One of his associates was Pablo Acosta (d. 1987), the criminal ruler over 200 miles of the US–Mexican border. In the mid-1980s he controlled as much as 60 per cent of the cocaine brought into the USA from Colombia. His own use of cocaine began to mar his judgement: a strike force including FBI agents eventually killed him.[25]

The greatest centre of cocaine enterprise was Medellín, the capital of Antioquia province in Colombia. Traditionally it was conservative, devout, and known for its large families and inflated civic pride. Its frugal, canny businessmen included Fabio Ochoa Vasquez, who smuggled alcohol and electrical equipment until around 1978, when he was induced by Pablo Escobar (1949–93) to adapt his smuggling organisation to the more lucrative drug business. Escobar had a successful career as a tombstone thief and dealer in stolen cars before venturing into drugs. Other traffickers were still focused on marijuana, but Escobar and his associates decided to substitute cocaine. The Ochoa family, together with Escobar and Carlos Lehder Rivas (b. 1947), launched a concerted smuggling campaign in 1981, and by the end of that year had smuggled about 19 tons of cocaine into the US. This was an auspicious moment to enter the cocaine business, just as the drug was becoming fashionable among affluent Americans. By chance, thousands of people from Antioquia province had settled in the US in 1965–75, and could be enlisted in the distribution network. Lehder organised a fleet of fast boats and small cargo planes to ship drugs into the US either by dropping them to waiting ships or leaving them at secret airfields. He oversaw operations from the Bahamas, where the long-serving Prime Minister Sir Lynden Pindling (b. 1930) was alleged to have received large payments from him. Lehder's organisation was tight and ruthless; its extensive ramifications were kept discrete to preserve security. The Medellín cartel's US power base was South Florida: Miami became a city of murders.

From 1984 the Medellín cartel waged a ferocious campaign in which their killer gangs, *sicarios*, murdered many thousands of people.

This narcoterrorism was particularly associated with Escobar and Jose Gonzalo Rodriguez (1947–89). In 1987 Lehder was captured near Medellín, extradited to the United States and sentenced there to a life sentence plus 135 years for drug-trafficking. In response his colleagues, under the motto 'Better in a grave than a jail in the United States', arranged kidnappings, car bombings and in 1989 blew up an airliner flying with 107 passengers. When, in 1989, the Medellín cartel rashly assassinated a presidential candidate, the Colombian President's retaliation included a new, unswerving commitment to extradition. Eduardo Martinez Romero (b. 1955), a crucial figure in the cartel's money-laundering, was captured shortly afterwards, and extradited to the US. After an appallingly bloody campaign of attrition and reprisals, Escobar surrendered to the Colombian authorities in 1991 conditionally on not being extradited to the US: he escaped in 1992, and was killed in a shoot-out a year later.

Escobar's organisation was not the only narcoterrorist gang based in Colombia. The Cali cartel, which positioned itself in the New York City market in the mid-1970s, was less confrontational than the Medellín gangsters, preferring bribery to murder as a first resort. It was nevertheless a ruthless organisation, which killed its junior members who failed. When the Medellín cartel was fighting the US and Colombian governments in 1984–91, the Cali cartel replaced it as the world's leading trafficking organisation. It transferred its cocaine-refining operations to Peru and Bolivia, and established new smuggling routes through Venezuela. It diversified substances. Opium was cultivated in Colombia, and heroin processed there was both cheaper and purer than that from South-east Asia. The Cali cartel was partially successful in suborning Colombian politics, but during 1995 six of its seven leaders were detained. Several smaller organisations in Colombia and elsewhere in Latin America filled the void. The Colombian gangs were cruel and disgusting beyond words. Nothing can be said to mitigate their behaviour. Yet their crimes did not occur in a historical vacuum and cannot be separated from US presidential tactics against illicit substances.

Ronald Reagan (b. 1911), US President from 1981 until 1989, surpassed Nixon as a wrong-headed drugs warrior. Marijuana supposedly sapped the middle classes' commitment to the Republican ideals of hard work and just rewards. Reagan therefore appointed as his first drugs czar Carleton Turner, a government chemist with an expertise in marijuana, who made suppression of this drug his first priority. Turner's reasoning, perhaps, was that junkies were far outnumbered by young pot-smokers, but it was crucial that the Republican leadership (perpetuating the assumptions of Anslinger's era) regarded inner-city heroin-users as vicious people who did not vote and might be left to decay and die. This approach reflected public opinion, which loathed urban squalor and feared drug-related crime. 'We have to start focusing on the users and make them pay the price, and we ought to have the death penalty for drug dealers,' Turner declared in 1985.[26] Notwithstanding the fear of the violence of armed drug-dealers, there was no proposal to restrict the gun supply—but then the 1980s were a period of transparent opportunism on drug issues. An East Harlem crack-dealer, reflecting on the Bush presidential campaign of 1988, said: 'I could be some dumb scumbag ho' that have a lot of money to push my campaign. And all I gotta say is "Drugs!" and they'll elect me immediately. Abortion and drugs is the best thing for politicians in America, man.'[27]

The Reaganite outlook aided and abetted dealers. It was not only that the administration supported Nicaraguan Contras who smuggled cocaine and protected other traffickers. Reagan's economic policies sanctioned the rampant operation of market forces: in a materialist society the dealer is the arch-materialist. 'Like most other people in the United States, drug dealers and street criminals are scrambling to obtain their piece of the pie as fast as possible,' one expert observer recorded in 1995. 'They are aggressively pursuing careers as private entrepreneurs; they take risks, work hard, and pray for good luck. They are the ultimate rugged individualists braving an unpredictable frontier where fortune, fame and destruction are all just around the corner, and where the enemy is ruthlessly hunted down.'[28] This was no new insight. Back in 1972 Graham Finney (b. 1930), Commissioner of Addiction Services in New York City, had given his view of the prevailing drug culture: 'The addict is a caricature of American society—the hedonism, the demand for instant gratification, the urge to get it now. He's a caricature of many, many businessmen ... in a funny way, the addiction problem brings into focus a lot of the unsolved business of this country.'[29] Addicts are archetypal of the ideal customer: they are the ultimate consumers, because they cannot give up and always want more. Finney was perhaps influenced by a classic article entitled 'Taking care of business:

the heroin user's life on the street' published in 1969. Reagan's policy-makers were oblivious to the lessons of this article:

> Heroin use today by lower-class, primarily minority group, persons does
> not provide for them a euphoric escape from the psychological and
> social problems which derive from ghetto life. On the contrary, it pro-
> vides a motivation and rationale for the pursuit of a meaningful life . . .
> If they can be said to be addicted, it is not so much to heroin as to the
> entire career of a heroin user. The heroin user is, in a way, like the com-
> pulsively hardworking business executive whose ostensible goal is the
> acquisition of money, but whose real satisfaction is in meeting the inor-
> dinate challenge he creates for himself.[30]

Reagan replicated the poor tactics of Operation Intercept. In 1982 his administration launched the South Florida Task Force, under the supervision of Vice-President George Bush (b. 1924), to co-ordinate nine federal law enforcement agencies in their fight against illegal drugs entering that state. During the Task Force's first year, there was a 64 per cent rise in drug-related prosecutions in South Florida, and $19 million in cash and property was confiscated. But while in 1983 government agents in South Florida seized 6 tons of cocaine and 850 tons of marijuana, by 1985 these figures were 25 tons and 750 tons respectively. As the amounts seized usually reflect the amounts being smuggled, this means that the quantities of cocaine had quadrupled, while quantities of the comparatively innocuous marijuana had fallen. The DEA estimated that in 1981 Americans used between 36 and 66 tons of smuggled cocaine annually, and that by 1984, following the intervention of the South Florida Task Force, this figure had risen to an estimated 61 to 84 tons. When the Force began, Florida dealers paid about $60,000 per kilogram of cocaine; by late 1985 this price had fallen by 40 per cent. At the end of the 1980s the kilogram price of cocaine was down to $15,000. The federal campaign to repress South Florida smuggling as the central feature of anti-drugs policy thus resulted in high-purity cheap cocaine becoming available in US inner cities, and fuelled the booming crack cocaine economy of the late 1980s. The foolishness of Florida state laws aggravated the problem by providing identical mandatory prison sentences for trafficking in either marijuana or cocaine. As one smuggler turned DEA informer observed in 1985, 'If you are going to get fifteen years for doing one and fifteen years for doing the other, you're going to go for the coke. It's easier to handle, easier to fly, and easier to hide.' One reporter described the symbiotic relationship between law enforcement officials in South Florida and traffickers. As a result of Washington's public relations needs, smugglers brought more cocaine into the USA,

> divided among several boats, one of which the smuggler considers expendable. If the police capture the decoy, they get some cocaine, a boat, a crew, statistics, and arrests. These may or may not lead to convictions or information, however. Most captures at sea involve not the drug trade's linchpins but its lowliest laborers, who are generally too ignorant and fearful of reprisals to be of use. In any case, the other boats get through. Both sides are reasonably content, but only the smuggler has accomplished his purpose.

A US government survey in 1977 found that 10 per cent of respondents aged eighteen to twenty-five had used cocaine in the past year; by 1985 one-third had used cocaine. Journalists proved reluctant to repeat the propaganda excesses of Anslinger's era, and somewhat complacently reported that the drug was not physiologically addictive. Although this was technically true, by the early 1980s there were nevertheless many users who found they could not control their cravings, and had a psychological dependence on the drug. The idea that cocaine was not dangerous if inhaled rather than injected was also fatally prevalent. This misconception was partly remedied by the widely publicised tragedy of the six-foot-eight-inches basketball player Len Bias (1963–86), who died of cocaine-induced heart failure while celebrating his signing with the Boston Celtics.

In the US some cocaine-users began 'freebasing'—that is, heating powdered cocaine, which was reduced to a pure crystallised form, crumbled and smoked through a water pipe. Encouraged by manufacturers of drug paraphernalia, freebasing became more prevalent around 1979. Many people with drug experience believed that smoking drugs—marijuana, or even heroin—was innocuous, and assumed this would be true of cocaine. Yet smoking cocaine intensified and accelerated psychological dependence. It might take years of regular snorting to develop a compulsion to use cocaine; it took only months, if not weeks, for a freebaser. The attraction for suppliers was that a freebaser might spend during one binge as much as a snorter in a week. The dangers of this technique of drug use were publicised when the American comedian Richard Pryor (b. 1940) was burnt in 1980 after his freebase kit exploded.

Crack cocaine was introduced in the USA around 1983 just as the younger, middle-class demand for cocaine began to fall. To obtain crack, cocaine was dissolved in water, mixed with baking soda and then heated until the water evaporated. When smoked, it reached the brain in four to six seconds. Chunks ('rocks') of crack were sold in small glass vials, originally from semi-derelict heroin 'shooting-galleries' until police raids on the 'crack houses' drove the dealers on to the streets. While a rock might seem cheap at $5, a crack high lasted only fifteen minutes, so one rock was never enough. Ten rocks were needed to stay high for an afternoon. Suppliers were marketing crack in such deprived districts as South Central Los Angeles and Miami's Overtown by 1984. During the following year it hit New York City's black and Latino neighbourhoods such as Harlem and Washington Heights. The escalated problem was indicated by a survey of forty-two NYC hospitals, which found seven deaths attributable to cocaine in 1983, ninety-one in 1984 and 137 in 1985. A CBS television documentary, *48 Hours on Crack Street*, presented the experience of New York City and Los Angeles slums as if the drug was prevalent in every American community, and disastrously raised the publicity stakes in 1985–6. Crack cocaine virtually replaced heroin in Miami, while in San Francisco users began smoking crack after injecting heroin-cocaine speedballs.

Every day in 1986 some 5000 Americans tried cocaine for the first time; 22 million Americans (one in eleven of the population) had used cocaine recreationally. Reagan, responding particularly to the crack crisis, in September 1986 issued an Executive Order known as the Drug-Free Federal Workplace Act. As a result, most federal employees have to undergo drug testing while other employers followed the government in requiring pre-employment urine tests. It is easy to beat urine tests for heroin and cocaine, whose traces clear from the body in days, although marijuana lingers for a month. Despite such measures, by the final full year of Reagan's presidency (1988), the US had an estimated 20 to 25 million marijuana smokers, 5.8 million regular users of cocaine and some 500,000 heroin-users, spending a total of some $150 billion annually on illegal drugs. Illegal drug enterprise was highly competitive. By 1988 85 per cent of crack-related crimes in New York City involved territorial disputes between rival dealers, or other tensions arising from the market culture.[31] The purity of heroin and cocaine sold on the streets continued to increase while prices fell. The retail price in New York City of a gram of cocaine fell from $70–$100 in 1986 to $50–$90 in 1991.

Philippe Bourgois is an anthropologist who gained the trust and friendship of some dozen Puerto Rican street dealers in East Harlem in the late 1980s and early 1990s. His book on the subject, *In Search of Respect: Selling Crack in El Barrio* (1995), makes almost unbearable reading; it quotes extensively from crack-house conversations, and depicts extremes of violence and human degradation that are unthinkable for most people. Like other immigrants to the USA, the crack-dealers compete to be part of the American Dream. 'We're supposed to struggle and make something of ourselves,' says Primo. 'You have to achieve in life in order to get somewhere ... the struggle is harder for the poor, but not impossible; just harder'. Primo is a self-sufficient man who believes that every American male is master of his own success. 'If I have a problem, it's because I brought in on myself. Nobody gotta worry about me; I'm gonna handle it.'[32] *In Search of Respect* is indispensable reading for anyone seeking to understand late twentieth-century drug habits. 'Self-destructive addiction is merely the medium for desperate people to internalise their frustration, resistance, and powerlessness,' Bourgois demonstrates. 'The contemporary exacerbation of substance abuse within concentrated pockets of the US population has little or nothing to do with the pharmacological properties of the particular drugs involved.'[33]

Crack attracted women because it was cheap and did not have to be injected. In many deprived urban communities young women prostituted themselves in order to earn the money to buy rocks, or got their drugs in crack houses in return for performing sex. The insistent sexualisation of the careers of women crack-users led to their vilification in the media, and their stigmatisation by some researchers. This adds to the injustice already oppressing the women, whose experiences of poverty, racism and sexism have been eloquently chronicled by Claire Sterk (b. 1957) and Lisa Maher.[34] Convinced that women crack-users are bad women who must be bad mothers, social workers in some US communities aggressively developed what has been called a 'harm maximisation programme' through 'user accountability'. Women, for example, were criminally prosecuted for neglect of the foetus after hospitals violated doctor–patient confidentiality and rights to non-disclosure of confidential information by reporting the results of toxicology tests to state agencies. Instead of working as allies of these disadvantaged women, medical professionals betrayed them. As many of these mothers were too poor to obtain ante-natal care, they were being penalised rather than supported in dealing with their social circumstances. Despite the proven success and cost-effectiveness of withdrawal treatment programmes, very few are available to pregnant women from the worst-affected communities. Instead, they are threatened with criminal penalties or loss of custody of their children. Punitive threats only deter them from seeking pre-natal care or drug treatment. Poor women and those from ethnic minorities are more likely to be denounced because of their reliance on public health clinics and because of the stereotypes held by some medical or social workers. The severity with which 'crack mothers' were punished served partly as a ruse to divert attention from the failures of US health provisions. Research has found that women who cannot abstain from drugs can give birth to healthy children especially if they can obtain pre-natal care. Crack-exposed infants are not doomed to suffer permanent mental or physical impairment. The toxic side effects are far less significant than poverty's impact on brain development.[35]

The Bush administration's unimpressive drugs czar William Bennett in 1989 attributed 'the intensifying drug-related chaos' to the fashion for crack, which was spreading 'like a plague'.[36] But, as the studies of Sterk and Maher show, it was poverty and deprivation that were truly pestilential. The demand for crack, cocaine and heroin during the 1980s and 1990s, which was so damaging to individuals and communities as well as qualitatively worse than earlier addiction crises, resulted from the social marginalisation of increasing proportions of the US population. Poverty in the US rose by one-third between 1968 and 1992 at a time when the rich were getting far richer and a few speculators were accumulating large fortunes.

Reagan's presidency eroded the citizenship of deprived people: inconvenient minorities were locked up on the pretext of achieving a drug-free America. The Anti-Drug Abuse Act, passed in 1986 by a huge majority, allotted $6 billion over three years for enforcement measures, education and treatment. It stipulated prison sentences for dealers who sold drugs near schools or recruited young people to peddle them. Possession of 5 grams of crack carried a mandatory five-year sentence, which was 100-to-1 more punitive than sentences for powder cocaine; a defendant would have to have possessed 500 grams of powder cocaine to earn a mandatory five years. This disparity, which was ostensibly because crack was reckoned more dangerous than powdered cocaine, was understandably perceived as racist. Eighty-nine per cent of crack cocaine defendants were black Americans and 7 per cent Hispanic. The comparable figures for cocaine powder were 27 per cent black and 39 per cent Hispanic. In 1986, before the Anti-Drug Abuse Act became effective, the average sentence under federal drug laws for blacks was 11 per cent higher than for whites; four years later the average was 49 per cent higher for blacks. Blacks in some cities were over twenty times more likely to be arrested on drug charges (and nationally four times as likely). This imbalance might be attributed to racism, search tactics based on minority profiling or the visibility of dealers from racial minorities. Whatever the explanation, 21 per cent of all state prison inmates in 1991 had been convicted on drug offences—subdivided between 8 per cent possession and 13 per cent trafficking. Black Americans were twice as likely to be imprisoned for drug offences than white. The US Sentencing Commission reported in 1997 that 90 per cent of offenders convicted in federal courts of crack cocaine distribution were black, although the majority of users were white. To the director of the British drugs charity Release, the Reagan–Bush war on crack resembled 'a war on black ghetto youth—a means of mobilising opinion against poorer people who are not covered by health and other insurance, and who are not part of mainstream society'.[37]

A study issued in 2000 by the Leadership Conference on Civil Rights noted that blacks represent 12 per cent of the US population and an estimated 13 per cent of drug-users, but despite the fact that equal arrest rates for minorities and whites are yielded by traffic stops and similar enforcement, 38 per cent of individuals arrested for drug offences and 59 per cent of those convicted are black. Black and Hispanic Americans are victimised by disproportionate targeting, unfair treatment by police and the DEA, racially skewed charging and plea-bargaining by prosecutors and discriminatory sentencing practices. It seems at times that judges and elected officials advance their careers by perpetuating or aggravating these flagrant inequities. One result of the racial bias in drug enforcement is the exclusion from the electoral system of a large proportion of racial minorities. Thirteen per cent of the total of 10.4 million adult black men had lost their right to vote owing to felony convictions in 1997. The advantage of this to Republicans in southern states such as Florida and Texas was well understood by the campaign advisers of George W. Bush (b. 1946) during the tarnished presidential election of 2000.

The US prison population increased threefold between 1980, the year of Reagan's election, and 1994. During the Bush presidency of 1989–93 the US had the highest per capita incarceration rate in the world, and more black men in their twenties in the criminal justice system than in college. One in three black men in their twenties was under correctional supervision or control in 1995. From the late 1990s low-level crack-dealers and first-time offenders sentenced in federal courts for trafficking crack received an average sentence of ten years and six months: this was 59 per cent longer than the average prison sentence received by rapists, and only 18 per cent less than the average of prison sentences for murder and manslaughter. Amnesty International reported in 1999 that in the US the rates of imprisonment for black and Hispanic women were respectively over eight and nearly four times higher than for white women. Thirty-two per cent of whites convicted of drug felonies received a prison sentence, compared with 46 per cent of blacks, according to US Department of Justice figures available in 2000. The 'three strikes, you're out' policy means that a large number of black and Hispanic men, with a history of untreated addiction and a small tally of drug-related offences, will be imprisoned for life. Within a few decades, states will have to construct expensive additional prisons serving as warehouses for large numbers of ageing, or geriatric, blacks and Hispanics whose lives will have been wasted in these futile and cruel institutions. In Western Europe incarceration rates stand at or below 100 per 100,000 of the population. In the US in 1999 the incarceration rate for black women was 212 per 100,000 and for black men 3408 per 100,000. The US incarceration rate for white men is 417 per 100,000 and for white women twenty-seven per 100,000.

The discrepancy between spending of state governments on prisons and education became glaring. Employment of instructors at public colleges rose by 28.5 per cent and of correctional officers by 129.3 per cent between 1982 and 1993. By 1997 only 50 per cent of federal drug-trafficking prisoners had graduated from high school, and only 3 per cent had graduated from college. Nevertheless, in a blunder of crashing stupidity, the Higher Education Act of 1998 denies student loan eligibility to individuals convicted of a drug offence. Even one charge of marijuana possession is penalised. Any individual with three or more drug possession charges is subject to a lifelong ban. No other type of offender faces such restrictions. This crass legislation prevents the rehabilitation of drug-users, and reinforces the discriminatory effect of US drug policing on African-Americans. Its cruel and irrational punishment typifies the US drug enforcement mentality. By perpetuating the disadvantages of the ghetto, it perpetuates the conditions that foster addiction.

Another aspect of the enforcement programmes of the Reagan presidency is underpublicised, but has had far-reaching consequences on international financial regulation. Profits from drug-trafficking constitute a real problem. Total global revenue from the illegal drugs trade considerably exceeded the annual turnover of the global alcohol industry by the 1980s. These huge transactions (estimated value in 1990 between $300 and $500 billion annually) escaped governmental supervision. As national sovereignty relies on a government's monopoly of taxation and citizens' obligations to pay taxes, so the illegal drugs trade presents a fundamental challenge to states. Ever since Rothstein's drug-running in the 1920s, traffickers have been keen to invest their money in legitimate enterprises. US legislation of 1984 empowered the government to seize assets upon probable cause as well as criminal indictment. The law further denied the accused the right to retain money with which to pay lawyers, arguing that the funds might derive from drug profits. These seized assets were sold by, and the profits shared among, law enforcement agencies. Local and state police welcomed the extra income, and were not always fastidious in collecting it. In March 1988 the Reagan administration launched the Zero Tolerance Policy Program, which sought to reduce the supply of illegal drugs into the US by targeting users as well as dealers. The Program was contrary to any civilised conception of justice: its operations were arbitrary, despotic, sometimes corrupt and often disproportionate. In a notorious incident of May 1988 the US Coastguard seized a $2.5 million yacht after finding one-tenth of an ounce of marijuana on board. Eighty per cent of US citizens who had property forfeited in 1991 were never charged with a crime. In 1993 property seized by the US Justice Department alone exceeded $600 million in value. It must be added that reforms enacted by the Clinton administration in 2000 reduced the possibilities of abusive procedures.

Offshore financial institutions are often used to launder money, although the CIA in 2000 officially listed London as a centre of drug money-laundering. The United States since 1985 has propelled the rest of the world towards co-ordinating and harmonising controls over black-market money. The US has sought to align all countries with the new control regime, preferably voluntarily but ultimately under international pressure. 'The fight against the laundering of drug-money will eventually lead to something that was never intended: a uniform global regulatory regime,' as one Dutch commentator noted. 'In this way the war on illegal toxicants is helping to produce a far-reaching and unlooked-for integration of the countries of the world.'[38]

Under a policy launched in 1986, the US government annually reviews whether or not to certify foreign governments as partners in its War on Drugs. Decertified countries lose foreign aid and are threatened with trade sanctions. This policy, which is intended to buttress the failed tactic of controlling drug supplies at source, demonstrates that the War on Drugs is not a war waged by allies, but an unequal partnership in which the USA judges, certifies, impoverishes and degrades human rights in the subordinate combatant nations. Washington continues to blame foreigners for nearly a century of failed US drugs prohibition.

In 1989 President George Bush allocated an additional $2.2 billion to fight 'the scourge of drugs'. Seventy per cent of that sum was allotted to enforcement in the US and overseas. Under the National Defense Authorisation Act of 1989, the US Department of Defense is the designated 'single lead agency' for drug interdiction under federal law. As a result, the US has provided counter-narcotic training that is barely distinguishable from counter-insurgency training to Latin American military units notorious for human rights abuses. Increased military aid was provided under Bush's 'Andean Strategy', a five-year plan to spend $2.2 billion eradicating cocaine sources in Colombia, Bolivia

and Peru. In 1996 the United Nations allotted £69 million in development aid to the world's poorest countries: the following year US
anti-drug aid granted to the Colombian army and police was nearly
$96 million. The most recent US military aid package to Colombia will
total $289 million. Such subventions are essentially anti-democratic in
their support of military powers, and aggravate corruption. The general
commanding Mexico's drug enforcement unit—hailed by General
McCaffrey, the US drugs czar, as 'an honest man and a no-nonsense
field commander'—was detained in 1997 for corruptly collaborating
with Amado Carillo Fuentes.[39]

The *National Drug Control Strategy* document published in 1989
contained a long introduction personally written by William Bennett,
whom Bush had appointed as Director of the Office of National Control Policy. Bennett's base rhetoric and false reasoning have been subjected to devastating analysis by Franklin E. Zimring (b. 1942) and
Gordon Hawkins (b. 1919) in *A Search for Rational Drug Control* (1992).
Bennett opened by claiming a 'dramatic and startling' fall in drug consumption: the estimated number of Americans using illegal drugs had
fallen by 37 per cent in four years from 23 million in 1985 to 14.5 million in 1988. After depicting the Nixon and Reagan wars on drugs as
successful, Bennett contradicted himself. 'Drugs are cheap, and . . . available to almost anyone who wants them,' he wrote. 'Fear of drugs and
attendant crime are at an all-time high.' Although strategies against foreign drug-suppliers were central in US foreign policy across the globe,
'drug trafficking, distribution and sales in America have become a vast,
economically debilitating black market'. Drugs thus constituted 'the
gravest present threat to our national well-being'. So grave was the
problem, Bennett argued, that drug enforcement officers should not be
fettered by democratic views of legality and justice. He dismissed the
notion that funds should be diverted from law enforcement to treatment of addicts or prevention programmes. Like Anslinger he insisted
that '*any* significant relaxation of drug enforcement—for whatever reason, however well-intentioned—would promise more use, more crime,
and more trouble'. Although he depicted the USA as suffering 'a crisis'
that had 'long appeared to spiral wildly out of control', he did not feel
that this was a reflection on the punitive policies that had characterised
American prohibition for seventy years: 'We should be tough on
drugs—much tougher than we are now.' Bennett strenuously insisted

that all types of drug use, and all levels of drug consumption, were equally pernicious. Accordingly the 'highest priority' must be to wage war on 'experimental first use, "casual" use, regular use, and addiction *alike*'. (Italics added). This sentiment beggars belief in its ignorance and crudity. Although a few pages earlier Bennett, understandably, had written 'our most intense and immediate problem is inner-city crack use', he would allow no distinction between drugs and their different levels of destruction on individuals and communities. Throughout 153 pages of *National Drug Control Strategy*, there is no definition of either 'drug' or 'drug problem', and no discussion of amphetamines, barbiturates and other substances. Perhaps this reflected official respect for the commercial interests of pharmaceutical companies. More probably it indicated the lack of finesse in the thinking of Bennett's office. The 1989 report's certainty that 'drug use is a moral problem' enabled it to proceed on all the failed old lines.[40]

This mentality resulted in men like Darryl Gates, chief of the Los Angeles Police Department, telling the Senate Judiciary Committee in 1990, 'the casual drug user ought to be taken out and shot'.[41] Bennett thought it acceptable to behead drug-dealers: he said that enforcement officers should be able to shoot down aircraft suspected of carrying traffickers, an act he likened to a traffic cop stopping a speeding motorist. His proposed punishments for drug-users included revoking driving licences, establishing militarised 'boot camps', evicting tenants from their homes, civil proceedings to force addicts into withdrawal treatment, and financial sanctions against colleges and universities that did not aggressively prohibit student drug use. The result of this attention was that 64 per cent of Americans cited drugs as the country's most urgent problem in 1989 compared with 3 per cent in 1986.

Bill Clinton (b. 1946), US President from 1993 until 2001, and his Vice-President Al Gore (b. 1948), in *Putting People First: How We Can All Change America* (1992), lumped drugs and crime together in a chapter that gave as much emphasis to policing streets and incarcerating criminals as to the more constructive strategies of education and treatment. This association in the American consciousness of illegal drugs with crime can be misleading. A survey by Columbia University's National Center on Addiction and Substance Abuse found in 1998 that 21 per cent of violent felons in state prisons committed their crimes under the influence of alcohol alone: only 3 per cent were high on crack or powder cocaine alone, and only 1 per cent were using heroin alone. Out of $13 billion allocated to drugs policy in Clinton's first budget of 1993, $8.3 billion was earmarked for law enforcement and interdiction with only $4.7 billion for treatment programmes and prevention. This emphasis persisted despite the RAND Corporation for the Office of National Drug Control Policy finding that treatment was ten times more cost-effective than interdiction in reducing US cocaine use. Domestic law enforcement cost fifteen times as much as treatment to achieve the same reduction in social costs. Yet, according to Bureau of Justice statistics issued in 1999, some 40 per cent of state and federal prisoners who were using drugs at the time of their offence reported participation in prison treatment programs in 1991, but only 15 per cent at the end of the decade.

Predictions that destructive patterns in the US would infect Europe proved false or exaggerated, as the panic over crack demonstrated. Britain's crack scare began in 1987 with the undeniable observation that the use of crack might increase. As the English criminologist Philip Bean has shown, the promoters of the scare hoped that by arousing fear and indignation, they would obtain a new system of prohibitions and exemplary punishments based on US drug enforcement measures. Politicians and journalists had little information on crack. American drug evangelicals exploited this ignorance to spread their sacred message: restrict supplies by aggressive policing. Both quality and tabloid newspapers regurgitated DEA statements. Detailed analysis of these reports by Bean shows they were abysmally misleading.[42]

In April 1989 Robert Stutman of the DEA, in the presence of the Home Secretary, Douglas Hurd (b. 1930), delivered what Bing Spear called 'a missionary address' to the Annual Drugs Conference of the Association of Chief Police Officers. 'In two years from now you will have a serious crack problem,' Stutman announced with a high-handed disregard of evidence. 'There ain't enough noses left to use the cocaine that's coming in [to the US]. It's got to go somewhere and where it is coming is right here.' Among other wild claims, he insisted that 75 per cent of crack-users entered 'virtually incurable addiction' after their third use of the drug.[43] Next month, Hurd regaled a conference of nineteen European nations with a version of Stutman's speech. He likened crack to a medieval plague—'a plague we are visiting on ourselves'—while vociferating Stutman's dubious assertions. 'The evidence is plain: the North American market having been saturated, the cocaine barons of Latin America are now driving their product into Europe.'[44] (Very little crack was used in Canada so in truth North America was far from saturated.) The Prime Minister, Margaret Thatcher (b. 1925), publicly supported 'firm action' and vowed that 'crack peddlers' would find 'no safe haven' in Britain.[45] Two months later the House of Commons Home Affairs Committee issued its self-indulgent report *Crack: the Threat of Hard Drugs in the Next Decade.* With the paranoid scaremongering so characteristic of the period, it declared that crack was 'more addictive and more damaging in its effects on society than any previously known drug'. There was 'no such person as a fully recovered crack addict'. This 'almost instantly addictive' substance was presented as 'an escalating problem . . . spreading into the shire counties of England'.[46] Such publicity was foolish. After the formation in July of a National Task Force on Crack, the criminologist Nicholas Dorn noted that the burgeoning 'crusade against crack is not without its winners. Constant prediction of a crack epidemic provides an emergency atmosphere within which institutions may be restructured and funds granted.' Once again pragmatic scepticism and an understated tone would have been preferable. 'At present the crack problem is small and localised, but police raids targeting the drug above all others are generating intense press interest and increased curiosity about it at street level,' Dorn warned. 'The publicity sparks in every bored and impressionable drug dealer the idea of using or dealing in these stimulating commodities. Dealers are told that they can make a fortune, and that crack is the world's greatest hit. More people seek out cocaine, pop it in the microwave with a few easily-obtained chemicals, and hey presto, there is an enlarged pool for the police to fish in.'[47] The nickname 'Crack City' bestowed on a housing estate in the London Borough of Lewisham was both inflammatory and misleading: it masked the fact that the most serious drug problem in the area was intravenous heroin use as a result of disastrous policies during the early 1980s. In many cases cocaine was part of a pattern of polydrug use by addicts whose primary drug was heroin.

The Metropolitan Police attitude to crack seemed tinged with racism. As the Lewisham study shows, about 75 per cent of arrests for cocaine and crack offences involved black people, whereas 80 per cent of cocaine and crack-users known to drug agencies and social services were white. The divisional police superintendent asserted that this reflected the fact that most dealers were black and most users white. For many years the police view of social issues in south London dominated the discourse on crack and cocaine. The eighteenth and nineteenth century fear of a roaming, lawless, untrammelled mob was refined by the police of the 1980s into something more focused and racist. The Metropolitan Police testimony to the House of Commons Home Affairs Committee in 1989 included tabloid images of inner-city depravity featuring the Yardies, Jamaican criminal gangs, as 'almost exclusively' supplying crack. 'Many of those involved are Jamaican illegal immigrants who have no fixed addresses but who are bound by their Jamaican origin and reggae culture and who travel from one location to another with regularity. Such is their nomadic lifestyle that serious offences, for example murders, have been and will continue to be committed wherever the cultural bandwagon happens to stop.' The Yardies served very well the need for extraneous, dangerous, almost inhuman antagonists on which the War on Drugs rhetorically relies. As late as 1997 the National Criminal Intelligence Service was still representing Yardies as threatening the 'security and stability of the nation'.[48] Some police statements about low-level cocaine and crack-dealing by people of Jamaican origin were correct; but larger white criminal gangs generally dominated large-scale distribution, especially at the safer end of the business. White gangsters informed on the small number of Yardies, whose activities were exaggerated by journalists. The relations between white gang-leaders in south London and some police officers were questionable.

The brouhaha that followed Stutman's speech was flawed in its emphasis. It stressed crack as in a class of its own, presenting a unique and unprecedented threat, rather than integrating it into the whole scene of polydrug abuse. The predicted massive crack crisis did not happen, as the winding up (after only thirteen months) of the National Task Force in August 1990 demonstrated. The British Crime Survey of 1994 found that three in every 100 people aged sixteen to twenty-four had used cocaine, fewer than one in 100 had used heroin and fewer than one in 200 had used crack. The limited use of crack had little to do with successful enforcement. Crack did not escalate in Britain because (unlike in the USA) there was a well-established market in amphetamines. Most English cities had a cheap, plentiful and stable supply of amphetamines serving as 'poor man's cocaine'. Crack could not compete with the established local business either on price or effects. In 1991 cocaine cost £80 per gram from which the user got, at most, a thirty-minute high; amphetamines cost £12–£15 per gram and provided a three to four-hour high.

The US influence on the British heroin scene of the 1980s was altogether more deleterious. Until 1967 the medical profession had been the only source of illicit supply, but after the institution of the treatment clinics, addiction spread by illicit supplies of heroin from abroad. The Home Office was notified of 1109 new cases of addiction in 1977. In 55 per cent of them, heroin was the principal drug at the time of first notification. By 1982, the annual total of new notifications had increased by over 150 per cent to 2793, of which heroin was the principal drug in 76 per cent of cases. The number of addicts notified to the Home Office rose from 2657 in 1970 to 5107 in 1980, 14,688 in 1985 and 17,755 in 1990. Dale Beckett in 1974 had described the predisposing elements that cause heroin addiction in terms of a plant: 'The seed is the drug and the availability, the soil is the stressed personality, and the climate is the microclimate of opinion about the drug. If all three are right, heroin addiction can take root. If one is wrong, it is almost impossible.'[49] The seed, the soil and supremely the climate encouraged the escalation of heroin use during the 1980s.

Availability should be considered first. The upsurge in London's illicit heroin market during the mid-1970s was partly attributable to the increasing policy of the official treatment clinics of prescribing methadone instead of heroin, and methadone only in oral doses. Although the Metropolitan Police had successes in confronting Chinese heroin-suppliers, South-east Asian producers put more effort into the European market after US troops left Vietnam in 1973. Following the overthrow of the Shah of Iran in 1979, Iranian exiles used heroin-trafficking as a way to export their capital from the ayatollahs' fundamentalist tyranny. By 1981 the numbers of notified heroin addicts, the numbers of heroin seizures and the quantities seized all indicated a serious escalation in heroin misuse. Cheap, abundant, high-purity heroin from Afghanistan and Pakistan dominated the British market during the 1980s. One kilogram of heroin costing £4,000 in Afghanistan or Pakistan was worth £20,000 once it reached Britain, and up to £40,000 once it had been broken into smaller units. Heroin would typically be sold on the streets in bags or wraps at £5 or £10 each; the final aggregate value of the original kilogram was thus about £100,000. Heroin's London street price fell by about 25 per cent during the early 1980s. Until 1978 British addicts were almost always initiated into heroin use by injection; but after 1979, crucially, much of the illicit traffic was in 'brown' heroin, used for smoking or sniffing rather than injecting. This enticed many drug experimenters who were frightened or repelled by injecting. The habit of 'chasing the dragon'—placing the heroin on aluminium foil, heating it and inhaling the vapour—became increasingly fashionable. A survey in the Wirral, where the number of heroin-users rose from under 100 in 1980 to over 5000 in 1987, reported 79 per cent chased the dragon and only 4 per cent were exclusive injectors. Similarly, a survey of 408 London heroin-users published in 1994 found 54 per cent injecting and 44 per cent chasing the dragon. Despite high daily doses, over long periods, many heroin-users did not progress to injecting.[50]

The soil for heroin addiction, in Beckett's formulation, was the stressed personality. These stresses were enormously aggravated by the dismantling of Britain's traditional heavy industrial base begun by the 1981 monetarist budget. Unemployment and an enveloping miasma of poverty and decay settled over many communities. Drugs became part of the hidden injuries of class discrimination. The link between heroin traffic and hopeless social deprivation (which had first been first evident in Scottish cities at the end of the 1960s) became increasingly evident during the 1980s. The illicit heroin business became the preserve of young working-class amateurs who saw it as one of their few opportunities in the new 'Enterprise Britain'. User-dealers, with low-level distribution networks, had worked in illicit drug markets in Europe and the US since the beginning of prohibition. But by the early 1980s, there was a distinction between the 'smack-heads', who dealt so as to raise money to buy their own drugs, and the 'bread-heads', who dealt for their own profit. Petty dealers must be conspicuous in their neighbourhood if they are to attract customers, and are therefore vulnerable to detection. They were nevertheless neglected as the objects of policing and rehabilitation in favour of the large-scale operators whose arrests would bring more kudos to policemen and their political masters.[51] Heroin problems were often highly localised. For example, after the collapse of coal-mining jobs in the Barnsley area of Yorkshire, whole streets of the Grimethorpe area were taken over by drug gangs. There was a 300 per cent increase in heroin use in the Barnsley area during 1992–5: one lorry was detained carrying heroin worth over £11 million.[52]

The third predisposing element towards heroin addiction, in Beckett's formulation, was the microclimate of opinion. This included expert opinion on prescribing to addicts. Medical disillusionment with long-term prescribing of drugs had set in during the late 1970s. An influential paper published in 1978 by Martin Mitcheson and Richard Hartnoll found that addicts who were prescribed heroin attended the clinic more regularly, were less likely to steal and had fewer difficulties with the police than those refused heroin. Nevertheless it also reported that 20 per cent of those refused heroin stabilised on oral methadone and another 20 per cent stopped using drugs. This contradicted the belief that the prescribing of heroin reduced the user's involvement with illegal drugs or improved their social stability. The London clinics' growing desire to change their prescribing patterns was thus reinforced, although Mitcheson and Hartnoll recognised that a confrontational approach—refusing heroin—would result in losing contact with some clients.[53] Griffith Edwards (b. 1928), Director of the Addiction Research Unit and a member of the Advisory Council on the Misuse of Drugs, had been monitoring heroin-users known to the Home Office in 1965. He concluded in 1979 that it was uncertain that maintenance prescriptions improved the careers of many addicts, and questioned whether abstinence was causally related to treatment.[54] In the same year, the venerable addiction expert Max Glatt was disturbed by finding cases of 'affluent and "smart set" youngsters' sniffing heroin and cocaine. 'Moreover, as the treatment centres were never set up to deal with the problem of non-narcotic yet addictive drugs (such as the "mainlining" of barbiturates, amphetamines, etc.) or with the prevalent polydrug misuser, no adequate provision exists for tackling these serious and common problems'. Glatt called for a thorough review of the clinics' management of opiate and other addictions.[55]

All these interventions reflected the revulsion of physicians at prescribing a drug like heroin. They did not like to be, in a phrase later coined by the novelist Will Self (b. 1961), 'drug dealers by appointment to H.M. Government'. After ten years of the clinic system, many of their medical staff felt with increasing strength that as medical practitioners they were concerned with treating patients, not social ills.[56] The number of addicts had remained fairly stable, but their behaviour remained intolerably disruptive, and clinicians resolved to confront their patients' continued misuse of drugs with more robust interventions. By the end of the 1970s, therefore, as a matter of clinical judgement, they were refusing to prescribe injectable drugs, substituting oral methadone, reducing doses and moving sharply towards a new regime of compulsory withdrawal. It is important to stress that these changes of medical attitude had begun before the Iranian revolution of February 1979 escalated the amount of Golden Triangle heroin flooding into Britain. The shift in attitudes had also started before the election of a new Conservative government led by Margaret Thatcher in May 1979. In other words, the change in the microclimate of medical opinion happened before political events led to a sharp rise in the number of people using heroin, and the number of new patients presenting at clinics.

The political temper of Britain during the 1980s is epitomised by the beliefs of the Cabinet Minister, Norman Tebbit (b. 1931), who regarded human beings as pack animals. 'There is no such thing as a multicultural pack; and a pack without hierarchy, shared values, a common identity, a single set of rules and a system of punishment for transgressors cannot survive,' he wrote. 'Advocates of multi-culturalism and of sexual licence, which undermines the family, are advocates . . . of perpetual instability and disorder.' He was an implacable drugs warrior. 'Dependence on drugs is a retreat from the obligations of society . . . into a sick, degraded criminal world.'[57] Like Nixon he used drugs as a rhetorical means to unify society in a paranoid temper: paradoxically the insistent reference to them in the political discourse of the 1980s had the effect of normalising drug-taking. Tebbit's hostility to multiculturalism and domestic diversity has its trans-Atlantic counterpart in the reaction of Barbara Bush (b. 1925) during a presidential visit of 1989 to a hospital treating troops wounded in Operation Just Cause against Noriega in Panama. 'I saw several rooms where the mother, father, and stepmother and stepfather were all there together reflecting, I guess, the new world,' she noted ruefully. 'There were many mixed marriages, many. A very handsome black man with two beautiful boys and a lovely Filipino wife told George, "I couldn't have better care if I had all Donald Trump's money." ' The First Lady reflected, 'It is hard being president.'[58]

The Conservative governments of 1979–97 headed by Margaret Thatcher and John Major (b. 1943) instituted penal policies on drugs modelled on the US war on drugs. They focused on law enforcement, and a system of heavier punishments, and apart from a few ill-conceived advertising campaigns, largely aimed at Middle England, ignored harm-reduction policies. They disregarded the marginal cost and marginal benefit of different policy alternatives. As with the Reagan and Bush administrations, the priority was cutting supplies rather than reducing demand. The Thatcher and Major governments were committed to introducing market forces into every aspect of British life, but were incapable of accepting that prohibitionist policies, according to market laws, were bound to make drug-trafficking more lucrative and stimulate the illicit drug economy. 'Much of the chaos that we now deal with', Kenneth Leech noted before the final defeat of the Conservatives in 1997, 'not least the escalation of the criminal market in heroin and cocaine, is the direct result of ill-thought out policy.'[59]

The New Right's drugs wars changed attitudes in Whitehall. Arthur Hawes in 1970 testified to his 'very deep debt of gratitude' to the Drugs Branch of the Home Office. 'Addicts would often turn to the Home Office for help and advice, as they were never hostile and always benevolent.'[60] Bing Spear, who became head of the Drugs Branch in 1977, perpetuated this tradition. He was a passionate, humane man who befriended addicts, disliked punitive American policies and resisted harsh policing. For many years he knew all the registered heroin-users in London. They trusted and consulted him, and went in numbers to his funeral. He was scrupulously helpful to physicians like Ann Dally (b. 1926), the London psychiatrist who as President of the Association of Independent Doctors in Addiction (AIDA) was Hawes's successor as an outspoken medical commentator on drugs policy. Spear described himself as 'the custodian of the Rolleston tradition' to Arnold Trebach, President of the Drug Policy Foundation. 'It was a startling vision for my American eyes to see the good friends he brought to several of my London seminars: long-time injecting heroin addicts,' Trebach recalled. 'It would be a sign from heaven if using addicts believed that they could go to the head of the DEA or FDA to get friendly advice—and even the name of a doctor who might prescribe injectable drugs to maintain their addictions within the law.'[61] Alas, by the time of Spear's retirement in 1986, the political climate was cajoling the Drugs Branch and other civil servants into a more aggressive, punitive and uncomprehending outlook. Dale Beckett regularly had meetings at the Department of Health, 'and there the climate certainly became more and more stringent, more and more closed down'. The DEA's influence was evident, particularly on beliefs about cannabis. As a result of the new temper of the times, British clinics adopted new and ill-advised anti-drug tactics based on punitive US models.[62]

Beckett had argued in 1979 that treatment centres should serve as maintenance centres for addicts who were unable to progress to withdrawal. There they could be prescribed appropriate doses of heroin together with sterile syringes and needles. 'While sheltered in one's drug cocoon, one can slowly learn how to handle life until one has gained sufficient wisdom to be able to leave the cocoon behind. It often takes years during which the numbed doctor is prescribing unremittingly a drug that he regards as a poison.' The training and humanitarian instincts of many doctors were opposed to indefinite prescriptions of opiates, but there were drawbacks when doctors imposed a withdrawal. 'The "ex" addict finds himself once again just as he was before he started his addiction; subject to the same pressures, misunderstandings, injustices, paranoia, complications and pain that made him reach out for heroin in the first place. But having once experienced the relief of heroin anaesthesia, he is more susceptible to addiction than he was before, and will try even harder to lay his hands on the drug.' In Beckett's experience it was harder to withdraw from methadone than from heroin. He acknowledged that heroin, like other sedative drugs including alcohol, produces depression if taken for long periods, and can accentuate the addict's sense of worthlessness. Intravenous use of heroin could lead to the injection of other harmful drugs. Yet he saw no valid argument against maintenance prescriptions of heroin. 'The addict with a not-too-generous but adequate legal supply of the drug is peaceful and relatively law-abiding': the addict scoring on the black market raised money by crime. 'Even on quite high doses, most heroin addicts are able to hold down responsible positions and sustain stable relationships. They keep out of prison, they aren't on social security, their children don't go into care. The saving to the nation is significant and the quality of their lives is unbelievably improved.'[63]

Despite such good advice, the campaign against drug misuse in

Britain during the 1980s was often akin to a campaign against drug-users. 'The main problem of heroin addiction is not the effect of heroin on the individual but the criminality associated with illicit consumption,' Beckett noted in 1983.[64] Yet the consultant psychiatrists were focusing on individuals—their patients—and disregarding the main problem, an expanding criminal market. Politicians, too, were wedded to Nixon's idea of drug-user as enemy. John Mordaunt (1958–95), who was deported from China to Britain in 1987 when he was found to be HIV positive, was the first active intravenous drug-user to address a plenary session of the International AIDS Conference—as late as 1993. 'There is no war on drugs,' he would say. 'There is and always has been a war on drug-users.'[65]

Ann Dally has described the consequences for an electrician aged twenty-nine who had been injecting heroin for fifteen years when his clinic abruptly changed its policy. The doctor did not bother to see him, but sent a message through the social worker that in future he would be refused injectable drugs and given liquid oral methadone instead. The electrician predicted that he could not continue working under this new regime (many heroin-users find that substituting methadone makes them lethargic). His time was soon dominated by his need to buy drugs illicitly. He lost his job, and lived by shoplifting and drug-dealing; honest work would never earn the sums he now needed for drugs. Dally accepted him as a patient, prescribed diminishing doses, and monitored his progress. Other addicts soon followed. Although many users could hold skilled or difficult jobs if their lives were not ruled by obtaining drugs, the clinical establishment seemed oblivious to this. 'One clinic refused to treat addicts *unless* they were unemployed. Others expected them to attend during working hours and refused to prescribe if they did not.' Yet for most adults both self-respect and one's coherent sense of identity rest on one's job. Like Beckett, Dally learnt that addicts would not renounce drugs when under coercion. 'A doctor has little or no control over this, though doctors who feel a need to be in control of their patients will deny this is so. This made nonsense of the current standard policy in the treatment of drug addiction which was either to insist on the addict giving up drugs immediately or else to put him onto a regime in which the dose was rapidly reduced so that, within a few weeks, he was "drug-free".'[66]

Dally felt that Connell had become one of the leaders of 'a sort of "mafia", acting in their own interests, largely concerned with power and prestige, including positions on important committees'.[67] Bing Spear quoted with approval Cindy Fazey's summary of how during the 1980s the moral high ground had been seized by an influential group within the medical establishment. 'Psychiatrists who took over treatment decided that the U.S.A. knew best, and addicts could be cured of their addiction. Abstinence became the universal goal to be enforced by only offering detoxification regimes, as in-patients or out-patients, and oral methadone in a few cases.' As a result, Spear complained, maintenance prescription practices 'were jettisoned for medico-political reasons . . . and not because they had failed'.[68] The senior members of this hierarchy insisted on their own superior prerogatives in treating drug-users while providing a service that few of their potential patients would tolerate. In 1984 under one-third of 7500 addicts notified to the Home Office were being treated by the clinics. The total number of addicts was five to ten times this figure. This was an indictment of the clinics, which, as Hartnoll observed in 1983, 'in their desire to move away from being seen as the prescribing centres they so deprecate in parts of the private sector, have yet to find a positive role and a set of creative alternatives to offer'.[69]

Connell complacently summarised the status quo in 1984. 'Many clinics now require that patients should attend the clinic on time and regularly if they are to receive a prescription and find that even "chaotic" patients are able to comply.' He explained that 'An increasing number of clinics operate a "contract" system, in which patients agree to define goals or objectives as part of treatment.' This meant that as a condition of treatment, the user agreed, usually by signing a contract, to reduce his dose of drugs at a specified rate, regardless of his need or ability to do so, undertaking to become drug-free within so many months, usually between two and six. The patient had to make this promise regardless of the length of the addiction, which in some cases exceeded twenty years. Many addicts agreed to contracts as an interim measure to extract prescriptions, but without any hope or intention of complying. Some addicts stopped presenting for treatment at official clinics, others abandoned the treatment regime unfinished and most

of those who completed treatment relapsed within weeks or months. The drop-out rate was higher because, as Connell noted, clinics seldom any longer prescribed sedatives as part of maintenance treatment.[70] His informal guidelines counted because he was influential in both the General Medical Council and the Royal College of Psychiatry. John Marks, who was in charge of the highly effective Liverpool Drug Dependency Clinic, was insistent that 'addicts give up when they are ready to and special detoxification units do little to expedite this. Probably all the units do is enable the addicts to survive until they are prepared to stop.'[71] This dissent cost Marks dearly: he lost his job, although he rebuilt a distinguished career in New Zealand. As a young drug-dependency consultant confided at this time, 'In drug dependency the most important thing is not to step out of line.'[72]

As late as 1982 the Advisory Council on the Misuse of Drugs, in a report on the treatment and rehabilitation of addicts, stated that 'The majority are relatively stable individuals who have more in common with the general population than with any essentially pathological subgroup.' One example was the English novelist Enid Bagnold (1889–1981), author of *National Velvet* and widow of the head of Reuters news agency. Her morphine habit had begun more than half a century earlier, when she was a voluntary nurse in the First World War; but despite an additional involvement with amphetamines, she survived to the age of ninety-one.[73] Similarly, Spear knew a doctor who had been introduced to cocaine around 1900 by a royal physician and was still receiving about 500 milligrams daily at his death aged almost a hundred.[74] Notwithstanding these productive lives, many consultant psychologists running clinics in the 1980s dismissed the needs of stable addicts, and often refused to prescribe at all. 'I would never prescribe methadone, I am in the business of changing people,' one of them told James Willis, who thought this remark showed 'monstrous arrogance: the track record of psychiatry is not that much to get excited about'.[75]

By targeting Mitcheson and Hartnoll's 20 per cent of addicts who stopped using drugs, and excluding from the system those patients who most needed help, clinics, as one of their staff declared, became 'much nicer places to work in'.[76] John Strang (b. 1950), then consultant psychiatrist at a Drug Dependence Unit in Manchester, claimed in 1984 that 'pragmatism' had forced the changes in clinic procedure. 'With the old model, the constant flow of new patients into the clinic system was not matched by any equivalent flow of patients out of the system. So with static or diminishing resources, the clinics found it necessary to look at shorter, more cost effective (and perhaps more appropriate) types of response.'[77] Such views put Strang on the fast-track to promotion: he became a consultant adviser on drugs to the Department of Health in 1986, and joined the Advisory Council on the Misuse of Drugs in 1989. But as Bing Spear observed, 'repeated unsuccessful detoxifications, as illustrated by an addict who recently underwent his 27th, hardly makes best economic use of available resources.' He supported, instead, 'a holding, harm-reducing operation to allow the addict, with professional help, sufficient time to acquire the motivation likely to result in a permanent break with his addiction.'[78] Spear, who 'was highly critical of Connell', was convinced 'that the policy of abrupt cutting down of heroin was disastrous.'[79]

Clients of the drug dependency institutions were increasingly compelled to accept counselling or group therapy as a condition of entering methadone maintenance programmes. 'This is both insulting and absurd,' James Willis believed. 'If someone asks for counselling, or is obviously in need of it, then it must be given. However, to make counselling a precondition of receiving methadone is as ridiculous as insisting that someone with gonorrhoea should have counselling in regard of their psychosexual problems as a necessary requirement for receiving antibiotic therapy.'[80] Attendance was obligatory: as meetings were usually held in normal working hours, it was impossible for most drug-users to retain their jobs. An addict in 1983 described his experience of being 'prescribed a totally inadequate amount of oral methadone and told to reduce to zero over six months'. This was conditional on attending 'a weekly meeting where we were "psychoanalysed" by a social worker and psychologist. These "experts" were two girls many years younger than I, yet they insisted "our" problems were the same as all other addicts: "Mummy didn't love you, Daddy was a drunkard," and so on. They were both arrogant and patronising.'[81]

When the new clinic policies were criticised during a committee meeting at the Department of Health, one of their consultants shouted, 'There is NOTHING wrong with the clinics except when these private doctors steal their patients!'[82] As the clinic system faltered, there were strenuous efforts to discredit physicians working outside the system. General practitioners had not been licensed since 1967 to prescribe heroin for addicts, but could prescribe other substances, notably methadone. As early as 1980 Thomas Bewley began attacking private doctors prescribing psychoactive drugs privately in return for fees. 'A doctor in private practice who prescribes for 20 such addicts could earn £500 a week or over £25,000 a year.' If twenty addicts were pre-scribed 5 methadone ampoules daily, their black market value would be £500 a day or over £180,000 a year.[83] Interestingly, he did not allude to those consultant psychiatrists who refused to prescribe for long-term maintenance of NHS patients in drug dependency units—and indeed made their reputations as authoritarian hard-liners—but were willing, quietly, to prescribe long-term maintenance doses to a small number of private patients. Bewley supported this campaign with a later article that summarised the views of sixty-nine addicts on the pre-scription habits of private practitioners—only half of whom had ever consulted a private doctor. Having juxtaposed the names of Lady Frankau and Ann Dally, he wrote of a black market in drugs 'from the Harley Street and Piccadilly Circus Golden Triangle'.[84] In fact, 'when addicts are charged with selling methadone ampoules', as Beckett noted, 'usually clinic sources are implicated, not those coming from independent doctors.'[85]

Dally became particularly unpopular because she never treated the new clinic policies as either sacrosanct or clinically neutral. Instead, she regarded them as integral to their political and social context. The con-sultant psychiatrists, she felt, were being

> encouraged indirectly by the press with headlines about the perils and
> wickedness of drugs and drug-taking. The new policies were causing a
> great deal of resentment and suffering among addicts and their families.
> They were also causing a lot of crime, which the authorities tried to
> conceal by arguing that most addicts had convictions before they
> became addicts so that depriving them of a legal supply of drugs made
> no difference to their criminality ... All this was in line with an increas-
> ingly repressive regime in the United States, from which the British
> Government clearly took its cues. Interest now lay not in helping the
> addicts but in the 'war on drugs', fortified by international operations
> with helicopters and the picturesque adjuncts of publicity stunts. British
> government ministers were seen participating in these and expressing
> their determination to 'beat this evil' or to 'conquer this wicked trade',
> while it was increasingly obvious that there was no chance of doing so.
> Yet in line with this political and publicity campaign, treatment for

addicts, where it was available, was becoming increasingly a question of instant abstention and appeals to moral fibre.[86]

Dally was recruited to a government committee preparing clinical guidelines for the treatment of addicts. At one of its meetings, a consultant from a drug dependency unit averred, 'The first essential in treating addicts is to make certain that no drugs can escape to the black market.'[87] This was tantamount to saying that there should be no prescription, although prescribed drugs form under one-tenth of 1 per cent of the black market. Some consultants were claiming 90 per cent success in withdrawing their clinic patients from opiate use. These claims were not credible. 'If they have 90 per cent success, I know all the failures twenty times over,' one addict said.[88] Many consultants ignored the fact that clinic figures showed what was prescribed rather than what was being obtained from an expanding black market. Among them, James Willis was unusual in believing (like Hawes twenty years earlier) that a small illegal 'grey' market in which addicts dealt among themselves from excess prescriptions was preferable to a black market of heroin smuggled from abroad by gangsters.

Under the *Guidelines of Good Clinical Conduct in the Treatment of Drug Misuse* published in 1984, patients were to be treated similarly, regardless of whether their addiction had lasted for weeks or decades. No patient's treatment should exceed a few weeks or months, by which time each patient should be drug-free. The maximum initial prescribed dose of methadone, 80 milligrams, was under 5 per cent of what the clinics had been prescribing at the start of the 1980s. The guidelines encouraged general practitioners to include addicts among their patients: as the number of addicts escalated, it was becoming harder to regard them as an excluded, abnormal minority requiring specialist services. There was instead a wish to bring them within the broader 'community care' approach that characterised British health and social services during the 1980s.[89] The first Community Drug Team (CDT) of health and social service workers had been formed in 1983, and by 1987 there were sixty-two CDTs serving individual health districts. Their performance was variable: some were overseen by political appointees whose opinions on drugs were formed by what they had seen the previous night on *The Bill*. The *Guidelines* advised physicians to refer long-term addicts to the clinics, although the clinics were unlikely (if they followed the *Guidelines*) to help long-term addicts. In fact, general practitioners resisted becoming involved in prescribing to addicts: it was not only that they feared the disruption of exigent patients demanding methadone. Parallel with the intolerant and aggressive medical regime taking control in the clinics, and supported by government, there was a use of *agents provocateurs*, often policemen, to catch physicians who prescribed methadone or other drugs that might reach the black market. *Agents provocateurs* were, of course, a technique that the DEA has been foisting on Europe since the agency's formation. This duress was intimidating. During 1984 several physicians who had been appalled by the new clinic policies, and had tried to help long-term addicts, stopped this work after 'hostile interviews' with Home Office inspectors who called at their surgeries or consulting rooms. This pushed more long-term addicts onto the black market.[90] General practitioners became increasingly wary of the disciplinary strictures of the General Medical Council.

During the Thatcher years, the availability of illegal drugs and the nature of illicit markets were transformed in Britain. Highly localised and poorly structured distribution networks were replaced by extensive, pervasive and tightly organised distribution systems. Increasingly drugs were brought into Britain by groups of professional criminals with no previous interest in drugs or by entrepreneurs trying a 'one-off' coup to enrich themselves. Both the gangs and the entrepreneurs found that the colossal potential profits created by prohibition outweighed the risks of being caught and punished.[91] Yet Thatcher attacked these exponents of her 'enterprise culture'. 'We are after you,' she threatened in 1985 during a well-publicised descent on the customs at Heathrow Airport to prove that her government was acting tough on drugs. 'The pursuit will be relentless. We shall make your life not worth living.'[92] In 1984 her government created a Ministerial Group on the Misuse of Drugs chaired by David Mellor (b. 1949), an ambitious Home Office minister who thought he could smell personal success far up the wind. Targeting heroin, Mellor's group devised a strategy to cut illicit supplies from abroad. This involved stricter law enforcement, increasing the deterrent effect of prohibitionist legislation, and as lower priorities, treatment, rehabilitation and preventive education. To fulfil the latter obligation, the government in 1985–6 mounted a mass-media advertising campaign, with the slogan 'Heroin screws you up', which was intended to eradicate drug use. Expert advisers warned the politicians that this shock campaign was likely to be counterproductive, and that a less dramatic strategy of harm reduction would be preferable. The campaign's grungy images of drugs seemed attractive to some young people, although older Conservatives were impressed by the advertisements. The government's emphasis, however, was on Reaganite policies of punitive legislation and overseas interventions. Among other provisions, the Controlled Drug Penalties Act of 1985 increased the maximum sentence for importing Class A drugs to life imprisonment.

In 1986 £10.8 million of overseas aid was committed to suppressing drug trafficking, including £3.4 million for a scheme to eradicate opium poppy production in the Dir district of Pakistan, and £1.5 million to combat cocaine production and trafficking in South America and the Caribbean. Mellor claimed credit for the Thatcher government that the growth of addict notifications had fallen from 42 per cent in 1983 to about 25 per cent in 1985. This was a classic example of politicians using drug statistics to mislead, for the addiction problem was escalating under the policies with which he was associated.[93] Amidst a fanfare of publicity Mellor visited South America in 1986–7. Anyone who hinted that £1.5 million aid to South America was wasted— indeed a pitiful example of 'gesture politics' given the size of the Colombian cartel's profits—was depicted as a subversive who was 'soft on drugs'. British politicians, like their American counterparts, were waging a fantasy war intended to boost their egos and popularity. The War on Drugs became a pretext for chauvinism and partisan sniping. 'Amsterdam is the cesspit of Europe,' huffed the Conservative politician Andrew Pearce (b. 1937) at a press conference in October 1986. 'The poison from there has spread around. It's like one man with a foul smell in his garden'. Pearce was a member of the European Committee of Enquiry into the Drugs Problem of the Member States. When a Labour MEP supported investigating the legalisation of certain drugs to curb the black market, Pearce demanded: 'Is that Labour party policy? Is Kinnock going to announce that the Labour party is going soft on drugs?'[94]

It was in this intemperate climate that the Drug Trafficking Offences Act of 1986 was enacted. Introducing the legislation the Home Secretary, Douglas Hurd, declared, 'There is no strand of public policy more important than the fight against drugs', yet there was 'only time for a short debate'.[95] In consequence this draconian legislation underwent minimal scrutiny or opposition. The DTOA empowered the courts to confiscate money and property accumulated in the five years before conviction. People not involved in crime who had received property from a convicted person were also subject to confiscation orders. The Act gave immunity from civil or criminal liability to those making disclosures about drug traffickers' profits. It made it an offence for anyone aware of an investigation to inform a suspect. Police were empowered to seize material from individuals not suspected of a crime. Furthermore, the Police and Criminal Evidence Act of 1986 empowered police to hold those suspected of drug-trafficking offences for up to thirty-six hours without access to lawyers and without informing relatives of their arrest. PACE also empowered police to search premises where the occupants were *not* suspected of crime. There had been for many years an idealisation by liberal Americans of the 'British System' of treating addiction as exclusively a medical and not a criminal problem. This had always been overstated: the Home Office and not the Ministry of Health had controlled the system since the first Dangerous Drugs Act in 1920; the response to the fashion for marijuana in the 1950s and 1960s had involved increased police activity and prison sentences. More than ever, after the legislation of 1986, the criminal justice system was central to British drugs policy.

It was anathema to the Conservative governments of 1979–97 to accept the relationship between drug use and deprivation. This relationship had been well documented in the USA by the 1950s, and was visible (although scarcely remarked) in Scotland by the end of the 1960s. Further British research in the early 1980s confirmed increasing heroin use among young unemployed people living on deprived council estates. After the heroin epidemic centred on London in the mid–late 1970s, there was a second upsurge in the mid-1980s. A number of studies—particularly those on the Merseyside borough of Wirral—showed that the sharp rise in household burglaries was associated with the escalating heroin misuse in the area. Research into these problems was marginalised or ignored by the authorities. This was in a period when the Archbishop of Canterbury's report on inner-city dereliction and social problems, *Faith in the City* (1985), was virulently denounced by Conservative politicians and newspapers as 'Marxist'.

The Prime Minister discounted the community consequences of high unemployment. 'There is no such thing as Society,' she told *Woman's Own* magazine in 1987. 'There are individual men and women, and there are families.' By 1990 the evidence was unmistakable, but it was not until late in the Major administration that the government's semi-independent Advisory Council on the Misuse of Drugs began investigating environmental influences on drugs. After the election of a New Labour government in 1997, the Advisory Council felt free to report unequivocally in 1998 'that on strong balance of probability deprivation is today in Britain likely often to make a significant causal contribution to the cause, contribution and intractability of damaging kinds of drug use'. It is doubtful whether such a conclusion would have been palatable under the Major administration: the Blair government, however, announced in 1998 a ten-year drug strategy with drugs, crime and social exclusion treated as equal and interrelated issues. This painfully belated change of tactics is promising. The Blair government, however, showed no interest in reforming the Misuse of Drugs Act of 1971, which took no account of environmental influences on illegal drug habits.

The 'New Right' administrations of Reagan and Thatcher crusaded against the 'permissive' morality identified with the 1960s and 1970s heedless that the new trends in citizens' private lives had in reality originated in the 1950s. The prevalent political ideology resulted in the US in a culpable reluctance by the administration to intervene when cases involving HIV began emerging in 1981. Instead, AIDS was stigmatised as a disease connected to homosexuality. Although the reaction among newspapers and the rank-and-file of the ruling Conservative Party in Britain was equally punitive, the British governmental response from 1985 was more humane and realistic. Politicians let their policies be fashioned by advice from professional elites: AIDS was treated as a medical issue, with doctors in charge, and the violence of populist ignorance was contained. Gay men working in voluntary organisations, although to a significantly lesser extent drug-users, were brought into the consensus. The prevalence of HIV among drug-users was crucial to the British strategy of presenting the virus as a threat to the general population rather than as a by-product of homosexuality. This strategy was partly adopted to reduce the likelihood of bigotry and violence directed against homosexuality, but aroused many tensions in policy-making.

The health risks of sharing needles were well established. A localised malaria epidemic caused by the sharing of contaminated needles had been one of the precipitating causes of the formation of the Egyptian Central Narcotics Intelligence Bureau in 1929. As early as 1934 three New York heroin-users were infected with malaria by sharing needles.[96] In 1968 Bewley co-authored a pioneering article on the transmission of hepatitis by dirty needles.[97] No research has ever shown that making needle possession illegal has reduced drug consumption. The role of needle-sharing in the transmission of HIV became evident in the early 1980s. The percentage of intravenous drug-users undergoing medical treatment for HIV in the US rose from about 3 per cent in 1981 to 17 per cent in 1984. By 1985 the reported frequency of infection with HIV in European drug-users varied from 6.4 per cent in England and 6 per cent in West Germany to 22 per cent in Italy, 32–42 per cent in Switzerland and 44–8 per cent in Austria and Spain.[98] In Italy there were eleven intravenous drug-users with overt AIDS in 1984, eighty-seven in 1985, 250 in 1986 and 639 in 1987. But in many countries the political authorities and medical hierarchy were reluctant to develop the necessary harm-reduction strategies. The Netherlands responded best. Dutch law permitted the sale of syringes without a prescription, and in 1984 the Amsterdam Municipal Health Service and the Junkie Union set up a needle-exchange programme intended to reduce hepatitis B infection rates. The Municipal Health Service rapidly expanded this government-funded needle-exchange system once the transmission of HIV by contaminated needles became well known. The Junkie Union and Amsterdam authorities doubted that total abstinence was a realistic aim and worked to reduce the health risks associated with intravenous drug use. The Dutch treated intravenous drug use as a chronic, relapsing condition, and provided medical and social services accordingly.[99]

It is easy to disinfect syringes with ordinary domestic bleach, but Edwin Meese III (b. 1931), US Attorney General in 1985–8, opposed teaching drug-users this disinfectant technique. He preferred drug-users to die rather than condone their habits by 'bleach and teach' programmes. Some authority figures believed that as intravenous drug-users would not change their conduct, their part in strategies to prevent HIV infection should be downplayed.[100] Street outreach bleach programmes often provided the first opportunity for public health workers to encounter intravenous drug-users outside treatment units, public health clinics or prison. They learnt—in some cases contrary to their assumptions—that many such users were concerned to preserve their health and prevent HIV transmission. However, needle-exchange schemes met aggressive political opposition in the USA: five laws passed by Congress between 1988 and 1991 prohibited federal funding of clean-needle programmes. This prohibition was renewed in 1998. Jon Stuen-Parker (b. 1954), who was the first to distribute sterile syringes publicly in the USA in 1986, had been arrested twenty-seven times in seven states by 1993. Some city-funded needle-exchange programmes began opening from 1988, although the programme in New York City was closed in 1990 in fulfilment of the campaign pledge of a newly elected mayor. A bill legalising needle-exchanges passed by the California legislature was vetoed in 1992 by the Republican Governor, Pete Wilson (b. 1933), who declared that there was 'insufficient evidence to demonstrate the efficacy of these programs' which 'threaten the credibility of our ongoing anti-drug efforts'.[101] This action is unforgivable in its ignorance or cynical callousness. Overall, the Reagan administration's response to AIDS showed its passionate feeling that fags, junkies and Haitians didn't matter. One can more easily respect the position of a senior official from a Third World country attending an AIDS forum in the early 1990s who told a counterpart from the British Department of Health, 'There is no point in our having needle-exchange clinics because we hang all our drug users.'[102]

The discriminatory attitudes to drug-users were grievous. Visiting New York City in 1987 on a fact-finding tour about HIV, the Minister of Health, Sir Norman Fowler (b. 1938), reflected, 'Many of the homosexual community were middle-class, well educated and certainly did not want to die. The intravenous drug-users were much more apathetic about their future.'[103] In other respects, it should be stressed, Fowler's response to the AIDS crisis was admirable (in 1969 he had written the first report in *The Times* of illicit powder heroin being smuggled from Hong Kong to satisfy the demand aroused by the disastrous launch phase of the drug dependency clinics). His limited sympathies with junkies were common. A Paris psychiatrist, explaining users' resistance to health education campaigns in 1987, declared: 'In shooting up, they already play with their own lives, and mock others.' An authoritative French *Histoire du Sida* (*History of AIDS*) (1989) similarly concluded, 'Too often the act of taking drugs is no more than acting out of their desire to destroy themselves.'[104] There is an element of wishfulness in such comments: if you believe that intravenous drug-users want to be dead, you feel less concerned about saving their lives or ameliorating their circumstances. In 1992 France, with an estimated 500 per cent more cases of HIV than Britain, still had no state-funded needle-exchange schemes. Although it is doubtless true that some intravenous drug-users are so demoralised or desperate as to be indifferent whether or not they live, this is emphatically untrue in other cases. It was not difficult, for those who cared to look, to find HIV positive intravenous drug-users in the late 1980s thirsting for life, and working to survive with courage and single-mindedness. Such people were often marginalised, or discriminated against, both as voluntary helpers and clients seeking the services of leading HIV charities in Britain, and no doubt the US. The repeated blanket denigration of them in written records seems a cruel and monstrous falsehood.

As part of the more punitive temper of the early 1980s, the Pharmaceutical Society had advised pharmacists to stop selling syringes to drug-users. Nevertheless some British drug workers by the mid-1980s were advocating the introduction of needle and syringe-exchange schemes. They were opposed by those who feared a policy of harm minimisation would legitimise intravenous drug use. The situation crystallised in Edinburgh. Roy Robertson, a general practitioner on the Muirhouse estate, treated many addicts because Scottish consultant psychiatrists were mostly unwilling to work in drug dependence clinics. Local police confiscated syringes from his patients as they left his surgery, and disrupted his policy of maintenance prescriptions. Edinburgh addicts therefore frequented 'shooting galleries', where twenty or thirty users would share a single syringe. When the HIV test became available in 1985, it was found that 50 per cent of 164 heroin-users from Robertson's practice were seropositive. In Glasgow, with less punitive policies, the comparable rate was under 5 per cent.[105] The ministers responsible for Scotland in the Conservative government were resolute in their commitment to a punitive drug-control policy, but in February 1986 an official committee to investigate drug use and HIV was appointed. Its members, *faute de mieux*, were predominantly Scottish haematologists and virologists rather than consultant psychologists from drug dependence clinics. 'We knew that prohibition didn't work,' one committee member recalled in 1993. 'If we'd been a lot of drug experts', commented a colleague, 'we'd have disappeared into our own navels.'[106] The committee's report concluded 'that on balance the containment of the spread of the virus is a higher priority in management than the prevention of drug misuse'. This proved unpalatable. The Advisory Council on the Misuse of Drugs was still reluctant in 1986 to endorse making sterile needles and syringes available, but such schemes developed in Britain from 1987 despite the residual opposition of some DDU consultants. Their hostility contributed to the dismissal at this time of John Marks as chief of Drug Dependency Services on Merseyside, although the needle-exchange scheme started by him resulted in Liverpool having a lower rate of HIV infection among drug-users.

Marks's needle-exchange programme was only part of his heroin minimisation strategy developed in 1985. He introduced a drug maintenance programme for addicts in Widnes whereby heroin, cocaine and amphetamines were prescribed for the respective users of those drugs. There was reportedly a 96 per cent drop in thefts in the Widnes area in the period to 1990 as addicts no longer needed to steal. The local black market withered away, and there were therefore no suppliers to recruit new users. Fatalities involving low-grade street drugs stopped. However, television reports in Britain and the USA on the Widnes Drug Dependency Clinic's successes broadcast during 1990 led to political pressure from London and DEA displeasure. After protracted manoeuvres, the Widnes clinic stopped prescribing heroin, and reverted to methadone, in 1995. Street dealing, drug-related thieving and deaths resumed. A controlled scheme of drug prescription, supervised by doctors, is surely preferable to a rampant black market. This could be achieved—as at Widnes—but for the influence achieved by American doctrinaires since the 1920s.

Throughout this period Ann Dally was targeted because she criticised the clinics for catering to young, single, recently employed men and ignoring addicts in their mid-thirties with long-standing habits. Despite enjoying the support of Spear at the Home Office, she was harried from 1986 until 1989 by the General Medical Council in a manner recalling the techniques of Beria and Stalinist show trials. Convoluted attempts to condemn her for serious professional misconduct are recounted in her memoir *A Doctor's Story*, which is a central text of this period. Although the GMC could not condemn her treatment methods, it successfully deterred other physicians from following her. Meanwhile Dally's patients were made the objects of petty spite.

> Either the Home Office inspectors or members of Scotland Yard's Drugs Squad had told pharmacists that if a patient was late in collecting his drugs, they were to dispense less than the amount prescribed. This was inhumane. An addict who was prevented from going to the pharmacy on time would be likely to develop withdrawal symptoms. If he went next morning, he would already be sick and in need. He would need yesterday's drug in order to restore his equilibrium. To deprive him of this made it more difficult for him to remain stable.[107]

Stupid, suspicious and envious policemen, indirectly influenced by the clinics' hostility to private practitioners, harassed other patients. 'She must be worth a bloody fortune,' said one police station officer.[108] The police trawled for evidence against her, badgered her patients and confiscated their legally prescribed drugs. 'Oh, she's been supplying you with sleeping pills, has she? And how much does she sting you for those?'[109] Her lawyers 'regarded the police as dishonest, crude and cruel'.[110]

If police behaviour was extreme, so too were the attitudes of some clinical psychologists. At a conference of the Royal College of Psychiatrists in 1987 one psychiatrist in charge of drug dependency services declared, 'If no one prescribes, no one requests. Let's not spoil our beautiful virgin territory.' As Dally recalled, another physician 'said complacently that we couldn't cope with all addicts so we should concentrate only on those who want to come off drugs. This was in fact the official line but was not usually described so openly.'[111] The policy implications of HIV were unwelcome to such people. A special committee of the Royal College of Psychiatrists, which in 1987 published its report entitled *Drug Scenes*, disavowed long-term maintenance prescriptions of oral methadone to keep patients away from injected drugs: 'It would certainly be wrong to take AIDS as an excuse for promiscuous prescribing.'[112] However, the committee, which included Griffith Edwards, Philip Connell and John Strang, had taken a position that was swiftly becoming untenable.

As a result of reappraisals necessitated by the mounting AIDS crisis, officials of the Department of Health and Social Services in 1987 urged consultants in charge of clinics to adopt greater flexibility in prescribing so that drug-users would not be deterred from attending. A working group of the Advisory Council on the Misuse of Drugs was formed in 1987 under the chairmanship of Ruth Runciman (b. 1936), afterwards Viscountess Runciman of Doxford. Their report's publication was delayed for some months as the Scottish Office opposed passages critical of the mistakes made in syringe policy in Edinburgh and Scotland generally. When finally issued in 1988, the Runciman report supported needle-exchange schemes, over-the-counter sales of syringes by pharmacists, and maintenance prescriptions as a way of attracting drug-users into medical services. Convinced that HIV posed worse social threats than heroin, the Runciman committee advocated harm-minimisation strategies and non-medical community treatment. Ministers rejected these recommendations as condoning drug use, but they marked a turning point against the punitive and inflexible policies of the early 1980s. 'AIDS', predicted Dorothy Black of the Department of Health in 1989, 'may be the trigger that brings care for drug users into the mainstream for the first time ever.'[113] By 1991 James Willis was able to write that the authoritarian approach of clinical psychologists—'I'm right and you're wrong'—'no longer commands after the failure of the penal approach'. The 'perfectly reasonable practice' of maintenance prescriptions of injectable heroin and methadone had 'almost been driven underground by an influential minority of psychiatrists. Fortunately, a degree of reality has now re-emerged with the need to control the spread of HIV infection, although it is sad that it has required a disaster to jolt the obdurate into a modicum of flexibility.'[114]

The lesson of HIV has been that preventive and treatment programmes are overwhelmingly more effective than the hugely expensive tactics of drug prohibition and supply eradication. According to one report in 1997, 'a year's heroin supply for U.S. users can be made from poppies grown on just 20 square miles of farmland. A year's supply of cocaine can be stashed in 13 truck trailers.'[115] Colombia in 1998 had 101,500 hectares under coca cultivation, according to CIA figures, and 6600 hectares of opium poppies. Peru and Bolivia had respectively an estimated 38,700 and 21,800 hectares under coca cultivation in 1999. Such figures make Pino Arlacchi (b. 1950) seem inexpressibly depressing. Arlacchi is the Italian anti-Mafia politician who in 1998 was appointed to head the UN Office for Drug Control and Crime Prevention. He has spearheaded a campaign to eradicate illegal poppy and coca cultivation by 2008 under the slogan: 'The war on drugs has not been won or lost. It has not even begun.'

Such intolerable nonsense has been created—the world's drug problems have been exacerbated—by the presidential Drug Wars. As the US government increased rather than reduced the imbalance between the rewards of the legal economy and those of the underground economy, narcotics retail sales became, in Bourgois's phrase, 'the biggest equal opportunity employer for males in the street economy'. To mitigate the problem, the obstacles to poor, ill-educated people from deprived communities entering the legitimate labour market needed to be reformed. This would require better education and training for the disadvantaged, but also compacts whereby employers undertook to provide jobs in communities and minimum wage agreements that were not insults to human dignity. The process of economic and social revival would be promoted by rebuilding the infrastructure and providing decent, affordable accommodation with access to a comprehensive system of public health care. A drug-orientated street life is an apprenticeship: young people find their role models, their sense of identity and their future expectations in the gangs. What the United States needs is to restore the pride, stability and role models of craft apprenticeships. The supreme aim, though, should have been to break the dynamism of the drug economy. 'In terms of concrete, short-term public policy, the single cheapest and simplest way to wipe out the material basis for the most violent and criminal dimensions of street culture is to destroy the profitability of narcotic trafficking by decriminalizing drugs,' Bourgois wrote in 1995. According to expert estimates the cost of producing an ounce of pure powder cocaine was about $8 to $10. Once this ounce had been adulterated and packaged in $10 quarter-gram vials, it was worth above $2000 in East Harlem. This $1990 profit represented the incentive to work in the violent, destructive illicit drug business. If drugs were decriminalised, prices would fall, there would be less incentive for dealers to sell on the streets, and the supply would decline by the laws of neo-classical economics. It is unlikely that the US government will take the huge profits out of trafficking by decriminalisation, simply because the drug issue has become dominated by spurious moral attitudinising and is the ruling justification of powerful, rapacious bureaucracies. But if drugs were decriminalised, Americans, as Bourgois concludes, would 'not have to waste billions of dollars prosecuting and confining drug users in ridiculously inefficient and expensive prisons. Violent crime, property theft, and medical costs would be dramatically reduced once addicts no longer have to pay exorbitant sums for their daily doses. Dealers would also no longer have high profits to fight over. The alternative, of course, is to lock everyone up.'[116]

FOURTEEN

So *Passé*

I never thought you'd be a junkie because heroin is so passé
—THE DANDY WARHOLS, 'IF YOU WERE THE LAST JUNKIE ON EARTH', 1997

Man is a make-believe animal—he is never so truly himself as when acting a part.
—WILLIAM HAZLITT

MCAFEE WAS A toothless, broken-limbed old jockey with a rasping Ulster accent and an interest in little girls. He made an assignation with one child, Caroline Blackwood, to meet in a lonely wood during the Second World War. He came out of the laurel bushes, wearing his best shiny bowler hat, rolling his eyes, whispering. There were white pills that he wanted her to take, and when she panicked and bicycled off he was aghast. 'Caroline, Caroline, what have I done?' he kept repeating. As she pedalled away, he called, 'Please, please, never breathe a word!'[1] In Nabokov's *Lolita* (1955) Humbert Humbert, deciding to marry Charlotte Haze so that he can ravish her daughter Dolores, procures forty amethyst-coloured capsules from his doctor. 'Visions of venery presented themselves to me swaying and smiling. I saw myself administering a powerful sleeping potion to both mother and daughter so I could fondle the latter through the night with perfect impunity.'[2] Fears of manipulative men stupefying their sexual victims are widespread in Western culture.

These anxieties have often been involved in media and political panics about new or newly publicised substances that have recurred since the Reagan inauguration of 1981. Some of these panics have worked up citizens' fears of a drug that would damage suburban white young people as crack wrecked young inner-city blacks and Hispanics. In certain instances they have exploited the understandable revulsion at latter-day McAfees and Humberts using drugs to subdue their sexual prey. In other cases again, substances have been condemned because they have fallen foul of pharmacological Calvinists who mistrust any substance that gives sensual, not to say sexual, pleasure without a retributive sequel. The florid fears of the US authorities have been exported to Europe, although often, as with crack cocaine, the terrors have proved exaggerated. Back in the mid-1970s, for example, there was concern about glue-sniffing among young Americans. The fashion waned, but never entirely vanished in some south-west states, especially among young and poor Hispanics. Americans responded with legislation: typically, in 1985, the Texas state legislature passed an act providing for the involuntary commitment of persons dependent on inhalants (including spray paint and cleaning solvents as well as glue). In Britain the Intoxicating Substances (Supply) Act of 1985 attempted to restrict the retail supply of inhalants but did not produce many prosecutions.

This chapter will survey some of the substances covered by the descriptive phrase 'designer drugs'. There has always been a demand for drugs to enhance the excitement of dancing—alcohol pre-eminently—and designer drugs were frequently dance drugs. Some of these substances had the appeal of renegade science, but the most significant of them—Ecstasy—brought a normalising influence to drug scenes. The young people who used Ecstasy did not consider themselves outlaws, and were concerned with a good night out rather than political defiance, social rebellion or adolescent naughtiness. This marked a momentous change. The success of Ecstasy in the clubs led to experimental use of other substances as dance drugs. Some were long-established (amphetamines, amyl nitrite) and others were novel (ketamine, GHB). Their use was essentially hedonistic. This distinguishes them from other drugs associated with disproportionate panics in the USA during the 1980s and 1990s, such as smokable methamphetamine and methcathinone, known as CAT.[3]

PCP was first synthesised in 1926. When the US pharmaceutical company Parke, Davis tested it during 1957 as a human anaesthetic, it was found to produce hallucinations, delirium, disorientation and manic episodes. Nevertheless, under the trade name of Sernyl (denoting serenity), it was marketed after 1959 for human medical use. In 1967 it was enlisted as a hallucinogenic during a San Francisco street festival, and quickly gained popularity as a street drug in the USA. It was usually smoked, but occasionally snorted, swallowed or taken in eye-drops. As a result of this burgeoning recreational use, Parke, Davis withdrew PCP from human consumption, although it was retained in veterinary anaesthesia. In small amounts PCP causes elation or carefree dreaminess; but larger amounts can induce catatonia, delirium, convulsions, coma and death. After the Controlled Substances Act of 1970 reduced the availability of barbiturates in the US, some Americans turned to PCP, which became known as 'angel dust'. The drug was comparatively easy and cheap to make in clandestine laboratories (notably in Los Angeles) and yielded high profits to organised crime. It was used to adulterate a variety of street drugs, but was also produced in a pure form sold under street names such as Angel Dust, Devil's Dust, Goon, Amoeba and Zombie. In 1977–8 it became the subject of concentrated political and media attention. 'It's a real terror of a drug,' declared the Director of the National Institute on Drug Abuse in 1977. 'Everything people used to say about marijuana is true about angel dust.'[4] By 1991 an estimated 7 million Americans had tried PCP at least once, but the drug never attracted a strong following outside the US. It was particularly prevalent in Washington DC, Detroit and Los Angeles, but receded after 1985.

The significance of PCP for the dance drugs lies in its derivative, ketamine (ketamine hydrochloride). First synthesised in 1962, ketamine was also marketed by Parke, Davis as an anaesthetic for animals (in poorer countries it is sometimes used as a human anaesthetic). Early in the 1970s it became a fashionable hallucinogenic in American gay dance clubs. It seems to sever the association between mind and body, and can make sexual contact seem bizarre and exciting, especially with strangers. There was a fad for ketamine in some British dance clubs of the late 1980s, and the drug retains a loyal following in both Britain and the US in the twenty-first century. It can induce heavy vomiting, loss of bodily co-ordination and other unpleasant traits. In large doses, like amphetamines, it can bring on schizophrenia-like psychosis. It was placed on Schedule III of the Controlled Substances Act in 1999.

Another dance drug of this period, which initially had particular devotees in gay dance clubs, was the hypnotic called Quaalude (known in Europe as Mandrax). As the prescribing of barbiturates plummeted, physicians substituted Quaalude. Some four million prescriptions were written annually in the US during the early 1970s. As more patients became dependent, it was put on Schedule II by the US authorities in 1973. This was the year in which David Bowie (b. 1947) sang in 'Time' of 'Quaaludes and red wine', for the drug was acquiring a sexual association. The American novelist Edmund White (b. 1940) wrote in 1977: 'The effect is a sort of twilight drowsiness, a lowering of the pain threshold and a stripping away of the defences and inhibitions. For this reason some men take quaaludes for heavy S&M sessions, but even occasional use can lead to addiction.'[5] Steve Rubell (1944–89) was 'the king of the lude', handing out the thick white tablets at his famous Studio 54 club in New York to customers and employees in the years after 1977. Quaaludes were ideal for dancers. 'Just the right mixture of lude and cocaine and alcohol gave the user the perfect, slippery, glimmering sensation for a night out.'[6] Quaaludes were promoted to Schedule I— wholly prohibited—under the CSA in 1984. A giant silver spoon suspended above the dance floor at Studio 54 shovelled invisible coke into the moon's nose, and cocaine with quaaludes was a popular combination of drugs.

The German film-maker Rainer Werner Fassbinder (1945–82), who destroyed himself with cocaine, depended on Quaalude under the European name of Mandrax. The mixture wrecked his days and nights. 'I'm left to invent the excuses and the lies,' wrote his lead actor Kurt Raab (1941–88).

I must also look after you like a child, to make sure nothing bad happens to you. All night long you've taken cocaine, and now it's four o'clock in the morning and you want to sleep. But you're too stimulated, so you have to take three Mandrax pills to calm you down. Then you remember you have to call Ingrid in Paris, to argue with her, so you take two more lines of coke, and then you're more awake than ever. More Mandrax. Suddenly the telephone receiver falls out of your hand and you collapse on the floor. My God, I think, now it's over.[7]

After the German authorities prohibited Mandrax in 1982, Fassbinder was prescribed a stronger drug, Vesperox, at a dose of half a tablet nightly. An actress in his household found that he was taking three pills nightly instead. 'I was furious and I cried and cried. "Don't worry," he said very calmly. "I know exactly what I'm doing. When I take something at a certain time, Juliane, you don't have to be afraid. I know what goes with what and what's really enough and what isn't." He spoke so confidently. It's hard to understand why, but I believed him. I imagined him like a racing driver or a sky diver.'[8] A few months later he was found dead in bed, beside a half-consumed line of cocaine, with a burnt-out cigarette in his hand.

In contrast to the 'downer' Quaalude, there was another substance that both gay men and dancers found made them excited or euphoric. Amyl nitrite had been used since the mid-nineteenth century but had become an increasingly popular inhalant among California gay men during the 1960s. Until 1969 it was available over the counter in US pharmacies. After the restriction of its supply, its function as a pleasure drug was replaced in the US by butyl nitrite, isobutyl nitrite and octyl nitrite: these vasodilators (widely known as 'poppers') were sold as an incense or as room-odorisers. The two most popular brands in the USA were Rush and Locker Room: other brands included Thrust and Lightning Bolt. Some 12 million bottles were reportedly sold between 1973 and 1978: Rush had 60 per cent of the market. These inhalants dilated blood vessels and increased heartbeat; users of 'poppers' found that the drugs prevented premature ejaculation, increased sperm, enhanced orgasm, relaxed the anal sphincter, made the identity of the sexual partner seem unimportant, or raunchier. Poppers could produce light-headed joy, wild abandon and a distorted sense of reality, which made them alluring for dancers. The after-effects included a thudding headache. By the late 1970s this group of drugs was engendering panic among puritans. A typically distorted report (in the New York *Daily News* of 16 May 1977) was headlined, 'Death trip—it's called butyl nitrite—it's legal—and it's lethal'. In the early 1980s there were persistent attempts to attribute the spread of HIV to the use of poppers. Its reputation as a killer drug was enhanced by such absurdities as the episode of *Quincy* (a television serial about a Los Angeles coroner) depicting the murder of an admiral. His death was achieved by substituting amyl nitrite for champagne in a bottle that he cracked open at a ceremony. Poppers had a strong identification with homosexuality. 'I could not be any more of a man if I shaved my head', reflected Will Self, 'shoved a rag soaked with butyl nitrite in my face and joined a conga line of buggery.'[9] The drugs' popularity was, however, not exclusive to homosexuality; nor has their possession been criminalised in most of Europe. The unpleasant English politician Alan Clark (1928–99) described some fun with his Conservative colleague Nicholas Soames (b. 1948) during Agricultural Questions in the House of Commons in 1990. Soames regaled him with stories of 'an incredibly powerful new aphrodisiac he has discovered', Clark alleged. 'I liked the sound of this, and after Prime Minister's Questions I drove him back to his flat and he brought down a "phial". It has to be kept in the fridge.'[10]

But quaaludes and poppers were not the most fashionable drugs of the 1980s and 1990s—still less the most lucrative for illicit suppliers. Chemists concocted new substances that were not covered by legislation. Because they were made in bespoke laboratories with cheap and easily procurable chemicals, traditional prohibitionist measures (such as customs surveillance, international law enforcement and the environmental vandalism of crop-spraying) were irrelevant. Often the laboratories had a one-off production run, and were then dismantled. In 1985 Senator Lawton Chiles (b. 1930) of Florida launched a vehement campaign, including Congressional hearings, against designer drugs. Until his intervention, designer drugs were marginal to the US drug scene. Only four laboratories had been seized—two in Hollywood, one in San Diego and another in Texas—and this was a reliable pointer to the limited extent of the designer-drug fashion. But Chiles interpreted these figures as indicating a failure by law enforcement agencies to appreciate the gravity of the crisis. He declared authoritatively—but incorrectly—that PCP had begun in Los Angeles before spreading through the nation, while others recalled how California had corrupted other states with LSD in the 1960s. The hearings instigated by Chiles were full of bogus rhetoric. In the event, the Anti-Drug Abuse Act of 1986 was acclaimed in the Senate by a voice vote, without debate; it included a Controlled Substance Analogue Enforcement Act, known as the Designer Drug Act, which introduced wide and strict prohibitions on analogues. The American publicity raised European anxieties about a new wave of illicit synthetic drugs. For example, the Royal College of Psychiatrists' report of 1987, *Drug Scenes*, noted 'acute concern about the possible spread of so-called "designer drugs" from North America'.[11]

Supremely important among the designer drugs was methylene-dioxymethamphetamine (MDMA), best known as Ecstasy. MDMA was first synthesised in the Merck pharmaceutical laboratories in Germany in 1912. Merck took out patents but little further attention was given to MDMA until the early 1940s when it was tested as a 'truth drug' at the behest of the CIA. MDMA was again neglected until Alexander Shulgin (b. 1922), an American biochemist who was fascinated by psychedelic drugs, tested it personally during the early 1960s. The drug releases serotonin from nerve endings, and therefore generates strong feelings of contentment. Shulgin began promoting MDMA's therapeutic possibilities, and from 1976 other practitioners used it in marriage therapy and psychotherapy. Shulgin's scientific investigations continued until his licence from the DEA was withdrawn in 1994 after a raid on his home. MDMA's early alternative name was Adam, supposedly because it was a catharsis for the rebirth of the innocent 'inner child' from Eden sought in therapeutic encounters. Like Hubbard, Huxley and Laing in the pioneering years of LSD, Adam's early missionaries hoped to confine its use to clinically supervised sessions, and to establish its therapeutic legitimacy.

However, the frivolous, euphoric effects of MDMA became widely known: it became fashionable, under the slang name of 'X' or 'X-T-C', in the Starck club, a venue that opened in Dallas in 1984 catering to gays and more tolerant Texas straights. From the Starck the fashion spread to other Dallas and Austin clubs. It was legal at this time in the US—although in Britain as early as 1977 MDMA had been included with other amphetamines as a Class A substance (along with heroin and cocaine)—and was sold over the counter in these clubs. 'This was the Reagan years, remember, so it was pure hedonism,' recalls Wade Hampton III, a rich Dallas teenager who used to charge his purchases to parental credit cards. X soon spread from the gay crowd to fratboys and jocks. 'You'd go into a bathroom and see Southern Methodist University football players wiping the mascara from their eyes. It was the first time [Dallas] men had their testosterone broken down.' But these rich straight boys 'fucked it up', says Hampton, who left Texas to become a leader of the California rave scene.[12] 'You'd see the odd one careening into the Starck—taking five, seven, 10 pills in one go, overdoing it in a way that there was no *possibility* that the police and the newspapers wouldn't get involved. They were *obvious*, having to be rolled into hospitals in ridiculous states, having gone temporarily blind from overactive eyelid fluttering . . . They were *politicians'* kids. Their parents were all friends with George Bush, for God's sake. They were the death knell for legal ecstasy.'[13]

In July 1984 the sale of MDMA was made illegal, although possession remained legal until June 1985. Despite a judicial recommendation that MDMA be put on Schedule III, the DEA insisted that it was listed on Schedule I (the most serious category) along with heroin. The Court of Appeals confirmed this status in 1988. Immediately after prohibition in 1985, the US dance scene went underground and MDMA's price soared as its quality deteriorated. 'The banning', according to Wade Hampton, 'while it degenerated the quality of the drug itself, also did something quite positive—it created a counterculture. It was the first sign I ever saw of these pampered kids saying "fuck the system" in a *big* way.' The prohibition of MDMA in 1984–5 provided 'a defining aspect of the rave movement: the fight-the-power side, people thinking "I'm doing the right thing, I'm doing it for my own reasons and I will do it by any means necessary".'[14] Traditionally, the club scene had been far less important in youth culture and drug history in the US than Britain. Middle-class American teenagers were motorists: in the evening they went out driving. Many had telephones in their bedrooms, and took advantage of cheap or free local call rates to talk interminably and unsupervised to friends. Few of their British counterparts had cars or telephones, and sought privacy and seclusion from parental monitoring in clubs. MDMA narrowed this distinction. After 1985 DJs began organising warehouse parties in large American cities. Ecstasy and rave subculture proliferated in California during 1991–2 (partly promoted by English and Irish expatriates). The combination of music, technology and chemicals created a new 'night-time economy'. By 1993 dealers were exploiting the market, and becoming increasingly aggressive. Party-promoters denounced each other to the police; corrupt busts and brutal protection rackets were rampant. MDMA-users substituted methamphetamine, and moved into the addict lifestyle, until some rave parties were more like hanging out in a crack den.

There are three phases after taking Ecstasy, as the journalist and self-styled 'White Brit Rave Aesthete' Simon Reynolds (b. 1963) has described. 'Depending upon the emptiness of your stomach, it takes approximately an hour to "come up": the senses light up, you start "rushing", and for a short while the experience can be overwhelming, with dizziness and mild nausea. Then there's the plateau stage, which lasts about four hours, followed by a long, gentle comedown, and an afterglow phase which can last well into the next day'. With a lover, therapist or close friend, the user loses his emotional reserve and becomes intimate, confiding and tactile. At a rave, this intimacy—what ravers call being 'loved-up'—is dispersed in a polymorphous communion. 'Anyone who's been to a rave knows the electric thrill of catching a stranger's eye, making contact through the shared glee of knowing that you're both buzzing off the same drug-music synergy. Part of what makes the classic rave experience so rewarding and so addictive are the superficial but touching rituals of sharing water, shaking hands, having someone a tad worse for wear lean on you as if you were bosom buddies.' The noise and flashing lights at a rave accentuate the experience because 'Ecstasy makes colours, sounds, smells, tastes and tactile sensations more vivid (a classic indication that you've "come up" is that chewing gum suddenly tastes horribly artificial).'[15] MDMA produces dry mouth, nervousness, slight nausea but above all jaw tension leading to teeth-grinding (bruxism) or grimacing in cases of high consumption. Ravers compensate by chewing gum or sucking dummies. The drug's after-effects include fatigue, irritability and volatile moods; long-term users may experience anxiety, panic, depression or feelings of persecution. If taken in excess, Ecstasy may damage nerve cells using serotonin, and reduced serotonin levels may cause depression.

The English singer Mark Almond (b. 1957) began using Ecstasy during the early 1980s, and estimates that he spent £250,000 on the drug. 'You meet someone, take Ecstasy, fall in love—for a while at least—and it's so intense that you believe it.' But the emotions were spurious and only sustainable by continuously taking the pills. 'I created a false world around me, mainly fuelled by the drug,' he wrote. He was rueful after his final detoxification and rehabilitation. 'How many false friends, how many bouts of bad health would I suffer—the liver damage, the blackouts, the mood changes, the insanity? Unable to communicate, love, live life itself without an Ecstasy.' His problems were not confined to illegal drugs: 'Through Harley Street I was soon to discover the great cache of legal drugs publicly available—and the long-term effects of addiction to Benzodiazapine (sleeping pills), to which I was a slave for over twelve years.'[16]

Certainly, if Ecstasy is taken daily, the blissful empathy soon wanes; some users increase the dose, and like Almond plummet from exhausting weekend binges into depression from which they may try to recover by using other drugs, such as amphetamines. A few users have died of an allergic reaction after taking one pill, but Ecstasy-related fatalities have usually involved binges, adulterated pills or polydrug use. In Britain there are around 100,000 deaths annually from tobacco-related illnesses, 30–40,000 from alcohol-related illnesses and accidents, and 500 from paracetamol. On average, heroin and solvent abuse each claim about 150 lives each year, while amphetamine's death toll is about twenty-five. In the first ten years of British rave, with at its peak 500,000 people taking E every weekend, it was implicated in approximately sixty deaths: an average of six per year. Some of these deaths involve secondary factors, such as overheating while dancing, or drinking too much water when one has not overheated.[17] According to the Office for National Statistics, between 1993 and 1996 there was on average one E-related death every three weeks in Britain, or an average of seventeen annually. Around a million E tablets were consumed each weekend. In the same period approximately 1000 people a year died in motoring accidents involving drivers under twenty-one, and some 600 were killed each year by drunk motorists. In the US in 1998 there was a total of nine Ecstasy-related deaths: only three involved Ecstasy alone.

The first British newspaper report about MDMA, headlined 'How the Evil of Ecstasy Hit the Streets', was published in the *Daily Express* (25 April 1985). In a follow-up story 'Ecstasy—the Latest Narcotic Menace', the *Daily Telegraph* (1 May 1985) claimed that the DEA were briefing British police and customs on the drug. Thereafter British newspapers were saturated with alarmist inanity. The *Sun* doctor warned readers about the 'Evil of Ecstasy' in 1988: 'If you're young enough, there's a good chance you'll be sexually assaulted while under the influence.' He warned that if the drug induced memory flashbacks, 'you could kill yourself'.[18] In fact, unlike some other dance drugs, Ecstasy, although it may make people more sexually receptive, does not increase the desire for sex. US journalists had known since the 1880s, and their British counterparts since 1918, that sensational reports about drugs sell newspapers, especially if heavily laden with moral indignation. The symbiotic and sometimes corrupt relationship between crime-reporters and the police led to an eruption of distorted or dishonest reports about Ecstasy and other designer drugs.

During the late 1980s two cultural movements converged in a new development of Britain's dance-drug scene. Electronic music, with a harsh, mechanistic sound reflecting the experience of young inner-city blacks, became popular in the mid-1980s as 'house' or 'garage' music (named after the Warehouse in Chicago and Paradise Garage in New York). In 1987 DJs on Ibiza, the Mediterranean hippie island resort, developed their own version of house/garage with a relentless throbbing beat. Ecstasy enhanced the experience of such music, and having hit the dance scene in Ibiza in 1987, was well entrenched by the following year. People returning from Ibiza brought a taste for the new sound and for Ecstasy back to Britain. The drug was part of the British (mainly underground) acid house music scene from 1987. It was central to the more popular and nationally dispersed rave scene of 1990–92. Since 1993 it has become more than ever entrenched in the commercial dance scene.

Britain had a long tradition of young people 'living for the week-end'—notably the trainee accountant Mods of the early 1960s—but hosts of young people reserving the weekend to go clubbing on drugs dates from the harsh final years of the Thatcher government (1988–90). Initially Ecstasy perhaps had a particular appeal to working-class young people who felt rejected, devalued and estranged by the dominant Conservative outlook. But there were increasingly tens of thousands of hedonists who were simply determined to enjoy themselves, and pursued that purpose with the voracious consumerism of the Thatcher and Major era. 'I want pleasure, and I want to win'—an extract from the Vegas manifesto of the English artist Dave Hickey—encapsulates the dance culture of the 1990s. Catchphrases like *'avin' it large* or *'avin' it major* convey the greedy materialism of the experience.

Thatcher's memoirs begin with the sentence 'My first distinct memory is of traffic,' and the most representative symbol of her long premiership was the M25, an orbital motorway encircling London that was officially opened by her in 1986.[19] Young entrepreneurs began organising large-scale outdoor raves within easy motoring distance of the M25, knowing that these parties could be reached from all over southern England. The authorities understood that this phenomenon could not be addressed in terms of drug prohibition—it was impossible to arrest every supplier or charge everyone in possession of Ecstasy—so they approached it as a public order issue. The police opened a Pay Party Unit to try to suppress these events, and by November 1989 were monitoring thirty raves weekly. Legislation was quickly drafted (recalling the Douglas-Home government's moves against amphetamines a quarter of a century earlier). The Entertainment (Increased Penalties) Act, which came into force in July 1990, empowered the courts to levy fines of up to £20,000 and sentence to six months' jail anyone organising an unlicensed party. By this time, however, the outdoor raves scene had receded. The police had monitored only ten raves in February 1990: the diminution was not attributable to successful policing, but rather to the unpleasantness when criminals began intimidating party-organisers in order to extort some of the profits. In July 1990, a week after the Entertainment (Increased Penalties) Act came into force, police arrested 836 people at a warehouse party near Leeds in Yorkshire. This was the largest mass arrest in Britain since 1819. Although, after a free festival at Castlemorton in Worcestershire in May 1992, twenty-three people were arrested, no convictions were sustained during two years of legal activity reportedly costing taxpayers almost £4 million.

In other ways the Ecstasy scene deteriorated in 1992. Dealers were improving their profits by adulterating their pills with cheaper drugs, such as amphetamines, LSD and tranquillisers. Crude combinations of speed and acid were also pushed. Because of Ecstasy's illegality, consumers did not know what they were buying, and sometimes received ketamine instead. MDA, a hallucinatory version of MDMA, was exported from Latvia. 'Perhaps because the demand was too great', as Mark Almond wrote of the period from 1992, the drug became 'eventually so adulterated that a whole generation would speak of Ecstasy but never have really had it'. After going clubbing in the mid-1990s, there would be chill-out parties in his London flat. 'More often than not I didn't know who the hell anyone was—strangers lay around, lines of coke, lines of nonsense being spoken, gibberish, babbling, prattling. Tablets were bitten on, chipped bits passed around. Speed. Rambling.

Acid drops placed on strangers' tongues. Strangers talking ten to a dozen. Chattering. Blurting. Bragging. Barely able to focus.'[20]

Perhaps partly in consequence of a momentary disillusion with Ecstasy, a new fashion emerged around 1992 for GHB (gamma-hydroxybutyrate), a salty, odourless clear liquid swigged from little bottles (or less commonly a powder dissolved in drink). This concentrated version of an amino acid occurring naturally in the human brain was synthesised in the 1960s. Initially used to treat insomnia, alcoholism and labour pains, it was reclassified by the FDA as a drug rather than a nutrient in 1990. This announcement that GHB was unsafe and illicit except under FDA-approved, physician-supervised protocols boosted its popularity in dance clubs in some states; a limited fashion for it, too, developed in Britain. Individual reactions to GHB vary considerably. Some people find that it enhances sexual contact, or at least changes the experience of being touched; other people are left without erotic charge. This corresponds with the considerable variation in individuals' reaction to doses. One person may be rendered dangerously comatose by a dose that makes another feel agreeably relaxed. If mixed with alcohol or certain other substances, GHB can cause respiratory failure or coma. There were obstacles to drug education about GHB in Florida. 'If we had given out safe drug-taking flyers in the club, we should have been shut down in a minute,' said the owner of the Firestone Club in Orlando. 'That's what it's like here.' Local Florida politicians and community leaders set up a Rave Review Task Force as a result of which clubs were closed and teenagers curfewed, but without eliminating the GHB fashion. 'There's still just as many drugs,' according to a member of the Orlando scene. 'The only difference is that people do it in places where you can't see 'em.'[21]

When the Hollywood actor River Phoenix (1970–93) died on the pavement outside the Viper Room in Los Angeles, the death was widely (and incorrectly) attributed to GHB. This raised the drug's media notoriety, as did the death in 1996 of a Texas teenager, Hillory Farias, which was confidently attributed to GHB, although the evidence is inconclusive. This publicity made it more fashionable, and its nicknames of 'liquid x', 'Georgia home boy', 'Goop', 'gamma-o' and 'grievous bodily harm' became journalistic catchphrases. Georgia and several other states made GHB a Schedule I substance carrying a mandatory minimum sentence for sale or possession of thirty years: a penalty far exceeding that for first-degree murder in most European jurisdictions. GHB received hysterically inaccurate television publicity on the *Oprah Winfrey Show* in 1998, which led to a nationwide panic about its potential as a 'date rape' drug. GHB stories began to be copied by European journalists at this time. Its little bottles had enjoyed a minority following on the gay scene for several years, but now became modish among the more adventurous British dance drug-users. At the same time, in 1998, the pharmaceutical company Pfizer launched its drug Viagra, for men with difficulty in achieving erections. Viagra began being used on the British dance scene at about the same time as GHB by similar sorts of clubber. GHB was promoted to Schedule I of the US Controlled Substances Act in 2000. Under a bill signed by Clinton, those convicted of possession, manufacture or supply of GHB became liable to up to twenty years and a fine of $1 million for a first offence, or 'not more than life', in the DEA's phraseology, in cases involving death or serious injury. This seems ludicrously disproportionate. In Britain, in an article headlined 'Be Sure of What You are Drinking', 'this unpleasant drug' was denounced by the medical correspondent of *The Times* as 'potentially very dangerous'.[22]

Another designer drug, Rohypnol (flunitrazepam), is a powerful benzodiazepine sold by Hoffman-La Roche. Originally used by body-builders, the FDA banned Rohypnol in 1990. At about the same time, body-builders began selling 'roofies' in the rave club scene around Orlando, Florida, touting the drug as having aphrodisiac properties. A small bottle or vial can make some people feel more tactile in a slightly drowsy way, and a few people horny. If mixed with alcohol, especially by people with a low body rate, it can cause unconsciousness, amnesia, respiratory problems and even coma. Rohypnol became known as a date rape drug around 1996. As one Florida DJ recalled, 'There was one guy that got sentenced to twenty years because he would slip roofies in girls' drinks, then take the chicks home and take videos of himself doing the chicks, with the chicks passed out.'[23] Florida and other states introduced thirty-year prison terms for possession. The attraction of GHB and Rohypnol for drug prohibitionists was that they could be called 'rape drugs'. They could be enlisted to undermine the libertarian argument that recreational drug use was a consensual, victimless crime. The vague but sensational publicity with which these drugs were cloaked by local politicians, journalists and Oprah Winfrey (b.

1954) gave the impression that rape by this method was prevalent. It was implied—quite erroneously—that every male taking either drug was intent on 'date rape'. There was seldom reference to the historically most entrenched date rape drug of all, alcohol.

The Rohypnol panic reached Britain in December 1997. In that month the Roofie Foundation was set up to provide a telephone helpline, legal advice and a safe house for 'victims' of Rohypnol. 'In America, women are being advised not to accept drinks from strangers,' the Foundation's director said. 'We have to let women here know that they are potential victims if they are having a drink out of an open glass in a pub or club, or even having a cup of tea in a private place.' Glossing this story, a Sunday newspaper reported, 'Hundreds of women are being attacked each year under the influence of a "date rape" drug which is freely available in Britain. Would-be rapists are able to slip the tiny purple tablets into drinks, inducing prolonged amnesia and a trance-like uninhibited state which leaves women incapable of resisting unwanted sexual advances.'[24] The claim that several hundreds had been raped with the drug was unsupported, and as dubious as the claim that Rohypnol was 'freely available'. It was a prescription drug that was not supplied under the NHS. A few days later reports surfaced of several Scottish teenage girls who had been raped in incidents which the police—perhaps correctly—related to Rohypnol. 'What we're seeing is just the tip of the iceberg,' Scotland Yard speculated. The Roofie Foundation's director averred in yet another interview that Rohypnol 'heightens a woman's sex drive in some cases and she can thus appear a willing participant, which makes it still harder in court to prove she was raped'.[25] It is doubtful if there were any rape trials in which the issue of Rohypnol consent had arisen: the Forensic Science Service tested for Rohypnol in eighteen rape cases in England and Wales during 1997 with negative results on every occasion. Nevertheless, with effect from May 1998, statutory controls were imposed on Rohypnol. Unauthorised possession (without prescription) became a criminal offence subject to a maximum penalty of two years' imprisonment, or an unlimited fine, or both.[26]

Following the expensive failure of the Castlemorton rave prosecutions, Britain's Criminal Justice and Public Order Act of 1994 targeted a range of marginal types—squatters, travellers, fox-hunt saboteurs and environmental activists—with new restrictions. Young people partying at raves and free festivals were also brought under legislative controls. Defining a rave as a hundred people playing amplified music 'characterised by the emission of a succession of repetitive beats', the Act empowered any police officer who 'reasonably believes' that people were assembling for a rave, to order them to disperse. Failure to comply became punishable by three months' imprisonment or a fine of £2500. The police were also empowered to stop anyone coming within a mile of an incipient rave. Though the law discouraged large-scale noisy outdoor parties, particularly in the countryside, smaller parties continued in desolate, brutalised urban settings.

The most egregious example of reactive legislation intended to gratify public prejudice was the Public Entertainments (Drug Misuse) Act of 1997. This despicable piece of stunt law-making empowered licensing authorities, acting on the advice of local police, to revoke the licences of clubs and other entertainment venues that failed to repress drug use on their premises. Apart from increasing the opportunities for police corruption, the Act is particularly objectionable because it raised the possibility that club-owners would begin excluding drug workers giving harm-reduction advice for fear that their presence would arouse police interest. This was misguided because clubbers are generally susceptible to health information and harm reduction information.[27] As with the prohibition of GHB education in the Florida clubs, this strategy seems intended to damage dance drug-users, so that occasional deaths can be publicised as reasons to abstain completely from drugs.

To take one example from 1997, a Scottish boy aged thirteen took three Ecstasy tablets while loitering in a wood, disliked the sensation and, having heard that water counteracted its effects, drank an immense amount of water. As water consumption is recommended to prevent dehydration during a night's dancing on drugs (including amphetamines), the child died of water poisoning. His grieving mother was duly produced on a public platform by David Macauley, Campaign Director of Scotland Against Drugs (SAD), to support opposition to drug education or harm-reduction projects. SAD had been launched in 1996 with partial government funding. Out of a total budget of £1.5 million, it spent £27,000 on harm-reduction (supporting a body supplying accurate information on drugs) and £900,000 on a glossy multi-media advertising campaign focused on dance drugs. The only drug named in the ensuing disinformation was Ecstasy, on to which was foisted the attributes of sundry other substances. SAD's campaign suggested that rat-poison was used to cut Ecstasy, although the only known cases of such adulteration involved heroin. It was suggested that women intoxicated on dance drugs would be easier prey to sexual attacks (which is untrue of Ecstasy but accurate about alcohol), or would develop amnesia and end up in bed with strangers (the occasional problem with Rohypnol). The advertisements even implied Ecstasy damaged lungs like tobacco. 'Hundreds of Scots died from drugs last year,' the campaign declared. The actual figure for 1995 was 251 comprising 155 opiate overdoses and ninety-six suicides using analgesics such as paracetamol. This compared with 20,000 Scots who had died of tobacco-related disease and 4000 of alcohol-related disease. SAD's lurid, slipshod publicity is not surprising given its resistance to less emotive but more precisely informed discourse on drugs. In 1997 Macauley of SAD denounced an academic report on socially integrated, functioning heroin-users as 'horribly irresponsible'. SAD's media adviser described drug workers involved in harm-reduction as 'pro-drug' and 'happy-clappy middle-class muesli eaters'. Another senior figure in SAD declared, 'If these people get their way, they are as good as giving kids an injecting kit with their pens and pencils when they start school.'[28]

The scare approach fails in anti-drugs propaganda. As Benedict King (b. 1970) explained to *Daily Telegraph* readers in 1997:

No one is going to listen to warnings about drugs being dangerous. Part of the attraction of drugs, motorbikes, and for all I know riding to hounds or being a war correspondent, rests on the same principle. Death does not cross the mind of most young people, and they are often keen to give the impression that they don't care if they live or die. The challenge is not to convince people that drugs are dangerous, but that they are uncool, and you can't do that while they are illegal.

Indeed it needs to be reiterated that for many adolescents, of both sexes, taking risks is central to the process of maturing. King's approach was bursting with good sense. 'What teenagers are genuinely scared of is embarrassment,' he wrote. 'If it was pointed out that ecstasy was extremely unlikely to kill you, but that it is guaranteed to make you grind your teeth together in an unattractive way and to talk gushing, sentimental drivel to people you don't like; if it was pointed out that it would make you a crashing bore, and that in the morning the memory of all this folly, combined with the hangover from hell, would make you wish you had died, then the anti-drugs campaign might strike a chord. As propaganda, it would at least have the benefit of being true.'[29] Instead there has been institutional dishonesty about the effects of Ecstasy. This method is futile in a society where so many young adults have taken drugs and lived unscathed. A 1996 survey concluded that 85 per cent of people who described themselves as 'clubbers' had used Ecstasy. With this level of Ecstasy consumption, it is claimed that illegal drugs have entered the mainstream; but this seems an exaggeration. Dance drugs are a normalised leisure activity among young people, but they are not yet a majority experience. The Health Education Authority's 1999 survey found that 39 per cent of people aged sixteen to nineteen and 33 per cent aged twenty to twenty-four had used illicit drugs during the previous year. It also indicated that among sixteen- to nineteen-year-olds, the age cohort with the largest proportion of drug-users, 54 per cent of respondents had *never* used an illicit drug. One would not suspect from the emphasis given during the 1990s to Ecstasy that the HEA found that among ten- to twenty-four-year-olds, amphetamine use as a dance drug was more than twice as common as that of Ecstasy. The rate of amphetamine consumption stood at about 16 per cent compared with 7 per cent for Ecstasy. This was hinted at, though, by a phrase in a Jarvis Cocker song, 'sorted for Es and Wizz'.

The British street price of E fell from £25–50 per tablet in the mid-1980s to under £10 by 2000. (A wrap of cocaine cost about £10 in 1999 compared with £30 in 1996; a wrap of 40 per cent heroin cost about the same.) A path-breaking study of the British dance drug scene of the 1990s found that clubbers using dance drugs at the weekend had a distinct profile. They had been more adventurous in early adolescence, and less inhibited by risks. Most smoked tobacco daily, drank regularly and used cannabis—and had started using these substances at earlier than average ages. Although in this respect their early histories resembled those of problem drug-users, and despite the British authorities resolutely keeping Ecstasy as a Class A substance, they did not fit into the opiate-addict classification. They avoided heroin and crack cocaine and reserved most Class A drug use for weekends. The vast majority held legitimate, even remunerative jobs; usually they were well educated; all social backgrounds (but especially the professional) were represented. Despite weekly violations of the Misuse of Drugs Act, they were not generally delinquent. These recreational drug-users represent about 10 per cent of the British young adult population, and their controlled, functional use of prohibited substances is not appropriately policed by drug enforcement techniques directed at opiate-dependent problem users.[30]

Opponents of this lifestyle have to convince that hedonism is deviant. Many of them mustered for the prolonged orgy of attitudinising that occurred during the House of Commons debate in January 1997 on the Public Entertainments (Drug Misuse) Act. The level of analysis is indicated by the contribution of Sir Michael Neubert (b. 1933). First he condemned Paul Flynn (b. 1935), the Welsh MP who at some cost to his career has been a stalwart critic of the stubborn failures of Wars on Drugs. 'Although he may rail against tabloid papers and so-called "tabloid politics", the great merit of tabloid newspapers is that they provide a clear, simple message that everyone can understand.' Neubert saw no dangers if that message was oversimplified or inaccurate. 'Emphasising all the technicalities which seem to cast doubt on the central proposition that drug abuse is essentially evil is against the best interests of the great mass of the British people.' Neubert claimed that his constituency, Romford, was 'the night-spot of the south' (Romford's US equivalent is Newark, New Jersey), which he thought gave him expertise. He had been to a club in Romford, watched the bouncers at work and was impressed by their door policy. 'Anybody wearing dirty jeans was rejected.' Evidently one can always tell a drug-user by their shabby clothes. Neubert regarded all such types as isolated, alienated, and probably jobless social deviants; he had no idea that dance drug-users were mainstream citizens in conventional employment. He could not grasp that dance drugs had become a leisure accessory functioning as just another commodity that helped to define a lifestyle. A young person's decision to use drugs did not depend on availability: it was a matter of consumer choice in a vibrant, variegated, albeit illegal, market. Neubert understood no difference between heroin and Ecstasy. 'Those of us who are fortunate to lead ordinary working lives cannot imagine the life of the drug-taker who lives by the day or by the hour, robbing in order to obtain easy money to pay for a quick fix,' he intoned.[31] His ignorance had its counterpart in another Essex man, the police officer Paul Betts, whose daughter died in 1995 after taking Ecstasy and gulping a vast amount of water. Betts once said, 'Being a copper and picking them up off the streets to take them to Accident & Emergency or to the morgue, to me, people who took drugs were all drop-outs. Either that or they were filthy rich.'[32]

Neubert's was not the silliest speech on the Public Entertainments Bill of 1997. A politician who had made a fortune from the privatisation of rubbish-bin collection thought that the strategies of Anslinger and Reagan were sure winners. He demanded 'zero-tolerance for drug-abusers' with mandatory imprisonment for everyone found in possession of drugs. Despite the protest of the Deputy Speaker, the Bill passed immediately from Second Reading to Committee, was immediately reported, read a third time without amendment, and passed. Both this procedure and the resultant Act vindicate the notion that politicians' legislation on drugs is the executive expression of human immaturity.

Part of the difficulty is that politicians gain their reputations for being practical by strenuously supporting what has already happened. Their language on drugs has steadily and intentionally narrowed the range of the thinkable. It has favoured moral abstractions that deter or dissipate thought, and muffle individual experience. The result has been a set of dodges rather than policies that command respect. In 1987, the year before acid house, 26,278 people were convicted or cautioned in Britain for drug offences. This figure rose from 47,616 in 1991 to 93,631 in 1995. Arrests for possession of marijuana increased by over 40 per cent between 1994 and 1998 while the number of arrests for dealing remained stable. Britain now has the most drug-experienced young population in Europe. It has proportionately as many young drug-takers as the USA. According to one authoritative estimate published in 2001, 'By the end of adolescence, accepting regional differences, between 50% and 60% will have tried illicit drugs, and up to 25% will be occasional to regular users.'[33] Despite the Blair government (elected in 1997) declaring that its drug strategy would focus on heroin and cocaine, cannabis possession accounts for up to 85 per cent of drug arrests.

Adults outside the Muslim world are entitled to buy, possess and use alcoholic drinks. They have, by custom, a right to be intoxicated in private. Someone who dislikes drunkenness in others is not entitled to interfere in another citizen's drinking as that person drinks in the privacy of their home, or somewhere appropriate such as a club. It seems irrational not to apply similar principles to Ecstasy. Admittedly its excessive use can lead to an aftermath of depression, but so do many other activities—having children too young, or too many children, or being isolated in the home—which the government does not seek to prohibit. It may cause brain damage in long-term heavy users, but so does alcohol, and adverse reactions to legal drugs administered in US hospitals kill around 100,000 Americans annually. Philip Jenkins (b. 1952) argues that puritanism is at the root of the prohibition problem. 'None of the regulating agencies accepts that a drug should have as its primary goal the elevation of mood, the giving of pleasure, the enhancement of sexual feeling or the refining of consciousness, at least for normally functioning people (as opposed to the clinically depressed). If none of these features is accepted as desirable or even tolerable, then the slightest evidence of harm automatically outweighs the (supposedly nonexistent) benefits of a given chemical, and it falls under the legal taboo as stringent as that imposed by any religion.'[34]

The War on Drugs launched by Nixon in 1969 has turned into the Thirty Years' War. With its aim of unconditional surrender, it is a war that cannot be won. Drugs remain dangerous, but they can also be rewarding to both suppliers and users: accordingly they remain ineradicable. Instead of resolutely narrowing the range of the thinkable, European politicians should evaluate the drug possibilities other than prohibition. One alternative would be to remove all controls on the production and marketing of drugs except the supply to children. A second alternative would be the state provision of drugs, or the commercial sale of drugs under strict governmental control of quantity and quality. The third would be government regulation of the production and sale of drugs, accompanied by treatment and harm-reduction programmes, and truthful drug education for children. The Dutch have provided an exemplary model of this. The first Amsterdam coffee shop licensed to sell cannabis under government regulations opened in 1978; there are now about 1500 such coffee shops in the Netherlands. Since 1978 there has been virtually no solvent abuse in the Netherlands, and after the taking of cannabis out of the black market, its use actually fell— although it revived in the mid-1980s as part of the house and rave music scenes. Dutch heroin use is lower than that in Britain or France as a result of separating the cannabis and heroin-suppliers: the Dutch junkie population is ageing, for there are not many new recruits. The licensed café system could be extended to other substances such as Ecstasy.

The European antithesis of the Dutch approach was provided in Scotland at the close of the twentieth century. In 1996, a year before a general election in which the number of Conservative MPs representing Scottish constituencies fell to zero, Michael Forsyth (b. 1954), Secretary of State for Scotland in the Conservative government, tried to rally his party behind a cause that he thought would unite Scottish opinion. He launched the Scotland Against Drugs campaign with these resounding words: 'Once again our way of life is threatened, this time by an enemy within. The drugs epidemic is a scourge as terrible as any medieval plague. Let us, as a nation, make a New Year resolution that 1996 is the year in which we will turn back the tide of drug abuse which is engulfing our young people and threatening our civilisation. Our aim is nothing less than to win back Scotland from the drug culture and liberate a generation.'[35] No acknowledgement here that drugs may be fun. No sense that their attraction is increased by such portentous yet trite slogans. No acceptance that the illicit drugs market is sustained by an economic reward system only made possible by prohibition. The paranoia, the overheated language, the mission to save civilisation, the huge and unrealistic policy targets with their implication that harm-minimisation targets are immoral, the political opportunism: everything is wrong-headed about Lord Forsyth of Drumlean's sound-bite.

The European powers can choose between Amsterdam and Edinburgh: between Regulation and Prohibition. Their decision should be taken in a temper of pragmatic scepticism. Depending on their choice, they will then confront either a minor chronic pest or an unbeatable and destructive adversary.

Acknowledgements

M Y FIRST DEBTS are to three exceptionally impressive individuals: Dr Dale Beckett, Dr Ann Dally and the Rev. Kenneth Leech who agreed to be interviewed by me and supplied papers and other material from their own collections. Readers of this book will realise how much I owe to their generosity and how admirable their example remains for those involved in British drug scenes. I have also received astute advice from my friend Dr Peter Nathan, and a trickle of literary references from another friend, Alan Bell. Jenny Davenport and Christopher Phipps criticised drafts of the book, and gave invaluable guidance. Toby Mundy gave rigorous comments on earlier chapters; later versions have been improved by the advice of Michèle Hutchison, Peter Tallack and Bill Hamilton. The sources of other comment and information must remain anonymous. Overall I should stress that although, as Charles Lamb said in similar circumstances, I have milked many cows, the butter I churn is my own.

I thank Professor Edward Mendelson for his permission to quote from the unpublished writings of W. H. Auden: these are copyright 2001 by the estate of W. H. Auden. The permission of the Earl of Derby and of the late Maureen, Marchioness of Dufferin and Ava, to use other unpublished diaries and correspondence is gratefully acknowledged. Douglas Mathews compiled the index and sanitised the proofs: it was a pleasure to have his help.

The resources and staff of the London Library and of the Wellcome Library for the History of Medicine were indispensable to the research of this book. I am also grateful to the archivists of the Berg Collection at New York Public Library (Auden correspondence); the Thomas Fisher Library at the University of Toronto (Bland papers); Lambeth Palace Library (Davidson papers); British Library (Gladstone and Curzon Viceregal papers); and the Public Record Office (for the papers of the Home Office, Foreign Office, Board of Trade, Directorate of Public Prosecutions, Law Officers and Premier's Office).

Notes

ABBREVIATIONS USED IN THE NOTES
BJA: *British Journal of Addiction*
BMJ: *British Medical Journal*
JAMA: *Journal of American Medical Association*

CHAPTER ONE

1. Sir Richard Carne Temple, ed., *A Geographical Account of Countries Round the Bay of Bengal, 1669 to 1679 by Thomas Bowrey* (1905), 80–81.
2. Ibid., 78–9.
3. Francisco Guerra, 'Sex and Drugs in the 16th Century', *British Journal of Addiction*, 69 (1974), 269–74.
4. Thomas Shadwell, *Complete Works*, III (1927), 38.
5. Sir John Chardin, *Travels in Persia* (1927), 246–7.
6. Ibid., 246.
7. John Pinkerton, *Voyages and Travels*, X (1811), 153.
8. Sir Clements Markham, ed., *The Letters of Amerigo Vespucci* (1894), 25–6.
9. Nicolás Monardes, *Joyfull Newes out of the Newe Founde Worlde, Englished by John Frampton, Merchant*, II (1925), 32.
10. Joseph De Acosta, *The Natural and Moral History of the Indies*, book IV, chapter 22; 1880 edition of Sir Clements Markham, vol. I, 245–6.
11. Antonio Julián, *La perla de la América* (Madrid, 1787), quoted 'The Narcotics We Indulge In', *Blackwood's Magazine*, 74 (1853), 626.
12. Chardin, op. cit., 243.
13. Virginia Berridge, *Opium and the People* (1999), xxii.
14. Homer, *The Odyssey*, book IV, lines 220–232, trans. E.V. Rieu, 1951 edition, 68.
15. A. S. F. Gow and A. F. Scholfield, eds., *Nicander* (1953), 123, 125.
16. Edward Gibbon, *The History of the Decline and Fall of the Roman Empire*, I (1776), chapter 3.
17. John Scarborough, 'The opium poppy in Hellenistic and Roman medicine,' in Roy Porter and Mikuláš Teich, eds., *Drugs and Narcotics in History* (1995), 17–18.

18. Robert Burton, *The Anatomy of Melancholy* (1621), part 2, section 4, subsection II.

19. Thomas Willis, 'Medicine in Man's Body', sec. VII, ch. 3, 139.

20. Louis Lewin, *Phantastica* (1931), 38.

21. Cristóbal Acosta, *Tratado de las drogas y medecinas de las Indias Orientales* (1582), 408–15.

22. [William Biddulph in] *Collection of Voyages and Travels Consisting of Authentic Writers in our Tongue . . . from the curious and valuable Library of the late Earl of Oxford*, I (1745), 797.

23. George Sandys, *A Relation of a Journey begun An: Dom: 1610* (1627), 66; Samuel Purchas, *Purchas His Pilgrimage*, IV (1905), 35.

24. Pinkerton, op. cit., IX (1811), 115.

25. Chardin, op. cit., 243–4.

26. Thomas Sydenham, *Works*, I (1848), 55.

27. Ibid., I, 173.

28. Willis, 'Mans Body', sec. VII, ch. 3.

29. Sydenham, op. cit., I, 173.

30. Ibid., I, 98.

31. Ibid., I, 180–81.

32. Willis, 'Mans Body', VII, i, 125–6.

33. Ibid., VII, i, 128.

34. Ibid., VII, ii, 133, 135.

35. Ibid., VII, i, 133, 135.

36. Kenneth Dewhurst, *Thomas Willis's Oxford Lectures* (1980), 58.

37. Samuel Pepys, *Diary*, V (1971), 151.

38. William Donaldson, letter in *Edinburgh Journal of Medical Science*, I (1826), 475–6.

39. Nicholas Lémery, *A Course of Chymistry* (1677), 278.

40. Pierre Pomet, *A Compleat History of Drugs* (1737 edition), 216–17.

41. Lémery, op. cit., 280–81.

42. Burton, *Anatomy of Melancholy*, part 2, section 4, sub-section 5.

43. Richard Davenport-Hines, *Vice* (1993), 161.

44. Davies, *Complete Poems*, I, 48–9, 53.

45. John Hayward, ed., *The Letters of Saint-Evremonde* (1930), 259.

46. M. Ageyev, *Novel with Cocaine* (1999 edition), 173–4.

47. John Locke, *Essay Concerning Human Understanding* (1690), book II, ch. I, § 6.

48. Locke, *Human Understanding*, book II, ch. I, ß 11.

49. Ibid., book II, ch. xxvii, § 23.

CHAPTER TWO

1. John Jones, *Mysteries of Opium Reveal'd* (1700), 170.

2. Ibid., 22.

3. Ibid., 24.

4. Ibid., 25.

5. Ibid., 34–5.

6. Ibid., 31.

7. Ibid., 245.

8. Ibid., 32.

9. Samuel Crumpe, *An Inquiry into the Nature and Properties of Opium* (1793), 12–13.

10. James Dallaway, *Constantinople Ancient and Modern* (1797), 77.

11. Martin Booth, *Opium* (1996), 111–12.

12. David Edward Owen, *British Opium Policy in China and India* (1933), 58.

13. Charles Ross, ed., *Correspondence of Charles, First Marquis Cornwallis*, II (1859), 1–2.

14. Peter Ward Fay, *The Opium War 1840–1842* (1975), 43.

15. Charles Alston, *Lectures on the Materia Medica, containing the natural history of drugs, their virtues and doses,* II (1770), 460.

16. For this observation, and throughout this chapter, I am indebted to Andreas-Holger Maehle, 'Pharmacological experimentation with opium in the eighteenth century', in Porter and Teich, *Drugs and Narcotics,* 52–70.

17. George Young, *Treatise upon Opium* (1753), 14.

18. Ibid., 28–9.

19. Ibid., iv–v.

20. Ibid., 38–9.

21. Sir Almroth Wright, 'Suffrage Fallacies', *The Times,* 28 March 1912, 7f.

22. Young, op. cit., 77–8.

23. Ibid., 79–80.

24. Ibid., 59, 61.

25. Ibid., 106–7.

26. George Cheyne, *The English Malady* (1733), 208–9.

27. Earl of Bessborough, *Lady Bessborough and her Family Circle* (1940), 40.

28. Earl of Bessborough, *Georgiana* (1955), 97.

29. James Boswell, *The Life of Samuel Johnson* (1791), 1341.

30. Ronald W. Clark, *Benjamin Franklin* (1983), 415.

31. Young, op. cit., 98–9.

32. Abraham Cowley, 'To Dr Scarbrough' (1656), stanza 6.

33. *The Lancet*, 23 August 1845, 202.

34. John Emsley, *The Shocking History of Phosphorus* (2000).

35. Alston, op. cit., II, 458–60.

36. Young, op. cit., 103.

37. John Parris, *Pharmacologia* (1843), 170.

38. Roger Lonsdale, *Eighteenth Century Women Poets* (1989), 318.

39. Horace Walpole, *Correspondence*, XVII, 295.

40. Alonzo Calkins, *Opium and the Opium Appetite* (1871), 142.

41. Ernest Lovell, ed., *Lady Blessington's Conversations with Lord Byron* (1969), 130.

42. Walpole, op. cit., XXXIX, 149.

43. Boswell, op. cit., 1271.

44. R. W. Chapman, ed., *Jane Austen's Letters* (1952), 9.

45. Bessborough, *Family Circle*, 99.

46. Lord Broughton, *Recollections of a Long Life*, III (1910), 204.

47. Viscount Furneaux, *William Wilberforce* (1974), 78.

48. Mark Bence-Jones, *Clive of India* (1974), 71, 191, 241, 247, 299.

49. Alethea Hayter, *Opium and the Romantic Imagination* (1968), 25.

50. Henri de Catt, *Frederick the Great*, trans. F. S. Flint, vol. II (1916), 40–2; Giles McDonough, *Frederick the Great* (1999), 280.

51. Bernard Mandeville, *The Fable of the Bees* (1934 edition), 49.

52. Ibid., 74.

53. Ibid., 45.

54. Baron de Montesquieu, *Persian Letters* (1721), letter 33.

55. Sir James Porter, *Observations on the Religion, Law, Government and Manners of the Turks*, II (1768), 96–9.

56. Alexander Russel, *The Natural History of Aleppo*, I (1794 edition), 126–7.

57. James Dallaway, *Constantinople Ancient and Modern* (1797), 77–8.

58. Russel, op. cit., I, 128–9.

59. Russel, op. cit., I, 129–30.

60. Baron de Tott, *Memoirs of the Turks and Tartars*, I (1786), 141–3 (translation of *Mémoires du Baron Tott sur les Turcs et les Tartares* (Amsterdam, 1784).

61. Boswell, op. cit., 1199.

62. Dallaway, op. cit., 78.

63. Walter Benjamin, *Baudelaire* (1997), 40.

CHAPTER THREE

1. Joseph Cottle, *Reminiscences of Samuel Taylor Coleridge and Robert Southey* (1847), 362–3.

2. Case of Delirium Tremens from Opium Eating', *Lancet*, 28 February 1846, 254–6.

3. House of Commons debates, 4 April 1843, vol. 68, column 412.

4. *Athenaeum*, 26 October 1839, 804.

5. Coleridge, *Notebooks*, III, 3539.

6. Bessborough, *Family Circle*, 134.

7. *Athenaeum*, 16 June 1838, 428.

8. Coleridge, *Letters*, III, 125–6.

9. Ibid., IV, 674–5.

10. Duke of Buckingham and Chandos, *Memoirs of the Court of England during the Regency*, I (1856), 145.

11. Castalia, Countess Granville, ed., *Lord Granville Leveson Gower: Private Correspondence*, II (1916), 422.

12. Duke of Wellington, ed., *Wellington and his friends* (1965), 70.

13. Lytton Strachey and Roger Fulford, eds., *The Greville Memoirs*, I (1938), 333.

14. Lord Colchester, ed., *A Political Diary, 1828–1850, by Edward Law, Lord Ellenborough*, II (1881), 34–5, 100, 167, 224–5.

15. Wellington, op. cit., 90; Brian Hill, *The Greedy Book* (1966), 24.

16. House of Commons debates, 4 April 1843, vol. 68, col. 400.

17. *The Times*, 28 June 1830, 3c.

18. Earl of Ilchester, ed., *Elizabeth, Lady Holland to her Son* (1946), 7.

19. Thomas De Quincey, *Collected Writings*, III (1897), 426–7.

20. *Lancet*, 28 January 1832, 614–17.

21. Jonathan Pereira, *Elements of Materia Medica*, II (1843), 1293.

22. G. R. Mart, 'Effects of the Practice of Opium Eating', *Lancet*, 11 February 1832, 711.

23. William Marsden, *The History of Sumatra* (1811), 278.

24. G. H. Smith, 'On Opium Smoking among the Chinese', *Lancet*, 10 February 1842, 709.

25. F. Robinson, 'On the Utility of a Knowledge of the Temperaments', *Lancet*, 28 March 1846, 360.

26. H. J. C. Grierson, ed., *The Letters of Sir Walter Scott*, V (1933), 29.

27. John Harriott, *Struggles through Life*, III (1815), 392.

28. De Quincey, op. cit., III, 389.

29. Lord Lytton, *Falkland* (1827), chapter 1; Knebworth edition, 24.

30. De Quincey, op. cit., III, 443.

31. Ibid., 388.

32. Ibid., 236.

33. Lord Lytton, *Lucretia* (1846), pt. III, ch. 12; 210–11 of 1853 edition.

34. Coleridge, *Notebooks*, III, 3407, 4272.

35. *Athenaeum*, 17 December 1859, 815.

36. Sir William Des Vœux, 'A Letter to the Opium Commission', *Nineteenth Century*, 35 (1894), 323.

37. H. H. Kane, *Drugs that Enslave* (1881), 3.

38. A. Richard Oliver, *Charles Nodier, Pilot of Romanticism* (1964), 38, 110.

39. Coleridge, *Letters*, V, 79–80.

40. Cottle, *Reminiscences*, 373.

41. Coleridge, *Letters*, II, 212.

42. Ibid., IV, 626.

43. Coleridge, *Essays*, II, 140–41.

44. Coleridge, *Notebooks*, III, 3431.

45. Coleridge, *Letters*, II, 110.

46. Mary Moorman, ed., *The Letters of William and Dorothy Wordsworth*, II (1969), 399.

47. Coleridge, *Notebooks*, II, 2091.

48. Earl Leslie Griggs, 'Samuel Taylor Coleridge and Opium', *Huntington Library Quarterly*, vol. 17 (1954), 366, 377.

49. Grierson, *Walter Scott Letters*, V, 97.

50. Prosper Mérimée, *Correspondance Générale*, III (1943), 134–5.

51. Ibid., 176, 255.

52. Ibid., 175.

53. Ibid., IV, 478.

54. Ibid., VIII, 529–30, 534.

55. *The Times*, 26 July 1841, 6a; Sir Alfred Lyall, *The Life of the Marquis of Dufferin and Ava*, I (1905), 25; Sir Harold Nicolson, *Helen's Tower* (1937), 66.

56. W. D. Chowne, 'Poisoning by Laudanum', *Lancet*, 20 August 1842, 706, 710.

57. *Annual Register* 1823, 1★–19★.

58. Harrison Ainsworth, *Rookwood* (1836), chapter V, p. 72.

59. Edward Bulwer-Lytton, *Lucretia*, part I, chapter X; p. 94 of 1853 edition.

60. Le Sténographie Parisien, *Affaire Castaing, Accusation d'Empoissonement* (1823), 190.

61. Anthony Todd Thompson, *The London Dispensatory* (1831), 479.

62. C. H. Phillips, ed., *The Correspondence of Lord William Cavendish Bentinck*, I (1977), 32–3.

63. *Cavendish Bentinck Correspondence*, I, 454, 483.

64. Sir Stamford Raffles, *The History of Java* (1817), 102–3.

65. Count Magnus Björnstjerna, *The British Empire in India* (1840), 199.

66. Charles Alexander Bruce, *Report on the Manufacture of Tea, and on the extent and produce of the tea plantations in Assam* (Calcutta, 1839), 32–3.

67. *Dictionary of National Biography: Missing Persons* (1993), 348.

68. Despatch of Captain Charles Elliot, 18 April 1838, quoted Sir James Graham, House of Commons debates, 7 April 1840, cols. 717–18.

69. Hosea B. Morse, *The International Relations of the Chinese Empire*, I (1910), 254.

70. Ibid., I, 659.

71. M. R. D. Foot and H. C. G. Matthew, eds., *The Gladstone Diaries*, III (1974), 29.

72. House of Commons debates, 8 April 1840, columns 813, 818.

73. House of Commons debates, 12 April 1886, vol. 304, column 1343.

74. Arthur Benson and Viscount Esher, eds., *The Letters of Queen Victoria 1837–1861*, I (1907), 261.

75. G. H. Smith, 'On Opium Smoking among the Chinese', *Lancet*, 10 February 1842, 708.

76. Smith, 'Opium Smoking', 709–10; James Hill, 'Opium Smoking in China', *Lancet*, 12 March 1842, 821.

77. Coleridge, *Notebooks*, III, 4406.

78. Thomas Carlyle, *Critical and Miscellaneous Essays*, II (1899), 59.

79. Edouard Foucard, *Paris Inventeur: Physiologie de l'industrie française* (Paris, 1844), 222.

80. Thomson, *Dispensatory*, 486.

81. J. A. Paris, *Pharmacologia* (1843), 75.

82. William Toynbee, ed., *The Diaries of William Charles Macready*, I (1912), 278, 396.

83. *Parliamentary Papers*, XIX (1834). Factories Inquiry Commission, Supplementary Report of the Central Board, part I, ordered by the House of Commons to be printed 25 March 1834; D.3, pp. 240–41.

84. Gladstone, *Diaries*, III, 487–93; Sir Philip Magnus, *Gladstone* (1954), 74–5, 84.

85. Violet Dickinson, ed., *Miss Eden's Letters* (1919), 45.

86. Samuel Flood, 'On the power, nature and evil of popular medical superstition', *Lancet*, 23 August 1845, 203.

87. Bessborough, *Family Circle*, 145–6.

88. Dickinson, op. cit., 132.

89. Greville, *Memoirs*, I, 375.

90. Margaret Forster, *Elizabeth Barret Browning* (1988), 97.

91. Daniel Karlin, *Barrett Browning Courtship*, xxx.

92. Ibid., 82.

93. Ibid., 210.

94. Ibid., 46, 210.

95. Ibid., 382.

96. Factory Inquiry Commission, Supplementary Report of Central Board, part I, 241.

97. Flood, 'Popular Medical Superstition', 203.

98. First Report of the Commissioners of Enquiry into the State of Large Towns (1844), appendix, 46, 48.

99. Factory Inquiry Commission, Supplementary Report of Central Board, I, 241.

100. John Rosselli, *Lord William Bentinck* (1974), 99.

101. Paris, *Pharmacologia*, 174.

102. Gustave Flaubert, *Correspondance*, I (1973), 279.

103. Charles Baudelaire, *Intimate Journals*, translated by Christopher Isherwood (1949), 50.

104. Graham Robb, *Victor Hugo* (1997), 122.

105. Flaubert, *Correspondance*, I, 278.

106. Walter Benjamin, *Charles Baudelaire* (1997), 98.

107. Mérimée, *Correspondance*, III, 283.

108. Balzac, *Correspondance*, III, 201.

109. Oliver, Nodier, 1.

110. Balzac, *Oeuvres Complètes*, XXVII (1962), 199.

111. Nassau Senior, *Conversations with Distinguished Persons*, II (1878), 398.

112. Joanna Richardson, *Théophile Gautier* (1958), 76.

113. Flaubert, *Correspondance*, I, 23–4.

114. Ibid., 570–72.

115. Ibid., IV (1927), 408.

116. Gustave Flaubert, *L'éducation sentimentale* (1869), pt. II, ch. 6.

117. Richard Davenport-Hines, *Vice* (1993), 168–72.

118. Théophile Gautier, *Correspondance Générale*, III (1988), 363–4.

119. Ibid., 35, 269–70.

120. Théophile Gautier, *L'Orient*, II (1877), 47–56.

121. Ibid., 49; Gautier, *Correspondance*, II (1986), *292–3*.

122. Honoré de Balzac, *Lettres à Madame Hanska,* III (1969), 112–13.

123. *Athenaeum*, 2 November 1872, 563.

124. *Athenaeum*, 30 March 1844, 292–3.

125. Report of the Indian Hemp Drugs Commission, I (1894), 175.

126. *Lancet*, 4 July 1840, 539–41.

CHAPTER FOUR

1. Edward Hyams, ed., *Taine's Notes on England* (1957), 255.

2. Eduard Levinstein, *Morbid Craving for Morphia* (1878), 9.

3. Gladstone *Diaries*, III, 489.

4. Berridge, *Opium*, 139.

5. Francis Anstie, 'The Hypodermic Injection of Medicines', *The Practitioner*, I (1868), 32–41.

6. Norman Howard-Jones, 'A Critical Study of the Origins and Early Development of Hypodermic Medication', *Journal of the History of Medicine*, II (1947), 217.

7. Otto von Niemeyer, *A Text-Book of Practical Medicine* (1871), 291.

8. Ziemssen, XVII, 876.

9. Levinstein, op. cit., 4; compare H. H. Kane, 'The Rapid Spread of Morphia by Subcutaneous Injection in Germany', *Maryland Medical Journal*, 8 (1881), 337–41.

10. Levinstein, op. cit., 6–7.

11. *The Practitioner*, III (December 1869), 342.

12. T. C. Allbutt, 'On the Abuse of Hypodermic Injections of Morphia', *The Practitioner*, V (1870), 327–31.

13. Levinstein, op. cit., 3.

14. Levinstein, op. cit., 126–31.

15. Berridge and Edwards, 118–22.

16. Courtwright, 46–8.

17. Horace Day, *The Opium Habit* (1868), 13.

18. J. Keith Anderson, 'On the Treatment of Spasmodic Asthma by the Subcutaneous Injection of Morphia', *The Practitioner*, XV (Nov. 1875), 321–2.

19. S. Weir Mitchell, *Characteristics* (1892), 14.

20. *Mérimée Correspondance*, VIII, 9.

21. Wilkie Collins, *The Moonstone* (1868), 3rd narrative, ch. X.

22. Courtwright, 49.

23. Levinstein, 4–5.

24. George Sand, *Correspondance*, XXIII (1989), 431.
25. Jacques Barzun, *Berlioz and the Romantic Century*, I (1969), 165.
26. Pierre Citron, ed., *Hector Berlioz Correspondance Générale*, I (1972), 310; Hugh MacDonald, ed., *Berlioz: Selected Letters* (1995), 64.
27. William Baker and William Clarke, eds., *The Letters of Wilkie Collins*, I (1999), 201.
28. Ibid., II, 319.
29. Ibid., II, 478.
30. Collins, *Armadale*, II, 59, 122.
31. Collins, *The Moonstone*, 4th narrative, ch. X.
32. Ziemssen, XI (1876), 20, 22–3, 37.
33. Hector Berlioz, *Correspondance Générale*, V (1989), 575.
34. George Eliot, *Felix Holt* (1866), ch. 12.
35. Francis Anstie, *Neuralgia and the Diseases that Resemble it* (1871), 125.
36. Hyams, op. cit., 290.
37. Anstie, *Neuralgia*, 21–2.
38. Ziemssen, XI, 25–6.
39. Ibid., 26.
40. Collins, *The Moonstone*, 1st narrative, chs. I and VIII.
41. Guy de Maupassant, 'Miss Harriet'.
42. Levinstein, op. cit., 76–7.
43. Anstie, *Neuralgia*, 224.
44. *Baudelaire Correspondance*, XIII (1948), 282.
45. F. F. Gautier, ed., *Œuvres Complètes de Charles Baudelaire*, III (1921), 192.
46. Ibid., 16–10.
47. Ibid., 231.
48. 232–3.
49. *Flaubert Correspondance*, IV (1927), 408.
50. *BMJ*, 24 April 1915, 744.
51. T. S. Clouston, 'Puberty and Adolescence Medico-Psychologically Considered', *Edinburgh Medical Journal*, XXVI (July 1880), 9–10.
52. Hugo von Ziemssen, ed., *Cyclopaedia of the Practice of Medicine*, X (1875), 331–3.
53. Anstie, *Neuralgia*, 219.
54. Jean Bruneau, ed., *Flaubert Correspondance*, III (1991), 742, 1527–8.
55. Levinstein, op. cit., 70, 73.
56. Ziemssen, X, 531–2.
57. Calkins, 155.
58. BL, Add ms. 46221, ff. 267, 270. Lady Cowell-Stepney to Gladstone, 17 October 1892.
59. Wilkie Collins, *Armadale*, II (1866), 139, 209.
60. Collins, *The Moonstone*, 3rd narrative, ch. IX.
61. 'Opium Taking in America', *Lancet*, 1 January 1881, 38.
62. *Lancet*, 19 July, 1851, 71.

63. Kane, *Drugs that Enslave*, 55.
64. *BMJ*, 18 December 1875, 764.
65. Sheridan Le Fanu, *The Wyvern Mystery*, II (1869), 80, 132, 194.
66. *Lancet*, 21 June 1851, 694.
67. Sir Squire Bancroft, *Empty Chairs* (1925), 104.
68. Levinstein, op. cit., 45.
69. Levinstein, op. cit., 112–13.
70. Ziemssen, XVII, 856.
71. T. S. Clouston, 'Diseased Cravings and Paralysed Control', *Edinburgh Medical Journal*, XXXV (May 1890), 995.
72. Ziemssen, XVII, 856.
73. Levinstein, 59.
74. Courtwright, *Dark Paradise*, 41.
75. Calkins, 80.
76. *BMJ*, 14 June 1873, 672–3.
77. James Crombie, 'A Simple Method for the Subcutaneous Application of Morphia', *BMJ*, 16 August 1873, 194.
78. *Lancet*, 8 December 1883, 1005.
79. 'Overdose of Morphia', *BMJ*, 25 October 1873, 490.
80. *Lancet*, 21 June 1851, 694.
81. Courtwright, 60.
82. C. W. de Kiewiet and F. H. Underhill, eds., *Dufferin-Carnarvon Correspondence 1874–1878* (1955), 94.
83. Calkins, 160.
84. Calkins, 57–8.
85. Anstie, *Stimulants*, 44–6.
86. Courtwright, 54.
87. J. C. Smith and Brian Hogan, *Criminal Law* (1978), 438.
88. Maurice Brett, ed., *Journals and Letters of Reginald, Viscount Esher*, I (1934), 23.
89. Sir George Higginson, *Seventy-One Years of a Guardsman's Life* (1916), 201–3.
90. *The Times*, 18 & 19 April 1861, both 11d; 12 October 1861, 4e.
91. Courtwright, 55.
92. Mitchell, *Characteristics*, 13, 14, 21–2.
93. Day, *Opium Habit*, 7.
94. Courtwright, 56.
95. Levinstein, op. cit., 1–2, 16, 66.
96. Levinstein, op. cit., 29.
97. Minutes of Evidence to Royal Commission on Opium, 8 September 1893, Q. 170.
98. H. L. Malchow, *Gentleman Capitalists* (1991), 191.
99. *Mérimée Correspondance*, VIII, 264.
100. Sir William Des Vœux, 'A Letter to the Opium Commission', *Nineteenth Century*, 35 (1894), 323.

101. Victoria Berridge, 'East End opium dens and narcotic use in Britain', *London Journal*, 4 (1978), 3–28.
102. Gustave Doré and Blanchard Jerrold, *London* (1872), 147–8.
103. Ibid., 20–1.
104. *Goncourt Journal*, VIII (1936), 59–60.
105. Kane, *Opium Smoking*, 17.
106. Evidence of Sir George Birdwood to Royal Commission on Opium, 15 September 1893, QQ. 1170, 1174.
107. Day, op. cit., 239.
108. Kane, *Opium Smoking*, 1.
109. Ibid., 12.
110. Ibid., 2.
111. Ibid., 3.
112. Ibid., 2.
113. Ibid., 72.
114. Aleister Crowley, *Confessions* (1969), 490.
115. Francis Steegmuller and Barabara Bray, eds., *Flaubert–Sand: the Correspondence* (1993), 252.
116. John Dos Passos, *The Big Money* (1936), 'Poor Little Rich Boy'.
117. Raymond Maude Lluellyn, *Occasional Contributions to 'The Globe'* (1889), 212–3; *The Times*, 28 June 1886, 6c and 9c.
118. Allbutt, *System*, II, 903.
119. Kane, *Opium Smoking*, 76–8, quoting *San Jose Mercury*, 8 October 1881.

CHAPTER FIVE

1. Brodie, *Works*, I, 656.
2. J. J. von Tschudi, *Travels in Peru during the years 1838–1842* (1847), 449–51.
3. 'Mr Weston on the use of Coca Leaves', *Lancet*, 18 March 1876, 447.
4. *Life of Christison*, II, 182–3, 242–3; Sir Robert Christison, 'Observations on the Effects of Cuca or Coca', *BMJ*, 29 April 1876, 527.
5. A. L., 'A New Use for Coca', *Lancet*, 23 September 1876, 449.
6. J. Hughes Bennett, 'The Therapeutical Effects of Chloral', *Edinburgh Medical Journal*, XV (June 1870), 1133–7.
7. George Balfour, 'Therapeutical Effects of Chloral', ibid., 1139.
8. 'Dr Richardson on Chloral Hydrate', *Lancet*, 11 February 1871, 209.
9. B. W. Richardson, *Druggists' Circular and Gazette* (November 1879), quoted Kane, *Enslave*, 156–7.
10. 'Death from hydrate of chloral', *BMJ*, 1 March 1873, 231.
11. 'Death from chloral', *BMJ*, 11 September 1880, 457.
12. 'The late Mr Amphlett', *BMJ*, 18 September 1880, 484.
13. Levinstein, 129–30.
14. Ziemssen, *Cyclopaedia of Medicine*, XVII, 448–9.

15. Thomas Inglis, 'Notes on a Case of Chronic Chloral Poisoning', *Edinburgh Medical Journal*, XXIII (1877), 211–16.

16. Kane, *Drugs that Enslave*, 150.

17. Liverpool Record Office, diary of 15th Earl of Derby, 23 February & 23 June 1891.

18. Alan Sheridan, *André Gide* (1998), 33.

19. *The Times*, 21 December 1878, 6e.

20. Lewin, *Phantastica*, 210–11.

21. Sir Hall Caine, *Recollections of Rossetti* (1882), 87–8.

22. Ibid., 169–70.

23. *Goncourt Journal*, VII (1936), 49–51.

24. Caine, op. cit., 198.

25. Ibid., 193–4.

26. Sir Launder Brunton, 'On the use of nitrite of amyl in angina pectoris', *Lancet*, 27 July 1867, 97–8; Brunton, *Pharmacology and Therapeutics* (1880), 141–2; Anstie, *Neuralgia*, 81–2.

27. George R. H. Dabbs, 'The Resuscitation of Infants', *BMJ*, 6 November 1880, 765.

28. J. Crichton Browne, 'Notes on the nitrite of amyl', *The Practitioner*, XIII (1874), 179–84.

29. F. Wellesley Kendle, 'Nitrite of Amyl', *Lancet*, 19 March 1887, 606.

30. 'Poisoning by Amyl Nitrite', *BMJ*, 27 November 1880, 859–60.

31. 'Clinical Society of London', *BMJ*, 26 February 1870, 221.

32. George Evans, 'Nitrite of Amyl in Facial Neuralgia', *The Practitioner*, XV (1875), 179–80.

33. George Painter, ed., *Marcel Proust: Letters to his Mother* (1956), 64; Philip Kolb, ed., *Marcel Proust Correspondance, II* (1976), 125.

34. Sir Robert Christison, 'The Wooler Poisoning Case', *Edinburgh Medical Journal*, I (1856), 709–10.

35. Craig Maclagan, 'On the Arsenic-Eaters of Styria', *Edinburgh Medical Journal*, X (1864), 202, 204.

36. Ziemssen, op. cit., XVII, 653–4.

37. D. M'N. Parker, 'Case of Death resulting from the Practice of Arsenic Eating', *Edinburgh Medical Journal*, X (1864), 116–23.

38. *The Times,* 11 March 1865, 5f.

39. *The Times,* 13 March 1865, 10a.

40. 'Sir Joseph Oliffe', *Lancet*, 20 March 1869, 416; *BMJ*, 20 March 1869, 274.

41. Robert Christophe, *Le Duc de Morny, 'Empereur' des Français sous Napoleon III* (1951), 237–8.

42. Alphonse Daudet, *Le Nabab*, I (1877), chapter 1 (London edition [1878], I, 1).

43. Ibid., I, chapter 4 (London ed., I, 109–10).

44. Ibid., bowdlerised in III, chapter 8 of English translations; published *circa finem* of penultimate chapter of French editions.

45. Ibid., I, chapter 1 (London ed., I, 27).

46. Ibid., I, chapter 4 (London ed., I, 124).

47. *Mérimée Correspondance*, XII (1958), 370–1.

48. Christophe, *Morny*, 241.

49. Daudet, op. cit., II, chapter 7 (London ed., II, 214).

50. Sir Richard Quain, *Dictionary of Medicine*, I (1882), 71.

51. Lewin, *Phantastica*, 322–4.

52. *The Times*, 5 August 1889, 5d.

53. J. H. Levy, *The Necessity for Criminal Appeal as illustrated by the Maybrick Case* (1909), 260.

54. Liverpool Record Office, diary of 15th Earl of Derby, 8 August 1889, folio 220; compare 10 August (folio 223), 21 August (folio 233) and 23 August (folios 234–5).

55. Levy, op. cit., 224–5.

56. Lord Broughton, *Recollections of a Long Life*, III (1910), 204. I owe this reference to Dr Arnold Harvey.

57. There is a good discussion of ether in Mike Jay, *Emperors of Dreams* (2000).

58. Dudley W. Buxton, 'Sleep and her Twin Sister, Death', *Contemporary Review*, 103 (1913), 105.

59. Buxton, 'Sleep and Death', 106.

60. *Correspondence of Charles Darwin*, IV (1988), 128, 303.

61. Daudet, op. cit., I, chapter 6 (London ed., I, 229–30).

62. Ziemssen, op. cit., XVII, 416.

63. 'Anaesthetics', *BMJ*, 5 July 1873, 11–12.

64. Ziemssen, op. cit., X, 536.

65. Lewin, op. cit., 200.

66. Ibid.

67. Ernest Hart, 'Ether Drinking', *BMJ*, 18 October 1890, 886.

68. Hart, 'Ether Drinking', 890.

69. Lewin, op. cit., 198–203.

70. Ibid., 194–5, 197.

71. Ziemssen, op. cit., XVII, 435–6.

72. James O. Robertson and Janet C. Robertson, *All Our Yesterdays* (1993), 330.

73. *The Times*, 12 February 1920, 17e.

74. Herbert Schueller and Robert Peters, eds., *The Letters of John Addington Symonds*, III (1969), 378.

75. Philip Harris, *A History of the British Museum Library 1753–1973* (1998), 307, 368.

76. Ann Thwaite, *Edmund Gosse* (1984), 64.

CHAPTER SIX

1. Mark Pendergast, *For God, Country and Coca-Cola* (1993), 26–7.
2. Robert Byck, ed., *Cocaine Papers by Sigmund Freud* (1974), 15–19.
3. Ibid., 20–21.
4. Tania and James Stern, trans., *Letters of Sigmund Freud 1873–1939* (1961), 29; *Cocaine Papers*, 155.
5. Stern, *Freud Letters*, 123; *Cocaine Papers*, 39–40.
6. Richard Webster, *Why Freud was Wrong* (1995), 46.
7. Stern, 128; *Cocaine Papers*, 41.
8. Ibid., 62.
9. Ibid., 71.
10. J. B. Mattison, 'Cocaine Doses and Cocaine Addiction', *Lancet*, 21 May 1887, 1025.
11. Louis Lewin, *Phantastica* (1931), 106–7.
12. Havelock Ellis, 'Mescal: A New Artificial Paradise', *Contemporary Review*, LXXIII (1898), 141.
13. *Cocaine Papers*, 73.
14. Ibid., 92.
15. Stern, 146; *Cocaine Papers*, 92.
16. *Cocaine Papers*, 117.
17. 'Erlenmeyer on the Effects of Cocaine in the Treatment of Morphinomania', *Journal of Mental Science*, XXXI (October 1885), 427–8.
18. Steven B. Karch, *A Brief History of Cocaine* (1998), 46.
19. *Cocaine Papers*, 171–3.
20. Ibid., 109.
21. James Strachey, ed., *The Complete Psychological Works of Sigmund Freud*, IV (1953), 115, 117.
22. 'Cocain [sic] as a local anaesthetic', *Lancet*, 4 October 1884, 608.
23. Sir Henry Butlin, 'Cocaine', *Lancet*, 29 November 1884, 975.
24. T. W. Carmalt Jones, 'Cocaine', *Lancet*, 6 December 1884, 1023.
25. G. H. Seagrave, 'The Value of Hypodermic Injections of Cocaine in the various Neuralgias', *BMJ*, 8 February 1896, 335.
26. 'Coca Pastils', *Lancet*, 13 December 1884, 1078.
27. *Cocaine Papers*, 186, 191.
28. T. C. Clouston, 'Diseased Cravings and Paralysed Control', *Edinburgh Medical Journal*, XXXV, pt II (March 1890), 809.
29. *Cocaine Papers*, 188–9.
30. Sir Clifford Allbutt, *A System of Medicine*, II (1897), 908–9.
31. Mattison, 'Cocaine Dosage', 1024–6.
32. Joseph Spillane, *Cocaine* (2000), 33, 160.
33. 'The Paris Universal Exhibition', *Lancet*, 31 August 1889, 451–2.
34. William S. McFeely, *Grant* (1981), 517.
35. Sir George Arthur, *Sarah Bernhardt* (1923), 143.
36. 'Nerve Exhaustion and Opium', *Lancet*, 12 October 1889, 754.

37. Ronald Hayman, *A Life of Jung* (1999), 94.
38. Eva Brabant et al., *The Correspondence of Sigmund Freud and Sándor Ferenczi*, I (1993), 154.
39. T. S. Clouston, 'Diseased Cravings and Paralysed Control', *Edinburgh Medical Journal*, XXXV, pt II (March 1890), 806–7.
40. Clouston, 'Diseased Cravings', 809.
41. Gootenberg, *Cocaine*, 29, 33.
42. Aleister Crowley, *Confessions* (1969), 180.
43. 'The Dangers of Cocaine', *Lancet*, 6 July 1895, 43.
44. Allbutt, op. cit., II, 907.
45. David T. Courtwright, 'The Rise and Fall and Rise of Cocaine in the United States', in Jordan Goodman, Paul Lovejoy and Andrew Sherratt, eds., *Consuming Habits* (1995), 208–9.
46. George Santayana, *The Last Puritan* (1935), 35, 63.
47. Spillane, op. cit., 154.
48. Ibid., 156–7.
49. Carl Sandburg, *The American Songbag* (1927), 206; another version in W. H. Auden, *The Oxford Book of Light Verse* (1938), 499 and W. H. Auden, *A Certain World* (1971), 130.
50. John M'Lennan, *Memoir of Thomas Drummond* (1867), 328–335.
51. Silas Weir Mitchell, *Characteristics* (1893), 13.
52. Pendergast, op. cit., 26.
53. Mitchell, *Characteristics*, 43, 71.
54. Fredson Bowers, ed., *The Works of Stephen Crane*, VIII (1973), 365.
55. 'What Has Become of Original Sin?', *Spectator*, 11 October 1890, 472.
56. Ouida, *Views and Opinions* (1895), 29.
57. Matthew Arnold, 'Heine's Grave'.
58. H. G. Keene, 'The Common Disorder of the Age', *National Review*, XI (1888), 796–7.
59. Alfred Binet, *Les Altérations de la Personnalité* (Paris, 1892), 39; Alfred Binet, *Alterations of Personality* (London, 1896), 41.
60. Max Nordau, *Degeneration* (1895), 34.
61. Ibid., 560.
62. *Goncourt Journal*, VI (1935), 225; G. V. Dobie, *Alphonse Daudet* (1949), 244.
63. Robert Baldick, *Pages from the Goncourt Journal* (1962), 296–7, 364.
64. *Goncourt Journal*, IX (1936), 10.
65. Oscar Wilde, *The Picture of Dorian Gray* (1891), chs. xi, xvi.
66. Octave Mirbeau, *Les Vingt et un Jours d'un Neurasthénique* (1901), ch. xxi; 263 of 1990 edn.
67. Sir Clifford Allbutt, 'Nervous Diseases and Modern Life', *Contemporary Review*, vol. 67 (1895), 210, 214–15, 217, 221, 226, 228–9.
68. 'Sulphonal in Diabetes', *Lancet*, 1 November 1890, 938; 'Poisoning by Sulphonal', *Lancet*, 8 November 1890, 1004; *Daily News*, 16 December

1890, 3; J. Thompson, 'Insomnia', *Lancet*, 17 January 1891, 179; J. R. Bradbury, 'Disorders of Sleep', in Allbutt, *System*, VII (1899), 753–4.

69. *Pall Mall Gazette*, 26 April 1889, 2.
70. William Henry Gilbert, 'Sulphonal', *Lancet*, 25 October 1890, 907.
71. *Lancet*, 4 April 1891, 787–8.
72. Israel Zangwill, *The Big Bow Mystery* (1892), 173.
73. Allbutt, op. cit., II, 912.
74. Dudley Bahlman, ed., *The Diary of Sir Edward Walter Hamilton 1885–1906* (1993), 296; Lewin, *Phantastica*, 213–14.
75. Lord George Hamilton to Lord Curzon of Kedleston, 5 March 1903, India Office Library, Mss Eur F 111/162.
76. 'Sale of Morphine in Berlin', *Lancet*, 20 April 1889, 804.
77. 'The Paris Universal Exhibition', *Lancet*, 31 August 1889, 451.
78. Sir James Lyall speaking during the evidence of Sir Joseph Peake, First Report of the Royal Commission on Opium, 8 September 1893, QQ. 116–17.
79. 'The Morphia Habit and its Treatment', *Journal of Mental Science*, XXXIV (April 1888), 117.
80. Sir Lauder Brunton, *Lectures on the Actions of Medicines* (1897), 640–41.
81. Augustine Birrell, *Sir Frank Lockwood* (1898), 191, 193, 196, 204.
82. *The Times*, 20 December 1897, 7a.
83. S. Weir Mitchell, *Doctor and Patient* (1887), 117.
84. 'British Gynaecological Society', *Lancet*, 23 March 1895, 750.
85. Robert Hichens, *Felix* (1902), 291–4.
86. *Journal of Mental Science*, XXXIV, 546.
87. Ibid., 547.
88. Ibid., 549–50.
89. Allbutt, op. cit., II, 880.
90. Minutes of the Royal Commission on Alleged Chinese Gambling and Immorality and Charges of Bribery against the Police Force (New South Wales), 14 December 1891, QQ. 14557, 14651.
91. 'Opium Smoking in New South Wales', *The Times*, 31 December 1888, 7f.
92. Lady Theodora Guest, *A Round Trip in North America* (1895), 97–8.
93. Allbutt, op. cit., II, 884.
94. *Crane Works*, VIII, 365–6.
95. Ibid., 366.
96. Ibid.
97. S. Weir Mitchell, *The Autobiography of a Quack* (1899), 7–8.
98. *Crane Works*, VIII, 366.
99. Angus Hawkins and John Powell, eds., *The Journal of John Wodehouse, First Earl of Kimberley for 1862–1902* (1997), 415.
100. India Office Library, Eur F 130/3, Earl of Kimberley to Marquess of Dufferin and Ava, 15 January 1885.

101. Booth, *Opium*, 156.
102. Sir Lepel Griffin, 'The Lotus Eaters', *Nineteenth Century*, 35 (1894), 515.
103. 'Obituary', *BMJ*, 29 April 1899, 1065.
104. Lord Newton, *Lord Lansdowne* (1929), 110.
105. Berridge, *Opium and the People*, 186.
106. Griffin, 'Lotus Eaters', 514, 519, 522.
107. *Review of Reviews*, XI (1895), 400.
108. A conspicuous exception is Virginia Berridge, who concluded in 1981 that 'the Commission was less of a cover-up than the anti-opiumists proclaimed'. Berridge, *Opium and the People*, 188.
109. Carl A. Trocki, *Opium and Empire: Chinese Society in Colonial Singapore 1800–1910* (1990), 237.
110. Allbutt, op. cit., II, 883.
111. RCO, 15 September 1893, Q. 872.
112. RCO, 20 January 1894, Q. 18150.
113. RCO, 15 September 1893, QQ. 1047–9.
114. RCO, 18 January 1894, Q. 16902.
115. RCO, 18 January 1894, Q. 16902.
116. RCO, 18 January 1894, Q. 16908.
117. RCO, 15 September 1893, Q. 1019.
118. RCO, 8 January 1894, Q. 12872.
119. RCO, 8 January 1894, QQ. 12876, 12878.
120. RCO, 8 January 1894, Q. 12893.
121. RCO, 10 January 1894, QQ. 13996, 14018–9, 14026.
122. RCO, 15 September 1893, QQ. 1175–6.
123. RCO, 15 September 1893, Q. 872.
124. RCO, 19 January 1894, QQ. 17529–30, 17543.
125. RCO, 19 January 1894, QQ. 17589, 17592, 17596, 17599.
126. Indian Hemp Committee, IV, 181.
127. IHC, IV, 440.
128. *Report of the Indian Hemp Drugs Commission* (Simla, 1894), para. 4351.
129. Report, para. 452.
130. Report, para. 467.
131. Report, para. 477.
132. Report, para. 490.
133. Report, para. 741.
134. IHC, IV, 304.
135. IHC, IV, 267–8.
136. IHC, IV, 270.
137. IHC, IV, 215.
138. IHC, IV, 6–7, 9.
139. IHC, IV, 17.
140. IHC, IV, 235–6.

141. IHC, IV, 76.
142. IHC, IV, 438.
143. IHC, IV, 287.
144. Report, para. 536.
145. T. S. Clouston, 'The Cairo Asylum—Dr Warnock on Hasheesh Insanity', *Journal of Mental Science,* 42 (1896), 795.
146. IHC, IV, 268.
147. IHC, IV, 438.
148. Merlin Holland and Sir Rupert Hart-Davis, eds., *The Complete Letters of Oscar Wilde* (2000), 629.
149. IHC, IV, 205.
150. IHC, IV, 110.
151. IHC, IV, 7.
152. IHC, IV, 285–6.
153. Lewin, *Phantastica*, 98; S. Weir Mitchell, 'Remarks on the Effects of Anhelonium Lewinii (the Mescal Button)', *BMJ*, 5 December 1896, 1627–8; Ellis, 'Mescal', 130, 138–9; John Kelly, ed., *The Collected Letters of W. B. Yeats,* II (1997), 95.
154. Allbutt, op. cit., II, 886, 888.

CHAPTER SEVEN

1. William Allison and John Fairley, *The Monocled Mutineer* (1978), 31.
2. Joseph McIver and George Price, 'Drug Addiction', *JAMA*, 12 February 1916, 476.
3. Richard Bonnie and Charles Whitebread II, *The Marihuana Conviction*, 47.
4. PRO FO 371/11713, minute of Sir Charles Orde, 17 June 1926.
5. André Gide, *Journal*, II (1997), 35.
6. Philip Ziegler, *Diana Cooper* (1981), 54–5, 116.
7. Horace Freeland Judson, *Heroin Addiction in Britain* (1973), 4.
8. Sir William Collins, 'The Work of the International Opium Conference at The Hague', *Contemporary Review*, 101 (1912), 324–5.
9. 'Heroin Hydrochloride', *JAMA*, 47 (1906), 1303.
10. 'Heroin', *Lancet*, 24 December 1898, 1744.
11. 'Creostal, Duotal and Heroin', *Lancet*, 3 December 1898, 1486.
12. W. O. Jennings, 'On the Physiological Cure of the Morphia Habit', *Lancet*, 10 August 1901, 363.
13. John Philipps, 'Prevalence of the Heroin Habit', *JAMA*, 14 December 1912, 2146.
14. Jennings, *Morphia Habit*, 335–7.
15. Sir Dyce Duckworth, 'The Opium Habit and Morphinism', *Lancet*, 15 August 1908, 440.
16. Oscar Jennings, *The Morphia Habit and its Voluntary Renunciation (A Personal Relation of a Suppression after Twenty-Five Years Addiction)* (1909), v.

17. Arthur Gamgee, 'On Chronic Morphinism and its Treatment', *Lancet*, 12 September 1908, 794.

18. Charles E. de M. Sajous, *Analytical Cyclopaedia of Practical Medicine*, III (1905), 506.

19. Joseph F. Spillane, *Cocaine* (2000), 92–3.

20. Ibid., 119.

21. Lambeth Palace Library, Davidson papers 433, Hamilton Wright to Davidson, 26 July 1910, f. 239.

22. Spillane, op. cit., 157.

23. C. W. Saleeby, 'The Cocaine Habit', *Daily Chronicle*, 19 July 1916.

24. Thomas S. Blair, 'The Relation of Drug Addiction to Industry', *Journal of Industrial Hygiene*, I (1919), 289.

25. W. D. Owens, 'The Importance of Eliminating the Cocaine *Habitué* from the Personnel of the United States Navy and Marine Corps', U.S. Navy Medical Bulletin, 4 (1910), 204–5, and Owens, 'Signs and Symptoms Presented by those Addicted to Cocaine', *JAMA*, 58 (1912), 329–30.

26. Graham Robb, *Rimbaud* (2000), 131–2.

27. Jad Adams, *Madder Music, Stronger Wine* (2000), 13–14, 81.

28. Stuart Creighton Miller, '*Benevolent Assimilation': the American Conquest of the Philippines*, 1899–1903 (1982), 256.

29. Edgar Wickberg, *The Chinese in Philippines Life* (1965), 115–19.

30. W. Cameron Forbes, *The Philippine Islands*, I (1928), 248.

31. *Report of the Philippines Commission*, II (1900), 35.

32. Lambeth Palace Library, Davidson papers 133, Sir Matthew Nathan to Rev. William Banister, 5 February 1907, f. 246.

33. James Blount, *The American Occupation of the Philippines 1898–1912* (1912), 580.

34. Elting Morison, ed., *The Letters of Theodore Roosevelt*, VII (1954), 437.

35. Lambeth Palace Library, Davidson papers 182, Brent to Davidson, St Thomas Day 1912, f. 348.

36. Lambeth Palace Library, Davidson papers 197, Charles Brent to Randall Davidson, 14 July 1904, enclosing memorandum 'Religious Conditions in the Philippine Islands', ff. 10–11, 18, 24.

37. Lambeth Palace Library, Davidson papers 379, Brent to Davidson, 20 June 1916.

38. Lambeth Palace Library, Davidson papers 161, Brent to Davidson, 12 September 1910, ff. 241–2.

39. Report of the Philippine Opium Committee, 49.

40. Peter Stanley, *A Nation in the Making* (1974), 164.

41. Lambeth Palace Library, Davidson papers 176, Brent to Davidson, 22 October 1912, f. 258.

42. Katherine Mayo, *The Isles of Fear* (1925), 134.

43. Herbert L. May, *Survey of Smoking Opium Conditions in the Far East* (Foreign Policy Association pamphlet, New York) (1927), 14, 15, 21.

44. Sir Lionel Phillips, *Transvaal Problems* (1905), 110.

45. Maryna Fraser and Alan Jeeves, eds., *All the Glittered* (1977), 156–8.

46. Peter Richardson, *Chinese Mine Labour in the Transvaal* (1982), 174–5.

47. House of Commons debates, 30 May 1906, columns 497–8.

48. House of Commons debates, 30 May 1906, columns 505–11.

49. Sir Frank Swettenham, 'India and Opium', *The Times*, 4 September 1924, 11e.

50. Lambeth Palace Library, Davidson papers 158, Brent to Davidson, 19 March 1909, f. 196.

51. Horace G. Alexander, 'Asia's Struggle with Opium', *Contemporary Review*, 127 (1925), 462.

52. Dame Edith Lyttelton, 'The Opium Question', *National Review*, 85 (1925), 107.

53. [Aleister Crowley], 'The Drug Panic', *English Review*, 35 (1922), 68.

54. Earl of Minto, speech on Indian Budget, 27 March 1907; Lambeth Palace Library, Davidson papers 133, f. 253.

55. Lambeth Palace Library, Davidson papers 147, John Morley to Davidson, 30 January 1908, f. 272.

56. Theodore Taylor, 'Opium: A Live Question', *Contemporary Review*, 103 (1913), 41.

57. Lyttelton, 'Opium Question', 106.

58. 'Opium and the Republic', *North China Daily News*, 11 May 1912.

59. 'Substance of a Sermon Preached by Bishop Brent at Trinity Cathedral, February 7, 1909', *Shanghai Times*, 9 February 1909; Lambeth Palace Library, Davidson papers 433, f. 49.

60. Collins, 'Opium Conference', 321.

61. Lambeth Palace Library, Davidson papers 158, Brent to Davidson, 19 March 1909, f. 196.

62. Sir Hugh Linstead, *Poisons Law* (1936), 135; Collins, 'Opium Conference', 317.

63. PRO BT 11/14/C353, minute of Sir Henry Fountain, 11 January 1912.

64. Collins, 'Opium Conference', 323–4.

65. Ibid., 325.

66. W. A. Bloedorn, 'Drug Addiction', *JAMA*, 25 January 1919, 262.

67. Jennings, *Morphia Habit*, 63.

68. Jill Jonnes, *Hep-Cats, Narcs and Pipe Dreams* (1996), 32–3.

69. Ibid., 33.

70. Lambeth Palace Library, Davidson papers 433, Hamilton Wright to Davidson, 26 July 1910, ff. 238–9.

71. PRO BT 11/14/C689, minute of Sir Henry Fountain, 22 January 1912.

72. PRO BT 11/14/C8059, Despatch 231 of Viscount Bryce, 8 September 1911.

73. PRO FO 371/10966, minute of Sir Basil Newton, 5 March 1925.

74. Thomas S. Blair, 'Narcotic Drug Addiction as Regulated by a State

Department of Health', *JAMA*, 17 May 1919, 1441–3.

75. Blair, 'Addiction to Industry', 295.
76. Courtwright, *Dark Paradise*, 95.
77. Spillane, *Cocaine*, 102.
78. Phillips, 'Prevalence of Heroin Habit', 2146–7.
79. McIver and Price, 'Drug Addiction', 478.
80. Pearce Bailey, 'The Heroin Habit', *New Republic*, 6 (1916), 314–16.
81. 'The Mental and Nervous Side of Addiction to Narcotic Drugs', *JAMA*, 2 August 1924, 325.
82. L. Kolb and A. G. du Mez, 'The Prevalence and Trend of Drug Addiction in the United States and the Factors Influencing It', US Public Health Service, *Public Health Reports*, vol. 39, no. 21, 23 May 1924, 1188.
83. May, *Survey of Smoking Opium,* 7.
84. Bonnie and Whitebread, *Marihuana*, 49.
85. 'Paris', *BMJ*, 25 January 1913, 193.
86. Arthur Gold and Robert Fizdale, *Misia* (1980), 110, 119–21.
87. Marek Cohn, 'Cocaine Girls', in Gootenberg, *Cocaine*, 108.
88. Hoare, *Wilde's Last Stand*, 36.
89. PRO HO 45/10813/312966, statement of Detective Inspector Francis Carlin, 5 May 1916.
90. PRO HO 45/10813/312966, statement by Phillip Dunn, 9 May 1916.
91. Blair, 'Addiction to Industry', 294.
92. Ibid., 295.
93. Lyttelton, 'Opium Question', 110.
94. 'Restrictions on the sale of cocaine', *BMJ*, 22 July 1916, 118.
95. PRO HO 45/11013/323566, evidence of Major General Sir Francis Lloyd, 30 November 1916.
96. Lambeth Palace Library, Davidson papers 379, Brent to Davidson, 20 June 1916.
97. 'Sale of Cocaine to Soldiers on Leave', *Daily Chronicle*, 19 July 1916; 'Canadian Officer on Trial', *The Times*, 5 February 1916, 3c; 'A Canadian's Crime', *The Times*, 7 February 1916, 3c.
98. PRO DPP 4/50, appeal before Lord Reading, 28 February 1916, ff. 19, 25.
99. 'Sale of Cocaine to Soldiers on Leave', op. cit.
100. 'The Cocaine Vice', *Daily Chronicle*, 19 July 1916.
101. PRO HO 45/10813/312966, minute of Sir Malcolm Delevingne, 22 July 1916.
102. House of Lords debates, 28 July 1925, vol. 125, cols. 460–61.
103. *The Times*, 8 December 1950, 8d.
104. Sir Malcolm Delevingne, 'Some International Aspects of the Problem of Drug Addiction', *British Journal of Inebriety*, 32 (1935), 149.
105. PRO FO 371/10970, minute of William Strang, 10 November 1925; PRO FO 371/11711, minute of Strang, 9 April 1926.

106. PRO FO 371/11715, minute of William Cavendish-Bentinck, 29 December 1926.

107. PRO FO 371/15524, minute of Hugh Dalton, 4 April 1931.

108. PRO HO 45/10813/312966, Sir Edward Henry to Home Office, 20 July 1916; H. B. Spear and Joy Mott, 'Cocaine and Crack within the British System', in Philip Bean, ed., *Cocaine and Crack* (1993), 33.

109. PRO HO 45/11013/323566, evidence of Sir Edward Henry, 30 November 1916.

110. 'Regulations with Respect to the Sale of Cocaine', *Lancet*, 5 August 1916, 238.

111. PRO HO 45/11013/323566, Sir Malcolm Delevingne, minute of 24 February 1917.

112. Bryan Connon, *Beverley Nichols* (1991), 54, 56.

113. 'International Control of the Sale of Narcotics', *JAMA*, 1 September 1923, 762; Berridge, 275; 'The Cocaine Habit', *BMJ*, 13 March 1926, 487; de Kort, 'Doctors, diplomats and businessmen', 126, 143.

114. Sir William Willcox, 'Drug Addiction', *British Journal of Inebriety*, 21 (1924), 14.

115. Sir Malcolm Delevingne, 'Some International Aspects of the Problem of Drug Addiction', *British Journal of Inebriety*, 32 (1935), 127–8.

116. See the forthcoming account of Billie Carleton by Philip Hoare in *New Dictionary of National Biography*.

117. John Grider (1892–1918), *War Birds, a diary of an unknown aviator* (1927), for 12 May 1918; D. Juniper, 'Correspondence', *BJA*, 65 (1970), 167–8.

118. Dr Donald Murray, House of Commons debates, 10 June 1920, vol. 130, col. 718.

119. A. B. Baxter, *The Parts Men Play* (1920), xviii.

120. Rohmer, *Dope*, 71.

121. Ibid., 171, 303.

122. Ibid., 291–2.

123. Ibid., 120.

124. Ibid., 186.

125. Ibid., 182.

126. Lady Dorothy Mills, *The Laughter of Fools* (1920), 3.

127. Sir Nöel Coward, *Play Parade*, I (1933), 497–8.

128. Philip Hoare, *Nöel Coward* (1995), 133–4.

129. Sir William Collins, 'The International Opium Convention and the Traffic in Cocaine and Opium', *BMJ*, 5 August 1916, 198.

130. PRO HO 45/11013/323566, evidence of Sir Edward Henry, 30 November 1916.

131. PRO HO 45/11013/323566, W. E. Jones to J. A. Johnston, 12 January 1917.

132. Report of the Committee on the Use of Cocaine in Dentistry, Cd. 8489 of 1917; 'Cocaine and Unregistered Dentists', *BMJ*, 17 March 1917, 367.

CHAPTER EIGHT

1. Edmund Wilson, *The American Earthquake* (1958), 91.
2. Spear and Mott, 'Cocaine and Crack', 37.
3. J. G. Lockhart and Mary Lyttelton (Lady Craik), *The Feet of the Young Men* (1928), 165–7.
4. Walter Elliot, House of Commons debates, 10 June 1920, vol. 130, col. 723.
5. Horace Freeland Judson, *Heroin Addiction in Britain* (1974), 16.
6. PRO FO 371/11715, minute of William Strang, 13 November 1926.
7. 'Self-Prescription of Dangerous Drugs', *Lancet*, 19 August 1922, 406.
8. Terry Parssinen, *Secret Passions, Secret Remedies* (1983), 166–7.
9. Kate Meyrick, *Secrets of the 43* (1933), 55–6.
10. PRO MH 58/277, Appendix I to Home Office memorandum, October 1924.
11. Bing Spear, 'The Early Years of the "British System" in Practice', in John Strang and Michael Gossop, eds., *Heroin Addiction and Drug Policy (1994)*, 13–14.
12. Pro Bono Publico, 'Abuse of Drugs', *The Times*, 29 February 1924, 8f.
13. Gamgee, 'Chronic Morphinism', 795.
14. Blair, 'Addiction to Industry', 285–6.
15. Willis Abbot, 'America and Europe', *The Times*, 15 January 1925, 15f.
16. 'Symposium on "The Doctor and the Drug Addict" ', *JAMA*, 4 December 1920, 1590.
17. 'Doctor and Drug Addict', 1589.
18. Alden Stevens, 'Make Dope Legal', *Harper's Magazine*, 205 (1952), 43.
19. 'Report on Narcotics', *JAMA*, 2 February 1924, 414.
20. PRO FO 371/10345, Despatch 1141 of Herbert Brooks, 10 July 1924.
21. Jonnes, *Hep-Cats*, 72–80.
22. 'Health Problems in New York State', *JAMA*, 14 April 1923, 1095.
23. Kolb and Du Mez, 1203.
24. Ibid., 1191.
25. Blair, op. cit., 292.
26. 'Narcotic Control in the State of Washington', *JAMA*, 5 May 1923, 1335.
27. Blair, op. cit., 288.
28. 'Doctor and Drug Addict', 1590.
29. W. E. Dixon, 'The Drug Traffic', *The Times*, 21 March 1923, 15e.
30. Crowley, 'Drug Delusion', 575.
31. Sir W. Norwood East, 'Obituary', *British Journal of Addiction*, XLII (1944), 52.
32. PRO MH 58/277, evidence of Dr F. S. D. Hogg.
33. PRO MH 58/277, evidence of Sir Maurice Craig.
34. 'Morphine and Heroin Addiction', *BMJ*, 27 February 1926, 391–3.
35. Report of Rolleston Committee, paragraph 24.
36. Delevingne, 'International Aspects of Drug Addiction', 127.

37. PRO MH 58/277, evidence of Sir Maurice Craig.

38. PRO MH 58/277, evidence of Sir Farquhar Buzzard.

39. PRO MH 58/278, evidence of Dr Alexander Forbes of Sheffield.

40. Abbot, 'America and Europe', 15f.

41. [Aleister Crowley], 'The Great Drug Delusion', *English Review*, 34 (1922), 572.

42. Ibid., 576.

43. J. F. C. Fuller, 'The Americans', *National Review*, 84 (1925), 736.

44. PRO FO 371/10345, memorandum of Sir Arthur Willert, 6 November 1924.

45. PRO FO 371/10345, Richmond Hobson to King George V, 11 October 1924, with enclosure.

46. Edward M. Brecher, *Licit and Illicit Drugs* (1972), 55.

47. Bonnie and Whitebread, *Marihuana*, 40.

48. Ibid., 43.

49. PRO HO 144/6073/436328/1, William Scott to Home Office, 9 August 1922.

50. PRO HO 144/6073/436328/ 2, minute of M. D. Perrins, 9 October 1922.

51. PRO HO 144/6073/436328/4, Delevingne, minute of 25 June 1923, and Delevingne to Dame Rachel Crowdy, 2 August 1923.

52. 'Hashish, Not Opium', *The Times*, 18 August 1923, 5b.

53. PRO HO 144/6073/436328/ 6, Delevingne to Sir Louis Kershaw, 27 August 1923.

54. PRO HO 144/6073/436328/ 6, memorandum of M. D. Perrins, 24 August 1923.

55. PRO HO 144/6073/436328/9, Sir William Horwood to Home Office, 6 September 1923; minute of J. H. Ashley, 24 August 1923.

56. HO 144/6073/436328/9, minute of 13 September 1923.

57. HO 144/6073/436328/32, minute of M. D. Perrins, 20 February 1924.

58. PRO HO 144/6073/436328/ 37, Egyptian Ministry of Interior, Report on Hashish Traffic in Egypt, 2 March 1924.

59. HO 144/6073/436328/58, memorandum of Dr A. H. Mahfooz Bey, 5 December 1924.

60. W. W. Willoughby, *Opium as an International Problem* (1925), 379.

61. House of Commons debates, 2 April 1925, vol. 182, cols. 1496–7.

62. House of Commons debates, 5 August 1925, vol. 187, cols. 1491–3.

63. House of Lords debates, 28 July 1925, vol. 125, cols. 457–9.

64. G. Fernandez Clarke, 'A Case of Veronal Poisoning', *Lancet*, 23 January 1904, 223–4.

65. Sax Rohmer, *Dope* (1919), 106.

66. Alfred Hind, 'A Case of Acute Sulphonal Poisoning', *Lancet*, 23 January 1904, 219.

67. James Burnet, 'What is Veronal?', *Lancet*, 30 January 1904, 335.

68. Sir William Willcox, 'Veronal Poisoning', *Lancet*, 25 October 1913, 1180.

69. Sir Thomas Clouston, *The Hygiene of Mind* (1909), 251.

70. Sam Whimster, ed., *Max Weber and the Culture of Anarchy* (1999), 45.

71. Davenport-Hines, *Vice*, 147; Stephen Twombley, *All that Summer She was Mad* (1981), 139–42.

72. Marcel Proust, *Correspondance*, V (1979), 283; ibid., XII (1984), 132.

73. Ibid., XVIII (1990), 534.

74. Ibid., XX (1992), 491.

75. Arnold Bennett, *Journals*, II (1932), 218.

76. Eric Hopkins, *Charles Masterman* (1999), 185, 199.

77. 'St John's Wood Veronal Poisoning Case', *The Times*, 31 December 1917, 10f; Hilary Spurling, *Ivy when young* (1974), 253–4; Marian McKenna, *Myra Hess* (1976), 75–6.

78. 'Sir Beauchamp Duff, Share in Mesopotamia Responsibility', *The Times*, 21 January 1918, 5a.

79. 'The Tragic Death of Gen. Duff Worried and Depressed by Criticism', *Daily Express*, 22 January 1918.

80. Lord Horder, *The Little Genius* (1966), 84.

81. 'The Use of Veronal', *The Times*, 23 January 1918, 4e.

82. 'The Use of Veronal', *The Times*, 8 March 1918, 4c.

83. 'VAD Nurse's Death', *The Times*, 12 December 1918, 5c; see also 'VAD Nurse's Death', *The Times*, 19 December 1918, 3a and 'Veronal Poisoning', *The Times*, 9 January 1919, 3a.

84. PRO HO 45/15597/354321/2, Sir John Ganzoni to William Bridgeman, 3 September 1923.

85. PRO HO 45/15597/354321/2, minute of 24 September 1923.

86. Willcox, 'Veronal Poisoning', 1178–81.

87. Filson Young, *The Trial of Hawley Harvey Crippen* (1933), 67–74.

88. 'William Henry Willcox', *Lancet*, 19 July 1941, 88.

89. PRO HO 45/15597/354321/2, minute of Sir Malcolm Delevingne, 1 December 1923.

90. PRO HO 45/15597/354321/2, minute of Sir John Anderson, 26 June 1924.

91. PRO HO 45/15597/354321/ 11, Home Office conference on the Barbitone group of drugs, 24 February 1925.

92. PRO HO 45/15592/354321/ 13, Willcox to Delevingne, 13 February 1926.

93. PRO HO 45/15597/354321/ 81, unsigned Home Office memorandum, January 1934.

94. PRO HO 45/15592/354321/ 81, unsigned Home Office memorandum, January 1934.

95. 'Barbituric Derivatives as Dangerous Drugs', *BMJ*, 22 May 1926, 875–6.

96. 'Poison for the Asking', *Spectator*, 26 January 1934, 107.

97. O. Bruns, *Münchener medizinische Wochenschrift* [Munich], 73 (1926), 977–8.

98. F. Scott Fitzgerald, *The Last Tycoon* (1941), chapter 1 (*The Bodley Head Fitzgerald*, I [1963] 168).

CHAPTER NINE

1. Delevingne, 'Drug Addiction', 129.

2. PRO FO 371/11711, Delevingne to Foreign Office, 10 May 1926.

3. PRO FO 371/12533, League of Nations memorandum 'Traffic in Opium', 23 February 1926.

4. PRO FO 371/12533, Delevingne to Foreign Office, 9 November 1927.

5. 'Paul Sacher', *The Times*, 27 May 1999, 27.

6. William McAllister, *Drug Diplomacy in the Twentieth Century* (2000), 79.

7. Henri de Monfreid, *Hashish*, 135.

8. Ibid., 14.

9. Ibid., 31.

10. Ibid., 113.

11. Ibid., 174.

12. PRO FO 371/12529, Clifford Plowman to Henry Dobinson, 22 June 1927.

13. PRO FO 371/12529, Delevingne to Sir George Mounsey, 17 August 1927.

14. PRO FO 371/11710, despatch 211 of Maclean, Addis Ababa, 26 October 1926.

15. Charles Nicholl, *Somebody Else* (1999), 190; Charles Nicholl, 'Diary', *London Review of Books*, 16 March 2000, 41.

16. Delevingne, op. cit., 127–8.

17. 'VAD Nurse's Death', *The Times*, 19 December 1918, 3a; compare Donald Carswell, *Trial of Ronald True* (1950), 104.

18. Pro Bono Publico, 'Abuse of Drugs', *The Times*, 29 February 1924, 8f.

19. Mills, *Laughter of Fools*, 180. Lady Wolverton in 1917 decided that as a war-time compromise she should travel by bus. She sat beside a woman who kept sniffing loudly, and eventually demanded if her neighbour hadn't got a handkerchief. 'Yes,' replied the woman, 'but I never lends it on a bus'.

20. 'Drug Addicts', *JAMA*, 16 February 1924, 561.

21. International Anti-Opium Association of Peking, *Morphia and Narcotic Drugs in China*, bulletin vol. V, no. 1 (February 1925), 15.

22. Vladimir Nabokov, *Tyrants Destroyed* (1975), 142, 148.

23. 'Restrictions of Sale of Drugs in Spain to Pharmacies', *JAMA*, 21 October 1916, 1238.

24. 'Cocaine Traffic', *Lancet*, 5 August 1922, 291.

25. 'International Control of the Sale of Narcotics', *JAMA*, 1 September 1923, 761.
26. Baron Harry D'Erlanger, *The Last Plague of Egypt* (1936), 143.
27. PRO FO 371/11714, minute of Kenneth Johnstone, 17 December 1926.
28. Paul Valéry, *Regards sur le Monde Actuel* (1945), 34; *Reflections on the World Today* (1951), 29–30.
29. PRO FO 371/12060, Annual Report for USA (1926), 84.
30. W. W. Willoughby, *Opium as an International Problem* (1925), 323.
31. Viscount Cecil of Chelwood, *A Great Experiment* (1941), 164–5.
32. PRO FO 144/6073/436328/ 60, Delevingne to Sir John Anderson, 22 November 1924.
33. Willoughby, op. cit., 349.
34. 'The Use and Abuse of Opium', *New Statesman*, 24 January 1925, 436–7.
35. Marcel de Kort, 'Doctors, diplomats and businessmen: conflicting interests in the Netherlands and the Dutch East Indies, 1860–1950', in Gootenberg, *Cocaine*, 136.
36. Willoughby, op. cit., 386.
37. H. J. Anslinger and William Tompkins, *The Traffic in Narcotics* (1953), 33.
38. Lord Olivier, 'Opium in America', *The Times*, 16 January 1925, 13e.
39. PRO FO 371/10967, minute of Sir Laurence Collier, 10 March 1925.
40. Willoughby, op. cit., 420–21, 425.
41. Delevingne, op. cit., 137.
42. PRO FO 371/11714, Viscount Cecil of Chelwood, memorandum 'Opium', 29 June 1925.
43. John Palmer Gavit, 'Uncle Sam Scores One on Opium', *Survey*, 15 January 1927, 485–6.
44. PRO FO 371/12530, minute of Frank Ashton-Gwatkin, 5 May 1927.
45. PRO FO 371/10345, Lord Crewe to Raymond Poincaré, 15 May 1923.
46. Delevingne, op. cit., 137.
47. PRO FO 371/10970, Sir Laurence Collier to Rowland Sperling, 3 September 1925.
48. Willoughby, op. cit., 348–9.
49. PRO FO 371/13973, Extract from an Agent of the Cairo City Police [1927?], f. 123.
50. PRO FO 371/13977, R. F. Wigram to Sir George Mounsey, 23 July 1927.
51. Delevingne, op. cit., 136.
52. PRO FO 371/15523, Delevingne to C. W. Orde, 27 June 1931.
53. Russell, *Egyptian Service*, 254.
54. Paul Gootenberg, 'Reluctance or resistance? Constructing cocaine (prohibitions) in Peru, 1910–50', in Paul Gootenberg, ed., *Cocaine: Global Histories* (1999), 46–55.
55. PRO FO 371/12528, despatch 157 of Sir Robert Michell, La Paz, 14 December 1926.

56. De Kort, 'Doctors, diplomats', 129–31.

57. PRO FO 371/10969, despatch 48 of F. G. Gorton, Saigon, 22 December 1924.

58. Sir Arnold Wilson, *South West Persia: a Political Officer's Diary 1907–1914* (1941), 244–5.

59. Sir Arnold Wilson, 'Opium in Persia', *The Times*, 20 January 1925, 8d.

60. PRO FO 371/10967, despatch OT(B)146, Sir Robert Hadow, 28 November 1924.

61. A. G. Lias, 'Drug Traffic in China', *The Times*, 8 May 1925, 15e.

62. PRO FO 371/12526, Sir Edward Cook to Sir Sydney Waterlow, 10 September 1927.

63. PRO FO 371/12526, minute of Kenneth Johnstone, 12 December 1927.

64. PRO FO 371/21046, minute of Milo Talbot, 23 November 1937.

65. PRO FO 371/10967, League of Nations memorandum 'Traffic in Opium: Cultivation of the Opium Poppy in Southern Serbia', 16 January 1925.

66. PRO FO 371/10344, despatch 410 of Sir Alban Young, Belgrade, 8 November 1924; PRO FO 371/10967, Despatch OT541, E. Murray Harvey, Belgrade, 4 November 1925.

67. PRO FO 371/12528, despatch 619 of Sir Reginald Hoare, Constantinople, 14 December 1927, and Delevingne to Mounsey, 24 December 1927; PRO FO 371/12527, Delevingne to Mounsey, 8 November 1927.

68. PRO FO 371/13973, minute of C. E. Minns, 17 October 1929.

69. Joseph C. Grew, *Turbulent Era*, II (1953), 883–4.

70. Russell, op. cit., 240.

71. Anslinger and Tompkins, *Traffic*, 280.

72. PRO FO 371/18203, S. Harrison (Sofia), report on 'Illicit Drug Traffic', 4 June 1932.

73. PRO FO 371/18203, Despatch 212 of John Balfour (Sofia), 19 August 1934.

74. Dame Rachel Crowdy-Thornhill, 'Ban on Heroin', *The Times*, 5 December 1955, 9e.

75. For the paragraphs that follow I rely on Kathryn Meyer, 'Japan and the World Narcotics Traffic', in Goodman, Lovejoy and Sherratt, *Consuming Habits*, 186–202.

76. Herbert L. May, *Survey of Smoking Opium Conditions in the Far East* (1927), 40–1.

77. Willoughby, *Opium*, 118–20.

78. Frederic Wakeman, Jr, *Policing Shanghai 1927–1937* (1995), 272.

79. Albert Fields and Peter Tararin, 'Opium in China', *BJA*, 64 (1970), 379.

80. Russell, op. cit., 252–3.

81. PRO FO 371/12526, memorandum on Opium Policy of Leopold Amery, March 1927.

82. PRO FO 371/12531, Sir Laurence Guillemard to Leopold Amery, 16 March 1927.

83. Herbert R. Robinson, *A Modern De Quincey* (1942), 105–8.

84. De Monfreid, *Hashish*, 168–9.

85. D'Erlanger, *Plague*, 284.

86. PRO FO 371/12532, Consul P. Grant Jones, 'Memorandum on the Traffic in Narcotics at Harbin', 25 July 1927.

87. PRO FO 371/13251, P. Grant Jones, 'The Drug Traffic in Harbin', 13 December 1927.

88. PRO FO 371/13251, P. Grant Jones, 'The Drug Traffic in Harbin', 30 April 1928.

89. Charles à Court Repington, *After the War* (1922), 143.

90. D'Erlanger, *Plague*, 121–7.

91. 'Statistical Data on Cocainism and Morphinism in Austria', *JAMA*, 13 December 1924, 1936.

92. PRO FO 371/11711, Delvingne to Foreign Office, 10 May 1926.

93. Jonnes, *Hep-Cats*, 79.

94. Anslinger and Tompkins, *Traffic*, 279.

95. Lyttelton, 'Opium Question', 111.

96. PRO FO 371/10969, Note on the Operations of a Syndicate for Importing Opium and Narcotics, [May 1925?].

97. PRO FO 371/10970, Home Office memorandum, 'MacDonald & Co of Riehen', 30 June 1925.

98. PRO FO 371/11711, Delevingne to Sir George Mounsey, 20 November 1926.

99. Arthur Gold and Robert Fizdale, *Misia* (1980), 280, 300.

100. 'Campaign against Cocainomania', *JAMA*, 20 August 1921, 633–4.

101. Russell, op. cit., 241.

102. 'Spread of Cocaine Traffic', *JAMA*, 12 August 1922, 569; Brenda Dean Paul, *My First Life* (1935), 89.

103. Judith Thurman, *Secrets of the Flesh* (1999), 402.

104. Laura Claridge, *Tamara de Lempicka* (2000), 91, 94.

105. Kate Meyrick, *Secrets of the 43* (1933), 127–8.

106. Pierre Drieu la Rochelle, *Le Feu Follet* (1931), 51–3.

107. Liane de Pougy, *My Blue Notebooks* (1979), 229–31.

108. John Richardson, *Sorcerer's Apprentice* (1999), 116.

109. De Monfreid, *Hashish*, 38.

110. Russell, op. cit., 255.

111. Ibid., 256.

112. PRO FO 371/11711, memorandum 'Opium' by Victor Cusden, 29 January 1926.

113. PRO FO 371/11711, despatch 219 of Sir John Sterndale Bennett, Santiago, 31 August 1926.

114. Delevingne, 'Drug Addiction', 141–2.

115. Anslinger and Tompkins, *Traffic in Narcotics*, 41.
116. D'Erlanger, *Plague*, 221–4; Jonnes, *Hep-Cats*, 99.
117. PRO FO 371/11715, despatch 139 of Herbert Brooks, 19 August 1926.
118. Anslinger and Tompkins, *Traffic in Narcotics*, 37–8.
119. PRO FO 371/11784, despatch 408 of Sir Robert Hodgson, Moscow, 31 May 1926.
120. PRO FO 371/11713, despatch 924 of Sir Robert Hodgson, Moscow, 16 December 1926.
121. PRO FO 371/11710, memorandum 'The Opium Habit in East Persia', by Henry Law, 21 July 1925.
122. D'Erlanger, *Plague*, 14–15; De Monfreid, *Hashish*, 175.
123. PRO FO 371/11710, memorandum 'The Opium Habit in East Persia', by Henry Law, 21 July 1925.
124. D'Erlanger, op. cit., 42.
125. Russell, op. cit., 228.
126. *Dictionary of National Biography*.
127. Russell, *Egyptian Service*, 223.
128. PRO FO 371/10970, Viscount Allenby to Sir Austen Chamberlain, 14 May 1925.
129. PRO FO 371/11714, memorandum 'Narcotics', by Douglas Baker of Cairo City Police Department, 28 January 1926.
130. Russell, op. cit., 223.
131. Central Narcotics Intelligence Bureau, Interim Report to June 1929 (Cairo Government Press, 1929), 7–8; copy in PRO 371/13974.
132. Russell, op. cit., 224.
133. Ibid., 225–6.
134. Ibid., 227.
135. Ibid., 236.
136. D'Erlanger, *Plague*, 129–32.
137. CNIB Report to June 1929, 2–4.
138 Ibid., 5.
139. Russell, op. cit., 234.
140. Ibid., 235.
141. Herbert Giles, *Some Truths about Opium* (1923), 30.
142. PRO FO 371/15523, J. Slattery, *Investigation of the Problem of Smuggling Cocaine into India from the Far East* (Government of India Press: July 1931).
143. 'Opium Trial at Shanghai', *The Times*, 16 February 1925, 12b; *North China Herald*, 24 January 1925; 'The Great Canton Road Opium Case', *North China Herald*, 7 March 1925.
144. Charles Walney, 'The Opium Traffic', *Morning Post*, 7 March 1925.
145. PRO FO 371/15523, Slattery, *Investigation*.
146. 'The Curse of China', *The Times*, 8 July 1924, 15f.
147. Thomas Fisher Library, University of Toronto, Rodney Gilbert to J. O. P. Bland, 22 August 1926, Bland microfilm 6.

148. PRO FO 371/13252, minute of Kenneth Johnstone, 17 February 1928.

149. PRO FO 371/13252, memorandum by G. S. Moss, Consul at Foochow, 22 August 1928.

150. Delevingne, op. cit., 145.

151. Anslinger and Tompkins, *Traffic*, 54–6; De Kort, 'Doctors, Diplomats and Businessmen', 134–5.

CHAPTER TEN

1. *Wine and Food*, I (1934), 1.

2. André L. Simon, 'First American Impressions', *Wine and Food*, II (1935), 6, 8.

3. Anthony Miles, Keith Waterhouse and Ronald Bedford, 'Drugs—are they a help or a menace?', *Daily Mirror*, 19 September 1955, 6–7.

4. Bruce Jackson, 'White-Collar Pill Party', *Atlantic*, vol. 218 (August 1966), 35.

5. Mark Amory, *Lord Berners* (1998), 216.

6. Jackson, 'White-Collar Pill', 36.

7. McAllister, *Drug Diplomacy*, 226.

8. Anslinger and Tompkins, *Traffic*, 67–8.

9. Miles, Waterhouse and Bedford, op. cit., 6.

10. Anon., 'Drugs: a *Help* or a *Menace*?', *Daily Mirror*, 18 September 1955, 16.

11. Richard Hunter, 'The Abuse of Barbiturates and other sedative drugs with special reference to psychiatric patients', *BJA*, 53 (1957), 95.

12. L. G. Kiloh and S. Brandon, 'Habituation and Addiction to Amphetamines', *BMJ*, 7 July 1962, 40.

13. Benjamin G. Schafer, ed., *The Herbert Huncke Reader* (1998), 26–7.

14. Theodor Adorno, *Minima Moralia* (1978), 54.

15. Grover Smith, ed., *Letters of Aldous Huxley* (1969), 722.

16 Frank Harris, 'Thoughts on Morals', *English Review*, 8 (1911), 442.

17. Cesare Pavese, *This Business of Living* (1961), 42.

18. Jackson, 'White-Collar Pill', 40.

19. T. S. Eliot, introduction to Djuna Barnes, *Nightwood* (1937 edition).

20. Alan Pryce-Jones, 'A Road With No Turning', *Listener*, 3 July 1958, 16.

21. Robin Murray, 'Minor Analgesic Abuse: the Slow Recognition of a Public Health Problem', *BJA*, 75 (1980), 9.

22. P. P. E. Savage, 'Abuse and Addiction—Man or Drug', *BJA*, 66 (1971), 289–9.

23. Murray, 'Analgesic Abuse', 10.

24. M. M. Glatt, 'Recent Patterns of Abuse of and Dependence on Drugs', *BJA*, 63 (1968), 118.

25. 'Headaches, a new approach', *Daily Mirror*, 12 September 1955, 6a.

26. Jackson, 'White-Collar Pill', 35.

27. Myron Prinzmetal and Wilfred Bloomberg, 'The Use of Benzedrine for

the Treatment of Narcolepsy', *JAMA*, 21 December 1935, 2051–4.

28. Eugene Davidoff and Edward Reifenstein, 'The Stimulating Action of Benzedrine Sulfate', *JAMA*, 22 May 1937, 1770–76.

29. Erich Guttmann and William Sargant, 'Observations on Benzedrine', *BMJ*, 15 May 1937, 1015.

30. Kiloh and Brandon, 'Addiction to Amphetamines', 40.

31. P. H. Connell, *Amphetamine Psychosis* (1958).

32. New York Public Library, Berg collection, W. H. Auden to Alan Ansen, 23 June 1952.

33. Richard Davenport-Hines, *Auden* (1995), 305–6, 318.

34. Jack Kerouac, *Vanity of Duluoz* (1969), 269.

35. Ann Charters, ed., *Jack Kerouc: Selected Letters 1940–1956* (1995), 100.

36. Ann Charters, ed., *Jack Kerouac: Selected Letters 1957–1969* (2000), 302.

37. Hugh Crichton-Miller, 'Subjective and Objective Observations on Benzedrine', *BJA*, 44 (1947), 46.

38. Burroughs, 'Letter from Master Addict', 128.

39. *Huncke Reader*, 340–1.

40. R. C. Browne, 'Amphetamine in the Air Force', *BJA*, 44 (1947), 70.

41. Hugh Trevor-Roper (Lord Dacre of Glanton), *The Last Days of Hitler* (1947), 66, 72–3.

42. Boyce Rensenberger, 'Amphetamines used by a physician to life moods of famous patients', *New York Times*, 4 December 1972, 1, 34.

43. F. Scott Fitzgerald, *The Last Tycoon*, 231.

44. Kerouac, *Duluoz*, 271.

45. Robert Rhodes James, ed., *Chips* (1967), 419.

46. Alice Echols, *Scars of Sweet Paradise* (2000), 44, 77.

47. Lord Segal, House of Lords debates, 30 June 1966, vol. 275, col. 825.

48. *Huncke Reader*, 341.

49. Ann Charters, ed., *Jack Kerouac: Selected Letters 1940–1956* (1995), 522–3; Jack Kerouac, *The Dharma Bums* (1959), 10.

50. *Huncke Reader*, 283.

51. Ibid., 341–2.

52. Report of Reference Committee on Hygiene, Public Health, and Industrial Health', *JAMA*, 13 July 1957, 1244; 'Use and Abuse of Drugs by Athletes', *Lancet*, 1 February 1958, 252.

53. Echols, *Scars*, 82–3.

54. John Clellon Holmes, *Go* (1952), 19, 36, 126.

55. Caroline Freud, 'Portrait of the Beatnik', *Encounter*, 12 (1959), 43.

56. Jackson, 'White-Collar Pill', 36–8, 40.

57. Abrahams, 'Drugs by Athletes', 23.

58. See Arnold Mandell, *The Nightmare Season* (1976); Tom Donohoe and Neil Johnson, *Foul Play: drug abuse in sports* (1987).

59. Julian Barnes, 'The Hardest Test', *New Yorker*, 21 August 2000, 97.

60. 'Cycling Ace Dies on Mountain Climb', *The Times*, 14 July 1967, 1g;

'Simpson Had Been Taking Drugs', *The Times*, 4 August 1967, 1h.

61. Ann Dally, *A Doctor's Story* (1990), 51–2.
62. Information from Ann Dally, 21 November 2000.
63. M. M. Glatt, 'Psychotherapy of Drug Dependence', *BJA*, 65 (1970), 51.
64. Kiloh and Brandon, 'Habituation and Addiction', 43.
65. Ibid., 41.
66. Miles, Waterhouse and Bedford, 'Drugs', 6.
67. MacDonald, 'Mood Modifying Drugs', 76.
68. S. Locket, 'The Abuse of the Barbiturates', *BJA*, 53 (1957), 106.
69. Jackson, 'White-Collar Pill', 36.
70. Sybille Bedford, *The Best We Can Do* (1958); Percy Hoskins, *Two Were Acquitted* (1984); Lord Devlin, *Easing the Passing* (1985).
71. Keith Waterhouse, 'Secrets of the Pill-Taker', *Daily Mirror*, 20 September 1955, 9.
72. Shelley Winters, *Shelley II* (1989), 14.
73. Diane Wood Middlebrook, *Anne Sexton* (1991), 34, 165, 210, 216.
74. Anne Sexton, *The Complete Poems* (1981), 165–6.
75. John Kenneth Galbraith, *Ambassador's Journal* (1969), 306.
76. H. Petursson and M. H. Lader, 'Benzodiazepine Dependence', *BJA*, 76 (1981), 135.
77. Private Information.
78. Interview with Kenneth Leech, 11 January 2001.
79. P. H. Connell, 'What To Do About Pep Pills', *New Society* (20 February 1964), 6–7.
80. Dale Beckett, 'Should We Legalise Pot?', *New Society*, 18 May 1967, 720.
81. PRO HO 305/8, Notes of Meeting on Drug Problems Held in Room 240, Home Office, on 22 November 1962.
82. P. D. Scott and D. R. C. Willcox, 'Delinquency and the Amphetamines,' *British Journal of Psychiatry*, 111 (1965), 868–9.
83. Neale Pharoah, 'He gets out of it', *New Society*, 20 February 1964, 8.
84. PRO Prem 11/4848, Sir Alec Douglas-Home to Henry Brooke, 4 February 1964.
85. PRO Prem 11/4848, Brooke to Douglas-Home, 18 February 1964.
86. PRO HO 305/4, T. C. Green of Home Office, circular letter to chief constables, 'Traffic in Drugs', 17 February 1964.
87. PRO HO 305/4, R. Walton to T. C. Green, 18 February 1964.
88. PRO HO 305/4, Sir Joseph Simpson to Green, 19 February 1964.
89. PRO HO 305/3, minute of Henry Brooke, 3 March 1964, on Selwyn Lloyd to Brooke, 28 February 1964.
90. 'A Bill Too Soon', *The Times*, 1 April 1964, 11b.
91. 'Drugs Industry in Trouble', *The Economist*, 4 April 1964, 66b.
92. Paul Barker, 'Brighton Battleground', *New Society*, 21 May 1964, 10.
93. 'A Bill Too Soon', 11b.

94. 'It's A Riot', *The Economist*, 4 April 1964, 20a.

95. Kenneth Leech, *Youthquake* (1973), 3.

96. Paul Barker and Alan Little, 'The Margate Offenders', *New Society*, 30 July 1964, 6–10.

97. Stanley Cohen, *Folk Devils and Moral Panics* (1972), 56, 135.

98. 'It's A Riot', 20a.

99. Kenneth Leech, *Keep the Faith Baby* (1973), 11–15.

100. Ibid., 35.

101. Ibid., 31–2.

102. 'Doctor signed for 43,000 purple hearts for himself', *The Times*, 21 July 1970, 2a.

103. 'Drugs made 5,500 guineas for doctor', *The Times*, 26 February 1970, 2f; 'Doctor says "junkies" were his friends', *The Times*, 29 February 1970, 3a; 'Striking off order on drug doctor', *The Times*, 29 February 1970, 3a.

104. David Hely, *The Anti-Depressant Era* (1997), 52. I am profoundly indebted to this excellent book.

105. Lord Kinross, *The Innocents at Home* (1959), 220.

106. Brian Inglis, 'A Little of What You Fancy', *Punch*, 5 March 1969, 340.

107. Kenneth Allsopp, 'Jazz and Narcotics', *Encounter*, 16 (1961), 57.

108. Matthew Lynn, *The Billion Dollar Battle* (1991), 48.

109. Macdonald, 'Mood Modifying Drugs', 78.

110. Miles, Waterhouse and Bedford, 'Drugs', 6–7.

111. Lord St Just, House of Lords debates, 30 June 1966, vol. 275, cols. 820–21.

112. Echols, *Scars*, 44.

113. Smith, *Huxley Letters*, 722.

114. Jay Stevens, *Storming Heaven: LSD and the American Dream* (1988), 176.

115. Ibid., 183.

116. Jonnes, *Hep-Cats*, 225.

117. Smith, *Huxley Letters*, 945.

118. Barry Miles, *Ginsberg* (1990), 99–105, 325–7.

119. Ibid., 276–9.

120. Smith, op. cit., 881.

121. Kenneth Leech, *Youthquake* (1973), 51.

122. William S. Braden, 'LSD and the Press', in Stanley Cohen and Jock Young, eds., *The Manufacture of News* (1981), 248–62.

123. Timothy Leary, *The Politics of Ecstasy* (1971), 38.

124. Stevens, *Storming Heaven*, 188.

125. Ibid., 269.

126. William Burroughs, *Last Words* (2000), 3, 44.

127. John N. Bleibtreu, 'LSD and the Third Eye', *Atlantic Monthly*, 218 (September 1966), 64–9.

128. Stevens, op. cit., 276.

129. Ibid., 278.

130. Jonnes, *Hep-Cats*, 239.
131. Echols, *Scars*, 157.
132. David E. Smith, John Luce and Ernest Dernburg, 'Love Needs Care: Haight-Ashbury Dies', *New Society*, 16 July 1970, 99.
133. Lord Stonham, House of Lords debates, 20 June 1967, vol. 283, col. 1271.
134. Lord Stonham, House of Lords debates, 5 July 1967, vol. 284, cols. 747–8.
135. David Black, *Acid* (1998), 4.
136. Bob Mullan, *Mad to be Normal* (1995), 220.
137. Ibid., 221.
138. Ibid., 222, 224–5.
139. Ibid., 225.
140. Adrian C. Laing, *R. D. Laing* (1994), 184–5.
141. Ibid., 196–7.
142. National Commission on Marijuana and Drug Abuse, *Drug Use: Problem in Perspective* (1973), 164, 224.
143. James Miller, *The Passion of Michel Foucault* (1993), 245, 248, 251.
144. Alasdair MacIntyre, 'The new superstition', *New Society*, 6 April 1967, 510.
145. McAllister, *Drug Diplomacy*, 220.
146. Ibid.
147. Ibid., 226.
148. House of Commons debates, 25 March 1970, vol. 798, col. 1455.
149. Lynn, *Billion Dollar Battle*, 57.
150. McAllister, op. cit., 229.
151. Ibid., 232.
152. Ian Hindmarch, 'Patterns of Drug Use in a Provincial University', *BJA*, 64 (1970), 401.
153. Hindmarch, 'Provincial University', 399–400.
154. Jackson, 'White-Collar Pill', 39.
155. House of Commons debates, 25 March 1970, vol. 798, col. 1469.
156. Franklin Zimring and Gordon Hawkins, *The Search for Rational Drug Control* (1992), 5–7.

CHAPTER ELEVEN

1. Stanley Meisner, 'Federal Narcotics Czar', *Nation*, 20 February 1960, 159–62.
2. Anslinger and Tompkins, *Traffic*, 295, 303.
3. Ibid., 282, 293.
4. *Huncke Reader*, xxii.
5. Harry Anslinger and Will Oursler, *The Murderers* (1961), 131.
6. John McWilliams, *The Protectors* (1990), 70.
7. Burroughs, 'Letter from Master Addict', 128.
8. McWilliams, op. cit., 70.
9. Harry Anslinger with Courtney R. Cooper, 'Marihuana: Assassin of

Youth', *American Magazine*, vol. 124 (1937), 19, 150.

10. John Kaplan, *Marijuana—the new prohibition* (1970), 89.

11. 'Federal Regulation of Medicinal Use of Cannabis', *JAMA*, 1 May 1937, 1543.

12. Bonnie and Whitebread, *Marihuana Conviction*, 174.

13. McWilliams, op. cit., 77–8.

14. Meyer Berger, 'Tea for a Viper', *New Yorker*, 12 March 1938, 49.

15. H. J. Anslinger, 'The Psychiatric Aspects of Marihuana Intoxication', *JAMA*, 16 January 1943, 212.

16. 'Recent Investigations of Marihuana', *JAMA*, 5 December 1942, 1128–9.

17. Eli Marcovitz, 'Marihuana Problems', *JAMA*, 29 September 1945, 378.

18. 'Marihuana Problems', *JAMA*, 28 April 1945, 1129.

19. Nathaniel West, *The Day of the Locust* (1939), chapter 22.

20. Anslinger and Tompkins, *Traffic*, 168.

21. Richard Nixon, *In the Arena* (1990), 133.

22. Benjamin DeMott, 'The Great Narcotics Muddle', *Harper's Magazine*, 224 (March 1962), 48.

23. H. J. Anslinger, 'Drug Addiction', *JAMA*, 23 September 1950, 333.

24. Anslinger and Tompkins, *Traffic*, 216, 218.

25. B. Dai, *Opium Addiction in Chicago* (1937). This observation was confirmed in later research on New York City: I. Chein, D. Gerard, R. Lee and E. Rosenfeld, *The Road to H: narcotics, delinquency and social policy* (1964).

26. Nelson Algren, *The Man With The Golden Arm* (1949), 17–18.

27. Anslinger, 'Drug Addiction' [1950], 333.

28. Kenneth Allsopp, 'Jazz and Narcotics', *Encounter*, 16 (1961), 54–56.

29. Jonnes, *Hep-Cats*, 125–6.

30. Alyn Shipton, *Groovin' High* (2000).

31. Peter Goldman, *The Life and Death of Malcolm X* (1974), 85.

32. Ralph Ellison, *Invisible Man* (1952), 15–17.

33. Jonnes, *Hep-Cats*, 140.

34. 'To grips with addiction', *New Society*, 12 March 1964, 19.

35. Jonnes, *Hep-Cats*, 160.

36. H. J. Anslinger, 'Drug addiction', *JAMA*, 23 September 1950, 333.

37. Jonnes, *Hep-Cats*, 119.

38. *Huncke Reader*, 268.

39. Alden Stevens, 'Make Dope Legal', *Harper's Magazine*, vol. 205 (1952), 42.

40. Anslinger and Tompkins, *Traffic*, 11–12.

41. Bonnie and Whitebread, *Marihuana Conviction*, 208.

42. Ibid., 213.

43. Harris Isbell, 'Perspective in Research on Opiate Addiction', *BJA*, 57 (1961), 18.

44. Henry L. Giordano, 'Marihuana—a calling card to narcotic addiction',

FBI Law Enforcement Bulletin, 37 (11) (1968), 2–5, 16.

45. Sir David Frost, *An Autobiography*, I (1993), 305.
46. Reginald Maudling, House of Commons debates, 16 July 1970, vol. 803, col. 1754.
47. Anslinger and Tompkins, *Traffic*, 19, 21–2.
48. Holmes, *Go*, 100–2.
49. Allen Ginsberg, 'The Great Marijuana Hoax', *Atlantic Monthly*, 218 (November 1966), 110.
50. 'Generations and Drugs', *New Statesman*, 7 July 1967, 1.
51. Gregory Corso, *Mindfield* (1992), 98.
52. Don Casto III, 'Marijuana and the Assassins', *BJA*, 65 (1970), 219; J. L. Simmons, ed., *Marijuana, Myths and Realities* (1967), 139, 183.
53. Lord Derwent, House of Lords debates, 20 June 1967, vol. 283, col. 1286.
54. Bonnie and Whitebread, *Marijuana*, 219–20.
55. Stevens, op. cit., 41.
56. Anthony Saper, 'The Making of Policy through Myth, Fantasy and Historical Accident', *BJA*, 69 (1974), 190.
57. Benjamin DeMott, 'The Great Narcotics Muddle', *Harper's Magazine*, vol. 224 (March 1962), 47.
58. Ibid., 48.
59. Ibid., 46.
60. Anslinger and Tompkins, *Traffic*, 186.
61. Ibid., 189.
62. Ibid., 226.
63. Stevens, op. cit., 42.
64. Oliver Harris, ed., *The Letters of William Burroughs 1945–1959* (1993), 83, 98.
65. Vincent P. Dole, Marie E. Nyswander and Mary Jeanne Kreek, 'Narcotic Blockade', *Archives of Internal Medicine*, vol. 118 (1966), 304–9. See also Vincent P. Dole and Marie Nyswander, 'Rehabilitation of the Street Addict', *Archives of Environmental Health*, vol. 14 (1967), 477–80.
66. Gertrude Samuels, 'Drug against drug', *New Society*, 17 October 1968, 554.
67. Horace Freeland Judson, *Heroin Addiction in Britain* (1973), 110.
68. Vincent P. Dole, 'What We Have Learned from Three Decades of Methadone Maintenance Treatment', *Drug and Alcohol Review*, vol. 13 (1994), 3–4.
69. David E. Smith, 'Love Needs Care', *New Society*, 16 July 1970, 100.
70. Alasdair MacIntyre, 'The cannabis taboo', *New Society*, 5 December 1968, 848.

CHAPTER TWELVE

1. Brenda Dean Paul, *My First Life* (1935), 92–3.
2. Ibid., 172–3.

3. 'Dangerous Drugs Prosecution', *The Times*, 7 December 1931, 7g.
4. Dean Paul, op. cit., 218.
5. Ibid., 204–5.
6. Ibid., 218–19.
7. 'Drug Charges', *The Times*, 6 September 1932, 9c.
8. Dean Paul, op. cit., 234.
9 Ibid., 237–8.
10. 'Miss Brenda Dean Paul To Go To Prison', *The Times*, 4 October 1932, 11b; 'Miss Brenda Paul's Appeal', *The Times*, 7 October 1932, 9d.
11. Dean Paul, op. cit., 244.
12. Ke Kort, 'Doctors, diplomats and businessmen', 127.
13. Dean Paul, op. cit., 252.
14. Ibid., 263–4.
15. W. H. Auden, 'Jean Cocteau', *Flair*, I (1950), 101.
16. H. B. Spear, 'The Growth of Heroin Addiction in the United Kingdom', *BJA*, 64 (1969), 248–9.
17. J. D. Caswell, *A Lance for Liberty* (1961), 251–4; 'Two unconscious in flat', *The Times*, 29 January 1947, 2d; 'Psychiatrist found dead', *The Times*, 6 March 1947, 2b.
18. Michael Sissons and Philip French, eds., *Age of Austerity* (1963), 88–99, 255–63.
19. Charlotte Mosley, ed., *Letters from Nancy* (1993), 233–4.
20. W. Norwood East, 'The British Government Report to the United Nations on the Traffic in Opium and other Dangerous Drugs', *BJA*, 46 (1949), 38–9.
21. Michael Banton, *The Coloured Quarter* (1955), 196.
22. Colin MacInnes, *England, Half English* (1961), 25–7.
23. Bernard Kops, *The World is a Wedding* (1963), 146–7, 149.
24. Ibid., 181, 183.
25. Spear, 'Growth of Heroin Addiction', 250.
26. George Lyle, 'Dangerous Drug Traffic in London', *BJA*, 50 (1953), 54, 56.
27. Ibid., 53.
28. Spear, op. cit., 251–3.
29. Bing Spear, 'The Early Years of the British System in Practice', in John Strang and Michael Gossop, eds., *Heroin Addiction and Drug Policy* (1994), 9.
30. Donald Johnson, *Bars and Barricades* (1952), 252–79.
31. Spear, op. cit., 254.
32. Colin MacInnes, *Out of the Way* (1979), 150–53.
33. Kops, op. cit., 233.
34. Colin MacInnes, *Absolute Beginners* (1959), 82–3.
35. Ibid., 64–5.
36. A. Kaldeeg, 'Heroin Addiction', *New Society*, 2 February 1967, 155.
37. Leech, *Keep the Faith*, 28; David Heisler, 'Stepney Worried About Young "Junkies" ', *Hackney Gazette*, 23 March 1967.

38. 'Manufacture of Heroin', *The Times*, 26 May 1955, 11e.
39. Earl Jowitt, House of Lords debates, 13 December 1955, vol. 195, cols. 10–27.
40. Lord Webb-Johnson, House of Lords debates, 13 December 1955, vol. 195, cols. 45–6.
41. Lord Amulree, House of Lords debates, 13 December 1955, vol. 195, col. 83.
42. Colin MacInnes, *Absolute Beginners* (1959), 54.
43. PRO HO 319/7, Sir Nigel Fisher, minutes of Joint Home Affairs and Health Parliamentary Committee, 5 December 1955.
44. 'Discussion Following the International Symposium', *BJA*, 53 (1956), 14.
45. William Burroughs, *Last Words* (2000), 3.
46. PRO LO/2/987, Sir Reginald Manningham-Buller and Sir Harry Hylton-Foster, 'Heroin: Note by the Law Officers', 12 December 1955.
47. PRO Prem 11/1438, Sir Norman Brook to Sir Anthony Eden, 'Heroin', 17 January 1956.
48. Sir Adolphe Abrahams, 'The Use and Abuse of Drugs by Athletes', *BJA*, 53 (1957), 23.
49. Colin MacInnes, *City of Spades* (1957), 73.
50. Spear, 'Early Years', 21.
51. Max Glatt, David Pittman, Duff Gillespie and Donald Hills, *The Drug Scene in Great Britain* (1967), 39–40.
52. Isabella Robertson, 'Studies in the Acid-Base Equilibrium in Psychoses', *Lancet*, 13 August 1927, 322–4.
53. Spear, 'Early Years', 18.
54. I. M. Frankau and Patricia Stanwell, 'The Treatment of Drug-Addiction', *Lancet*, 24 December 1960, 1377–9.
55. Spear and Mott, 'Cocaine and Crack', 47.
56. Lady Frankau, 'Treatment of Heroin and Cocaine Addiction', *Nursing Times*, 9 June 1961, 737–8.
57. Lady Frankau, 'Treatment in England of Canadian Patients Addicted to Narcotic Drugs', *Canadian Medical Association Journal*, vol. 90, 8 February 1964, 421.
58. Frankau, 'Treatment in England', 423.
59. Spear, 'Early Years', 19.
60. Glatt, *The Drug Scene*, 84.
61. Vyner, *Groovy Bob*, 152–3.
62. Spear and Mott, 'Cocaine and Crack', 49–50.
63. Lady Frankau, 'Heroin and Cocaine Addiction', 737–8.
64. Henry Matthew, 'The Second Report of the Interdepartmental Committee on Drug Addiction', *BJA*, 61 (1966), 174.
65. Dally, *Doctor's Story*, 104.
66. Michael Nyman, 'Birmingham tackles addiction', *New Society*, 9 February 1967, 202.

67. Glatt, op. cit., 82–9.
68. Frankau, 'Canadian Patients', 49–50.
69. Leech, *Keep the Faith*, 28.
70. 'Make Marijuana Legal, Says Curate', *The Times*, 8 March 1966; Kenneth Leech, 'Facts and Figures About Addiction', *Guardian*, 3 November 1967.
71. 'Conversation with Max Glatt', *BJA*, 78 (1973), 241.
72. Spear, 'Early Years', 16.
73. Kenneth Leech, *Youthquake* (1973), 34.
74. Lord Stonham, House of Lords debates, 20 June 1967, vol. 283, cols. 1271–2.
75. H. R. George and M. M. Glatt, 'A Brief Survey of a Drug Dependency Unit in a Psychiatric Hospital', *BJA*, 62 (1967), 147.
76. H. Dale Beckett, 'Hypotheses Concerning the Etiology of Heroin Addiction', in Peter G. Bourne, ed., *Addiction* (1974), 39.
77. N. C. Lendon, 'Drugs Causing Dependence', *BJA*, 61 (1965), 124.
78. Viscount Amory, House of Lords debates, 30 June 1966, vol. 275, cols. 813–17.
79. Kenneth Leech, 'Danger on the Drug Scene', *Daily Telegraph*, 8 December 1966.
80. DeMott, 'Narcotics Muddle', 53.
81. Sally Trench, *Bury Me in My Boots* (1968), 66–7.
82. Judson, *Heroin Addiction*, 53.
83. Brain, 'British System', 17.
84. Alan Glanz, 'The fall and rise of the general practitioner', in Strang and Gossop, *Heroin*, 155.
85. Thomas Bewley, 'Heroin and Cocaine Addiction', *Lancet*, 10 April 1965, 808–10.
86. Private information.
87. Spear, 'Early Years', 24.
88. Thomas Bewley, 'Heroin Addiction in the United Kingdom (1954–1964)', *BMJ*, 27 November 1965, 1284–6.
89. Brenda Jordan, Kenneth Leech and Judith Piepe, 'Drug addicts: authoritarian methods doomed to failure', *Guardian*, 4 February 1967.
90. Bestic, *Turn Me*, 251–2.
91. P. H. Connell, 'Centres for the treatment of Addiction: Importance of Research', *BMJ*, 20 May 1967, 500. See also Connell and John Strang, 'Creation of the Clinics', in Strang and Gossop, *Heroin*, 167–75.
92. Connell, 'Amphetamine Misuse', 23–4.
93. Thomas Bewley and Stephen Lock, 'Philip Henry Connell', *BMJ*, 31 October 1998, 1255.
94. John Owens, 'Integrated Approach', *BMJ*, 20 May 1967, 501; Michael Nyman, 'Maintaining heroin addicts', *New Society*, 21 September 1967, 409.
95. Dale Beckett, 'Maintaining heroin addiction', *New Society*, 14 September 1967, 360.

96. 'The debate on drugs', *New Society*, 2 December 1965, 4.

97. Bestic, *Turn Me*, 248.

98. Burroughs, Letters, 317, 345.

99. A. J. Hawes, 'A Year After The Drugs Report', *The Times*, 15 November 1966, 11c.

100. Interview with Ken Leech, 11 January 2001.

101. A. J. Hawes, 'Goodbye Junkies', *Lancet*, 1 August 1970, 258–60.

102. Kenneth Leech, 'The London Drug Scene in the 1960s', in David Whynes and Philip Bean, eds., *Policing and Prescribing* (1991), 43–4.

103. 'Addicts in search of treatment', *The Times*, 8 July 1967, 1a.

104. Leech, *Keep the Faith*, 45.

105. B. A. R. Smith (Ministry of Health) to K. Leech, 19 August 1966, Leech papers; K. Leech, 'Treating Drug-addicts', *New Statesman*, 8 September 1967; 'Ministry accused of deceit', *The Times*, 15 January 1968, 2a.

106. Dale Beckett, 'Maintaining heroin addicts', *New Society*, 14 September 1967, 360; interview with Dale Beckett, 13 December 2000.

107. Arthur Hawes, 'Growing Black Market', *The Times*, 27 June 1967, 9c.

108. 'Dr Petro is arrested by drug squad', *The Times*, 12 January 1968, 1d; 'Dr Petro remanded on £1500 bail', *The Times*, 13 January 1968, 2d.

109. 'Dr Petro will continue treatments', *The Times*, 15 February 1968, 1c; 'Dr Petro fined £1,700 on drug charges', *The Times*, 15 February 1968, 4a.

110. Tripp, 'Petro', 12.

111. Cindy Fazey, 'The Consequences of Illegal Drug Use', in Whynes and Bean, *Policing and Prescribing*, 30.

112. Kenneth Leech, 'John Petro, the junkies' doctor', *New Society*, 11 June 1981, 431.

113. Tripp, 'Petro', 17.

114. 'Dr Swan guilty on 13 charges', *The Times*, 3 January 1969, 2c; 'Professional assassin was really a policeman', *The Times*, 4 January 1969, 2a; 'Strong-arm man of Dr Swan in dock', *The Times*, 7 January 1969, 2d; 'Dr Swan sentenced to 15 years' gaol', *The Times*, 11 January 1969, 2e.

115. Judson, *Heroin Addiction*, 39–40, 92.

116. Ibid., 91.

117. Tripp, 'Petro', 13.

118. James H. Willis, 'Unacceptable face of private practice', *BMJ*, 13 August 1983, 500.

119. Lord Stonham, House of Lords debates, 5 July 1967, vol. 284, cols. 744, 750.

120. James Stansfield, 'The Pushers', *Daily Mail*, 26 August 1965.

121. Lord Stonham, House of Lords debates, 5 July 1967, vol. 284, col. 737.

122. 'Find Out First', *New Society*, 16 December 1965, 4; Peter Chapple, 'Treatment in the Community', *BMJ*, 20 May 1967, 500–1.

123. H. Dale Beckett, 'Obituary', the *Lancet*, 13 December 1975, 1219; Tripp, 'Petro', 12; interviews with Dale Beckett, 13 December 2000 and Kenneth Leech, 11 January 2001.

124. Interview with Dr H. Dale Beckett, 13 December 2000.

125. Alan Bestic, *Turn Me On Man* (1966), 220–23.

126. Interview with Dr H. Dale Beckett, 13 December 2000.

127. Colin MacInnes, 'The Problem', *New Society*, 2 March 1967, 321.

128. Jonnes, *Hep-Cats*, 268.

129. Bruce Jackson, 'Exiles from the American Dream', the *Atlantic*, 219 (January 1967), 51.

130. Richard Neville, *Hippie Hippie Shake* (1995), 351.

131. Judson, *Heroin*, 87.

132. 'Conversation with Max Glatt', 241.

133. Leech, 'Voluntary Agencies', 135.

134. Dally, *Doctor's Story*, 91.

135. 'Bench call on doctor to explain', *The Times*, 7 October 1969, 4g.

136. 'Conversation with Max Glatt', 242.

137. Edgar May, 'Drugs without Crime', *Harper's Magazine*, 243 (July 1971), 63–4.

138. Kenneth Leech, 'The Role of the Voluntary Agencies in the Various Aspects of Prevention and Rehabilitation of Drug Users', *BJA*, 67 (1972), 131.

139. 'Who Breaks a Butterfly on a Wheel?', *The Times*, 1 July 1967, 11a; Ray Connolly, ed., *In the Sixties* (1995), 143–5; Lord Montagu of Beaulieu, *Wheels within Wheels* (2000), 275.

140. Vyner, *Groovy Bob*, 112.

141. Ibid., 219.

142. Ibid., 198, 227.

143. Lord Stonham, House of Lords debates, 30 June 1966, vol. 275, col. 830, and 20 June 1967, vol. 283, col. 1271.

144. Tony Parsons, *Dispatches from the Front Line of Popular Culture* (1994), 110.

145. Harry Shapiro and Caesar Glebbek, *Jimi Hendrix, Electric Gypsy* (1995); Jerry Hopkins and Danny Sugarman, *No One Gets Out Of Here Alive* (1980); David Dalton, *Piece of my Heart* (1985); Ellis Amburn, *Pearl: The Obsessions and Passions of Janis Joplin* (1992).

146. Robert Power, 'Drug trends since 1968', in Strang and Gossop, *Heroin*, 31.

147. Kenneth Leech, 'The natural history of two drug cultures', *New Society*, 1 June 1972, 466.

148. James Willis, 'Prescribing to Addicts' in David Whynes and Philip Bean, eds., *Policing and Prescribing* (1991), 72.

149. Leech, *Keep the Faith*, 86–7.

150. Lord Sandford, House of Lords debates, 26 March 1969, vol. 300, col. 1339.

151. 'Theatre of the Drugged', *New Society*, 19 March 1970, 467.

152. Richard Neville, *Playpower* (1970), 119.

153. Martin Plant, 'The Escalation Theory Reconsidered', *BJA*, 68 (1973), 312–3.
154. N. H. Rathod, 'The Use of Heroin and Methadone by Injection in a New Town', *BJA*, 67 (1972), 115, 120–1.
155. Interview with Dr H. Dale Beckett, 13 December 2000.
156. E. H. Bennie, P. Mullin and Balfour Sclare, 'Drug Dependence in Glasgow 1960–1970', *BJA*, 67 (1972), 101.
157. Moya Woodside, 'The First 100 Referrals to a Scottish Drug Treatment Centre', *BJA*, 68 (1973), 240.
158. Tripp, 'Petro', 17.
159. Leslie Iversen, *The Science of Marijuana* (2000), 246.
160. James Callaghan, House of Commons debates, 27 January 1969, vol. 776, col. 959.
161. Tom Iremonger, House of Commons debates, 27 January 1969, vol. 776, cols. 990, 995.
162. Quintin Hogg, House of Commons debates, 27 January 1969, vol. 776, col. 956–8.
163. Hogg, House of Commons debates, 27 January 1969, vol. 776, cols. 950, 957.
164. Patrick McNair-Wilson, House of Commons debates, 27 January 1969, vol. 776, cols. 968–70.
165. A. S. Lynch, E. R. Lake and J. L. McClure, 'A Report of a Series of Meetings Between Addicts and their Parents', *BJA*, 66 (1971), 231.

CHAPTER THIRTEEN

1. Dan Baum, *Smoke and Mirrors: the War on Drugs and the Politics of Failure* (1996), 7.
2. Anthony Summers, *The Arrogance of Power* (2000), 317–18, 449.
3. Richard Nixon, *In the Arena* (1990), 133.
4. Ibid., 134–5.
5. Humberto Fernandez, *Heroin* (1998), 214.
6. Patricia Adler, *Wheeling and Dealing* (1993), 196–7.
7. Tony Smith, 'How dangerous is heroin?', *BMJ*, 25 September 1993, 807.
8. Fernandez, op. cit., 218.
9. Alfred W. McCoy, *The Politics of Heroin: CIA Complicity in the Global Drug Trade* (1991).
10. Gore Vidal, *Collected Essays 1952–1972* (1974), 374.
11. Judson, *Heroin Addiction*, 147.
12. John Marks, 'Opium, the Religion of the People', *Lancet*, 22 June 1985, 1439.
13. Philip Jenkins, *Synthetic Panics* (1999), 22.
14. Erich Goode, 'How the American Marihuana Market Works', *New Society*, 11 June 1970, 992–4.

15. Marks, 'Opium', 1439.

16. Richard Crossman, *The Diaries of a Cabinet Minister*, III (1977), 836–7.

17. Fernandez, op. cit., 223.

18. Gary Indiana, *Horse Crazy* (1989), 133–4.

19. Ethan Nadelmann, *Cops across Borders* (1993), 129.

20. Ibid., 276.

21. David Kline, 'How to Lose the Coke War', *Atlantic Monthly*, 259 (May 1987), 27.

22. Peter Eisner, *America's Prisoner* (1997).

23. Nadelmann, op. cit., 471–2; or 285.

24. Ibid., 474–5.

25. Terence Poppa, *Drug Lord* (1990).

26. James Lieber, 'Coping with Cocaine', *Atlantic Monthly*, 257 (January 1986), 47.

27. Philippe Bourgois, *In Search of Respect* (1995), 345.

28. Ibid., 326.

29. Judson, *Heroin Addiction*, 147.

30. E. Preble and J. Casey, 'Taking care of business: the heroin user's life on the street', *International Journal of Addiction*, 4 (1969), 21.

31. P. J. Goldstein, H. H. Brownstein, P. J. Ryan and P. A. Bellucci, 'Crack and Homicide in New York City', in C. Reinarman and H. Levine, eds., *Crack in America: Demon Drugs and Social Justice* (1997), 113–130.

32. Bourgois, op. cit., 54.

33. Ibid.

34. Claire E. Sterk, *Fast Lives: Women who use Crack* (1999); Lisa Maher, *Sexed Work: Gender, Race and Resistance in a Brooklyn Drug Market* (1997).

35. 'Pregnant Women and their Babies: Drug War Casualties', *New Republic*, 5 March 2001, 7.

36. Office of National Drug Control, *National Drug Control Strategy* (1989), 3–5.

37. Jane Goodsir, 'Cocaine and Crack', in Strang and Gossop, *Heroin*, 132.

38. Jan Willem Gerritsen, *The Control of Fuddle and Flash* (2000), 232–4.

39. Kevin Williamson, *Drugs and the Party Line* (1997), 30.

40. Franklin Zimring and Gordon Hawkins, *The Search for Rational Drug Control* (1992), 5–8.

41. Jenkins, *Synthetic Panics*, 97; Darryl E. Gates with Diane Shah, *Chief* (1992), 286.

42. Philip Bean, 'Cocaine and Crack: the Promotion of an Epidemic', in Philip Bean, ed., *Cocaine and Crack*, 59–60.

43. Geoffrey Pearson, Heidi Safia Mirza and Stewart Phillips, 'Cocaine in Context: Findings from a South London Inner-City Drug Survey', in Bean, *Cocaine and Crack*, 99, 110–11.

44. 'Illegal Drug Menace is like a Medieval Plague, Says Hurd', *The Times*, 19 May 1989, 5a.

45. Margaret Thatcher, House of Commons debates, 25 May 1989, vol. 153, col. 1118.

46. Spear and Mott, 'Cocaine and Crack', 54–55.

47. Nicholas Dorn, 'A Dangerous Crackdown', *The Times*, 26 July 1989, 6f.

48. Karim Murji, 'White Lines: Culture, "Race" and Drugs', in Nigel South, ed., *Drugs: Cultures, Controls and Everyday Life* (1999), 59.

49. Beckett, 'Hypotheses', 53–4.

50. H. Parker, R. Newcombe and K. Bakx, 'The new heroin users: prevalence and characteristics in Wirral, Merseyside', *BJA*, 82 (1987), 147–57; Michael Gossop, Paul Griffiths and John Strang, 'Chasing the dragon: characteristics of heroin chasers', *BJA*, 83 (1988), 159–62; P. Griffiths, M. Gossop, Beverley Powis and J. Strang, 'Transitions in patterns of heroin administration: a study of heroin chasers and heroin injectors', *Addiction*, 89 (1994), 301–9.

51. Mark Gilman and Geoffrey Pearson, 'Lifestyles and Law Enforcement', in Whynes and Bean, *Policing*, 100.

52. John Sweeney, 'Miners' children in the pits of heroin', the *Observer*, 6 October 1996.

53. Martin Mitcheson and Richard Hartnoll, 'Conflicts in deciding treatment within drug dependency clinics', in D. J. West, ed., *Problems of Drug Abuse in Britain* (1978), 74–7; Hartnoll and Mitcheson, 'Evaluation of Heroin Maintenance in a Controlled Trial', *Archives of General Psychiatry*, 37 (1980), 877–84; Martin Mitcheson, 'Drug Clinics in the 1970s', in Strang and Gossop, *Heroin Addiction*, 182–3.

54. Edwards' reports on his follow-up study of all heroin users known to the Home Office in 1965 are in PRO MH 166/935 (not yet released for consultation); see 'Recent Trends in Opiate Dependence', *BMJ*, 7 April 1979, 911; Edna Oppenheimer, Gerry Stimson and Anthony Thorley, 'Seven-year follow-up of heroin addicts', *BMJ*, 15 September 1979, 627–9.

55. Max Glatt, 'Recent trends in opiate dependence', *BJA*, 12 May 1979, 1279.

56. Interview with Dr H. Dale Beckett, 13 December 2000.

57. Norman Tebbit, 'There is such a thing as society', *Spectator*, 25 November 2000, 16.

58. Barbara Bush, *A Memoir* (1994), 321–3.

59. Kenneth Leech, 'Drug Use: prevention and education', paper of February 1997.

60. Hawes, 'Goodbye Junkies', 258.

61. Arnold Treebach, 'Bing Spear: the Passing of a Legend', Drug Policy Foundation announcement, 15 July 1995: accessed www.hoboes.com/pub/Prohibit.

62. Interview with Dr H. Dale Beckett, 13 December 2000.

63. Dale Beckett, 'Heroin, the gentle drug', *New Society*, 26 July 1979, 181–2.

In places I have quoted from the original typescript of this article kindly supplied by Dr Beckett.

64. Dale Beckett, 'Prescription of controlled drugs to addicts', *BMJ*, 9 July 1983, 127.

65. Andria Efthimiou-Mordaunt, 'The user's voice', *Inside Out*, vol. 14 (2000), 9.

66. Dally, *Doctor's Story*, 60–2.

67. Ibid., 69.

68. Spear, 'Early Years', 26.

69. Richard Hartnoll and Roger Lewis, 'Unacceptable face of private practice', *BMJ*, 13 August 1983, 500.

70. P. H. Connell and M. Mitcheson, 'Necessary safeguards when prescribing opoid drugs to addicts', *BMJ*, 10 March 1984, 768.

71. Marks, 'Opium', 1440. See Cindy Fazey, *The Evaluation of Liverpool Drug Dependency Clinic: the first two years 1985 to 1987* (Mersey Health Authority, 1987).

72. Dally, op. cit., 66.

73. Anna Sebra, *Enid Bagnold* (1986), 176, 184, 248, 257, 263–4.

74. Spear and Mott, 'Cocaine and Crack', 46.

75. James Willis, 'Prescribing to addicts', in Whynes and Bean, *Policing*, 72, 75.

76. Dally, op. cit., 92.

77. John Strang, 'Abstinence or Abundance—what goal?', *BMJ*, 8 September 1984, 664.

78. H. B. Spear, 'Management of Drug Addicts', *Lancet*, 6 June 1987, 1322.

79. Interview with Fr Ken Leech, 11 January 2001.

80. Willis, 'Prescribing to Addicts', 75.

81. A. B. Robertson, 'Prescription of controlled drugs to addicts', *BMJ*, 9 July 1983, 126.

82. Dally, op. cit., 130.

83. Thomas Bewley, 'Prescribing psychoactive drugs to addicts', *BMJ*, 16 August 1980, 497.

84. Thomas Bewley and A. Hamid Ghose, 'Unacceptable face of private practice: prescription of controlled drugs to addicts', *BMJ*, 11 June 1983, 1876–7.

85. Beckett, 'Prescription', 127; A. Burr, 'The Piccadilly Drug Scene', *BJA* (1983), 5–19.

86. Dally, op. cit., 86.

87. Ibid., 128.

88. Interview with Dr Ann Dally, 16 November 2000.

89. Alan Glanz, 'The Fall of the General Practitioner', in Strang and Gossop, *Heroin*, 155–63.

90. Dally, op. cit., 133, 135.

91. Ruggiero and South, *Eurodrugs*, 109.

92. Gerry Stimson, 'Can a War on Drugs succeed?', *New Society*, 15 November 1985, 276.

93. Ruggiero and South, *Eurodrugs*, 133; 'The campaign against drug misuse', *Lancet*, 26 July 1986, 235.

94. Tim Malyon, 'Towards a no-win Vietnam war on drugs', *New Statesman*, 17 October 1986, 7.

95. House of Commons debates, 21 January 1986, vol. 90, cols. 241, 243.

96. Emanuel Apfelbaum and Ben Gelfand, 'The artificial transmission of malaria among intravenous diacethylmorphine addicts', *JAMA*, 102 (1934), 1664.

97. Thomas Bewley, Oved Ben-Arie and Vincent Marks, 'Relation of Hepatitis to Self-Injection Techniques', *BMJ*, 23 March 1968, 730–32.

98. P. P. Mortimer et al., 'HTLV-III Antibody in Swiss and English Intravenous Drug Abusers', *Lancet*, 24 August 1985, 449–50; J. F. Peutherer et al., 'HTLV-III Antibody in Edinburgh Drug Addicts', *Lancet*, 16 November 1985, 1129–30.

99. Sandra D. Lane et al., 'The Coming of Age of Needle Exchange', in James A. Inciardi and Lana Harrison, eds., *Harm Reduction* (2000), 49. I am indebted to this first-class source for the passage that follows.

100. Ibid., 52.

101. Ibid., 60.

102. Richard Davenport-Hines and Christopher Phipps, 'Tainted Love', in Roy Porter and Mikulás Teich, eds., *Sexual Knowledge, Sexual Science* (1994), 373.

103. Sir Norman Fowler, *Ministers Decide* (1991), 263.

104. Mirjo Grmek, *History of AIDS* (1990), 168.

105. Roy Robertson, 'Epidemic of AIDS related virus (HTLV-III/LAV) infection among intravenous drug abusers', *BMJ*, 22 February 1986, 527–9; E. A. C. Follett et al., 'HTLV-III antibody in drug abusers in the West of Scotland: the Edinburgh Connection', *Lancet*, 22 February 1986, 446–7; R. Robertson, 'The Edinburgh Epidemic', in John Strang and Gerry Stimson, eds., *AIDS and Drug Misuse* (1990), 95–107. For anecdotal evidence on the introduction of HIV to Edinburgh's drug-using population, see R. Robertson, 'The arrival of HIV', in Strang and Gossop, *Heroin*, 95–6.

106. Virginia Berridge, *AIDS in the UK* (1996), 96.

107. Dally, op. cit., 219.

108. Ibid., 191.

109. Ibid., 255.

110. Ibid., 265.

111. Ibid., 227.

112. Royal College of Psychiatrists, *Drug Scenes* (1987), 189.

113. Berridge, *AIDS*, 222.

114. Willis, 'Prescribing', 71, 76.

115. Glenn Frankel, 'US War on Drugs Yields Few Victories', *Washington Post*, 8 June 1997, A1.

116. Bourgois, op. cit., 320–21.

CHAPTER FOURTEEN

For a general introduction to this subject, see Nicholas Saunders, *Ecstasy and the Dance Culture* (1995) and Matthew Colin & John Godfrey, *Altered State: the Story of Ecstasy Culture and Acid House* (1997).

1. Lady Caroline Blackwood, *For All That I Found There* (1973), 117–25.
2. Vladimir Nabokov, *Novels 1955–1962* (1996), 65–6, 88.
3. For this formulation, and for much other information, I am indebted to a first-class analysis of the politics of designer drugs, Philip Jenkins, *Synthetic Panics* (1999).
4. Ibid., 54.
5. Charles Silverstein and Edmund White, *The Joy of Gay Sex* (1977), 65.
6. Steven Gaines, *Simply Halston* (1991), 200.
7. Robert Katz and Peter Berling, *Love is Colder than Death* (1987), 128–9.
8. Ibid., 185.
9. Will Self and David Gamble, *Perfidious Man* (2000), 7.
10. Alan Clark, *Diaries* (1993), 273.
11. Royal College of Psychologists, *Drug Scenes*, 22.
12. Simon Reynolds, *Energy Flash* (1998), 280–81.
13. Push and Mireille Silcott, *The Book of E* (2000), 19.
14. Ibid., 20–21.
15. Reynolds, op. cit., xxv.
16. Mark Almond, *Tainted Life* (1999), 144.
17. Nicholas Saunders, *Ecstasy and the Dance Culture* (1995).
18. Push and Silcott, op. cit., 43.
19. Margaret Thatcher, *The Path to Power* (1995), 1.
20. Almond, op. cit., 351–2.
21. Push and Silcott, op. cit., 104–6.
22. Thomas Stuttaford, 'Be Sure of What You are Drinking', *The Times*, 21 December 2000, 2/9.
23. Push and Silcott, op. cit., 103.
24. Zoe Brennan, 'Fight to stop rape drug as hundreds fall victim', *Sunday Times*, 7 December 1997, 10.
25. Daniel McGrory, 'Schools alert over date rape drug', *The Times*, 15 December 1997, 8.
26. Richard Ford, 'Date-rape pills to be outlawed', *The Times*, 1 April 1998, 8.
27. Fiona Measham, Judith Aldridge and Howard Parker, *Dancing on Drugs: Risks, Health and Hedonism in the British Club Scene* (2001), 127, 131, 188.
28. Kevin Williamson, *Drugs and the Party Line* (1997), 53–9; Allan Brown, 'Taxpayers fund research into "respectable" heroin use', *Sunday Times*, 9 March 1997, A/7; Lucy Adamson, 'Labour's drug policy under fire', *Sunday Times*, 19 October 1997, A/30.

29. Benedict King, 'Fight drugs the lampoon way', *Daily Telegraph*, 4 February 1997; David Twiston Davies, *The Daily Telegraph Book of Letters* (1998), 219–20.

30. Meacham, Aldridge and Parker, *Dancing on Drugs*, 181–3.

31. House of Commons debates, 17 January 1997, vol. 288, cols. 538–40.

32. Push and Silcott, op. cit., 119–20.

33. Measham, Aldridge and Parker, op. cit., 16.

34. Jenkins, *Synthetic Panic*, 195–6.

35. Williamson, op. cit., 46.

Bibliographic Note

THE INTERNET CONTAINS so much information on drugs history and drugs policy that it seems superfluous to provide a traditional bibliography. Moreover, the footnotes to my chapters show the chief sources on which my book is based. It will be more helpful, I think, to provide a guide to further reading.

Edward Brecher's authoritative and comprehensive *Licit and Illicit Drugs* (Boston: Little, Brown, 1972) can be accessed on the Internet (at www.druglibrary.org/schaffer/Library/studies/cu/cumenu.htm). *The Encyclopaedia of Psychoactive Substances*, compiled by Richard Rudgley (New York: St. Martin's Press, 1999), is weighted toward traditional societies. Although the German toxicologist Lewis Lewin's *Phantastica: A Classic Survey on the Use and Abuse of Mind-Altering Plants* (Rochester, Vt.: Park Street Press, 1998) was first published in 1924, it remains both readable and informative. A more recent treatment is David T. Courtwright's impressive *Forces of Habit: Drugs and the Making of the Modern World* (Cambridge, Mass.: Harvard University Press, 2001). Philip Jenkins has written a sane and elegant book containing ideas that transcend its ostensible subject: *Synthetic Panics: The Symbolic Politics of Designer Drugs* (New York: New York University Press, 1999). It is also worth consulting essays in Jordan Goodman, Paul E. Lovejoy, and Andrew Sherratt (editors), *Consuming Habits: Drugs in History and Anthropology* (New York: Routledge, 1995), and in Roy Porter and Mikulás Teich (editors), *Drugs and Narcotics in History* (New York: Cambridge University Press, 1995).

Michael Massing's *The Fix* (New York: Simon & Schuster, 1998; Berkeley: University of California Press, paperback edition, 2000) is an excellent survey of recent US drugs history. A helpful but not unflawed historical introduction is Jill Jonnes, *Hep-Cats, Narcs, and Pipe Dreams: A History of America's Romance with Illegal Drugs* (New York: Scribner, 1996; Baltimore: Johns Hopkins University Press, paperback edition, 1999). Other information is provided by Alfred W. McCoy, *Politics of Heroin: CIA Complicity in the Global Drugs Trade* (Brooklyn: Lawrence Hill Books, 1991), and by Gary Webb, *Dark Alliance: the CIA, the Contras, and the Crack Cocaine Explosion* (New York: Seven Stories Press, 1998).

Two studies of drugs and cinema deserve to be noticed: Michael Stark's *Cocaine Fiends and Reefer Madness: An Illustrated History of Drugs in the Movies* (New York: Cornwall Books, 1982) and Jack Stevenson's *Addicted: The Myth and Menace of Drugs in Film* (London: Creation Books, 2000). There are numerous literary anthologies describing drugs and the experiences of their users. For those who enjoy this sort of book, I should mention Michael Jay's *Artificial Paradises: A Drugs Reader* (New York: Penguin, 1999).

One of the great books of narcotics history is David T. Courtwright's *Dark Paradise: Opiate Addiction in America before 1940* (Cambridge, Mass.: Harvard University, 1982). Hardly less valuable is David Courtwright, Herman Joseph, and Don Des Jarlais (editors), *Addicts Who Survived: An Oral History of Narcotic Use in America, 1923–1965* (Knoxville: University of Tennessee Press, 1989).

There is a huge body of literature on cocaine. Possibly the best introductions are Joseph F. Spillane's *Cocaine: From Medical Marvel to Modern Menace in the United States, 1884–1920* (Baltimore: Johns Hopkins University Press, 2000) and Paul Gootenberg (editor), *Cocaine: Global Histories* (New York: Routledge, 1999). Gabriel García Márquez's *News of a Kidnapping* (New York: Knopf, 1997) is a book of urgent moral commitment depicting the effects on Colombia of the

Medellín cocaine cartel. An account of the Colombian terrorist gangster Pablo Escobar written from the standpoint of the US Special Forces is Mark Bowden's *Killing Pablo: The Hunt for the World's Greatest Outlaw* (New York: Atlantic Monthly Press, 2001).

Patricia Adler's *Wheeling and Dealing: An Ethnography of an Upper-Level Drug Dealing and Smuggling Community* (New York: Columbia University Press, 2nd edition, 1993) and Philippe Bourgois's *In Search of Respect: Selling Crack in El Barrio* (New York: Cambridge University Press, 1995) deserve special attention and praise. Lisa Maher's *Sexed Work: Gender, Race, and Resistance in a Brooklyn Drug Market* (New York: Oxford University Press, 1997) and Claire E. Sterk's *Fast Lives: Women Who Use Crack Cocaine* (Philadelphia: Temple University Press, 1999) are also valuable.

Richard J. Bonnie and Charles H. Whitebread published a classic study of marijuana in 1974 that was republished in 1999 by the excellent Lindesmith Center of New York as *The Marijuana Conviction: A History of Marijuana Prohibition in the United States.* Another valuable historical introduction is David Solomon (editor), *The Marihuana Papers* (New York: Bobbs-Merrill Co., 1966). The pharmacologist Leslie L. Iversen, a Foreign Associate of the US National Academy of Sciences and a Fellow of the Royal Society in London, has written *The Science of Marijuana* (New York: Oxford University Press Inc., 2000), which scrupulously examines the health benefits and risks of the drug.

Different aspects of drug trafficking and international drug enforcement are covered by the University of Virginia's William B. McAllister in *Drug Diplomacy in the Twentieth Century: An International History* (New York: Routledge, 2000), Ethan A. Nadelmann's *Cops across Borders: The Internationalization of U.S. Criminal Law Enforcement* (University Park: Pennsylvania State University Press, 1993), and Ron Chepesiuk's *Hard Target: The United States War against International Drug Trafficking, 1982–1997* (Jefferson, N.C.: McFarland & Company, 1999).

Probably the best introduction to harm-reduction policy is James A. Inciardi and Lana D. Harrison (editors), *Harm Reduction: National and International Perspectives* (Thousand Oaks, Calif.: Sage Publications, 2000). Another authoritative academic study has been published under the auspices of the Earl Warren Legal Institute: Franklin E. Zimring and Gordon Hawkins's *The Search for Rational Drug Control* (New York: Cambridge University Press, 1992).

After Prohibition: An Adult Approach to Drug Policies in the 21st Century (Washington D.C.: Cato Institute, 2000), edited by Timothy Lynch, is essential reading—not least for the pithy foreword by Milton Friedman and rousing personal manifesto of Gary E. Johnson, governor of New Mexico. Ten years of research by Robert J. MacCoun, professor of public policy and law at the University of California, and Peter Reuter, professor of public policy at the University of Maryland, into punitive prohibition policy has resulted in *Drug War Heresies: Learning from Other Vices, Times, and Places* (New York: RAND Studies in Policy Analysis and Cambridge University Press, 2001), which is highly authoritative but sometimes rather technical. Other opinions are usefully collected in James A. Inciardi (editor), *The Drug Legalization Debate* (Thousand Oaks, Calif.: Sage Publications, 1999). The British antiprohibition case is presented in Selina Chen and Edward Skidelsky (editors), *High Time for Reform: Drug Policy for the 21st Century* (London: Social Market Foundation, 2001).

Index